Longbridge Deverill Cow Down

An Early Iron Age Settlement in West Wiltshire

by Sonia Chadwick Hawkes with Christopher Hawkes

with contributions by

Rebecca Annable, Rose Annable, Frederick Anderson, Collin Bowen, Don Brothwell, Lisa Brown, B. Denston, Eric Freeman, Guy Grainger, Ralph Harcourt, Shirley Jarman, Peter Marshall, Alison MacDonald, David McOmish, Graham Morgan, M.E.S. Morrison, Daphne Nash, Michael Smith, Wendy Smith, Ronald Tylecote, Elizabeth Wesley, Duncan Wilson

Drawings by Marion Cox, David McOmish and Edward Impey

Photographs by Sonia Chadwick Hawkes

Edited by Lisa Brown

Oxford University School of Archaeology

Monograph No. 76

2012

Published by the
School of Archaeology
36 Beaumont Street, Oxford OX1 2PG

ISBN 978-1-905905-25-6

This volume has been prepared for publication by Oxford Archaeology on behalf of Oxford University School of Archaeology and edited by Lisa Brown.

The publication of this volume was made possible by a grant from English Heritage.

Every attempt has been made to identify the copyright holder of the aerial photographic image shown in Fig. 1.3. We would be grateful for any information regarding provenance and ask that the publisher be notified.

Printed in Great Britain

Contents

List of Figures

List of Tables

Sonia Hawkes with Jennifer Nicholson (© The Wiltshire Times 1960)

Summary

The early Iron Age settlement at Longbridge Deverill Cow Down, Wiltshire was excavated between 1956 and 1960 by the late Sonia Chadwick Hawkes. Funding was provided by the then Ministry of Works to investigate a well-defined D-shaped enclosure on the Down in advance of tree plantation. The enclosure was known from vertical photographs taken by the RAF for the national air survey shortly after WWII, but aerial survey carried out by J.K. St. Joseph at the start of the excavation, after the Down had been ploughed, revealed that it was one of a complex of three enclosures. The results of the survey and of the initial excavation prompted a continuation of the fieldwork in order to establish the stratigraphic and chronological sequence of the settlement.

A field survey of the site and surrounding area undertaken during the excavation by Collin Bowen of RCHM was continued over several years by David McOmish of English Heritage, and the results were drawn together for this volume. The excavation programme involved digging trenches across the earthworks of the three enclosures and an investigation of their interiors. The D-shaped enclosure proved to be a later enhancement or addition to a major early Iron Age enclosure, which probably served as a stock pen well into the medieval period. The well preserved remains of four roundhouses that lay within two of the enclosures represent a settlement occupied between the 9th and 6th centuries BC. At least two of these structures were burnt out, possibly deliberately, preserving abundant pottery and other artefacts. Some 70 excavated pits that post-dated the roundhouse settlement, probably by about 200 years or more, must have been associated with a later settlement that lay largely beyond the excavated areas. Unusually for the time, basic environmental sampling was carried out and organic material was submitted for radiocarbon dating.

Sonia and Christopher Hawkes spent many years following the excavation bringing together elements of the stratigraphic and specialist reports with the assistance of students and specialists. The site archive was ordered during the 1990s but at the time of Hawkes' death in 1999 this important site remained largely unpublished. The publication of this volume has been supported by the Hawkes Estate, overseen by Professor Helena Hamerow of the School of Archaeology at the University of Oxford, and funded by English Heritage, within the scope of their *Implementation Plan for Exploring our Past 1998*.

Résumé

L'habitat du premier âge du Fer sur la Colline de Longbridge Deverill Cow Down, Wiltshire a été fouillé entre 1956 et 1960 par feu Sonia Chadwick Hawkes. Cette opération avait été financée par le Bureau des Monuments historiques du `Ministry of Works' d'alors afin de rechercher un enclos en D bien défini sur la Colline, préalablement à la plantation d'arbres. L'enclos était connu grâce à des clichés verticaux pris par la RAF dans le cadre d'une reconnaissance aérienne nationale peu après la Seconde Guerre mondiale, mais celle effectuée par J.K. St. Joseph au début de la fouille, après le labour de la Colline, a révélé qu'il faisait partie d'un complexe de 3 enclos. Les résultats et la fouille initiale ont motivé la poursuite des travaux de terrain pour permettre d'établir la séquence stratigraphique et chronologique de l'habitat.

Une étude des lieux du site et des environs, entreprise durant la fouille opérée par Collin Bowen de RCHM (la Commission royale des monuments historiques) a été poursuivie sur plusieurs années par David McOmish de l'agence du patrimoine britannique, English Heritage ; les résultats ont été rapprochés pour ce volume. Le programme de fouille a impliqué l'ouverture de tranchées dans les fossés et les remparts des trois enclos et une recherche de leurs intérieurs. L'enclos en D s'est avéré être une revalorisation plus tardive ou l'ajout à un enclos majeur du premier âge du Fer, qui a probablement servi de parc à bestiaux bien dans l'époque médiévale. Les vestiges bien conservés des structures circulaires qui se trouvaient dans deux des enclos représentent un habitat occupé entre le IXe et le VIe av. J.-C. Au moins deux de ces structures ont été brûlées, peut-être délibérément, permettant la préservation d'une abondance de céramique et d'autres artefacts. Quelque 70 fosses excavées qui post- dataient l'habitat, probablement d'environ 200 ans ou plus, ont sûrement été liées à un habitat plus tardif qui s'étendait en grande partie au-delà des zones fouillées. Exceptionnellement pour l'époque, un prélèvement paléoenvironnemental basique a été exécuté et du matériel organique a fait l'objet d'une datation radiocarbone.

A la suite de la fouille, Sonia et Christopher Hawkes ont passé nombre d'années à rassembler les éléments des rapports stratigraphiques et spécialistes avec l'assistance d'étudiants et de spécialistes. L'archive du site a été commandée durant les années 1990 mais, à la mort de Hawkes en 1999, cet important site demeurait en grande partie non publié. La publication de ce volume a été appuyée par le `Hawkes Estate', sous l'égide du Professeur Helena Hamerow de la `School of Archaeology at the University of Oxford' et par English Heritage, dans le cadre de leur *`Implementation Plan for Exploring our Past' - 1998* (Plan de mise en application pour l'exploration de notre passé).

Zusammenfassung

Die früheisenzeitliche Siedlung bei Longbridge Deverill Cow Down in Wiltshire wurde zwischen 1956 und 1960 von der verstorbenen Sonia Chadwick Hawkes ausgegraben. Finanziert wurde die Grabung vom Ministerium für Arbeit zur Freilegung einer gut definierten D-förmigen Anlage in den Downs, auf einem Gebiet, auf dem Bäume angepflanzt werden sollten. Die Anlage war von senkrecht aufgenommen Photos der Royal Air Force bekannt, welche kurz nach dem 2. Weltkrieg im Zuge einer landesweiten Gebietsaufnahme gemacht wurden. Es stellte sich jedoch auf weiteren Luftaufnahmen, die von J.K. St. Joseph im Vorfeld der Grabung aufgenommen wurden nachdem das Gelände gepflügt wurde, heraus, dass es sich nicht um eine, sondern um einen Komplex von drei Anlagen handelte. Das Resultat dieser Aufnahmen und der ersten Grabung führten zu einer Fortführung der Grabungsarbeiten zur Festlegung der stratigraphischen und chronologischen Gliederung der Siedlung.

Eine Felduntersuchung des Geländes und der Umgebung, durchgeführt während der Ausgrabung von Collin Bowen (RCHM), wurde im Folgenden mehrere Jahre von by David McOmish (English Heritage) weitergeführt. Die Resultate wurden für diesen Band ausgewertet. Die Ausgrabung beinhaltete Sondagen durch die Erdwerke und Innenräume der drei Anlagen. Es stelle sich heraus, dass die D-förmige Anlage eine Verstärkung oder Erweiterung einer früheisenzeitlichen Hauptanlage war, welche wahrscheinlich als Vieheinzäunung bis weit hinein ins Mittelalter genutzt wurde. Die sehr gut erhaltenen Überreste von vier Rundhäusern, welche innerhalb von zwei der Anlagen nachgewiesen werden konnten repräsentieren eine Siedlung, die zwischen dem 9. und 6. Jahrhundert v. Chr. bewohnt war. Mindestens zwei der dort nachgewiesenen Gebäude waren, möglicherweise absichtlich, ausgebrannt worden. In ihnen wurde eine große Menge Keramik und andere Artefakte gefunden. Etwa 70 untersuchte Gruben, welche ca. 200 Jahre nach den Rundhäuser angelegt wurden gehörten scheinbar zu einer Siedlung, welche größtenteils außerhalb des Untersuchungsgebiets lag. Ehr ungewöhnlich für die Zeit in welcher die Ausgrabung stattfand wurden Bodenproben genommen und organisches Material C14-datiert.

Sonia and Christopher Hawkes, mit der Hilfe von Studenten und Spezialisten, verbrachten viele Jahre nach der Ausgrabung damit die Stratigraphie sowie die Auswertungen der Proben zu verbinden. Die Grabungsunterlagen wurden in den 1990er Jahren archiviert, doch als Hawkes 1999 starb war diese so wichtige Ausgrabung noch größtenteils unpubliziert. Die Publikation dieses Bandes wurde unterstützt von Hawkes Estate und betreut von Professor Helena Hamerow (School of Archaeology, University of Oxford), sowie von English Heritage, im Rahmen des *Implementation Plan for Exploring our Past 1998* Projektes.

Editorial Preface

Over 50 years has elapsed since the final season of excavation at Longbridge Deverill, Cow Down in 1960. During the 40 years between the completion of fieldwork and the death of Sonia Chadwick Hawkes in 1999, she and Christopher Hawkes, together with research assistants and students from the Oxford University Institute of Archaeology, volunteers and specialists from various institutions carried out a range of post-excavation work. Survey fieldwork on Cow Down initiated by Collin Bowen during the excavation was continued by David McOmish of the then Royal Commission on Historical Monuments

The initial priorities of the post-excavation work were the processing and cataloguing of finds, submission of samples for radiocarbon dating and petrological and archaeobotonical analyses. A number of specialist reports were commissioned between the 1960s and 1980s as funding for the project was intermittently procured. During the 1980s Christopher Hawkes, with the assistance of Guy Grainger and Duncan Wilson, completed a typology and illustrated catalogue of the large pottery assemblage, and the artefact reports were drafted at about the same time. Shortly thereafter the finds were deposited with Devizes Museum (now the Wiltshire Heritage Museum). The paper archives remained in Oxford but will be transferred to the Museum in due course.

In 1993 the archive was ordered and key elements of it digitised. The archive includes original site plans and records, illustrations, photographs and slides, reports, superseded drafts, along with letters and memos covering the period from the excavation until Sonia Hawkes' final illness. These represent an important archaeological resource, but also a glimpse into the sometimes arcane workings of various institutions involved in the work and funding of the project. Shortly thereafter, Sonia Hawkes collated the various components of six chapters and drafted the framework of a publication report. A comprehensive series of artefact and site illustrations prepared by Marion Cox during the 1970s are a mainstay of the publication. One of four of the Longbridge roundhouses was published in the Oxford Journal of Archaeology (Hawkes 1994), illustrated with one of a set of reconstruction drawings by Edward Impey.

The opportunity to publish the site in full arose when English Heritage agreed in 2007 to fund the publication within the scope of Programme 4 of English Heritage's *Implementation Plan for Exploring our Past 1998*, which seeks to bring important unpublished sites into the public domain. At the time Hawkes were working towards publication, the Longbridge Deverill site had few noteworthy parallels, particularly for the four impressive roundhouses, then matched only at Pimperne, and the substantial, fine early Iron Age pottery assemblage, unique at the time of its discovery. A number of important early Iron Age settlement and midden sites have since been investigated and published, offering an opportunity to review the Longbridge Deverill settlement in a broader regional and national context.

Although Sonia Hawkes' original framework was broadly adhered to in preparing the publication draft, much of the existing text was clearly out of date in the light of comparative data accumulated since her death. This was particularly the case for the environmental and artefact reports, some of which were bare catalogues or incomplete drafts. Although the studies of the human and animal remains had largely stood the test of time, it was necessary to recalibrate the radiocarbon dates and to reconsider the analysis of a particularly important archaeobotonical sample. Where feasible, the specialist authors were contacted and offered the opportunity to comment of their original reports. The overviews of the pottery and other artefacts have been revised to take into account similar material from recently published sites. Finally, because elements of the existing structural report were quite meagre, and unbalanced by the more fulsome artefact reports, the sections describing the enclosure earthworks and pits have been revised and expanded. Numerous anomalies in the records, including duplication of feature numbers, have been resolved as far as was possible and the main text underpinned by detailed catalogue descriptions in appendices inserted at the back of the volume.

Preface

For those of us learning our Iron Age archaeology in the 1960s the site of Longbridge Deverill, Cow Down, excavated in a series of short campaigns between 1956 and 1960, was legendary. Our knowledge was based essentially on two lectures given by the excavator, Sonia Hawkes, one to the CBA conference on the Iron Age of Southern Britain in December 1958 and the other to the Prehistoric Society in 1966. It was enough to show that the site, with its large timber houses and huge assemblage of early Iron Age pottery, was exceptional and was clearly to be one of the type sites of the British Iron Age, but without a report it was difficult to say more.

The publication has been a long time coming. There are many reasons for this. The original excavation was undertaken at the instigation of the Ancient Monuments Division of the Ministry of Works in the pioneering days when the idea that post-excavation work needed funding would have been greeted with surprise. Without funds the sheer volume of material recovered was overwhelming. It was also a time when Sonia was swept into a busy and demanding academic life at the Institute of Archaeology at Oxford, there to develop new research interests and teaching responsibilities. Yet the work on Longbridge Deverill continued, albeit sporadically. A succession of research assistants was given specific tasks of preparation, experts were cajoled into producing specialist reports and the redoubtable Marion Cox turned out a series of incomparable drawings, which now illustrate this volume. By the mid-1990s the report was nearing completion and Sonia felt confident enough to tease the expectant audience with a discussion of one of the houses published in the Oxford Journal of Archaeology (1994), but her death a few years later brought the project to a temporary end.

That we now have the material before us in full is due in very large part to the determination of Helena Hamerow, Sonia's successor at Oxford, who shouldered the responsibility of seeing Sonia's important research excavations through to full publication. It has been a demanding task but one which, with the publication of this volume, has now been successfully completed. All those working in Iron Age and Saxon archaeology are greatly in Helena's debt. The other partner in the enterprise is English Heritage, the successor body to the Ancient Monuments Division who initiated the original excavations. Under a far-sighted initiative to ensure that key excavations undertaken in the past are made publicly available they provided funds for the last phase of post-excavation work leading to this publication.

The pulling together of the disparate texts and specialist reports to create a cohesive publication has been the work of Lisa Brown of Oxford Archaeology. Her deep and expert knowledge of the British Iron Age, and especially of its pottery, and her sympathy for the project, has ensured that the report matches the demands of modern scholarship. It has been no easy task but we now have before us an array of new data which can be brought fully into the continuing debate. The legend of Longbridge has at last become a reality.

Barry Cunliffe

Acknowledgements

I would like to thank David McOmish for his contribution to this book and also for his general enthusiasm, assistance and some wonderful anecdotes of his involvement with Collin Bowen and Sonia Hawkes. Thanks are also due to the Wiltshire Times for allowing, with unqualified delight, the reproduction of photographs taken by the newspaper while the excavation was in progress.

I greatly appreciate the contributions of the Oxford Archaeology Graphics Officers, especially Magdalena Wachnik and Georgina Slater, who were involved in all stages of preparation of the text and figures. Magdalena Wachnik offered helpful advice on the overall design of the volume and designed the cover. The French and German translations are by Nathalie Haudecoeur-Wilks and Markus Dylewski respectively. Nicola Scott prepared the archive for deposition. Anne Dodd and Alex Smith have been a consistent source of useful advice and support during the preparation of the volume.

Helena Hamerow of Oxford University Institute of Archaeology, acting as Sonia Hawkes' literary executor, provided the opportunity for me to be involved in bringing the book to publication, and gave constructive advice and support along the way. I would also like to thank Barry Cunliffe for writing the preface and for commenting on the first draft, although responsibility for the final content is entirely my own.

The volume has been funded by English Heritage, and we are grateful to Barney Sloane of the Strategic Planning and Management section of English Heritage's National Heritage Protection Commissions Programme, along with Kath Buxton, Caroline Howarth and Charlotte Winter, who all provided assistance during the course of the project. We owe special thanks to Helen Keeley, the Project Officer for English Heritage, who has been directly involved at all stages of the project.

Lisa Brown

A break during excavation (© The Wiltshire Times 1960)

Introduction

by Sonia Chadwick Hawkes

'From Longbridge Deverill I again ascend the chalky district, to an insulated eminence, called on the Map of Wiltshire, Whiten-Hill, where we again find ourselves among the Britons. Near the north-west point of this hill, is a small earthern work of a very singular form, resembling the letter D, with an entrance on the straight side, and towards the east. Its area contains about one acre and a quarter, and the ditch of the rampart is on the inside. On the east side of this work, we have found the usual marks of British population, and in the ditch on the left side of the entrance to it, we dug up some rude fragments of coarse pottery, together with a large piece of fine red Samian, but the whole of this ground having been in tillage, few important discoveries can be made without the use of the spade.'

Sir Richard Colt Hoare *The Ancient History of South Wiltshire* (1812,103)

This earthwork, which remains still a markedly visible monument, is situated about one mile east-south-east of Longbridge Deverill at 198m O.D. on the flat top of a spur of downland enclosed by a loop of the River Wylye, just west of Whiten Hill (ST 887405). The opportunity to excavate arose in the autumn of 1956 when the farmers, Keith and Roger Stratton, announced their intention of planting the D-shaped enclosure with trees. The officers of the then Ancient Monuments Division of the Ministry of Works in charge of the case, John Hurst and Michael Thompson, had no grounds for doubting that this symmetrical enclosure was indeed a minor Roman earthwork, as Colt Hoare's discoveries suggested. Maud Cunnington (1930-2, 196) had classified it as Roman and it was to appear as such in the forthcoming *Victoria County History of Wiltshire, I, part 1* (1957, 83), although an alternative view that it might have been a post-medieval copse enclosure had been suggested.

Nonetheless, it was felt that the task of excavating and recording the earthwork could be managed in, at most, a couple of seasons by the young graduate student entrusted with the task. The setting of the enclosure amongst the lynchets of a large complex of 'celtic fields' had been recognised from a series of high-level Air Ministry photographs taken during the autumn of 1946, before the down was brought under the plough, but initially this was seen as a minor complication. My brief was to excavate the enclosure, date it and establish its character and its relationship with the lynchets abutting it in advance of plantation. The complications that were to ensue were not anticipated, though, with hindsight, the early air photographs should have been more closely studied from the outset.

The excavation of the D-shaped enclosure, which took place over three separate months during October 1956 and April and September 1957, included sectioning the ditches and causeway and trial trenching most of the interior. All were very small scale campaigns with just myself in charge of four labourers from a building firm in Warminster, who worked in the old way with spade, pick and shovel, with interventions by myself with a trowel whenever anything interesting turned up. But they were very skilled at following layers and spotting pottery or anything else unusual, so the quality of the excavation was good. During the last season we were helped by a few volunteers who mostly worked on the excavation of an earlier roundhouse just inside the enclosure entrance. Otherwise, trial trenching revealed no contemporary occupation of the interior of the D-shaped enclosure, which, from pottery in its primary ditch silts, appeared to date from the 'saucepan pot' phase of the Iron Age, perhaps the 2nd or 3rd century BC. Roman activity on the site seems to have been confined to ploughing. By December 1957, with excavation complete, the D-shaped enclosure was duly planted with beech trees, but these subsequently died and were not replaced, so there is no copse there today.

The first excavation was carried out under the illusion that, except for the fields, this enclosure was an isolated feature, perhaps a stock enclosure, but suspicions that the situation might be otherwise were aroused already during the 1956 season. Large amounts of burnt flint and weathered pottery were picked up in the stubble on the field to the east of the earthwork. Before the second season of excavation, therefore, I acquired new aerial photographs from Dr. J.K. St Joseph. These obliques had been taken under excellent conditions during 1955, shortly after the down around the earthwork had been ploughed for the first time within living memory, possibly for the first time since Colt Hoare recorded ploughing during the Napoleonic Wars. They clearly revealed that the D-shaped enclosure lay within a much larger settlement complex. A large area to the east was occupied by a ditched enclosure resembling Little Woodbury (Bersu 1940), some 2.4ha in extent, surrounded by a silted-up ditch, visible during Easter 1957 as a strip of darker soil in the newly ploughed field. The area inside the ditch could be seen, both in the air photographs and on the ground, to be pockmarked with darker patches of soil, which by analogy with Little Woodbury were interpreted as pits and working hollows. This new enclosure corresponded with the area in which the sherds and burnt flints had been found. The D-shaped enclosure (henceforth Enclosure III) appeared to lie across the western end of this new enclosure (henceforth II), and its incurving ditches at this point met exactly the corners of Enclosure III. Yet another enclosure (I), of the same type as II, but smaller, and with no wide opening, lay a little over 100m northwest of Enclosure II. It was only partly exposed in the air photographs since a large part of it was in an adjoining field still under thick downland turf at that time.

It was now clear that this was a site of first importance. There was a major field system and within it, and in close proximity to each other, were three enclosures apparently of early Iron Age date, two of which at least appeared to have contained farmsteads of Little Woodbury type. Although the excavations of 1957 were still doggedly concentrated on searching the interior of Enclosure III in advance of tree planting, cuttings were also placed at the intersections of the ditches of Enclosures II and III to establish their relationship. It became clear that Enclosure III had been constructed across the open end of the silted up Enclosure II and that the construction of Enclosure II predated it by some centuries.

During the excavations of April 1957 a small single-engine aircraft circling the site proved to be Dr St. Joseph taking more photographs of the area. At the Council for British Archaeology Conference on the Iron Age of Southern Britain in December 1958 (Frere 1958) both St. Joseph and I lectured on Longbridge Deverill. He showed photographs of the site with the excavation trenches clearly visible, which I was able to add to the site archive.

In the summer of 1958, exploration of the site entered a new phase, with the focus of interest transferred to Enclosures I and II. As before, the excavation lasted for only a month. An assistant, Peter Addyman, eight workmen and a number of volunteers were added to the workforce. We sectioned the ditches of the enclosures to determine their precise location on the ground, their date and character, and opened up part of the interior of Enclosure II to determine the nature of the occupation. Stripping plough and topsoil by hand using a 20 foot grid (though it might seem quaint now) was an immense advantage on a site where there had been so little modern ploughing that large quantities of pottery survived not only in pits but also the tops of postholes. Many of the postholes belonged to two of a sequence of four big roundhouses and the quality and quantity of the dating and occupation evidence from them remains noteworthy in Wessex Iron Age archaeology. When we returned to the site in 1960 and reopened the excavated parts of Houses I and 2 it was already evident that, even during such a short interval, the plough had bitten deeper and was doing more damage. Today the site must be severely plough damaged and any houses not excavated in 1958 and 1960 largely or totally destroyed. In 1960, however, conditions of preservation were still relatively good.

The season lasted six weeks during August and September, and the workforce consisted of eight workmen, 12 volunteers, one site assistant, Jennifer Nicholson, with my husband, Professor Christopher Hawkes, as finds assistant. We explored more of the interior of Enclosure II and also opened a small area in the accessible part of Enclosure I. We were housed in three small huts, and personnel and resources were totally inadequate to cope with the huge volume of finds we turned up. As in 1958, the senior staff found themselves working till nightfall on the site to complete planning, and Christopher was overwhelmed by the mass of material he had to process in and around our shared directorial hut. I remember the astonishment of the Ministry official in this year, Reay Robertson-McKay, as he gazed aghast at the trays and trays of pottery, bones and stone Christopher was carefully listing and packing. 'If we had realised that there would be so many finds from this site, you could have had the Stonehenge hut'. We had recently seen this very large and superior hut in use by Paul Ashbee for the excavation of just a Bronze Age barrow with minimal finds, and had envied him its spaciousness and peace and quiet compared with the hurly-burly of Longbridge Deverill, where site planning and finds processing competed for space in one small hut, and tempers frequently frayed.

The result of such inadequate resources during the excavation was that not all finds could be marked or even washed on site and many had to be dealt with on return to Oxford. As there was no post-excavation funding to pay an assistant, I myself washed, marked and restored pottery during several years in the early 1960s. However, by 1966 the site plans were finalised and most of the finds drawn by Marion Cox, so that we were able to give a major lecture about the site to the Prehistoric Society. Having shown the richness of the site to the assembled company, we hoped that we might persuade them, where we had failed with the Ministry of Works, of the importance of someone completing the excavation before time and the plough made it too late to get a good result. But it was not to be, and the Iron Age enclosures on Longbridge Deverill Cow Down were left to their fate with only a fraction of their story told. Even the ploughing, sometime later in the 1960s, of the field containing most of Enclosure I failed to provoke any further response from official quarters, and a wonderful chance at least to excavate that small enclosure fully under optimum conditions was lost.

However, in some quarters fieldwork on the site continued. Dr Collin Bowen of the then Royal Commission on Historical Monuments at Salisbury, who had been in touch about the field system during the excavation, continued surveying and working on the photographs of the site for many years until the early 1980s. He lay the groundwork for the final plan of what turned out to be a remarkably interesting and well-preserved system of fields and trackways. After his retirement the work was completed, with his assistance, by David McOmish.

As with so much else about this site, not only has the work on it been protracted and episodic, but the whole publication has needed time to mature. It is regrettable that the final publication has been so long delayed, but the circumstances described above should give an inkling why. After a great burst of post-excavation work on the site during the earlier 1960s, progress was slowed down by the non-production of specialist reports and the lack of funds for assistance with the pottery. By the time these omissions began to be remedied during the early 1970s and again during the early 1980s both Christopher and I had acquired many competing obligations and lacked the time to sit down for enough long consecutive periods to pull all the elements of the report together. In his last active years, 1988-9, he was able to write up the small finds in the intervals of finishing his report on the Colchester Dykes, and he very much wished to write the discussion of the pottery too, but he was by now in his 85th year and suddenly it all became too much. He was taken ill and died in 1992.

After tidying up the archive in 1993 I realised that practically all the report was there in some form or another, in draft, on record cards, in specialist reports, in memoranda and that with a little paid assistance and the total sacrifice of every other academic commitment for several months, there was nothing to prevent the final completion of the report. The saving grace was a grant in 1993 from the British Academy to employ an assistant, the indefatigable Alison MacDonald, to put all the various records on computer and thus produce the very substantial skeleton that I could flesh out to produce a finished report..

I dedicate it to Christopher Hawkes, of course, in love and gratitude for everything we shared together. My excavation of Longbridge Deverill Cow Down was one of the causes, and I hope its publication will be seen as one of the major fruits of, our marriage. Christopher's contribution is incalculably great, not so much for what he actually wrote but what he inspired in me and others through the generosity of his personality and scholarship.

Oxford, 14 February 1994

Chapter 1: The Site in Context – Field Survey and Air Transcription

by Collin Bowen and David McOmish

INTRODUCTION

The complex of prehistoric enclosures and field systems at Longbridge Deverill on Cow Down, Wiltshire lies at approximately 200m above OD on an undulating spur whose slope falls away steeply below the site to the north, west, and south. It is located at the generally higher north-western end of the Grovely Great Ridge, an Upper Chalk formation capped in places by Clay-with-Flints. Immediately to the north, the valley of the River Wylye separates the ridge from the main body of Salisbury Plain (Fig 1.1). The position of the settlement is slightly below the summit of the spur and on ground falling very gently to the south. The Longbridge Deverill site occupies a place within a rich prehistoric landscape of linear earthworks, hillforts and settlement sites (Fig. 1.2).

A small D-shaped earthwork enclosure (Enclosure III) on Cow Down was known, planned and described in the early 19th century by Sir Richard Colt Hoare (1812, 103), having previously appeared on the first edition of the 1" OS map of 1810. Routine vertical photographs taken by the RAF for the national air survey shortly after World War II, when the whole area was under pasture, showed it to be notably distinct and of an unusual shape – a backward D – set among a close web of 'Celtic' fields extensively overlaid by plough ridges of medieval and later form (Figs 1.3-1.4). Since Sonia Hawkes' 1956–1960 excavations, aerial photography and fieldwork have gradually yielded additional information about the site and its environs. Much of this work was carried out by the staff of the former Royal Commission of the Historical Monuments of England (RCHME), which merged with English Heritage in 1999, but the comments and interpretation in the following

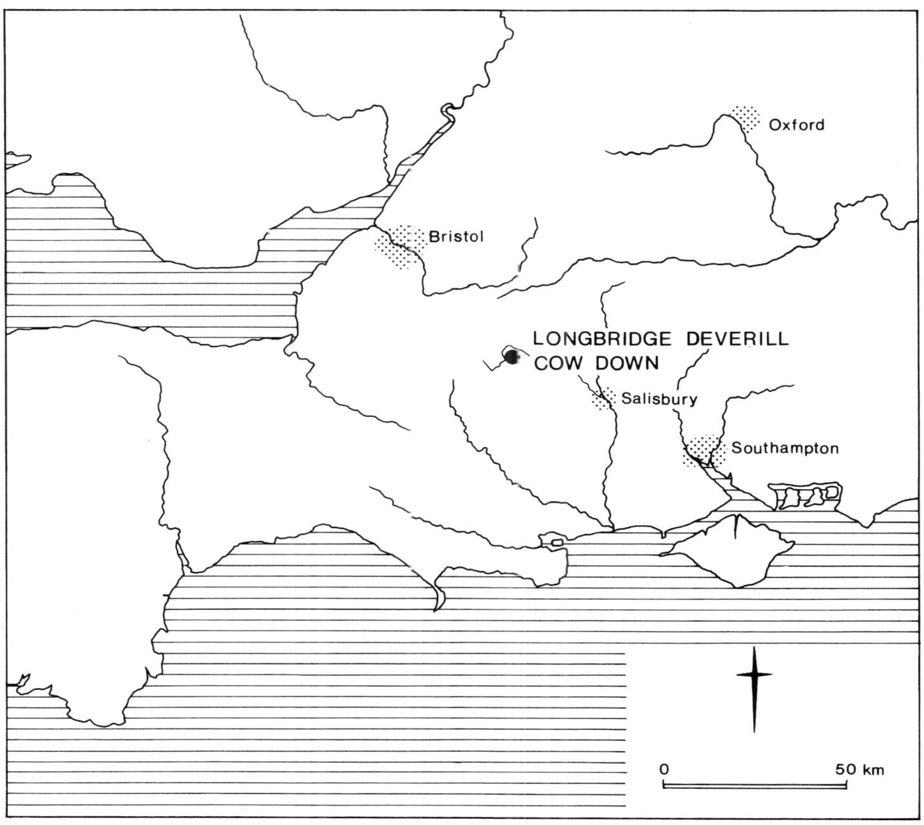

Fig. 1.1 Location of the site

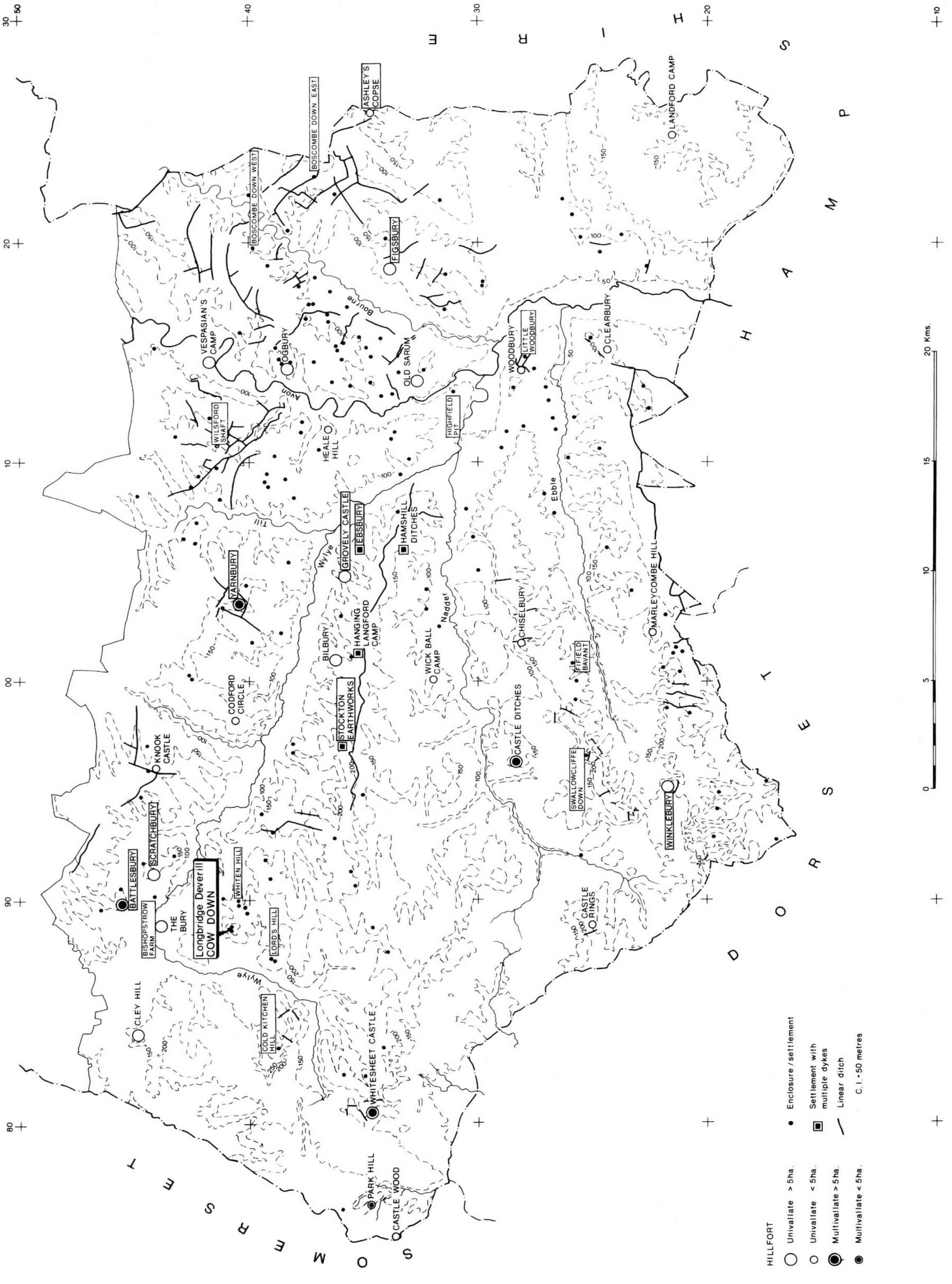

Fig. 1.2 Iron Age sites in south Wiltshire

account are the sole responsibility of the authors.

RCHME involvement sprang from a particular interest in Wiltshire around 1956, when the opening of an office at Salisbury for Central Southern and South-West England was under consideration. Contact was made with Sonia Hawkes, whose recent finds had suggested the possibility of an early Iron Age date for Enclosure III. No similar site was known to RCHME staff and it was, therefore, thought that the finds might relate to a pre-enclosure settlement that had been flattened beyond ground recognition.

Dr R. M. Butler, who had visited the site with Collin Bowen, searched the records of the Cambridge University Committee for Aerial Photography for any possible relevant prints. Due to a quirk in the

Fig. 1.3 Vertical aerial photograph of Cow Down showing Enclosure III and field systems

Fig. 1.4 Vertical aerial photograph of Cow Down showing Enclosure III and field systems (Crown copyright Ordnance Survey 002: 63-083. License agreement English Heritage)

nomenclature used in filing, none could be found. Shortly after, some startling oblique air photographs, then recently taken by St. Joseph, came to light (Fig. 1.5-1.6). These remain the most dramatic of all known of this much photographed place and these, together with some other fine vertical photographs, made it possible to produce a transcription plan (Fig. 1.7). The photographs showed the D-shaped enclosure covering *c.* 0.6ha (1.5 acres) as an 'island' among new arable, a remarkable survival in a landscape much denuded by agricultural activity. The photographs also revealed that the enclosure is only one of three located in an area of *c.* 25ha (62.0 acres) on the spur top. Indeed, Enclosure III was seen to have the soil marks of another enclosure (II) contiguous with it on the east (Fig. 1.5).

Enclosure II is 2ha (5.0 acres) in size and defined on three sides by a continuous ditch. The presence and position of a western side is uncertain due to the interlocking with Enclosure III. No definite entrance to Enclosure II is visible but there is the suggestion of a diminished width of ditch at its the south-east angle. This might be significant in relation to the featureless area between it and a double lynchet trackway (SE DL) which seems to approach it from the south (Fig. 1.7). Plentiful smear marks of occupation within the line of the ditch, but virtually none outside it, suggest that this was the limit of occupation. Also, given that these indications of occupation extend up to the settlement perimeter, it is plausible that the accompanying bank was located externally. However, since 'Celtic' fields and broad as well as narrow ridge and furrow cultivation overlie the enclosure, all traces of upstanding earthworks have been obliterated. A further 100m to the north-east of Enclosures II and III is a third ditched enclosure (I), ovoid in shape and 1.4ha (3.0 acres), with smear marks of occupation within the interior. A 'Celtic' field system was laid out over this enclosure with the sides of one of the fields lying against the remains of an internal bank on the eastern side. Broad ridge and furrow cultivation lies unconformably over the whole.

Clasping Enclosure III were other soil marks of elliptical form. These, however, were explained as a distortion, though unusual, caused by the earthwork in the 'envelope' pattern made by 'round and round' ploughing or cropping (Bowen 1975).

Fig. 1.5 Cow Down photographed by J.K. St. Joseph 13 April 1955 (original photograph held at Cambridge University Collection of Aerial Photography: PM43)

Enquiry of the then current farmer, Mr Keith Stratton, confirmed that the ground had been freshly broken up in this way by a heavy plough with digger share drawn by caterpillar tractor. The furrows thus made were up to 0.6m deep. In addition to the enclosures the air photographs showed a striking pattern of 'Celtic' fields, their razed lynchets glaringly white (Figs 1.5 and 1.6). Over most of the northern parts shown by these photographs is a superincumbent weave of broad ridge and furrow on both recently ploughed and unploughed areas.

The establishment of an RCHME office in Salisbury made the site more accessible, but priorities for the small number of staff there lay outside Wiltshire and visits were made only when individuals could find the time. However, some ground survey corrected an initial error in a plan made for the excavator and the relationship of Enclosure III to the 'Celtic' fields was examined, as was that between the barrows and the 'Celtic' field system.

The site continued to be treated as a watching brief but under purposeful surveillance from the air. RCHME's Air Photographic Unit, under the direction of John Hampton, organised sorties over the site and collected a variety of photographs from other sources. The result of NMR involvement and of technical advances in transcription was the production of a plan much more accurate than that initially produced by RCHME, and with a considerable enhancement of detail, some of it very significant. This new base plan (Fig. 1.7) was itself annotated following intensive examination and interpretation of the air photographs, together with select ground survey. The stippled convention used by the Air Photographic Unit of RCHME for the delineation of the lynchets, however, reflects the difficulty of portraying accurately the overall fall of the lynchets by the more desired 'hachure' convention.

Fig. 1.6 The enclosures at Cow Down photographed By J.K St. Joseph 13 April 1955: Enclosure I (left centre); Enclosure II (top centre); Enclosure III (centre) (original photographs held at Cambridge University Collection of Aerial Photography: PM55)

LAND USE

The oldest known settlement at Longbridge Deverill is that dated by Christopher and Sonia Hawkes to the early Iron Age, but it is likely that some arable cultivation predated this settlement. Part of the 'Celtic' fields were certainly laid out with reference to two round barrows (Fig. 1.7, (a) and (b)). These are clearly respected by and are earlier than the fields, but by an unknown margin. The relationship between the field system and the enclosures is considered below. Cultivation took place in the Roman period, as is made clear by scatters of pottery presumably sent out with manure. There is also a scatter of small pieces of 'foreign stone'. From what settlement this may have come is unknown. In post-Roman times a form of strip cultivation was carried out, which in places overlaid parts of Enclosures I and II, but not III as well as some of the 'Celtic' fields, though the linear features were generally avoided. W LIN and N LIN were with little doubt used as ways up to and across the Down. The double lynchet track contemporary with the 'Celtic' fields running south-east from Enclosure II , SE DL, may also have been used by those following the N LIN across Enclosure II, even into quite recent times.

In the last 200 years there is evidence that the Down was used to pasture horses as well as cattle. Some arable cultivation took place other than by ridged techniques, as evidenced by the fragments of 'Celtic' fields that can only have been degraded by such ploughing, perhaps following preliminary levelling. A dewpond of relatively recent date near the summit to the west of Enclosure I emphasises the need for water for stock and one of the ways it was met. The linears were very likely also used to get animals to and from the waterside meadows.

It is obvious that there is an extensive history of agrarian exploitation on Longbridge Deverill Cow Down. Glimpses of the sequence can be shown by fieldwork and air photographic observations but the situation is so complex and the remains so fragmentary that only the broadest statements of association and development can be advanced.

EARTHWORK ENCLOSURE III

The D-shaped enclosure is *c.* 0.6ha (1.5 acres) in size and defined by a ditch and external bank (Fig. 1.8). The ditch is 1.0m-1.2m deep, the greater dimensions generally relating to the straight eastern side. The ditch has a flattened U-shaped profile, varying in width from *c.* 2m-3 m at the base, to *c.* 6m-8m at the

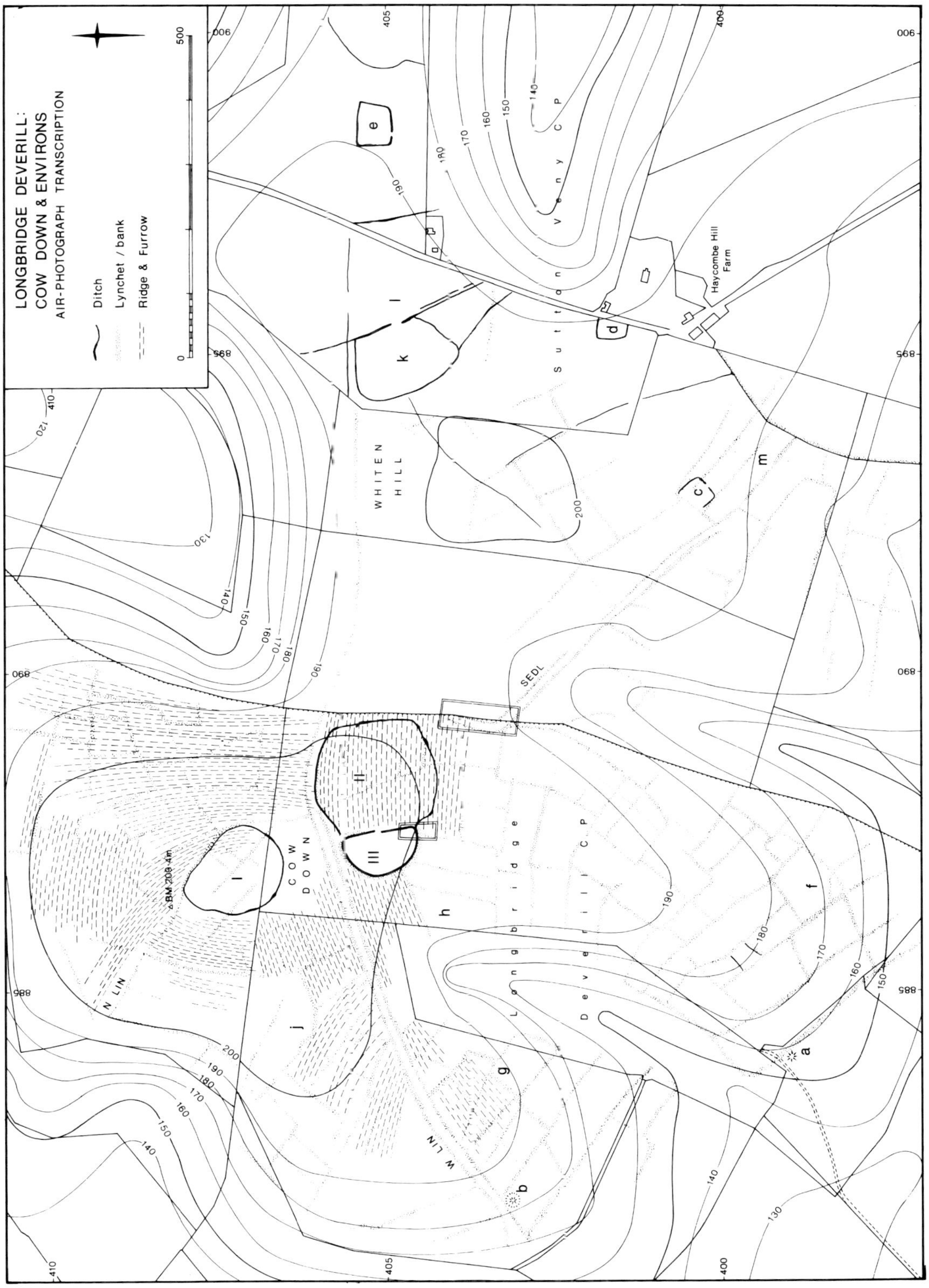

Fig. 1.7 Longbridge Deverill Cow Down and environs: air photograph transcription

top. There is one entrance, on the east side of the enclosure, across a causeway *c.* 6m wide. The ditches on either side of the entrance do not share the same alignment.

The external bank now visible is a curiously slight construction, less than 0.5m wide and standing to a height of only *c.* 0.3m-0.5m above the modern plough lynchet. It is absent along the east side. Traces of a possible internal bank have been recorded in the south-east corner of the enclosure. Here, there is a mound *c.* 13.0m long, *c.* 1m-2m wide and *c.* 0.4m high. The insignificant size of the remaining bank structure, so disproportionate to the ditch, suggests either original spreading or robbing, perhaps for top dressing. Slight ledging is visible at approximately 0.4m-0.5m above the ditch bottom on the outer face of the ditch, except along the eastern side.

Survey indicates that the enclosure overlies 'Celtic' fields. Its external bank cuts a 'Celtic' field lynchet meeting it from the south, just short of its southern tip (Fig.1.9). It is therefore certain that, at that point, the outside bank is later than the 'Celtic' field lynchet. Since this lynchet is as developed as others in the area, it can be said that the enclosure is subsequent to or very late in the history of the field system there. The northern side of the field, of which the lynchet is the western edge, is obviously somewhere beyond the earthwork bank and could be represented by the mounded area referred to previously. Two more lynchets, with corresponding slight steps in the circuit of the external bank, meet the enclosure from the south. The curve in the inner side of the ditch opposite the junction with the south-western lynchet may suggest contact with and subsequent alteration of a pre-existing structure. These two features again indicate that the enclosure is later than the 'Celtic' field system, already long established.

Apart from slight and regular undulations near the entrance that resulted from the excavations, the interior is featureless. Levelled profiles (Fig. 1.10 suggest that it was deliberately flattened. 'Celtic' field positions discussed above suggest that fields covered the whole area at one time before the enclosures were built.

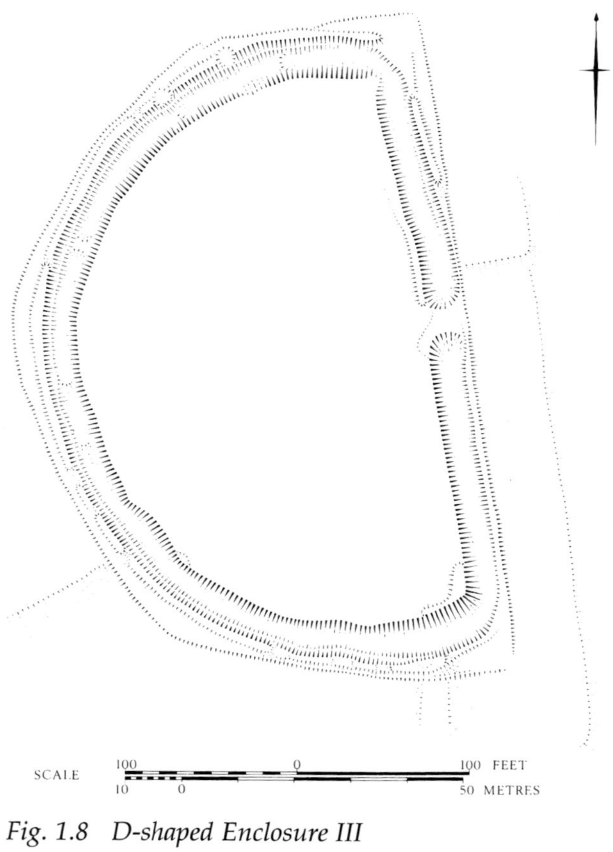

Fig. 1.8 D-shaped Enclosure III

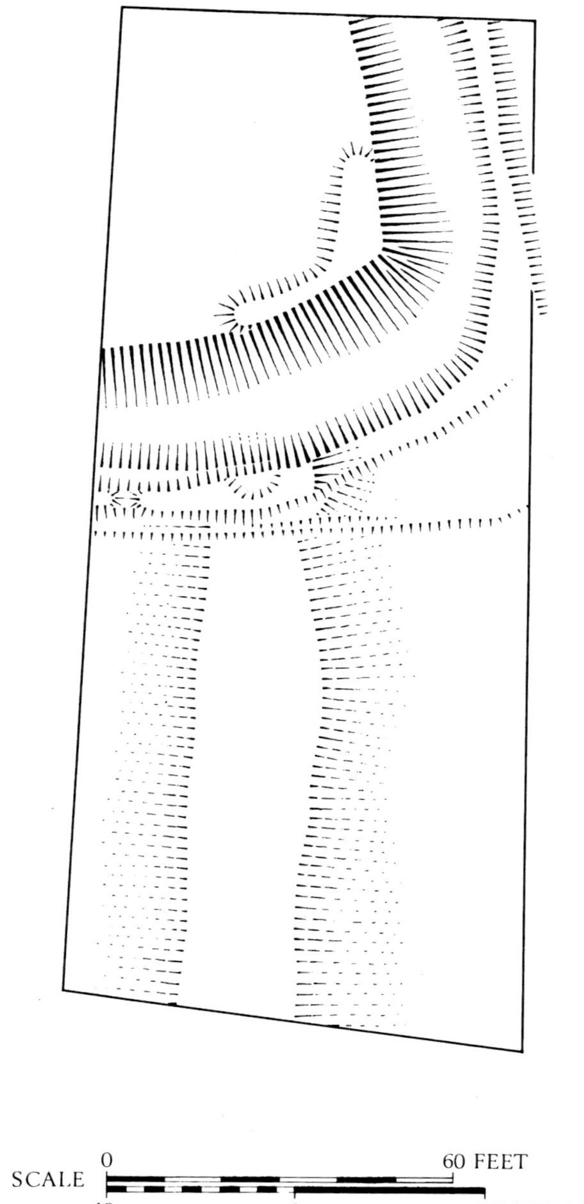

Fig. 1.9 'Celtic' field lynchet cut by Enclosure III

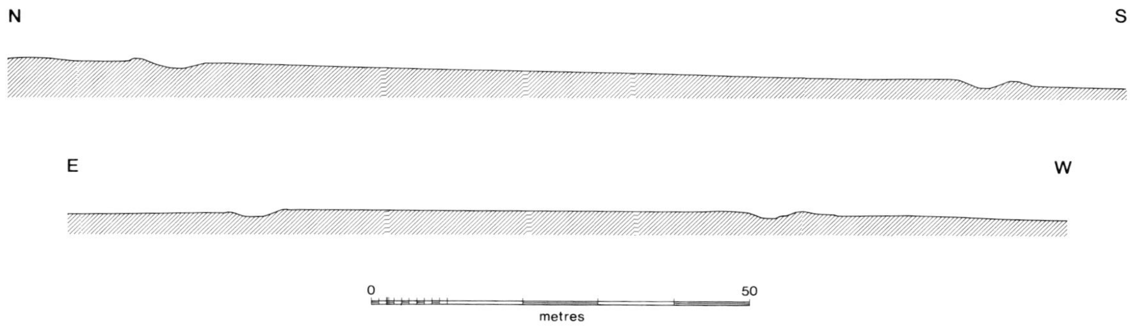

Fig. 1.10 Levelled profiles of Enclosure III

CONTEXT AND ANALOGY

Enclosures

The pattern of settlements – their spacing and grouping, the shapes of individual enclosures and the location of surviving 'Celtic' fields – is very incomplete. It should be stressed that, while the bigger enclosures may point to the existence of settlement, they may themselves have been but a transient part of such settlement. In addition, some other lesser enclosures are outliers and not adjacent to true settlement areas, rather like downland buildings, hay-guards or pounds in recent historic periods. The small rectangular enclosures (c), (d) and (e) shown on Fig 1.7 and such rare features as the scarped triangle tucked into a 'Celtic' field at (f)) on plan, may be examples of this.

The shape and size of individual enclosures are clearly significant, reflecting particular answers to specific needs and to the forces of tradition and status as well as to the resources available. The original form of Enclosure II is obscured by its elision with III, but it is likely that it comprised two opposed and curved, and two straight sides. If there was a west-facing entrance to Enclosure II, as the surviving causeway might suggest, then it is unusual. It has been estimated that fewer than 15% of known Iron Age enclosures in southern England have a west orientated entrance (Hill 1995, 12). Conversely, there is another form of enclosure rather more rectilinear in construction with a 'humped' projection. Enclosure I also has a suggestion of this type of projection.

Enclosure III could represent the western end of such a humped enclosure, taken up and preserved when the rest of Enclosure II was abandoned. However, its form is apparently without known parallel in a prehistoric context. It is the only surviving enclosure of the Longbridge Deverill complex visible at ground level. The earthworks survive where almost everything else has been flattened during prehistoric and later periods, retaining an unexpectedly sharp outline, given its once presumed age and subsequent history of use. The enclosure's survival is perhaps due to its use for some farming purpose in medieval and later times, the bank possibly reduced to provide marl for the fields, as is known to have happened elsewhere. Enclosure II is unlikely, on analogy with other contemporary sites, to have lacked a western side so, considering the remarkably revealing aerial photography, Enclosure III surely masks, incorporates or follows the line of the former western element of Enclosure II. Enclosure III overlies a relatively well preserved 'Celtic' field lynchet at its south-east point but other slight lynchets are truncated by its curved western side.

The enclosures on Cow Down and Whiten Hill are uncomplicated ditched features and contrast with other settlements usually of Roman date, where the addition of subsidiary enclosures has led to elaboration, as is the case on nearby Lord's Hill (Fig. 1.11).

'Celtic' Fields and Linear Ditches

'Celtic' fields covered the hilltop at different times and it is apparent that some form of organic development of the system took place (Fig. 1.12). There has been too much alteration in individual field size to make useful statistics, but it is apparent that field length varied between about 40m and 130m. One particular block south-west of Enclosures II and III was established later than the construction of round barrow (a)). The east face of an unploughed lynchet cut by a track at this location was cleaned, photographed and drawn by D. J. Bonney and Collin Bowen in the 1950s. It was clear that this was a positive accumulation only and no ancient fields beyond it are now identifiable with any certainty, in an area where a strip system probably extended before modern rearrangement. What seems most likely is that this lynchet represents the terminal line of a coherent hilltop block of prehistoric fields separate from and probably earlier than any 'Celtic' fields that may once have existed below it.

Linear ditches were an integral part of land management on Cow Down. Trackway W LIN provided access to the Deverill Valley to the west. It is now mostly marked by a degraded low bank or lynchet on either side of a fairly broad way, deeply

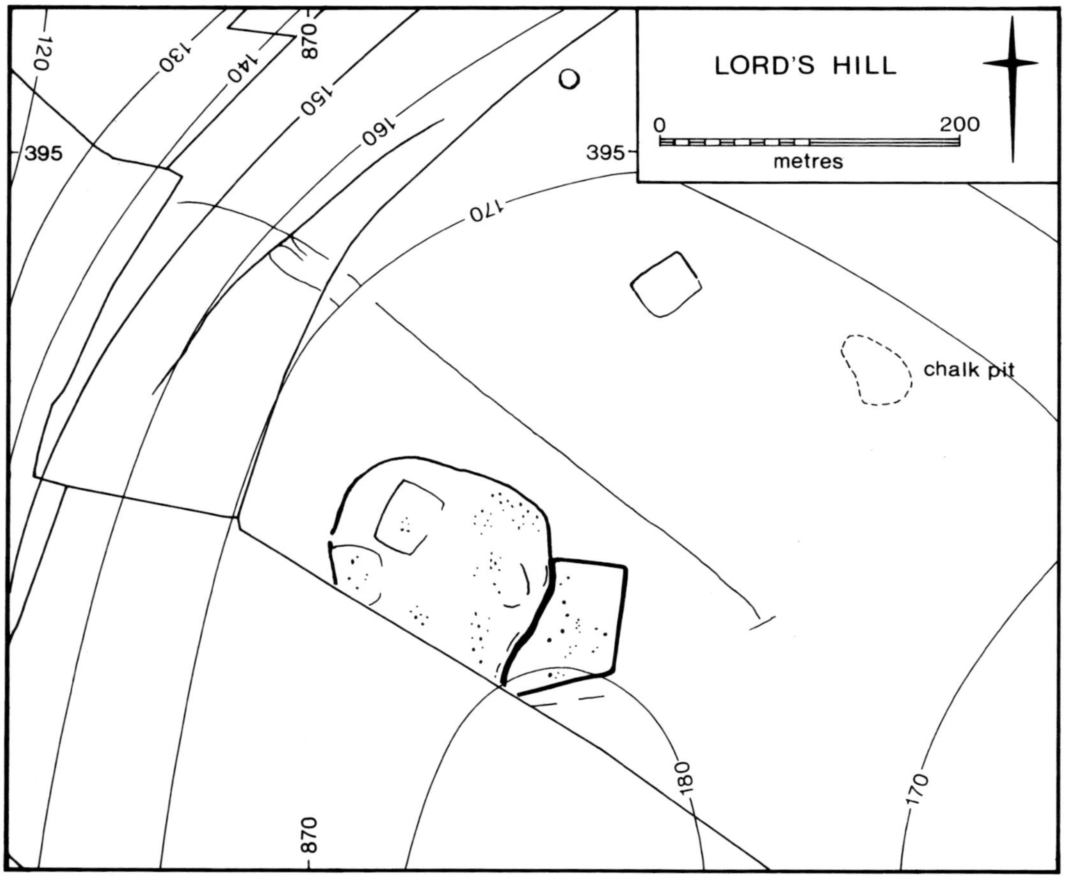

Fig. 1.11 The enclosure on Lord's Hill

hollowed in places, testifying to long wear. It may have been contemporary with a phase of Enclosure II since its course appears to incorporate the northern sector of the ditch of that enclosure. Local re-laying of the 'Celtic' field system is noticeable at the western end of the trackway, immediately to the east of the round barrow (b). There, a block of fields laid out axially from the track, and therefore probably contemporary with it, consists of three, possibly four, long divisions running south-east from W LIN to the edge of the coombe escarpment. Within each of these lines lateral subdivisions parallel to the main spine create smaller field plots averaging *c.* 100 m x 50 m in area. These smaller fields are superimposed upon earlier elements of the system, which are oblique to W LIN, (g). A 'Celtic' field lynchet abutting Enclosure III at the south-west is parallel to the W LIN, and may thus also be part of the new layout.

To the south of Enclosures II and III, there is further evidence for the amalgamation and alteration of existing fields. Lateral divisions within fields have been deliberately removed to create a longer form (h). This can also be seen north of the trackway, W LIN, south-west of Enclosure I. Amongst fields with an axial relationship to the track, there is one block on a different alignment, where the fields average *c.* 25 m in breadth and more than *c.* 70 m in length. These may represent the vestiges of earlier fields, subsequently re-laid. Indeed, the attempt to accommodate the earlier system south-west of Enclosure I created a very irregular pattern (j). Enclosures I and II were, therefore, possibly contemporaneous with the trackway and an adapted field system. If so, then one agricultural unit perhaps embraced Enclosure II and its contiguous fields to the south of W LIN, another comprised Enclosure I and fields north of the track. The position and function within such a framework of the double lynchet trackway SE DL, which approached Cow Down from the south-west is unknown. This is now generally seen on the ground as one abnormally long scarp, the usual result of ploughed infill of such a feature, which funnels into the possible open space south-east of Enclosure II. It is also likely that at different times it led up to the hill and also across it. To the south-east it runs out south of the small square enclosure to the west of Haycombe Hill Farm (c). However, SE DL does post-date the 'Celtic' field system south-east of Enclosure II, since its orientation alters markedly where they meet. Its destination is unascertainable, any northward continuation masked by later ridge and furrow cultivation.

The trackways were clearly important as a means of communication across the ridge. W LIN

Fig. 1.12 'Celtic' fields on Cow Down (1956)

continues east from Enclosure II and passes north of the enclosure on Whiten Hill (Fig 1.7 (k)). Significantly, this sub-oval enclosure of *c.* 1.6ha (4 acres), is bounded to the east by a linear ditch, another subdivision of the ridge top (l)). This ditch line, in part double, which may reflect its usage as a track, is aligned roughly NW-SE, its northern limit terminating at the sharp edge of the escarpment overlooking the Wylye Valley. Both this ditch and the northern linear N LIN further to the west intersect W LIN, suggesting perhaps that there was a major reorientation in the axis of communication at some point. Two smaller, sub-rectangular enclosures are located to the south and to the south-west of the Whiten Hill enclosure (c) and (d)). They are separated by another linear ditch, again aligned on a NW-SE axis. At the south, this and another linear ditch form a butt junction. Long 'Celtic' fields were developed axially to the west from this ditch (Fig. 1.7 (m). To the east other ditches, also aligned NW-SE, testify to a regular and well-structured division of the landscape. A sub-rectangular enclosure, *c.* 0.4ha (1 acre) in area (Fig. 1.7 (e)), is located in the most easterly subdivision on the escarpment edge approximately 300m to the east of Whiten Hill.

The hollowed trackway N LIN runs in a sinuous course from the foot of the chalk escarpment in the north-west (ST 884409) to a point where it becomes indistinguishable from the fields south of Enclosure II *c.* 800m to the south-east. Its final destination may have been SE DL. This track is flanked by associated 'Celtic' fields. These are perhaps clearest in the area formerly occupied by Enclosure I. The track changes direction approximately 30m before it reaches the enclosure. This change in direction may indicate an attempt to avoid a barrier left by the enclosure. Here, the track cannot be clearly isolated from the fields which overlie the enclosure. The remains of 'Celtic' fields to the north-east of Enclosure I have been severely mutilated by ridge and furrow, but there are suggestions that lynchets developed axially from the trackway. To the south of the intersection with W LIN, the track traverses the interior of the presumably by then abandoned Enclosure II. This arrangement presupposes that the enclosure is earlier than the track. This track must once have been a substantial earthwork. In 1956 its course was marked by a linear scarp *c.* 0.6m high, but today it survives to a height of no more than *c.* 0.2m. It is worth noting that the trackway crossed an area in Enclosure II which excavation showed was devoid of domestic structures and that it in fact passed between two of the houses. Within the enclosure, and east of the track, elements of 'Celtic' fields can be identified from air photographs. There is no lynchetting immediately to the west of it, although ridge and furrow in that area adds to the difficulty in interpreting the remains. However, 'Celtic' fields may indeed have been absent there, for they would have impeded access to Enclosure III. The external 'bank' of the enclosure is possibly only upcast from ploughing the adjacent 'Celtic' fields during this phase of activity. It is not present along the east side of the enclosure, which corresponds to the field free zone.

The Post-Roman Context

There is no record of archaeological finds of pre-conquest Saxon date around the D-shaped enclosure complex. There are no recorded pre-Conquest charters for the manor, and so it is impossible to ascertain the line of the early estate boundary. However, other better attested manors in the Wessex chalklands suggest the likelihood that the present parish boundary may indeed follow the Saxon boundary and date back at least to the 5th or 6th century AD, or probably earlier given the proximity of significant prehistoric features such as linear earthworks (Bonney 1979). The earliest reference to the manor of Longbridge Deverill occurs in Domesday Book, but its distinguishing prefix is not recorded until 1239 (Gover *et al.* 1939, 166). Cow Down itself is first documented in 1655. The manor formed part of the estates of the Abbey of Glastonbury from the Conquest until the Dissolution when it passed to the Thynnes of Longleat. Its inclusion within Glastonbury Abbey's estates has resulted in extensive surviving documentary evidence for customs, disputes and agricultural practices within the manor. Although these have not been examined in detail, the historical evidence does illuminate some aspects of the archaeology.

The prehistoric enclosures and field system are extensively overlain by ridge and furrow, which can be assumed to be of post-Roman date. The earliest documentary evidence for the open field system occurs in Wessex in the 7th century AD. It is, however, unlikely that the remains on Cow Down are as early as this. Indeed, it has been demonstrated that the Saxon land use in the Wessex chalk valley estates is likely to have adhered closely to a pattern of valley meadowland, hillside arable and downland pasture (Hooke 1988). It is in fact most likely that the ridge and furrow forms part of a post-Conquest and possibly sporadic expansion of the arable onto land which is best, and traditionally, suited to pasture. Rental documents record an increase in the frequency of ploughing of the demesne in the early 13th century (VCH Wilts 4, 13), and this evidence of an attempt to increase production may also provide a context for the extension of the arable onto previously unploughed land. A fairly short episode of medieval ploughing is suggested by the good preservation of the underlying prehistoric fields. It is clear that the Down had been returned to pasture well before 1748, when an estate map shows the area to be completely free of any vestiges of relict field or strip boundaries (map in possession of Marquis of Bath at Longleat). The Down ceased to be ploughed much earlier, most probably in the late 14th or 15th century when there is extensive evidence in Wiltshire, as elsewhere, for arable land being taken out of cultivation and turned over to pasture, commonly for sheep.

The use of the Down for pasture continued until the 20th century, and successive air photographs chronicle the degradation of the earthwork remains after the resumption of cultivation. Two prominent features appear to be associated with earlier pastoral activities. The first is the dew pond (ST 882406) sited on the crest of the natural scarp, *c.* 500m to the south-west of the enclosures, and which would have provided a source of fresh water for animals grazing on the downland pasture. The second is the D-shaped enclosure itself. Morphological, stratigraphical and locational criteria all suggest that this was probably in use in the late/post-medieval period. This construction or refurbishment clearly post-dates the ridge and furrow as it is in no way degradedby it.

CONCLUSION

In summary then, our understanding of the origins, history and use of the D-shaped Enclosure III remain somewhat enigmatic. Anomalies in the character of Enclosure III as a prehistoric earthwork include the relatively small area enclosed, a very small external bank, a substantial and wide ditch and a very wide entrance gap. The fieldwork demonstrated that the field system is clearly complex and that it developed and changed over a long time. Thin scatters of Roman pottery indicate arable manuring during that period, though associated settlement evidence has not been found. There is clear evidence for extensive ploughing of the Down in medieval-type broad ridge and furrow, and some of the tracks noted on the plan were with little doubt used in this phase. The position of the enclosure in this context indicates at least that it was respected and that it was almost certainly being used and perhaps enhanced during the medieval period, possibly as a stock pen. There is a final possibility that a former landowner deliberately refurbished the enclosure as part of an ornamental garden landscape feature. If some prehistoric version of Enclosure III had existed, perhaps as an element of Enclosure II, its remains do not correspond to the now extant earthworks that were investigated during fieldwork and excavation.

Collin Bowen sadly died on 25th October 2011. I feel enormously privileged to have worked with Collin, and still remember, vividly, following in his wake as we ascended the slope to Cow Down. Mini-tape recorder to hand, noting his thoughts as he climbed the hill and then me, mesmerised by his ability to make sense of the slightest archaeological features – all of which helped build the detail of this report. A remarkable archaeologist.

Chapter 2: The Structural Remains – Method of Excavation and Recording

by Sonia Chadwick Hawkes and Christopher Hawkes

A 1956 proposal to undertake tree plantation of the D-shaped enclosure (later designated Enclosure III) prompted the Ancient Monuments Division of the Ministry of Works to commission a small scale excavation at Longbridge Deverill Cow Down. The enclosure was generally believed at that time to be

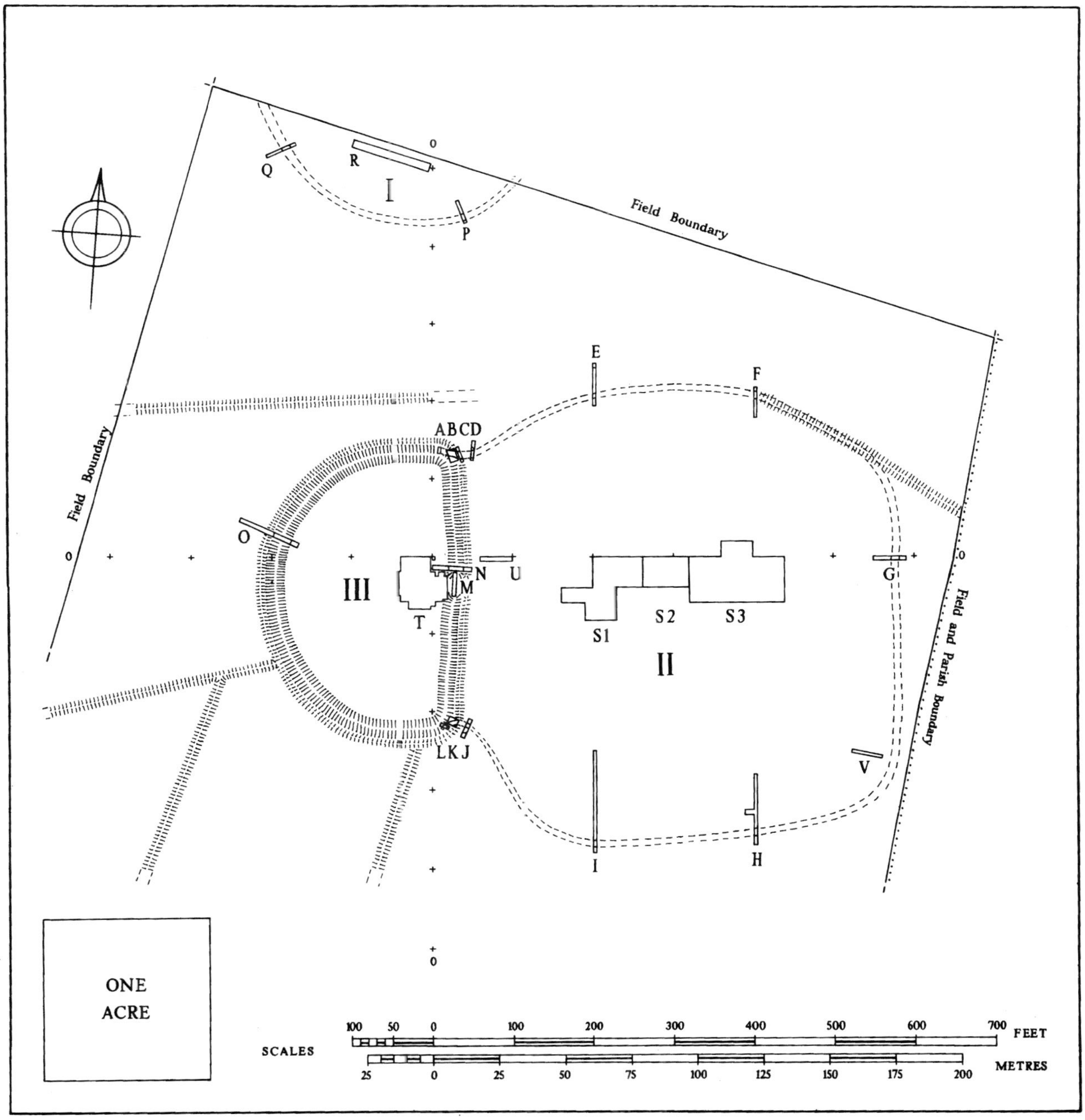

Fig. 2.1 Enclosures I, II and III and trench locations

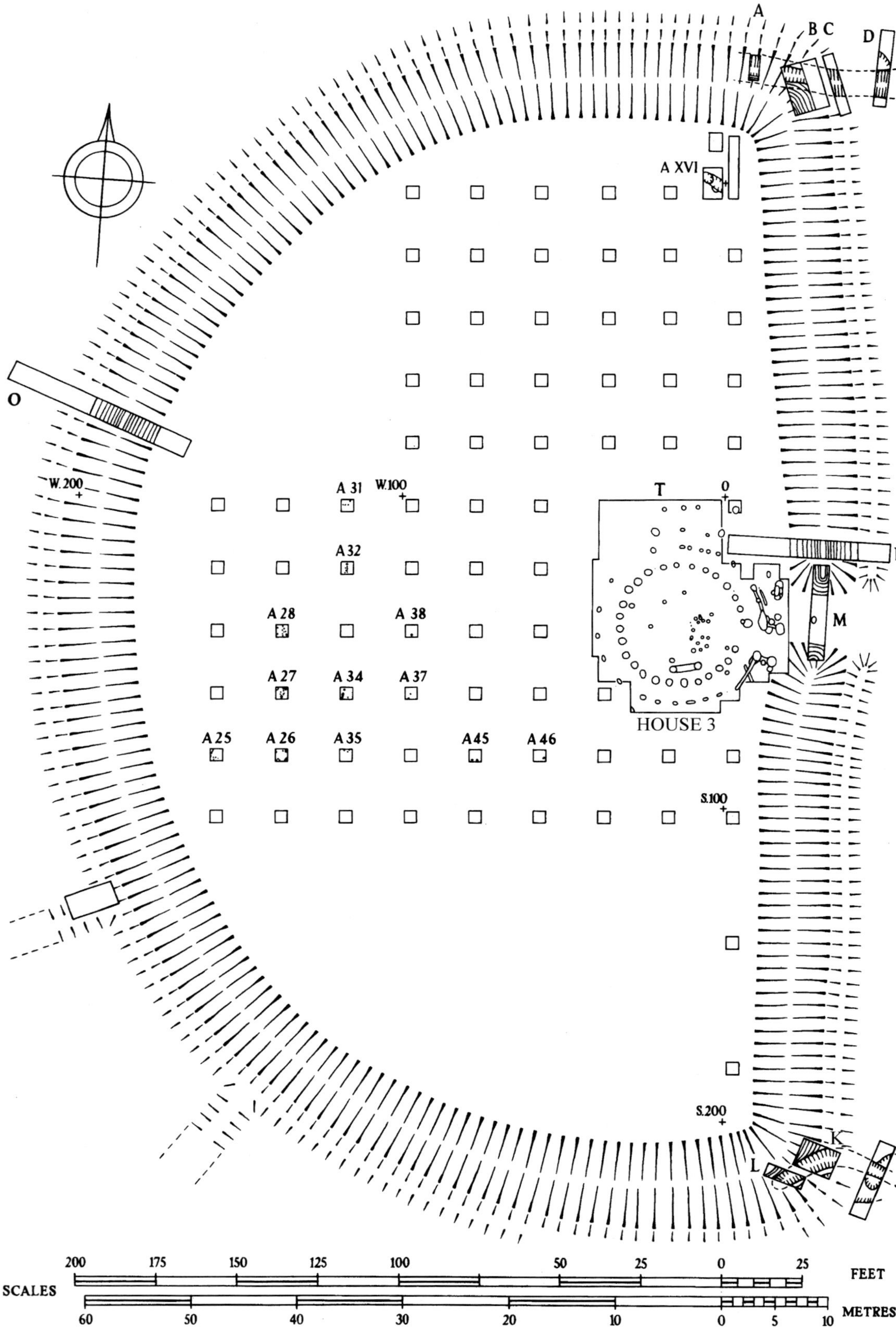

Fig. 2.2 Trial trenching in Enclosure III

Fig. 2.3 Cutting trial trenches in Enclosure III

a Roman earthwork and was described as such in the *Victoria County History* for Wiltshire (1957, 83). Air Ministry photographs taken in 1945 and 1946 showed that the enclosure lay within a 'Celtic' field system (Chapter 1, Figs. 1.3-1.4).

The 1956 brief instructed excavation of the enclosure in order to date it, establish its character and its relationship with the field system. The ditches and causeway were sectioned (Fig. 2.1, Cuttings M, N, O) and most of the interior investigated by trial trenching of the topsoil down to the natural in 0.91m (1 yard) box trenches (Figs 2.2-2.3). The trenches are visible in J.K. St. Joseph's 1957 aerial photograph (Fig. 2.4). The trial trenching exposed numerous features, including the remains of a large roundhouse (House 3).

During the first season significant quantities of burnt flint and abraded pottery were recovered from the field to the east of Enclosure III, prompting Sonia Hawkes to examine aerial photographs taken in 1955 by St Joseph before she engaged in a second season of excavation. These revealed that the enclosure formed part of a larger settlement complex within the 'Celtic' fields. The outline of a large ditched enclosure (Enclosure II) and internal features were visible in the photographs and also on the ground of the recently ploughed fields (Figs. 1.5-1.6). The location of Enclosure II corresponded with a concentration of pottery and burnt flints. A third enclosure (Enclosure I) lying approximately 100m north-west of Enclosure II was also visible in the aerial photographs (Fig. 1.6 – left bottom of ploughed field; Fig. 2.1, top left).

The 1957 excavations of what was, by then, recognised to be a major Iron Age complex, focussed on the interior of Enclosure III. The roundhouse recognised in the trial trenches was fully exposed just inside the east-facing entrance of Enclosure III and the structure was excavated as House 3 in Cutting T (Fig. 2.2), using a grid system shown in Fig. 2.5. The intersections of the ditches of Enclosures II and III were examined in Cuttings B and K (Figs 2.1, 2.2, 2.11, 2.17), demonstrating that Enclosure III post-dated Enclosure II by several centuries and that House 3, therefore, actually lay within the western part of Enclosure II and predated the construction of Enclosure III.

In 1958 the ditches of Enclosures I and II were sectioned and a large open area, S 1-3 (Figs 2.1 and 2.6), was opened in the interior of Enclosure II. The trench was stripped by hand using a 6.1m grid in order to recover as much evidence as possible from the as yet only lightly ploughed soils (Figs. 2.7-2.8). The well-preserved remains of three addtional roundhouses (Houses 1, 2 and 4) were exposed in Areas S1-3, along with numerous pits and postholes.

Fig. 2.4 Enclosure III under excavation, photographed by J.K. St. Joseph 15 April 1957 (original photograph held at Cambridge University Collection of Aerial Photography: UN88)

In 1960 the previously excavated parts of Houses I and 2 were re-opened for further excavation and a 30m by 2.8m trench (Cutting R) was opened in the interior of Enclosure I (Figs 2.1 and 2.9).

No further excavation was undertaken on the site after 1960 but the Royal Commission on Historical Monuments continued a survey programme in the wider area of the site until the early 1980s. This work was subsequently continued by David McOmish of English Heritage, who describes the results in Chapter 1. During 1882-83 a small scale fieldwalking exercise undertaken by Peggy Guido and Eve Machin on the interior of Enclosure II adjacent to Enclosure III revealed that, based on the quantity of finds recovered from the ploughsoil, plough damage during the previous 20 years had been extensive (Appendix 1).

In the following descriptions of the structural remains, archaeological features (cuts) are designated by prefixes assigned by Hawkes: PH-posthole; P-pit; D-ditch; H-hollow. Rather than using a sequential numbering system for the fills of features, these were in every case assigned numbers 1-n, prefixed by the feature abbreviation (*eg* P25, 'layers' 1-9), as was standard practice at the time.

THE ENCLOSURES

by Lisa Brown (based on notes by Sonia Chadwick Hawkes)

The earthworks of the three enclosures were investigated in narrow trenches, referred to in the records as 'Cuttings I, II and III' (Fig. 2.1). Only the southern part of Enclosure I was accessible to the excavators, and two Cuttings, P and Q, were made across this stretch. The three extant sides of Enclosure II were exposed in Cuttings C-J, the intersections between Enclosures II and III in Cuttings A, B, L, and K, the western side of Enclosure III in Cutting O, and its entrance in Cuttings M and N. The trench dimensions were not consistent and were not always accurately recorded, but most were only 1-1.5m wide.

Enclosure I

Only the southern end of oval Enclosure I was available for excavation (Figs 1.6 and 2.1). Two trenches, Cuttings P and Q, both measuring *c.* 12.5m long x *c.* 1m wide, were dug across the enclosure ditch and Cutting R, measuring 5m x 2.8m, focussed on the southern interior (Figs 2.9-2.10).

Enclosure I Ditches

The ditch sections were drawn (Fig. 2.9) but no written record of the fills exists in the archive, nor were the position of finds indicated. The fill sequences can be summarised on the basis of the section drawings, which are fortunately quite detailed.

The south-west facing section of Cutting P was exposed in a ditch *c.* 1.25m deep and some 3m wide. The ditch had a U-shape profile and had, on the south-east side, either been cut by another feature, widened out by quarrying or similar activity, or had cut an earlier feature *c.* 0.50m deep. The initial fill (5) appears to have been composed of small chalk pieces, probably eroded from the upper sides of the ditch. The drawing shows (5) filling the hollow on the south-east side of the ditch, but this was probably unrelated material. Fill (4) represented a conflation of two deposits, chalky soil created by erosion from both sides of theditch and a chalk mass

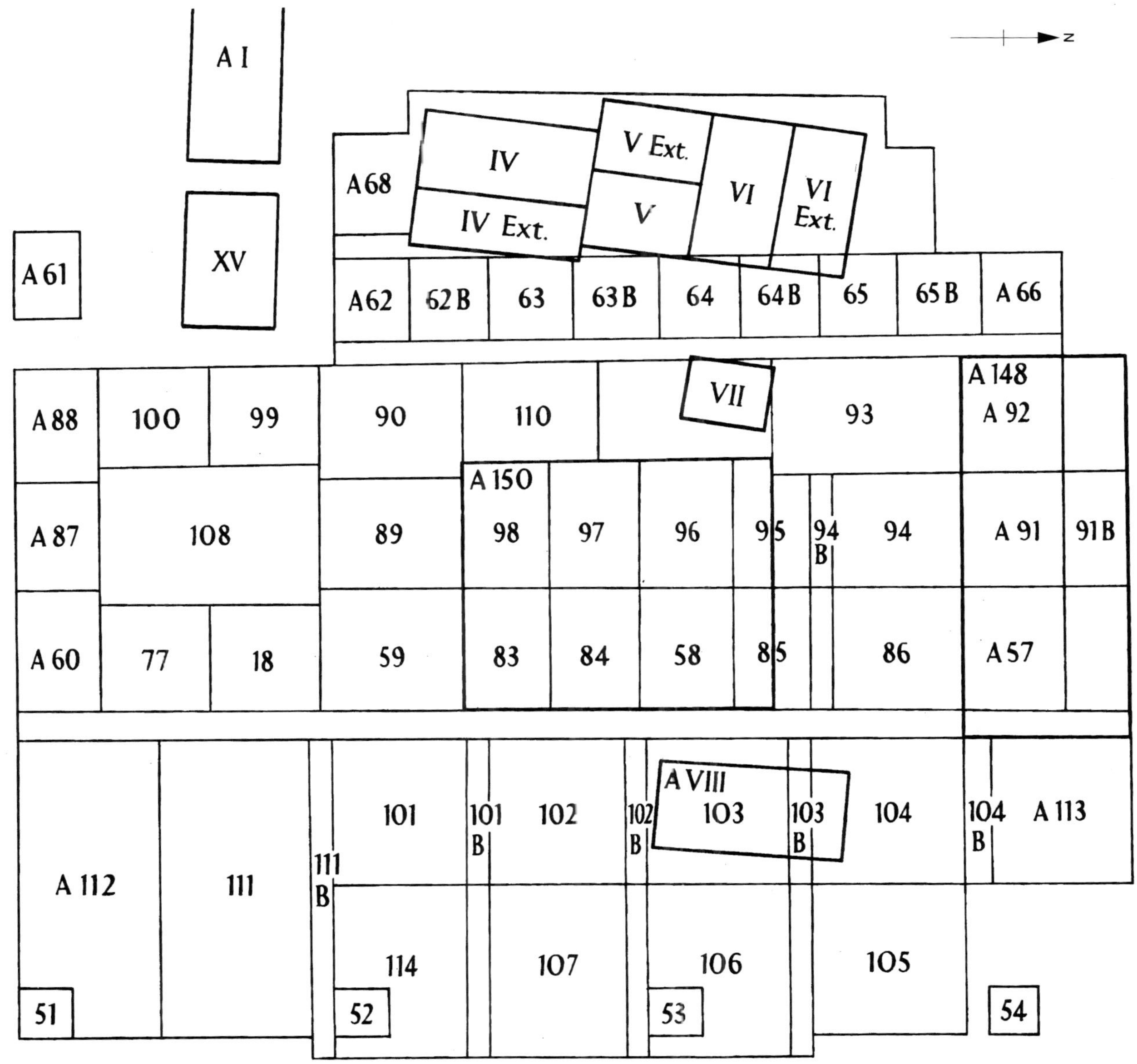

Fig. 2.5 Enclosure III Cutting T: plan of original cuttings

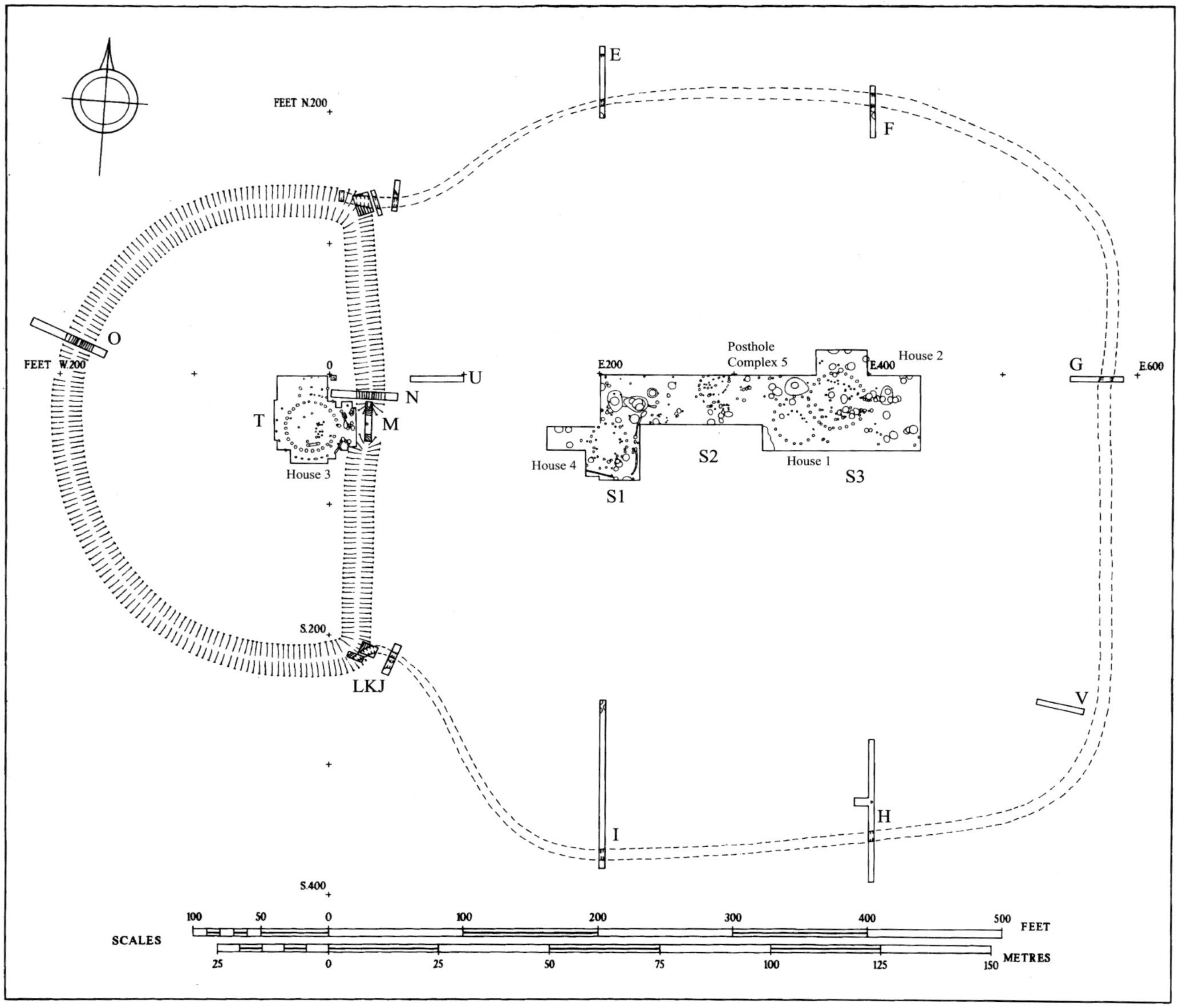

Fig. 2.6 Enclosures II and III: plan of cuttings

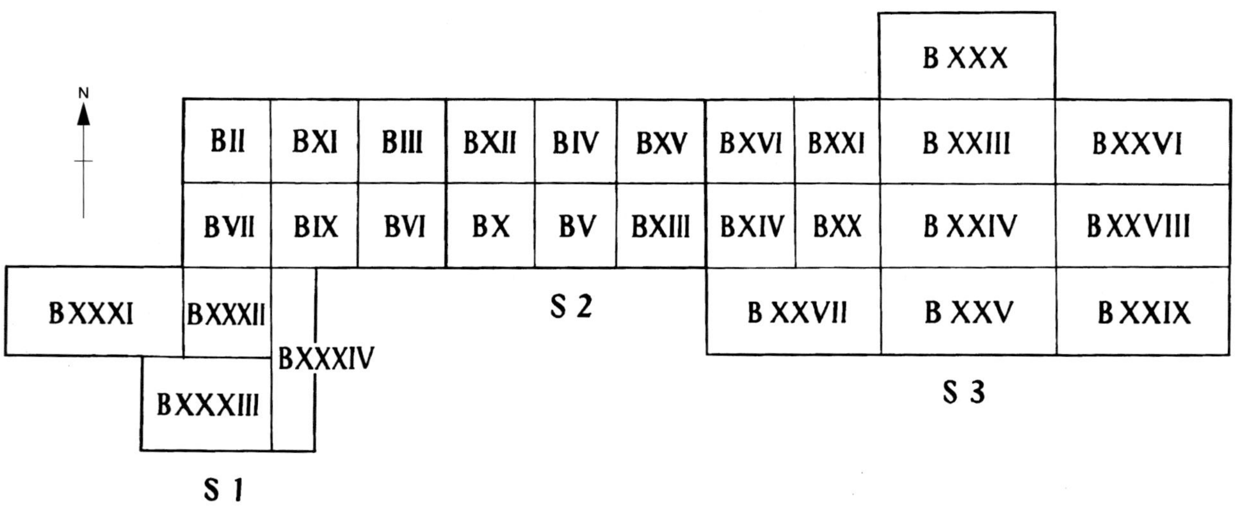

Fig. 2.7 Enclosure II Area S1-3: plan of original cuttings

Fig. 2.8 Enclosure II Area S1-3 under excavation

filling the central hollow, which may have derived from a bank. It was at this stage that the south-east side of the ditch may have been dug into. Once (4) had accumulated, the shallow hollow above was filled by (3), a sterile looking chalky soil. The overlying layer (2), which runs both across the ditch and the shallow feature on the south-east side was probably a deliberate levelling dump incorporating flint and chalk rubble.

The south-western stretch of the ditch, exposed in Cutting Q, is quite distinct to that in Cutting P. The profile suggests that an original V-shape ditch *c.* 1.20m deep, containing chalky fill (4) was recut as a broader, shallower feature, leaving the narrow base of the original intact (Fig. 2.9). A large stone, indicated by the drawing conventions and a photograph (Fig. 2.10) to be a massive flint block, occupied the base of the recut. Shattered chalk and soils (3) accumulated above from both sides of the ditch edge. Fill (2), apparently a clean soil with minimal chalk content, differs from the clearly deliberate fill of occupation-rich soil (2) in Cutting P. The contrasting profiles and fill sequences of the two stretches of the enclosure ditch appear to testify to a complex history of recutting, natural erosion and deliberate backfilling.

Enclosure I Interior

Cutting R proved too small an area to adequately characterise settlement or other activity within the enclosure. A number of pits, working hollows and postholes were exposed but no specific structures identified (Fig. 2.9). However, aerial photography and field survey evidence (see Chapter I) suggest that Enclosures I and II were probably occupied by separate farms. The ceramic evidence (Chapter III) indicates that Enclosure I was probably occupied from sometime between the 9th-8th century BC, on the evidence of a short-rim furrowed bowl from the fill of Pit 1 (Chapter 3, Fig. 3.17, no. 5), a type comparable to those from House 1 in Enclosure II. The bowl fragment is likely to have been residual in the pit, as a complete situlate jar (Fig. 3.17, no.1; Table 2.1), probably of 6th-5th century BC date, lay on the base, but it nonetheless testifies to earlier activity in the vicinity.

Altogether five pits were exposed in this small trench, four of which (Pits 1-4) were fully or partly excavated. The section drawings of Pits 1-3 demonstrate that they were of cylindrical form and relatively shallow at *c.* 1m deep, a typical feature of this pit type, as recognised at Danebury, Hampshire (Whittle 1984, 131). Pits 1 and 2 contained small chalk shatter that may have eroded from the pit edges following the accumulation of thin deposits of primary silts. The upper fills of both appear to have been deliberate levelling dumps incorporating quantities of burnt flint (Fig. 2.9). Pit 3 was only 0.50m deep and just over 1m in diameter and appears to have been deliberately backfilled with small chalk and burnt flint rubble. There is no

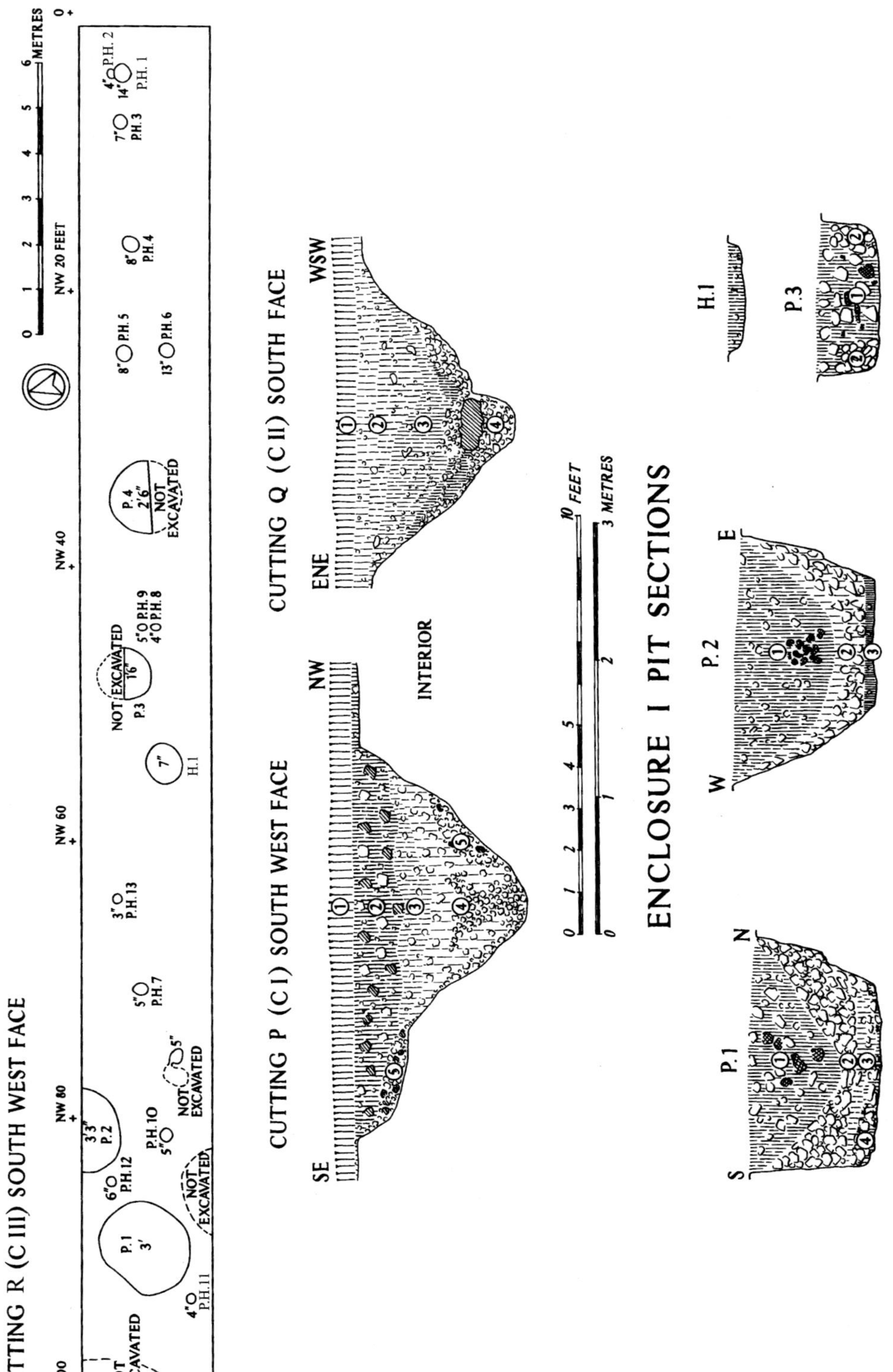

Fig. 2.9 Enclosure I Cuttings P, Q and R

Table 2.1 Enclosure I pits

Pit	Form	Dia m	Depth m	No. fills & description	Finds
1	cylindrical	1.67	0.92	4 – chalk shatter; burnt flint	186 sh pottery; pyrites; bone (a)
2	cylindrical	1.78	0.9	3 – chalk shatter, burnt flint	Pyrites; bone (a) (h)
3	cylindrical	1.12	0.46	2 – chalk and flint rubble	-
4	Not illus.	1.60	0.76	2 – not recorded	Pyrites; bone (a)

Key: a-animal bone; h-human bone

Table 2.2 Enclosure I postholes

PH	Dia m	Depth m	Morphology	Finds
1	0.43	0.35	Vertical sides, flat base	-
2	0.18	0.10	-	-
3	0.35	0.18	Vertical sides, flat base	-
4	0.38	0.21	Vertical sides, flat base	Bone (a)
5	0.38	0.21	Rounded profile	Unspec charcoal
6	0.35	0.33	Vertical sides, flat base	-
7	0.33	0.13	-	-
8	0.18	0.13	Rounded profile	-
9	0.21	0.23	Rounded profile	-
10	0.28	0.13	Rounded profile	-
11	0.21	0.15	Rounded profile	-
12	0.21	0.15	Vertical sides, flat base	
13	0.21	0.75	-	

Fig. 2.10 Enclosure I Cutting Q: south face of ditch section (1958)

extant section drawing of Pit 4 but the records indicate that it was 1.60m across and only 0.76m deep, filled with soil containing chalk and burnt flint overlying a layer of chalk rubble (Appendix 2B). Only Pit 1 yielded pottery, Pits 2, 3 and 4 only animal bone and pyrites. The fragmented jar found in Pit 1 had been placed close to or directly on the base, clearly reflecting a deliberate act.

Summary details of the pits are presented in Table 2.1.

The few other features exposed in Cutting R included a feature described as a hollow (H1). It measured 0.74m wide 0.18m deep and was filled with chalky soil and produced no finds (Fig. 2.9). A number of postholes appear in plan on Fig. 2.9 but no section drawings exist and little detail was recorded apart from dimensions (Table 2.2). The brief fill descriptions (Appendix 2 C) suggest that none of the postholes contained substantial or obvious packing material, nor were post dimensions discernable. The shape of PH2, 7 and 13 was not recorded, but the others are of two shapes, some with vertical sides and a flat base (PHs 1, 3, 4, 6, 12), the others with a rounded profile (PHs 5, 8-11). The two deepest (PHs 1 and 3) were of the vertical sided variety, but there seems otherwise to be no particular correlation between shape and depth. PH2 may have recut PH1, or was ancillary to it. A fragment of animal bone and charcoal of unknown species were the only finds from the postholes.

Enclosure I may have contained houses similar to those in Enclosure II but, unfortunately, the opportunity was not taken when ploughing afforded the first modern threat to this smaller enclosure to explore it more fully. There is not only the whole unanswered question of when Enclosure I was abandoned and given over to the plough, but also the question of if and how it related functionally and socially to its larger neighbour. That could perhaps have been answered by comparison of roundhouse structures as well as artefacts.

Enclosure II

The Enclosure II ditch defined an area roughly 160m x 175m. In plan the western terminals merge into the earthworks of D-shaped Enclosure III, which was shown in excavation to post-date it. The ditch defining Enclosure II was sectioned in 12 Cuttings (A-L) (Figs. 2.1; 2.11-2.18).

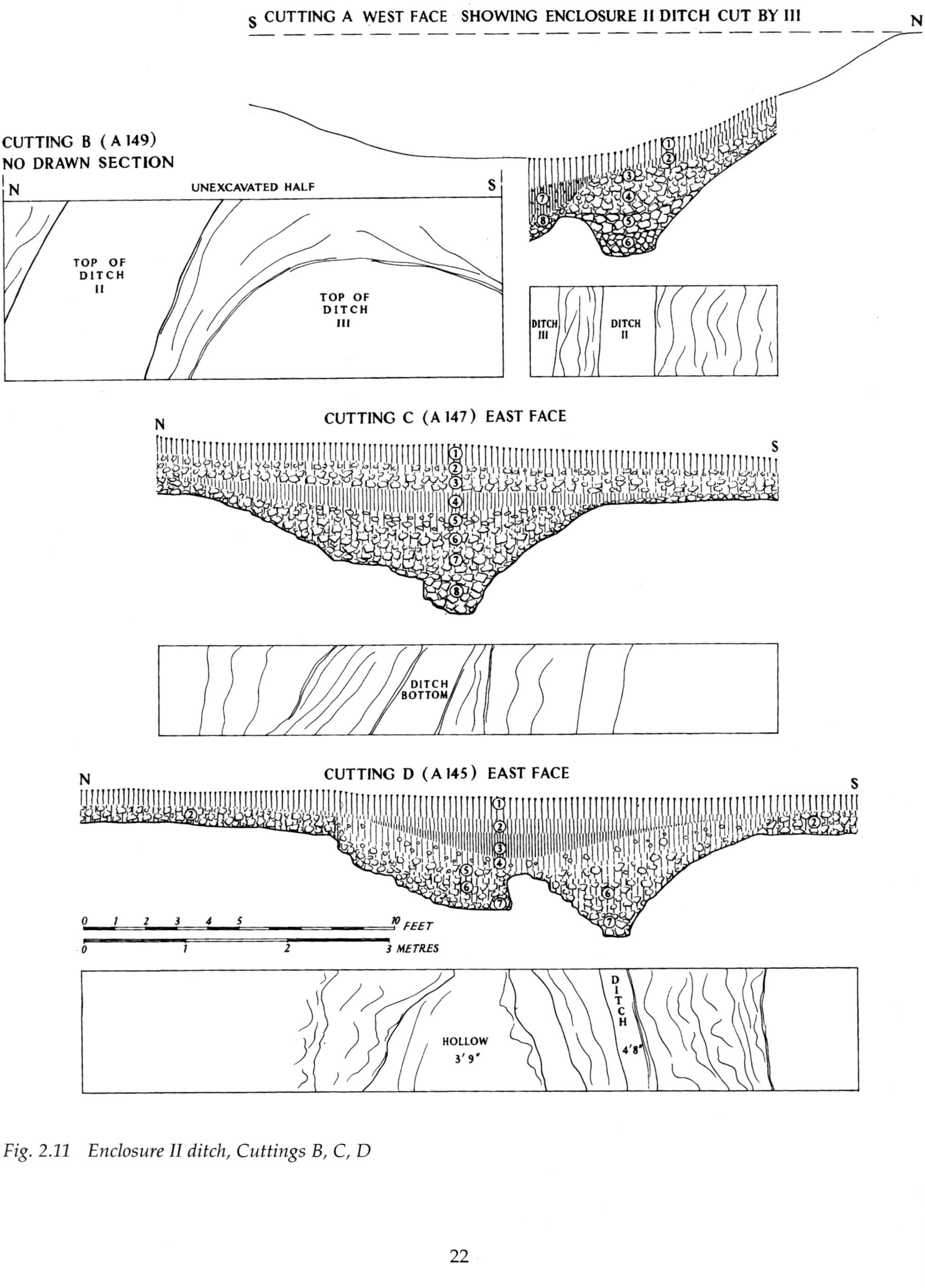

Fig. 2.11 Enclosure II ditch, Cuttings B, C, D

Enclosure II Ditches

Cuttings A and B and Cuttings K and L, at the north-east and south-east junctions with Enclosure III, were positioned to investigate the relationship between Enclosures II and III. The results clearly demonstrated that the ditch of Enclosure III cut that of Enclosure II.

The section drawings and photographs of the group of cuttings (A-D) across the north-west corner of Enclosure II show a fill sequence dominated by chalk rubble and very chalky soil, possibly material from a no longer extant bank (Fig. 2.11-2.13). Alternatively, the chalk rubble, which appears in some of the sections (especially Cutting A) to be carefully positioned rather than slumped or

Fig. 2.12 Enclosures II/III Cutting B: view of ditch sections from the southeast

Fig. 2.13 Enclosure II Cutting D: east face of ditch section

fallen, may represent an operation to level this part of the Enclosure II ditch prior to excavating the ditch of Enclosure III. A deep hollow to the north of the ditch, exposed in Cutting D, may have been the result of chalk quarrying at some point. A fragment of a burnished bowl with a sharply carinated body (Fig. 3.32, no.1) was recovered from the primary fill (6) of the ditch in Cutting D.

The ditch sections exposed in Cuttings E and F (Fig. 2.14), on the northern side of the enclosure, also show chalk rubble as components of the fills (eg Cutting E (5) and Cutting F (8)), but interspersed

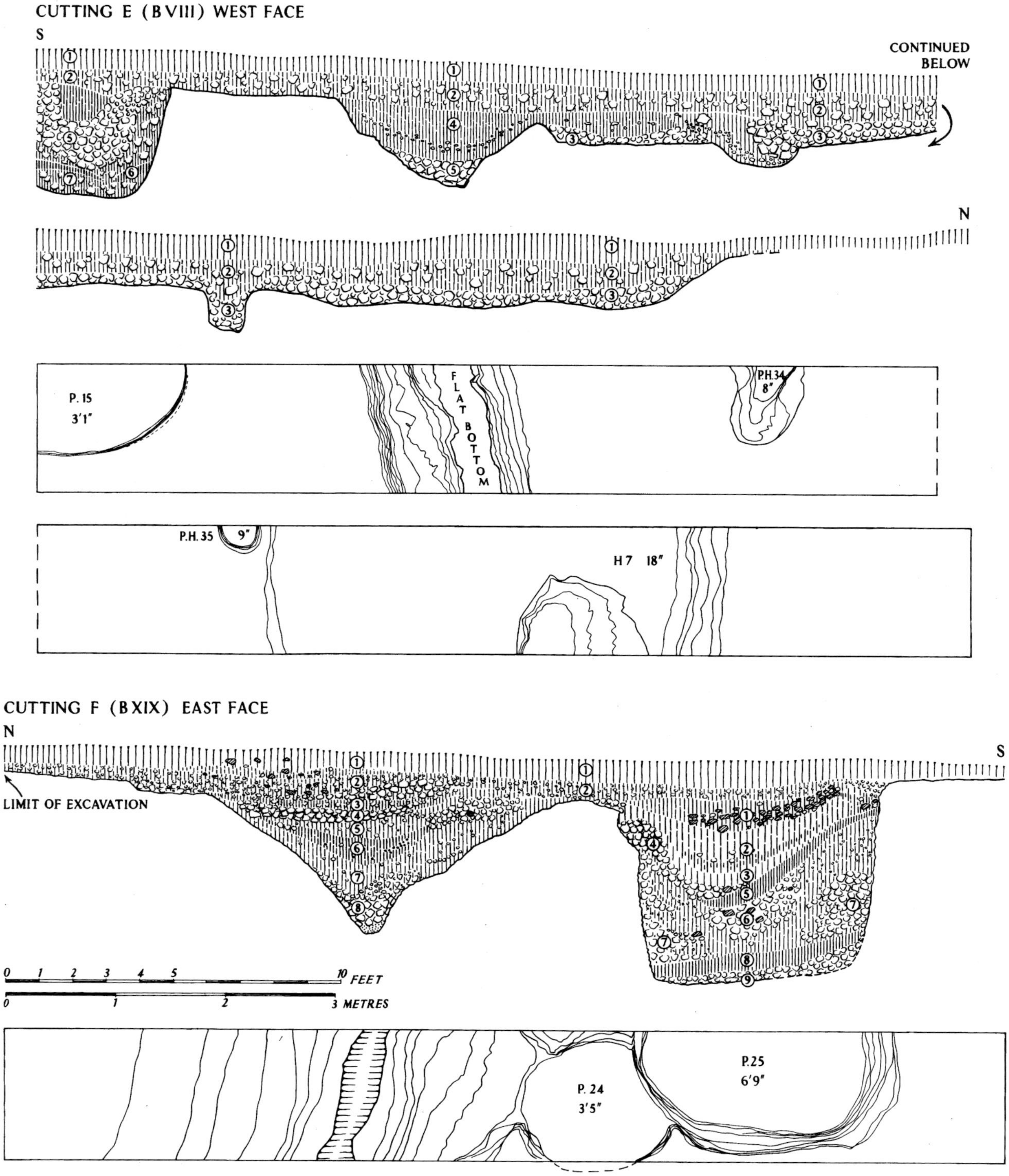

Fig. 2.14 Enclosure II Cuttings E and F

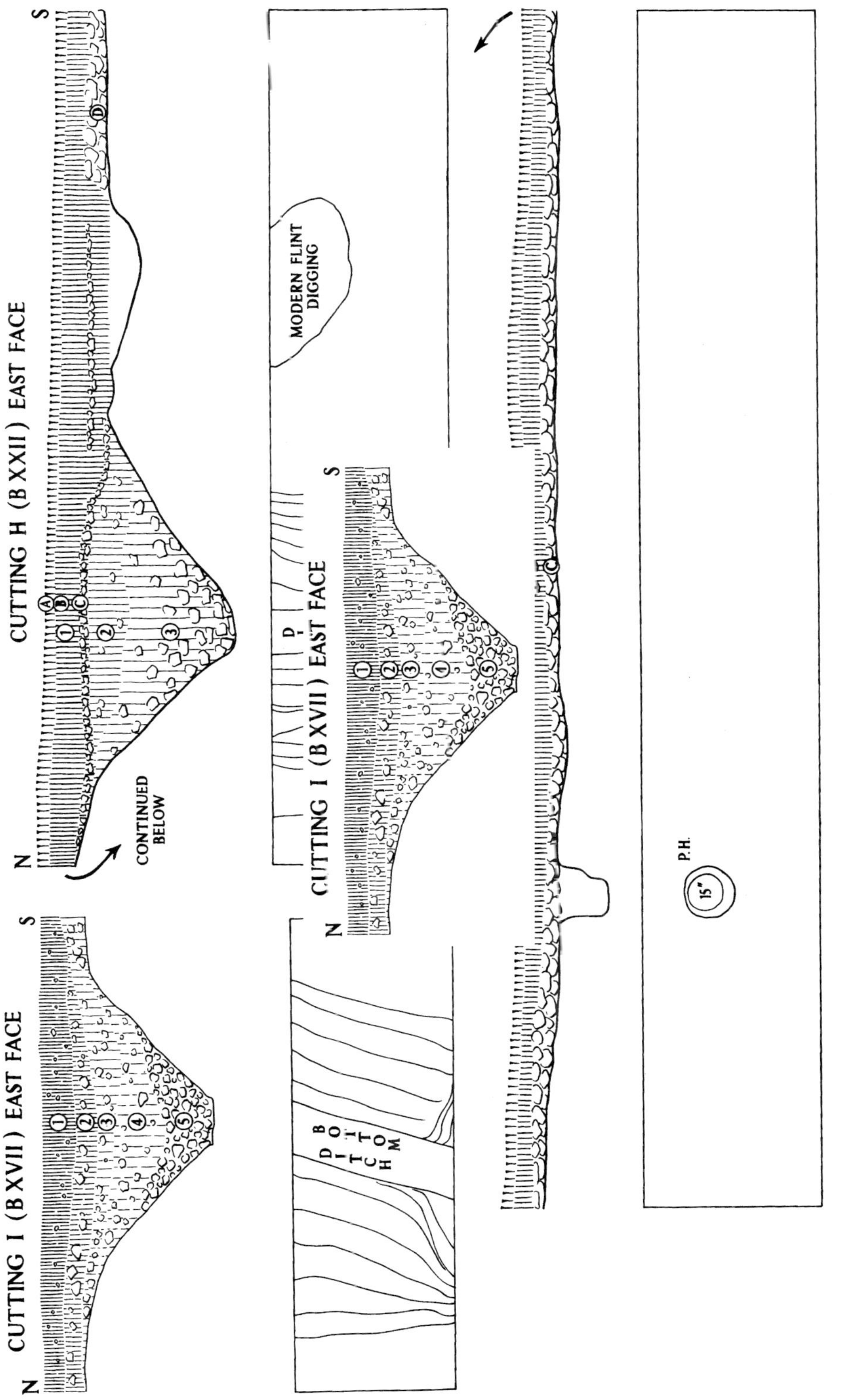

Fig. 2.15 Enclosure II Cuttings H and I

with soil. This pattern could be indicative of bank erosion. The profile varies a great deal in these two cuttings, that of Cutting F showing a classic V-shape, much deeper than that of Cutting E. The fill sequences are also very different. The top of the ditch in Cutting F appears to have been deliberately levelled by chalk rubble (4), whilst ditch Cutting E accumulated a final layer of thick soil (4). No diagnostic pottery was recovered from the ditch fills in these trenches.

The southern part of the enclosure ditch was investigated in Cuttings H and I (Figs 2.15-2.16). The existing section drawing (Fig. 2.15) lacks a scale and seems to have been somewhat botched, probably due to problems with the original site drawings. However, assuming the scale is the same as for the other section drawings and, on the basis of the imperial scale shown in the photograph of the ditch in Citting I (Fig. 2.16), it was at this point *c.* 2.5 – 3.0m wide and 1.3m deep. The profile was V-shaped with a flat base, again containing much chalk in the lower fills. Again, the paltry and fragmentary pottery from these ditch sections is not very informative. A small, slack-shouldered jar from top fill (2) of ditch Cutting I (Fig. 3.32, no. 2) was incorrectly classified by CFC Hawkes as a 'saucepan' pot and also inaccurately assigned to the primary fill. However, this vessel, in limonite-rich fine sandy fabric (F12) could date to the early part of the middle Iron Age, contemporary with some of the pits close to the roundhouses in Cutting S.

The section of Cutting J (Fig. 2.17) suggests a similar possibility of quarrying at the ditch edges as was observed in Cutting D, and these two excavation events were likely to have been contemporary. A bipartite furrowed bowl rim (Fig. 3.32, no. 15) recovered from top fill of the ditch in this trench and a fingertip decorated sherd (Fig. 3.32. 4), from the fill of the adjacent quarry, are not helpful in dating these feature, as both are likely to be residual.

The relationship between Enclosures II and III is best demonstrated in the section of Cutting L (Fig. 2.17) where, although the two ditches did not directly impinge on each other, the fill sequence clearly shows the V-shaped Enclosure III ditch to post-date the flat-bottomed ditch of Enclosure II. Both were largely filled with chalk rubble, again probably bank material. The profile of the Enclosure II ditch in Cuttings J and K both show the same distinctive flat base and chalk dominated fills. A small fingertipped jar rim found in layer (7), just above the primary fill of the ditch in Cutting K (Fig. 3.32, no.3), provides more convincing evidence for an earliest Iron Age date for the Enclosure II ditch.

Fig. 2.16 Enclosure II Cutting I: south face of ditch (1960)

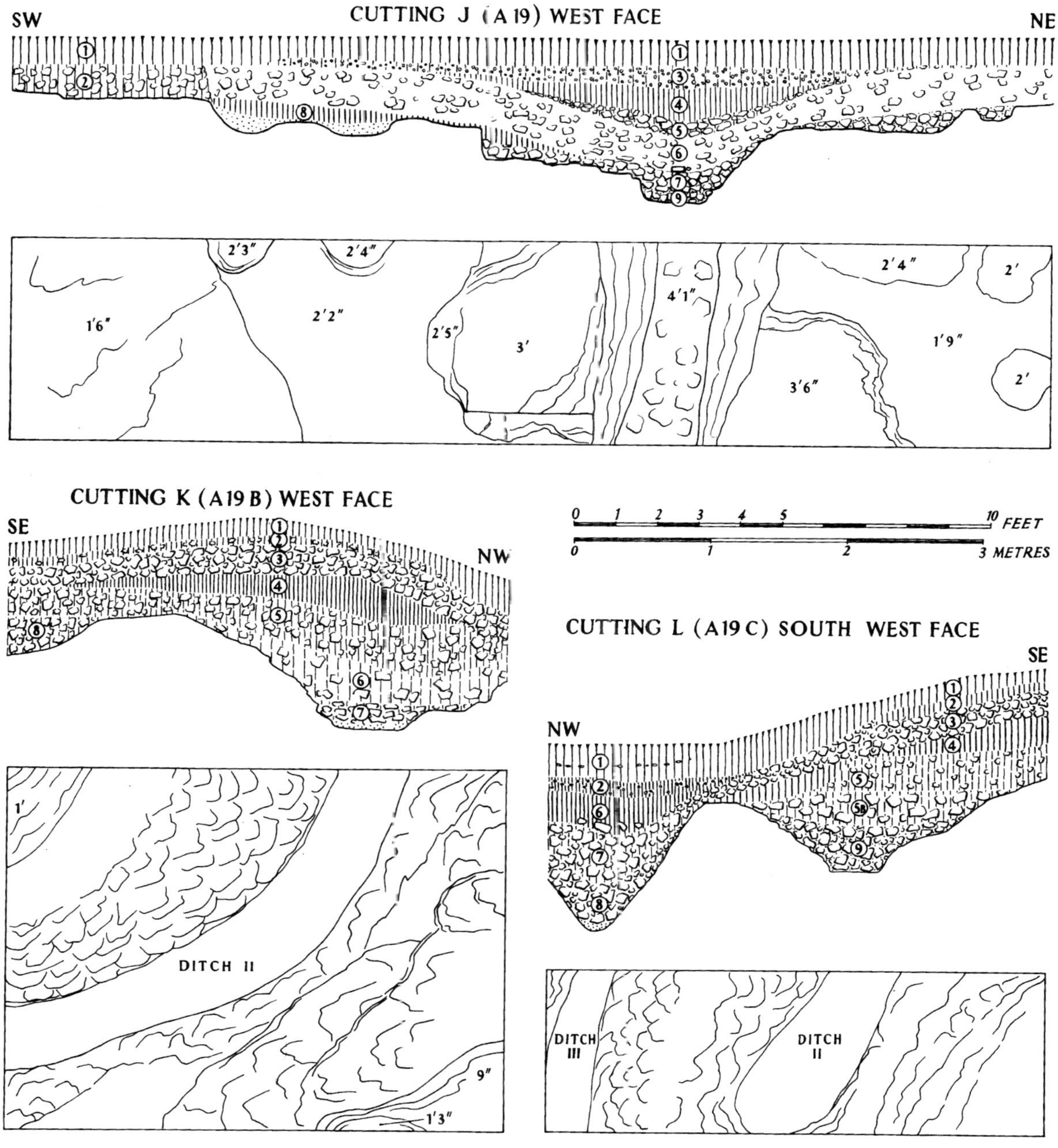

Fig. 2.17 Enclosures II/III Cuttings J, K, L

The investigation of the eastern ditch of the enclosure in Cutting G was evidently neither described nor drawn and no finds were recorded.

Enclosure II Interior

Part of the interior of Enclosure II was investigated in a large open area excavation (Areas S1-3) and in the two narrow Cuttings U and V (Fig. 2.1). No records were found for Cuttings U and V and it may be that no features were found in these areas. The three roundhouses (Houses 1, 2 and 4), post-hole complexes, pits and hollows exposed in Areas S1-3 are described below in various sections: The Houses, The Pits, The Hollows and The Postholes.

Areas S1-3 was an open area excavation approximately 4,572 m^2 in size within the centre of Enclosure II. Much of the trench was occupied by Houses 1, 2 and 4 (Figs 2.6 and 2.19). The roundhouses had all apparently been burnt, their sites abandoned and no structures rebuilt in the same location, as was the case at Little Woodbury, Wilts. (Bersu 1940, figs. 20-21) and Pimperne, Dorset (Harding, Blake and Reynolds 1993). The custom at

Fig. 2.18 Enclosures II/III Cutting K: ditch underlying Enclosure III bank

Fig. 2.19 Enclosure II: excavation of interior Area S1-3 (copyright: The Wiltshire Times 1960)

Longbridge Deverill seemed to involve respecting the destroyed houses by 'tidying up' the site, not least by packing much of the broken and burnt pottery that survived the fire into the tops of the nearest postholes. The amount of pottery recovered during the excavation of the postholes of the three major houses is remarkable by any standard. It was particularly impressive in the case of Houses 1 and 2, where the fragments were very large. During excavation of these two houses very often the first sign of a posthole was the appearance, in the top of the broken chalk subsoil, of masses of pottery.

The survival of the pottery was another piece of good fortune. In 1958 and 1960, when Houses 1, 2 and 4 were excavated, their sites had been under the plough for only a very few years, and that probably for the first time since the early 19th century. Moreover the farming method was still traditional, ploughing was rotational, the land being put periodically down to grass, and a plough in the 1950s was a modest affair compared with its modern successors. So the site had not been intensively ploughed as it has since. However, between 1958 and 1960 a year's ploughing intervened between excavations and we noticed that postholes of House 1, reopened for plan checking, had lost up to 0.05m in depth. We felt then that time was running out and that within a very few years all that precious pottery and much structural data would have been destroyed. So, from that point of view, the timing of the excavation was lucky.

Enclosure III

D-shaped Enclosure III is described in some detail in the Introduction and in Chapter I. It is clearly not of Iron Age construction, but there was a physical link between its eastern side and the wesern side of Enclosure II. Enclosure III was *c.* 0.6ha (1.5 acre) in area and was defined by a ditch and external bank with a single entrance located on the east side, across a 6m wide causeway (Fig. 2.2).

Enclosure III Ditches

The western profile of the enclosure was examined in Cutting O, the eastern profile in Cutting N and the entrance in north-south Cutting M (Figs 2.20-2.22). The ditch was 1.2m deep in Cutting O and some 2.0m deep on the eastern side, near the entrance in Cutting N. Its widest point was explored in Cutting N, where it was 6m – 8m across with a U-shaped profile deepened along the base with a straight-sided flat-based trench 0.2m – 0.3m wide. There is no record of the ditch fills, but the section drawings indicate that a thin primary silting deposit (Cutting O (12)) was overlain by a mass of small chalk rubble (Cutting N (6); Cutting O, (11)). This may have accumulated, at least in part, through collapse and erosion of the chalk bank. There followed what was probably a period of natural silting (Cutting N (5); Cutting O (10)). Subsequently, a load of flint rubble was thrown in (Cutting N (3B); Cutting O (9)) before another soil deposit accumulated, possibly again through natural slippage and weathering (Cutting N (4); Cutting O (8)). Thin soil overlying this might have been a turf line (Cutting N (18); Cutting O (5)) but, without the benefit of a soil description, this remains uncertain.

Enclosure III Interior

The interior of Enclosure III was initially examined in a series of trial trenches (Fig. 2.2). The features, mostly postholes and stakeholes (SH), exposed during this exercise are shown in Figs 2.23-2.25. There is no other detailed record in the archive of these or of any associated finds, apart from a mention of two pottery sherds, one from topsoil and one from Trial Trench A32 (Fig. 2.25), and a scrap of animal bone from PH26.

The remains of House 3 were located during trial trenching just inside the entrance of the enclosure and were subsequently fully exposed in Cutting T. House 3 clearly pre-dated Enclosure III by a considerable period and was at least broadly contemporary with one of the occupation phases of Enclosure II. The structure is fully discussed below (see The Houses).

Table 2.3 Enclosure III Trial Trenches postholes

PH	*Trench*	*Depth m*	*Figure*
17	A32	0.15	Fig. 2.25
18	A32	0.12	Fig. 2.25
19	A32	0.75	Fig. 2.25
20	A31	0.10	Fig. 2.24
21	A31	0.18	Fig. 2.24
22	A28	0.23	Fig. 2.25
23	A28	0.21	Fig. 2.25
24	A28	0.25	Fig. 2.25
25	A28	0.41	Fig. 2.25
26	A28	-	Fig. 2.25
27	A28	0.10	Fig. 2.25
28	A27	-	Fig. 2.25
29	A27	0.20	Fig. 2.25
30	A27	0.25	Fig. 2.25
31	A25	0.50	Fig. 2.24
32	A25	0.12	Fig. 2.24
33	A25	0.10	Fig. 2.24
34	A26	0.12	Fig. 2.25
35	A26	0.10	Fig. 2.25
36	A26	-	Fig. 2.25
37	A26	0.12	Fig. 2.25
38	A26	0.12	Fig. 2.24
39	A35	0.12	Fig. 2.24
40	A34	0.23	Fig. 2.24
41	A34	0.15	Fig. 2.23
42	A38	0.23	Fig. 2.23
43	A45	0.12	Fig. 2.24
44	A45	0.15	Fig. 2.24
45	A6	0.15	Fig. 2.23

Table 2.3 presents the location and details of the postholes in summary form. No section drawings of the postholes were found in the archive, but profiles of some of the stakeholes appear on the plans.

THE HOUSES

by Sonia Chadwick Hawkes

Introduction

Strictly speaking, all four of the roundhouses at Longbridge Deverill were contemporary with Enclosure II and are, therefore, referred to in text and catalogues as Enclosure II, House 1, and so on. The apparent location of House 3 within Enclosure III is coincidental, as the construction of Enclosure III post-dated the roundhouse, probably by many centuries. In a small number of instances feature numbers relating to the roundhousess have been duplicated because numbering from 1-n was repeated in the second and subsequent seasons of excavation. Renumbering in the years following the fieldwork largely resolved this problem but a few duplications were noted during editing (eg PH101 and PH102 assigned to both Houses 1 and 2 and Gully1 (G 1) assigned to both Houses 3 and 4). These have not been renumbered but the allocation of features to specific structures or enclosures should allay confusion.

The houses were proven to have formed part of a sequence, the earliest, House 1, dating back perhaps to the 9th-8th century BC. House 2 stratigraphically post-dated House 1 and was constructed possibly a century or so later. House 4 may have been broadly contemporary with House 1 but produced slightly later radocarbon dates of 810-370 cal BC and 780-

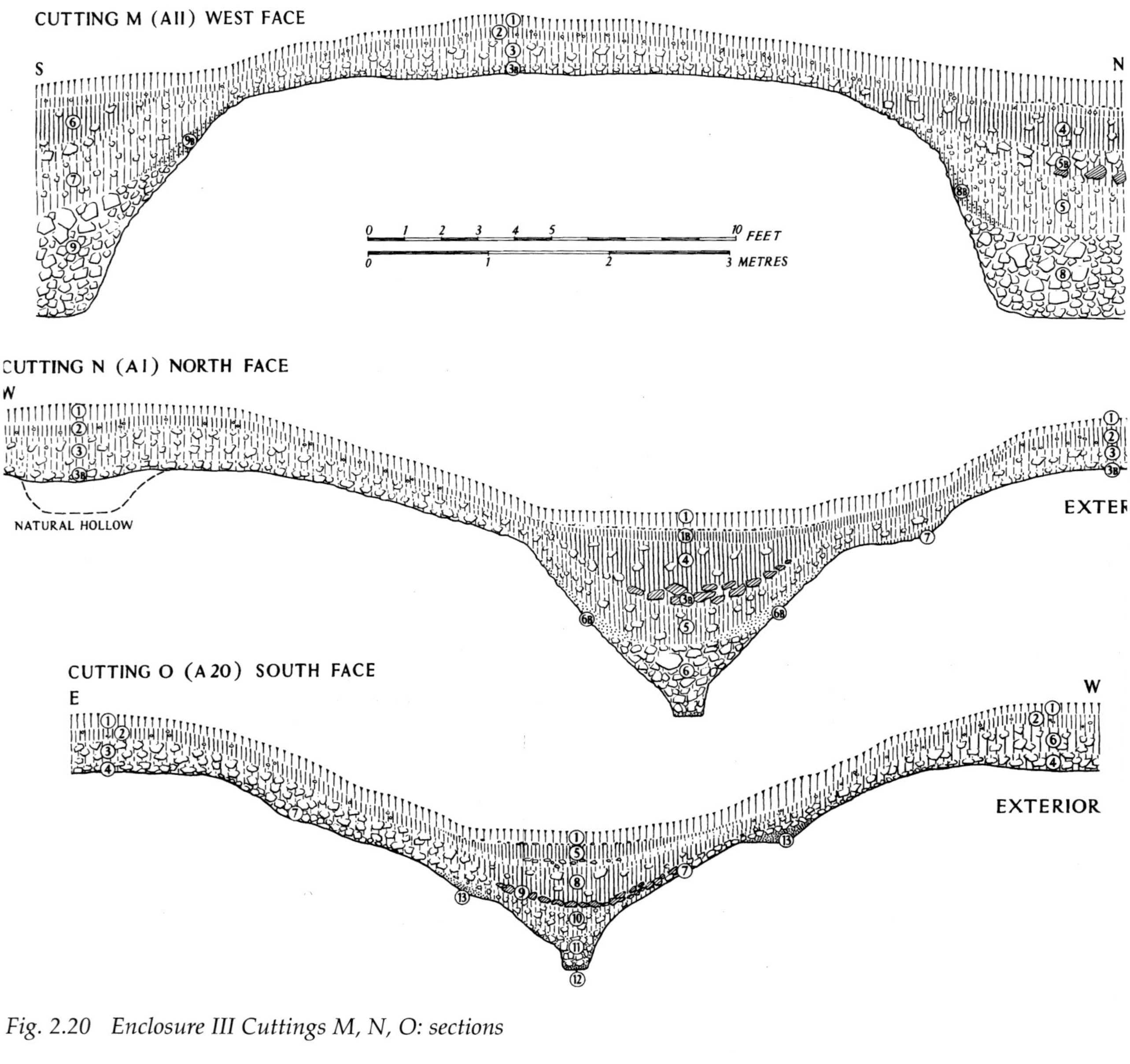

Fig. 2.20 Enclosure III Cuttings M, N, O: sections

Fig. 2.21 Enclosure III Cutting N: north face of ditch section (1956)

Fig. 2.22 Enclosure III Cutting O: south face of ditch section (1957)

380 cal BC, and it was just as likely to have been in use at broadly the same time as House 2 (see Chapter 6). The latest house in the sequence, House 3, was by far the best preserved and thus allowed for a tentative reconstruction of its original appearance and the use of the huge space within its interior and exterior parts.

House 1

House 1 was 11m in diameter, with 18 principal posts forming a circuit interrupted by a doorway a little over 3m wide, located between PH141 and PH165 (Fig. 2.26-2.27). The opposing pair of postholes, PH167 and PH139/140, indicate the probable position of a porch, evidently repaired at some stage with the recutting of PH140. The size of the main ring postholes suggest that they formed a wall strong enough to support the roof and high enough to give a maximum of useful space inside the house. As with House 4, there is no real evidence for a second post ring, nor would this have been structurally necessary. If the height of this wall were estimated to have been 1m, the apex of the roof could have been about 5.7m off the ground, and appreciably more if either the roof pitch was more than the suggested 45° angle or so, or if the wall itself were taller.

Evidence remains only for the use of oak, hawthorn and hazel in construction of the house or activity within it (see Chapter 5) but other timbers such as ash may have been used, and it is unlikely that hawthorn was used as a main structural element. The main ring postholes were of oak and it seems likely that much of the roof was of the same wood, and probably cut from coppiced stools. Much of the small timber in the roof to which the thatch was attached and the wattling in the walls

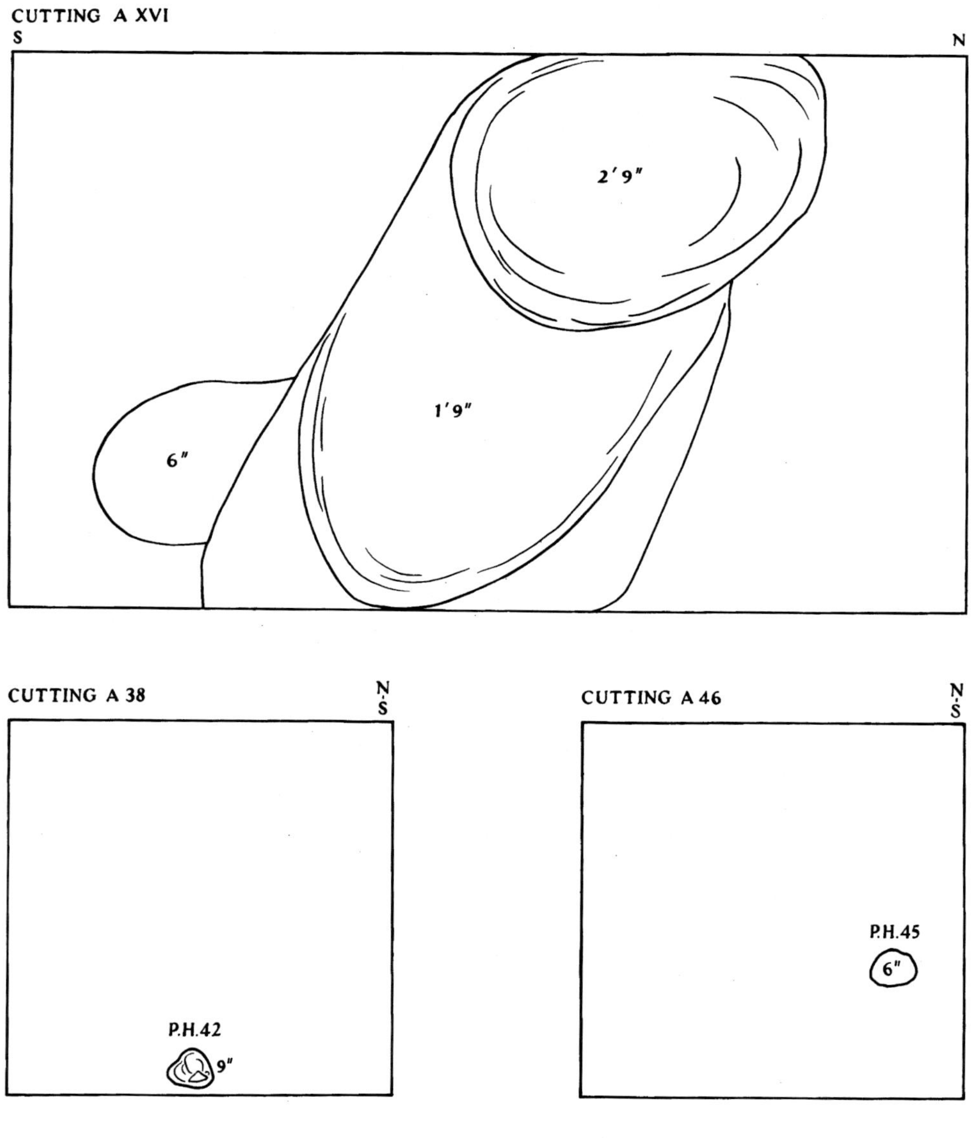

Fig. 2.23 Enclosure III trial trenches

was probably hazel. The enormous lateral thrust exerted by the weight of the roof at the top of the walls may have been reduced if the builders had increased the rigidity of the cone by the insertion of horizontal rings of posts encircling the rafters at perhaps three or four levels inside the roof. These could have been pegged and lashed to the rafters. The poles in the horizontal ring were possibly scarfed and pegged to each other. If some of the rafters were allowed to extend beyond the eaves to rest on the ground this would have contributed greatly to the inherent stability of the structure. This was shown to be the case at Butser and also proved to be a useful feature in the process of construction.

The tops of the main postholes are likely to have been linked together to form a continuous wallplate capable of taking a still considerable lateral pressure, probably by means of horizontal timbers fixed by mortise and tenon to the upper. If the tenon passed right through the mortises of the two horizontal timbers scarfed and joined above the top

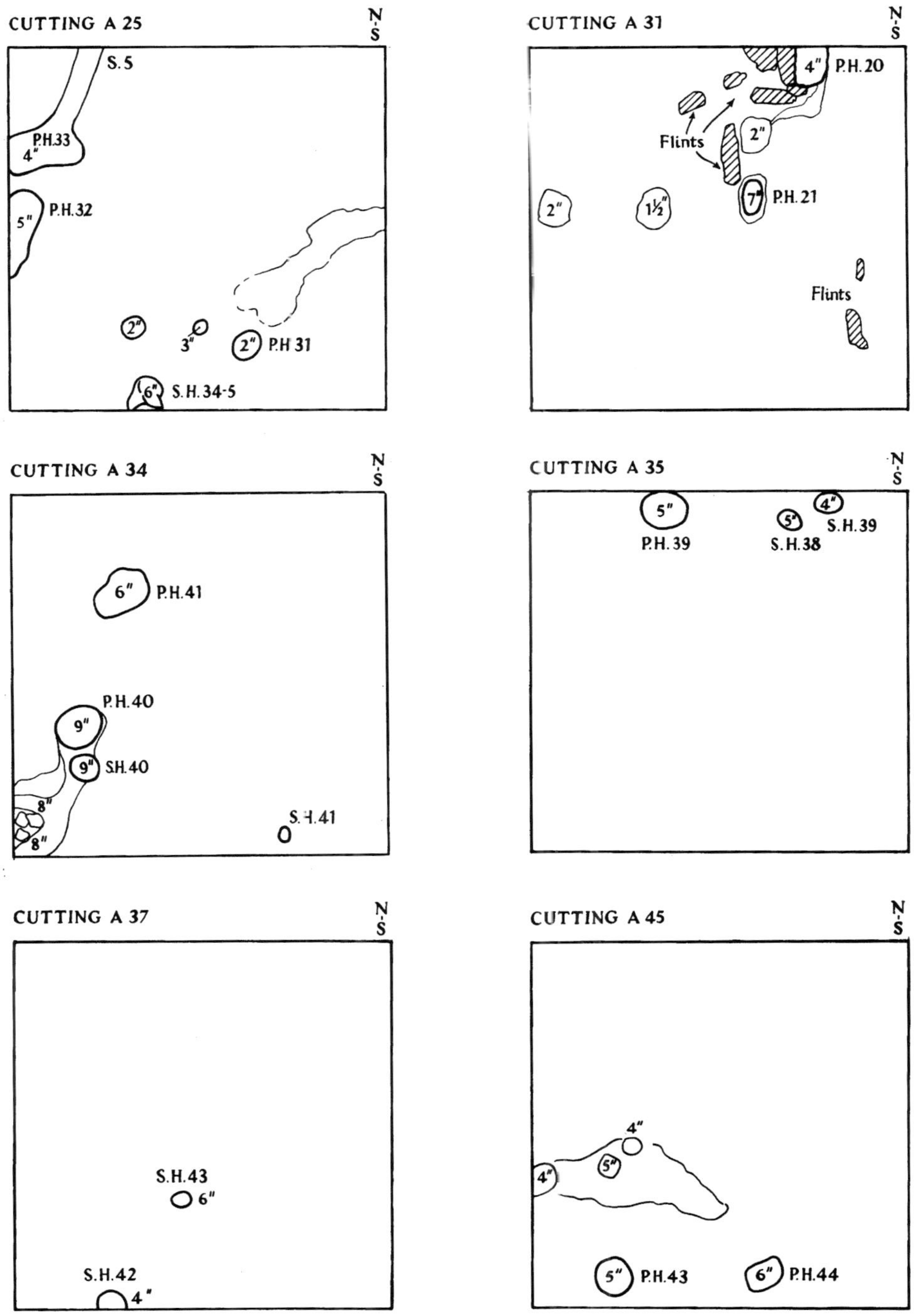

Fig. 2.24 Enclosure III trial trenches

of the upright this would create a very strong chain line ringbeam on to which the butt end of the rafters could be fixed. Any point of weakness caused by the interruption of the porch opening could be compensated by the buttress-like action of the structure itself, and perhaps also by a long rafter on either side resting on the ground.

A porch considerably taller than the wall would have allowed light into the interior and provided a useful covered working space. It could also possibly have been sealed by one or two sets of double doors, socket hinged at the top and bottom. Impressions in the carefully recovered daub, especially from PHs 151 and 165, clearly show that the spaces between the posts were filled in with a substantial wall of chalk cob reinforced by a wattle framework. This was probably either constructed *in situ* or made as a separate piece and firmly pegged

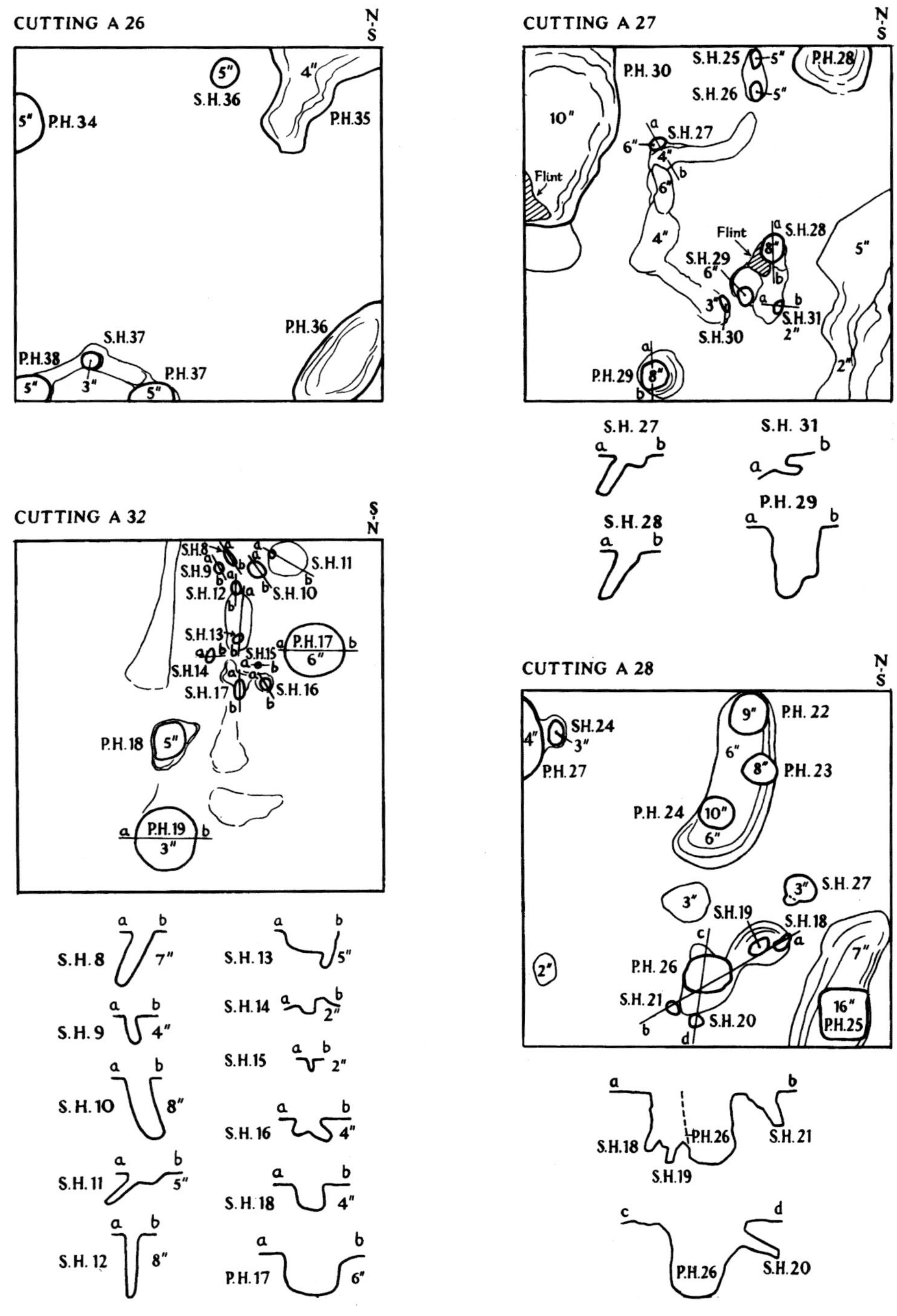

Fig. 2.25 Enclosure III trial trenches

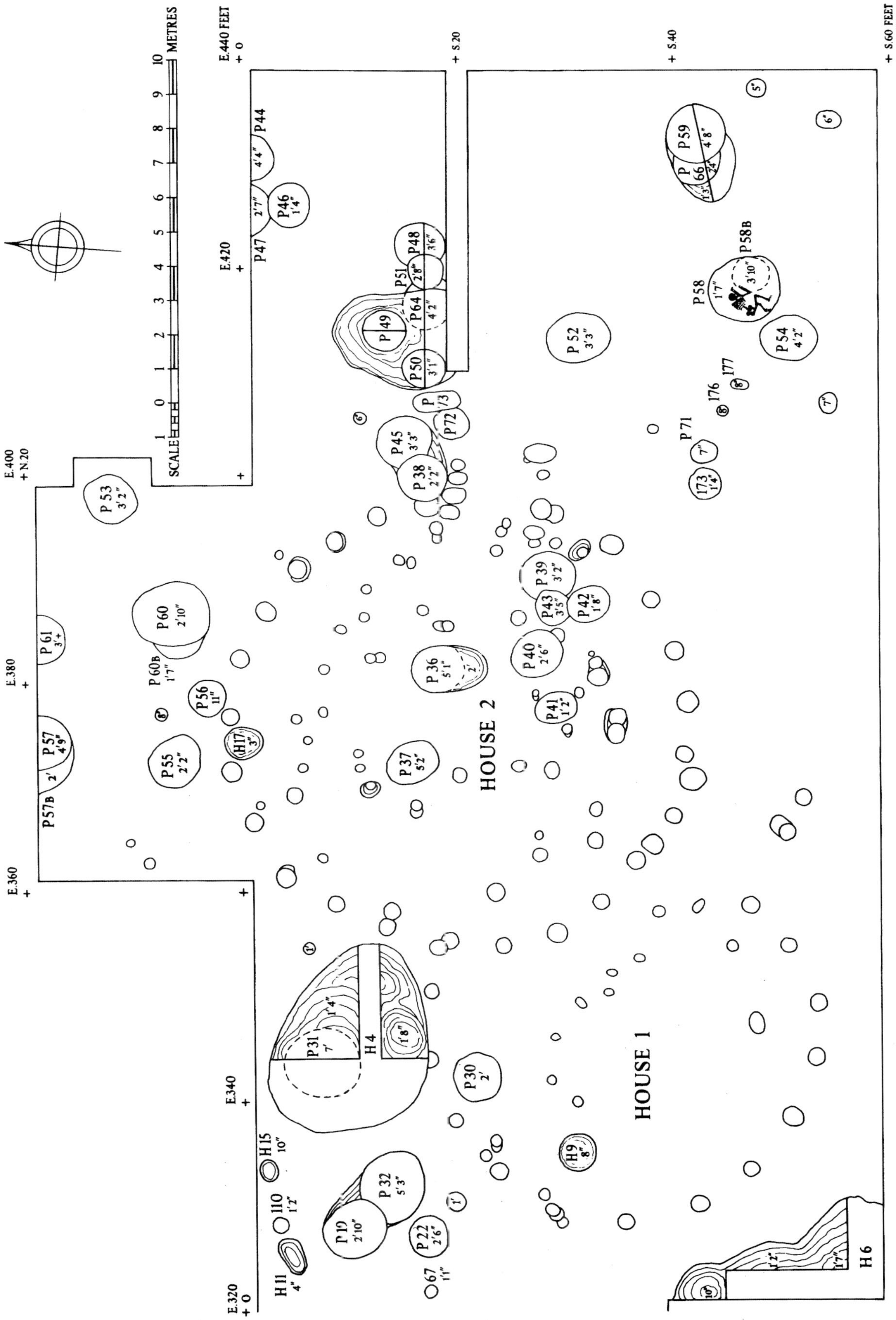

Fig. 2.26 Enclosure II Area S3: Houses 1 and 2

into place. The wall would almost certainly have been protected from the weather by overhanging eaves, although in this case no trace of a resulting drip gully survived.

Cob daub samples were recovered from many of the main ring postholes. Most were burnt orange with no surviving wattle impressions. The only unburnt samples, both well preserved with good wattle impressions, were from PHs 151 and 165, both in the south-east sector of the structure, the latter being the inner porch posthole on the south side. The construction implied is of wattle coated with a good thickness of daub filling in the spaces between the main upright posts. The daub, where unburnt, consisted of an extremely solid and well preserved chalk cob, apparently a puddled mixture of chalk and straw (straw impressions were visible in the fabric). This was a much finer and harder mixture than that used for House 2. The facing, where it survived, was a roughly smoothed surface with what may be keying for plaster facing. Most pieces were too small to show the pattern of the wattling, but fragments from the corner posthole showed evidence of sticks or withies passing across, up and down and through. This was also observed at the porch corner of

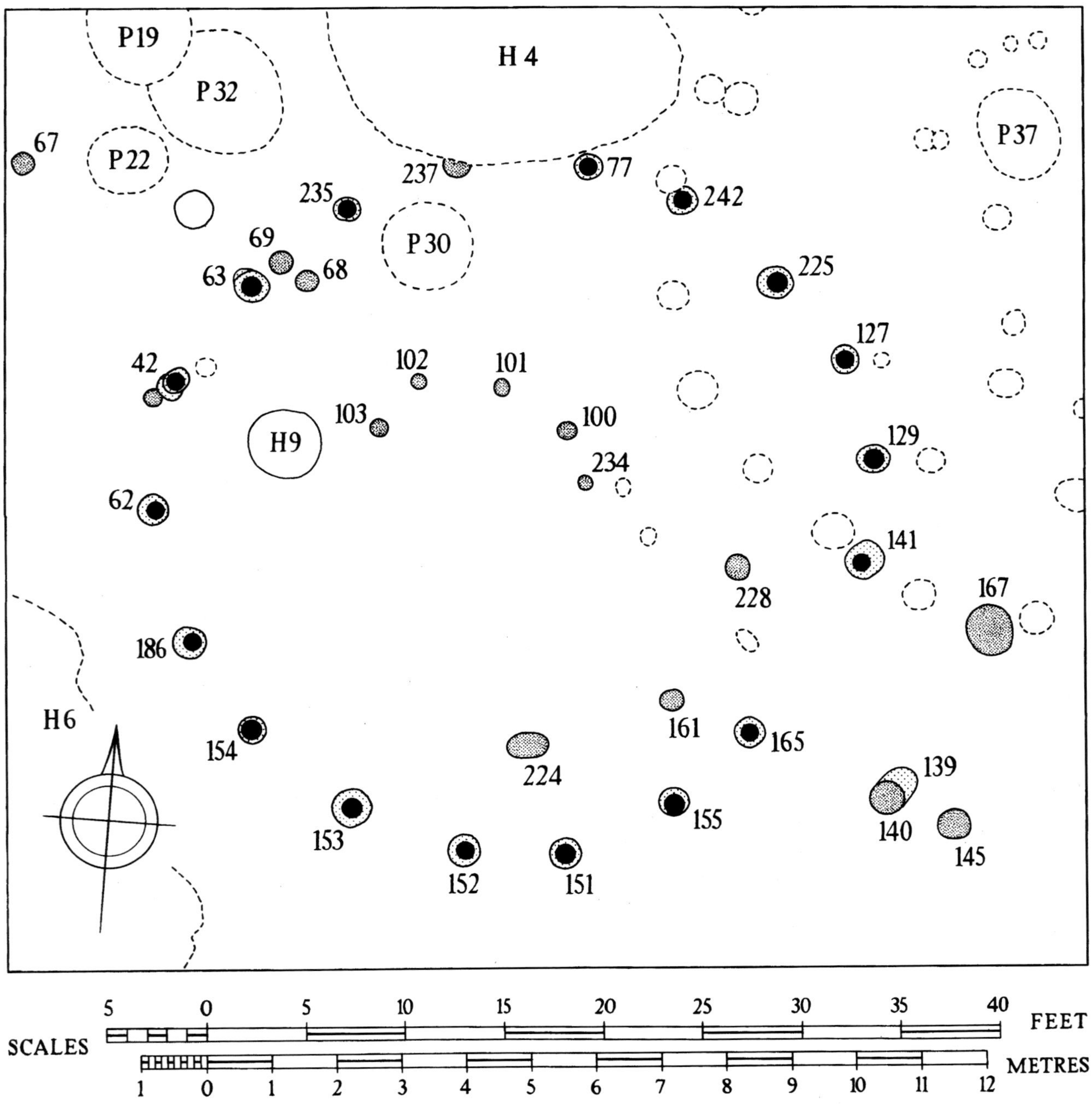

Fig. 2.27 Enclosure II Area S3: House I

Table 2.4 House 1 postholes and contents (Fig. 2.28)

PH	*Dia m*	*Dia post*	*Depth m*	*Packing*	*Pot*	*Artefacts (Fig ref)*	*Ecofacts*
Main ring							
42	0.43	-	0.23	Flint	25	-	Wall daub
62	-	-	-	-	-	-	-
63	0.61	0.38	0.76		8	-	Daub; oak
69	0.28	-	0.31	-	-	-	-
77	0.33	-	0.46	-	-	-	Charred post, unspec
127	0.46	0.26	0.31	Chalk	3	-	Oak; bone a
129	0.46	-	0.31	Chalk	2	-	Unspec
141	0.59	-	0.28	Chalk, flint	-	-	Oak (NPL-105); bone a
151	0.51	0.38	0.21	Chalk, flint	233	-	Wall daub; hawthorn; bone a
152	0.46	0.21	0.23	Chalk, flint	592	-	Oak, hazel; bone a
153	0.53	0.33	0.26	Chalk	76	-	Oak; bone a
154	0.41	-	0.23	Greensand quern	184	Hammerstone, spindle whorl, AE object	Daub; bone a
155	0.38	-	0.18	Greensand, chert	1	Chert hammerstone (4.10,8)	-
165	0.46	-	0.25	Greensand, chalk	5	Quern, antler tine (4.5,5)	Wall daub; oak hazel; bone a
186	0.41	0.23	0.21	-	5	Spindle whorl	Daub; oak
225	0.46	0.33	0.33	Chalk	33	Chalk spindle whorl/weight	Daub; hawthorn
235	0.41	-	12.5	-	42	Chalk weight	Oak (NPL-104); bone a
237	0.38	-	0.41	-	3	-	Daub; unspec
241	0.43	-	0.41	Chalk, flint	-	-	Unspec
242	0.43	-	0.31	Chalk, flint	-	-	-
Porch							
139	-	-	0.38	-	-	-	Oak hawthorn
140	0.41	-	0.41	-	4	AE pin (4.1,3)	Burnt bone a
145	0.51	-	0.18	Chalk	6	-	Burnt bone a
167	-	-	-	Sstone quern	11	-	Bone a
Internal							
100	0.53	-	0.41	-	-	-	-
101	-	-	0.26	-	-	-	-
102	-	-	0.18	-	-	-	-
103	-	-	0.23	-	-	-	-
161	0.33		0.13	-	1	-	Unspec
224	0.1	-	0.15	Flint	1	-	Fired clay
228	0.46	-	0.13	Chalk	-	-	-
234	0.21	-	0.10	Chalk	-	-	-
External							
128	0.43		0.28	Chalk	-	-	-

Bone a = animal bone; Bone h = human bone

House 2 and may be a special way of constructing corners. Samples of unburnt and burnt daub were taken to see if they were the same, or whether the orange daub was different in composition (see Chapter 4, Freeman).

The crescent shape formed by the internal postholes, PH101, PH101 PH102, PH103 and PH234, suggest that together they formed some interior fitting, conceivably a screening hearth. The majority of both coarse and fine pottery came from the tops of the postholes on the south side of the house. This may have served as a division of the interior into areas with different functions, although positioned as it is it is difficult to see how such a screen could be useful. From their position neither of these postholes nor any of the others surviving seem likely to have had an integral structural function. PH68 and PH69 should probably not be considered as structurally integral in the house and, although associated with the house, their purpose is unclear.

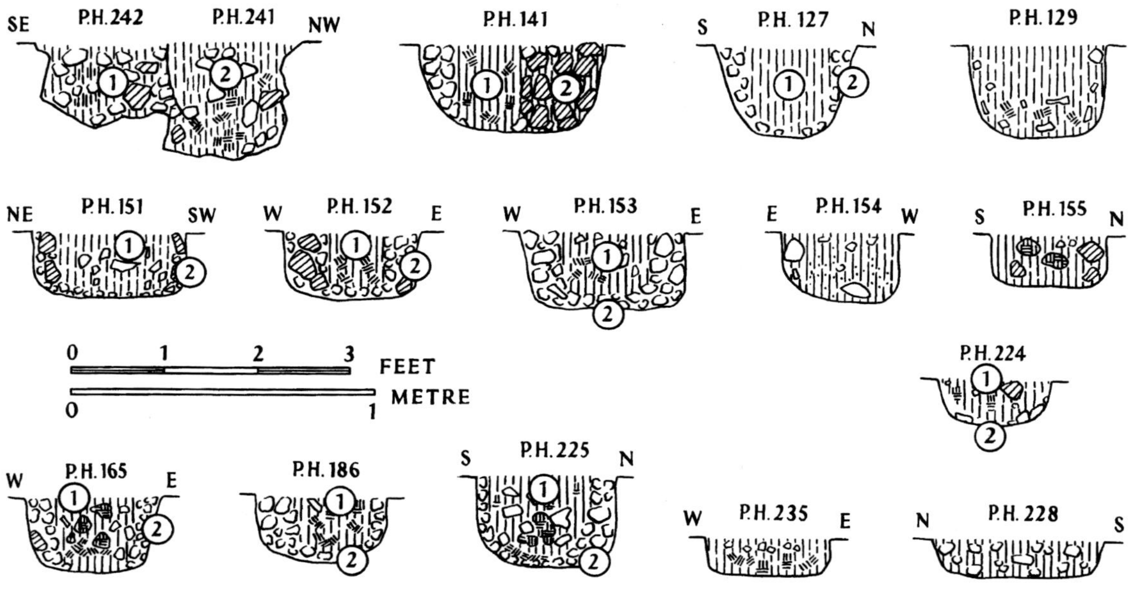

Fig. 2.28 House I postholes

House 2

The diameter inferred from the main ring postholes of House 2 is the largest of the four houses, and this itself raises some problems as to the reconstruction (Fig. 2.29; right of photo 2.30). It is not entirely clear whether it was a single ring or a double ring roundhouse. It has been convincingly suggested that many apparently single ring roundhouses were in fact built with an outer ring that carried the wall itself (Guilbert 1981), with two concentric rings of posts, the outer and less substantial ring carrying the wall. This could have been the case with House 2 if postholes PH226, PH227 and PH233 on the south-west side are seen as the only surviving evidence for an outer ring and the massive main ring posts bore the main stress exerted by the roof. This would have given the house an internal diameter of almost 17m.

The size of the very shallow outer ring postholes discounts them as sockets for rafters (Figs 2.31-2.32/ Table 2.5). However, a building of this size would have been extremely difficult to construct, and coupled with the form of the porch, it seems more likely that it was a single ring house. It may be that postholes PH266, PH227 and PH233 represent the remains of a veranda inserted under the eaves in the manner suggested for House 3. The asymmetrical position of PH172 indicates that the porch structure was carried by opposing posts

Table 2.5 House 2 postholes and contents (Fig. 2.31- 2.32)

PH	*Dia m*	*Dia post*	*Depth m*	*Packing*	*Pot*	*Artefacts (Fig ref)*	*Ecofacts*
Main ring							
90	0.41	-	0.51	'stone'	7	-	Hazel; bone a
91	-	-	-	Chalk	13	-	Hawthorn
112	0.41	-	0.46	Chalk, flint	-	-	Unspec
113	0.48	-	0.51	Chalk, flint	-	Iron	-
114	0.51	0.26	0.51	Chalk	-	-	Unspec
126	0.51	-	0.56	-	51	-	Wall daub; hazel; bone a
132	0.48	0.21	0.43	Chalk	3	-	Daub; oak
133	0.48	-	0.41	'Stone'	3	-	-
134	0.46	028	0.38	Chalk	44		Hazel; bone a
135	0.6	0.38	0.41	Chalk	117	Slingstone	Daub; hazel ash
142	0.46	-	0.48	Chalk	5	-	Wall daub; oak
144	0.43		0.48	-	27	-	Fired clay; oak
146	0.51	0.28	0.41	Chalk	19	-	Oak
147	0.41	0.26	0.38	Chalk	55	-	Unspec
149	0.23	-	0.51	Chalk	2	-	Daub; oak hazel

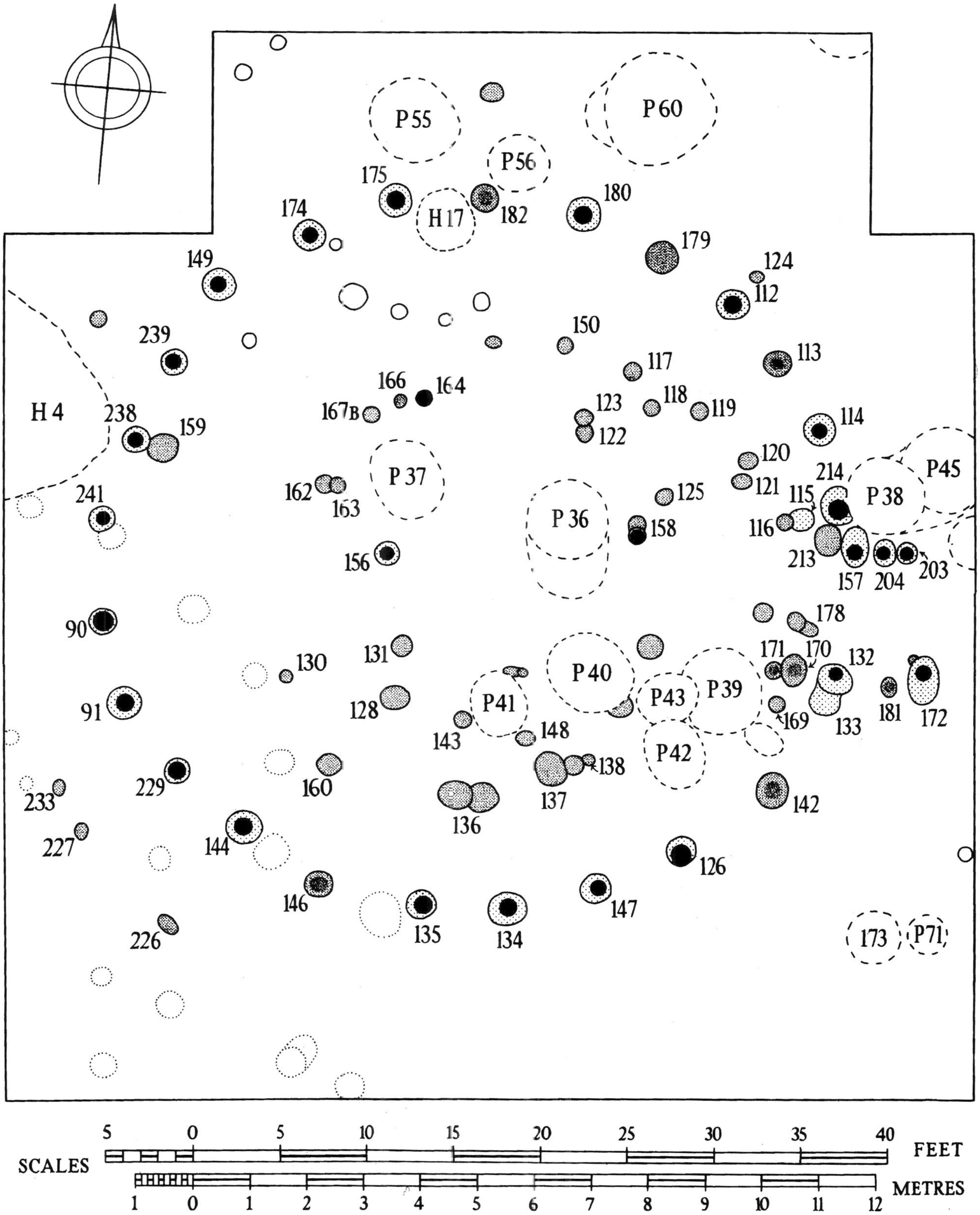

Fig. 2.29 Enclosure II Area S3: House 2

Table 2.5 House 2 postholes and contents (Fig. 2.31- 2.32) (continued)

PH	Dia m	Dia post	Depth m	Packing	Pot	Artefacts (Fig ref)	Ecofacts
157	0.61	-	0.51	Quern frag	17	-	Daub; oak, hazel
172	0.92		0.46	-	15	-	Wall daub; oak hawthorn hazel
174	0.51	0.23	0.46	Chalk	4	Horn core (4.5,4)	Oak hazel
175	0.56	.36	0.43	Chalk	2	-	-
179	0.56	-	0.43	Chalk, flint	5	-	Oak hawthorn hazel ash
180	0.46	-	0.43	Chalk	2	-	Oak hazel
182	0.46	-	0.43	Chalk, flint	5	-	Wall daub; hazel ash; burnt bone a
203	0.28	-	0.18	-	1	-	-
204	0.41	0.23	0.36	-	12	-	Daub; unspec
213	0.53	-	0.51	-	-	-	Hazel
214	0.69	0.38	0.46	Chalk	2	-	-
229	0.43	-	0.59	Chalk	26	-	Oak hazel
238	0.53	-	0.28	-	5	-	unspec
239	0.63	-	0.41	Flint	3		unspec
241	0.43	-	0.41	Chalk, flint	1	-	Fired clay; unspec
Internal							
115	0.33	-	0.18	-	-	-	-
116	0.31	-	0.31	-	-	-	Fired clay
117	0.31	-	0.21	Chalk	-	-	-
118	0.26	-	0.21	-	-	-	-
119	0.28	-	0.28	-	-	-	-
120	0.31	-	0.33	-	-	-	-
121	0.33	-	0.26	-	-	-	-
122	0.28	-	0.26	Chalk	-	-	-
125	-	-	shallow	-	1	-	-
128	043	-	0.28	-	7	-	-
130	0.36	-	0.28	-	1	-	-
131	0.36	-	0.28	-	-	-	-
136	0.61	-	0.36	Chalk	98	-	Unspec; bone a
137	-	-	-	-	208	Red deer antler (4.5,1)	-
138	0.21	-	0.18	-	-	-	-
143	0.28	-	0.41	-	4	-	-
148	-	-	-	Chalk	-	-	-
150	0.31	-	0.23	-	-	-	-
158	0.31	-	0.38	quern frag, chalk	1	-	-
159	0.46	-	0.13	Chalk, flint	-	-	-
160	0.31	-	0.15	-	-	-	-
162	0.21	-	0.10	-	7	-	-
163	0.26	-	0.15	-	-	-	-
164	0.23	0.23	0.23	-	-	-	-
166	0.21	-	0.31	-	-	-	-
167	0.66	-	0.41	Chalk, flint	15	-	-
169	0.31	-	0.13	-	-	-	-
170	0.51		0.38	Quern frag, chalk	1	-	Daub; oak hazel
171	0.28	-	0.23	-	-	-	Daub, oak
178	0.51	-	0.31	-	-	-	Burnt clay
213	0.53	-	0.56	-	-	-	-
External							
181	0.31	-	0.13	-	1	-	Unspec
226	0.53	-	0.71	-	-	Ceramic spindle whorl	-
227	0.31	-	0.5	-	-	-	-
233	0.23	-	0.1	-	-	AE earring (4.1,2)	-
234	0.21	-	0.71	-	-	-	-

Bone a = animal bone; Bone h = human bone

PH181 and PH 203 and that PH 204 was placed there as a reinforcement. PH181 and PH203 may have formed the front of the porch, possibly linked at the top by a lintel supporting the gable end. This would have been built with the king post supporting the ridgepole and the interstices weatherproofed with a light wattle and daub screen.

The asymmetric position of substantial PH172 suggests that it was not structural, but its situation has a close parallel in PH145 of House 1, the function of which is not clear. Within the interior the group formed by PH136 and PH137, apparently a pair of posts replaced once and twice respectively, must represent an important interior fitting. This feature has an exact parallel in PH62 and PH73 of House 3, positioned in exactly the same part of the interior. The remaining 34 postholes suggest no obvious explanation, although it is conceivable that some supported a form of raised platform towards the edges of the building, again as postulated for House 3. The relationship of PH170, PH171 and PH178 with the porch is puzzling as PH178 would have obstructed the doorway. It may indicate a reduction in the size of the opening but it need not have been contemporary with the house.

Considerable quantities of chalk cob daub were found in the postholes of the main structural posts of both the main ring and porch, especially on the south and south-east sides. The daub retained good impressions of hurdle or wattle-work, indicating that the 0.9-1.4m spaces between the timber uprights were filled by panels of wattling, presumably lashed in place both to the uprights, the wall plate, and probably secured at the bottom by stakes driven a short way into the ground (see Chapter 4, Fig. 4.14). The wattling was plastered with a considerable thickness of daub, consisting of fine chalk lumps and soil, perhaps mixed with a little clay, and probably puddled to a stiff paste with water. This chalk cob does not seem to have had the usual admixture of straw for binding, since straw impressions were not visible either in the fabric or on the surface. Possibly it was more of a *terre pisé* or simply a chalky mud. It survived well, although was sometimes rather crumbly, and preserved the casts of the wattling very clearly.

This wattling seems to have been of the usual over and under woven pattern but a few pieces from the corner where the house wall met the porch show variations of pattern, with withies and sticks passing through the mixture. This was possibly localised, something to do with the manner of attaching the wattled panel to the posts in the corner. Many pieces of the cob showed the outside surface still preserved, as a rather irregular, roughly smoothed surface apparently coated for protection against the

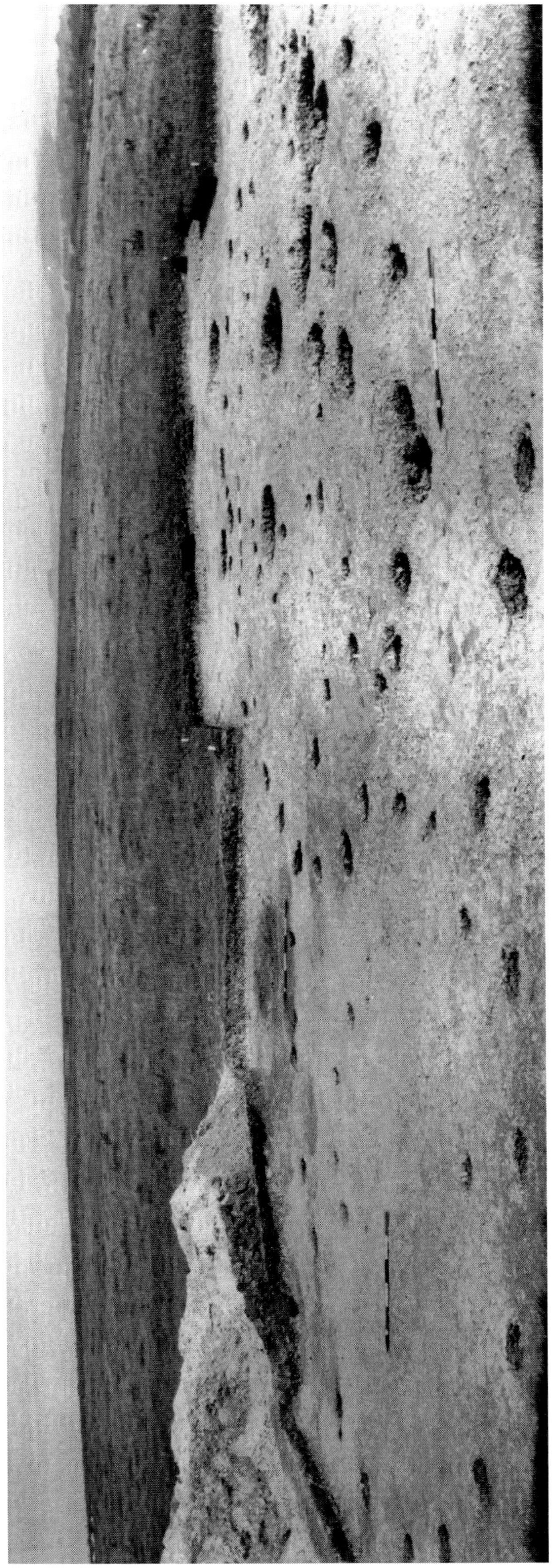

Fig. 2.30 Enclosure II Area S3: House 1 (left) and House 2 (right)

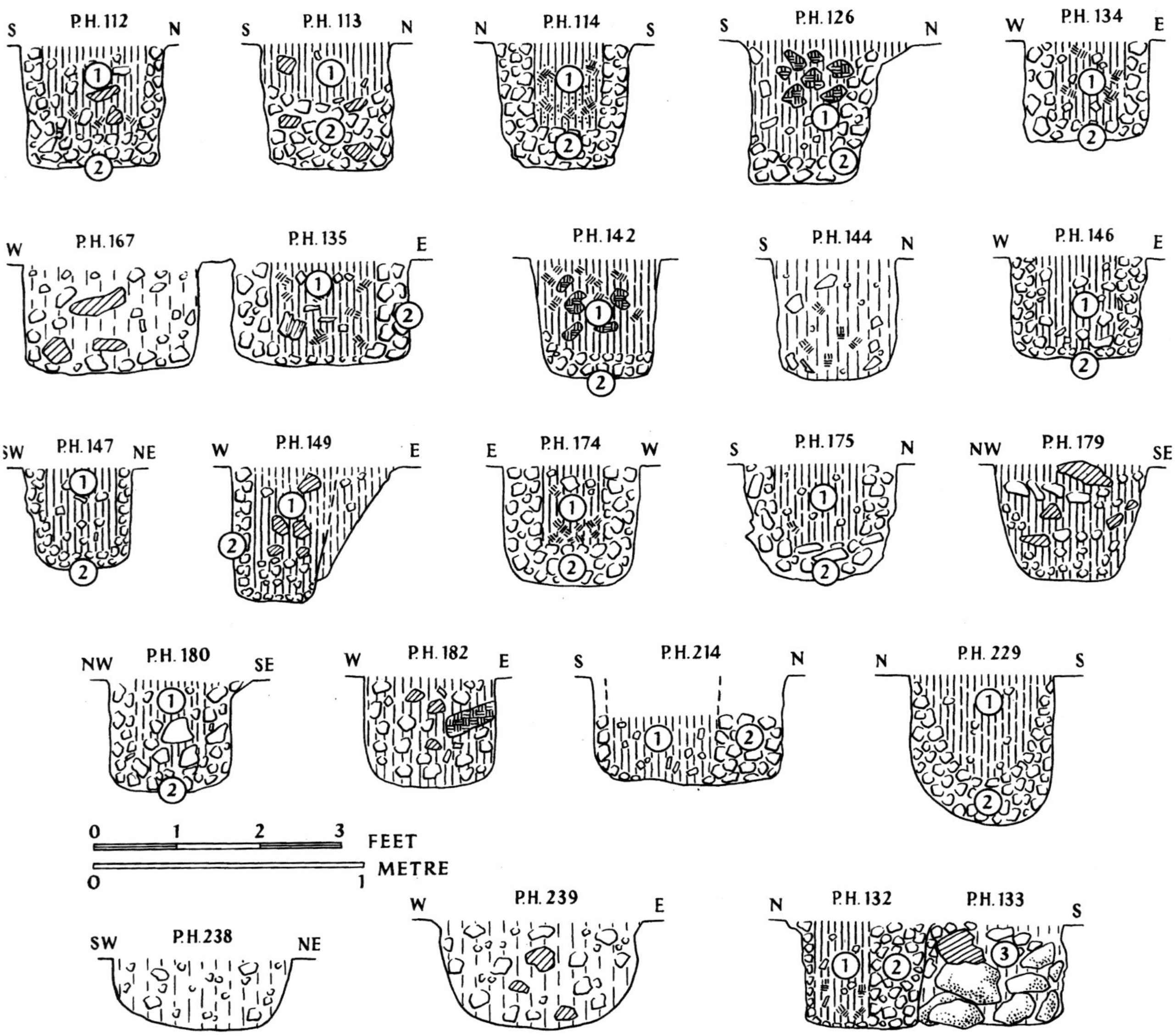

Fig. 2.31 Enclosure II House 2: sections of main ring postholes

elements with a crude lime plaster. Some pieces showed this outer skin as a white or yellow plaster 1mm or so thick on top of a grey or dark grey cob. Thie greyness did not extend to the parts with wattled impressions, and were perhaps the result of staining with smoke from the fire on a surface that was occasionally renewed with a fresh layer of plaster. However, it would be more likely for the cob to have been on the outside of the building as a weather proofing. It was at 40mm – 6mm thick, with at least 20mm of this on top of the wattlework. Cob was possibly used inside as well, but there was no evidence of this.

The best preserved daub came from the main ring postholes on the south-east side and from the south side of the porch. This was not apparently burnt and seems, therefore, to have escaped the fire that destroyed the house. Possibly this side of the house was not badly burnt owing to the wind direction, and the daub fell off when the house was levelled, or else the daub fell off before the house became too hot. Burnt daub, very cindery and broken to small pieces, occurred on the north side of the porch where the fire may have been hotter.

House 3

House 3 was published in 1994 (Hawkes) ahead of this site report, chiefly to release the evidence about it in the light of the final publication of the nearly contemporary house excavated about the same time on Pimperne Down, Dorset (Harding 1963 and 1974; Harding, Blake and Reynolds 1993). The Pimperne house, already widely known because it formed the subject of a major reconstruction

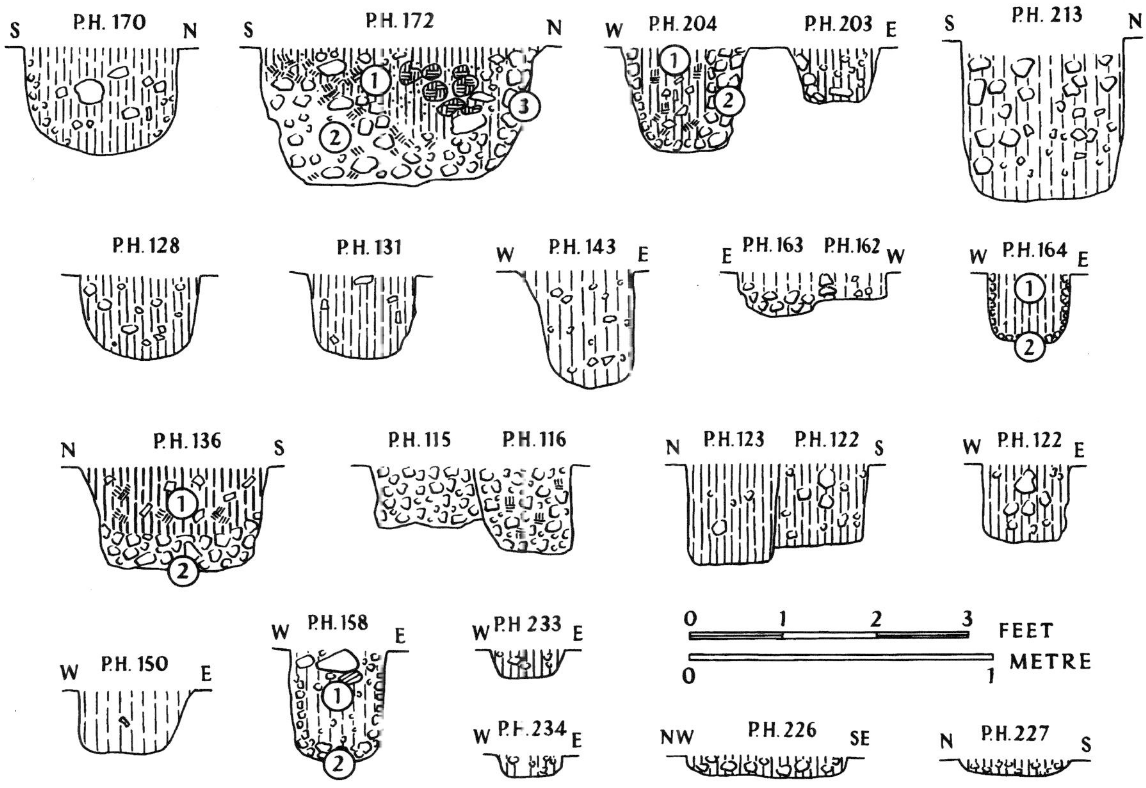

Fig. 2.32 Enclosure II House 2: sections of ancillary postholes

(Reynolds 1979), was similar in scale but different in detail. So House 3 presents us with an alternative model dwelling house for the period in question (Fig. 2.33).

Edward Impey, now of English Heritage, produced a series of fine reconstruction drawings based on the structural evidence recovered from the excavation of House 3, postulating various details of construction, decoration and activity. A selection of these is presented in Figs 2.34-2.37.

Situation on the Site

House 3 was situated immediately inside the causeway of D-shaped Enclosure III. Some of its porch postholes were encountered in the first season during excavation of the entrance of Enclosure III, and were then interpreted as gate posts. One of them, the several times recut PH3 on the north side of the causeway close beside the ditch terminal, may have been a gate post but there was nothing to date it to the period of Enclosure III. Indeed, the only find recovered from it, a fragment of Late Hallstatt type bronze bracelet in its upper filling (Fig. 4.1,5), clearly derives from the occupation of House 3, which is of this date. PH3, therefore, can more plausibly be interpreted as a much modified element in the outermost ring of postholes belonging to this house (Fig. 2.33). Placed as it is beside the porch of House 3, it could have been the emplacement for some such thing as a totem pole or even a hitching post for a pony as illustrated in a reconstruction drawing by Edward Impey (Fig. 2.34).

House 3 was excavated piecemeal during three seasons, with the result that the structure was never seen as a whole on the ground, let alone from the air, so no overall photographs exist. Moreover, the impossibility of opening up a large enough area around it meant, almost certainly, that part of the outermost ring of posts and other peripheral features remain unexcavated and unplanned. However, by the end of the second season in 1957 there existed on paper an accurate plan of the major part of the house in relation to the entrance of Enclosure III, and by then it was quite clear that the two could not have co-existed. The ditch terminal south of the Enclosure III causeway would effectively have blocked entrance to the house and the lack of House 3 debris in the ditch is another cogent argument for attributing house and ditch to different periods. The only pottery from the primary silts of the Enclosure III ditch, from the cuttings north of its entrance, is of quite another type, the so-called 'saucepan pot', which taken at face value, could date the enclosure about three centuries later than the house.

Confirmation of a later date for the construction of Enclosure III was forthcoming in 1957, when excavation following new evidence from air photographs revealed it to have been constructed across the wide open end of Enclosure II. This earlier enclosure must still have been visible, perhaps because of a hedge around it, but the ditches were by then fully silted. The latest of the ditch fills contained Phase B pottery, some of it of saucepan type. The primary silts of the Enclosure II ditches contained nothing as early as the pottery from House 1, but sherds of fingertipped storage jars and tall necked furrowed bowls like those from Houses 2 and 3. The ceramic evidence alone is insufficient to enable us to determine for which of these two closely successive major structures the enclosure was constructed, but the position of House 3 is very suggestive. It lay precisely in the middle of the wide western opening of Enclosure II, so that, if one stretched a line from antenna to

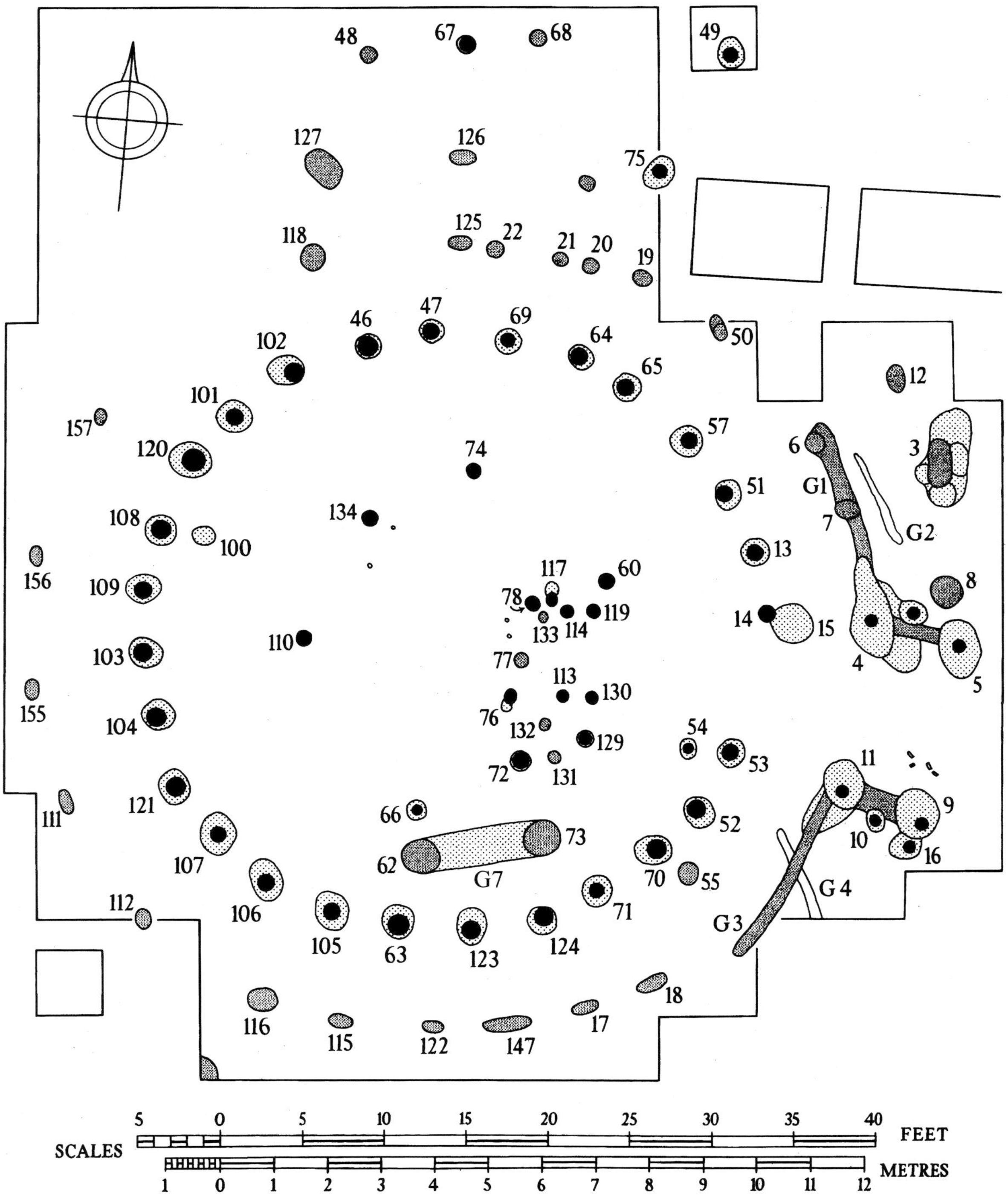

Fig. 2.33 Plan of Cutting T: House 3

Fig. 2.34 Reconstruction drawing of House 3 (artist: Edward Impey)

Fig. 2.35 Reconstruction drawing of House 3 (artist: Edward Impey)

Fig. 2.36 Reconstruction drawing of House 3 interior (artist: Edward Impey)

Fig. 2.37 Reconstruction drawing of House 3 (artist: Edward Impey)

Fig. 2.38 Excavating House 3 (1957)

Fig. 2.39 Excavating House 3 (1957)

antenna, House 3 is placed centrally but outside the enclosure, though with its porch facing in. In 1957, these antennae were explored as far and fully as time and resources permitted and, though no real terminals to the Enclosure II ditches were found either to north or south of the big opening, the indications were that the ditches were becoming shallower and their ends could be expected not far beyond the limits of excavation.

Collin Bowen suggested that the Enclosure II ditch may originally have continued all around the outer edge of the line of the Enclosure III ditch, with the effect that Enclosure II may have been 'cottage loaf'-shaped, and House 3 contained within its smaller 'top-knot'. Inspection of the section in Cutting O through the western side of the Enclosure III ditch, shows that there is indeed a slight step towards the top of the outer slope, which might be the remains of an earlier ditch, now largely destroyed by that of the present Enclosure III. If so, the earlier ditch would have been very slight, not more than 0.76 – 0.92m deep, much shallower than the main Enclosure II ditch, and more likely, to have been a marker ditch for the imposing final ditch of Enclosure III. The fact that a similar step exists on the outer edge of the Enclosure III ditch immediately north of the causeway in Cutting N tends to reinforce the idea of a marker ditch. However, it throws no real light on the original physical relationship of House 3, in terms of ditches or fences across the opening, to Enclosure II. That the western opening, with House 3 at its centre, must have been protected in some way seems certain, but the 1956-1957 excavations did not resolve the problem. It is possible, though, that the single posthole found in the middle of the causeway of Enclosure III originally formed part of a line of fence posts across the mouth of Enclosure II.

Trial trenches in the enclosure interior north and west of House 3 revealed no other major structural or ceramic occupation traces of its period beyond its immediate area. Here there were only postholes to the north of the house that may represent screens or drying racks (Fig. 2.33). But pottery contemporary with that from House 3 was found in a disturbed pit in the working hollow complex (H3) approximately 75 m to the east near the centre of Enclosure II (Fig. 2.43). This suggests that the occupants of House 3 were active within Enclosure II, and it seems likely that it was they who were responsible for its construction. The excavation was insufficient to tell exactly how they used this large sack-shaped enclosure, or what motivated them to make it, but it enclosed the whole area previously occupied by the ancestral dwellings, Houses 1, 2 and 4, and their ancillary features. Subsequently it served to contain all later domestic occupation on the site in the culturally distinct Phase B, down to at least the 3rd century BC.

Description of the Structural Remains

Houses 1, 2 and 4 were situated in the middle of Enclosure II, where the air photographs show clear evidence of medieval ploughing, and where in 1958 and 1960 modern ploughing was already nearly scraping the chalk bedrock. In contrast, the remains of House 3 had been protected for a long time before excavation by a blanket of undisturbed thick downland turf. Despite some evidence for medieval and later activity within Enclosure III, there was no definite evidence that it had been ploughed since Roman times. The typical soil profile above House 3 showed at least 0.15m of turf above a further 0.15m of humis soil and ancient ploughsoil. The tops of the postholes appeared in a layer of broken chalk between 0.80-0.15m above solid chalk bedrock. Since Roman ploughing had gone deep enough to destroy any trace of floor and hearth, the depth of the ploughsoil should be added, so that the original posthole depths can be estimated to have been 0.30m greater than the depths from the top of the chalk bedrock, maybe more allowing for some soil erosion caused by ploughing in Roman times. Thus the major structural posts must originally have been sunk into the ground at the least to depths of between 0.60 – 0.90m (Figs 2.40-2.42). This situation applies also to the other houses, and one should imagine their structural timbers being planted originally comparably deeper than appeared at the time of excavation.

Like the other houses, House 3 had been destroyed by fire and never rebuilt in the same place. In this respect there is a marked contrast with other similar and broadly contemporary great roundhouses excavated in Wessex, at Little Woodbury, Wilts. (Bersu 1940, fig. 20), Pimperne Down, Dorset (Reynolds 1979, fig. 3b; Harding, Blake and Reynolds 1993, figs. 16-18), and Balksbury Camp, Hants (Guilbert 1981, fig. 1), where the corresponding major dwelling houses were rebuilt on the same site. At Longbridge, a certain amount of tidying up appears to have taken place after the fires, but as with the other houses, the ruins of House 3 and its contents seem to have been left on the site, explaining the unusual amounts of pottery and other finds recovered during excavation. In the case of House 3 the fire must have been particularly fierce, for the majority of cob daub surviving from the house wall had been reduced to cinders and the pottery from the interior mostly severely burnt. The main structural timbers seem to have burned right down into their postholes, and the resulting scorched post sockets and fillings of fine burnt earth and charcoal were very noticeable at the time of excavation. The majority of main structural timbers left measurable post casts so that, not only the depths of the original posts, but also their diameters could be recorded.

The excavation took place at a time when even such a now routine procedure as keeping charcoal for identification was in its infancy. It was to be almost ten years before the charcoals were finally dealt with and when dating Iron Age timbers by the radiocarbon method was not considered viable at all. Thus, few charcoal samples were kept from House 3, the first to be excavated, compared with the larger selection from the three houses dug a year or two later. However, enough was kept from House 3 to suggest that, as with the other houses, the main ring timbers were of oak (PH104, PH106 and PH107), although ash may have been used in the porch (PH11) and for the rafters, and that the cob daub had been plastered on withies of hazel.

The artefacts from House 3 make it clear that chronologically it is the latest of the four excavated

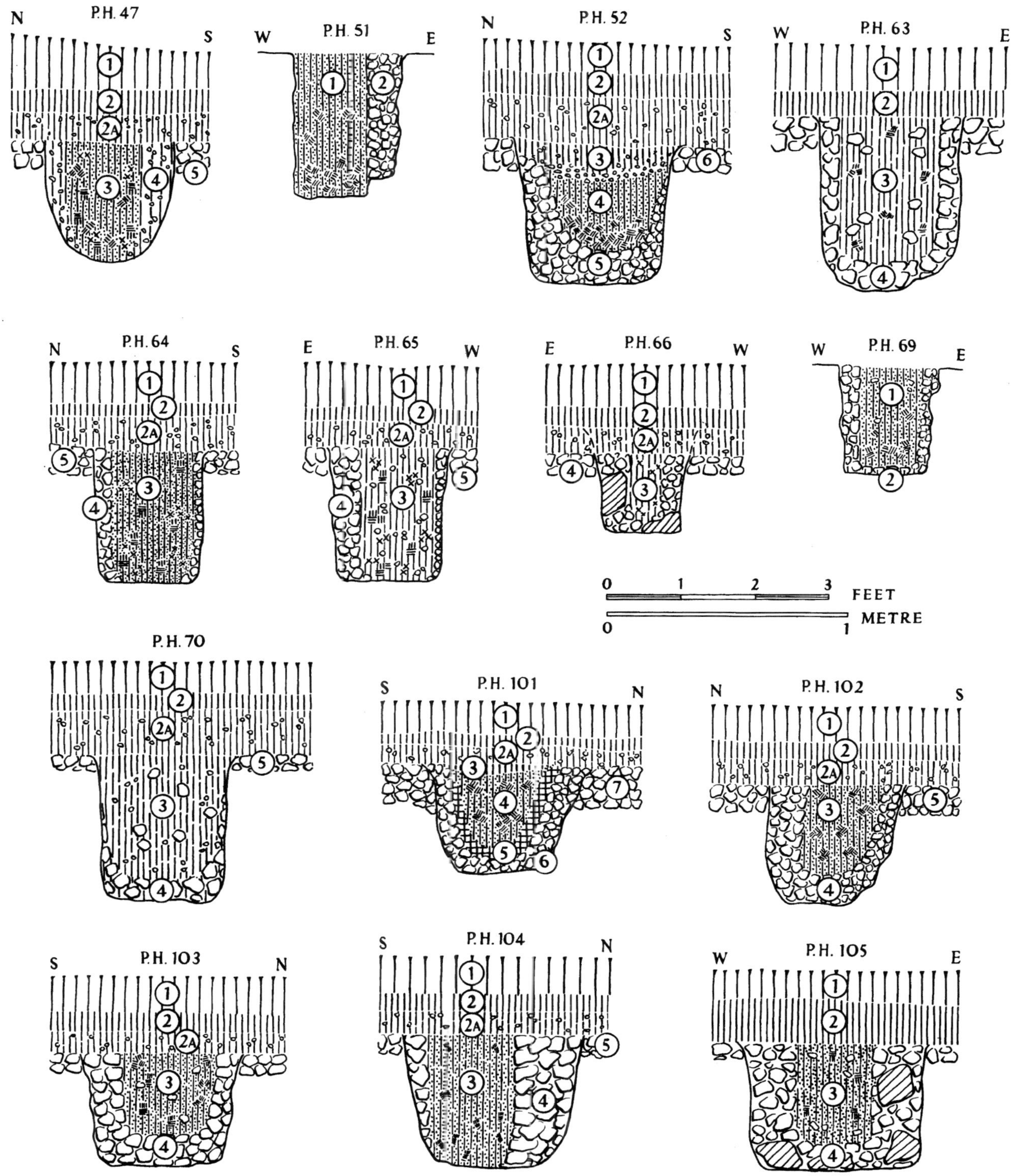

Fig. 2.40 House 3: sections of main ring postholes

and the single radiocarbon date, obtained from the remains of a burnt oak post in PH104 bears this out, though it should not be taken at face value. This is the only one of the Longbridge radiocarbon samples that was not taken or stored under controlled conditions and it may be contaminated. The pottery from House 3 is contemporary with, or even slightly earlier than, the Ceramic Phases 1-3 at Danebury, Hampshire, which were dated there by calibration of a long series of radiocarbon dates, to 550-450 BC (Cunliffe 1984,190-8), and appear marginally earlier than the pottery from the Pimperne House, tentatively dated by Harding to around 500 BC (Harding, Blake and Reynolds 1993, 57). The suggested absolute date for Longbridge Deverill House 3 is around the second half of the 6th century *BC [Editor's note: calibration in 2010 provides a broad date range of 710-210 cal. BC (see Chapter 6)]*.

Structurally, House 3 is the most sophisticated of the roundhouses, showing more elaboration than its predecessors, and a greater consumption of timber. It had a main structural ring of 27 posts which measures, from post centre to post centre, 11.60m in diameter. The posts were cut from the trunks of trees averaging 0.30m in diameter, some measuring as little as 0.25m and some as much as 0.38m. These massive, heavy timbers had been seated in large postholes, usually oval with a maximum diameter between two and three times bigger than the posts. They were dug between 0.38m and 0.59m deep into the chalk bedrock, and the posts had been carefully adjusted as to position and then tightly packed around with rammed chalk and flint rubble. Whether the different post sizes and depths were structurally significant was hard to tell. Probably the cut trunks were taken at random from a waiting stack, but the depths to which they were sunk would have been dictated by the need to even up their heights above ground, to enable the construction of the continuous lintel or wallplate, which would have joined the individual elements in the main post circle and made a rigid structure strong enough to support the rafters and the great weight of the thatched roof. As with House 2, the care and skill involved in this initial phase of the house's construction should not be underestimated – it shows clearly in the nearly perfect circle the builders achieved.

The only major mistake shows at the northern side of the entrance, where PH15 had been dug out of alignment and backfilled, and PH14, specially tailored to fit the actual post, had to be constructed alongside it. Presumably, enlarging PH15 further would have run the risk of the post slipping. A post in this position at the entrance must have been particularly vulnerable to the outward thrust of the weight of the roof since between it and its counterpart PH53 on the other side of the entrance there was an unusually large gap of nearly 2.40 m for the lintel to bridge.

The main ring posts in House 3 were set closer together than in its predecessors. Their spacing is not absolutely precise, but the gaps between them average about 1m. For internal support posts, these would have been awkwardly close set, allowing little room for movement between them, though admittedly the spacing at Pimperne was little greater. As in House 2, however, as indeed already in House 1, the surviving daub was nearly all recovered from these main ring postholes or around the porch, indicating that in House 3, too, this main structural ring is likely to have been the exterior wall. With postholes so close set, the withies forming the wattle-work could have been woven directly between and around the main structural timbers. This would have added further strength, reinforcing the wallplate at the top of the posts. As in House 2, however, it would perhaps have been speedier and more efficient to have used specially prepared wattle panels and simply lashed them into place.

About 1.85m outside the main post ring was another concentric circle of much slighter postholes, with an overall diameter of about 15.5m. Around the back and sides of the house this outer ring of posts left irregular traces, their postholes being shallow, varying from 0.75 – 0.28m deep, irregularly spaced (perhaps partially due to non-excavation or plough damage), and variously shaped, those on the SSE side being predominantly long oval, while others were oval or round. However, all were round bottomed with an earthy fill, few contained any domestic debris and none any remains of daub or burnt timbers. It is in line with this secondary post ring that the innermost posts of the massive porch were located.

This arrangement of features is best paralleled in House 1 at Little Woodbury (Bersu 1940, fig. 20; Guilbert 1981, fig. 7,G) and Winklebury Camp, House 3888 (Smith 1977, fig. 6; Guilbert 1981, fig. 1), broadly contemporary in date, where this second ring of slighter postholes appeared to represent the outermost ring of structural timbers. However, House 3 was better preserved than either of these and, incomplete though the excavation was, it showed that approximately 1.85m beyond this secondary ring were the remains of yet another intermittent ring of postholes, which, level with the outermost porch posts, achieved a maximum diameter for the house of 18.30m. This outermost ring of posts is represented by PH12, PH126, PH127, the unexcavated segment of a posthole in the corner of Cutting A113, and perhaps PH8 and PH16 on either side of the porch. Very possibly there are others beyond the limits of excavation to the west and south. All postholes excavated in this third ring were relatively shallow, not more than 0.30m deep, round bottomed and with an earthy fill. Only PH16 contained any trace of a burnt post *in situ*, and this may in fact have been part of the outer porch structure.

The others are best interpreted, as Reynolds interpreted the similarly placed posts of the contemporary house on Pimperne Down, Dorset, as emplacements for the butt ends of the long rafters used in the initial stages of constructing the conical roof (Reynolds 1979, 93-103; Harding, Blake and Reynolds 1993, 98-9). There are a number of these postholes in the two period ground plan of the Pimperne House (Harding 1974, pl. III; Reynolds 1979, pl. on p. 94, fig. 3a,b; Harding, Blake and Reynolds 1993, fig. 16), but Reynolds selected six symmetrically placed oval holes which would have been ideal for grounding the longest rafters used in his own reconstruction. To reach the apex of the roof at the 45° angle which is the optimum for thatch, these needed to be coppice grown timbers over 11m long. To erect such heavy and unwieldy rafters, it

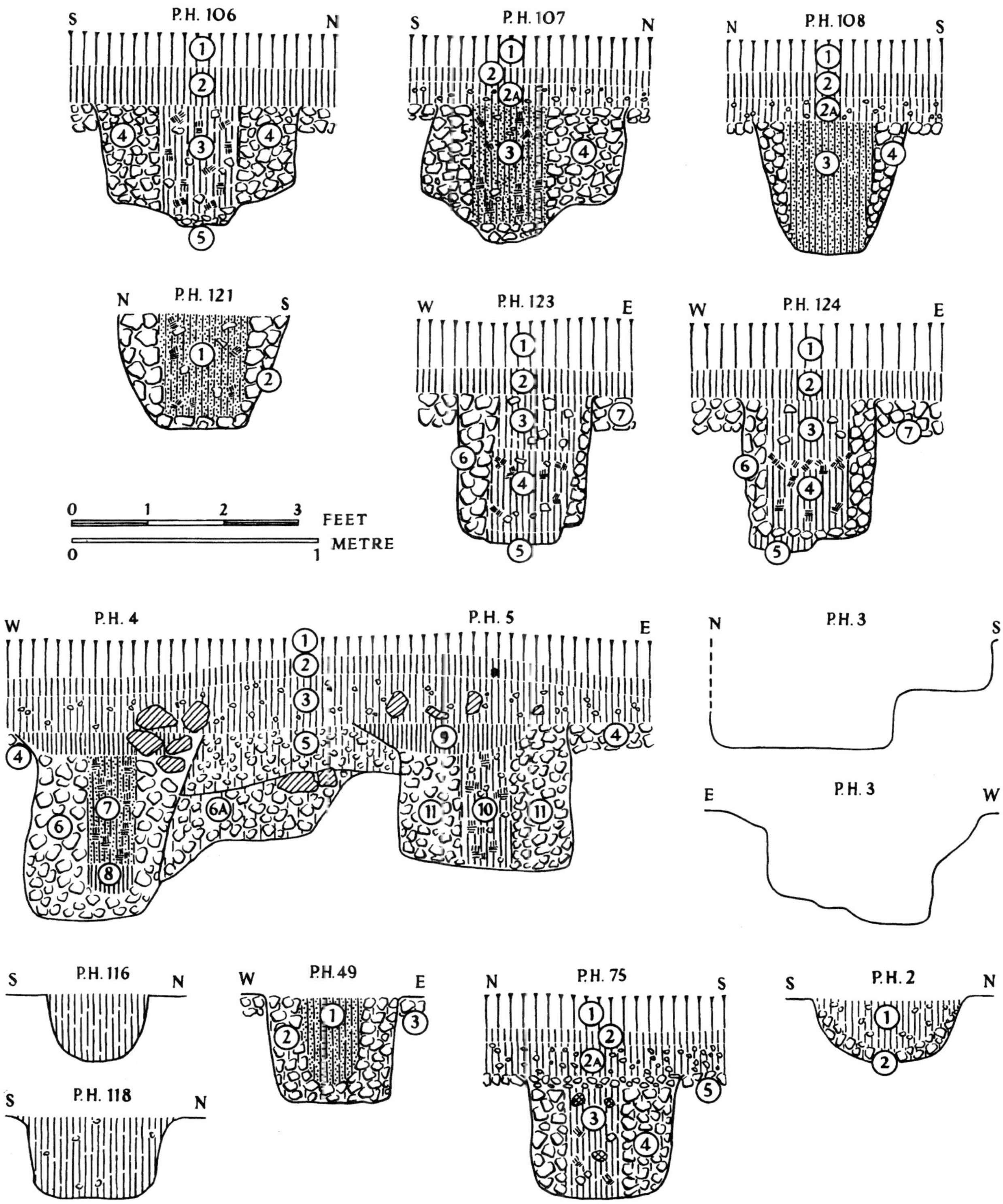

Fig. 2.41 House 3: sections of main ring postholes

proved practical to bed them in the ground and lean them against the lintels of the main structural post ring while adjusting their positions before making them secure.

Assuming that the builders of House 3 aimed at the same angle of 45°, the 18.30m diameter of the circle of bedding postholes implies a total height for the house, from ground to apex, of 9.15m, and a height of 3.66m for the circle of main ring support posts. The main rafters running from ground to apex would have been about 13.7m long and, since such very long timbers must have been difficult to obtain as well as to handle, presumably as few as possible were used. If we include the outer ring

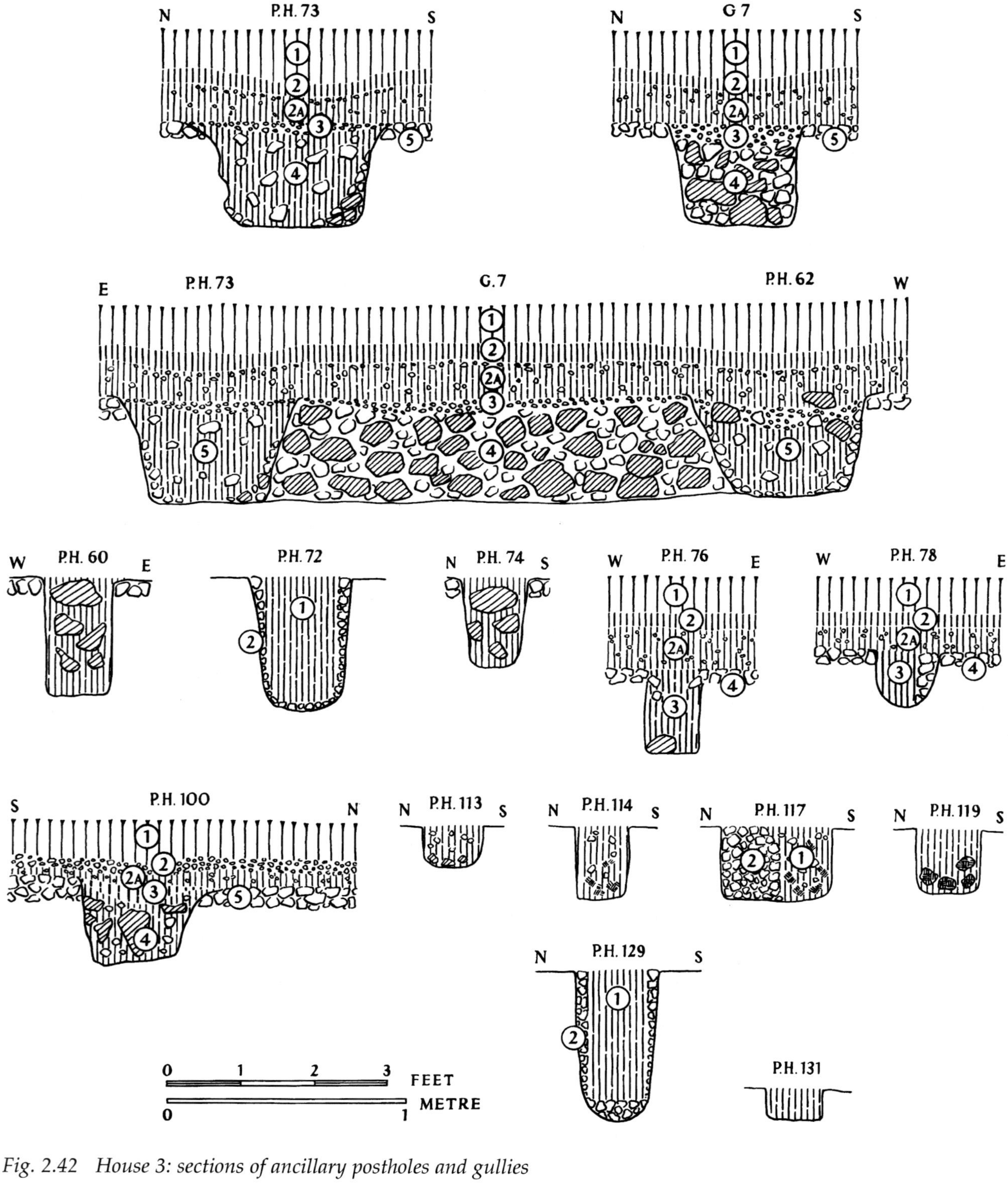

Fig. 2.42 House 3: sections of ancillary postholes and gullies

postholes beside the porch, what we know of the layout suggests that there need have been no more than 10 such very long rafters. Excluding the porch side rafters, which must have been too close for comfort if left projecting at ground level so would anyway have had to be sawn off at the eaves after the building was complete, there could have been as few as five or six grounded rafters originally. In the Pimperne reconstruction the original six were left bedded in the ground to give extra stability to the house.

Whether Iron Age master builders would have followed the same procedure is matter for speculation. Since such projecting post ends could have tripped people up and would anyway have eventually rotted, as proved the case at Pimperne, one suspects that all these posts may have been sawn off neatly at the level of the eaves once the house was completed, to bring them back into line with the rest of the rafters. The reconstruction drawings show these major rafters left projecting (Figs 2.34-2.37). The final choice would have depended on whether they were efficient as stabilisers. Such massive and heavy houses, built on a flat-topped and completely exposed site at the height of 200m above sea level, would have had on occasion to stand up to hurricane force winds such as were experienced by the excavators in 1960, when the site huts were blown down. One supposes that these great roundhouses were precisely designed to withstand such extreme weather conditions and their builders would have had experience, or at least received tradition, in how best to ensure their stability. Certainly the reconstructed Pimperne house survived the great hurricane of 1987 with little damage, but in its valley situation it hardly replicates the exposed situation of the Longbridge houses.

The whereabouts of the eaves in Longbridge Deverill House 3 is no mystery thanks to the preservation of drip gulley G2 to the north of the porch, the least plough damaged part of the house. It indicates that the thatch projected for up to 0.61m beyond the secondary ring of support posts. The area of the house covered by thatch would thus have been as great in diameter as 16.75m. Reynolds commented that drip gullies form only where there is bare earth below the eaves (Harding, Blake and Reynolds 1993, 108). At Longbridge the presence of such gullies tends to support the notion that much activity took place on either side of the porch, especially around PH3, which has already been mentioned as a much used and replaced external feature of the house.

The secondary ring of posts may have been erected at the same time as the main ring post circle, but the shallowness and variety and, above all, the oval shape of some of the holes, argues against it. The impression they give is that these posts were relatively slight, and had been inserted under the eaves at a fairly advanced stage in the construction of the house. The shallow, sometimes oval, postholes would have enabled them to be manoeuvred into position. If so, the full complement of rafters, presumably made of coppice grown oak or ash, must have been positioned independently of this secondary post ring. They would have been adequately supported by the main post ring with its stoutly constructed lintel, by a ringbeam erected around the original group of long rafters near the apex of the roof, and by one or more extra ringbeams fashioned around the full compliment of rafters before the building was thatched.

Edward Impey, the creator of the reconstruction drawings, envisaged an outer ringbeam supported by this post ring under the eaves of the thatch. The posts in this secondary ring can be calculated as standing about 1.83m high under the eaves and Impey, considering the practicalities of reconstruction, was tempted to locate the main daubed outer wall here. He was unhappy about the height and weight of the wattle and daub infilling if it had been placed, as the position of the surviving daub suggested, between the main ring posts. However, I witnessed daub being successfully applied to a wattled wall of this height during the reconstruction of a Viking farmhouse in Jutland. Everything about House 3 suggests that one should not underestimate the skills of its builders, so to have constructed 3.66m high walls of wattlework would surely not have been beyond their capabilities.

The secondary post ring in House 3 is very different in character from that in the Pimperne House, where its function as support for the main daubed outer wall was not in question, and it is not at all well suited to the support of wattle and daub panels except perhaps in certain sectors. It seems therefore to have functioned in a relatively minor, perhaps ornamental as well as utilitarian, way. As well as serving as props for the ring beam supporting the thatch, the posts in this second ring could have served as supports for light screening around a low verandah or storage area around the exterior of the house. The not inconsiderable space below the eaves could have been very useful for protecting farm implements, vehicles, the domestic woodpile, animals and, in summer, even humans from the elements. It could have been partitioned to serve any number of purposes and carried outer screens of varying character, including lightly daubed panels.

For comparison we should look at the Crickley Hill house, where there had apparently been daubed outer screens surviving as a ring of burnt daub, supported by outer ring posts that had not been dug down into the ground and thus left no trace in the form of postholes (Dixon 1976, 174, fig. 8; Guilbert 1981, fig. 8,N). Clearly, once the main ring posts and their lintels were in position, the placing and construction of main walls and screens in these great roundhouses was a matter for personal choice or local tradition, or both. But if the Longbridge Deverill houses are typical at all as a series, the builders and users were clearly capable of innovation and improvements in the light of experience.

In the Longbridge Deverill house series the creation in House 3 of a secondary ring of posts to provide screened external space around the main wall of the house was itself an innovation. It seems to have been absent in House 2. On either side of the inner porch posts, the secondary post ring gave way to a continuous curving slot or gully about 3.66m long. G1 to the north of the porch was round bottomed, 0.13m deep and incorporated PH6 and PH7, which may have been earlier features. They were both filled with dark earth but G1 also contained burnt earth and charcoal. By contrast G2, the drip gully alongside it, contained only chalky silt. G3, to the south of the porch, had a rounded bottom 0.23m deep and was filled with dark earth and pottery. Here there were no earlier or integral postholes. G1 and G3 seem both to have belonged to an early, though not the first, version of porch construction and these two gullies presumably functioned as bedding trenches for some fairly substantial form of screening, either for timber planking or, more likely, for daubed wattlework. Either or both these 3.66m lengths of solidly protected outside space could have been partitioned off from the rest of the 'verandah' area, to make 'vestibules' on either side of the inner porch.

The uses for such vestibules could have been legion, but that to the south of the porch provides a clue. In its final form G3 cut through a pre-existing drainage gully G4, with a chalky silt fill like G2, which ran out from the under eaves area in a south-easterly direction into unexcavated ground. This looks like a gully caused by running water. There may simply have been a leak in the roof here, which seems unlikely since there are no other such gullies, or there may be some other explanation. Might this have been a place for human ablutions, or even for stalling a milk cow in this covered and convenient position outside the house proper but beside the inner entrance? Certainly one should not forget the variety of human needs that must have been met within the scope and purlieus of such a sophisticated and evidently practical great dwelling structure as House 3. As perhaps the ultimate or penultimate development in a long history of roundhouse building on the site, it must have incorporated in its design the answer to the experience and needs of many ancestral generations of builders and inhabitants. In its heyday it must have been a very impressive dwelling indeed.

The ESE facing porch in particular commands our attention. It was an imposing affair that projected from the secondary post ring for 1.52m and had an internal width of 3.40m. The posts that supported it, as an essentially freestanding structure abutting the house, are noticeably smaller than the main ring posts, not exceeding 0.23m in diameter. Reinforced as they must have been by lintels, tying them together and to the main ring posts in the house interior, these porch posts carried only the weight of the porch itself and presumably could afford to be less massive. Nonetheless, their recut postholes suggest that the innermost porch posts had both been replaced during the lifetime of the house.

The fact that the outer posts were apparently not replaced suggests that the porch was only partly rebuilt, and only the inner posts requiring renewal. This, the only evidence in the house for rotten timbers, is easily explicable. Whereas the posts in the house interior would have been well insulated from the weather and the external posts protected by the deep eaves of thatch and the drying effects of sun and wind, the inner porch posts were perhaps the most vulnerable timbers in the building. The sharp angles between the roof of the main house and its gabled porch would have been the weakest parts of the whole great expanse of thatch, becoming veritable watercourses in wet weather, and thus liable to waterlogging. In extremes of bad weather enough rain could have seeped through and trickled down the inner porch posts to soak the ground there and eventually rot the bases of these timbers. A visit in August 1985 to the 'Pimperne House' at Butser (Reynolds 1979, 93-103), which is similar in scale if not in exact constructional detail, provided confirmatory evidence on this point. Less than ten years after it was built, the thatch where its projecting porch adjoined the main roof had become sodden and moss grown. Indeed major rethatching was under way to reduce the sharp angles at the back of the porch.

Even partially dismantling House 3 porch must have been a major undertaking, given that it could have stood anything up to 5.50m high at the gable and had its side walls and gable clad in wattle work and daub plaster. The shallow gullies connecting the pairs of porch postholes presumably served as foundations for infill panels of wattle, which would have been daubed. These gullies seem not to have survived the reconstruction of the porch, and it seems likely that the secondary posts which slightly cut them, PH10 and its (unnumbered) counterpart on the north side, set mid-way between the main pairs of posts, were introduced to help support the weight of extra thatch on top of wattle and daub walls 1.5m wide and up to 3.65m high. It was of course impossible to determine the original height of the porch, but a distance of 3.65m at the sides assumes that the porch lintels were at the same height as those of the main ring posts. In the 'Pimperne House' reconstruction, the lintel of the porch was deliberately lowered, presumably as a protection against bad weather.

However, Longbridge House 3 was more sophisticated, with an outer porch and a kind of inner lobby between it and the entrance through the main ring wall into the interior of the house itself. There could thus have been a progressive diminution of the height of the doorways, but this may not have been regarded as aesthetically pleasing or even necessary since the entrance arrangements allowed for at least two places where light doors, screens or curtains could have been interposed between the snug interior and the elements outside. An imposingly big porch introducing the maximum of light may well have been considered more important than draught exclusion. Otherwise, why make the porch so very wide? In the interior there were anyway several pairs of postholes between the entrance and the supposed central position of the fireplace, which could have supported further screens against draughts as well as such things as racks for drying clothes or working skins indoors.

The large projecting porch is a feature of all the major post built roundhouses (Guilbert 1981) and they must have provided a great amenity to their inhabitants in the form of a well-lit antechamber. At Longbridge, as elsewhere, the porches of all the houses faced ESE, away from the prevailing wind and into the early morning sun. They thus provided a sheltered place to enjoy the first draughts of fresh clean air after a night spent sleeping in a smoky interior. Very probably they provided a place to sit and talk during the daytime away from the hubbub around the hearth, and a place in which to work in a good light at tasks such as carving and weaving. It is not impossible to imagine the household loom being carried out into the porch in summer. Within the south side of the porch of House 3 was a little group of rectangular stakeholes. If these belonged to the period of the house, and it is difficult to interpret them otherwise, they could be the traces of some activity requiring sticks being driven into the ground. For example, one could imagine a woman sitting with her back to the porch wall doing tablet weaving.

And one could certainly imagine people sitting in the porch keeping an eye open for visitors. Visitors, except for friends and kin from Enclosure I close by to the north, were most likely to approach from the downs to the east and south-east, where Bowen found traces of a double lynchet track and further enclosures on Whiten Hill (see Chapter 1). Doubtless there were other settlements on the downs yet further off to the south and east where the Longbridge settlement, on its northern extremity, could be approached from the rest of the block of downland between the rivers Wylye and Nadder. The entrances to the Longbridge houses, therefore, commanded approaches from the community's most vulnerable quarter.

It is clear, from the nature of the hillfort sites of Crickley Hill, Winklebury Camp, Balksbury Camp and the enclosed settlements at Little Woodbury, Pimperne Down and Longbridge Deverill, that the occupants of our great roundhouses were people of substance, some of them perhaps ranking as chieftains or even regional overlords. While not claiming anything more for the 'top man' at Longbridge than that he belonged to the landed gentry of his day; the extent of his fields, about 100 acres (40ha) under plough, in addition to unknown amounts of land used for meadow and rough grazing, suggesting affluence, and the quality of his pottery, and above all that of his ancestors, that he prided himself on the appearance of his dinner service, it is clear that he must have occupied a position in society that could have involved such traditional exploits as cattle raids on the one hand and ceremonial visits and entertainment on a lavish scale on the other. The porch of his roundhouse is likely to have been an important feature in his social life, as lookout post when visitors were predatory, and as reception area when visitors came seeking hospitality. The larger and more imposing the porch the better it would have fitted its ceremonial role, therefore, which is why the reconstruction drawings favour a high gable. And the porch is likely to have been handsomely decorated, so one would expect the woodwork of the jambs and lintel to have been carved all over, with the addition of decorative finials, and the plaster-work painted or impressed with ornament.

In reconstructing these fine houses it is all too easy to be cautious as to the extent of the decoration displayed, for of course it is impossible for us to reconstruct its precise character. The modern tendency, displayed in the 'Pimperne House' at Butser, to play safe and recreate only the basic minimalist structure, denying it sophisticated carpentry, comeliness and practical features such as a well-made and well polished earth floor, devalues the grandeur of the finish of the originals. Houses such as Longbridge House 3, which used large resources of timber in their construction, would have been finished externally and internally to the highest quality. Internally they are likely, within the concept of their day, to have been sophisticated.

As has already been remarked, the hearth of House 3 was ploughed away probably in Roman times, but it is likely to have been placed centrally. Between it and the door were postholes, mostly paired, which probably supported screens and/or drying racks. In addition to these there were seven postholes which were tailor made to contain deep-set structural posts about 0.30m in diameter. They formed an irregular circle approximately 2.75m inside the main structural post ring, were as deeply bedded and clearly were themselves structural and intended to carry a considerable weight. At the time of excavation, when less was known about the plans of other great roundhouses and no practical experiment had been made into their construction, it was thought that they might have supported a scaffold erected to help in the construction of the roof. This remains a possibility, but Reynolds has shown that such a scaffold would probably not have been necessary. Another possibility, included in Impey's reconstructions of the house interior, is that these timbers were positioned to support a platform level with the top of the main post ring, thus making use of some of the huge amount of 'dead' space in the house above floor level. Such a platform would still have left up to 5.20m of clearance around the open hearth and would therefore probably not have created a fire hazard or problems with dispersal of smoke. It might have been useful for extra sleeping accommodation and certainly for storage. The porch being wide enough to have driven a cart through, there is no practical limit to what might have been stored aloft, including hay and seed corn, except of course the untested question of fire hazard and the inadequate information about ancillary structures. The suggested platform, 3.66m above the ground, might have served to make the domestic quarters below somewhat snugger and better protected from swirling smoke in windy weather.

There is evidence from such a fully excavated site as Crickley Hill, as well as strong presumptions from Little Woodbury and Longbridge Deverill itself, that, some possible but much slighter ancillary structures notwithstanding, the great roundhouses existed singly at any one time as the chief social and residential structure for the whole community. We therefore have to reckon with the fact that these huge houses would presumably have been partitioned internally into different functional areas; communal cooking, eating and working areas, being presumably separated from sleeping quarters for individual units within the whole larger unit occupying the structure. Perhaps the innermost ring posts had the additional function of helping support radial partitions of such a flimsy character – of wattlework, daub, hides or blankets – that no other trace of them survives. In writing about the internal organisation of a small round shepherd's hut near Veii in northern Italy, Close-Brooks described the division between the cooking area and the shepherds's bunk-beds (Close-Brooks 1966, 350). Bunk-beds have been encountered by Edward Impey, too, in the context of the communal roundhouses of Papua, New Guinea (pers. comm.). Perhaps they also existed in House 3 and its predecessors, but the proof will have gone up in smoke and now escapes us. Nonetheless, House 3 still has precious information to give us about other aspects of its domestic economy.

The distribution of its pottery, for example, despite Roman ploughing, remained very distinct at the time of excavation. The bulk of it was confined to the southern sector of the house, inside the main post ring (surely another indicator that this was the site of the main wall), and to the area of the porch, with a much smaller scatter in and around the postholes on the north side. Other finds, such as loomweights, spindle whorls and bone tools were also confined to the southern half of the house interior. This combined evidence suggests that the south side and porch of the house were the areas of major domestic activity, whereas the other side of the house was given over to other activities, such as sleeping.

Finally we come to the problem of the internal feature consisting of a pair of very substantial postholes, PH62 and PH73, set at the ends of a chalk filled trench 2.9 m long, at the very heart of the scatter of pottery. A pair of recut postholes in a similar position in the southern sector of House 2, again in the thick of a dense concentration of pottery, looked to have been a predecessor. Though interpreted at the time of excavation a 'loom-structure', it was always apparent that this was a most unlikely function. The upright warp-weighted loom does not require to be set vertically into postholes, but rather to be propped against a suitable wall. I am indebted to Philip Dixon for what now seems the obvious explanation – that these were probably the postholes for a fixed piece of furniture such as an earth-fast table or dresser, such as can still be seen in some medieval great halls, on which the family table service and festal meal would be displayed on grand occasions. When the houses burnt down, therefore, the family 'plate', in the form of fine haematite-coated drinking vessels, as well as more utilitarian containers for liquor and food and perhaps their contents, were destroyed with them. This could explain the spread of broken pottery around this posthole feature in House 3, as well as House 2, and possibly also House 1.

The coincidence that a series of at least three great roundhouses were burnt to the ground with their contents over several centuries and were never rebuilt on the same site, as elsewhere in Wessex in this period, raises questions which cannot satisfactorily be answered. Nevertheless the suspicion remains that the fires which destroyed the houses so thoroughly may not have been accidental at all. There are tantalising suggestions of a possible funeral rite, apparently unique to the people on Longbridge Deverill in this latest Bronze/earliest Iron Age phase of culture in Wessex, which involved the deliberate burning of a dead man's house with its contents and respecting the site for all time thereafter. Indian funerals in the North American subcontinent involved similar rituals, but on nothing like so grand or so extravagant a scale.

The sacrifice, if such it was, on a remote piece of downland in Wiltshire, of a whole succession of great roundhouses, with all the investment of timber and possibly professional labour that had been involved, and with their contents set out as for a funeral feast, represents conspicuous waste on a scale to equal princely burial custom in the late Iron Age, with the difference perhaps that there may have been no body involved. Though remains of bone were carefully kept throughout the excavations, no traces of human bones were found in any of the roundhouses. This need not signify. While their lodges burned, the bodies of the Indian chiefs were wrapped in skins and placed in trees, and some comparable rite may have been going on in latest Bronze/early Iron Age Wessex. In the later, 'B' phase of the Iron Age at Longbridge Deverill, certainly, when bits and pieces of human skeletons are a regular feature of the contents of rubbish pits, exposure of the dead, rather than cremation, seems to have been the regular funeral rite. With the burning of the great roundhouses we may be faced with a rare survival of a grander rite, known also in Late Hallstatt Europe.

Table 2.6 House 3 postholes and contents (Figs 2.40- 2.42)

PH	*Dia m*	*Dia post*	*Depth m*	*Packing*	*Pot*	*Artefacts (Fig ref)*	*Ecofacts*
Main ring							
13	0.53	-	0.31	-	-	-	Unspec
14	0.31	-	0.46	-	-	-	Unspec
15	-	-	0.46	'packing'	-	-	-
46	0.41	-	0.36	chalk	-	-	Burnt daub
47	0.53	0.31	0.51	chalk	1	-	Burnt daub; unspec; burnt bone a
51	0.46	0.31	0.53	Chalk			Unspec; bone a
52	0.61	0.38	0.61	Flint	10	-	Daub; unspec; bone a
53	0.61	0.31	0.38	Chalk, flint	-	-	Unspec
57n	-	-	0.41	Chalk	6	Bone spatula (4.4,5)	Unspec
63	0.61	0.38	0.74	-	28	-	Burnt daub; unspec
64	0.46	0.33	0.59	chalk	1	-	Burnt daub; unspec
65	0.46	0.31	0.59	Chalk	1	-	Fired clay
69	0.46	0.31	0.59	Chalk	-	-	Unspec
70	0.69	-	0.64	Chalk	9	-	daub
71	0.61	0.26	0.56	-	15	-	Daub; unspec; bone a
101	0.69	0.38	0.46	Chalk	2	-	Unspec; burnt bone a
102	0.69	0.28	0.51	Chalk	1	-	unspec
103	0.69	0.33	0.38	Chalk	5	-	Daub, unspec charcoal, burnt bone a
104	0.66	0.36	0.48	Chalk	7	-	Daub; oak (HAR-255); burnt bone a
105	0.76	0.31	0.53	Chalk, flint	35	-	Daub; unspec
106	0.76	0.33	0.51	Chalk	38		Daub; oak
107	0.84	0.31	0.59	Chalk	20		Fired clay; daub; oak
108	0.61	0.36	0.56	Chalk		Chalk spindle whorl (4.12,7)	Daub; unspec
109	0.92	0.38	0.46	Chalk	-	Antler gouge/beater (4.4,10)	Daub; unspec; bone
120	0.84	0.36	0.56	Chalk, flint, sstone	12	-	Daub; bone
121	0.69	0.31	0.51	Chalk	5	-	Unspec; bone a
123	0.76	0.33	0.64	-	50	-	Unspec; bone a
124	0.53	0.36	0.59	-	40	-	Daub; fired clay, unspec; bone
Porch							
3	-	-	0.51	Flint		Ae bracelet frag (4.1,5)	Unspec
4	-	0.66	0.76	chalk	16	Iron bracket angle (4.2,3)	Daub; unspec; bone a
5	0.87	0.53	0.61	Chalk	1	2 loomweights (4.8,2-3)	daub
8	0.61	-	0.18	-	-	-	-
9	0.92	-	0.31	-	-	-	-
10	0.31	-	0.15	-	-	Sstone rubber (4.11,5)	Burnt post stump
11	-	-	0.66	-	52	-	Burnt daub, hawthorne hazel
12	-	-	0.31	-	-	-	-
16	0.46	0.23	0.23	-	-	-	Burnt post stump
Outer ring							
17	0.46	-	0.23	-	3	-	-
18	0.61	-	0.23	-	7	Burnt, polished bone	Bone a
19	-	-	0.13	-	-	-	-
20	-	-	0.13	-	-	-	-
21	-	-	0.71	-	-	-	-
22	-	-	0.10	-	-	-	-
50	0.46	-	0.21	-	-	-	-
111	0.26	-	0.76	-	-	-	Unspec
112	0.31	-	0.18	-	-	-	Unspec
115	-	-	0.15	-	-	-	-
116	0.41	-	0.28	-	-	-	-
118	0.53	-	0.33	-	-	-	-
125	0.46	-	0.15	-	-	-	-
126	0.46	-	0.71	-	-	-	-
147	0.92	-	0.21	-	-	-	-

Table 2.6 House 3 postholes and contents (Figs 2.40- 2.42) (continued)

PH	*Dia m*	*Dia post*	*Depth m*	*Packing*	*Pot*	*Artefacts (Fig ref)*	*Ecofacts*
155	-	-	0.21	-	-	-	-
156	-	-	0.15	-	3	-	-
157	-	-	0.71	-	-	-	-
Roof support							
54	-	-	-	-	16	-	-
55	-	-	-	-	32		
60	0.28	-	0.51	Flint	-	-	-
74	0.28	-	0.41	Flint	-	-	-
100	0.46	-	0.36	Flint	-	-	-
110	0.31	-	0.18	Chalk	-	-	Unspec
134	0.31	-	0.61	-	-	-	-
Internal							
66	0.38	0.15	0.33	Flint, chalk	-	-	Unspe
72	0.41	0.31	0.59	Chalk	19	-	-
76	0.31	-	0.33	Flint	-	-	-
77	0.31	-	0.23	-	-	-	-
78	0.31	-	0.23	Chalk	-	-	-
113	0.23	-	0.18	-	-	-	-
114	0.21	-	0.31	-	-	-	Unspec
117	0.21	-	0.31	Chalk		-	-
119	0.28	-	0.28	-	-	-	daub
129	0.36	0.26	0.66	Chalk	4	-	-
130	0.21	-	0.10	-	-	-	-
131	0.23	-	0.13	-	-	-	-
132	0.21	-	0.71	-	-	-	-
133	0.21	-	0.10	-	-	-	-
External							
48	-	-	0.28	Flint	5	-	Bone a
67	0.36	0.31	0.33	Chalk	-	-	-
68	0.31	-	0.33	Chalk, flint	-	-	-
Fitting							
Gully 7	0.71	-	0.38	Chalk, flint	-	-	-
62	0.66	-	0.46	Chalk, lint	59	-	-
73	0.66	-	0.46	Chalk, flint	44	-	Bone a
Rack							
2	0.61	-	0.28	Chalk	-	-	-
49	0.53	0.26	0.43	Chalk	3	-	Unspec
75	0.56	0.21	0.51	Chalk	5		Daub; unspec

Bone a = animal bone; Bone h = human bone

House 4

At 8m in diameter House 4 was the smallest of the Longbridge houses. It was a single ring round-house (Figs 2.43-2.46), markedly less sophisticated than House 2, which preceded it, or House 3, which succeeded it. Including PH209, PH219 and PH220 (but not PH195 or PH196) the ring includes 17 posts. A few pieces of daub were recovered from three postholes, one of the main ring, one interior posthole near the south-west side, and one of the porch postholes. Most was too fragmented for comment, but where unburnt it seems to have been cob daub of chalky composition, similar to that from Houses 1 and 2. Once again, the house seems to have been wattle walled with cob plastering. Some of the daub was very orange in colour, perhaps burnt. The wattle and daub panels would have filled the gaps between the posts, and the joinery of the roof and porch was probably of the pattern suggested for House 1.

Table 2.7 House 4 postholes and contents (Fig. 2.47)

PH	*Dia m*	*Dia post*	*Depth m*	*Packing*	*Pot*	*Artefacts (Fig ref)*	*Ecofacts*
Main ring							
183	0.46	0.21	0.21	Chalk	-	-	Unspec
184	0.41	0.23	0.23	Chalk	1		Daub, oak
185	0.38	-	0.26	Chalk	1	-	-
193	0.33	-	0.28	-	3	-	-
194	0.64	-	0.31	-	-	-	Unspec
195	0.46	-	0.28	Flint	-	Ceramic sling bullet (4.13,6)	daub
196	0.61	-	0.38	Flint, chalk	18	-	Daub, unspec
197	0.41	0.10	0.21	Chalk	1	-	Daub, oak
198	0.41	0.21	0.21	Chalk	20	-	Wall daub, oak (HAR-254)
199	0.51	-	0.26	Chalk	4	-	Daub, oak
200	0.46	0.21	0.23	Chalk	-	Ceramic spindle whorl (4.12,4)	Unspec
207	0.41	-	0.33	Chalk	35	-	Daub, unspec charcoal
208	0.51	0.26	0.36	Chalk	1	Antler weaving comb (4.4,2)	Wall daub, oak & hawthorn
209	0.46	0.28	0.48	Chalk, flint, Sstone	-	-	-
210	0.26	-	0.31	Chalk	3	-	Wall daub, unspec
230	0.48	-	0.31	-	-	-	-
232	0.41	-	0.43	Chalk	2	-	Unspec
Internal							
187	0.41	-	0.13	-	1		
188	0.26	-	0.13	-	-	-	-
191	0.33	-	0.10	-	-	-	-
192	0.36	-	0.26	Chalk, flint			
202	0.48	-	0.15	Chalk	-	-	bone
205	0.28	-	0.15	-	-	-	-
211	0.41	-	0.31	Chalk flint	3	-	-
219	-	-	-	-	-	-	-
220	0.36	-	0.23	-	-	-	-
231	0.31	-	0.23	Chalk	-	-	-
External							
189	0.26	-	0.10	-	-	-	-
201	0.28	-	0.13	Chalk	1	-	-
206	0.31	-	0.10	Chalk	-	-	-
212	0.31	-	0.21	'stone'	-	-	-
215	0.31	-	0.18	Chalk	-	-	Oak
216	0.69	0.48	0.38	Chalk	14	Chert rubber	Daub, oak, hawthorne, hazel
217	0.71	0.18	0.41	-	1	-	Unspec (HAR-256)
218	0.81	-	0.53	Chalk,flint	-	Sstone rubber (4.11,4)	-
221	0.31	-	0.23	Chalk, flint	-	-	-
222	0.15	-	0.18	Chalk	2	-	-
223	0.48	-	0.23	Flint	-	-	-
226	0.66	-	0.51	Chalk, flint	-	-	-
236	0.33	-	0.18	-		-	-
240	0.26	-	0.10	-	-	-	-

Bone a = animal bone; Bone h = human bone

In contrast to the other houses it is possible that at some stage House 4 was partially surrounded by a fence formed of slender poles set within gullies G1-3 (Fig. 2.44). However, as PHs 208, 210, 216 and 217 seem likely to have supported porch posts, this phase of the house and the gullies and fence may not have been contemporary. The gap between PHs 218 and 226 looks like a break in the fence corresponding to a house doorway represented by PHs 208 and 209. Therefore, if the fence and house were standing at the same time, the doorway was probably narrowed by the insertion of post PH209

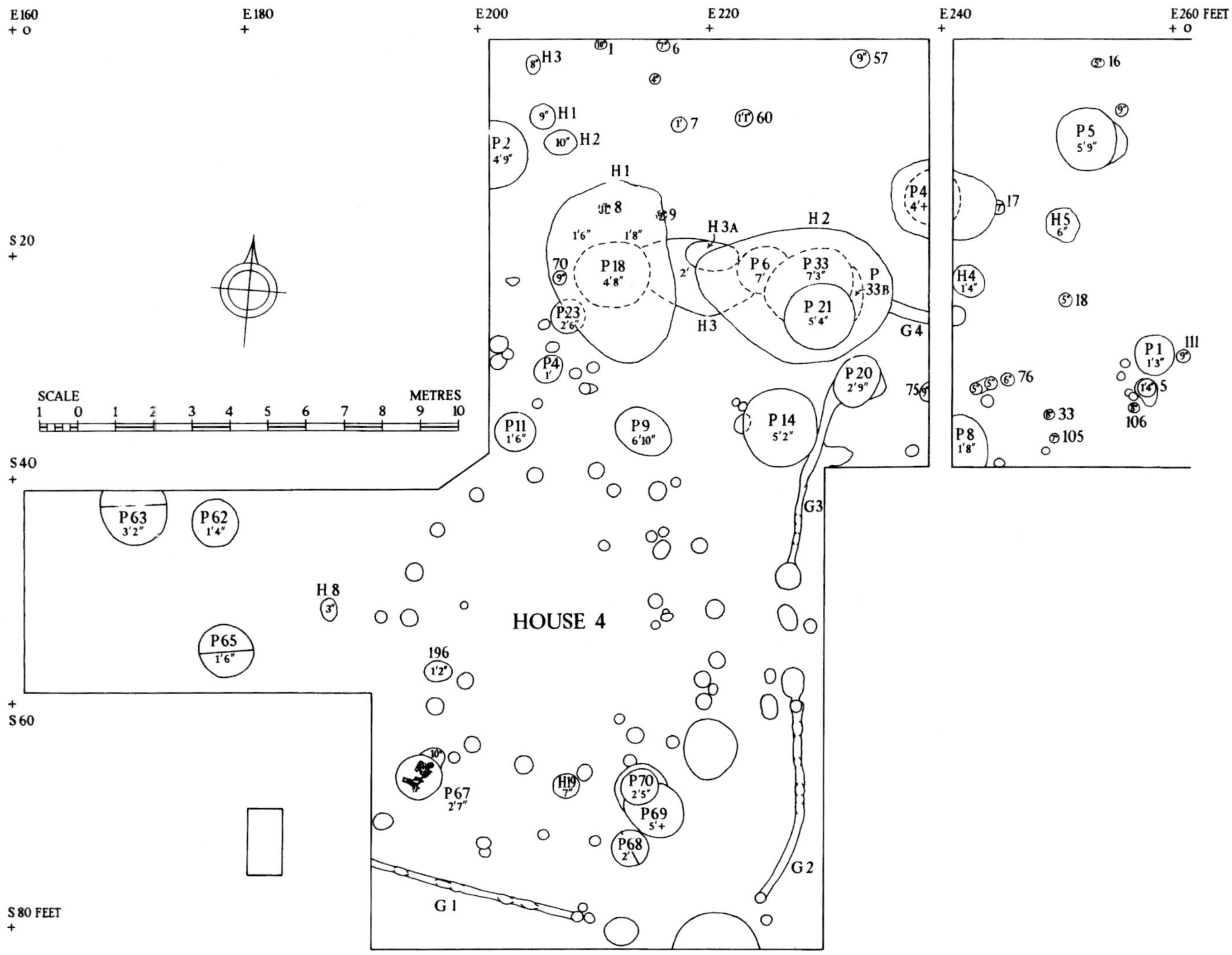

Fig. 2.43 Enclosure II Area S1: House 4

and the removal of posts PH216 and PH217, leaving it without a porch. At this stage, either earlier or later than the porch phase, the fence was created with an entrance corresponding to the door of the hut. The arrangement of the postholes in the gullies is curious, especially in G 1 and 2. The apparently paired postholes would not have been ideally placed for a wattle fence built *in situ* and are perhaps more likely to have been supports for hurdles fixed between them, although the large gap at the south-east corner of the fence may indicate that its purpose was more as a windbreak than a barrier.

The internal postholes show no obvious pattern and at best can probably only be said to have been part of various indoor fittings, either temporary or permanent. The group PH187, PH188 and PH192 was possibly associated with the entrance during either of its supposed phases, perhaps supporting a screen to the north side of the entrance. Just on the exterior, PH189, PH236 and PH240 might have held small posts intended to buttress up the daub wall from the outside.

The Longbridge Deverill roundhouses – an afterword

by Lisa Brown

When Sonia Hawkes published her paper on House 3 in 1994, she would have been scarcely aware of a resurgence of interest within the archaeological arena in British prehistoric roundouses. The mechanisms of investigation and interpretation of these structures had evolved, and cosmological approaches became a popular method, championed by Parker Pearson (1996), Oswald (1997) and Fitzpatrick (1997). In the very year that House 3 was published, Fitzpartrick presented a study of the social space of a 7th-6th century BC roundhouse excavated in 1989-1991 at Dunstan Park in Berkshire

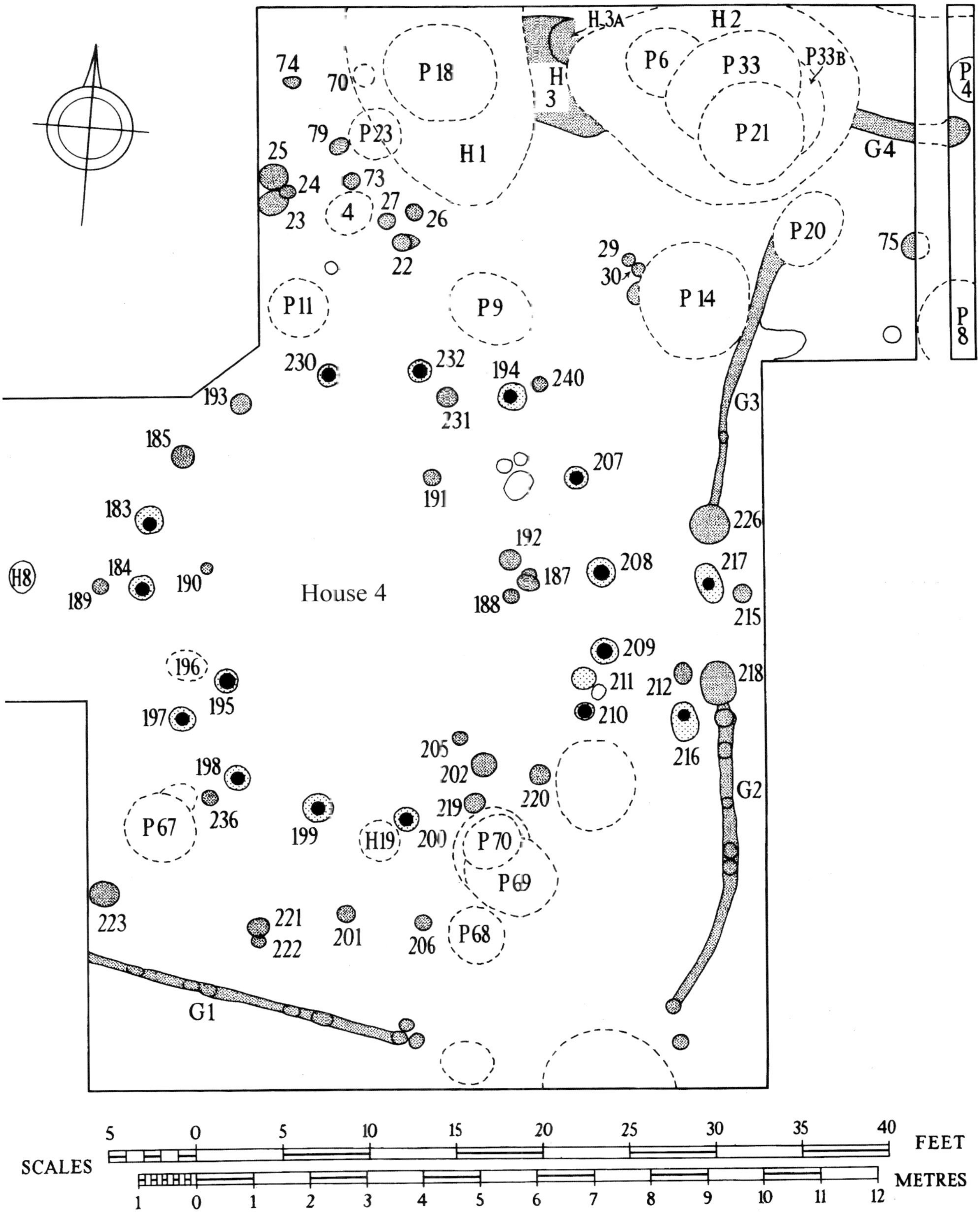

Fig. 2.44 Enclosure II Area S1: House 4

(Fitzpatrick 1994). Just a year earlier a paper by Coe and Newman (1993) examined various aspects of a burnt-out roundhouse at Brighton Hill South, Hampshire, reprised in a monograph shortly thereafter (Fasham *et al.* 1995). A pertinent study by Webley (2007) included the evidence from the Longbridge Deverill excavations in an examination of use and abandonment of roundhouses during the late Bronze Age-early Iron Age period in southern England. Rachel Pope's extensive research on the use of domestic space, especially roundhouses, published in the same year, seeks to contextualise, mainly through functional interpretations, routine behaviours and activities in prehistoric Britain (Pope 2007; 2008). Sharples even more recent consideration of later prehistoric Wessex pays particular attention to the the character of houses, and the late Bronze Age to early Iron Age transitional period to which the Longbridge settlement belongs.

With the benefit of hindsight, aspects of Sonia Hawkes' interpretation of, for example, the spatial distribution of pottery within House 1 may appear naïve (see Chapter 3, Catalogue of Illustrated Pottery, Enclosure II House 1), but she was working in the context of an earliest Iron Age Britain comprehended at the time from the results of a very few excavated sites of this period. The recent studies mentioned above were conducted against a background of prolific and growing evidence for the construction, use and decommissioning of roundhouses accumulated over several decades of excavation in Britain, and especially in the Wessex

Fig. 2.45 House 4: palisade entrance viewed from the north (1960)

region. Hawkes attention to detail during and following the Longbridge excavations, and her obvious enthusiasm for the subject, have provided us with an impressive body of evidence for the four 'great' roundhouses, enhanced by the admirable site plans of Marion Cox and reconstruction drawings of Edward Impey.

THE ENCLOSURE II PITS

by Lisa Brown (based on catalogues by Sonia Chadwick Hawkes)

Over 70 pits in Areas S1-S3 were full or partially excavated, and most of them were drawn in section (Figs 2.48-2.50; 2.57). Judging by the stratigraphic and ceramic evidence, the majority of the pits post-dated the earliest Iron Age settlement represented by Houses 1-4, some of them slighting structural features or cutting through floor levels of the abandoned houses.

Most of the pits were cylindrical in shape, the exceptions being three beehive pits – P7, P21 and P32. A number of others were too shallow to judge their original shape and a few were of irregular profile, hybrids of cylindrical and beehive shapes (Table 2.8). In a study by Alasdair Whittle of the pits at Danebury, cylindrical pits were characterised as having a 'circular mouth, sometimes oval or squarish, equal or greater in diameter to a flat base of similar form and sides thus vertical or steeply sloping. In the completely uneroded examples the sides are straight, and slightly concave examples are most probably

Fig. 2.46 House 4: palisade entrance viewed from the south (1960)

slightly weathered below the mouth' (Whittle 1984, 131). In contrast to Longbridge, cylindrical pits represented a much smaller proportion of all the 1707 pits excavated at Danebury, accounting for only 13% (Poole 1991, 160). It seems that at Danebury, at least, the beehive form increased in popularity at the expense of the cylindrical shape by the late 5th century or thereabouts, possibly due to their greater efficiency for storage purposes (Whittle 1984, 131).

The Longbridge Deverill beehive pits are not especially well-dated, certainly not sufficiently to place them in a later phase than the numerous cylindrical pits, a class to which, in fact, the only certain example of a later middle Iron Age pit (P22) belongs. Although a radiocarbon date was obtained on material from 'well down' in the fill of beehive P7 (Appendix 2B), located to the south of Posthole Complex 5, the broad range of 830-170 cal BC was not helpful in defining its place in the chronological sequence. The longevity of the cylindrical form at

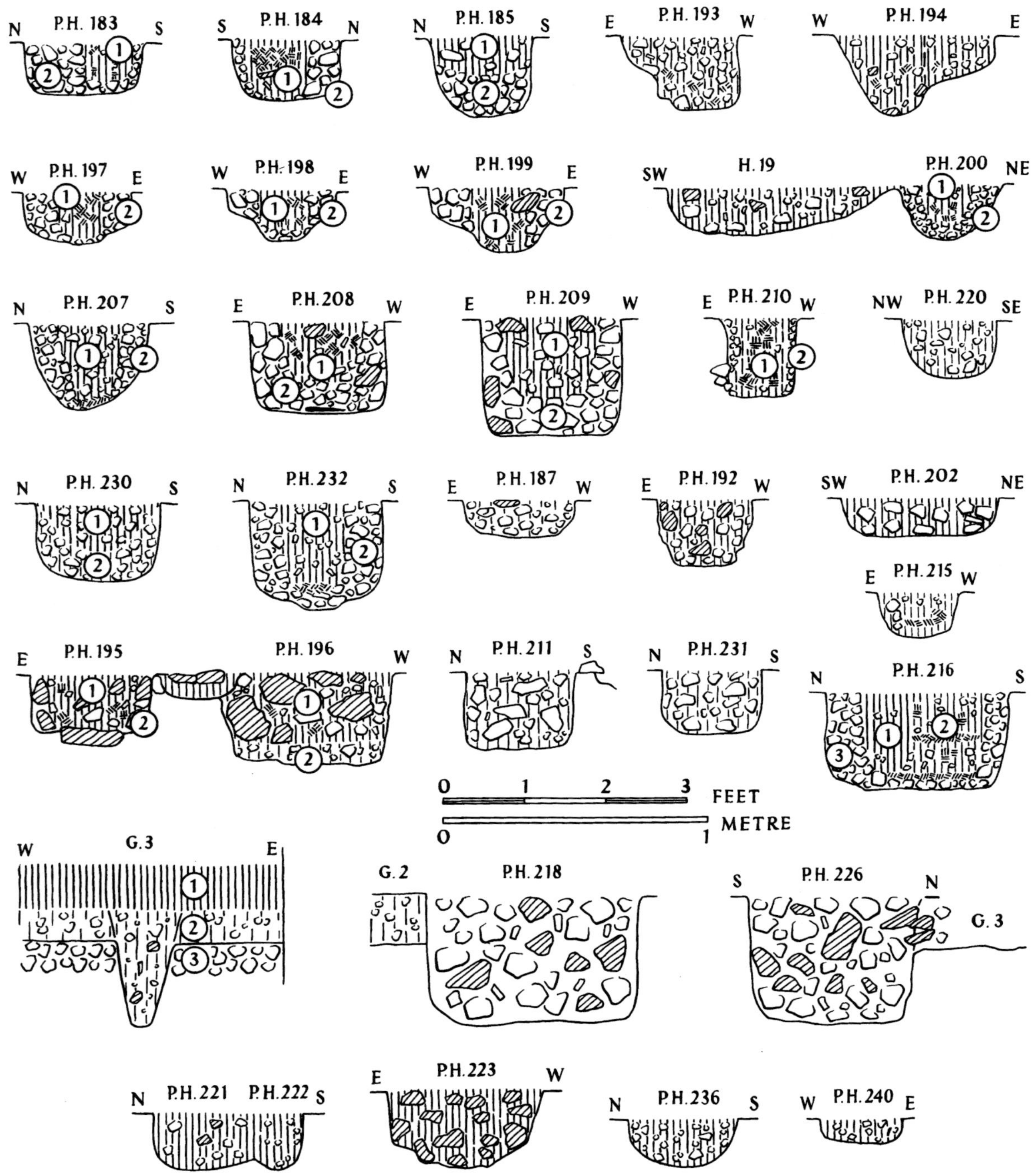

Fig. 2.47 House 4: sections of postholes and gullies

Longbridge may reflect differences in settlement function and agricultural practices to sites like Danebury and Winnall Down, Hants, where beehive forms were also predominant by the middle Iron Age (Winham 1985, 22). The continuing preference for the cylindrical form throughout the life of the early to late Iron Age settlement at Gussage All Saints, Dorset, for example, indicates that the the pattern of displacement by beehive pits was not a consistent one across southern England (Jefferies 1979, 9-15).

The stratigraphic and ceramic evidence indicates that most of the Longbridge pits were backfilled sometime bewteen the end of early Iron Age and beginning of the middle Iron Age – between the 5th-early 3rd centuries BC. It is difficult to be more precise as many of the pottery forms had a long currency and, unfortunately, scientific dating was limited to three very broad radiocarbon dates – two from P37 (770-360 cal BC and 810-370 cal BC) and one from P7 (830-170 cal BC). The dates were all subject to the limitation of the wide standard deviation associated with the radiocarbon ages of plateau-affected deposits of this part of the Iron Age (see Chapter 6).

Nonetheless, a helpful chronological indicator is provided by a total absence in the pit assemblages of a key element of an important local early Iron Age ceramic tradition based in the Wiltshire region – scratched-cordoned bowls dated to the 5th-early 4th centuries BC (see Chapter 3). Their absence at Longbridge, apart from a single sherd from PH235 associated with House 1, must signify that the Longbridge pits belonged to the period later than the currency of these bowls, perhaps the mid-late 4th-early 3rd centuries BC. This suggests a gap of at least 100 years between the abandonment of earlier settlement, probably no later than the 6th century BC, and the reoccupation of the site by the pit-digging community. The alternative explanation, that the later settlement simply did not import and use scratched-cordoned bowls, seems highly unlikely considering the proximity of Longbridge Deverill to the manufacturing centre, and the widespread distribution of these particular wares within the Wessex region.

Although none of the pits appear to have been contemporary with the early settlement, the plethora of these features in Area S indicates intensive settlement activity within the enclosure following the abandonment of the roundhouses. Yet no evidence of structures contemporary with the majority of these pits was found in the excavated area, so it it seems likely that the focus of the later settlement lay elsewhere and that the pits were concentrated, perhaps in zones, at a remove from its domestic heart.

In summary, them, the pottery assemblages from many of the pits confirm that they post-date the earliest Iron Age settlement represented by Houses 1-4, some by several centuries, and that most were backfilled during a period somewhere within the 4th-early 3rd centuries BC. In Table 2.8 below, the date range provided by these forms is indicated as EIA-MIA, suggesting a broad and transitional phase between the currency of the distinctive forms of the earliest Iron Age (but after the scratched-cordoned bowl horizon) and the fully-developed middle Iron Age tradition.

One of the pit assemblages that perhaps best typifies the transitional early Iron Age-middle Iron Age (late 4th-3rd century BC) stylistic range was recovered from P37. This was a relatively deep (1.58m) cylindrical pit cut through the floor of burnt-out House 2. The fill profile shows a deliberate rather than gradually accumulated fill sequence (Fig. 2.48). On the base of the pit was a concentration of charred barley that had evidently been placed in a bag set on the pit base (see Morrison, Hawkes and Smith, Chapter 5). An iron sickle (Fig. 4.2, 11) had been placed on top of the grain, perhaps sealing the bag. A radiocarbon date of 810-370 cal BC was obtained on charred hazel wood from the pit, but the wood may well have been residual debris, along with burnt wall daub, from the house fire. A second, slightly later date of 770-360 cal BC on the barley itself allows for a mid 4th century date for the backfilling.

A number of other artefacts recovered from the pit include an iron knife and a bone handle, stone loomweights and a ceramic slingshot in addition to almost 200 sherds of pottery (Fig. 3.19). Notably, very little pottery contemporary with the house was recovered apart from from a furrowed cup sherd (Fig. 3.7, 14), which Hawkes quite rightly illustrated with the House 2 assemblage, understanding that it was contemporary with the occupation of the building and not the filling of the pit. The absence of other earliest Iron Age pottery can no doubt be attributed to the post-destruction clearance practices seen more clearly in the case of House 3 (Webley 2007). In contrast, however, P40, which also lay within House 2, produced a small assemblage made up almost entirely of earliest Iron Age pottery (Fig. 3.22)

Some other pits that yielded assemblages of reasonable size, incorporating some elements diagnostic of an early Iron Age- middle Iron Age transitional style, are cylindrical pits P11 (Figs 2.50 and 3.28), P53 and P59 (Figs 2.49, 2.50 and 3.23); beehive pit P21 (Figs 2.48 and 3.25); and P33/33B (no section, Fig. 3.25). Cylindrical P69/70 contained a range of metal atrefacts, including a bronze punch (Fig. 4.1, no. 1), an iron socket (Fig. 4.2, no. 5) and a bone tool (Fig. 4.4 no. 7) associated with a pottery assemblage of over 120 sherds that included a complete vessel (Fig. 3.21, no.7), which seems to fit within transitional ceramic phase.

Nonetheless, a number of pit assemblages may be somewhat later than those described above. These include P14, P18, P33, P43, P46, P54, P55, and P 69/70. Most of these produced, in addition to pottery of consistently more rounded shape or well-finished quality, other artefacts : P14 – shale ring; P33 – crucible; P43- chalk weights; P54 – bronze and iron artefacts and pyrites; P69/70 – bronze and iron objects and a bone tool. One pit produced a pottery assemblage that certainly must belong to the later part of the middle Iron Age, probably to some point after the mid 3rd century BC (Figs 2.50 and 3.29). It contained at least one near complete decorated saucepan pot and a second with a perhaps related type of decoration (Fig. 3.29, Pit 22, nos 1 and 2). P22 was a small feature, cylindrical in form and only 0.76m deep, located just to the north-east of House 1, close to intercutting Pits 19 and 32. It is clear from the section drawing that P22 was deliberately backfilled with an occupation-rich deposit that made up the primary fill. Although the site records do not record the position of the pots within the pit, they most likely were incorporated within this fill

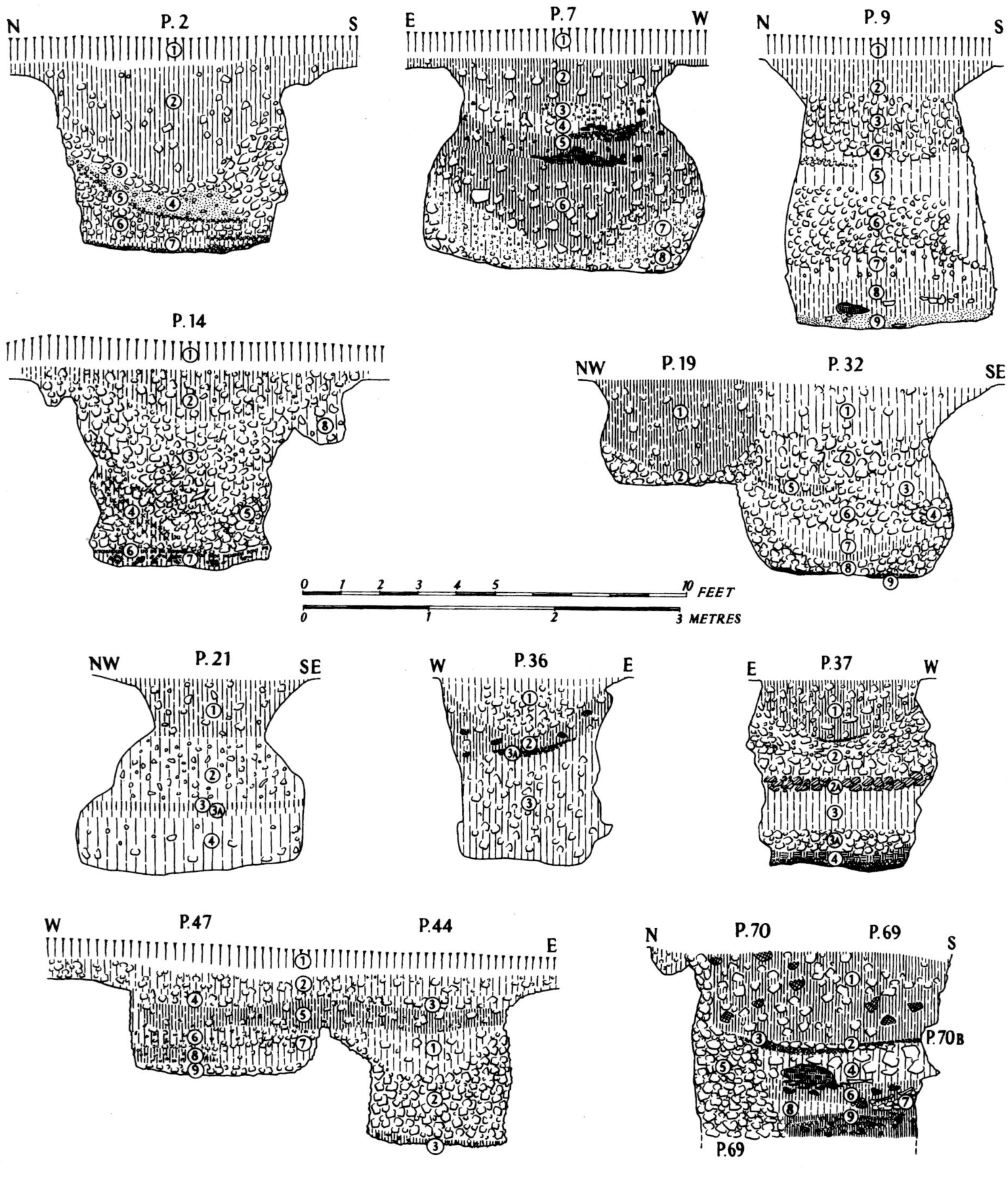

Fig. 2.48 Enclosure II pit sections

(3), and may have been especially selected for deposition. This ceramic group seems out of keeping with the other pit assemblages, and could point either to continual occupation of the site between the 4th and 2nd-first centuries BC, or to a very limited later middle Iron Age presence.

Several of the pits contained deposits of artefacts, natural stone and animal and human remains that were obviously specially selected for deposition, rather than representing chance components of backfill material. The contents of the very productive P37 have been discussed above. Complete or near-complete pots were found in P22, P37, P64 and P69/70, the large jar in P64 (Fig. 3.22) accompanied by a penannular brooch (Fig. 4.1, no. 9), probably of 4th century date (see Chapter 4).

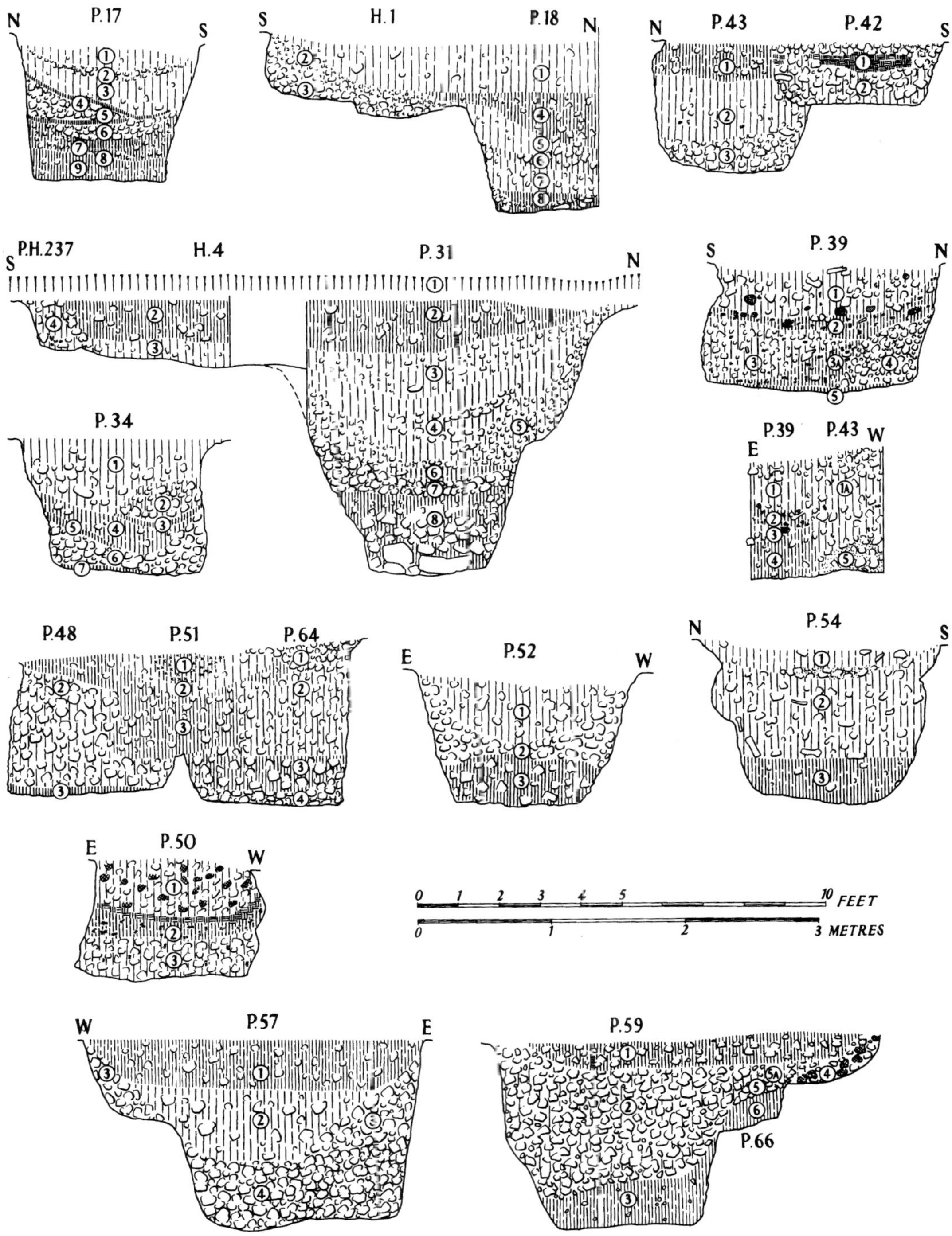

Fig. 2.49 *Enclosure II pit sections*

Complete animals were buried in P5 (not illustrated) and P53 (see Chapter 5). In the case of P5 a lamb burial was accompanied by pyrites and a sizeable collection of 145 sherds of pottery, including substantial fragments of jars and bowls (Fig. 3.18). A dog skeleton (Fig. 2.52) was found in P53, again associated with a large pottery collection, possibly of slightly later date (Fig. 3.23), fuel ash slag, probably the remains of an oven, and loomweights. Other examples of articulated animal bone were photographed *in situ* during excavation but not drawn and, in most cases the pit numbers are not recorded on the photographs, so a level of detail is lost. A cattle skull was photographed in P31, with a probably related long bone visible (Fig. 2.53) and horse skulls and mandibles in P39 (Figs 2.54-2.55).

Three human burials were also associated with pits. An infant of about six months had been placed just below the uppermost fill of P63, to the west of House 4 in Area S1 (Figs. 2.43 and 2.50), but few details were recorded (Appendix 2B) and no plan or

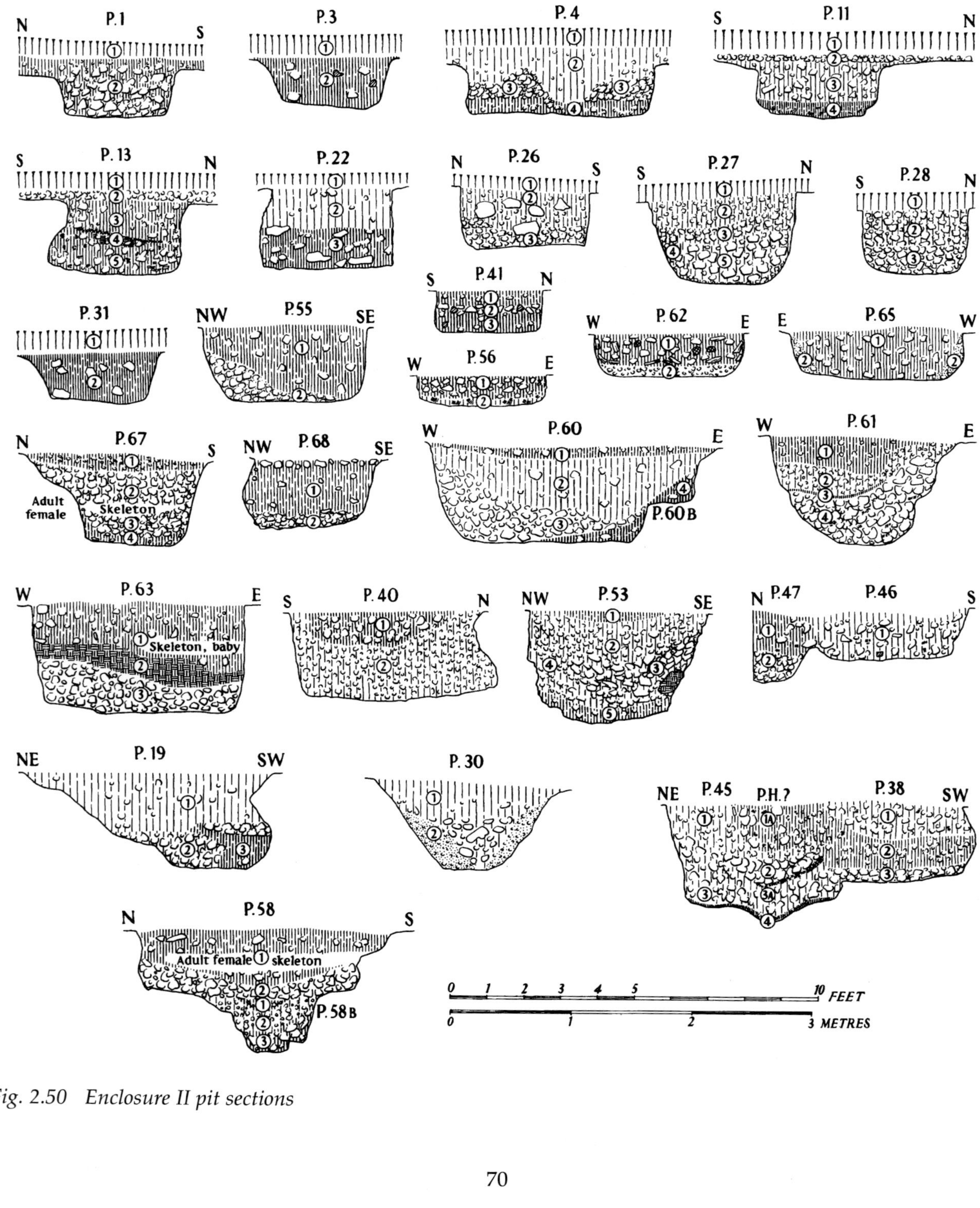

Fig. 2.50 Enclosure II pit sections

Table 2.8 Enclosure II Pits and contents

Pit	Form	Dia	Depth	Fills	Pot	Artefact	Ecofacts	Deposit	Date
1	Cylindrical	0.97	0.38	1	-	Chalk loomwt (4.7,1); daub	bone a,h	-	-
2	Cylindrical	2.44	1.45	6	23	Iron tool (4.2,8)	Bone a, oak hawthorn hazel		EIA-MIA
3	Cylindrical	1.12	0.41	1	15		Bone a		EIA-MIA
4	Cylindrcal	1.58	0.43	3	4	'clay object'	daub	-	-
5 (ni)	-	1.60	1.75	-	145	pyrites	Hazel, bone a	Complete lamb	EIA-MIA
6 (ni)	= H4	-	2.13	-	-	-	-	-	-
7	Beehive	1.67	1.60	7	38	Slag, hearth botton, chalk loomwt (4.9,2); daub; fired clay	bone a		830-170 cal BC
8 (ni)	-	-	0.51	-	2	-	Bone a, h	-	EEIA-MIA
9	Beehive	1.93	2.08	8	33	-	Bone a	-	EIA-MIA
10 (ni)	-	1.2	0.26	-	29	-	-	-	-
11	Cylindrical	1.42	0.46	3	50+	-	Ash	-	EIA-MIA
12 (ni)	= H4	-	0.41	3	-	-	-	-	-
13	Cylindrical	0.99	0.61	4	1	Slag, bone gouge/beater, iron pin (4.1,10)	Bone a,	-	EIA-MIA
14	Cylindrical	2.64	1.58	6	100+	Shale ring (4.2, 15)	Hazel, oak, hawthorn; bone a	-	MIA
15 [E]	Cylindrical	-	0.94	6	-	-	-	-	-
16 (ni)	-	0.69	0.38	-	-	-	-	-	-
17	Cylidrical	1.37	1.07	9	29	AE bracelet (4.1,6); Bone gouge/beater (4.4,11)	-	-	EIA-MIA
18	Cylindrical	2.47	1.42	5	150	-	Bone a,h	-	MIA
19	Irregular	2.03	0.87	2	81	Shale ring (4.2,14)	-	-	EIA-MIA
20 (ni)	-	1.50	0.84	1	7	-		-	EEIA-EIA
21	Beehive	1.42	1.63	4	38	Lump unfired clay; daub	bone h	-	EIA-MIA
22	Cylindrical	0.97	0.76	2	50	Chalk loomwt (4.7,4)	Bone a	Decorated pots	Late MIA
23 (ni)	-	-	0.76	-	9	-	-	-	EIA-MIA
24 (ni)	-	-	1.04	-	2	-	-	-	EIA-MIA
25 [F]	Cylindrical	2.44	205	9	5	-	-	-	?EIA
26	Cylindrical	1.07	0.53	2	6	-	Bone a	-	?EIA
27	Cylindrical	1.22	0.71	4	8	Chalk loomwt (4.9,1)	-	-	EIA-MIA
28	Cylindrical	0.87	0.53	2	1	-	-	-	-
29 (ni)	-	0.66	0.46	-	9	-	Oak	-	?EIA
30	Conical	1.45	0.61	2	2	-	-	-	-
31	Cylindrical	2.44	2.13	7	22	-	Bone a	-	-
31	Cylindrical	1.17	0.43	2					
32	Beehive	1.30	1.60	9	-	-	-	-	-
33/33B (ni)	-	-	2.121	-	52	Crucible (3.25,4;4.13,2)	-	-	MIA
34	Cylindrical	1.42	0.92	7	3	-	Bone a	-	EIA
35 (ni)	-	-	0.71	-	-	-	-	-	-
36	Cylindrical	1.42	1.53	3	57	Iron awl (4.2,6);chalk loomt (4.8,3); stone wt	Oak hawthorn hazel; bone a	-	?MIA

Table 2.8 Enclosure II Pits and contents (continued)

Pit	Form	Dia	Depth	Fills	Pot	Artefact	Ecofacts	Deposit	Date
37	Cylindrical	1.27	1.58	6	187+	Fe brooch (4.1,8A); Fe knife (4.2,7); Fe sickle (4.2,11); stone wts (4.9, 10-11); bone handle (4.4,1); ceramic slingshot (4.13,8); chalk loomwt (4.9,1); stone loomwts (4.9,2-3); burnt clay; wall daub	hawthorn hazel oak; bone a h	Charred grain; iron tools, brooch; weights, pots	810-360 cal BC
38	Cylindrical	1.37	0.66	3	19	Wall daub	oak hazel; bone a	-	-
39	Cylindrical	1.67	0.97	5	89	Iron rod (4.2,1); chalk loomwts (4.7, 5-6); bone comb (4.4,3); daub	hazel oak; bone a	-	MIA
40	Cylindrical	1.53	0.53	2	62	Ceramic spndle whorl (4.12,4)	Oak hawthorn hazel; bone a	-	EIA-MIA?
41	Cylindrical	0.87	0.36	3	77	-	Hawthorn oak ash; bone a	-	EIA-MIA
42	Cylindrical	1.24	0.51	2	11	-	Oak hazel; bone a	-	-
43	Cylindrical	0.76	1.04	3	32	Chalk loomwts (4.6,2-3)	Oak; bone a	-	MIA
44	Cylindrical	1.42	1.32	3	5	Chalk loomwt (4.8,5), Sstone frag, pyrite	Bone a	-	EIA-MIA
45	Cylindrical	1.30	0.99	4	35	Chalk loomwt; rubber (4.11,1); furnace bottom; daub	hawthorn hazel; bone a	-	-
46	Cylindrical?	1.27	0.41	1	66	-	Bone a	-	MIA
47	Cylindrical	1.50	0.79	3	24	Daub; Pyrites; haematite lump	bone a	-	EIA-MIA
48	Cylindrical	1.20	1.07	2	9	Daub; Cone of pyrites	oak hazel; bone a	-	EIA-MIA
49 (ni)	-	2.39	0.21	3	30+	-	Bone a	-	Early MIA
50	Cylindrical	1.17	0.94	3	42	Bone needle (4.4,6); Crucible (4.13,1); all daub; pyrites	bone a	Dog elements	MIA
51	Irregular	1.00	0.82	3	17	'Stone'; pyrites	Bone a	-	EIA-MIA
52	Cylindrical	1.60	0.99	3	28	Wall aub;Pyrites	bone a	-	EIA-MIA
53	Cylindrical	1.45	0.97	5	100+	Chalk loomwts (4.6.4); fuel ash slag; daub	bone a	Complete dog (2.52)	EIA-MIA
54	Cylindrical	1.83	1.27	3	66	AE collar (4.1,7); Fe strip (4.2,4); pyrites; daub (frog embedded)	bone a	Pots	MIA
55	Cylindrical	1.32	0.66	2	60	Chalk spindle whorl (4.12,10); pyrites	Bone a	Dog elements	MIA
56	Cylindrical?	1.07	0.28	2	7	Slag	-	-	EIA-MIA
57B	Cylindrical	2.54	1.45	4	25	Flint hammerstone (4.10,9); pyrites; daub; fired clay	bone a		-
58	Irregular	2.03	0.48	2	27	Bone implement (4.13,4); pyrites	Bone a, h;	Human burial	-
58B	Irregular	0.92	1.17	3	-	-	-	-	-
59	Cylindrical	2.90	1.42	3	63	Pyrites; fired clay; daub	oak hazel; bone a;	-	EIA-MIA
60	Cylindrical	2.39	0.87	4	155	Burnt daub; Fe frag (4.2); chalk loomw (4.8,4); pyrites	Bone a	-	EIA-MIA
60B	-	-	0.48	1	-	-	-	-	-
61	Irregular	1.50	0.92	4	3	-	-	-	-
62	Cylindrical?	1.25	0.41	2	4	-	Bone a	-	EIA-MIA
63	Cylindrical	1.73	0.97	3	23	Ceramic slingshots (4.13,9-10); daub	Bone h	Infant bural in top fill	EIA-MIA
64	Cylindrical	1.20	1.27	4	12	Fe brooch (4.1,9)	-	Near complete pot	Early MIA
65	Cylindrical?	1.42	0.46	2	47	-	-	-	EIA-MIA

Table 2.8 Enclosure II Pits and contents (continued)

Pit	Form	Dia	Depth	Fills	Pot	Artefact	Ecofacts	Deposit	Date
66	Cylindrical?	-	0.71	2	3	Sstone rubber (4.10,1)	-	-	-
67	Cylindical	.50	0.79	3	107	Fe obj (4.2,9); chalk loomwt; stone loomwt; smithing slag	Bone a, h	Human inhumation burial	EIA-MIA
68	Cylindrical	0.99	0.61	2	4	-	Bone a	-	-
69/70	Cylindrical	2.44	1.53	9	120+	AE punch (4.1,1); Fe socket (4.2,5); bone tool (4.4,7)	Bone a	Near complete pot (3.21,7)	EIA-MIA
71 (ni)	-	0.92	0.18	1	-	-	-	-	-
72 (ni)	-	-	-	1	3	-	Bone a	-	EIA?
73 (ni)	-	-	-	1	10	-	-	-	EIA?

Bone a = animal bone; Bone h = human bone (ni) = not illustrated in section (D) = number duplicated [F] = Cutting F etc.

photograph were found in the archive. Close by, in P67 immediately to the south-west of House 4, a crouched adult inhumation burial was positioned about halfway up the pit (Figs 2.43 and 2.50). A second adult burial was found in P58 across the site in Area S3 (Figs 2.26 and 2.50). Although also crouched, the circumstances of burial seem to differ from burial P67. The body had been placed in the hollow of a nearly filled irregular feature (P58B), perhaps an unfinished pit or, alternatively, the grave was dug across the top of P58B, enlarging the pre-existing feature for ease of digging. There was insufficient evidence to determine whether the burials were contemporary, but the P67 pit is tentatively dated to the early Iron Age- middle Iron Age transition on the basis of the pottery (Fig. 3.22). The small ceramic assemblage from P58 included a rim that could be from a vessel of the same broad date (Fig. 3.31), but of insufficient size to be certain.

Details of the pits and their contents are presented in Table 2.8.

THE HOLLOWS

by Lisa Brown

Sonia Hawkes described a number of shallow, irregular features as 'working hollows' (prefixed H on the plans). Their function is uncertain, and probably varied, but they are common features of Iron Age settlements, including many on chalkland. Some may have originated as quarries for chalk, clay or other subsoil material, others perhaps created to accommodate minor industrial or craft activities such as metalworking or pottery produduction, and subsequently levelled with dumps of occupation-rich deposits, less often left to fill in through natural processes.

Cutting E

H 7 was partly exposed in the southern end of Cutting E, in the northern area of Enclosure II (Fig. 2.14). It was over 2m wide, 0.46m deep and filled with soil incorporating lumps of chalk. No other details were recorded and it produced no finds.

Enclosure II Areas S1-S3

Details of the hollows excavated in the Areas S1-S3 are summarised in Table 2.9 below and section drawings in Figs 2.56-2.57. The site plans of Enclosure II show several cases of duplication of working hollow numbers, some of which were otherwise unrecorded. The worst of the confusion affects hollows excavated in Area S2, within and around Posthole Complex 5, and Area S3, in the vicinity of Houses 1 and 2. However, the duplication is reflected in the records only in the case of H11, for which two separate sets of data exist (see Appendix 2D). In the other cases, only a single set of data has been recorded and the duplicate feature recorded only on plan, as shown in Table 2.9. Duplication of recorded hollows catalogued below has been highlighted (D) in the table below and their locations described.

Fig. 2.51 Enclosure II Area S1: Pit 14 ash and charcoal deposits (1958)

Fig. 2.52 Enclosure II Area S3: Pit 53 dog burial

Fig. 2.53 Enclosure II Area S3: Pit 31 cattle skull

Fig. 2.54 Enclosure II Area S3: Pit 39 horse skull and mandibles

Fig. 2.55 Recovery of horse skull from Pit 39 and excavation of adjacent Pit 43

One of the hollows merits specific mention. The designation H3 is duplicated in the records and the details listed in Appendix 2D clearly refer to a very shallow feature containing a few scraps of pottery, in common with most of these features. H3 as recorded in plan (Fig. 2.43) and section (Fig. 2.57) is clearly something altogether different, and produced an enormous amount of well-preserved pottery of earliest Iron Age date, broadly similar to that from House 2 (see Chapter 3, Figs 3.15-3.16). Notably, this assemblage also contained two examples of what appear to be prototypes of burnished scratched-cordoned bowls, (Fig. 3.15, nos 16 and 17), with unpronounced cordons and no (surviving) white infill. Similar vessels found at New Buildings, near Longstock, Hants. have been

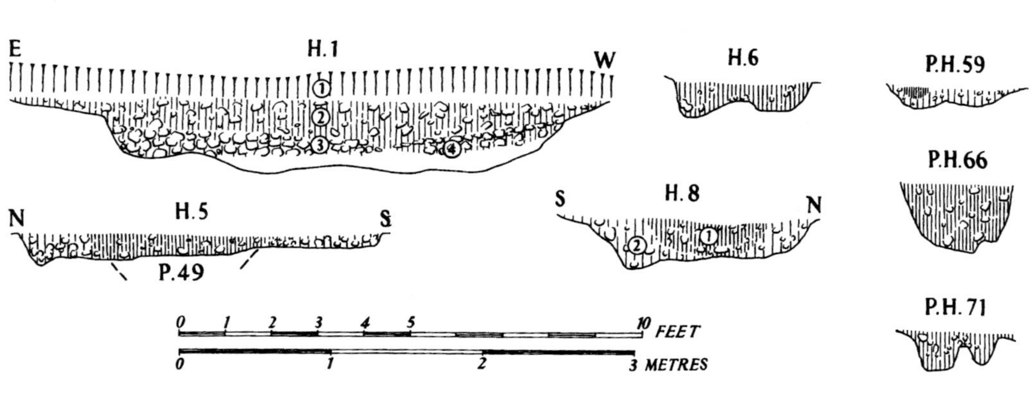

Fig. 2.56 Hollows: H1 (location uncertain); H5 (Area S3, with P49, unlabelled on Fig. 2.26:); H6 (Area S2, south of Posthole Complex 5, Fig. 2.58:): H8 (east of Posthole Complex 5, Fig. 2.58), and adjacent postholes

Table 2.9 Enclosure II Hollows

Hollow	*Dia m*	*Depth m*	*Fill*	*Artefacts*	*Location*	*Figure*
H1	3.86	0.48	Chalky soil			Fig. 2.56
H2	-	0.26	Dark soil	pottery		2.43-2.44; Section 2.57
H3 (D) / 3A	-	0.21	Brown soil	pottery	Area S1 north of House 4, cut by Pits 18 & 33,	Fig. 2.43-2.44; Section Fig. 2.57; pottery Fig. 3.15-3.16
H4	-	0.41	(2) Dark soil (3) chalky soil (4) loose chalk & flint		Adjacent P 31	Figs. 2.26; Section Fig. 2.49
H5	2.39	0.15	Chalky soil			Fig. 2.26; Fig. 2.56 (section); Fig. 2.58
H6 (D)	0.87	0.28	Brown soil	pottery		Fig. 2.26; Fig. 2.56 (section)
H8		0.08	Not recorded		Area S1 west of House 4	Fig. 2.58; Fig. 2.56 (section)
H8 (D)	1.65	0.31	(1) dark soil (2) chalky soil	pottery	Adjoining PH59	Fig. 2.65; Fig. 2.63 (section)
H9		0.21	Ashy soil		Area S3 House1	Figs 2.26; 2.58
H10		0.26	Clayey soil with chalk		Area S2	Fig. 2.58
H11(D)		0.21	Dark soil		Area S3 adjacent H10	Figs. 2.26; 2.58
H11 (D)		0.10	Brown soil		Area S3	Fig. 226; Fig. 2.58
H12	-	-	-	-	-	-
H13	-	-	-	-	-	Recorded as 'near Pit 4', not on plan
H14	-	-	-	-	-	Not recorded
H15	-	0.26	Soil with chalk & flint	-	North of House 1	Fig. 2.58
H16		0.21	Brown soil	-	-	Not illustrated
H17	-	0.08	Dark soil	pottery	Within House 2	Figs. 2.26; 2.29
H18	0.61	0.08	-	-	-	Not illustrated
H19	0.71	0.18	Dark soil with flint & chalk	Pottery; Hone (Fig 4.13, 3)	South of House 4	Figs. 2.43-2.44

interpreted as early varieties of this tradition (Brown 2000, 66). The only clear example of the type came from PH235 associated with House 1 (Fig. 3.6, no. 91).

H3 lay to the north of House 4, in a complex of features that include H1 and H2, which cut its western and eastern sides. H3, which was possibly recut as H3A, if the plan is accurate (Fig. 2.43), may in fact have been a pit, as the fill sequence suggests (Fig. 2.57). It was in turn recut by P18 and P33A. If the pottery assemblage is correctly attributed to H3, then this may have been the only pit open in the excavated part of Enclosure II during the occupation of one or other of the earliest Iron Age houses. It could equally be the case that when House 4 (or indeed House 1 or 2) was demolished, much of the pottery was cleared out and redeposited in this feature, which was later mangled by recutting.

ENCLOSURE II POSTHOLES NOT ATTRIBUTED TO STRUCTURES

Posthole Complex 5

by Lisa Brown

Posthole Complex 5 is shown on the site plans as a concentration of postholes lying within Area S2 of Enclosure II (Figs 2.6 and 2.58-2.59). The group of 27 numbered postholes forms a semi-circle or, if it is assumed that truncation was no more severe on the western side than the eastern, an oval shape. The northern part of this concentration appears to have continued beyond the excavated area. The unnumbered postholes shown on the plan were presumably unexcavated, although the records do not make this clear. Although Hawkes did not include PHs 10, 19, 20 and 21 in this group, or the shallow trench within which they appear to lie, their location in relation to PH 11, 12, 61 and 89 suggests a circuit, so their details are included here. PH20 and PH21 are the most substantial features, and may represent a replacement or a double post setting, perhaps belonging to a doorway.

The group almost certainly represents or includes at least one structure, which Hawkes interpreted as oval in shape. The distribution of features, however, allows for a range of possibilities – a roundhouse of *c.* 10m diameter, of which the western postholes did not survive: an oval structure 8+m across; a small circular structure *c.* 5 – 6m in diameter, perhaps a structure ancillary to one of the main roundhouses, the eastern arc representing a fence. However, few of the postholes were recorded in any detail and no section drawings are extant. A few small pottery sherds recovered from five of the postholes (Fig.

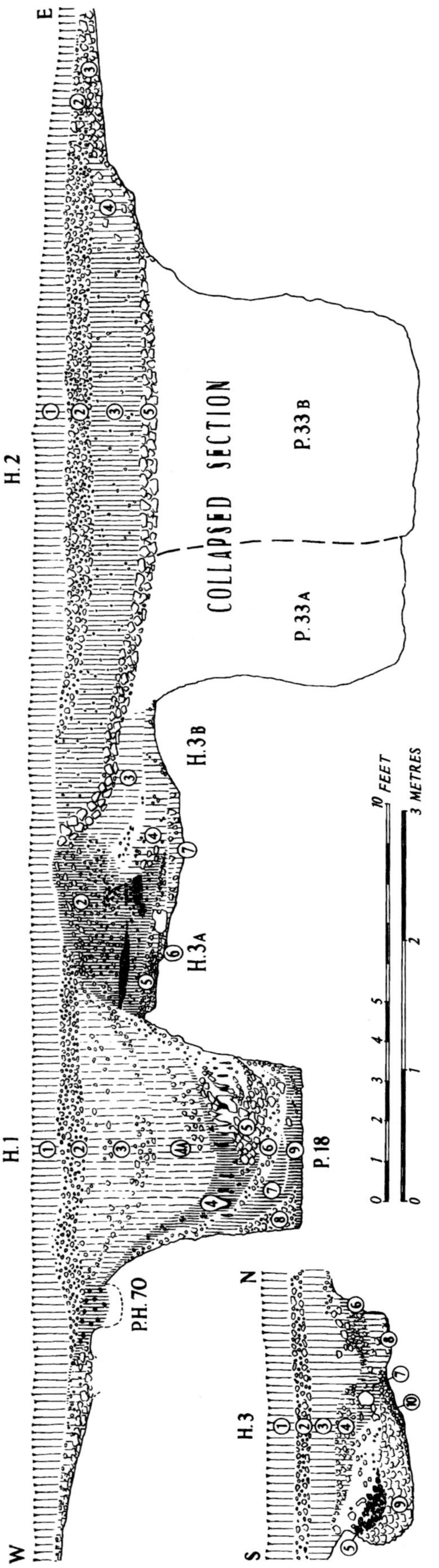

Fig. 2.57 Enclosure II Area S1: Hollows complex H1, H2, H3 north of House 4

Table 2.10: Posthole Complex 5 postholes

PH	*Dia m*	*Depth m*	*Characteristics*	*Finds*
10	0.31	0.43		
11	0.30	0.20		
12	0.30	0.20		
19	0.33	0.33		
20	0.41	0.43		
21	0.68	0.48		
44	-	-		
45	-	-	Flint/chalk packing	pottery (Fig. 3.14, 16)
46	-	-		
48	-	-	Chalk packing	pottery
50	-	-	-	-
51	-	-	-	-
52	-	-	-	-
53	-	-	-	-
54	-	-	-	-
55	-	-	-	pottery (Fig. 3.14,12)
56	-	-	Chalk/flint packing	bone a
57	-	0.23	Burnt flint	
58	-	-	-	-
61	-	'shallow'	-	Pottery; Bone a
80	-	-	-	Pottery
84	-	'shallow'	-	-
85	-	-	Cut by PH86	-
86	-	'shallow'	Cuts PH85	-
87	-	-	-	-
88	-	'shallow'	-	-
89	-	-	Flint packing	-

Table 2.11 Posthole Cluster in Area S2

PH	*Dia m*	*Depth m*	*Fill*	*Finds*
16	0.33	0.12	Dark soil with flints	
28	0.35	0.38	Dark soil	Bone a
31	0.66	0.23	Brown soil	pottery
32	0.46	-	Dark soil	
36	-	-	Chalky soil	Bone a
39	-	-	Brown soil	Pottery (Fig. 3.14, 5-6, 10)
40	-	-	Brown soil	Pottery (Fig. 3.14,4)
41	-	-	Brown soil	
81	'small'	-	Fine chalky soil	Pottery
82	-	'shallow'	Chalky soil	Pottery (3.14, 2)
93/94	-	-	Chalky grey soil	Pottery

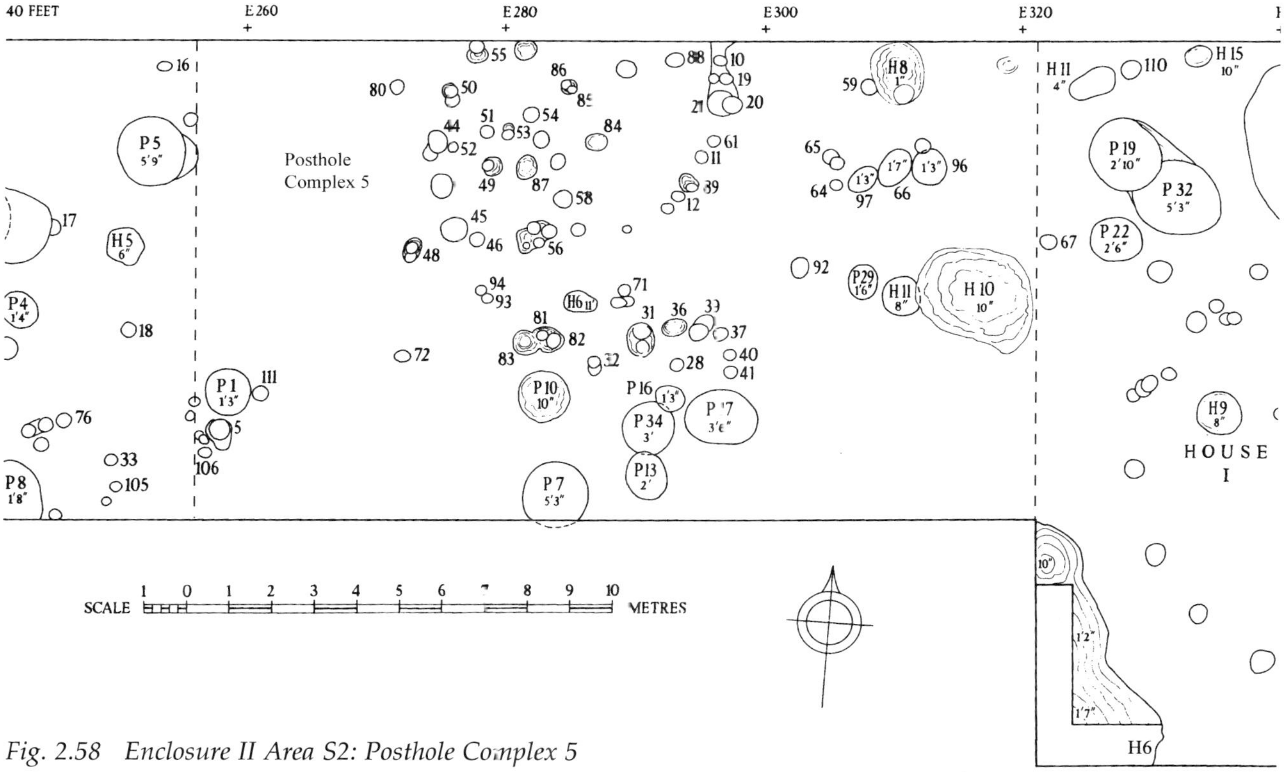

Fig. 2.58 Enclosure II Area S2: Posthole Complex 5

Fig. 2.59 Enclosure II Area S2: Posthole Complex 5 viewed from the south (1958)

Table 2.12 Enclosure II Areas S1-3 Postholes

PH	*Dia m*	*Depth m*	*Fill*	*Finds*	*Figure*
4	-	0.31	-	pottery (Fig. 3.14, 1)	-
5	0.66	0.41	Brown soil, chalk rubble at base		Fig. 2.48; 2.65
8	0.25	0.28	Fine dark soil		Fig.2.48
9	0.31	0.23	Brown soil		Fig.2.48
10	0.31	0.43	Brown soil		-
13	0.15	0.75	Chalky oil		-
14	0.18	0.75	Chalky soil		-
15	0.23	0.75	Chalky soil		-
17	0.25	0.18	Chalky soil	pottery	Fig.2.48
18	0.33	0.12	Dark grey soil	pottery	Fig. 2.48; 2.65
19	0.33	0.33	Brown soil		-
20	0.41	0.43	Brown fill		-
21	0.68	0.48	Chalk rubble		-
22	-	-	Dark grey chalky soil		Fig. 2.49
23	-	0.20	Dark soil with chalk		Fig. 2.49
24	0.28	0.28	Dark chalky soil		Fig. 2.49
25	0.48	0.35	Brown soil	pottery	Fig. 2.49
26	0.25	0.15	Dark soil	bone a	Fig. 2.49
27	0.30	0.33	Dark chalky soil		Fig. 2.49
29	-	-	Chalky soil		Fig. 2.49
30	-	-	Chalky soil		Fig. 2.49
33	0.30	0.20	Dark grey soil		Figs. 2.48; 2.65
37	-	-	Chalky soil		-
38	0.38	0.38	Dark grey soil		-
43	-	-	Chalky dark soil	pottery (Fig. 3.14, 11)	-
47	-	-	-	-	-
49	-	-	Grey soil with chalk rubble below	pottery (3.14, 15)	-
59	0.92	0.12	Brown chalky soil		Fig. 2.65
60	-	0.33	Fine chalky soil		Fig. 2.48
64	0.33	0.12	Clky soil		-
65	0.46	0.21	Chalky brown soil		-
66	0.71	0.48	Chalky broown soil		Section Fig.2.63
67	0.41	0.33	Chalky soil		-
68	0.48	0.46	Dark chalky oil		-
70	0.43	0.23	Brown soil		Figs 2.49; 2.64
71	0.71	0.23	Chalky soil	pottery	Fig. 2.63
72	-	-	Brown soil		-
73	0.1	0.25	Grey chalky soil		Fig. 2.49
74	-	-			Fig. 2.49
75	0.56	0.23	Grey soil with large flints		Fig.2.48-9
76	0.35	0.15	Grey soil		Fig. 2.48; 2.65
78	-	-	Chalky soil		-
79	-	-	Dark soil		Fig. 2.49
83	-	-	Chalky brown soil	pottery	
92	-	-	Brown soil	pottery	-
95	-	-	Dark soil with flint and chalk	pottery (3.14, 3)	-
96	-	0.38	Dark grey soil		-
97	-	0.38	Dark soil with large chalk and flints	pottery; bone a	-
98	-	-	Chalky soil		-
99	-	-	Brown soil		-
104	0.38	0.23	Brown soil chalk rubble at base		-
105	0.25	0.18	Brown soil chalk rubble at base		Fig. 2.48; 2.65
106	0.35	0.21	Brown soil with large flints		Fig. 2.48; 2.65
107	0.38	0.21	Gravelly brown soil		-
108	0.28	0.12	Gravelly brown soil		
109	0.31	0.13	Gravelly brown soil		-
110	-	0.35	Brown soi with large flints		Fig. 2.32

Table 2.12 Enclosure II Areas S1-3 Postholes (continued)

PH	*Dia m*	*Depth m*	*Fill*	*Finds*	*Figure*
111	0.36	0.23	Brown soil with chalk and lint		Fig.2.48
124	-	-	Brown soil		-
156	0.43	0.41	Chalky soil		-
168	0.51	0.12	Brown soil	pottery	-
173	0.46	0.41	Chalky soil	pottery (3.14, 14)	Fig. 2.32
176	0.26	0.21	Brown soil		Fig. 2.32
177	0.46	0.21	Brown soil		Fig. 2.32
190	0.21	0.10	Brown soil		-
196	0.61	0.35	Chalky soil with large flnts		Fig.2.48-49; Section Fig. 2.52

3.14, 12 and 16) suggest a date contemporary with House 2.

Posthole cluster to the south of Posthole Complex 5

The postholes in this group are recorded in plan in Fig. 2.58, but no section drawings are extant in the archive.

Other Postholes in Enclosure II Areas S1-3

Isolated postholes and small posthole groups for which no interpretation has been provided were recorded only in catalogue form (Appendix 2C). They are known only from their position on plans Figs 2.43-2.44 and 2.58 and, in a few cases, from section drawings including those relating to Houses 1-4. The numbers of the figures on which these postholes appear are provided below in Table 2.12, which presents summary data taken from the catalogues in Appendix 2C.

Table 2.13: Enclosure II Cuttings U and E postholes

PH	*Dia m*	*Depth m*	*Fill*	*Cutting*
1	0.23	0.25	Chalky soil	U
2	-	'shallow'	Chalky soil	U
3	0.56	041	Dark soil, large flint packing	U
6	0.36	0.21	Fine chalky soil	U
7	0.38	031	Chalky soil	U
34				E
35	0.38	0.23	Chalk lumps	E

Postholes in Enclosure II Cuttings U and E
(see Fig. 2.6 for Cutting location. Table 2.13)

Cutting E PH34 and PH35 are illustrated in plan and section in Fig. 2.14. The position of Cutting U is shown on Figs. 2.1 and 2.6 but no plan or section drawings exist of the postholes found in the trench.

Chapter 3: The Pottery

INTRODUCTION

by Lisa Brown

Christopher Hawkes evidently intended to draw together the specialist reports, catalogues and various other strands of pottery analysis and interpretation that had been undertaken over a number of years, and to write a general discussion of the results. This he never achieved. Thin-section and heavy metal analyses were carried out by, respectively, David Williams and P.T. Partridge during the 1970s. A great deal of additional work on the pottery was continued during the 1980s following Christopher Hawkes' retirement from the project by Guy Grainger and Duncan Wilson, research assistants to Sonia Hawkes.

Some elements of the early pottery analysis are now so out-dated that they have been omitted from the publication and replaced with editorial comments and summaries. The method statement, fabric and form typologies and expansive illustrated catalogue of the pottery have been retained. Also presented in this chapter are Grainger's analyses of fabric quantification and discussions on the finewares by Daphne Nash and Sonia Hawkes. Details of the scientific analyses are presented in Appendix 3A.

The pottery illustrations by Marion Cox represent a valuable resource for in their own right. It appears that most of the diagnostic sherds, at least those from the most important and productive features, were illustrated, and to a high standard. The illustrated catalogue provides a useful resource for comparative research on late Bronze Age and Iron Age pottery from southern Britain.

The Longbridge Deverill pottery assemblage spans the period now commonly referred to as the 'earliest Iron Age' to the middle Iron Age. A few scraps of Roman pottery found in the top fill of the Enclosure III ditch are listed in the catalogue but were not considered further.

CLASSIFICATION AND TYPOLOGY

by Christopher Hawkes (based on a draft report by Duncan Wilson)

Method of Recording

Printed forms were used to record the pottery, on which were entered numerical codes representing its various characteristics. The codes were then systematically grouped into categories. Time did not permit more than a beginning to be made in comparative analysis by context of information about the pottery thus recorded. But Guy Grainger used the data in his formal analysis by context of the main characteristics of the pottery, namely Fabric, Profile and Decoration. The original forms were checked, revised where necessary, and deposited in the site archive. The system is as follows:

Column	*Category*	*Code-letter Prefix*
Column 1:	Context of Discovery	
Column 2:	Pottery Fabric	F
Column 3:	Technique of Potting/ Surface Treatment	T/ S
Column 4:	Form and Profiles	P (and handles H)
Column 5:	Decoration	D
Column 6:	Surface impressions/ or concretions, *etc*	E
Free field:	References to text, Comments, Drawing References	

Column 1: Context of Discovery

The contexts are stratigraphic wherever possible. For those in postholes, most often of the houses, this is effected, where feasible, by distinction between finds from the packing around the post when erected, and finds in the post socket. The former should relate to construction, the latter to abandonment. The records of such details are the same as those used in the account of the excavations. For those in pits, working hollows and ditch sections, it is given by the numbered layers within them. Of Enclosures I, II, III, each surrounded by its ditch, that of D-shaped Enclosure III had its interior less exposed to modern ploughing. Its topsoil, therefore, was sampled by a grid of 0.91 m² box trenches, except in the area where the emplacement of House 3 was discovered beneath and the ground opened up in a sequence of cuttings to expose the whole structure. Pottery from the topsoil of Enclosure III, most from the area of House 3, has been recorded *in toto*, as has that from the small scale trenching of Enclosure I. In the case of Enclosure II, however, the subject of a much larger area excavation, time did not permit full processing of the pottery from the topsoil of its central area, Areas S1-3, though all that was recovered has been preserved as part of the site archive.

The recording forms specify the contexts of pottery throughout as reflected in the account of the excavations. Pottery from the house emplacements, mostly from postholes, is in broad terms distinctively homogeneous. Later the Enclosure II settlement site was put into different use, after the last of the houses had been abandoned. The foundations of House 3 were not disturbed, but the central area of Enclosure II, and more especially the site of House 2, was given over to pits, some of a type appropriate for grain storage. Except where residual, the pottery from these pits differed from that of the houses, being again mostly distinctive and broadly homogeneous.

Column 2: Pottery Fabrics

The left-hand numbers in Column 2 of the records are those given to the Fabric Types. These types were established using 10x magnification, which usually allowed correct attribution of further specimens to be made without binocular microscope or hand lens. Inclusions of limestone or shell were identified with a 10% solution of hydrochloric acid. The middle numbers of Column 2 give the total of sherds from each context of each Fabric Type and the right hand numbers their total weight in grammes. The prefix F is used to denote 'Fabric Type' on the recording forms and throughout the text.

This identification of fabrics took its start from the analysis during the early 1980s by David Williams (Appendix 3A). He worked on 104 samples chosen by visual inspection by Sonia Hawkes, representing obviously distinctive fabrics from key contexts and selected to answer a number of specific questions posed by her. Williams identified, classified and described the analysed fabrics as nine, calling them A to E and H to K. Being limited by the choice of samples submitted, this total accordingly could not be exhaustive, but each of the nine has its correlated place in the fuller fabric list (below). Its units were defined as Fabric Types, and each was given a number, with the prefix F. Williams also analysed the white inlay on a decorated haematite-coated jar and a limited programme of heavy mineral analysis on five haematite-coated sherds was also undertaken by P.T. Partridge at about the same time (Appendix 3A).

The number series, at several points, was purposely made discontinuous, but all were grouped into broader Fabric Groupings by Duncan Wilson, numbered 1 to 14 in unbroken sequence. In the following list of the Fabric Groupings, and of the Fabric Types contained in each, every Type has been defined by a brief description, followed, where required, by its correlative Williams Fabric. In the wording of these descriptions, 'sand' or 'sandy' denoted the main tempering (of the clay, which itself need not be specified). Where the fabric contains inclusions described as grains, grits or shell, these are defined by size as follows:

Fine:	Grains (or other) not discernible by naked eye.
Medium:	Grains (or other) of less than 1mm diameter.

Fabric Groupings and Fabric Types:

Groupings	*Types*	*Description and Williams Fabric correlation*
Grouping 1 (Roman or later)	F1	miscellaneous
	F2	sandy 'greyware', normally Roman
	F3	samian
Grouping 2	F11	very fine micaceous sandy fabric with occasional flint fragments or grog (Williams Fabric A)
Grouping 3	F13	fine sand, not as smooth as F11 (Williams Fabric D)
Grouping 4	F12	medium sand with abundant grains (Williams Fabric C)
	F15	coarse sand with abundant grains
Grouping 5	F14	fine sand, between F11 and F12, with small flint chips (< 1mm) and occasional ochreous grog (Williams Fabric B)
	F16	fine sand and vegetable matter and grog
	F19	fine sand with abundant voids left by vegetable matter (Williams Fabric E)
Grouping 6	F20	miscellaneous limestone inclusions
	F22	abundant medium angular limestone tempering and medium fossil-shell grits (included in Williams Fabric I)
	F23	coarse angular white crystalline grits with coarse chalky limestone pieces
	F27	coarse chalky limestone tempering with some ochreous inclusions
Grouping 7	F24	abundant angular white crystalline grits, mostly medium or coarse
Grouping 8	F21	abundant rounded medium limestone grains with some shell (included in Williams Fabric I)
	F25	occasional rounded limestone grains and medium sand
	F26	rounded limestone grains and coarse grog
Grouping 9	F30	miscellaneous shelly fabrics
	F31	abundant coarse shelly inclusions (included in Williams Fabric J)
	F33	sparse coarse shell, fine sand and some vegetable matter

Grouping 10	F32	medium-sized shelly inclusions with some medium sand (included in Williams Fabric J)
Grouping 11	F40	miscellaneous flinty fabrics
	F41	very coarse flint tempering in a sandy fabric (Williams Fabric H)
Grouping 12	F50	miscellaneous ochreous grog
	F52	medium to fine ochreous grog with medium sand
Grouping 13	F51	coarse ochreous grog with some medium to coarse flint
	F43	coarse flint and ochreous grog in medium and coarse sandy fabrics
	F44	coarse flint and ochreous grog in a fine sandy fabric
Grouping 14	F42	sparse medium/coarse flint in a medium sandy fabric (Williams Fabric K)

Coarse: Grains (or other) of more than 1mm diameter.

The final treatment of the pottery by Fabric Groupings, each Grouping under its number, with tabulation by context of discovery, is presented in Appendix 3B.

Column 3: Technique of Potting; Surface Treatment

Potting technique (T0) was recorded in cases where it could be discerned, although this was rare. These techniques were recorded for information on particular pots, but being visible on only very few sherds, have not been used in any comparative analysis of sherds by context.

The following types of technique may be distinguished:

T01 miscellaneous / not discernible
T02 coil built
T03 slab built
T04 pinched
T05 pinch marks and vertical working marks on inside of pot
T06 horizontal working or finishing marks inside the pot
T07 joint between base and wall of pot very obvious; vertical smoothing on inside of pot

Surface treatment is included in this column, though two of its types, coating with haematite and burnishing, could perhaps be called decorative rather than technical. The code prefix S0 covers the eight types recognised. Of these, only five were considered potentially significant for overall analysis by context:

Group 1 (haematite-coated) S04 haematite coating
Group 2 (grass-wiped) S05 vertical grass wiping externally
S06 vertical grass wiping and horizontal finishing marks around base.
S08 horizontal grass wiping externally
Group 3 (burnished) S02 burnishing

Not grouped for analysis were:
S01 miscellaneous/not discernible
S03 smoothing or wiping
S07 external knife-trimming

Column 4: Form

Form was recorded in seven categories. The prefix P denotes profile, where extant complete or unmistakably restorable; H denotes any lesser sherd with a handle. Where the extant parts are only from the **base**, or from the **body**, **neck** or **rim**, these words serve as prefixes respectively for each. The compartments in the column, stating the types of all these by their serial number only, thus are six; the category of the seventh is diameter of vessel at the rim, where it could be measured. Where referred to in the text, this is coded 'dia'. The information thus presented was collated with that from Column 3 (Technical) and Column 5 (Decoration), by Grainger, and compared by him with the pottery groupings already defined by Fabric, thus producing a formal analysis of the ceramic material from the site.

The following list starts with the profiles. These, with their prefix P, have been divided into Groups. Beginning with Group 1, every Group has a number of its own number and this numeration extends into the categories to be listed farther on: those of Base, Body, Neck, Rim and Handle. Thus the numbers given to the Groups that cover the Profiles do not always follow each other in serial order. Those missing are used for Groups of the ensuing other categories.

Group 1 P0i Furrowed keg jar
Group 2 P0ii Furrowed vessel, probably keg jar
Group 3 P0iii Undecorated keg jar
Group 4 P01 Carinated bowl or cup with furrowed decoration, everted rim
P02 Carinated bowl or cup with furrowed decoration, upright rim
P03 Carinated bowl or cup with furrowed decoration, vertical neck
P04 Carinated bowl or cup with

		furrowed decoration, widely splayed basin
	P04a	Carinated bowl or cup with furrowed decoration, deep basin
Group 5	P05	Carinated bowl or cup with furrowed decoration, tall everted rim
	P09	Carinated bowl or cup with grooved decoration
Group 7	P06a	Carinated bowl or cup with grooved decoration, tall concave neck
	P06b	Undecorated carinated bowl or cup, tall concave neck
	P07a	Carinated bowl or cup with grooved decoration, wide mouth
	P07b	Undecorated carinated bowl or cup, wide mouth
	P08a	Carinated bowl or cup with grooved decoration, tall vertical neck
	P08b	Undecorated carinated bowl or cup, tall vertical neck
	P10	Carinated vessel with everted rim
	P11	Vessel with everted rim
	P14	Carinated cup with everted rim, upper neck vertical, lower part outward-curved to sharp shoulder carination.
	P18	Vessel with concave neck
Group 9	P12	Carinated bowl with rounded body
	P13	Carinated bowl with rounded body, particularly curved above carination
	P15	Carinated bowl with deep rounded body
	P16	Bowl with rounded body
Group 11	P19	Tall carinated jar
	P20	Jars decorated like P19, but not carinated
	P21	Jars decorated like P19, but sherd too small for positive identification.
Group 12	P23	Jar with rounded body
Group 18	P25	Carinated jar with wall of body slanted straight
	P26	Carinated jar with wall of body rounded
	P27	Carinated jar like P25-P26, but sherd too small for positive identification
	P28	Carinated jar with everted rim
	P30	Sharply carinated jar with wall of body slanted straight, everted rim.
	P32	Carinated jar with inward-sloping neck
	P33	Carinated jar with wall of body slanted straight, everted rim
Group 20	P29	Small vessel with flaring rim
Group 25	P17	Barrel jar
	P31	Miniature barrel jar
	P38	Rounded bowl
	P39	Barrel jar, probably like P17, but sherd too small for positive identification
	P51	Jar with convex barrel body
	P52a	Jar with convex barrel body, upright or everted rim
	P52b	Jar with convex barrel body, short rim
	P55	Jar, possibly with cylindrical body, too small for positive identification
Group 26	P22	Jars with rounded shoulder, 'situla' form
	P56	Jars with rounded shoulder, 'situla' form, barrel body.
	P46a	Jars or bowls with 'flower-pot' profile
	P46b	Jars or bowls with 'flower-pot' profile, distinct rim
Group 31	P36a	Globular jar, rim with rounded tip
	P36b	Globular jar, rim with flattened tip
	P37a	Jar with rounded shoulders, rim with rounded tip
	P37b	Jar with rounded shoulders, rim with flattened tip
Group 32	P34	Large barrel jars
Group 33	P40	Dish with rounded sides
	P44	Shallow dish with splayed sides
	P45	Shallow dish as P44, possibly lid, sherds too small for positive identification
	P53	Dish like P40, sherd too small for positive identification.
Group 34	P35	Pear-shaped jar
	P41	Pear-shaped jar like P35, sherd too small for positive identification.
	P47	Pear-shaped jar with rounded shoulder
Group 35	P43	Pedestal vase
Group 36	P42	'saucepan' vessel with gently curved sides
	P49	'saucepan' vessel with straight, almost vertical sides
	P50	'saucepan' vessel with gently curved, almost vertical sides

(NB P24, P48, P54 not used)

Base codes:

01. Omphalos base (miscellaneous)
02. Omphalos base, oblique wall
03. Omphalos base, sharply oblique wall
04. Flat base (miscellaneous)
05. Flat base, oblique wall
06. Flat base, sharply oblique wall
07. Flat base, vertical wall

08. Flat base, splayed or straightened edge, oblique wall
09. Pedestal base, oblique wall
10. Flat base, straightened edge, oblique wall
11. Oblique wall (miscellaneous)
12. Vertical wall (miscellaneous)
13. Flat base with hole(s) in the bottom (miscellaneous)
14. Curved base, vertical wall
15. Splayed edge, vertical wall
16. Sharply oblique wall (miscellaneous)
17. Flat base, rounded edge, oblique wall
18. Miscellaneous
19. Foot ring, oblique wall
20. Foot ring, sharply oblique wall
21. Flat base with hole(s) in the bottom, oblique wall
22. Rounded edge (miscellaneous)
23. Omphalos base with hole(s) in the bottom, sharply oblique wall

Body Codes:
01. Miscellaneous
02. Carinated shoulder
03. Rounded profile
04. Shoulder (miscellaneous)
05. Straight-sided

Neck Codes:
01. Narrows slightly from shoulder
02. Sharply constricted
03. Straight-sided, tall
04. Concave from shoulder to rim
05. Angular
06. Concave from shoulder to rim and narrow

Rim Codes:
01. Vertical with plain, squared rim
02. Vertical with plain, rounded rim
03. Vertical with 'lens-shaped' rim
04. Everted with 'lens-shaped' rim
05. Sharply everted with 'lens-shaped' rim
06. Everted with plain, squared rim
07. Not used
08. Vertical with furrow immediately below rim
09. Everted, rounded rim
10. Up-turned, short, rounded rim
11. Everted rim with slight external lip
12. Up-turned rim with short, squared top
13. Incurving rim with interior thickened
14. Everted rim (miscellaneous)
15. Everted rim with smooth curved profile
16. Up-turned rim with neck slightly thickened
17. Flat-topped rim with exterior thickened
18. 'Proto-bead' rim
19. Rim with groove on top
20. Tall, slightly everted rim
21. Flat-topped rim, exterior and interior thickened
22. Interior chamfer
23. Plain, incurving rim, rounded wall
24a. Exterior chamfer
24b. Flat-topped, incurving rim
25. Slightly up-turned rim
26. Up-turned rim, exterior thickened
27. Incurving rim, interior chamfer
28. Flat-topped rim with interior thickened and chamfered
29. Slightly everted rim
30. Sharply everted rim, grooved on top
31. Vertical with exterior turned round on itself
32. Interior thickened
33. Rim turned up and inwards
34. Squared and thickened rim
35. Flat-topped rim, exterior thickened
36. Rounded and thickened rim
37. Turned up and pointed rim
38. Incurving rim, squared
39. Incurving rim, squared and with slight thickening
40. Turned up rim, with exterior flanged

Handle Codes:
01. Rod-shaped, miscellaneous
02. Rod-shaped, transverse
03. Miscellaneous

Key to Comments:
01. Illustrated
02. Limey deposit on inside of sherd
03. Carbon deposit on inside of sherd
04. Carbon deposit on outside of sherd
05. Grain impression
06. Sherd burnt, discoloured or distorted: post deposition
07. Drawn on reverse of sheet
08. Grain impression on bottom of base
09. Fabric type sherd (removed)
10. Probably same vessel
11. Food remains on inside
12. Cross join
13. Heavily abraded, possibly residual

Column 5: Decoration

The various styles of decoration are as follows:

D01. Furrowed (miscellaneous)
D02. Furrowed on neck with 2 or 3 broad, shallow furrows
D03. Furrowed on neck with 4 or more broad, shallow furrows
D04. 2 or 3 separate grooves on neck
D05. 4 or more separate grooves on neck
D06. Grooved (miscellaneous)
D07. Incised (miscellaneous)
D08. Incised decoration (miscellaneous) with white inlay
D09. Incised circles with white inlay
D10. Incised hatching with white inlay
D11. Incised dots in a strip with linear border and white inlay
D12. Incised/stabbed isosceles triangle dots with linear border and white inlay

D13. Shallow incised lines, roughly parallel, with associated dots
D14. Deeply incised dots with associated hatching
D15. Incised / stabbed triangle dots with linear border at 45° angle to line of pattern
D16. Vertical line of dots with parallel incised ladder pattern and associated stabbed triangles
D17. Incised ladder pattern
D18. Incised dots in a strip with linear border with associated strip of hatching at an oblique angle
D19. Finger tip and nail impressions on neck
D20. Finger tip and nail impressions on rim edge and shoulder
D21. Finger tip and nail impressions on side of rim edge
D22. Finger tip and nail impressions on shoulder
D23. Finger tip and nail impressions on shoulder but not on rim
D24. Broad furrow below rim, finger impressions on top of rim
D25. Finger tip and nail impressions (miscellaneous)
D26. Finger tip and nail impressions on neck and shoulder
D27. Incised diagonal lines on top of rim
D28. Slashes on rim edge
D29. 'Stick' impressions on rim edge, curved incised lines on shoulder
D30. Shallow incised lines 'eye-brow' pattern with horizontal incised line immediately below rim
D31. Single shallow incised line
D32. Hatched area with border
D33. Curved parallel incised lines
D34. Deep hatched area
D35. Diagonal, shallow incised lines
D36. Zig-zag pattern of shallow incised lines
D37. Parallel incised lines (miscellaneous)
D38. Random roughly horizontal shallow furrows below rim (possibly burnishing marks)
D39. Deep incised lines
D40. Finger nail impressions on shoulder
D41. Vegetation (straw or twig) impressions on rim
D42. Finger nail impressions on rim
D43. Finger nail impressions on rim edge and shoulder
D44. Finger tip and nail impressions around base
D45. Diagonal slashes on shoulder
D46. Finger nail impressions (miscellaneous)
D47. Very shallow intersecting incised lines
D48. Diagonal lines
D49. Knobbed shoulder
D50. Strip of hatching separated by angle of 45 degrees
D51. Strip of incised vertical lines
D52. Strips of hatching with incised line border separated by angle of 45 degrees
D53. Combination of diagonal hatched strips and vertical strips of dots
D54. Vertical zig-zag hatched strips, sometimes with lines of dots with or without border
D55. Vertical strip of dots with adjoining diagonal strips of dots
D56. Vertical strips of hatching and horizontal line of dots
D57. Vertical strip of dots and horizontal zig-zig strips of incised lines
D58. Diagonal strips of dots with white inlay
D59. Shallow grooves above shoulder
D60. Stabbed decoration in horizontal lines
D61. Stabbed decoration in horizontal line on shoulder
D62. Stabbed decoration in horizontal line on rim
D63. Triangle of deep hatching
D64. Curved rilling
D65. Diagonal ladder pattern of shallow grooves
D66. Fingernail marks below rim
D67. Horizontal incised zig-zag
D68. Hatching on carination, stabbed decoration below
D69. Deep, parallel incised lines
D70. Horizontal strip of dots
D71. Diagonal incised lines / finger nail slashes and horizontal furrows
D72. Horizontal furrows and lines of punched roundels
D73. Deep incised lines
D74. Diagonal hatching and incised lines
D75. Parallel lines of finger tip impressions on body
D76. Strips of diagonal, deep incised lines and dots
D77. Vertical incised zig-zag
D78. Dot encircled by single ring
D79. Horizontal zig-zag incised lines and vertical dots
D80. Diagonal slashes on rim
D81. Combination of vertical, curved and diagonal strips of dots and horizontal line of dots.
D82. Combination of curved and vertical strips of dots
D83. Hatched triangles, white inlay on shoulder, line of dots on carination and diagonal strips of dots below carination
D84. Double row of hatched triangles on shoulder, lines of dots on and below carination, and more hatching further below
D85. Combination of diagonal and vertical strips of hatching and horizontal strip of dots.
D86. Hatched strips (miscellaneous)
D87. 4 or more grooves on rim side, 4 or more grooves on neck above carination
D88. Very shallow grooves, almost vertical, above carination
D89. Dot encircled by double ring
D90. Combination of vertical strips of dots and 2 vertical lines of hatched triangles, with white inlay, which form a plain vertical zig-zag area in between

Vessel Forms

by Christopher Hawkes

Jars are taller than their width. Bowls are wider than their depth. Cups resemble bowls at small size: rim diameter less than 100-110mm.

Keg Jars

Group 1. Furrowed Keg Jars

P0i. Tall, like a keg with gently swelling profile, flat base and flat-topped rim, which is very short and only marked by being bounded on the upper edge by a broad band of furrowing. This is 'wave-furrowing', shallow, with intervening ridges low and rounded ; *cf.* that of Furrowed Bowls, Groups 4 and 5.
Fig. 3.1, no. 1, from House 1, alone is a complete profile, and has five furrows in a band 30mm broad; fabric is fine F11, and surface haematite-coated, orange brown, and brightly burnished, S04/2. Fig. 3.1, nos. 2 and 3 are similar but rim sherds only.

Group 2. Furrowed Sherds

(Apparently related to Group 1)
P0ii. Gently incurved neck with furrowing like Group 1, occurring also on the gentle curve out to the flat-topped rim.
Fig. 3.1, no. 4, flat rim and furrowed short neck, and Fig. 3.1, no. 5, gentle shoulder and neck, rim missing, have the same surface treatment as Group 1, S04/2, but are made in the slightly coarser fabric F14; both from House 1, they are the sole examples from the site.

Group 3. Plain Keg Jars

P0iii. Profile as Group 1 but not furrowed.
Fig. 3.6, no. 83, House 1, profile inferred from upper part, flat-topped rim; fabric medium F42, with burnished haematite externally, S04/2; could be a simplified, coarser variant of P0i; no other examples found.

Carinated Bowls and Cups

The distinction between Bowls and Cups is in size, most obviously diameter, the divide being respectively more or less 100 – 110mm at the rim. Vessels of both sizes probably made for liquid or for semi-liquid contents and for imbibing – though the smaller bowls and the cups could have been filled by dipping into larger containers, probably Group 11 Jars.

In Groups 4 and 5 the furrowing is 'wave-furrowing': the furrows are shallow, 5 or 6mm wide, with the intervening ridges low and rounded. The 'groove-furrowing' of Group 7 is narrower and sharper. Where some authors call examples of either kind 'rilled', they are influenced from the Continent: 'rilled' translates the German *gerillte* (French *cannelée*, or sometimes *côtelée*, 'ridged'). We shall here call the first kind 'furrowed', the second 'grooved'.

Group 4. Carinated Bowls and Cups with Furrowed Decoration

[Short rim, typically everted, very seldom upright]
P01. The base is raised and hollowed with an omphalos. The vessel walls expand into a basin with a carination at the maximum diameter, the shoulder angle, which in P01 is fairly sharp. The straight portion above is the neck, slanted slightly inward or almost vertical and horizontally furrowed. The rim, which sometimes has a tapered section, everted and rounded, or in some cases squared and distinctively short. The fabric is invariably fine, even for the largest bowls, usually F11 or F14. Exterior and interior surfaces are haematite-coated and highly burnished, S04/2.
In Enclosure II all examples are from House 1: in Fig. 3.1, nos. 12 and 18 with the basin deep and diameter large, and the medium-sized nos. 9, 13 and 19. The type appears in Enclosure I also, as a residual sherd in Pit 1: Fig. 3.17, no. 5.

P02. Rare: as P01 but with blunt carination and upright, tapered rim. House II.1, Fig. 3.1, no. 6; F11, S04/2.

P03. The furrowed neck is slanted at a near vertical angle, the carination thus more obtuse than P01, but the profile otherwise similar. Fabric fine, F11, F13 and F14, and exterior coated with burnished haematite, S04/2.
All are from House 1: Fig. 3.1, cups nos. 7, 14 and 16; bowls (small) no. 8, (medium) no. 10; and sherds nos. 11, 15 and 17.

P04. Basin more widely splayed than P01, furrowed neck slanted in from a sharp carination; rim sharply everted and short or medium; overall shape thus normally shallower than in P01. Fabric always fine, usually F11, and externally and internally coated with burnished haematite, S04, or burnt and/or weathered, S01.
All from House 1: Fig. 3.2, nos. 23-33, and sherd no. 36, with two furrows between a pair of rows of punched impressed ring with central dot. If no. 35, with oblique slashing in this position, is thought slanted, not vertical as shown, it could be added to this group.

P04a. Bowl with deep basin, neck slanted sharply in from carination; broad band of furrows. The prevailing overall size is very large, with everted rim less short than in P01-4, except in one case where the bowl more nearly resembles P01 in proportions. Fabric fine, F11 and F14, with haematite-coating, S04.
Three from House 1, Fig. 3.2, nos. 20-22: the smaller one is no. 21; no. 22 may have been even larger than the type example no. 20, which preserves all of the profile but the base.

Group 5 Carinated Bowls and Cups with Furrowed or Grooved Decoration

[Tall, everted rim]
P05. Furrowed. The only example, from House 1, Fig. 3.2, no. 34, is a haematite-coated Cup. The neck has one furrow close beside the carination; above, where its inward slant is gently hollowed, the rim is bent out from a shallow offset, and its slightly tapered section approaches a lens shape, as the rim shape on some of the Jars of Group 11, presumed containers of the liquids into which such cups would be dipped. Those jars are all from House 1, in equivalent contexts.

(Due to rearrangement of the numbered profile series, the profile described next is P09. As forms intermediate between P05 and P09 may be identified in the future, the notional Group 6 which might comprise them is here omitted. Such forms might belong to some interval after the end of House 1, which produced P05, and before the start of House 2, which produced P09 along with Group 7. Occupation in this interval could be expected elsewhere on the site.)

P09. Grooved. The only example, from House 2, Fig. 3.7, no. 1, is a fine Cup, F13. The base is missing; the basin was very shallow; the neck, slanting up from a carination, almost straight but faintly convex, and with a band of seven horizontal grooves (narrower than furrows). Within the plain portion above them begins the outward slant of the rim, which becomes a sharp eversion bearing a band of six horizontal grooves. The mouth diameter equals the carination at slightly over 120mm, a maximum size for a Cup.

Bowls of Profiles of Group 7 (Normal and Abnormal) and Group 9

[Showing varied patterns of grooving and/or furrowing]
These, with some smaller sherds, (*e.g.* House 3, Fig. 3.11, nos. 3-5), are listed under probable P06a profile, Fig. 3.15, no.5; normal P12 profile, Fig. 3.15, no. 17; normal P13 profile, Fig. 3.15, no. 16; from WH3. Abnormal variant of P06a, extremely large, from House 2, Fig. 3.8 no. 23, with broad omphalos base, sharp carination, flat-topped rim. From House 3, Fig. 3.12, no. 18 was probably a bowl, abnormally deep; but surviving upper profile resembles that of a carinated jar (P33) though ware not coarse, F21, and surface must originally have been burnished; decoration D65.

Group 7. Bowls and Cups with Concave Profile of Neck and Rim

a) Grooved; b) Plain
P06a. Bowl with omphalos base, basin shallow, carination usually sharp. The concavity above carination has three to five, or rarely seven or nine grooves on the lower part. Above this the concavity is plain and curves to the rim. The diameter of the mouth is less than or equal to the carination. Fabric usually fine, F11, F13 and F14, surface usually coated with burnished haematite, S04/2, or burnt and/or weathered, S01.
Many examples from House 2, Fig. 3.7, nos. 3, 5, 8-10, 13, 15; Fig. 3.8, no. 16 (three grooves set abnormally apart) and the abnormal no. 23; rarer from WH3, Fig. 3.15, nos. 1 and 2 and the abnormal no. 5; rarest from House 3, Fig. 3.11, nos.1 and 2.

P06b. Plain, but otherwise similar to P6a, though carination may be blunter. Fabric usually fine, F11, F13, and F14, and coated with burnished haematite, S04/2, or burnt and/or weathered.
Two from House 2, Fig. 3.8, no. 25 sharp, no. 26 blunt; two, but also sherds, from WH3 Fig. 3.15 nos. 7 and 10, and from House 3, Fig. 3.11, no. 10 and no. 12.

P07a. Bowl, profile as 6a but with rim diameter greater than the carination. Cup similar though carination may be blunter, as Fig. 3.7, no. 2 from House 2, which like Fig. 3.7, no. 1 has grooves arranged in two bands, lower band six grooves, upper band four. Fabric usually fine, F11 and F13, coated with burnished haematite, S04/2, or burnt and/or weathered, S01.
Other cups from House 2 are Fig. 3.7, no. 14 and Fig. 3.8, no. 18, each with three grooves; bowls are Fig. 3.7, nos. 6, 7, 11, and Fig. 3.8, no. 19. In both sizes, flare of rim varies.

P07b. Plain bowls and cups, otherwise like P7a.
From WH3, bowl Fig. 3.15, no. 9; from House 3, Fig. 3.11, nos. 6, 7, 9, carination respectively sharp, less sharp, blunt. From Enclosure II. Area S.2 are Fig. 3.14, nos. 1 – 3.

P08a. Bowl as 6a but neck tall and vertical above band of four grooves; everted rim short. House 2, Fig. 3.7, no. 12.
P8b. Like 8a but plain. House 3, Fig. 3.11 , no. 11.

P10. Other carinated vessels with everted rim, various.
Includes WH3, Fig. 3.15, no. 13; House.3, Fig. 3.11, no. 13.

P11. Other vessels with everted rim, various but not carinated.

P14. Plain cup with small omphalos base, carination equal in diameter to mouth of flaring rim, neck concavity slightly flattened. House 3, Fig. 3.11, no. 8 (F13, S04/2).

P18. Sherds of bowls with concave neck, whether or not carinated, of Group 7 but not distinguished further. House 4, Fig. 3.13, no. 2; and perhaps also WH3, Fig. 3.15, no. 14.

Group 9. Carinated Bowls with Rounded Body

P12. Bowl with blunt carination; base perhaps was flat, rim probably everted. WH3, Fig. 3.15, no. 17.

P13. Bowl as P12 but with complete flat base, and carination still blunter. WH3, Fig. 3.15, no. 16; House 3, Fig. 3.11, no. 14.

P15. Bowl with rounded body thickening to a straight flared rim; surface plain throughout.
House 3, Fig. 3.11, no. 15 only (F14, S04/2), unless the body sherd from WH3, Fig. 3.15, 15, with small stab decoration D60, belonged to another of the same type.

P16. Bowl (incomplete profile) with rounded body curving into a constriction from where the rim stood up; just below constriction is a cordon in low relief.
Fig. 3.6, no. 91, intrusive in House 1; sherd only, exterior haematite-coated and burnished, S04/2.

Carinated Jars – A: in Fineware Fabrics 11, 13 and 14

Group 11. Tall Carinated Jars

[With everted rim; decoration incised and often with punch-dotted bands, whitened with inlay]
All from House 1, apart from a few residual sherds found elsewhere.
P19. Jar with flat base, wall of body slants steeply up in the middle steepening further to a gently convex curve, more rarely almost straight, to reach the shoulder. Shoulder is almost always at the maximum diameter; carination is blunt or nearly rounded more often than sharp, but neck is more often bent in sharply, and is straight or slightly curved. The bend leads to a sharp constriction, rim everted at 60 to 45 degree angle. Rim is tall and slightly tapered up or down to approach a lens shape. Rim is rounded or squared and always kept free of the decoration which appears on the neck, shoulder or body. Decoration ceases only towards the base. The form recalls Continental classes of jar with everted rim, though the shoulder with its blunt or rounded carination, shows here a modification of the Continental profiles and a likeness to bronze buckets, probably significant for chronology.
Jars of undoubted P19, exclusively from House 1. Fig. 3.3, nos. 37-39; Fig. 3.4, nos. 43 and 47; Fig. 3.5, nos. 48, 53-54, 56-57, 60; Fig. 3.6, 61-62, 71-72 and probably 78. Fabric nearly always the fine F11.

P20. This is reserved for possible pieces like P19, except in suggestion of a body without the carinated shoulder. Sherds from House 1 that might represent a similar form are Fig. 3.6, nos. 81 and 82.

P21. This includes all sherds like P19 in decoration, but too small for representation of profile (Fig. 3.3, nos. 40-42; Fig. 3.4, nos. 44-46; Fig. 3.5, nos. 49-52, 55, 58-59; Fig. 3.6, nos. 63-70, 73-75, 80); a few such sherds occur in contexts later than House 1, where they are certainly intrusive.

Group 12. Fineware Jars with Rounded Body (cf. Bowls of Group 9)

P23. Jar with rounded body and shoulder, base flat, short rim gently curving to near vertical, slightly flattened top. Thick walled from base to mouth, exterior surface coated with burnished haematite; House 1, Fig. 3.6, no. 79, S04/2, plain, might be corresponding Jar form to bowl P15; both are from House 3, Fig. 3.11, no. 15, bowl (P15); no. 17, jar (P23). A comparable jar sherd, not illustrated, is from the internal cutting R in Enclosure I.

Carinated Jars: B – in Coarseware

P27. As Group 18 (see below), but either varying from its profiles or with profiles indeterminate; crudely potted: sherds only.

P28. As P27 but everted rims: body sherds only.
House 1, Fig. 3.6, no. 77 (was larger than a P33); also no. 92 .

- Group and Profile number series is here interrupted, allowing for new, as yet undiscovered types to be inserted (*CFC Hawkes*) -

Group 18. Carinated Jars

[Normally with fingertip decoration in horizontal row on carination and usually another along exterior of rim; flat base]

P25. Jars with wall slanted straight, at 100-110 degree angle from base, rarely with protruding foot as Fig. 3.9, no. 44, or near vertical wall, to a normally sharp shoulder carination; neck is concave, rim normally flat on the top and sometimes slightly thickened or rolled outwards.
Examples from House 2, Fig. 3.9, nos. 38 and 44; House 3, Fig. 3.12, no. 25; these show the range of size.

P26. As P25 with body rounded out, carination may be blunt or even rounded.
House 2, Fig. 3.8, no. 34; Fig. 3.10, nos. 51 and 53; House 3, Fig. 3.12, no. 24; House 4, Fig. 3.13, no. 5; WH3, Fig. 3.16, no. 22 and very large no. 21.

P30. Jar with wall apparently very straight, sharp carination, short inturned neck and sharply everted rim, tapered, rounded and proportionately tall; upper row of fingertip decoration on the constriction at neck.; the impressions are unevenly spaced and, as at the carination, abnormally shallow.
From House 4, Fig. 3.13, no. 1; an exceptional case.

P32. Jar with tall neck above carination in-turning; rim either distinguished only by row of fingertip decoration, or bent gently upwards and slightly tapered.
House 2, Fig. 3.8, nos. 28 and 29; House 3, Fig. 3.12, no. 27 and 43; A single further example, not illustrated from the internal cutting R in Enclosure I.

P33. Jar as P25 but rim everted or standing nearly upright from slant of neck; wall of body may be slightly rounded; top of rim normally flat, sometimes slightly thickened outwards.
There are many examples: from House 2, Fig. 3.8, nos. 31-33; Fig. 3.9, nos. 37 and 43; House 3, Fig. 3.12, nos. 41 and 45; WH3, Fig. 3.16, nos. 19-20, 23, 26. One special variant is Fig. 3.10, no. 55, from House 2, which has no finger-tipping, but only a row of very shallow broad hollows on exterior of rim and eight equally spaced, pinched up lugs like warts on the shoulder. Fabric unusually fine, F14; surface burnished, S02.

Carinated Bowls in Coarseware

Group 20. Wide-mouthed Bowls

[With finger-tip decoration]
P29. Any small vessel with flaring rim as in Group 7, but in coarseware and with weakly carinated shoulder; sides splayed outwards from a narrow flat base, making it a wide-mouthed bowl and not a jar. Only the shoulder and flaring rim sherd found in this ware, Fig. 3.14, no. 8, from the Enclosure II posthole complex, Area S2. This example has a row of fingertip ornament along the shoulder and the exterior of its rim. Most other finger-tipped sherds from this complex are from jars. A small rim sherd (Fig. 3.14, no. 10), may be of wide-mouthed bowls. If so, the form is rare.

Jars with Rounded Profiles

Group 25. Barrel jars

[Also others with similar body]
P17.Barrel jar, crudely made, in-turning rim with diameter equalling the plain flat base. Pit II.53, Fig. 3.23, no. 3; Pit II.5, Fig. 3.18, no. 7, though base is missing; both with rim-top rounded; variant with flat-topped rim, Pit II.50, Fig. 3.26, no. 2.

P31. Miniature jar, barrel-shaped body sloping to meet a narrowed base, thickened downwards to a solid foot. Above a slightly constricted neck, rim has two varieties of profile: P31a, with everted lip and flattened top; P31b, upstanding, top rounded and on either side pinched slightly into a lug, each with small round horizontal perforation.
P31a. Pit II.21, Fig. 3.25, no. 3.
P31b. Pit II.33B, Fig. 3.25 , no. 4.

P38. Bowl with rounded sides, base flat and less in diameter than the mouth; flattened rim-top. Pit II.33B, Fig. 3.25, no. 1.

P39. Sherds of rims suggesting barrel-like bodies; rims upright and with top either rounded or flat (seldom inwardly bevelled). Pit II.7, Fig. 3.30, no. 4; Pit II.59, Fig. 3.23, nos. 3-4; WH5, Fig. 3.31, no. 3.

P51. Jar with barrel-like body, maximum diameter at shoulder height, giving a pronounced curve inward to mouth; rim not defined nor thickened, top rounded. Pit II.55, Fig. 3.28, no. 1.

P52a. Jar with flat base and body profile like P51 until above the shoulder, where (from slight constriction, hardly a neck) the rim stands up or is slightly everted; it is short and may be slightly thickened, top rounded or, very rarely, flattened. Diameter at mouth is somewhat greater than at base. Pit II.53, Fig. 3.23, no. 1; Pit II.59, Fig. 3.23, no. 1; Pit II.43, Fig. 3.24, no. 2; Pit II.11, Fig. 3.28, no. 3; Pit II.46, Fig. 3.26, no. 1; Pit II.49, Fig. 3.20, no. 1; Pit II.5, Fig. 3.18, no. 6.
With rim-top flattened, Pit II.64, Fig. 3.22, no. 1; Pit II.30, Fig. 3.30, no. 1.
P52b. Jar, like P52a except for rim, which is even shorter, and thickens only inwards, sharply turned above into a bevel, slanting to the lip.
Pit II.14, Fig. 3.27, no. 5; the bevelled rim on this body form is rare: Pit II.46, Fig. 3.26, no. 4; Pit II.43, Fig. 3.24, no. 3 and Pit II.54, Fig. 3.24, no. 6, Pit II.9, Fig. 3.30, no. 4. No other illustrated sherds but *cf.* The bevel in Group 31, P36b.

P55. Some crudely made jars, which below the inward curve to their rim may have had truly cylindrical body: for example, Pit II.33B, Fig. 3.25, no. 5, suggests this. But no sherds sufficiently preserved to demonstrate form with certainty.

Group 26. Rounded-Shoulder jars of 'Situla' Form

[With neck and everted rim]
P22. Jars with this profile are either large and heavy vessels, as if for storage, or medium-small or (rarely) smaller. In the large size, the sides slant steeply up from a flat base as far as the shoulder, very slightly convex but at a mean outward angle of some 105 degrees; the roundness of the shoulder varies, and the neck varies from a simple constriction to an inward-curved or taller straightened form. The mouth is greater in diameter than the base, the rim is everted either gently, with an outward-thickened lip, or thickened both inward and out, with lip more prominent or bent sharply outward and flattened on the top.
Three of this size are restorable complete: Pit I.1, Fig. 3.17, no. 1; Pit II.5, Fig. 3.18, no. 4; and Pit II.37, Fig. 3.19, no. 6, with the flat-topped rim lipped sharply out. Rim sherds: Pit II.69/70, Fig. 3.21, no. 3; and three with flat-topped rim lipped outward: Pit II.21, Fig. 3.25, no. 1; Pit II.33B Fig. 3.25, no. 10. Medium small: Pit II.5, Fig. 3.18, no. 5; Pit II.37, Fig. 3.19, nos. 8-9; Pit II.40, Fig. 3.22, no. 2. Pit II.11, Fig. 3.28, no. 2, is a variant having evidently had a broad shoulder, no neck but a simple constriction, and the rounded lip of its flattish-topped rim folded over it (no match has been found).
Smaller size with slant of sides steeper, as implied by Fig. 3.30, no. 5, from Pit II.9; probably Pit II.34, Fig. 3.31, no. 1, lacking neck and rim but with

rounded shoulder showing 'situla' form, but unique in having fingernail decoration; also Pit II.21, Fig. 3.25, no. 7, though with shoulder rounded very weakly and neck relatively tall, rim plain and everted only slightly; size small but form still reminiscent of the 'situla'. A squat version may be suggested from Pit II. 64, Fig. 3.22, no. 2.

P56. Like P22 but sides more barrel-shaped below a neck more markedly constricted; rim is everted straight with lip is squared off or flattened. The size ranges from medium to small. Pit II.37, Fig. 3.19, no. 4 (strong shoulder inferred) and no. 5; Pit II. 69/70, Fig. 3.21, no. 1 and no. 8 which has rim externally lipped.

P46. Thick-walled jars or possibly bowls of 'flower-pot' shape; mouth evidently wider than the base inferred by slope of body. Two varieties recognised, 46a and 46b, both very rare.
P46a. The one certain example from Enclosure II, Ditch (primary silt), Fig. 3.32, no. 3, has a flattish-rounded rim upstanding from weakly formed shoulder.
P46b. Two examples recognised. That from Pit II.41, Fig. 3.20, no. 2, has a heavy rim, flat on the top, with squared lip protruding outwards, a very short concave neck above a weakly-rounded shoulder (less in diameter than the lip), and body below it gently concave. That from Pit II.60, Fig. 3.31, no. 1, has a heavy flat-topped rim, with lip protruding outwards and rounded off; no neck, but a weakly rounded shoulder..
All examples apparently large: P46a example has a calculated rim diameter of 230mm; P46b from Pit II.41, 300mm.

Group 31. Jars of Barrel-Like but Globular Form

[Round-bellied or round-shouldered; rims various]
P36a. Round-bellied globular jars, rims plain, upstanding or slightly everted, top rounded. Restored with most of profile: Pit II.54, Fig. 3.24, no. 3, small and rather less fine, Encl. III, Fig. 3.33, no. 2. Sherds including rim: Pit II.41, Fig. 3.20, no. 3; Pit II.69/70, Fig. 3.21, no. 4; Pit II.51, Fig. 3.24, no. 2.
P36b. Round-bellied globular jars, rims plain, upstanding or slightly everted, top flattened: or rarely, with inward-slanting bevel, one with a pair (opposed) of vertically-perforated lugs at shoulder height: Pit II.14, Fig. 3.27, no. 6. Profile near complete: Pit II.53, Fig. 3.23, no. 2; smaller but finer, Pit II.22, Fig. 3.29, no. 2. Sherds including rim: Pit II.49, Fig 3.20, no. 3; Pit II.50, Fig. 3.26, no. 1; Pit II.62, Fig. 3.31, no. 1, of vessel large and very `globular'; Pit II.72, Fig. 3.31, no. 1; WH5, Fig. 3.31, no. 1. A large flat base from Pit I.1, Fig. 3.17, no. 3 appears to have belonged to a large jar of this group.

P37. Round-shouldered ovoid jars with diameter greatest at shoulder height; globular shape distinguishes them from P22. Rims, as in P36, are of two kinds, a and b.
P37a. Rims plain, upstanding or slightly everted, top rounded. Profiles complete: Pit II.53, Fig 3.23, 7; Pit II.14, Fig. 3.27, no. 1. Sherds: Pit II.59, Fig. 3.23, no. 2; Pit II.44, Fig. 3.24, no. 1; Pit II.50, Fig. 3.26, no. 4; WH II.6, Fig. 3.31, no. 1. One not illustrated, from WH3, has rim short and inwardly thickened.
P37b. Rims plain, upstanding or slightly everted, top flat. Profiles complete: Pit II.14, Fig. 3.27, no. 4. Sherds: Pit II.41, Fig. 3.20, no. 1, large size; Pit II.33B, Fig. 3.25, no. 2; Pit II.14, Fig. 3.27, no. 3; Pit II.11, Fig. 3.28, no. 1.

Group 32. Very Large Jars

[With flat base and barrel body]
P34. Profile almost complete: Rim with rounded lip, everted with groove around the top (to hold a lid such as Pit II.46, Fig. 3.26, no. 2, P45 of Group 33). Pit II.69/70, Fig. 3.21, no. 7, the sole example. In the same layer (6) of this pit were found numerous sherds of a thicker walled jar, Fabric F21, with a flat and perforated base. Though of a bigger jar than no. 7, they deserve mention here as showing a second such storage jar, discarded at the same time.

Dishes or Shallow Lids and Wide-mouthed Bowls

Group 33. Plain Shallow Dishes and Wide-Mouthed Bowls

[Some sherds being possibly of lids, one certainly]
P40. Dish with rounded sides, rim lipped both outwards and inwards or inwards only; Pit II.37, Fig. 3.19, no. 1; lipped inwards only are a sherd from Pit II.33B, Fig. 3.25, no. 8 and Pit II.5, Fig. 3.18, no. 8; drooping lip from Pit II.47, Fig. 3.22, no.1.

P44. Shallow dish with splayed and barely convex sides; rim, above a slight exterior offset, is thickened and heavy, lipped prominently outwards and inwards. Pit II.5, Fig. 3.18, no. 1.

P45. Sherds perhaps of P44 but too small for identification, including however, some possible and one certain lid sherds, with shallow groove on underside, to fit a jar rim (such as Pit II.69/70, Fig. 3.21, no. 7, P34 of Group 32): this is Pit II.46, Fig. 3.26, no. 2.

P53. Sherds perhaps of P40 but too small for identification, including base sherd from Pit II.30, Fig. 3.30, no. 2.

Pear-shaped Jars and Pedestal Vases

Group 34. Jars Represented by Rim and Neck Implying Pear-Shaped Body

['vases piriformes']
P35. Among the four vessels of various forms in Fig. 3.29, no. 3 from Pit II.22 represents this form by the curve of its everted rim and hollowed neck, running smoothly out to a pear-shaped body, of medium to large, and probably tall, size. Similar rim/neck sherds, from Pit II.19 and Pit II 37 (not illustrated). A small version is Pit II.18, Fig. 3.29, no. 6; Pit II.7,

Fig. 3.30, no. 3; and perhaps Pit II.39, Fig. 3.31, no. 2; the medium-sized one is unmistakeable, as is Fig. 3.32, no. 5, from primary silt in Enclosure II Ditch. These examples represent a graceful form appearing in these contexts as a much rarer type than it later became.

P41. A similar body is represented by two pieces with only a constriction for the neck, and an everted rim with a slanting interior bevel. In Pit II.18, Fig. 3.29, no. 9 the shoulder bulge is evident, while in WH5, Fig. 3.31, no. 7, the pear shape may be inferred from the distinctive rim and neck form. This profile is rarer than P41.

P47. This profile bears less resemblance to P35 and P41. The shoulder bulge is usually less pronounced, and in some examples drooping, so that their profile may closely resemble P37a, as shown by Pit II.67, Fig. 3.22, no. 1. In neck construction, however, the profile resembles P41, while the rim is a near bead-rim: Pit II.3, Fig. 3.30, no. 2 with a shoulder more bulging, (as also one not illustrated from Pit II.2). Our examples with the narrower shoulder bulge tends also towards the bead-rim jar or bowl, itself however not a regular standardised form on this site: (see the two rims mentioned below).
In Fig. 3.24, Pit II.43, no.1 has the simplest rim, with a slight interior thickening, but otherwise similar to those of P36a or P52; Pit II.51, Fig. 3.24, no. 5 has a near bead-rim, as in Pit II.21, Fig. 3.25, no. 4 (weak), and Pit II.18, Fig. 3.29, no. 3. Pit II.7, Fig. 3.30, no. 2 has the same large and fully rounded lip.

Group 35. Pedestal Vases

[All examples are in finely-burnished dark ware]
P43. The pedestal, a gracefully heightened form of everted foot-ring, is thicker than the sides of the vase for the sake of stability; as is the raised base that it supports. The sides are no more than 2mm thick and the shoulder is rounded, the neck concave, and the rim either gently everted and plain or rather more everted, with a slight outward lip, flattened mildly.
From Pit II.5, Fig. 3.18, no. 3 shows the profile with the more everted rim; Pit II.5, Fig. 3.18, no. 2, shows the shoulder and the less everted rim. Fig. 3.20 shows two pedestals: Pit II.41, Fig. 3.20, no. 4 and Pit II.49 no. 2, part of the side but incomplete beneath; Pit II.37, Fig. 3.19, no. 7 produced one fragment; a small rim sherd in similar fineware, Fig. 3.19, no. 2, may belong to another P43 as may Pit II.55, Fig. 3,28, no. 2.

The best example, Pit II.5, Fig. 3.18, no. 3, has an internal depth of 105mm and an internal width of 138mm across the mouth. Such 'vases' would have been suitable for drinking from, no less than the haematite covered bowls (and similar cups) of Groups 4, 5, 7 and 9, though in shape so different. But their rarity must suggest that their use was limited to a minority, which their elegance and the burnish of their smooth dark surface should imply was a socially high one. Among the larger vessels from the Pits, some could have held the beverage ready to be served for drinking; but those most graceful in the form, namely the pear-shape of Group 34, and especially P35, never came from Pits that contained sherds of the pedestal form P43. There was apparently therefore a difference of time between the vogue of P43 and the pear-shaped jars. This matter, of the serial chronology of the Pits, is considered elsewhere.

Saucepan Vessels

Group 36. Vessels of the 'Saucepan' Form

[Sides gently swelling or very nearly vertical; no neck, but a slight hollowing or groove beneath a rim normally rounded, swollen inwardly if at all]
P42. Vessel having a base presumed flat and body with a gentle and even swelling, continued or straightened upwards to a simply rounded rim swollen out or seldom inwards, demarcated only by a slight hollowing below it. Examples found are only sherds, but the base is as P50. The form seems a standardised development from Group 25 and 31, but is not very common. Examples from Pit II.54, Fig. 3.24, nos. 1 and 7; Pit II.33B, Fig. 3.25, nos. 3 and 6, Pit II.55, Fig. 3.28, no. 6; Pit II.18, Fig. 3.29, no. 8; Pit II.22, Fig. 3.29, no. 4 and Fig. 3.32, no. 2, from primary silt in Enclosure III Ditch.

P49. This version of the 'saucepan' has the thickness of the side narrowing upwards to a thin plain rim, top simply rounded off. Fig. 3.33, nos. 7 and 8, stray sherds from Enclosure III, one found in ditch, one in interior, seem the only two examples.

P50. 'Saucepan' vessel with near vertical walls, flat base; the rim, not marked unless by a horizontal groove, simply rounded or with a slight internal swelling and/or a flattened top. Pit II.22, Fig. 3.29, no. 1, with burnished surface, has this groove and 'eyebrow' decoration; Pit II.18, Fig. 3.29, no. 2 is a plain and coarser rim sherd; Fig. 3.32, no. 6 from the primary silt in Enclosure II Ditch, is another example. Pit II.2, Fig. 3.30, no. 3 has the flat-topped rim; rim of a sherd not illustrated from Pit II, 60, was another P50.

Thus all our three versions of the 'saucepan' form are rare, least rare being P42; this is nearest to the forms that seem tending towards it in Groups 25 and 31.

ANALYSIS OF THE FABRIC GROUPS

by Guy Grainger

The pottery assemblages from all contexts as recorded have been considered on the basis of the 14 groups recognised by Wilson (see above). The pottery is grouped by fabrics in context of discovery, with inferences drawn for relative chronology. The totals by sherd count of pottery by fabric and context within archaeological groupings relating to Enclosures I-III are presented in Appendix 3B: Tables 3B1a-3B1l.

The 328 contexts examined by Wilson produced a total of 6038 sherds (whole or partial vessels were counted as one sherd). The number of sherds in each Fabric Group is listed in descending order with percentage of total sample in Table 3.1.

A breakdown of the numbers of sherds occurring in each context (Table 3.2) reveals that almost 50% of these contexts contained 1-5 sherds, while fewer than 10% contained more than 50 sherds. The contexts were therefore generally examined in groups, based either on features, as with the houses and enclosing ditches, or on feature type/area (*ie* pits in Enclosure II). Where possible, they were assessed in chronological order (Phases 1-5), based on the strategraphic sequence.

Table 3.1 Distribution of total site sherds by Fabric Group

Fabric Group	*No. sherds*	*% total sample*
9	962	15.9
11	826	13.7
3	735	12.2
5	690	11.4
14	651	10.8
8	583	9.7
2	540	8.9
4	354	5.9
13	265	4.4
10	241	4.0
6	90	1.5
12	53	0.9
1	43	0.7
7	5	<0.1

The Houses

The emplacements of the roundhouses were the earliest pottery-producing contexts encountered at the site and, therefore, provide the natural starting point for an examination of fabric trends. The number of sherds in each Fabric Group is given for each house in Table 3.3. The postholes and cuttings above the postholes associated with House 3 are considered separately.

Enclosure II, House 1 – Phase 1

This assemblage is dominated by Group 2 (63%) with a noticeable proportion of Group 5 (17.9%), and lesser amounts of Group 3 (4.6%), Group 11 (5.1%) and Group 14 (6.0%). The handful of sherds of Group 4, 8 and probably 9 are most likely intrusive.

Table 3.2 Distribution of pottery in contexts listed in Table 3.4

No. sherds per context	*No. contexts*	*% total no. of contexts*
1-5	156	47.6
6-10	44	13.4
11-30	67	20.4
31-50	32	9.8
51-100	20	6.1
101+	9	2.7

Table 3.3 Houses 1-4. Distribution of sherds by Fabric Group *House 1 (contexts 9-34), House 2 (contexts 35-76), House 3 cuttings (contexts 231-268), House 3 postholes (contexts 269-311), House 4 (contexts 77-98).*

	House 1		*House 2*		*House 3 Cuttings*		*House 3 Postholes*		*House 4*	
Fabric Group	*No.*	*%*	*No.*	*%*	*No.*	*%*	*No.*	*%*	*No.*	*%*
1	--	--	--	--	2	0.3	--	--	--	--
2	271	63.0	44	8.7	44	6.5	33	7.1	7	9.2
3	20	4.6	54	10.7	108	15.8	57	14.0	8	10.5
4	1	0.2	4	0.8	21	3.1	--	--	4	5.2
5	77	17.9	136	27.0	157	23.0	63	15.5	27	35.5
6	--	--	5	1.0	--	--	--	--	9	11.8
7	--	--	--	--	--	--	1	0.2	--	--
8	5	1.2	1	0.2	7	1.0	2	0.5	--	--
9	8	1.9	58	11.5	50	7.3	31	7.6	4	5.2
10	--	--	2	0.4	4	0.6	1	0.2	--	--
11	22	5.1	140	27.8	114	16.7	67	16.5	11	14.5
12	--	--	--	--	3	0.4	2	0.4	--	--
13	--	--	7	1.4	71	10.4	62	15.2	--	--
14	26	6.0	52	10.3	101	14.8	87	21.4	6	7.9
Total	430		503		682		406		76	

Enclosure II, House 2 – Phase 2

The sample from House 2 is in many respects similar to that from House 1, with Groups 2, 3, 5, 11 and 14 making up 84.5% of sherds recovered. However, the most common pottery is that of Groups 5 (27%) and 11 (27.8%). Group 2 is much less common than in House 1, accounting for only 8.7% of the total. Quantities of Groups 3 (10.7%) and 14 (10.3%) are, as in House 1, small but still significant. In contrast to House 1, Group 9 accounts for a sizeable proportion of the sherds (11.5%).

The mean sherd weights of the sherds of the main Fabric Groups in Houses 1 and 2 are considered below (Table 3.4). This measurement is important as it is influenced by the presence or absence of large sherds/partial vessels and can, therefore, provide a general impression of the overall size of sherds under consideration.

The dominant Fabric Groups in each house, Group 2 in House 1, Groups 5 and 11 in House 2, have mean sherd weights markedly above the other groups, suggesting that most of the large sherds/ partial vessels tend to belong to these Fabric Groups. A glance at the illustrated pottery from these houses confirms this. Fabric Groups 3, 5 and 11 have similar mean sherd weights in both houses, but by contrast, the mean sherd weight of Group 2 is much lower in House 2 than in House 1.

Consideration of Tables 3.3 and 3.7, therefore, indicates that House 2 has a much smaller proportion of Group 2 pottery than House 1, and that on average the sherds are noticeably smaller. Both points suggest that the Group 2 pottery found in House 2 is residual. The very small amounts of pottery from Groups 4, 6, 8, 10 and probably 13 (19 sherds, 3.7% of total) must be intrusive.

Table 3.4 Mean weights of sherds by Fabric Group

Fabric Group	*House 1 Mean weight*	*House 2 Mean weight*
2	34.1 g	11.7 g
3	11.0 g	14.4 g
5	20.1 g	15.0 g
9	--	32.5 g
11	24.3 g	35.5 g
14	17.6 g	19.5 g

Enclosure II, House 4 – Phase 2

Although the sample is small, it exhibits a very similar distribution to that of House 2. Group 5 is the most common fabric type (35.5%), followed by Group 11 (14.5%). Groups 2, 3, 9 and 14 are also present in generally similar proportions to those of House 2, and are probably residual. Group 4 (4 sherds, 5.2% of total) and Group 6 (9 sherds, 11.8% of total) both occur rather more frequently than the supposedly intrusive elements of the assemblages from Houses 1 and 2. Reference to Appenxix 3B, Table 3B.1 shows that all Group 6 sherds and one Group 4 sherd came from a single context, PH 198 (context 82).

Enclosure III, House 3 – Phase 3A and 3B

Almost all the contexts designated as parts of House 3 could be classed either as cuttings or postholes. These two types of context have been examined separately, as it is likely that the cuttings would have been more susceptible to contamination by later pottery than the postholes.

Postholes – Phase 3A

Five major groups occur in broadly similar quantities, four of which are familiar from Houses 1, 2 and 4: Group 14 (21.4%), Group 11 (16.5%) Group 5 (15.5%) and Group 3 (14.0%). The new Group is 13 (15.2%): the 7 sherds of this type from House 2 may therefore represent the very beginning of use of this type. There is still a fair quantity of residual Group 2 (7.1%) and also Group 9 (7.3%) in the sample. A very small amount (1.5%) of intrusive pottery of Groups 7, 8, 10 and 12 was also recovered.

Cuttings – Phase 3B

The fabric type distribution is almost identical to that of House 3 postholes. The same five major Groups (3, 5, 11, 13 and 14) and two minor Groups (2 and 9) account for 94.6% of the sample, and are in the same proportions except for Group 5, which is higher, and Groups 13 and 14 which are lower. Groups 2, 8, 10 and 12 account for 2.3% of the total and again represent the intrusive fringe. The 21 sherds of Group 4 make up the remaining 3.1% of the sample. It is clear from the low degree of contamination by other, later, pottery types that the fill in the cuttings is almost contemporary with that of the postholes. It seems, however, that there was time for some Group 4 pottery to get into the cuttings after the postholes were sealed.

Enclosure II, Working Hollows

The distribution of fabric types by percentage is given below for each of the hollows together with the distribution from House 3 cuttings (taken from Table 3.3) for comparison.

Working Hollow 3 – Phase 3C; Working Hollows 1 and 2 – Phase 4

Overall the pottery from H3 and the stratigraphically later hollows H1 and H2 is similar to that from House 3 cuttings. There is a continued occurrence in considerable, though varying, quantities of Groups 3, 5, 9, and 11, and in smaller numbers Groups 13, 14 and the residual Group 2. Although Group 8 pottery is present in slightly greater numbers than before, it is still a rarity. Group 4, missing from the assem-

Table 3.5 House 3, cuttings and working hollows Fabric Group distribution by percentage

Fabric Groups	House 3 % Cuttings	WH.3 %	WH.1 %	WH.2 %	WH.6 %	WH.5 %	WH.4 %
1	0.3	0.3	--	--	--	--	--
2	6.5	6.2	9.0	4.0	--	4.2	--
3	15.8	21.0	12.0	10.1	41.2	--	--
4	3.1	--	17.3	7.1	--	2.1	3.3
5	23.0	13.6	11.3	7.1	--	--	6.6
6	--	--	--	2.0	--	--	3.3
7	--	--	--	--	--	--	--
8	1.0	3.3	0.7	4.0	11.8	20.8	50.8
9	7.3	14.5	12.8	25.3	11.8	70.8	16.4
10	0.6	2.1	2.3	18.2	5.9	--	9.8
11	16.7	23.7	21.1	8.1	--	--	--
12	0.4	--	--	--	29.4	--	--
13	10.4	8.6	3.0	6.1	--	--	--
14	14.8	6.8	10.5	7.1	--	2.1	9.8
Total no. sherds	682	338	133	99	17	48	61

blage in H3, is however, present in reasonable quantities in both H1 and H2. The latter context also contains a sizeable proportion of Group 10 pottery. Analysis of the pottery from these hollows suggests that H3 is a little later than House 3 and that H1 and H2 are slightly later than H3.

Working Hollows 4 and 5 – Phase 5; Working Hollow 6 – Possibly Phase 5

H5 and H4 both produced assemblages that are markedly different from those already considered. Most of the pottery in H5 belongs to Group 9 (70.8%), but a fairly large proportion (20.8%) of Group 8 pottery is also present. In H4, Group 8 is most common (50.8%), the majority of the remainder is Group 9 (16.4%), 10 (9.8%) and 14 (9.8%). This major change in fabrics indicates that H4 and H5 are later than H1 and H2. The small size of the sample from H6 makes it impossible to comment on the pottery, beyond noting the dominance of Group 3 and the rare Group 12.

Enclosure II Pits and Postholes (Contexts 99-193) – Phase 5

In the following text Enclosure II postholes treated with the pits are those with no apparent relation to any house. The pottery from the 15 pits, each containing at least 40 sherds, (P5, P14, P19, P36/36B, P37, P39, P40, P41, P46, P53, P54, P60, P65, P67 and P69/70) was initially examined in isolation in an unsuccessful attempt to discern any patterns or trends at context level.

The Fabric Group distribution for the pits and postholes together is given below in Table 3.6. The major Fabric Groups in the pits and postholes are 9, 8 and 3 together with smaller amounts of Group 4 and 10. The decline of residual Group 2 pottery continues, but more significant is the marked decline of Groups 5, 11 and 14, compared with the House 3 cuttings, and the virtual disappearance of Group 13. The pottery from the pits and postholes indicates that they are later than H1 and H2, and belong to the same phase as H4 and H5. Certain variations in the occurrence of some of the less common Fabric Groups were detected in the pits. Group 2 is normally only represented by the odd sherd in each context but a few, notably in P65 P67 and, to a lesser extent P69/70, just to the south of House 4, and P40 and P60 in the area of House 2, have rather larger concentrations. Pits with a higher than average proportion of Group 4 pottery, (7, 9, 12, 19, 22, 34, 36/36B, 38, 41, 44, 54 and 55) and Group 10 pottery (7, 11, 14, 18, 21, 22, 23, 31, 39, 42, 43, 52, 54, 55, 56 and 65) were isolated but, compared to the remaining pits in each case, failed

Table 3.6 Enclosure II, pits and postholes Fabric Group distribution

Fabric Groups	No. sherds	% sherds
1	--	--
2	66	3.0
3	329	15.1
4	184	8.4
5	101	5.0
6	43	2.0
7	4	0.2
8	440	20.1
9	519	23.8
10	177	8.1
11	118	5.4
12	25	1.1
13	25	1.1
14	153	7.0

to highlight major change in the other Fabric Group, except that the high Group 10 assemblage has virtually no Group 14 material. It is, therefore, reasonable to treat the pottery from the pits and postholes in Enclosure II as a single group. A small number of pits contained relatively high concentrations of the rare Fabric Groups: P21, P29, P37, P46, P48 and P59 – Group 6; P22 – Group 7 and P53 – Group 12. PH79 also contained 3 sherds of Group 12 (and no other pottery).

Enclosure II Hollows

The very small quantity of pottery found in these features makes any assessment difficult. The Group 13 pottery in H8 suggests that it belongs to phase 3 or 4, and Groups 8 and 10 in H7 is indicative of phase 5. The Group 12 sherds in H19 could indicate phases 3-5.

Enclosure II, Ditch (Contexts 205-230)

The layers recorded in the enclosure ditch sections were amalgamated into three groups:

1. Topsoil/subsoil
2. Top layer of the ditch fill
3. All lower layers of ditch fill

The distribution of the Fabric Groups is given in Table 3.7.

The pottery from the top ditch fill layer is mostly from Cutting H2 (context 212), the remainder coming from Cutting J3 (context 216). Cutting H2 contains mostly Group 8 pottery with lesser amounts of Groups 3, 9 and 14, and clearly belongs to phase 5. The lower ditch fills, not surprisingly, appear to be earlier. The presence of quite a high proportion of Group 13 pottery and a noticeable amount of Group 4 pottery tends to suggest that this assemblage fits into phase 4. This is reinforced by the high levels of Groups 11 and 14 and the small amounts of Groups 8 and 10.

Enclosure III, Ditch

Pottery was recovered from Cutting M5 and Cutting M8, Cutting N5 and Cutting O8 (contexts 323-5, 327). The Fabric Group distribution for these contexts is given in Table 3.8. The presence of quantities of Groups 4, 10 and 13 fabrics tends to point to phase 4, but there are a number of Group 8 sherds, which could place this assemblage as late as phase 5.

Enclosure I

The pottery from pits 1-4, the ditch and a group labelled 'Enclosure I' (contexts 01-08) is collected together in Table 3.9. The high proportion of Groups 4, 11 and 14, and the fairly small amount of Group

Table 3.7 Enclosure II Ditch, Distribution of Fabric Group

Fabric Groups	*Topsoil*	*Upper Layer Ditch Fill*	*Lower Layers Ditch Fill*	*%*
1	--	--	--	--
2	--	1	3	2.1
3	--	12	10	6.8
4	2	12	9	6.2
5	1	21	12	8.2
6	1	1	15	10.3
7	--	--	--	--
8	1	32	7	4.8
9	1	22	17	11.6
10	--	--	3	2.1
11	4	19	26	17.8
12	--	--	6	4.1
13	8	--	22	15.1
14	--	--	24	16.4

Table 3.8 Enclosure III Ditch, distribution of Fabric Groups

Fabric Groups	*No. of sherds*
1	2
2	6
3	2
4	10
5	--
6	--
7	--
8	5
9	2
10	7
11	1
12	--
13	6
14	--

Table 3.9 Enclosure I, distribution of Fabric Groups

Fabric Groups	*No. sherds*	*%*
1	2	0.5
2	23	5.6
3	23	5.6
4	66	16.2
5	14	3.4
6	13	3.2
7	--	--
8	24	5.9
9	65	15.9
10	10	2.5
11	95	23.3
12	9	2.2
13	10	2.5
14	54	13.2

8, are indicative of phase 4. There is nothing in any of the individual contexts which contrasts with this overall view, so it is likely that all the Enclosure I contexts belong to phase 4.

Enclosure III – Surface Finds (Context 328) – after Phase 5

The pottery from this context belongs to Group 1, made up of various Roman fabric types and represents the latest assemblage considered.

Summary

Phase 1:

Enclosure II, House 1 (Contexts 09-34)
Group 2 is dominant, but there is also a sizeable amount of Group 5 pottery and smaller quantities of Groups 3, 11 and 14 sherds. The very small amount of Group 9 pottery may either be intrusive or mark the beginnings of its use.

Phase 2:

Enclosure II, House 2 (Contexts 35-76), House 4 (Contexts 77-98)
The proportion of Group 2 has dropped away sharply, and those sherds that do occur appear to be residual. The major Fabric Groups are 5 and 11, with 3, 9 and 14 also present in significant numbers.

Phase 3:

Enclosure III, House 3. 3A Postholes (Contexts 269-311), 3B Cuttings (Contexts 231-268). 3C Enclosure II, Working Hollow H3 (Context 201). In both 3A and 3B the major Groups are 3, 5, 11, 13 and 14, together with the slightly less common Group 9. There is still a reasonable amount of the residual Group 2. The Cuttings (3B) also contain a small amount of Group 4. The majority of the pottery from H1 also comes from Groups 3, 5, 9, 11, 13 and 14, with, in addition, a residual presence of Group 2. There are also small amounts of Groups 8 and 10.

Phase 4:

Enclosure II, H1 and H2 (Contexts 199, 200), Enclosure I, (Contexts 01-08), Enclosure II, Ditch (Contexts 205-230, except 212 and 216), and Possibly Enclosure III, Ditch (Contexts 323-325, 327).
The most indicative features of this rather transitional phase is the emergence of Groups 4 and 10 while Group 8 remains very much a minor presence. There is considerable variation among what were the major Groups of phase 3, the overall impression being that Group 9 is increasing in importance, that Groups 3, 11 and 14 continue unchanged, and that Groups 5 and 13 are in decline.

Phase 5:

Enclosure II, Remaining Pits and Postholes (Contexts 99-193), Enclosure II, Ditch (Contexts 212 and 216)
The major Groups in Phase 5 are 3, 8 and 9, with Groups 4 and 10 also present in significant numbers. Groups 11 and 14 have fallen away, Group 5 continues to decline, and Group 13 has virtually disappeared. Groups 5, 11, 13 and 14, with Group 2 all appear to be residual.

DISCUSSION OF THE POTTERY
by Lisa Brown

Sonia and Christopher Hawkes, with the assistance of several colleagues and research assistants, worked intermittently on the Longbridge Deverill pottery for more than three decades following the end of the excavations in 1960. Nonetheless, even as late as 1994, when Sonia Hawkes published an interim site report featuring House 3 (Hawkes 1994), there were very few pottery assemblages of late Bronze Age and earliest Iron Age date available to consider in the light of her own. The major comparative collection was that from All Cannings Cross, published by Maud Cinnington in (1923), a site and an asemblage which was quite different to the Longbridge assemblage in some respects. Fineware bowls and jars of the kind and condition recovered from Houses 1 and 2 were still rare, and the correlation between the burning of roundhouses and the ritual redepositon of their contents (often fire-affected pots), a phenomenon highlighted at Brighton Hill South, Hants by Coe and Newman (1993; Fasham *et al.* 1995), had scarcely registered on the archaeological conscience before the 1990s.

The past decade or so has seen the publication of an increasing number of examples of the deliberate placement in postholes and other structural features of earliest Iron Age pottery, often decorated and sometimes burnt. This practice was identified at Houghton Down (Brown 2000, 79-81) and Flint Farm (Brown 2008, 70 and fig. 6.52,1) in Hampshire, and Cockey Down, Wiltshire (Lovell *et al.* 1999, 33-8), amongst other locations in the Wiltshire/Hampshire region. Casual collection of a sizeable group of large fresh sherds of similar pottery thrown up by badgers on Bathampton Down signals the location of a possibly significant settlement of the same date on Bathampton Down, Somerset (Brown forthcoming).

Neither, at the time of Sonia Hawkes' death, had the 100,000 sherds recovered from four seasons of excavation between 1982-85 at the Wiltshire midden site of Potterne yet been published. In fact, it was not until 2000 (Gingell and Morris) that this material was disseminated, and then, due to financial constraints, only in very summary fashion compared to the Hawkes' extensive illustrated catalogue (below). The proliferation of ceramic evidence for the earliest Iron Age (or, as some prefer, late Bronze Age/early Iron Age transition) has gone hand in hand with an effort to understand the archaeology of midden sites. Excavations carried out in 1992-1993 at a rediscovered enclosure and midden at East Chisenbury, Wiltshire (McOmish *et al.* 2010) produced pottery broadly akin to that recovered at Longbridge, Potterne and All Cannings Cross (Raymond 2010, 66-9), but this assemblage has yet to be fully published. Yet more pottery and other artefacts have been recovered very recently from badger setts at East Chisenbury during 'Operation Nightingale', a rehabilitation project that engages wounded British military personnel in the archaeological process (Walshe *et al.* 2011, 40-43). If, as has often been proposed, midden sites represent favoured locations at which 'human values' were expressed through feasting, destruction and deposition (Waddington 2008; 2010), then it is easy to imagine the settlement at Longbridge Deverill and the midden sites at All Cannings Cross, Potterne and East Chisenbury were linked in a social and cultural network that spanned the western and northern edges of Salisbury Plain during the late Bronze Age and earliest Iron Age. The very same occupants of the Longbridge houses may have repeatedly travelled to those nearby sites (and vice-versa) to celebrate special occasions of the calendrical year or to reaffirm bonds of kinship or political affiliation.

The Longbridge Deverill pottery represents, for the most part, two phases of occupation of the site. The most impressive is that remarkable collection of material noted above from the four roundhouses and associated features, dating to the earliest part of the Iron Age. It was this group that prompted the most attention from Sonia and Christopher Hawkes and their colleagues. A second group, which was recovered from the pits, is a much less conspicuous, simple coarseware range, perhaps dating to a transitional phase between the end of the early Iron Age or beginning of the middle Iron Age, most likely separated in time by at least several generations of inhabitants of Cow Down.

The forms represented in this second, later group are mostly barrel-shaped jars that lack the emphasising characteristics of the pronounced shoulders, long upright rims, or finger-impressed decoration of the *earliest* Iron Age Longbridge coarseware jars that were associated with fine bowls. They also lack similar charactierstics of the *early* Iron Age assemblages from a multitude of Wessex sites. Jars of this second group were dated at Danebury originally to a 'ceramic phase' 4-5 (360-310 BC), but were found also, on further examination, to occur commonly in deposits dating to 'ceramic phase' 6, a century or so later (Brown 1995, 246-8). Similar vessels were found at the Easton Lane settlement near Winchester (Fasham *et al.* 1989).

A single Longbridge pit, P22 (Fig. 3.29) contained pottery of the 'developed' middle Iron Age, including a saucepan pot decorated in the 'Yarnbury-Highfield style', generally dated to the 3rd – 1st centuries BC (Cunliffe 2005, 104, fig. A:17). That this pit was an isolated feature constructed after all the other pits had been decommissioned, as could be argued on ceramic style, seems unlikely. It may be the case simply that there was something particularly notable about this pit, or about the circumstances surrounding its filling that the decorated vessels were selected to accompany its closure.

House 1 and 2 Finewares

by Daphne Nash

The finewares in both Houses 1 and 2 consist of two types, bowls (or cups) and jars. Bowls/cups are more numerous than jars, though House 1 seems to have more bowls relative to jars than House 2. If not the result of accident of preservation, this deviation could be interpreted in a number of ways, including a change in eating or feasting practices in the interval between the occupation and destruction of the two houses. A majority of bowls and jars in each house resembled each other closely in fabric, decoration and technique, while there were a few 'outsiders'.

Disposal

Most of the fine pottery of Houses 1 and 2 came from postholes and virtually all was burnt, some to cinders. Some House I ware in particular was reduced to a solid powder. In both houses the ware was broken both before and after the fire, possibly suggesting that it broke or exploded at the time of the fire. The fact that a significant number of the sherds join or belong to known bowls and jars suggests that the houses were well stocked at the time of destruction or that they had been the scene of feast-related activity prior to the conflagrations. Some of the pottery got ground into the floor and left, more or less where they were broken and it seems clear that other pieces, including many of the largest fragments, were repositioned following the fire.

In both houses, pottery was mostly confined to a few postholes, all on the same side of the houses in both cases, on the south immediately to the left of the entrance from the outside. Other postholes did, however, contain sherds, often (and notably in House 1) from vessels different from those in the main postholes. An unusual ring-decorated sherd in Williams fabric F11 came from PH167, otherwise not a rich source of sherds. A notable difference between the distribution of sherds in the two houses is that in House 1 joining sherds came only from any one posthole, though unjoined parts of the same jar might come from two (*eg* PH151 and 152). In House 2, however, joining sherds of bowls were commonly recovered from up to four different postholes and/or the overlying soil. Also there were far more jar bases from House 2 than from House 1. This placement seems to have been'rational', that is, a whole section such as rim or the left hand portion of a piece is from one feature, and the rest from another. This also suggests stages in the breakage, confirmed by the way in which some sherds were blackened or cinderised and others adjoining them not. The reason for the inclusion of fragments of the same vessels in several postholes in House 2 but not in House 1 is a matter of speculation. There were arguably different causes of breakage: falling from different heights, deliberate smashing, differential redeposition.

House 1

Short-rimmed furrowed bowls and tall 'situla' jars are made of approximately or exactly the same fabric, fine and micaceous with moderate to abundant grit, not always coarser in the jars, suggesting the same source. There was apparently less use of grog than was found in the fine House 2 wares, but this is not certain. Both jars and bowls were sometimes coated with haematite and polished. A feature shared by some was the frequent appearance of impressions from seeds and other vegetable debris, even on the finished surfaces. This is also true of House 2 wares, suggesting they were made under similar conditions, possibly in the vicinity of food preparation because of the cereal grains incorporated in the clay as well as on the surface. A mouse caught inside one vessel as it dried is an appropriate visitor around a food store or kitchen (*editor: no record identifying this vessel was found in the archive*). If they were made indoors, the impressions might suggest the presence of straw on the floor and poor light might partly account for the apparent paradox of blemishes on otherwise carefully finished surfaces.

Whether made indoors or out the debris around the workplace could be turned to good use. One of the finest House 1 jars has its plain panels apparently deliberately left rough, or even roughened, by wiping straw and general roughage across the wet clay, possibly for ease of gripping as much as variation in texture for decorative reasons. The fine polished surface must have been slippery, the jars were heavy even when empty, and the inlaid decoration was fragile, so blank panels, and especially rough ones, would have been practical.

House 1 bowls are of a fairly uniform pattern with a short rim, wide deep furrows above the carination and a well-rounded base with omphalos. The jars also form a coherent group – tall, situlate with carinated shoulders and a rim which bent outward at a remarkably constant angle. Both bowls and jars (equally true of House 2) are irregular in shape and have, where visible, internal finger sweeps in various directions. Just as the bowls had a single general type of decoration, so the fine haematite-coated jars had a general type, but with more variations in detail. The basic design was alternating blank and decorated panels running from the base of the rim to about two-thirds down the body or rather lower. The panels were bordered by vertical strips of dots, possibly inspired by the rivets on bronze buckets. There is conflicting evidence as to what these strips originally looked like. Probably the row of holes appeared as a row of white dots, but the stripes either side of them sometimes have a penumbra of debris of white paste, suggesting that some of the field around the dots was filled in. Unfortunately it is not easy to distinguish white paste from chalk from burial when there are only traces of it. There were also linear or occasionally curved strip or ribbon patterns within the fields in various geometric arrangements, or sets of triangles.

The main vessels from the south part of the house seem to have formed a set. Two at least are of seemingly identical fabric, and the rest very similar. There are variations, however, which might point to the activity of different potters working more or less together. There is a sufficient body of sherds with white paste still adhering in solid patches to suggest that the ribbons and triangles were not in their final form, a hatched or dotted pattern, as they now seem, but were solid patterns of white, the hatching or nicks representing 'keying' to hold the none-too-sticky white paste. If this is so, then the type of keying may well have been individual to each potter, who used whatever they found worked, as do plasterers. Two common and different techniques were noted – the little oblique and roughly parallel lines and the multiple rows of nicks made with a pointed instrument which left cuneiform marks. For the triangle pattern the potter(s) seem to have stuck to lines rather than nicks or holes. One of the minority sherds (not from the main pottery postholes) had a herringbone arrangement while simple parallels were normally preferred.

Therefore a tentative conclusion about the main body of jars is that they were from a single 'school', if not sometimes even the same hand, and that they were probably not made far from the bowls that accompany them because of the close similarity in fabric and in the quality of the haematite. Furthermore the pots were not mended in their lifetimes, perhaps because they did not come from an excessive distance, and could be replaced easily. It would not be difficult to see the bowls and jars of House 1 as a 'service'.

House 2

Here there are contrasts with House 1. The bowls are clearly related to those of House 1 but are of significantly different design, notably in the constant appearance of a long tall neck. There are no short necked House 2 bowls, but a couple from House 1 (Fig. 3.2, nos 33 and 34) have started to lengthen. The furrows are still a constant feature of the House 2 bowls, and some of them are still broad and fairly deep, but many have only scratches, sometimes not even very carefully aligned. The quality of the haematite is still often very high, and in fact it is extremely difficult in many cases to tell apart the fabrics of House 1 and 2 without the aid of the decoration. But some of the bowls have slightly more visible inclusions than would normally be found in House 1 wares, and in some cases the haematite slip was of lower grade, containing quite a lot of sand which gravitated to the bottom. But this is not by any means constant.

There are some forms from House 2 made of a completely different fabric, probably from another source, and of a different shape, though in the same general tradition. It seems that although there was a hard core of bowls of very similar type and design from both houses, there were more 'rogues' from House 2 than 1, suggesting perhaps a different pattern of supply. This suspicion is heightened by the most obvious difference in the House 1 and 2 wares, *ie* the difference between the bowls and jars in House 2. While these two types of vessel formed a 'set' in House 1, they are completely different in House 2. In House 1 the jars were certainly the most elaborate and fancy of the finewares, in House 2 they are coarse and decorated in a very simple fashion, and such haematite as they may have had was not of the fine polished quality found on House 1 jars.

Furthermore, the fabrics of the House 2 bowls and jars are different. The inclusions are different, and it is difficult to imagine them coming from the same source in the way in which the House 1 bowls and jars may have. On the other hand, the bowls are so similar in fabric and general technique to House 1 wares that it suggests they were from the same general source, though later on. There may have been a potting community of some sort lasting for several generations, with a peak in its creativity in the lifetime of House 1, and a decline thereafter, with House 2 receiving the 'tail'. Alternatively, the community may have progressed to specialised production of bowls. Arising from the vast difference in quality between the House 2 bowls and jars comes the question: were House 1 jars and bowls from the same source, which lost the art or market for fine jars in the interval between the houses, or were there two sources, bowl potters whose wares continued to be acceptable for a number of generations and jar potters whose finewares became obsolete? Or did Longbridge Deverill simply not continue to take fine jars, though they still existed? Whatever the case, it is clear that the crude House 2 jars, often decorated with fingertip and fingernail impressions, did not originate from the same source as the fine House 1 jars.

On looking closely at the All Cannings Cross pottery (Cunnington 1923), it seems there are not the Longbridge Deverill House 1 type jars at all. Bowls and many jars are more like House 2, or the bowls, more precisely still, like the long-necked variety in House 1. Perhaps All Cannings Cross falls chronologically between House 1 and 2. Their white inlaid jars have rounded contours rather than the angular ones of House 1.

House 1 / 2 overlaps

It has not been possible to establish the absolute interval between the Houses by means of calibrated radiocarbon dates, but there are a few points of direct comparison. A chronological break between Houses 1 and 2 is proven by stratigraphic evidence, and their different pottery styles may be a product of this interval. Yet there are continuities between the bowls. Examples are the taller rim appearing on some House 1 sherds; some of the 'best' House 2 bowls still present furrows like those of House 1, though with the high neck. The fabrics are extremely similar. To take one example (which incidentally is not particularly typical of either house's mainstream fabrics), House 1, Fig. 3.2, no. 33 (PH186) is a rough dark red bowl with the incipient elongated neck. It is extremely similar in feel, colour and the way it has weathered, to House 2, Fig. 3.8, no. 17. And bowls from both House 1 and 2 have burnt to a very similar yellow-grey powdery quality, suggesting similar manufacture. Grittiness is perhaps more characteristic of House 2 wares than 1, though it may be that House 1 potters were simply more skilled at disguising it. House 1, Fig. 3.1, no. 8 has as much grit as anything normal in House 2 . So for the bowls there was certainly continuity in the general source of supply, while in jars there was complete change.

Note on the Furrowed Bowls

by Sonia Chadwick Hawkes

The recovery of masses of sherds of fine tableware which had been stuffed into the tops of postholes or left lying around on the floor of the three major early houses after their destruction by fire enabled us to perceive clearly, as nowhere else excavated to date, that the Wessex furrowed bowls form a long sequence, manufactured over many generations and varying considerably in their form and significantly in their technique of decoration. The situation was conveniently summed up by Harding (1974, 148), who was familiar with the Longbridge evidence, but a good deal of research remains to be done.

The haematite bowls from the earliest house excavated at Longbridge, House 1 are distinguished not only by their very fine clay fabric and good quality haematite slip coating, but by their characteristic form. Bowl size and depth of body/base may vary considerably, suggesting variety of function – not just drinking cups as the bowls from the later houses, perhaps – but all have necks short in proportion to the body/base, ranging from markedly insloping to nearly upright, decorated by broad horizontal furrowing/rilling, above an often sharply carinated shoulder and surmounted by a normally everted lens shaped rim. Where the base survives, there is a well-made, often large, omphalos which must have given the completed bowl great stability in use.

Note on Scratched-Cordoned Bowls
by Lisa Brown

Scratched-cordoned bowls can be seen as a stylistic development of early Iron Age furrowed bowls, often red-finished ('haematite-coated'), tracing a progression from short- and then long-rimmed furrowed bowls, through to flaring rim bowls with shallow-tooled diagonal lnear decoration, and then on to the distinctive form in which angles of the body were accentuated by cordons between which geometric decoration was scratched with a sharp tool after firing. The scratched decoration was sometimes filled with a calcareous white chalk paste similar in composition to that used on the decorated jars associated with furrowed bowls. Present knowledge suggests that the currency of scratched-cordoned bowls spanned the 5th to early 4th centuries (Cunliffe 2005, 99).

The only certain example of a scratched-cordoned bowl from Longbridge Deverill is a small body sherd found in the fill of main ring posthole PH235 of House 1 (Fig. 3.6, no. 91), a structure otherwise associated with a very large assemblage of short-rimmed furrowed bowls (Figs 3.1-3.2). This small sherd was interpreted by Christopher Hawkes as intrusive in this feature (see Appendix 3A, sample B35) and it does seem reasonable to regard it as a later stray, possibly associated with an early Iron Age settlement that lay beyond the excavated area of the site, or much further afield. Although Hawkes cites other possible fragmentary examples of scratched-cordoned bowls (archive report) these apparently had no trace of a cordon, or indeed, of scratched decoration, and he did not identify their context. Two examples of incised-decorated bowls with unpronounced cordons and no white infill found in 'working hollow' H3 (Fig. 3.15, nos 16 and 17) are uncommon types in the Longbridge assemblage. Another similar body sherd from House 3 (Fig. 3.11, no. 3) may be of the same general tradition. These resemble bowls of the 5th-3rd centuries BC 'All Cannings Cross-Meon Hill' group, with shoulder decoration of shallow-tooled diagonal lines (Liddell 1933, 1935; Cunliffe 2005, 99-100; fig. A:8, 5;), but are generally not well-dated.

The scratched-cordoned sherd has no obvious context within the history of the occupation of the Longbridge settlement. Although corresponding in tradition to the Later All Cannings Cross-Meon Hill ceramic style group (Cunliffe 2005, 99) it is apparent that House 1 was not extant as late as the 5th century BC. The short-necked furrowed bowl form that dominates the House 1 assemblage was dated to the 10th/9th-7th centuries BC at nearby Potterne (Gingell and Morris 2000, 150: Bowl Type 3.4, fig. 49) and regarded as pre-dating Ceramic phase 1-3 material from Danebury, Hampshire (Cunliffe 198, 242).

Early-Middle Iron Age Pottery From the Pits
by Lisa Brown

The character of the pottery recovered from the Longbridge Deverill pits suggests that backfilling occurred at the end of the early Iron Age and beginning of the middle Iron Age, perhaps between the 5th-early 3rd centuries BC. From the absence of scratched-cordoned bowls from deposits associated with both the houses and the pits it can reasonably be inferred that the Longbridge pits post-dated the currency of these wares. Neither, however, do the pits appear to have been contemporary with the occupation of Houses 1-4.

The pottery recovered from many of the pits indicates that these features were backfilled during the 4th-early 3rd centuries BC. The ovoid jars, proto-saucepan pots, burnished pots with pedestal bases and shallow flat-rimmed dishes are forms that first appeared in the Wessex region during the end of the early Iron Age proper. One pit in particular, P37, produced around 200 sherds of pottery (Fig. 3.19). Stylistically the pottery sits on the cusp between the early and middle Iron Age. Fig. 3.19, 1 is a dish dated at Danebury (form DA1) to Cp5-7, allowing an earliest date at about the mid 4th century BC. The Longbridge example is in oolitic fabric F21, resembling Danebury examples in Fabric H, perhaps the preferred regional fabric for the production of these vessels prior to the proliferation of glauconitic sandy ware versions. Large shouldered jars of of the slack variety, several corresponding to type JB4 at Danebury, dated to Cp4-5 (360-310 BC) (Cunliffe 1984, 261 and fig. 6.34; Brown 1991, fig. 6.6) or somewhat later (Brown 1995, 246), mark a transition from more angular types of the 5th – early 4th centuries BC.

Some of the pit assemblages – notably P14 (Fig. 3.27), P18 (Fig. 3.29), P33 (Fig. 3.25), P43 (Fig. 3.24), P46 (Fig. 3.26), P54 (Fig. 3.27), P55 (Fig. 3.28) and P 69/70 (Fig. 3.21) – exhibit characteristics suggesting a more developed middle Iron Age stylistic tendency. The vessel forms are more rounded or ovoid, the developed saucepan form more common, and surface finishes on the whole more refined. It is certainly possible that these pits are contemporary with those assigned an EIA-MIA date (see Chapter 2, Table 2.8) but incorporating finer, more sophisticated vessels.

However, it is also possible that these pit groups were contemporary with that from P22, the single incontrovertible example of a pit filled during the developed (or late) part of the middle Iron Age, probably to some point after the mid 3rd century BC. Distinctive characteristics of the this later middle Iron Age stylistic tradition are an especial attention to finish, particularly burnishing, on a range of standardised vessels that include saucepan pots of developed form, curved or S-profile jars and bowls, alongside a set of decorative motifs of generally limited range within any given regional assemblage. P22 (Fig. 3.29) produced pottery of this type, the small assemblage of 16 sherds largely making up parts of a burnished saucepan pot in glauconitic fabric (F12), decorated with the tooled arc motif characteristic of Yarnbury-Highfield style (Cunliffe 2005, 104; fig. A:17). A globular jar in fine shell-tempered ware (F32) from the same pit was decorated with a, perhaps related, wave motif (Fig. 3.29, Pit 22, nos 1 and 2). The precise position of these vessels in the fill is not clear from the records but their selection for deposition must have been a considered choice. Although the P22 assemblage stands out from the others, it need not necessarily have signified a very limited later middle Iron Age presence in this part of the site. Some of the other pits in Area S may have warranted in their decommissioning the inclusion of only conservative and undecorated varieties of more ostentatious counterparts selected for deposition in P22. Nonetheless, these simple vessels do completely dominate the ceramic assemblage left by the pit-digging community at Longbridge Deverill, and appear to form a coherent group, whether chronologically or culturally.

CATALOGUE OF ILLUSTRATED POTTERY

by Sonia Hawkes, Daphne Nash, Rose Annable and Alison MacDonald

In the descriptions that follow the abbreviations used are:

PS = Petrological Sample.
F = Fabric.
P = Profile.
D = Decoration.
S = Surface.
dia. = diameter.

All entries use the following format:

Sherd No. Description of sherd(s) drawn
Context
No. sherds. Form. Decoration. Colour.
Surface treatment and appearance
Fabric. PS number (where applicable)
Code for profile, decoration and surface treatment

Enclosure II House I

Figs. 3.1 – 3.6

Copious quantities of pottery, much of it in large fragments, were recovered from the House 1 and, to a lesser extent, from the overlying ploughsoil. Much had been burnt in the conflagration that destroyed the building and amongst the fineware vessels were examples of everything from the total reduction of sherds to cinders, warping and distortion through heat, to mere smoke blackening of red haematite. A good deal of the pottery escaped the intense heat, however, and retained its pristine form and decoration.

The survival of so much pottery from a house of this type and date is unusual, though a similar phenomenon occurred in the case of House 2, and, less spectacularly, in that of House 3. Unlike the Little Woodbury and Pimperne houses, none of the Longbridge houses was rebuilt on the same site, so total clearance of debris was not undertaken. The ruins seem to have been tidied up to some extent, however, and the broken pottery was deliberately packed into the tops of major postholes where the removal or destruction of large timbers had left cavities. The large amounts of pottery found in some postholes and the large size of some fragments make it impossible that their presence was due to natural causes. In considering the human agencies at work, Nash, in her analysis of pottery from Houses 1 and 2, remarks that, whereas in House 2 sherds from a single vessel might occur in up to four different postholes, with significant numbers joining between features, in House 1 joining sherds occurred only in single features, though non-joining parts might come from two. Whatever the reason for this difference, it is quite clear that most of the pottery was disposed of after the fire by careful reburial on site. This custom at Longbridge Deverill, its results left largely undisturbed by the relatively slight amount of plough damage prior to excavation, compared with Little Woodbury and Gussage All Saints, has preserved a remarkably large sample of the domestic vessels in use when each of these great roundhouses was destroyed.

From House 1 there are very few sherds of medium or coarsewares, and such as can be illustrated (Fig. 3.6, nos. 84-89) are mostly small and weathered pieces, evidently later intrusions which worms or small animals had carried down into its postholes from the old ground surface. Some at least appear to derive from the occupation of the partly overlying House 2, while at least one (Fig. 3.6, no. 92) derives from even later occupation of the site. The nearly total absence of contemporary cooking pots or coarse storage vessels, except for the base of an unusually large and heavily gritted, though still haematite-coated, vessel (Fig. 3.6, no. 78), and a few sherds which had perhaps already been trodden into the floor or incorporated in existing posthole fills at the time of the fire, gives the House 1 assemblage a very special character.

The predominance of fine haematite-coated bowls or drinking cups and the equally fine white inlaid large carinated jars strongly suggest some unusual circumstance: House 1 appears to have been cleaned out very thoroughly, swept and garnished as for a feast. The cups and jars seem to represent a set of fine tableware, evidently the very best available at the period, which had been standing on shelves, or more probably on a festal table, when the fire broke out. The size of many of the sherds, the nature of the breakages and the fire damage, the fact that burnt and unburnt sherds can be joined together, and above all the high percentage of vessels which could be substantially reconstructed, all testify to this set of tableware having been intact before the fire. Nash noted that breakages had occurred before and during the conflagration, some perhaps resulting from the urgency of the feasters to escape or, depending on interpretation of events, through deliberate breakage; some occurring as the jars and their presumed liquid contents exploded in the heat; some undeniably occurring while people were picking over and tidying the remains afterwards. The distribution of the pottery chiefly in the southern sector of House 1, a situation repeated in Houses 2 and 3, gives us the likely location of the main assemblage of pottery within the house interior. From the distribution of finds generally, this seems to have been the principal living area.

The bulk of pottery from House 1 is clearly not totally representative of the whole range of forms and fabrics used during its lifetime, and some apparently atypical sherds may belong to earlier phases of its occupation. A case in point is Fig. 3.2, no. 35 from PH139, the earlier of two re-cut postholes belonging to the porch, which is different in detail from anything used at the time of the fire. So, indeed, is Fig. 3.2, no. 36, represented by just two weathered sherds from PH 151, which has white inlaid punched roundels like those on the carinated jars of the houses's final phase, but which do not occur on their accompanying final phase carinated bowls. It is uncertain how long the house was in use, but one must surely reckon that, during its span of occupation, even if only for a generation, potters must more than once have furnished its owners with sets of fine tableware, of which the latest and most fully represented may be only one specific variation. It is noticeable that none of the pottery represented shows signs of ancient repair. Since at least the big jars must have been both vulnerable and precious, their good condition at the time of the fire suggests that the set was newly acquired. Of course the earlier, or apparently earlier, sherds than the generality from House 1 may have derived from an earlier house yet again, somewhere close by.

The fact that the site was not totally excavated cannot be overstressed: the incompleteness of the occupation sequence may include its beginning. Certainly we can be sure that there was at least one house, probably several, intervening in time between Houses 1 and 2 . Some of the atypical cup sherds, like the singletons in Fig. 3.2, nos. 32 and 33, which have unusually tall rims for the early period, may have come from a nearby house intermediate between 1 and 2. This is almost certainly true of Fig. 3.2, no. 34 with its very tall rim and marked waist above exiguous furrowing. Finally, Fig. 3.6, no. 91, again a very weathered single sherd, from a cordoned bowl, must have come from yet another phase of the occupation, the latest in the A phase, whose main house may also have been nearby, somewhere in the unexcavated parts of the centre of Enclosure II. So the assemblage from House 1 is complex and suggestive of structures that may have existed elsewhere on the site.

However, the fine vessels used during the last days and hours of House 1 is a very precious archive indeed. In its bias towards luxury and entertainment it is interesting both socially and economically, representing as it does one aspect of the material goods of a prosperous, evidently high-ranking farmer and landowner. However, in this present context it is the types and numbers of fine pottery vessels and their technology, which must command our attention.

The decorated tablewares, whether bowls, cups or jars, are all made in very similar fabrics. The finest, used for jars as well as cups and bowls, is a well-levigated clay with natural inclusions of fine quartz grains and mica flecks (Williams Fabric A: Wilson Fabric 11), which Williams considers to have been derived from the local Gault clay at Crockerton, site of kilns in medieval times, situated just 3km north-west of the Longbridge Deverill site (Appendix 3A). Some bowls and jars were made in a slightly coarser fabric, with a few larger quartz grains and some deliberate flint temper (Williams Fabric B: Wilson Fabric 14), and a very few contained ill-sorted quartz and much flint (Williams Fabric H: Wilson Fabric 41) or flint and some limestone (Williams Fabric K: Wilson Fabric 42). All are handmade, but the potting is uniformly good, and the firing, in an oxidising atmosphere producing red wares, must have been done in a strong updraught kiln. The end products are not only fine but hard and durable, and far superior to anything that succeeded them on the site. As containers for liquids, for example, they must have been much more satisfactory than the cups and jars of La Tène form, which were fired to a much lower temperature in a blackening smother kiln, and which, when their superficially glossy burnished surfaces are penetrated, can be both porous and soluble. The early pottery from House 1 was practically and technologically far superior to anything from the centuries following. It is a pity no trace of a kiln was found, for all the evidence suggests it was produced on site, either by a resident or by an itinerant professional potter. It is not just that the clay source was local or even that haematite, used on all the early Phase A finewares, is known to have been ground and used on the site, but Nash's perceptive remarks about the various similarities between decorated jars primarily, but also between jars and bowls, convince us of a table service which must have been made locally.

The service contains three major forms – the keg jar, with furrowed ornament below the rim; the carinated bowls or cups with wave-furrowed decoration; and the large fineware carinated jars with everted rim and white inlaid, incised decoration. The paste of white calcite used on the latter must have been applied after firing, or else it would have burnt off in the kiln, whereas haematite, used to a greater or lesser degree on all three forms, was applied as a slip to the pots when leather hard before firing, and subsequently burnished. It is a commonplace that polished haematite was intended to imitate bronze, and no surprise to find bronze models for the carinated bowls and jars from this early, essentially Late Bronze Age (Phase Ai) occupation of Longbridge Deverill.

Fig. 3.1

Keg Jars

1. Complete profile of furrowed keg jar
PH 151.
21 joining sherds. Flat-topped rim, diameter a little less than that of body, flat base. 5 broad, shallow furrows below rim. Exterior grey-brown, patched with red, with remains of orange brown haematite, highly burnished, fire damaged and eroded. F11. PS 44.
P0i, D03, S04/2.
Rim dia. 160mm; height 255mm.

2. Rim of furrowed keg jar
PH 42.
Flat-topped rim. At least 4 broad, shallow furrows below rim. Exterior bears traces of haematite; interior orange-buff. F11. PS 22.
P0i, D03, S04.

3. Rim of furrowed keg jar
PH 152.
Upright, flat-topped rim. At least 1 broad furrow below rim. Exterior bears traces of red-brown haematite, interior buff. F11. PS 46.
P0i, D01, S04.

4. Rim from furrowed keg jar (or bowl)
PH 151.
Flat-topped rim, slightly everted from neck. At least 2 broad, shallow furrows below rim. Red-brown, burnt but probably once haematite coated and burnished. F14. PS 23.
P0ii, D02, S04/02.

5. Body sherds from furrowed keg jar (or large bowl with exceptionally deep basin)
PH 42.
4 joining sherds. Gently curving shoulder carination and slightly convex neck. At least 6 broad, shallow furrows below rim. Exterior orange brown, interior grey-brown; once haematite coated and burnished, burnt. F14.
P0ii, D03, S04/02.

Carinated Bowls and Cups

These were very numerous and only those which could be reconstructed to produce at least a major part of a profile, and a few single sherds which show divergent form or decoration, have been drawn. The illustrations show that there must have been at least 30 bowls or cups in use in House 1 at the time of the fire. They vary greatly in size, ranging in diameter from 285mm down to less than 88mm, with the majority between 125-150mm across. There is also considerable variation in depth in relation to diameter, with some noticeably deep bowls represented, notably Fig. 3.1, nos. 6 and 20. Probably they varied in function, with the smaller bowls serving mainly as drinking cups, but doubling as soup or porridge bowls, while the larger ones could have been serving dishes for food or containers for liquids. The small cups could have been dipped into some of the larger bowls, and, of course, into the big decorated jars. Another possibility is that there was an age and sex distinction at work, with the tiny bowls for children and the large bowls for men. This size variation is confined to the bowls from this house. Those from the later houses show greater uniformity.

The forms of the House 1 cups and bowls are also distinctive. Above the omphalos base and basin of variable depth, there is normally a sharp shoulder carination, above which the insloping neck is generally short in proportion. Rims are short and range from nearly upright to markedly everted. Decoration, above the carination, invariably takes the form of broad, shallow, horizontal wave-furrows. Form and decoration both set the House 1 bowls apart from their successors in Houses 2 and 3. They share only the use of haematite inside and out, to give a fine red burnish. Nash noted numerous impressions from seeds and other vegetable debris even on the finished surfaces, indicating that they had been made in a domestic context, rather than in a professional workshop elsewhere.

6. Almost complete profile of carinated bowl with furrowed decoration
PH 152.
Upright tapered rim, shoulder carination blunt, basin quite deep. 2 broad, shallow furrows above shoulder. Burnt and smoke fumed, burnished haematite on interior and exterior. F11.
P02, D02, S04/2.
Rim dia. *c.*145mm; height *c.*80mm.

7. Complete profile of carinated bowl with furrowed decoration
PH 153.
5 sherds, 3 joining. Slightly everted tapered rim, neck upright, shoulder carination blunt, basin quite deep and thick with omphalos. 2 broad, shallow furrows above shoulder. Exterior orange to buff, haematite eroded; interior fumed by smoke, but still burnished; burnt. F13.
P03, D02, S04/2.
Rim dia. *c.*96mm; height *c.*55mm.

8. Almost complete profile of carinated bowl with furrowed decoration
PH 235.

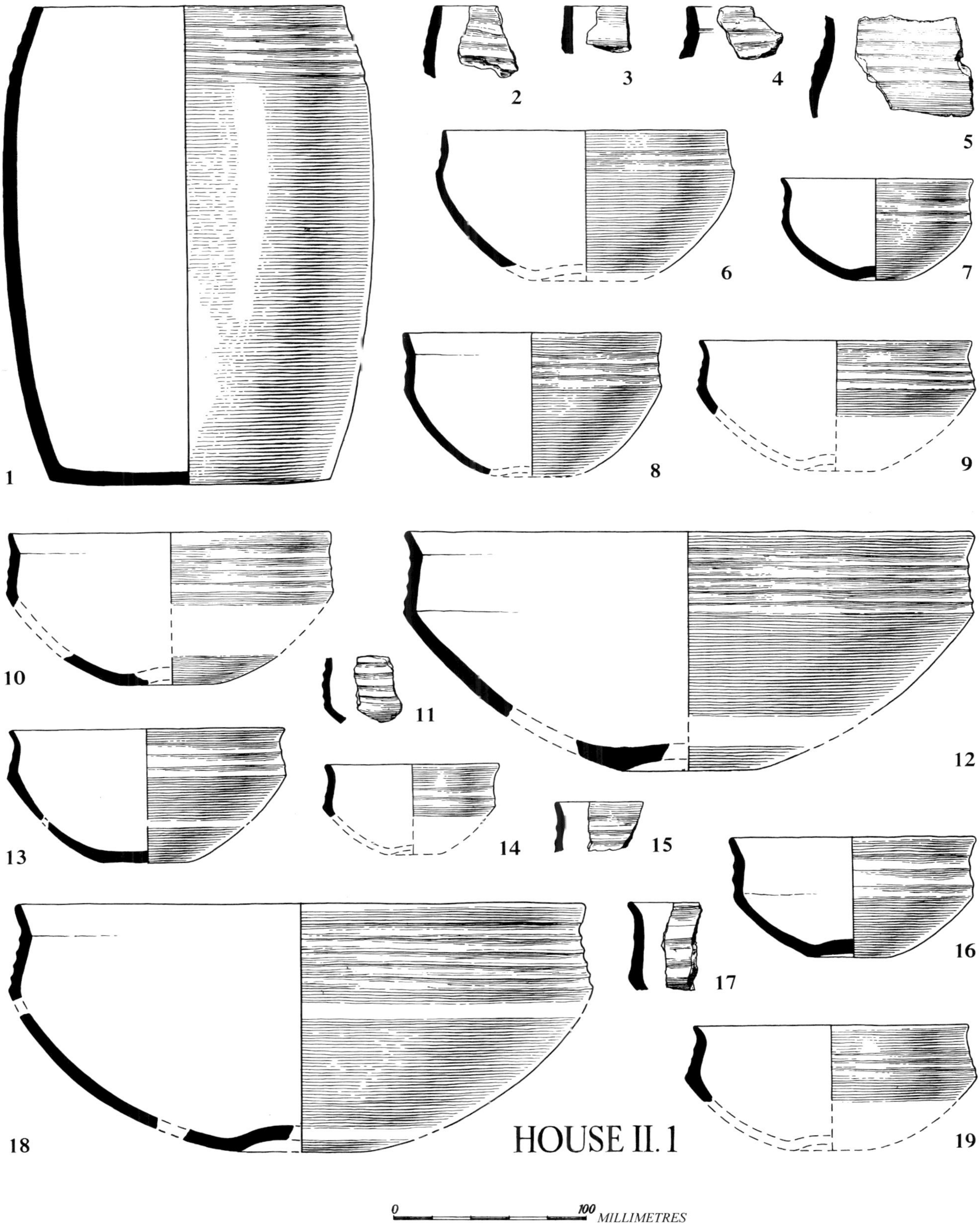

Fig. 3.1 Pottery from Enclosure II House 1 (scale 1:3)

13 joining sherds. Rim slightly everted, neck almost upright, shoulder
carination blunt, basin quite deep. 3 broad, shallow furrows above shoulder. Burnt; exterior and interior both orange to brown fumed by smoke, once haematite coated and burnished. F14.
P03, D02, S04/2.
Rim dia. *c*.130mm; height *c*.75mm.

9. Rim and shoulder profile of carinated bowl with furrowed decoration
PH 165.
Rim slightly everted, neck slightly inturned, shoulder carination quite sharp, basin shallow. 3-4 broad, shallow furrows above shoulder. Exterior and interior haematite coated and burnished, burnt and weathered. F14. PS 24.
P01, D02/3, S04/2.
Rim dia. *c*.135mm.

10. Partially complete profile of carinated bowl with furrowed decoration
PH 154.
28 sherds. Rim slightly everted, neck nearly upright, shoulder carination quite sharp, basin apparently shallow, omphalos base. 4 broad, shallow furrows above shoulder. Exterior and interior blackened but retain burnish, presumably on haematite. F14.
P03, D03, S04/2.
Rim dia. *c*.165mm

11. Body sherd of carinated bowl with furrowed decoration
PH 154.
Below rim to below rounded shoulder carination. 4 broad, shallow furrows above shoulder. Exterior and interior purplish red to brown with smokey patches, remains of haematite coating in the furrows, burnished; burnt and weathered. F14.
P03, D03, S04/2.

12. Almost complete profile of large carinated bowl with furrowed decoration
PH 154, 42 & 167.
7 joining sherds from PH 154; additional rim and base sherds from PH 42 & 167. Rim everted with internal carination, neck short and slightly inturned, shoulder carination quite sharp, basin quite deep, omphalos base. 4-5 broad, shallow furrows, spirally made, above shoulder carination. Exterior and interior red with some smoke blackening; haematite-coated and burnished, but burnt and weathered. F14. PS 78 (PH 167 base sherd).
P01, D03, S04/2.
Rim dia. *c*.290mm; height 130mm

13. Almost complete profile of carinated bowl with furrowed decoration
PH 235.
11 sherds, 10 joining. Rim everted, neck inturned, shoulder carination sharp, basin quite deep, base nearly flat. 3 broad, shallow furrows above carination. Exterior and interior red to brown, haematite coated and burnished inside and out; burnt and weathered. F14.
P01, D02, S04/2.
Rim dia. *c*.140mm; height *c*.72mm.

14. Rim and shoulder profile of carinated cup with furrowed decoration
PH 235 & 63.
2 sherds. Rim slightly everted, neck gently sloping, shoulder carination quite sharp. 2 broad, shallow furrows above shoulder. Exterior and interior discoloured brown, haematite coated and burnished; burnt. F11.
P03, D02, S04/2.
Rim dia. *c*.90mm.

15. Rim and neck sherd from carinated bowl with furrowed decoration
PH 152.
Rim slightly everted, neck almost vertical. At least 3 broad, shallow furrows below rim. Exterior and interior haematite coated and burnished; burnt black and weathered. F11.
P03, D02/3, S04/2.

16. Complete profile of carinated cup with furrowed decoration
PH 152.
9 sherds making up almost complete bowl. Rim slightly everted, neck almost vertical, shoulder carination quite blunt, basin fairly deep, base thick with shallow omphalos. 3 very broad, shallow furrows on neck. Exterior and interior haematite coated and burnished but subjected to intense heat, causing warping and discolouration. F11.
P03, D02, S04/2.
Fully restored. Rim dia. 126mm, height 63mm.

17. Rim and shoulder sherd from carinated bowl with furrowed decoration
PH 154.
Rim slightly everted, neck almost vertical, shoulder carination blunt. 2 very broad, shallow furrows above shoulder. Exterior and interior light brown with traces of orange haematite, and burnishing. F14.
P03, D02, S04/2.

18. Almost complete profile of large carinated bowl with furrowed decoration
PH 152.
8 sherds, 2 from the rim joining. Rim everted

with internal carination, neck inturned, shoulder carination blunt, basin quite deep, base with large, well indented omphalos. 5 broad, shallow furrows above the shoulder. Exterior and interior orange-brown, discoloured by smoke; traces of haematite and burnish. F11.
P01, D03, S04/2.
Rim dia. *c*.293mm; height *c*.130mm.

19. Rim and shoulder profile of carinated bowl with furrowed decoration
PH 151.
1 sherd. Rim everted, neck inturned, shoulder carination sharp, basin probably shallow. 3 broad shallow furrows above shoulder. Exterior and interior haematite coated and burnished, burnt and blackened. F11.
P01, D02, S04/2.
Rim dia. *c*.140mm.

Fig. 3.2

20. Almost complete profile of deep carinated bowl with furrowed decoration
PH 154, 151 & 167.
30 sherds, 24 joining from PH 154. Rim relatively tall, slightly everted, with sharp internal carination where it joins the sharply inturned neck, shoulder carination blunt, basin deep. 4-5 broad, shallow furrows spirally made above the shoulder. Exterior uniformly reddened but no haematite survives, interior smoke-grey; burnt and weathered. F14. PS 79 (PH 167 body sherd).
P04a, D03, S01.

21. Rim and shoulder sherds from deep carinated bowl with furrowed decoration
Area S3, BXXV Layer 2.
2 joining sherds. Rim everted with internal carination, neck inturned, shoulder carination blunt, basin probably deep. 3-4 broad, shallow furrows above shoulder. Exterior burnt and eroded with traces of haematite, interior red-brown. F11.
P04a, D03, S04.

22. Rim and shoulder sherds from large, deep carinated bowl with furrowed decoration
PH 135 (House 2 main ring post, closely adjacent to porch post 167: their upper fills have pottery of the two occupations mingled).
2 sherds nearly joining. Rim everted with internal carination where it joins the markedly inturned neck, shoulder carination sharp, basin probably deep. At least 7 broad, shallow furrows on neck. Burnt and weathered, surfaces eroded. F14.
P04a, D03, S01.

23. Rim and shoulder profile of carinated bowl with furrowed decoration
PH 151.
4 joining sherds. Rim sharply everted with internal carination, neck short and markedly inturned, shoulder carination sharp, basin probably shallow. 2 broad, shallow furrows above shoulder. One sherd retains burnished haematite on exterior, one is blackened, other two burnt orange with surfaces eroded. F11.
P04, D02, S04.
Rim dia. *c*.165mm.

24. Rim and body profile of carinated bowl with furrowed decoration
PH 151.
2 joining sherds. Rim short and everted, neck short and markedly inturned, shoulder carination sharp, basin shallow. 3 broad, shallow furrows above shoulder. Exterior and interior burnt and smoke-blackened, burnished haematite on exterior. F11.
P04, D02, S04.
Rim dia. *c*.138mm.

25. Rim and body profile of carinated bowl with furrowed decoration
PH 151.
6 sherds, 3 joining. Rim short and everted, neck short and inturned, shoulder carination sharp, basin shallow. 3 broad, shallow furrows above shoulder. Mostly blackened but remains of red-brown haematite on exterior of basin. F11.
P04, D02, S04.
Rim dia. *c*.162mm.

26. Almost complete profile of carinated bowl with furrowed decoration
PH 151.
3 joining sherds. Rim relatively tall and sharply everted with internal carination, neck short and inturned, shoulder carination sharp, basin quite deep. 2 broad, shallow furrows above shoulder. Interior and rim very burnt and eroded, exterior bears trace of burnish and haematite, partially discoloured by smoke. F11.
P04, D02, S04/2.
Rim dia. *c*.123 mm; height *c*.70mm.

27. Partially complete profile of carinated bowl with furrowed decoration
PH 154 & 186.
14 sherds, 13 joining from PH 154. Rim everted, neck short, sharply inturned, shoulder sharply carinated, basin quite shallow, base with shallow omphalos. 2 broad, shallow furrows above shoulder. Exterior and interior haematite coated and burnished, burnt and weathered. F11. PS 10.

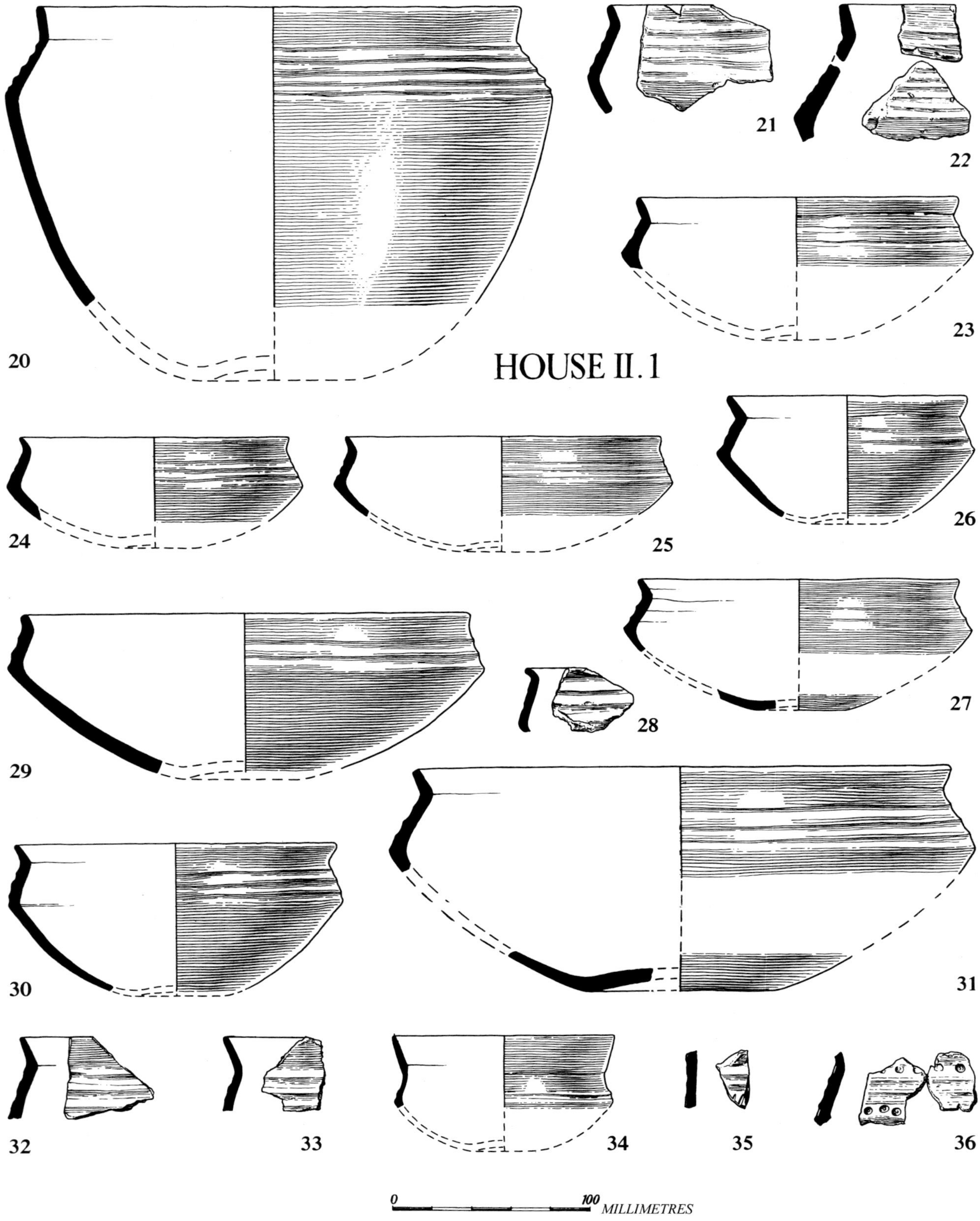

Fig. 3.2 Pottery from Enclosure II House 1 (scale 1:3)

P04, D02, S01.
Rim dia. *c*.165mm; height *c*.70mm.

28. Rim and shoulder sherd from carinated bowl with furrowed decoration
PH 154.
1 sherd. Rim very short and sharply everted, neck inturned. 2 very broad, shallow furrows above shoulder. Exterior and interior burnt black and weathered. F11.
P04, D02, S01.

29. Almost complete profile of carinated bowl with furrowed decoration
PH 152.
5 sherds, *c*. 25% of bowl. Rim very short, slightly everted, neck very short and inturned, shoulder sharply carinated, basin shallow. 2 broad, shallow furrows above shoulder. Exterior and interior deep red-brown with burnished haematite remaining, burning has caused erosion of slip, warping and discolouration. F11.
P04, D02, S04/2.
Fully restored. Rim dia. 228mm; height 90mm.

30. Almost complete profile of carinated bowl with furrowed decoration
PH 151 & 167.
6 sherds, 5 joining from PH 151, *c*. 33% of bowl. Rim sharply everted with internal carination, neck inturned, shoulder carination sharp, basin quite deep. 3 broad, shallow furrows above the shoulder. Interior burnt and eroded, exterior burnished; haematite coated but smoked grey. F13. PS 80 (PH 167 rim sherd).
P04, D02, S04/2.
Rim dia. *c*.165mm; height 80mm.

31. Partially complete profile of carinated bowl with furrowed decoration
PH 151.
6 sherds, none joining. Rim sharply everted with internal carination, neck inturned, shoulder sharply carinated, basin probably not deep, base with large omphalos. 3 broad, shallow furrows above shoulder. Most sherds burnt and eroded, but burnished haematite on exterior and interior. F11.
P04, D02, S04/2.
Rim dia. *c*.275mm.

32. Rim and neck sherd from carinated bowl with furrowed decoration
PH 42.
1 sherd. Rim tall, sharply everted, neck inturned. At least 3 broad, shallow furrows below rim. Exterior orange to red, interior buff to orange, both haematite coated and burnished. F11.
P04, D02/3, S04/2.

33. Rim and neck sherd from carinated bowl with furrowed decoration
PH 186.
1 sherd. Tall everted rim, neck slightly convex. At least 3 broad, shallow furrows below rim. Exterior purplish brown, interior orange brown with burnished haematite; burnt and weathered. F12.
P04, D02/3, S04/2.

34. Rim and shoulder profile of carinated cup with furrowed decoration
PH 152.
1 sherd. Rim taller than usual, gently everted, neck concave, shoulder carination blunt. Single narrow furrow on shoulder. Exterior and interior pale orange, haematite coated and burnished; weathered. F11.
P05, D01, S04/2.
Rim dia. *c*.113mm.

35. Body or neck sherd from carinated bowl with furrowed decoration
PH 139.
1 sherd from neck or body. Decorated by two broad, shallow furrows flanked by zones of diagonal finger nail slashes. Exterior and interior pale orange to buff, haematite coated and burnished; weathered. F11. PS 2.
P04, D71, S04/2.
?Residual.

36. Neck and shoulder from carinated bowl with furrowed decoration.
PH 151.
2 sherds, not joining. Neck inturned. Decorated by 2 broad, shallow furrows flanked by lines of punched roundels, dia. 5mm, made by stick or bone with a central hole which has left a small bump in the centre of the impression. Burnt and weathered, traces of white calcitic inlay in the roundels. F13.
P04, D72, S01.
?Residual.

Fig. 3.3

Large Carinated Fineware Jars

These fine large vessels, average height *c*. 380mm, clearly formed a set, but just how many there were in the service is something of a problem. They are all made in a very similar fine fabric (Williams Fabric A: Wilson F11) and they are very similar in form. Each has a flat base from which the walls of the body were built up at a steep angle, sometimes slackening to a curve before joining the sharply insloping neck at a very oblique shoulder angle. The tall lens-shaped rims are always sharply everted, and in diameter wider than their corresponding base, though less than the maximum girth of the jar.

Each appears to have been decorated in a similar panel style, in which six bands with central lines of roundels divide the body vertically into six major fields. From the best preserved pieces it seems that two of these fields were left plain and the other four filled with geometric ornament.

There is a great mass of sherds from these pots, many of them decorated, and a great diversity of ornamental styles, but unfortunately in very few cases was it possible to join enough of the same pot to find out the overall design. Only in one case, Fig. 3.3, no. 39, were enough sherds present to allow a convincing restoration, but this was useful as it showed that the potter had used very similar ornament on the opposite sides of the vessel, in this case hatched chevrons. On another pot, Fig. 3.4, no. 47, of which there were ornamental pieces from both sides, the potter used hatched bands forming large chevrons. From these it was possible to conclude that a potter was unlikely to use dissimilar patterns on the same vessel, and thus useful to separate the sherds into groups according to ornament. These, and the slight variations in form and texture amongst the large jars, make it reasonably safe to estimate that there were at least eight of them in use in House 1 when it burnt down.

These big, handmade jars were probably coil built, and their interiors show the impressions of finger sweeping in various directions which indicate that the potter worked without the benefit of any constantly moving turntable. The exteriors were smoothed and the rim area inside and out and the decorated panels were coated with haematite and burnished. The plain panels were not always treated in the same way and there is at least one clear case (Fig. 3.5, 56) where the plain panel was only summarily smoothed by hand and apparently deliberately left rough or even roughened, by sweeping straw and general roughage across the wet clay. This may have been done to make the pot easier to grip. The fine polished surfaces must have been slippery, and as the jars were heavy and unwieldy even when empty, the plain panels on either side may have been considerably practical. Except for the common feature of the six vertical bands with their rows of punched roundels, the large carinated jars show considerable ornamental variation. This includes hatched triangles arranged in various ways, pendent or standing (Fig. 3.3, no. 37, Fig. 3.5, no. 53) or set sideways (Fig. 3.3, no. 39); linear strips with hatching arranged in geometric patterns (Fig. 3.4, nos. 43-47, Fig. 3.5 no. 54); linear or curved strips containing punched roundel ornament (Fig. 3.6, nos. 61-75); and treble-outlined chevrons (Fig. 3.5, no. 57). There is conflicting evidence about the original appearance of this ornament.

In the case of the vertical bands, the rows of roundels were probably intended to look like rows of white spots, apparently inspired by the rows of rivets on bronze buckets. In the case of the hatched triangles and hatched or nicked strips, there are sufficient sherds with remains of white calcite paste adhering in solid patches to suggest that the hatching or nicking served as keying to attach a solid coat of white paste to these parts of the ornament, so that the original effect would have been of shiny red jars with panels decorated with plain white triangles or white strips, alternating with vertical bands of white 'rivets', and with plain red or natural coloured panels.

In considering the different forms of decoration and keying used on the different jars, Nash wondered whether there had been more than one potter at work producing the set of vessels. If so, she considered that the similarities in fabric, form and technique over-rode the differences, and felt that, if not by the same hand, the whole assemblage, jars and bowls as well, had been made by members of the same 'school' or workshop. The fact that none of the bowls or jars showed signs of ancient repair reinforces the impression that the bulk of the pottery was not an accumulation but a relatively new set of tableware for a special occasion.

37. Rim and body profile of large carinated jar.
PH 151 & 152.
10 sherds, 7 joining, 3 not joining. Everted, lens shaped rim, neck angular, shoulder carination blunt. Decorated below the rim by white inlaid incised decoration: a vertical band with median line of dots, with one plain and two decorated panels. The largest sherd shows a line of 4 pendant triangles below the rim, and the tip of a triangle from another row of standing triangles above the shoulder. This part of the decoration is apparent on another sherd, where below the triangles are two bands of horizontal punched dots, separated by a plain narrow band. Beneath the dots is more triangle ornament, indicating that this pot had similar decoration on the body as on the neck. Exterior red brown, interior orange red, haematite on exterior, interior shows finger sweeps; burnt and weathered. F11.
P19, D84, S04.

38. Body sherd from large carinated jar.
PH 151.
1 sherd. Decorated with punched dots (and probably a hatched triangle) as on previous vessel; possibly same jar. Exterior buff to orange, interior buff to black; haematite coated burnt and weathered. F11.
P19, D84, S04.

39. Almost complete profile of large carinated jar (Fig. 3.34)
PH 154.
35 sherds, some joining. Rim tall and sharply everted, angular neck, slightly carinated shoulder, base flat. Originally decorated with 6 vertical bands, each with punched dots

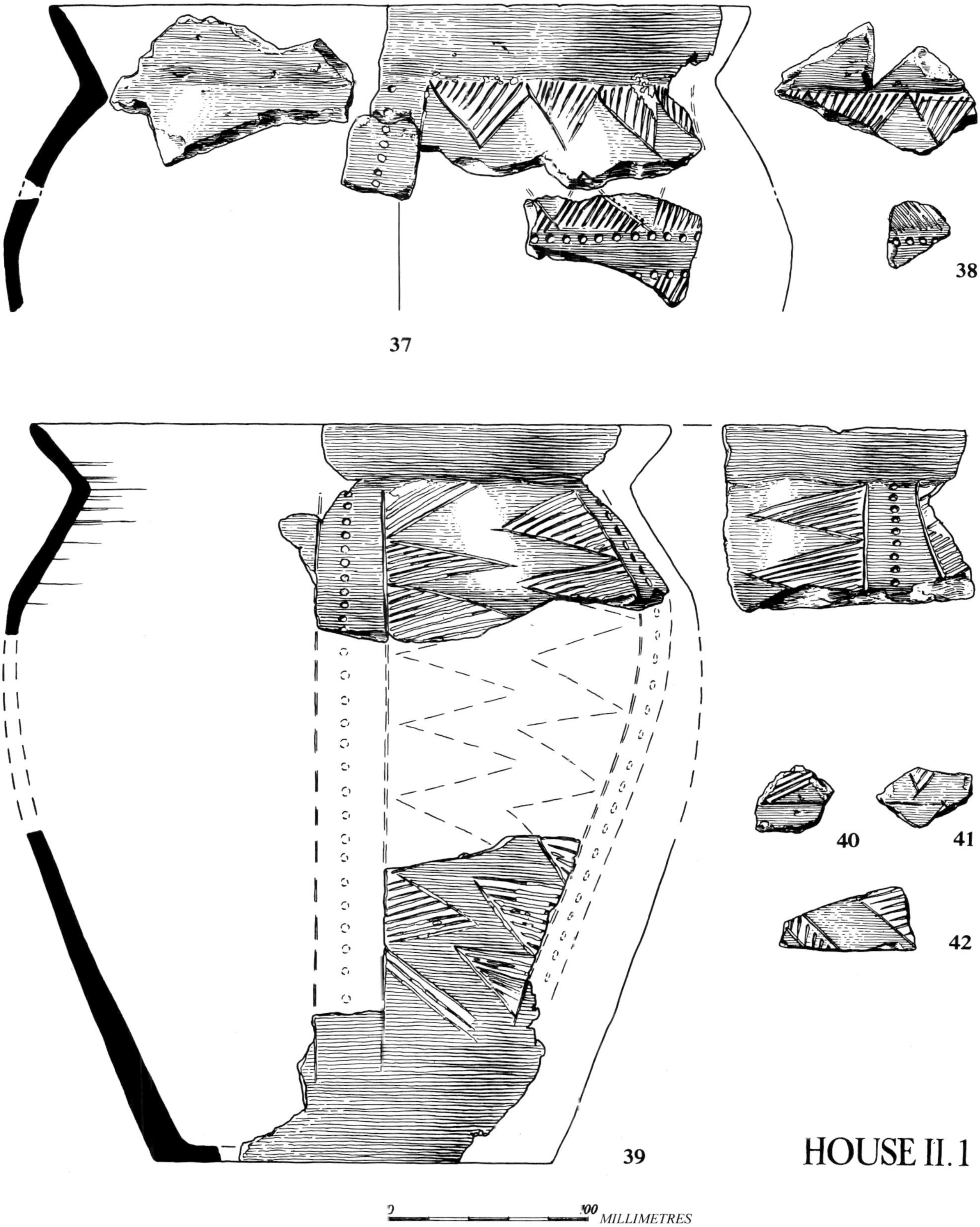

Fig. 3.3 Pottery from Enclosure II House 1 (scale 1:3)

down the centre. The intervening panels appear to have been alternatively decorated: 1 decorated, 2 plain, 1 decorated, 2 plain. Decorated panels comprised two vertical strips of hatched triangles. White calcitic inlay in the triangles and dots. Exterior and interior patched grey brown and red black, weathered; exterior haematite coated and burnished. F11.
P19, D90, S04/2.

40. Body sherds from large carinated jar.
PH 151.
2 joining sherds. Hatched decoration with single horizontal incised line. Exterior grey black, interior buff; burnt and weathered. F11.
P21, D74, S01.

41. Body sherd from large carinated jar.
PH 151.
1 sherd. Hatched decoration with single horizontal incised line. Exterior grey black, interior buff; burnt and weathered. F11.
P21, D74, S01.

42. Body sherd from large carinated jar.
PH 152.
1 sherd. Decorated with area of hatching (possibly from vertical strip of hatched triangle), separated from narrow ribbon of vertical incised lines by plain band. White calcitic inlay in the grooves. Exterior haematite coated and burnished; weathered. F11.
P21, D54, S04/2.

Fig. 3.4

Forty-four sherds from a large carinated jar, 24 joining to form rim, neck and shoulder (no. 43), some others joining. Nos. 44, 45 and 46 are single decorated body sherds probably from this vessel. PS 14.

43. Top of large carinated jar
PH 151.
24 joining sherds. Rim tall, shoulder slightly carinated. Decorated in panels below rim; one blank panel and two adjacent decorated panels apparent, The main decorated panel bordered by vertical bands with punched dots down the centre; and comprises a large cross of hatched ribbon, with its centre on the shoulder angle. Part of a similar ribbon visible on adjacent panel, and another incised cross may have been the decoration here. Exterior orange to grey and black, interior orange to grey; burnt and weathered; interior shows marks of finger sweeps. F11.
P19, D53, S04.

44. Shoulder sherd from large carinated jar (possibly 43)
PH 151.
Hatched ribbon decoration forming part of a cross, white calcitic inlay. Exterior buff, interior buff to orange; burnt and weathered. F11.
P21, D53, S01.

45. Decorated sherd from large carinated jar (possibly 43)
PH 151.
Two bands of hatched ribbon decoration, white inlay. Exterior buff to black, interior orange to grey; weathered. F11.
P21, D52, S01.

46. Body sherds from large carinated jar.
PH 151.
2 joining sherds probably from vessel above. One vertical band of hatched ribbon decoration, with a second meeting it at an oblique angle, below this point is a horizontal band of punched dots bordered by incised lines. White inlay in the grooves and dots. Exterior and interior brown to grey; weathered. F11.
P21, D85, S01.

47. Almost complete profile from large carinated jar
PH 154.
15 sherds, 14 joining. Rim flaring, shoulder slightly carinated. Decorated with incised and impressed white inlaid ornament: diagonal bands arranged in chevron pattern with horizontal lines through the angles of the pattern occupy the decorated panels on body and shoulder; the bands have internal oblique lines or wedges incised to hold the white paste. A row of impressed dots at very short intervals runs below the shoulder in the decorated panel, a similar row runs down the centre of the two vertical borders to the decorated panels. These borders are *c* 40mm wide, bounded by vertical incised and inlaid lines, one of which was carelessly executed and divides into two. Abundant remains of white paste in all incisions. Number of decorated panels unknown: a blank panel apparent on either side of decorated panel. Exterior haematite coated and burnished, interior preserves sweep marks from potter's fingers. Sherds burnt before and after breakage; blackened patches, and part of shoulder badly warped. F11. PS 13.
P19, D54, S04/2.

Fig. 3.5

48. Rim, neck, shoulder and part of body profile of large carinated jar
PH 151.
18 sherds, 13 joining to form major part, another 4 join. Rim flaring, carination at the

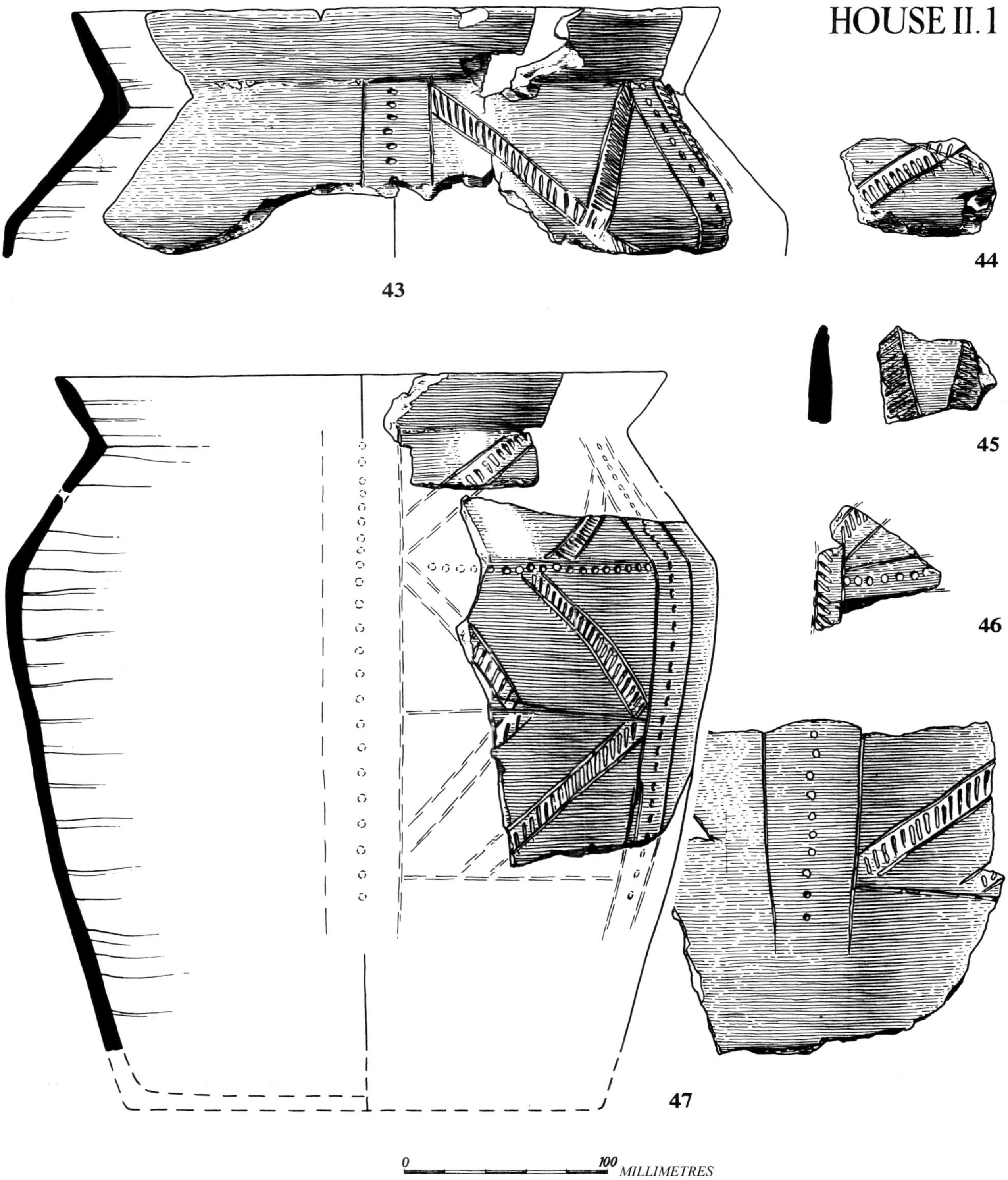

Fig. 3.4 Pottery from Enclosure II House 1 (scale 1:3)

neck and shoulder. Decorated by lines of dots inside widely spaced parallel vertical lines, with a horizontal row of dots below shoulder carination. Running down from the rim is a semicircle of parallel lines inside which are dots, an uncommon pattern at Longbridge. Exterior black, interior beige to black; haem - atite coated but burnt and weathered. F11.
P19, D81, S04.

49. Shoulder or body sherd from large carinated jar.
PH 152.
Decorated by curved pair of lines, inside which are dots with white inlay (similar decoration to no. 48). Exterior orange to black, interior buff to orange; red haematite exterior; burnt and weathered. F11.
P21, D82, S04.

50. Shoulder or body sherds from large carinated jar.
PH 152.
2 joining sherds. Decorated by curved line and white inlaid dots (decoration as no. 48). Exterior black to red and haematite coated, interior grey worn; burnt and weathered. F11.
P21, D82, S04.

51. Shoulder or body sherds from large carinated jar.
PH 152.
2 joining sherds. Decorated by two bands which curve in a semi-circule; white inlaid dots inside the incised lines. Exterior black with red patches, haematite, buff interior, smooth wiped; burnt and weathered. F11.
P21, D82, S04.

52. Shoulder or body sherds from large carinated jar.
PH 151.
2 joining sherds. Decorated by three vertical lines and a vertical line of white inlaid dots. Exterior and interior orange to black, exterior haematite coated; burnt and weathered. F11.
P21, D51, S04.

53. Rim, neck, shoulder and part of body profile of large carinated jar.
PH 154.
4 joining sherds. Rim flaring, shoulder slightly carinated. Groove below neck. Shoulder decorated by hatched, inverted triangles, white inlay; with a row of closely spaced dots below the carination. On the body there are two narrow strips in upright chevron or diamond pattern, white inlaid dots inside the incised lines. Exterior and interior light red to brown-grey, exterior haematite coated; burnt and weathered. F11.
P19, D83, S04.

54. Body sherds from large carinated jar.
PH 42.
3 joining sherds from body below shoulder carination. Decorated by vertical strip with oblique incisions along its length; white inlay in the grooves. A row of narrowly spaced, white inlaid dots below shoulder carination. An incised and white inlaid line runs at right angle to the vertical strip, 73mm below the shoulder dots. Haematite coated, partly blackened and distorted by fire. F11.
P19, D56, S04.

55. Shoulder or body sherd from large carinated jar.
PH 42.
Decorated by two parallel incised and white inlaid lines, possibly forming part of a large vertical zig-zag pattern. Exterior orange to grey, interior grey. Haematite on exterior, interior shows finger sweeps. Distorted by fire; burnt and weathered. F11.
P21, D77, S04.

56. Body sherds from large carinated jar.
PH 42.
2 sherds from body below shoulder carination. Vertical strip of white inlaid dots bordered by incised lines; two parallel bands comprising double row of dots inside incised lines, branching off main vertical strip at oblique angles. Exterior and interior red, exterior haematite coated, interior wiped, slight traces of burning. F11.
P19, D55, S04.

57. Body sherds from large carinated jar.
PH 153.
4 joining sherds. Vertical strip of white inlaid dots and incised line, next to roughly horizontal zig-zag pattern of three closely spaced incised lines. Exterior red, interior orange to grey, exterior haematite coated; burnt and weathered. F11.
P19, D57, S04.

58. Body or shoulder sherd from large carinated jar.
PH 151,
At least two parallel grooves, probably forming part of a zig-zag pattern. Exterior red, interior brown; exterior haematite coated. F11.
P21, D76, S04.

59. Body or shoulder sherd from large carinated jar.
PH 153.
Incised, white inlaid lines, possibly forming part of zig-zag pattern. Exterior and interior orange to buff, with black traces on the interior; burnt and badly weathered. F11.
P21, D76, S04.

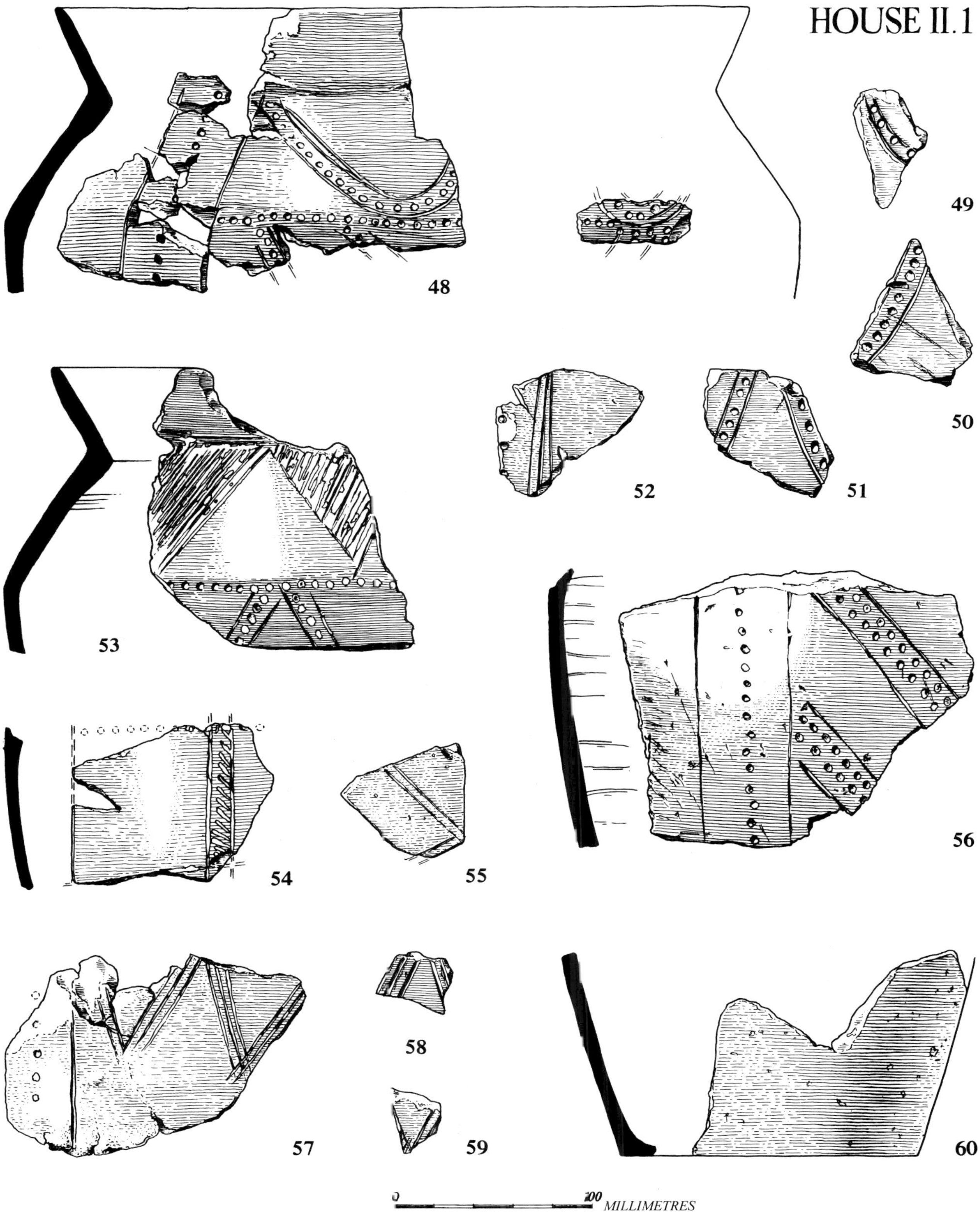

Fig. 3.5 Pottery from Enclosure II House 1 (scale 1:3)

60. Lower body and base profile of large carinated jar.
PH 152.
17 sherds of base and lower body. Base flat with sharp edge, dia *c* 150mm; body walls fairly steep. Undecorated. Exterior orange, interior orange grey; haematite on exterior. F14. PS 182.
P19, D00, S04.

Fig. 3.6

61. Rim, neck and part of shoulder profile of large carinated jar.
PH 152 and 153.
2 sherds, not joining. Flaring rim. Vertical strip of white inlaid dots bordered by incised lines, diagonal band of dots with incised line border. Exterior red-orange to grey, interior orange, haematite coating on one sherd, other burnt black. F11.
P19, D12, S04.

62. Shoulder and body sherds from large carinated jar.
PH 153.
2 joining sherds. Undecorated. Exterior and interior orange to black, exterior burnished; burnt and weathered. F11.
P19, D00, S02.

63. Body sherd from large carinated jar.
PH 157 (House 2).
Incised line and indentations with white inlay. Exterior brown to black, interior black; exterior burnished. F11.
P21, D12, S02.

64. Body sherd from large carinated jar.
PH 153.
Horizontal incised lines at top and bottom of sherd, possible traces of white inlay. Exterior and interior black; burnt and weathered. F11.
P21, D37, S01.

65. Body sherds from large carinated jar.
PH 152.
2 joining sherds. Vertical strip of white inlaid dots with one incised line border remaining, next to area of diagonal hatching, white inlaid, parallel. Exterior black, interior buff to black, haematite on exterior; burnt and weathered. F11.
P21, D14, S04.

66. Body sherd from large carinated jar.
PH 152.
Incised diagonal line across sherd, group of white inlaid, stabbed indentations on one side of line. Exterior and interior buff to black, exterior haematite coated; burnt and weathered. F11.
P21, D15, S04.

67. Body sherds from large carinated jar.
PH 154.
2 joining sherds. Incised diagonal line across sherd, two rows of stabbed indentations on one side of line. Exterior and interior black, exterior burnished; burnt and weathered. F11.
P21, D12, S02.

68. Body sherds from large carinated jar.
PH 152.
4 sherds, forming two pieces. Vertical strip of white inlaid dots bordered by incised lines beside a series of short horizontal incised lines with another vertical incised line, forming a ladder pattern. To the right is a horizontal incised line with indentations below. Exterior and interior buff with areas of black, haematite on the exterior. F11.
P21, D16, S04.

69. Body sherds from large carinated jar.
PH 152.
2 joining sherds. Vertical incised line with a series of short horizontal incised lines, forming a ladder pattern. Exterior red to black, interior black, haematite on exterior; burnt and weathered. F11.
P21, D17, S04.

70. Body sherd from large carinated jar.
PH 154.
Bottom section decorated with vertical strip of dots bordered by hatching with white inlay remaining. Exterior buff to grey, interior orange; weathered. F11.
P21, D14, S01.

71. Lower body and base profile of large carinated jar.
PH 153.
4 joining sherds. Flat base, body fairly steep. Undecorated. Exterior and interior grey to black. F11.
P19, D00, S01.

72. Rim and neck sherds from large carinated jar.
PH 154.
6 joining sherds. Flaring rim and angular neck. Triangle pattern formed by rows of indentations bordered by incised line, white inlay. Exterior and interior orange grey; burnt and weathered. F11.
P19, D12, S01.

73. Body sherd from large carinated jar.
PH 154.
Triangle pattern formed by rows of indentations bordered by incised lines, white inlay. Exterior and interior orange, haematite on the exterior; weathered. F11.
P21, D12, S04.

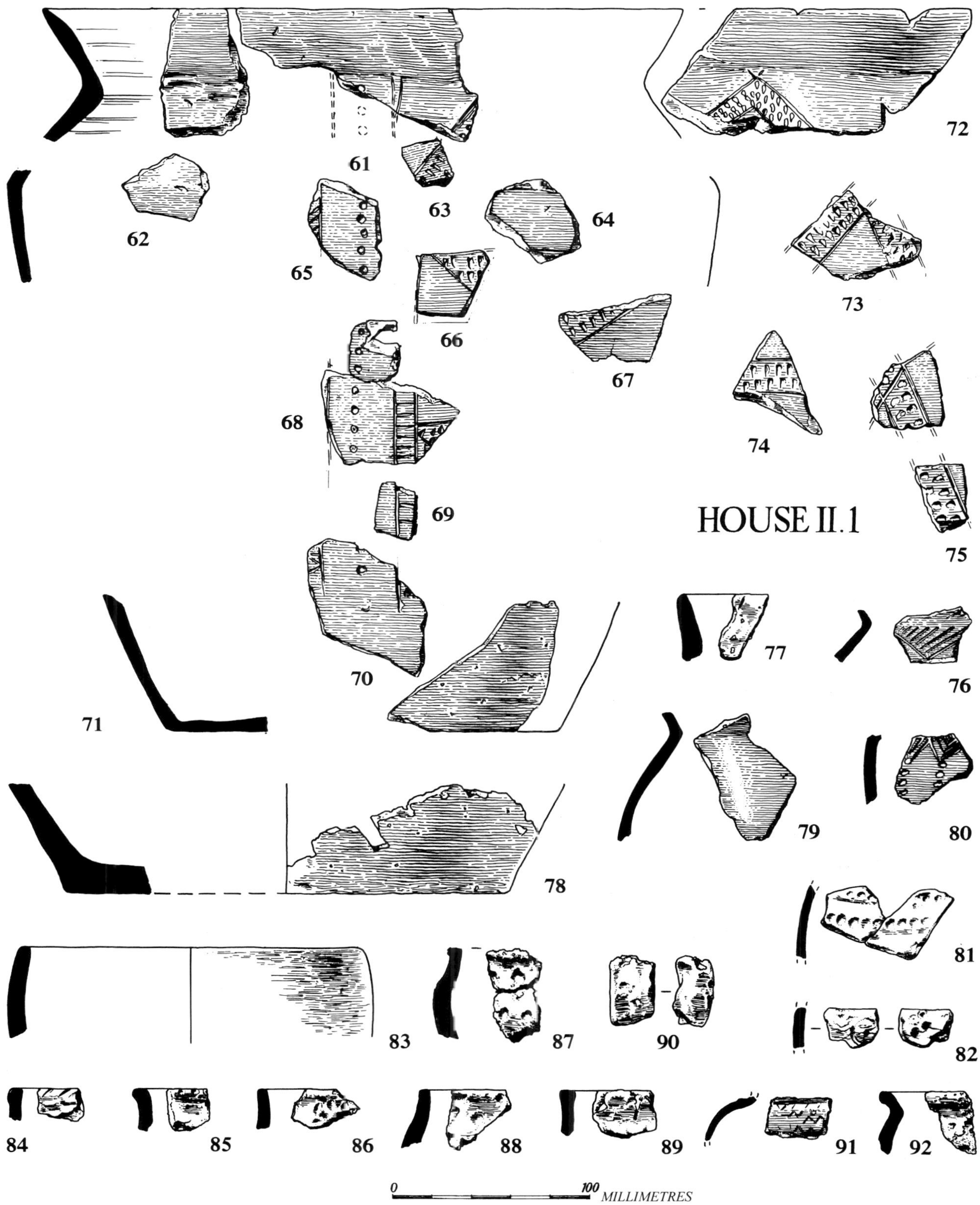

Fig. 3.6 Pottery from Enclosure II House 1 (scale 1:3)

74. Body sherd from large carinated jar.
PH 152.
Horizontal band of two rows of indentations bordered by incised lines. Exterior buff to red, interior black, haematite on exterior; burnt and weathered. F11.
P21, D12, S04.

75. Body sherds from large carinated jar.
PH 151.
2 sherds, not joining. Band comprising two rows of indentations bordered by incised lines, white inlay. At the top end of one sherd another strip of dots and incised lines crosses the main band. Exterior red to brown, interior black, haematite exterior; burnt and weathered. F11.
P21, D12, S04.

76. Neck and shoulder sherd from large carinated vessel.
PH 165.
Inverted triangle with deep hatching on shoulder; probably part of a row. Exterior and interior red to brown, exterior once haematite coated; burnt and weathered. F11.
P10, D63, S01 (S04).

77. Rim sherd from large carinated vessel.
PH 165.
Plain, everted rim. Undecorated. Exterior red to brown, interior grey to brown; weathered. F14.
P30, D00, S01.

78. Lower body and base profile of large carinated jar.
PH 154.
18 sherds, most joining. Flat base, 16mm thick; dia. 230mm. Sharp angle base, body walls fairly steep. Undecorated. Exterior red to brown, interior grey to brown; burnished haematite exterior. F41. PS 27.
?P19, D00, S04/2.

Miscellaneous Forms

79. Neck and shoulder sherd from jar with body rounded out.
PH 186.
Incurving sharply at neck, rounded shoulder carination. Undecorated. Exterior and interior pale orange to buff, haematite coated and burnished. F14.
P23, D00, S04/2.

80. Body sherd from large jar.
PH 237.
Row of inverted triangles below shoulder, filled by 'herring-bone' incised lines with white inlay, in concentric triangles. Below triangles a vertical row of dots. Exterior and interior black, exterior haematite coated and burnished. F11.
P21, D07, S04/2.

81. Shoulder sherd of thin walled rounded jar.
PH 151 and 153.
2 joining sherds, curving shoulder. Two rows of fingertip impressions. Exterior and interior orange buff, exterior probably haematite coated; very weathered. F11.
P20, D75, S04.

82. Body sherds from vessel.
PH 167.
2 sherds, not joining. One sherd with dot encircled by a ring, other with fingertip impressions. Haematite coating exterior. F11.
NB. Possibly intrusive.
P20, D78+D25, S04.

83. Rim profile of vessel, possibly plain keg jar.
PH 235.
Straight rim, wall thickness *c*10mm. Undecorated. Burnished haematite exterior; burnt and weathered. F42. PS 34.
P0iii, D00, S04/2.
Rim diam. *c*170 mm.

84. Rim sherd from vessel.
PH 154.
Flat-topped rim with slight external thickening. Diagonal nail slashing on rim. Exterior buff brown, interior dark brown; interior shows close set, horizontal sweep marks. F13.
P00, D80, S01.

85. Rim sherd from vessel.
PH 154.
Rim flat, groove on the top; slight external projection. Fingernail impressions on rim. Exterior and interior grey brown. F14.
P00, D42, S01.

86. Rim sherd from vessel.
PH 145.
Fingertip and nail impressions on rim. Exterior and interior grey black, burnt and weathered. F42.
P00, D21, S01.

87. Rim and shoulder sherd from vessel.
PH 151.
2 joining sherds. Rim slightly flattened with external projection, shoulder rounded. Fingertip impressions on neck and shoulder. Exterior and interior brown. F41. PS 29.
P00, D26, S01.

88. Rim sherd from vessel.
PH 154.
Flat-topped rim, slight external thickening.

Shallow fingertip impressions on neck.
Exterior grey brown, interior grey black. F13.
P00, D19, S01.

89. Rim sherd from vessel.
PH 151.
Flat rim, slightly thickened. Undecorated.
Exterior red brown, interior black: burnt and weathered. F42.
P00, D00, S01.

90. Part of handle from vessel.
PH 151.
Handle with ovoid section; wide and flat on top, pointed below, somewhat irregular; length *c*35mm. Undecorated. Exterior and interior brick red; burnt and weathered. F42.
PS 33.
P00, D00, S01.
Maximum dia. in section 17mm.

91. Shoulder sherd of decorated bowl with rounded body.
PH 235.
Scratched-cordoned bowl fragment. Curved shoulder with two or more furrows leaving cordon-like ridge between them, above the curve of the shoulder; thin walled *c* 4-5mm. Four rows of horizontal zig-zags, scratched lightly onto burnished surface. Exterior and interior black apart from traces of red haematite; burnt and weathered. F14.
PS 35.
P16, D67, S04/2.
In shape and decoration unlike any other House I vessel.
NB. Intrusive in this house series. Indicates late Early Iron Age 'Second A' occupation elsewhere on the site (Liddell 1935, Pit 1, Pl. 25 and 26).

92. Rim sherd from carinated jar.
PH 151.
Rounded, everted rim with pronounced lip, curving shoulder. Undecoratd. F42. PS 45.
P28, D00, S01.
NB. Probably intrusive.

Enclosure II HOUSE 2

Figs 3.7 – 3.10; 3.35

Carinated Bowls and Cups with Grooved Decoration or Undecorated

Carinated bowls and cups constitute a notable proportion of the material from House 2. The form is characterized by a tall, concave neck and sharply carinated shoulder. Decoration usually comprises a band of grooves above the carination. The clay is fine in texture, and traces of haematite often remain on the exterior.

Fig. 3.7

1. Almost complete profile of carinated cup with grooved decoration.
PH 134 and PH 147.
8 sherds, some joining. Tall, concave neck, sharp shoulder carination and shallow base. 2 bands of 6 evenly spaced grooves, probably drawn by a comb or other pronged instrument, above shoulder. Bands separated by 14mm, with plain area between them at waist. Sherds from PH 134 were burnt black and cindery, the others were partially red; all coated with burnished haematite on the exterior, possibly also on the interior. F13. PS 48.
P09, D87, S04/2.

2. Almost complete profile of carinated bowl/cup with grooved decoration.
PH 134, PH 135 and Pit 43.
9 sherds, some joining. Tall, concave neck, rounded shoulder carination, shallow base. 2 bands of narrow grooves above shoulder. Similar to Fig. 1 (above). Instrument of decoration may have been the same, and two vessels possibly a pair. Two sherds from 134 burnt black, the others had an orange red exterior, and a darkened interior; those from PH 135 had a partially black interior; sherd from Pit 43 was red. Burnished haematite on exterior and interior of all sherds. F13. PS 47.
P07a, D87, S04/2.

3. Complete profile of carinated bowl with grooved decoration.
PH 136 and PH 137.
21 sherds, some joining. Tall, concave neck, rounded shoulder carination, omphalos base. Band of 9 closely set, shallow, narrow grooves above shoulder. Exterior and interior deep red to brown, haematite coated and burnished; burnt and weathered. F14.
P06a, D05, S04/2.

4. Neck and shoulder profile of carinated bowl with grooved decoration.
PH 135.
Concave neck, carinated shoulder. Band of 7 broad grooves, shallow and slightly irregular above shoulder. Exterior and interior burnt dark grey; exterior haematite coated; burnt and weathered. F11. PS 56.
P07a, D05, S04/2.

5. Almost complete profile of carinated bowl with grooved decoration.
PH 135 and PH 126.
10 sherds, some joining. Tall, slightly concave neck, sharp shoulder carination and shallow base. Band of 7 grooves above shoulder incised with pointed instrument. Exterior grey, interior buff, burnished on both

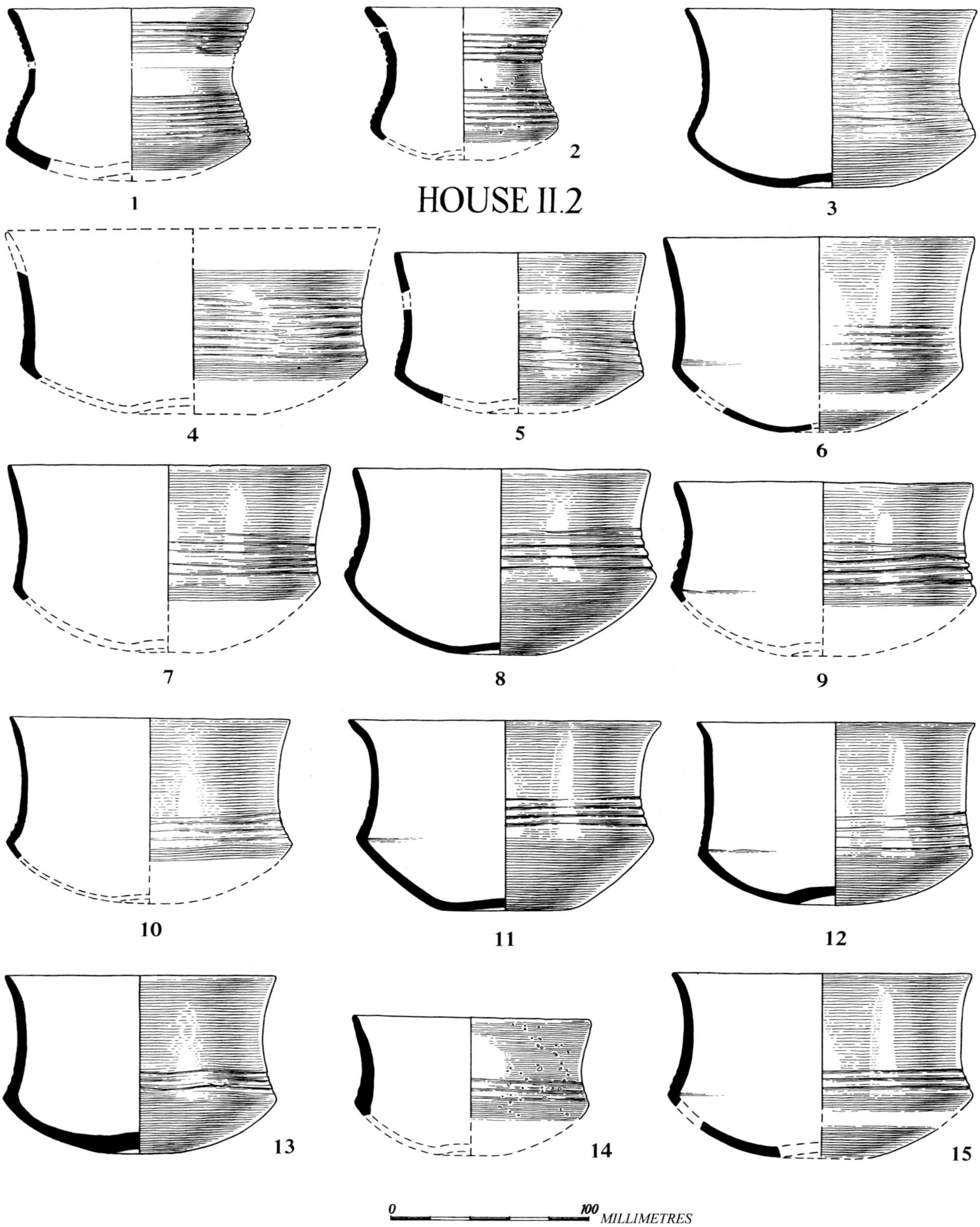

Fig. 3.7 Pottery from Enclosure II House 2 (scale 1:3)

surfaces, haematite coated; fire damaged and weathered, surface flaking. F11. PS 57.
P06a, D05, S04/2.

6. Almost complete profile of carinated bowl with grooved decoration.
PH 134 and PH 137.
36 sherds, some joining. Tall, slightly concave neck, fairly sharp shoulder carination, deep base. Band of 4 broad, shallow grooves, well-spaced above shoulder. Exterior red to yellow, interior grey to brown; burnished haematite exterior and interior; badly burnt and weathered. F11. PS 55.
P07a, D05, S04/2.

7. Rim, neck and shoulder profile of carinated bowl with grooved decoration.
PH 136, PH 137, and PH 144.
22 sherds, some joining. Tall, slightly concave neck, fairly sharp shoulder carination. Band of broad, shallow grooves above shoulder. Burnished haematite exterior and interior; fire damaged and weathered. F11. PS 50.
P07a, D05, S04/2.

8. Complete profile of carinated bowl with grooved decoration.
PH 134, PH 136 and PH 137.
28 sherds, some joining. Tall, concave neck, carinated shoulder, curved lower body, deep base with slight omphalos. 3 or 4 wide grooves above shoulder (top line roughly executed), drawn with a rounded instrument. Burnished haematite slip exterior and interior; fire damaged and weathered. F11.
P06a, D04/5, S04/2.

9. Rim, neck and shoulder profile of carinated bowl with grooved decoration.
PH 126, PH 135 and PH 137.
6 sherds, some joining. Tall, concave neck, carinated shoulder. Band of 5 broad, shallow grooves above carination, deeply drawn. Exterior red to brown and patched grey, interior red to brown. Burnished haematite exterior and interior. F11. PS 52.
P06a, D05, S04/2.

10. Rim, neck and shoulder of profile of carinated bowl with grooved decoration
PH 134, PH 135, PH 137, PH 147 and topsoil.
15 sherds, some joining. Tall, slightly carinated neck, sharp shoulder carination; thin walls. Band of 4 shallow grooves above shoulder. Exterior red, interior grey to black; interior burnished, once haematite coated; weathered and eroded. F14. PS 61.
P06a, D05, S04/2.

11. Complete profile of carinated bowl with grooved decoration
PH 154 (House 1).
11 joining sherds. Rim flared, neck concave, sharp shoulder carination, base with slight omphalos. Band of 4 narrow and rather scratchy grooves above shoulder. Exterior purple red, interior dark brown; traces of burnished haematite on exterior and interior; burnt and weathered. F11.
P07a, D05, S04/2.

12. Complete profile of carinated bowl with grooved decoration.
PH 126, PH 136, PH 137 and PH 146; top of PH 135 and PH 167.
29 sherds, some joining. Rim everted, neck almost straight, sharp shoulder carination, omphalos base. Band of 4 irregularly-spaced grooves above shoulder; drawn with instrument which leaves a striated impression, possibly twig. Exterior brick red, interior grey; exterior and interior burnished and haematite coated; burnt and weathered. F14. PS 54.
P08a, D05, S04/2.

13. Complete profile of carinated bowl with grooved decoration.
PH 126, PH 135 and PH 172.
12 sherds, 6 joining. Rim everted, upper neck fairly straight, lower neck concave, sharp shoulder carination, base shallow, slight omphalos. Band of 3 broad, shallow grooves above shoulder. Exterior red to brown, interior grey to brown; haematite on exterior and interior; exterior burnished, interior smooth. F14. PS 51.
P06a, D04, S04/2.

14. Rim, neck and shoulder profile of carinated cup with grooved decoration.
PH 156 and Pit 37 (1).
2 joining sherds. Neck slightly concave, sharp shoulder carination. Band of 3 broad, shallow grooves above shoulder. Exterior and interior buff and grey brown in patches; burnt and weathered. F42. PS 81.
P07a, D04, S01.

15. Almost complete profile of carinated bowl with grooved decoration.
PH 126, PH 135 and PH 137.
9 sherds, 4 joining. Neck slightly concave, sharp shoulder carination. Band of 3 shallow grooves above shoulder. Exterior red, smoke patches on rim, interior smoked grey and burnished, haematite coated; weathered. F14. PS 49.
P06a, D04, S04/2.

Fig. 3.8

16. Rim, neck and shoulder profile of carinated bowl with grooved decoration.

PH 182.
3 sherds; 1 from rim, 2 joining from shoulder. Tall, concave neck, sharp shoulder carination. Band of 3 or more irregular grooves above shoulder. Exterior and interior grey to orange; burnt and weathered. F11.
P06a, D04, S01.

17. Rim, neck and shoulder sherds from carinated bowl with grooved decoration.
PH 136, PH 137 and PH 143.
18 sherds, some joining. Tall, slightly concave neck, sharp shoulder carination. Band of 3 broad grooves above shoulder. Exterior and interior purplish burnished haematite coating; burnt and weathered. F13.
P08a, D04, S04/2.

18. Almost complete profile of rilled carinated cup with grooved decoration.
PH 126 and PH 147.
8 sherds, some joining. Tall, slightly concave neck, blunt shoulder carination, shallow base with slight omphalos. 3 narrow, shallow grooves above shoulder. Exterior red to orange, interior orange to brown and grey; burnished haematite exterior; burnt and friable. F13.
P07a, D04, S04/2.

19. Almost complete profile of carinated bowl with grooved decoration.
PH 135, PH 136 and PH 137.
5 sherds. Tall, slightly concave neck, sharp shoulder carination, shallow base, slight omphalos. Band of irregular grooves above shoulder, probably with same sort of instrument as Fig 3.7 no. 12. Burnished haematite on exterior and interior; burnt and weathered. F11.
P07a, D04, S04/2.

20. Rim, neck and shoulder sherds from carinated bowl with grooved decoration.
PH 147.
2 joining sherds. Tall, slightly concave neck. Band of 3 or 4 widely set shallow grooves above shoulder. Exterior red to brown, interior grey; burnt and weathered; burnished haematite exterior and interior. F13.
P08a, D04/5, S04/2.

21. Rim, neck and shoulder sherds from carinated bowl with grooved decoration.
PH 179.
4 sherds, 2 joining. Tall, almost straight neck, gentle shoulder carination. Band of at least 4 shallow wide grooves above shoulder. Interior blackened by fire; burnished haematite exterior and interior. F11.
P08a, D05, S04/2.

22. Rim and neck sherd from carinated bowl with grooved decoration.
PH 137.
Slightly concave neck. Top part of a band of grooves evident. Exterior and interior brick red, core dark grey; traces of burnished haematite exterior and interior; burnt and weathered. F11.
P08a, D04/5, S04/2.

23. Partially complete profile of large, carinated bowl with grooved decoration.
PH 134, PH 135 and PH 146.
26 sherds, 11 joining. Neck concave, sharp shoulder carination, slight omphalos base. Alternating panels of horizontal and vertical grooves on neck. Burnished haematite exterior and interior; burnt and weathered. F14. PS 58.
P06a, D59, S04/2.

24. Rim and neck sherds from carinated bowl with grooved decoration
PH 147.
5 joining sherds. Tall, concave neck, fairly thin-walled. Decorated by shallow, diagonal grooves. Exterior and interior light orange to brown, haematite coated; weathered. F14.
P06, D88, S04.

25. Complete profile of undecorated carinated bowl
PH 136 and PH 137.
16 joining sherds. Tall, concave neck, sharp shoulder carination, shallow base with neat omphalos. Undecorated. Exterior and interior deep red-brown haematite slip, highly burnished; burnt and weathered. F14.
P06b, D00, S04/2.

26. Partially complete profile of undecorated carinated bowl.
PH 157.
11sherds, 5 joining. Slightly concave neck, blunt shoulder carination. Undecorated. Exterior and interior patchy grey and buff, surfaces badly eroded; burnt and weathered. F14.
P06b, D00, S01.

27. Body sherd from vessel.
PH 174.
Decorated by impressed double ring with central dot. Exterior and interior red to brown; smooth surfaces. F11.
P00, D89, S01.
This sherd is unlike anything in House 2, but similar to a sherd in House 1 (Fig. 3.6 no. 82). Both may be associated with earlier occupation material lying on the surface.

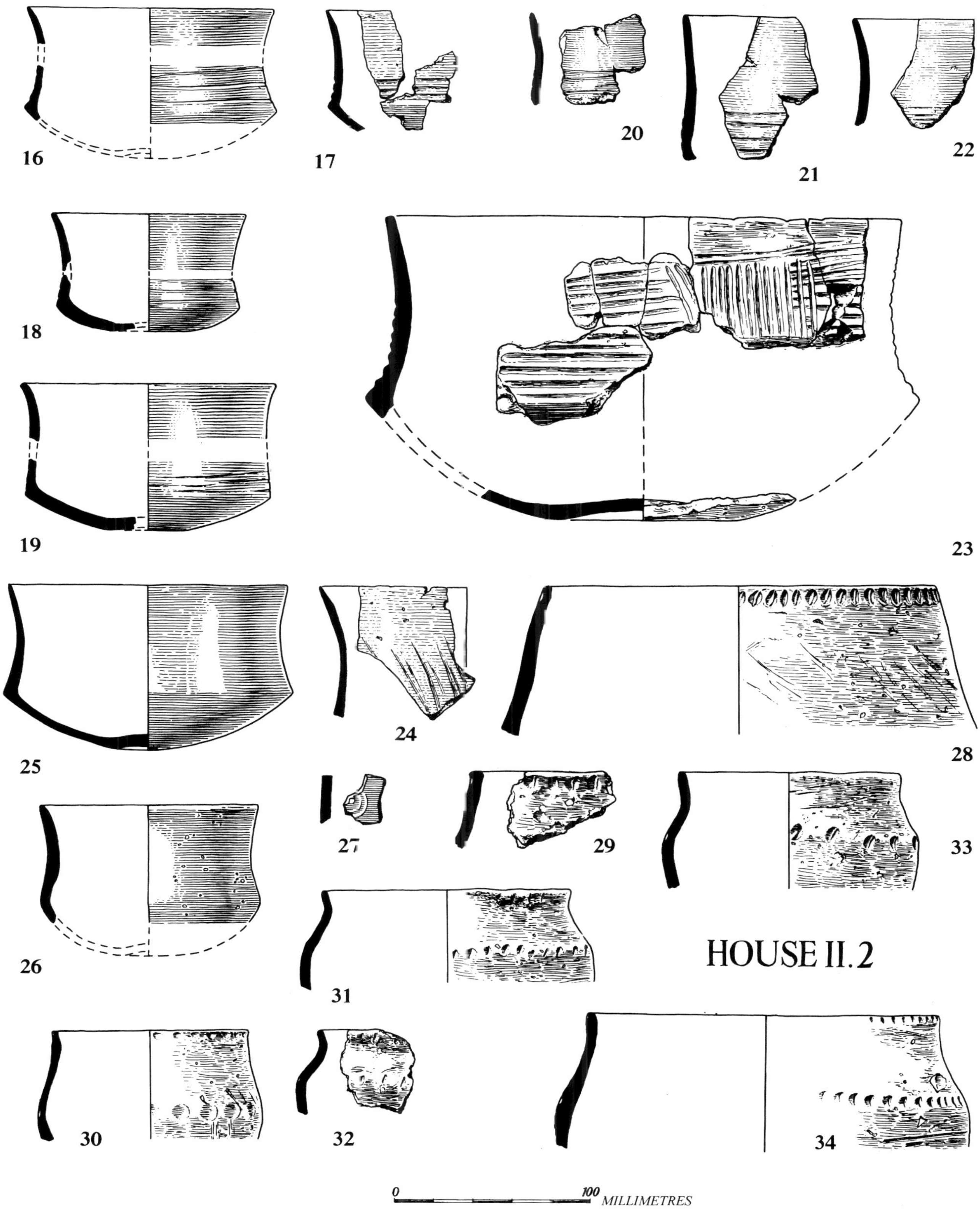

Fig. 3.8 Pottery from Enclosure II House 2 (scale 1:3)

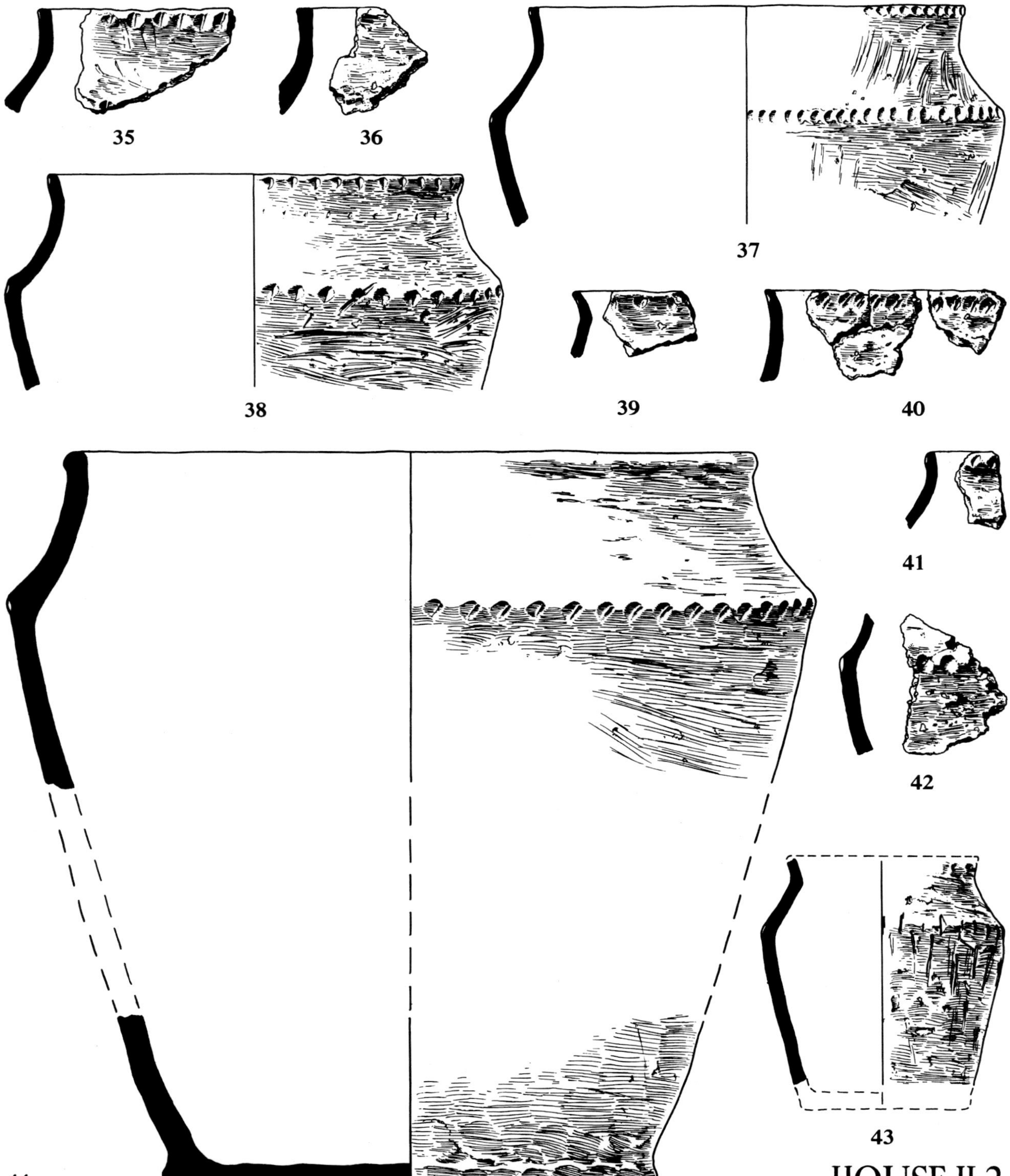

Fig. 3.9 Pottery from Enclosure II House 2 (scale 1:3)

Carinated Jars with Fingertip and Fingernail Decoration

These vessels constitute the remaining pottery assemblage for House 2. They are usually large, thick-walled jars, although some smaller examples were made (*e.g.* nos. 30-33), and were probably for domestic storage. Decoration comprises finger and nail impressions often on the rim and shoulder. The clay is fine with many inclusions, and surfaces smoothed.

28. Rim and part of body profile of large carinated jar.
PH 126, PH 137, PH 144, PH 146 and PH 147.
11 sherds, 7 joining. Inturned rim and body, slight thickening below rim; closed form. Fingertip and nail impressions on rim. Exterior light brown, interior light grey. F41.
P32, D21, S01.

29. Rim and part of body sherds from large carinated jar.
PH 126.
Inturned rim and body; closed form. Fingertip and nail impressions on rim. Exterior light brown, interior grey; surfaces weathered. F41.
Probably part of same vessel as Fig. 3.9 no. 42.
P32, D21, S03.

30. Rim, neck and shoulder profile of carinated jar.
PH 204.
10 sherds, 9 joining. Flat-topped rim, slightly rounded shoulder. Small fingertip impressions on the rim and shallow fingertip impressions on shoulder; also above the shoulder by diagonal nail scoring and below by vertical nail scoring. Inside the vessel are finger imprints below the rim and horizontal nail scoring at the shoulder. Exterior and interior patched black and orange; burnt. F31.
P32, D20, S01.

31. Rim, neck and shoulder profile of carinated jar.
PH 134 and PH 136.
10 sherds, 6 joining. Slightly everted rim, concave neck and gentle shoulder carination. Fingertip and nail impressions on rim and shoulder. Exterior light red to grey, interior grey; smooth finish. F14.
P33, D20, S01.

32. Rim, neck and shoulder sherd from carinated jar.
PH 137.
Everted rim, concave neck, gentle shoulder carination. Fingernail impressions on the rim and shoulder. Exterior light brown to grey, interior grey. F42.
P33, D43, S01.

33. Rim, neck and shoulder profile of carinated jar.
PH 134.
2 joining sherds. Upright rim, concave neck and gentle shoulder carination. Irregular fingertip and nail impressions on shoulder. Exterior and interior red to light grey; surfaces roughly smoothed. F31.
P33, D23, S01.

34. Rim, neck and shoulder profile of carinated jar.
PH 135.
4 sherds, not joining. Upright rim, gently sloping neck. Fingertip and nail impressions on rim and shoulder. Exterior light red to brown, interior light brown; surfaces roughly smoothed. F41.
P26, D20, S01.

Fig. 3.9

35. Rim, neck and shoulder sherds from carinated jar.
PH 134.
4 joining sherds. Straight rim, concave neck and slight thickening to the shoulder. Fingertip and nail impressions on rim and possibly shoulder. Exterior light red, interior light grey; surfaces smoothed. F14.
P25, D20, S09.

36. Rim and neck sherd from carinated jar.
PH 135.
Straight rim and concave neck. Undecorated. Exterior light red, interior light brown; smooth surfaces. F41.
P25, D00, S01.

37. Profile from rim to below shoulder of carinated jar.
PH 126 and PH 239.
8 sherds, 6 joining. Slightly flattened rim, concave neck, sharp shoulder curvature, rounded body. Small fingertip impressions on the rim edge and shoulder. Exterior light brown to red, interior grey; smoothed surfaces. F14. PS 61.
P33, D20, S03.

38. Profile from rim to below shoulder of carinated jar.
PH 229.
8 sherds, 5 joining. Rounded and slightly everted rim, concave neck and sharp shoulder curvature. Fingertip and nail impressions on rim and shoulder. Exterior light red to grey, interior grey; smoothed surfaces. F41. PS 63.
P25, D20, S03.

39. Rim and neck sherd from carinated jar.
PH 135.
Rounded, everted rim, concave neck. Fingertip impressions on rim. Exterior and interior light red; smooth but slightly uneven surfaces. F41.
P33, D21, S01.

40. Rim and neck sherds from carinated jar.
PH 126 and PH 142.
4 sherds, 3 joining. Plain rim, concave neck. Fingertip and nail impressions on rim. Exterior light grey, interior light brown; roughly smoothed surfaces. F41.
P25, D21, S01.

41. Rim and neck sherd from carinated jar.
PH 146.
Rounded, everted rim, gently sloping neck. Fingertip and nail impressions on rim. Exterior and interior light grey; smooth surfaces. F13.
P25, D21, S01.

42. Neck to below shoulder profile of carinated jar.
PH 126, PH 132 and PH 147.
4 sherds, 2 joining. Concave neck, curved shoulder. Fingertip and nail impressions on the shoulder. Exterior and interior light red; smoothed, well finished surfaces.F41.
P25, D22, S03.
Probably part of vessel Fig. 3.8 no. 29.

43. Almost complete profile of carinated jar.
PH 136.
19 sherds, 16 small sherds from body joining. Rim slightly everted, neck inverted, fairly sharp shoulder curvature. Fingernail impressions on shoulder. Exterior and interior dark grey; even surfaces, possibly vegetable smoothing on the exterior. F14.
Probably part of same vessel as Fig. 47.
P33, D40, S01.

44. Partially complete profile of carinated jar.
PH 134, PH 137, PH 144, PH 146 and PH 229.
21 sherds, some joining. Rounded rim, sharp shoulder curvature, base flat with slightly protruding foot. Fingertip and nail impressions on shoulder. Exterior and interior light red to grey; smooth surfaces, burnt and weathered. F31. PS 59.
P25, D23, S01.

Fig. 3.10

45. Rim sherds from vessel, probably carinated jar.
PH 137 and PH 147.
2 joining sherds. Flat top rim with fairly straight profile. Small fingertip impressions on rim. Exterior and interior dark grey; smooth surfaces. F14.
?P25, D21, S01.

46. Rim sherds from vessel, probably carinated jar.
PH 135.
2 sherds, not joining. Flat top rim with straight profile and fingertip impressions. Exterior light red to brown, interior grey; smooth surfaces. F41.
?P25, D21, S01.

47. Rim sherd from vessel, probably carinated jar.
PH 136.
Plain rim with curved profile and fingernail impressions. Exterior and interior dark grey; rough surfaces. F14.
Probably part of same vessel as Fig. 43.
?P33, D42, S01.

48. Rim sherd probably from vessel, probably carinated jar.
PH 134.
Rounded rim, slightly everted, small fingernail impressions. Exterior and interior brown; smooth surfaces. F13.
?P25, D42, S01.

49. Rim sherd from vessel, probably carinated jar.
PH 147.
Everted rim with fingernail impressions. Exterior and interior grey; rough surfaces. F14.
?P25, D42, S01.

50. Shoulder and body sherds from carinated jar.
PH 136 and PH 137.
5 sherds, none joining. Curved shoulder with small fingernail impressions. Exterior and interior light grey.; smooth surfaces. F14.
P33, D40, S01.

51. Shoulder and body sherds from carinated jar.
PH 147.
5 joining sherds. Concave profile, curved shoulder, rounded body. Fingernail impressions on shoulder. Exterior light red to grey, interior grey; surfaces smoothed. F14.
P26, D40, S03.

52. Neck and shoulder sherds from carinated jar.
PH 126, PH 135 and PH 136.
3 sherds, not joining. Curved shoulder. Fingertip and nail impressions on shoulder and indication of similar above neck. Exterior and interior light grey; smooth, finely finished surfaces. F14.
P25, D22, S03.

53. Partially complete profile of carinated jar.
PH 126, PH 134, PH 135, PH 136, PH 137, PH

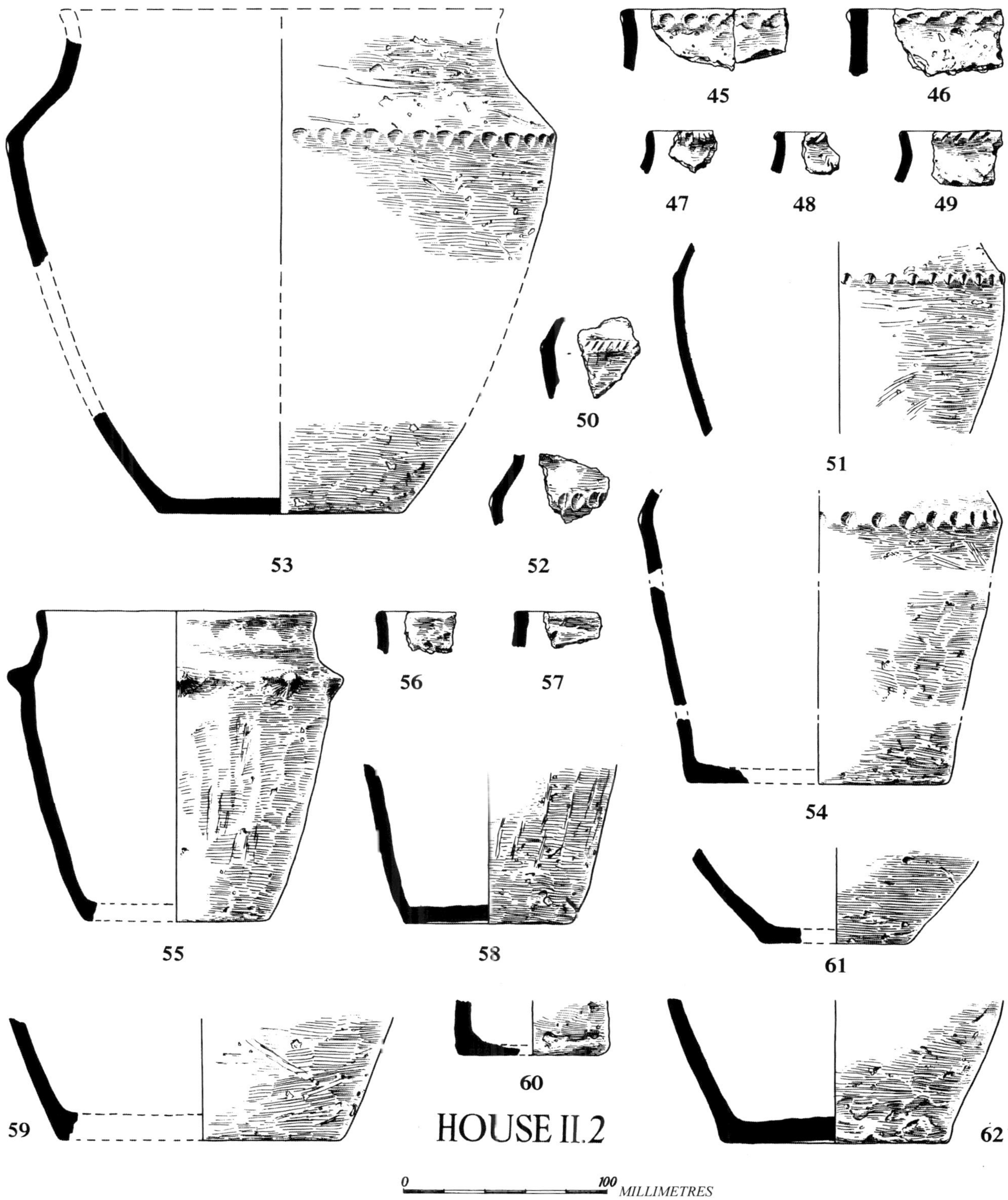

Fig. 3.10 Pottery from Enclosure II House 2 (scale 1:3)

147 and PH 167.
53 sherds, many joining. Slightly everted rim, fairly sharp shoulder curvature, rounded body, flat base. Fingertip impressions on shoulder. Exterior red to grey, interior grey; smoothed surfaces. F41. PS 65.
P26, D22, S03.

54. Partially complete profile of carinated jar.
PH 137.
11 sherds, some joining. Curved shoulder, fairly straight body profile, flat base. Fingertip impressions on shoulder. Exterior and interior red to brown; smoothed surfaces. F31. PS 60.
?P33, D22, S03.

55. Almost complete profile of carinated jar.
PH 136.
2 joining sherds. Slightly flattened, upright rim, concave neck, high shoulder, fairly straight body profile, flat base. Projecting bosses on shoulder. Exterior dark grey, interior light brown to grey; roughly smoothed surfaces, very slight burnish. F14.
P33, D49, S02.

56. Rim sherd of vessel.
PH 162.
Plain rim, almost straight profile. Fingertip impression on rim. Exterior and interior light grey with red core; smoothed surfaces. F42.
P00, D21, S03.

57. Rim sherd of vessel.
PH 143.
Plain rim with straight profile. Undecorated. Exterior and interior light red; smoothed surfaces. F31.
P00, D00, S03.

58. Body and base sherds of vessel, probably carinated jar.
PH 135 and PH 137.
7 sherds, 6 joining. Straight body profile, flat base. Undecorated. Exterior and interior light grey; rough surfaces. F43.
?P25, D00, S01.

59. Body and base sherds of vessel.
PH 136 and PH 137.
4 joining sherds. Base flat, body profile gently everted. Exterior light red, interior grey; smoothed surfaces. F41.
P00, D00, S03.

60. Base sherd of vessel.
PH 126.
Flat base, straight body. Undecorated. Exterior and interior light grey with light brown core; rough surfaces. F31.
P00, D00, S01.

61. Body and base sherd of vessel, probably carinated jar.
PH 137.
Base flat, body profile everted. Undecorated. Exterior light red, interior patchy light red to grey; rough surfaces. F14.
?P26, D00, S01.

62. Body and base sherd of vessel, probably carinated jar.
PH 147.
Base almost flat, body profile gently everted. Undecorated. Exterior and interior light red to grey; rough surfaces, burnt and weathered. F42. PS 83.
?P26, D00, S01.

Enclosure II House 3

Figs 3.11 – 3.13; 3.36

Carinated Bowls

Fine carinated bowls form part of the assemblage of House 3. The form is characterised by a tall, concave neck and sharply carinated shoulder. Often these bowls are not decorated, but if decoration does appear, it usually comprises shallow grooves above the carination. The clay is fine in texture, and traces of burnishing and haematite appear on many examples.

Fig. 3.11

1. Profile from rim to below shoulder of carinated bowl with grooved decoration.
A 94 (2B).
3 sherds, not joining. Tall, concave neck, sharp shoulder carination and shallow base. At least 3 horizontal grooves on neck. Exterior and interior red with grey core; smooth surfaces, once haematite coated and burnished. F11. PS 84.
P06a, D04/5, S04/2.

2. Neck and shoulder sherd from carinated bowl with grooved decoration.
PH 124.
Fairly tall neck, sharp shoulder carination. 4-5 shallow grooves on neck. Exterior and interior red with grey core; smooth surfaces, possibly haematite coated and burnished; weathered. F13.
P06a, D05, S04/2.

3. Neck and shoulder sherd from carinated bowl.
A 93 (2B).
Concave neck, sharp shoulder carination. Diagonal, shallow incised lines on neck. Exterior and interior red, smooth surfaces, possibly haematite coated and burnished. F14.
?P06a, D35, S04/2.

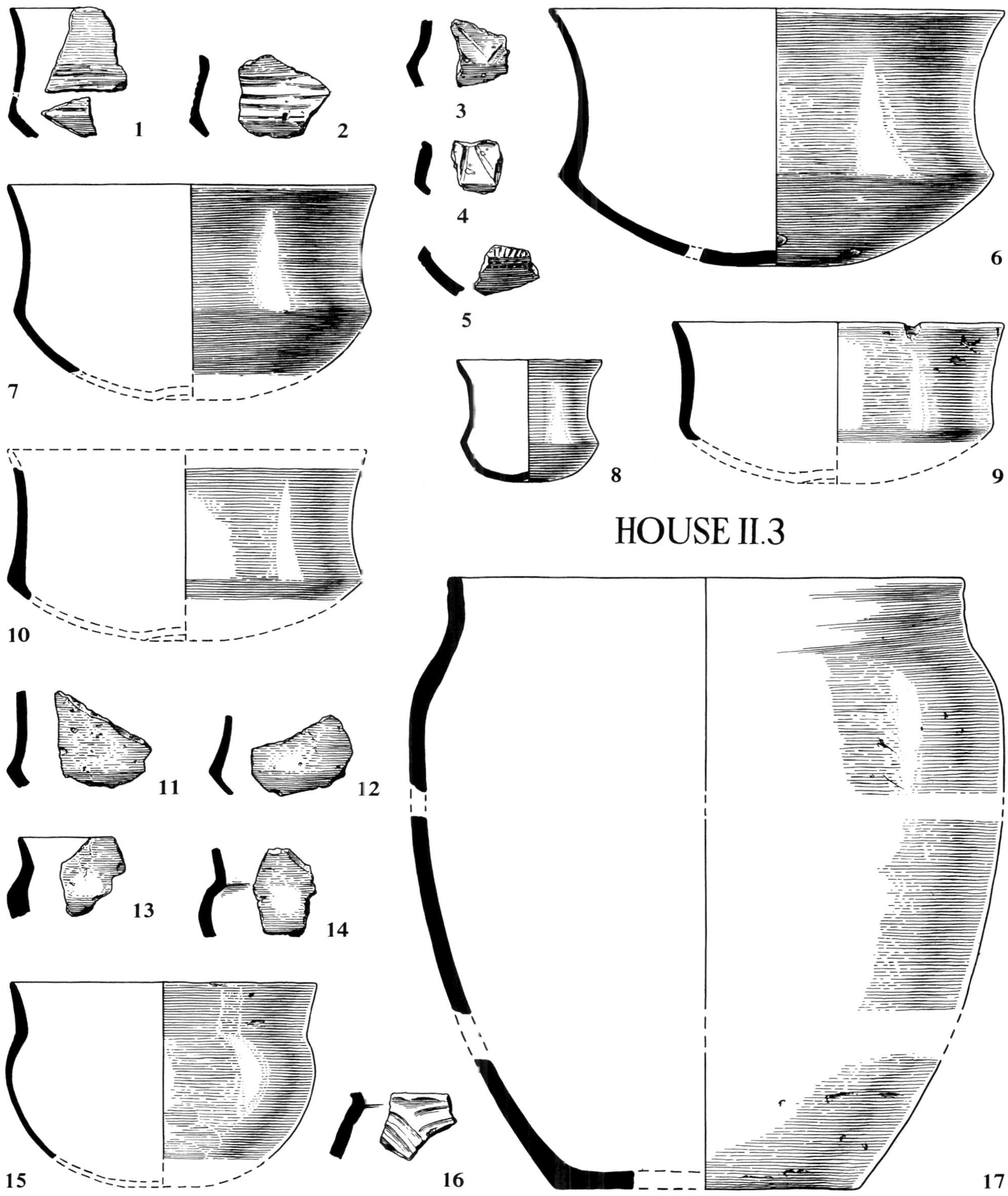

Fig. 3.11 Pottery from Enclosure II House 3 (scale 1:3)

4. Neck and shoulder sherd from carinated bowl.
A 65 B (2B).
Short neck, sharp shoulder carination. Diagonal lines on neck. Exterior and interior brown. F42.
?P06a, D48, S01.

5. Shoulder and body sherd from carinated bowl.
A 91 (2B).
Part of body immediately below sharp shoulder carination. Hatching, with double row of stabbed ornament above shoulder. Exterior and interior grey; smoothed surfaces. F11.
?P06a, D68, S03.

6. Almost complete profile of carinated bowl.
PH 73, PH 120.
9 sherds, joining in 2 groups. Tall, concave neck, sharp shoulder carination, shallow base with slight omphalos. Undecorated. Base perforated after firing with 4 or more roughly circular holes. Exterior and interior red; smoothed surfaces; exterior burnished and haematite coated. F11.
P07b, D00, S04/2.

7. Almost complete profile of carinated bowl.
A 65 (2B).
34 sherds, many joining. Tall, fairly concave neck, fairly sharp shoulder carination, fairly shallow base. Undecorated. Exterior light red, interior light brown; haematite and burnishing exterior; areas blackened by fire. F11. PS 85.
P07b, D00, S04/2.

8. Complete profile of carinated cup
PH 55.
8 joining sherds. Everted rim, upper neck almost straight, sharp shoulder carination, shallow base with slight omphalos. Undecorated. Exterior and interior grey to red; burnished haematite on exterior; burnt and weathered. F13.
P14, D00, S04/2.

9. Rim, neck and shoulder profile of carinated bowl.
PH 72.
Tall, slightly concave neck, gentle shoulder carination. Undecorated. Exterior and interior grey; burnishing on exterior, haematite coated; exterior smooth, interior rough; both surfaces show traces of vegetable matter. F14.
P07b, D00, S04/2.

10. Neck and shoulder profile of carinated bowl.
PH 62a.
4 joining sherds. Tall, slightly concave neck, sharp shoulder carination. Undecorated. Exterior and interior light orange to brown, partly fire blackened; burnishing and haematite on exterior; interior smooth. F14.
P06b, D00, S04/2.

11. Neck and shoulder sherd from carinated bowl.
PH 71.
Tall, upright neck, sharp shoulder carination. Undecorated. Exterior and interior red to brown, burnishing and haematite on exterior. F14.
P08b, D00, S04/2.

12. Neck and shoulder sherds from carinated bowl.
A 63 B (2B).
2 sherds. Part of curved neck, sharp shoulder carination. Undecorated. Exterior and interior red; burnishing and haematite on exterior; interior smooth. F11.
P06b, D00, S04/2.

13. Rim, neck and shoulder sherd from carinated bowl or cup.
A 94 (2B).
Everted rim, short neck, curved shoulder. Undecorated. Exterior and interior red, grey core; haematite on the exterior; smooth surfaces. F13.
P10, D00, S01.

14. Neck and shoulder sherds from carinated bowl or cup with body rounded out.
A 94 B (2B).
2 joining sherds. Everted neck, rounded shoulder. Undecorated. Exterior and interior red, grey core; burnishing and haematite on exterior, interior smooth. F13. PS 84.
P13, D00, S01.

15. Almost complete profile of carinated bowl with deep, rounded body
PH 72.
5 joining sherds. Tall, slightly flared rim, rounded shoulder and body profile. Undecorated. Exterior dark brown, interior orange brown; burnishing and haematite on exterior; burnt and weathered. F14.
P15, D00, S04/2.

16. Neck and shoulder sherd from jar.
PH 120.
Everted neck, part of shoulder. Wide, shallow grooves in the shape of interlocking arcs which overlap at the centre on shoulder. Exterior and interior red; exterior haematite coated and burnished; interior blackened and weathered. F11.
P21, D06, S04/2.

17. Almost complete profile of large carinated jar with rounded body.
PH 63 and PH 123, A 94 & 95 (2B).
11 sherds. Upright rim, curved shoulder, rounded body, flat base. Undecorated. Exterior red to black, interior buff to brown; burnishing and haematite on exterior; smooth surfaces. F13. PS 86.
P23, D00, S04/2.

Fig. 3.12

18. Neck and shoulder profile of vessel
PH 62 and A 94 (2B).
3 sherds, 2 joining. Tall, inverted neck, curved shoulder. Shallow, oblique lines in between widely spaced, near vertical grooves above carination. Exterior and interior light brown; smoothed surfaces. F21.
P33, D65, S03.

19. Neck and shoulder sherds from vessel, probably carinated jar.
PH 105.
2 joining sherds. Slightly concave neck, curving shoulder. Diagonally hatched chevron design above carination, bordered on the top by a horizontal line. Exterior and interior dark brown; smoothed surfaces. F41.
P21, D63, S03.

20. Neck sherd from vessel.
A 67 (2).
Slightly concave neck. Zone of hatching (probably chevron), bordered on the top by a horizontal line. Exterior and interior dark brown; smoothed surfaces. F14.
P00, D63, S03.

21. Body sherd from vessel.
A 92 (2B).
Probably from neck/shoulder area. Closely set diagonal grooves, bordered on the top by a horizontal line. Exterior and interior brown; smoothed surfaces. F42.
P00, D69, S03.

22. Body sherd from vessel.
A 92 (2B).
Probably from neck/shoulder area. 2 horizontal grooves. Exterior and interior dark brown; smoothed surfaces. F14.
P00, D69, S03.

23. Body sherd from vessel.
A 92.
Vertical line with 2 stabbed dots on one side. Exterior and interior dark brown; smoothed surfaces. F14.
P00, D70, S03.

24. Rim, neck and shoulder sherds from carinated jar.
A 148 (2A).
3 joining sherds. Upright rim, outward-sloping neck, gently curving shoulder. Fingertip impressions on shoulder. Exterior and interior orange to red; very weathered. F41.
P26, D22, S01.

25. Profile from rim to below shoulder of carinated jar
PH 73 and A 95 (2B).
4 sherds, 3 joining. Flat-topped rim, gently curving shoulder. Large, round fingertip impressions on neck and shoulder. Exterior dark grey to brown, interior light brown to grey; smoothed surfaces.F13.
P25, D26, S03.

26. Rim and neck profile of carinated jar.
PH 129.
Upright rim, slightly concave neck. Oblique finger nail impressions below rim. Exterior and interior red; burnt and weathered. F13.
P32, D66, S01.

27. Profile from rim to below shoulder of carinated jar.
PH 73 and A 94 (2B).
3 sherds, 2 joining. Upright rim, fairly sharp shoulder carination. Fingertip and nail impressions on rim and shoulder, also some fingernail striations between the rim and shoulder. Exterior and interior red with brown core; burnt and weathered. F14.
P32, D20, S01.

28. Rim to shoulder sherds from carinated jar.
A 93 (2B).
2 joining sherds. Upright rim, concave neck, gentle shoulder carination. Fingertip and nail impressions on rim and shoulder. Exterior and interior grey to brown; smooth surfaces. F42.
P27, D20, S03.

29. Rim and neck sherds of carinated jar.
PH 129.
2 joining sherds. Flat-topped rim, concave neck. Fingertip impressions on rim. Exterior and interior light brown; rough surfaces. F43.
P27, D21, S01.

30. Rim and neck sherd of vessel.
PH 123.
Roughly rounded rim, slight ledge on interior, straight neck. Widely set fingertip and nail impressions on rim. Exterior and interior dark brown. F41.
P00, D21, S01.

31. Rim and neck sherd of carinated jar.

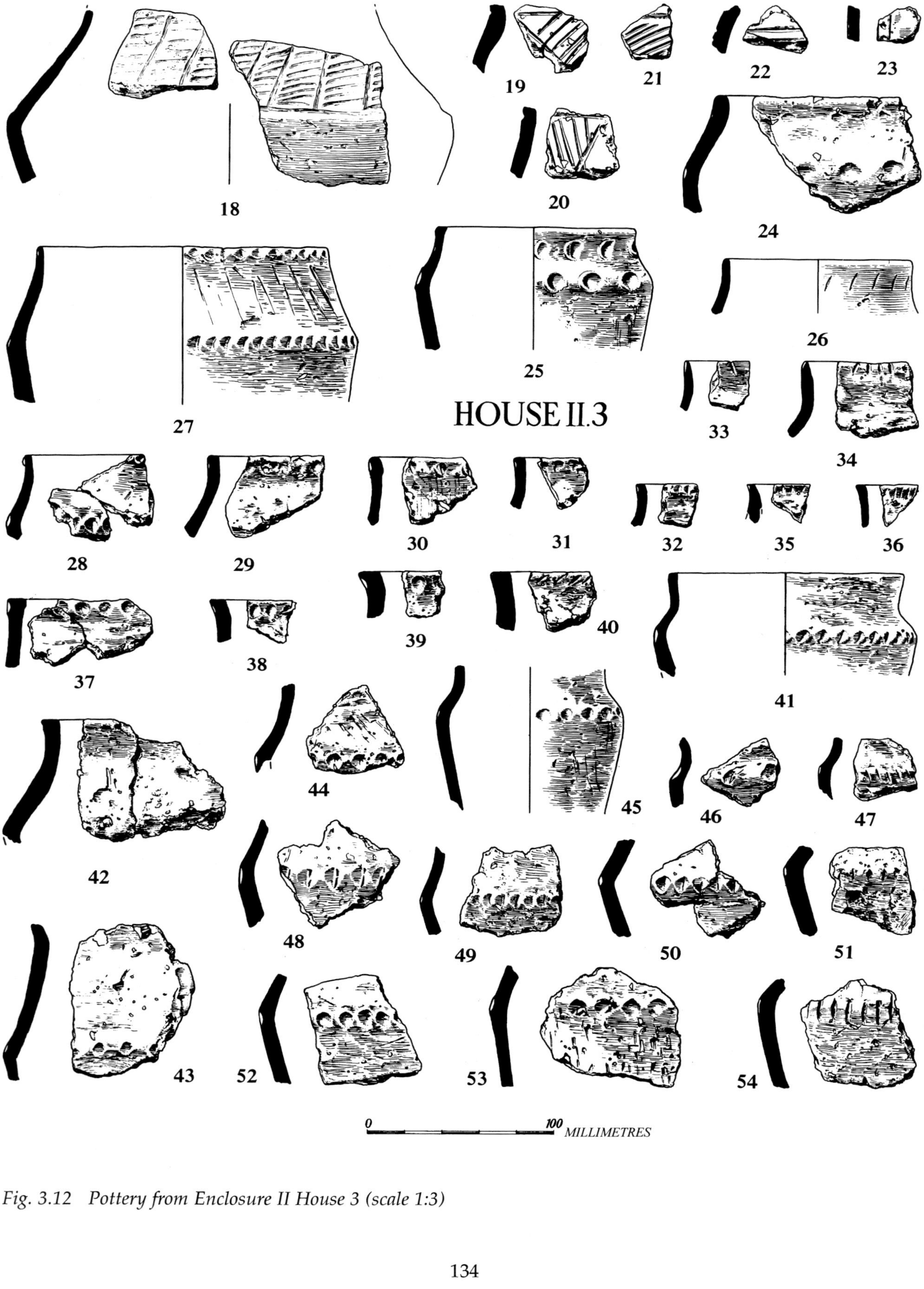

Fig. 3.12 Pottery from Enclosure II House 3 (scale 1:3)

PH 123.
Flat-topped rim, slightly concave neck. Fingertip and nail impressions on rim. Exterior and interior grey to brown; rough surfaces. F13.
P27, D21, S01.

32. Rim and neck sherd of carinated jar.
PH 123.
Flat-topped rim, slightly concave neck. Fingertip and nail impressions on rim. Exterior and interior grey to brown; rough surfaces. F42.
P27, D21, S01.

33. Rim and neck sherd of vessel.
PH 55.
Thin, plain rim, slightly concave neck. Oblique finger nail impressions or slashes on rim made by small tool. Exterior and interior brown; smooth surfaces. F42.
P00, D42, S03.

34. Rim and neck sherds of vessel.
PH 123.
3 sherds, not joining. Upright rim, concave neck. Horizontal lines on rim. Exterior red, interior grey to black. F42.
P00, D62, S01.

35. Rim and neck sherd of vessel.
PH 55.
Plain rim, slightly concave neck. Fingernail impressions on rim. Exterior and interior grey. F42.
P00, D42, S01.

36. Rim and neck sherd of vessel.
A 65 B (2B).
Slightly flared rim, straight neck. Fingernail impressions on rim. Exterior and interior grey to brown. Rim sherd from 65 B (2B) possibly from same vessel. F42.
P00, D42, S01.

37. Rim and neck sherds of vessel.
A 65 B (2B).
2 joining sherds. Flat-topped, upright rim, straight neck. Fingertip impressions on rim. Exterior and interior brown; rough surfaces. F42.
P00, D21, S01.

38. Rim and neck sherds from vessel
PH 105.
2 sherds, not joining. Flat-topped rim, straight neck. Small finger tip impressions on rim. Exterior and interior dark brown. F41.
P00, D21, S01.

39. Rim and neck sherd from vessel.
A 94 (2B).
Thick, flat-topped rim with fingertip impressions. Exterior and interior light yellow to brown. F43.
P00, D21, S01.

40. Rim and neck sherd from carinated jar.
A V ext PH 4.
Thick, flat-topped rim with oblique fingernail slashes. Exterior and interior grey to red. F41.
P25, D42, S01.

41. Rim to below shoulder profile of carinated jar.
A 94 (2B).
3 joining sherds. Flat-topped rim, straight neck, prominent shoulder carination. Fingertip and nail impressions on shoulder. Exterior light red to brown, interior brown to grey; smooth surfaces. F31.
P33, D23, S01.

42. Rim, neck and shoulder sherds from carinated jar.
PH 123.
2 joining sherds. Flat-topped rim, shoulder carination. Undecorated. Exterior and interior brown to grey; smooth surfaces, eroded and weathered. F43.
P25, D00, S01.

43. Neck and shoulder of carinated jar.
A 148 (2A).
Tall, slightly concave neck, sharp shoulder carination. Small finger tip impressions on shoulder. Exterior and interior red; hard fabric; weathered and probably burnt. F41.
P32, D22, S01.

44. Neck and shoulder sherd from carinated jar.
PH 63.
Concave neck, part of shoulder carination. Fingertip and nail impressions on shoulder. Exterior and interior light red. F43.
P27, D22, S01.

45. Shoulder and upper body profile of carinated jar.
A 148 (2A).
3 sherds. Rounded shoulder carination with fingertip and nail impressions. Exterior and interior light red. F14.
P33, D22, S01.

46. Neck and shoulder sherd from carinated jar.
A 65 (2B).
Concave neck, rounded shoulder carination with fingertip and nail impressions. Exterior and interior brown. F14.
P27, D22, S01.

47. Shoulder sherd from carinated jar.
PH 124.

Rounded shoulder carination with oblique fingernail slashes. F14.
P27, D40, S01.

48. Shoulder sherds from carinated jar.
PH 73 and A 94 S7.
3 sherds. Rounded shoulder carination with large fingertip and nail impressions. Exterior light brown to red, interior grey; rough interior surface. F21.
P27, D40, S01.

49. Shoulder sherds from carinated jar.
A 65 B (2B).
4 joining sherds. Rounded shoulder carination with small fingertip and nail impressions. Exterior and interior brown. F41.
P27, D22, S01.

50. Shoulder sherds from carinated jar.
A 91 (2B).
3 joining sherds. Sharp shoulder carination.with fingertip and nail impressions. Exterior and interior brown; smoothed surfaces. F41.
P27, D22, S03.

51. Shoulder sherd from carinated jar.
PH 123.
Sharp shoulder carination with small fingertip and nail impressions. Exterior and interior light red to brown; eroded and weathered. F31.
P27, D22, S01.

52. Shoulder sherd from carinated jar.
PH 105.
Fairly sharp shoulder carination with fingertip impressions. Exterior and interior buff to grey. F43.
P27, D22, S01.

53. Shoulder sherds from carinated jar.
PH 62 a.
2 joining sherds. Gentle shoulder carination with large finger tip impressions. Exterior and interior light brown to grey; roughly wiped with cloth or grass. F43.
P27, D22, S01.

54. Shoulder sherd from carinated jar.
PH 123.
Rounded shoulder carination with close-set slashes. Exterior red, interior brown to red; smooth interior surface; weathered. F41.
P27, D61, S01.

Fig. 3.13

55. Rim and neck profile of vessel.
PH 105.
Upright rim. Undecorated. Exterior and interior red to black. F13.
P00, D00, S01.

56. Rim and neck sherd from vessel.
PH 73.
Uneven, flat top rim with internal and slight external projections. Undecorated. Exterior and interior dark brown to grey. F13.
P00, D00, S01.

57. Rim and neck sherd from vessel.
A 95 (2B).
Upright rim, concave neck. Undecorated. Exterior and interior black. F41.
P00, D00, S01.

58. Rim and body sherd from vessel.
A VI (3).
Flat top rim, straight body. Undecorated. Exterior and interior orange. F31.
P00, D00, S01.

59. Rim and body sherd from vessel.
A 65 B (2B).
Flat top rim, straight body. Undecorated. Exterior red brown, interior brown, blackened rim. F31.
P00, D00, S01.

60. Rim and body sherd from vessel.
Cutting IV, 2.
Upright rim, straight body. with diagonal, shallow incised lines. Exterior orange, interior brown. F32.
P00, D35, S01.

61. Shoulder sherd from carinated jar.
PH 73.
Fairly gentle shoulder carination. Undecorated. Exterior and interior brown to grey. F31.
?P25, D00, S01.

62. Rim sherd from vessel.
PH 123.
Flat top rim with exterior projection. Undecorated. Exterior brown to dark grey, interior black. F41.
P00, D00, S01.

63. Rim sherd from vessel.
Cutting V, P II C.
Outward sloping rim. Undecorated. Exterior and interior brown to grey. F21.
P00, D00, S01.

64. Rim sherd from vessel.
Cutting V, 3.
Flaring rim. Undecorated. Exterior brown, interior red brown. F31.
P00, D00, S01.

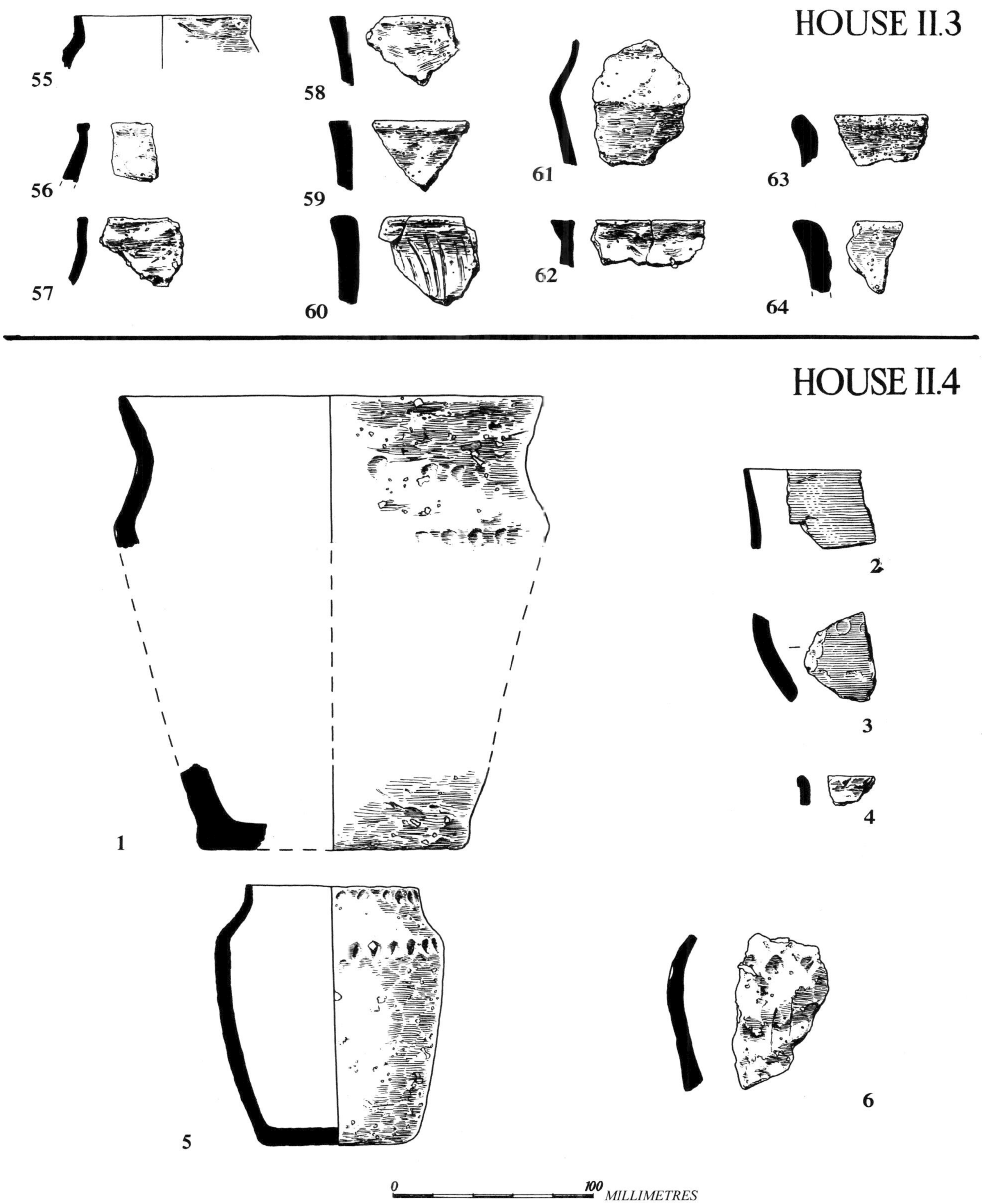

Fig. 3.13 Pottery from Enclosure II House 3 and Enclosure II House 4 (scale 1:3)

Enclosure II House 4

1. Partially complete profile of carinated jar.
   PH 198.
   14 sherds, some joining. Everted rim, sharply carinated shoulder, flat base. Fingertip impressions on the neck and shoulder. Exterior buff to orange, interior buff to dark brown. F22. PS 88.
   P30, D26, S01.

2. Rim sherds from vessel, probably carinated bowl.
   PH 216.
   2 joining sherds. Plain, upright rim. Undecorated. Exterior and interior orange, burnished and haematite coated. F11.
   P18, D00, S04/2.

3. Body sherd from vessel.
   PH 187.
   Gently sloping body with incised circles, with traces of white inlay. Exterior dark brown to orange red, interior dark brown to black. F13.
   P00, D09, S01.

4. Rim sherd from bowl.
   PH 216.
   Upright rim with out-turned lip, fingernail impressions. Exterior and interior buff to orange. F12.
   P00, D42, S01.

5. Complete profile of small carinated jar.
   PH 207.
   35 sherds, many joining. Upright rim, rounded shoulder carination, flat base. Fingertip impressions on rim edge and shoulder. Exterior orange to buff exterior, orange to dark brown interior. F41.
   P26, D20, S01.

6. Shoulder and upper body sherd from vessel.
   PH 210.
   Rounded shoulder carination with fingertip impressions. Exterior and interior orange to grey. F41.
   P27, D22, S01.

Enclosure II Area S2 Posthole Complex

Fig. 3.14

1. Rim to below shoulder profile of carinated bowl.
   PH 32.
   3 sherds, not joining. Tall, concave neck, sharp shoulder carination. Undecorated. Exterior red to black, interior red to brown; burnt and weathered. F14.
   P07b, D00, S01.

2. Rim to below shoulder profile of carinated cup.
   PH 82.
   Everted rim, upper neck almost straight, lower part outward-curved to sharp shoulder carination. Undecorated. Burnished haematite on exterior. F52.
   P07b, D00, S04/2.

3. Rim and neck sherd from carinated bowl.
   PH 95.
   Flaring rim Undecorated. F42.
   P07b, D00, S01.

4. Rim and neck sherds from vessel.
   PH 40.
   2 joining sherds. Flat-topped upright rim. Fingertip and nail impressions on neck. Exterior brown, interior buff to brown. F42.
   P00, D19, S01.

5. Body sherd of vessel.
   PH 39.
   Decorated by two shallow incised lines in zig-zag pattern. burnished haematite on exterior. F14.
   P00, D36, S04/2.
   Part of Fig. 6 below.

6. Rim to shoulder sherd of vessel.
   PH 39.
   Everted rim, sloping shoulder with two diagonal shallow incised lines. Burnished. F14.
   P00, D35, S02.
   Part of Fig. 5 above.

7. Rim sherd of vessel.
   PH 80.
   Flat-topped rim with fingertip impressions. F42.
   P00, D21, S01.

8. Rim to shoulder sherd of carinated bowl.
   PH 32.
   Everted rim, curved shoulder carination. Shallow fingertip impressions on rim and shoulder. F14.
   P29, D20, S01.

9. Shoulder sherds from vessel, probably carinated jar.
   PH 18.
   2 sherds. Gentle shoulder carination with fingertip impressions. F41.
   P27, D22, S01.

10. Rim and neck sherd from vessel, possibly carinated bowl.
    PH 39.
    Flared rim with fingertip impressions. Exterior black, interior dark grey. F42.
    ?P29, D21, S01.

11. Rim and neck sherd from vessel.
PH 43.
Slightly everted rim with thin tip with fingernail impressions. Exterior and interior orange; smooth, wiped surfaces. F42.
P00, D42, S03.

12. Neck and shoulder sherds from carinated jar.
PH 55.
2 joining sherds. Rounded shoulder carination with fingernail impressions. Exterior red brown to black, interior orange to brown; smooth, wiped surfaces. F41.
P32, D40, S03.

13. Rim sherd from vessel.
PH 4.
Upright rim, gentle shoulder carination. Undecorated. smooth, wiped surfaces. F31.
P00, D00, S03.

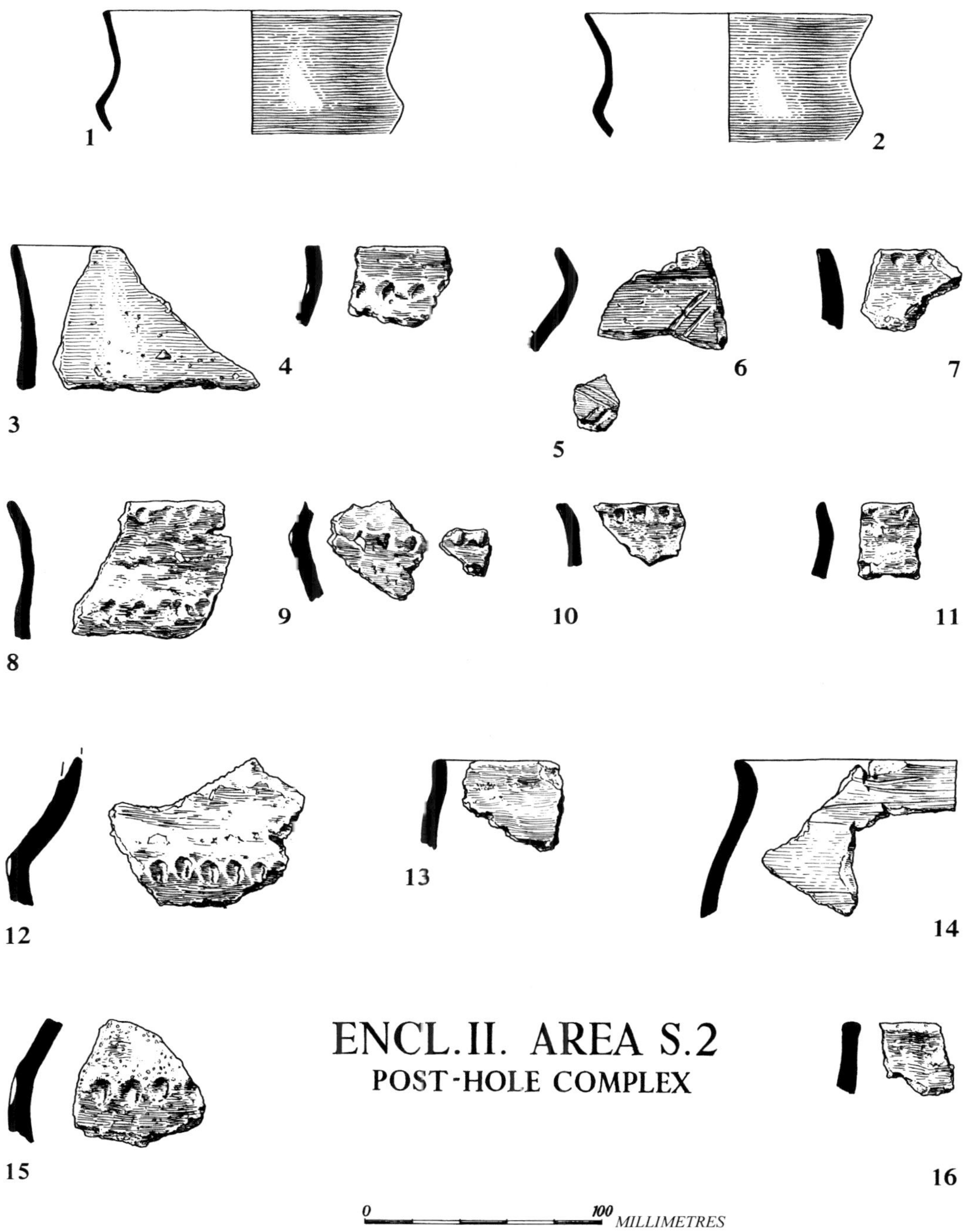

Fig. 3.14 Pottery from Enclosure II Area S2 Posthole Complex (scale 1:3)

14. Rim sherd of rounded bowl.
PH 173.
Rounded, everted rim, sloping shoulder. Roughly horizontal shallow furrows below rim (possibly burnishing marks). Smooth, wiped surfaces. F32.
P38, D38, S03.

15. Shoulder sherd from carinated jar.
PH 49.
Rounded shoulder carination with fingertip and nail impressions. Exterior brown to orange, interior red to black, burnt. F21.
P32, D22, S01.

16. Rim and neck sherds from vessel.
PH 45.
2 sherds, not joining. Flat-topped rim, straight neck. Undecorated. Exterior black, interior brown to black; burnt and weathered. F32.
P00, D00, S01.

Enclosure II Working Hollow 3

Fig. 3.15 – 3.16

1. Neck and shoulder profile of carinated bowl with grooved decoration.
22 sherds. Tall, concave neck, sharp shoulder carination. 6 evenly-spaced grooves on neck. Exterior dark orange red, interior brown. F13.
P06a, D05, S01.

2. Neck and shoulder profile of carinated bowl with grooved decoration.
Tall, concave neck, sharp shoulder carination. 3 evenly-spaced grooves on neck. Exterior dark orange, interior orange; exterior smooth-wiped. F14.
P06a, D04, S03.

3. Neck and shoulder sherd from carinated bowl with grooved decoration.
Part of concave neck, sharp shoulder carination. 4 evenly spaced grooves on neck. Exterior and interior orange; exterior haematite coated. F14.
P06a, D05, S04.

4. Neck and shoulder sherd from carinated bowl with grooved decoration.
Concave neck, sharp shoulder carination. 4 evenly-spaced grooves on neck. Exterior and interior orange; exterior haematite coated. F13.
?P06a, D05, S04.

5. Neck and shoulder profile of carinated bowl with grooved decoration.
2 sherds. Tall, concave neck, sharp shoulder carination. Groups of vertical grooves alternating with groups of horizontal grooves on neck. Exterior and interior orange to brown; exterior smooth-wiped. F13.
P06a, D59, S03.

6. Neck sherd from carinated bowl with grooved decoration.
Part of tall neck with groups of vertical grooves alternating with groups of horizontal grooves. Exterior light brown grey, interior grey; exterior smoothed. F13.
P06a, D59, S03.

7. Almost complete profile of carinated bowl.
8 sherds. Tall neck, sharp shoulder carination. Undecorated. Exterior orange to dark orange, interior dark orange to dark grey; burnished haematite on exterior. F13.
P06b, D00, S04/2.

8. Almost complete profile of carinated bowl.
4 sherds. Tall neck, sharp shoulder carination. Undecorated. Exterior and interior red to dark orange; exterior haematite coated. F14.
P07b, D00, S04.

9. Partially complete profile of carinated bowl.
2 sherds. Tall neck, sharp shoulder carination. Undecorated. Exterior orange to grey, interior grey; burnished haematite on exterior. F13.
P07b, D00, S04/2.

10. Rim to below shoulder profile of carinated bowl.
5 sherds. Tall neck, sharp shoulder carination. Undecorated. Exterior and interior dark grey to black; exterior burnished and haematite coated. F14.
P06b, D00, S04/2.

11. Neck and shoulder sherd from carinated bowl.
Tall neck, sharp shoulder carination. Undecorated. Exterior and interior orange to dark red; exterior smoothed. F13.
P07b, D00, S03.

12. Neck and shoulder sherd from carinated bowl.
3 sherds. Tall neck, sharp shoulder carination. Undecorated. Exterior grey, interior buff to grey; exterior smoothed. F13.
P07b, D00, S03.

13. Rim to below shoulder profile of carinated bowl.
2 sherds. Everted rim, sharp shoulder carination. Undecorated. Exterior and interior black; exterior burnished, haematite coated. F14.
P10, D00, S04/2.

14. Shoulder sherd from carinated bowl.
Fairly sharp shoulder carination.
Undecorated. Exterior and interior orange;

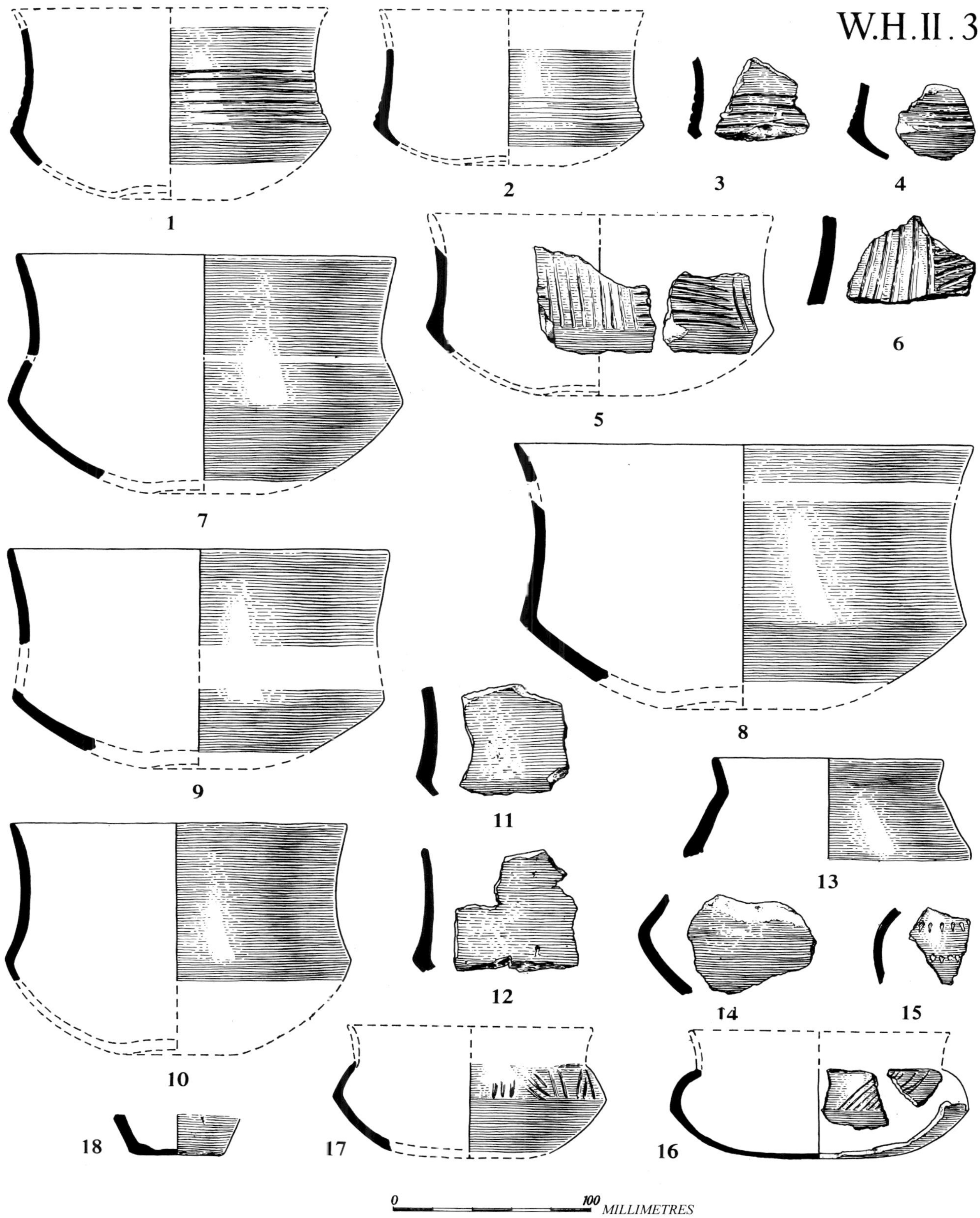

Fig. 3.15 Pottery from Enclosure II Working Hollow 3 (scale 1:3)

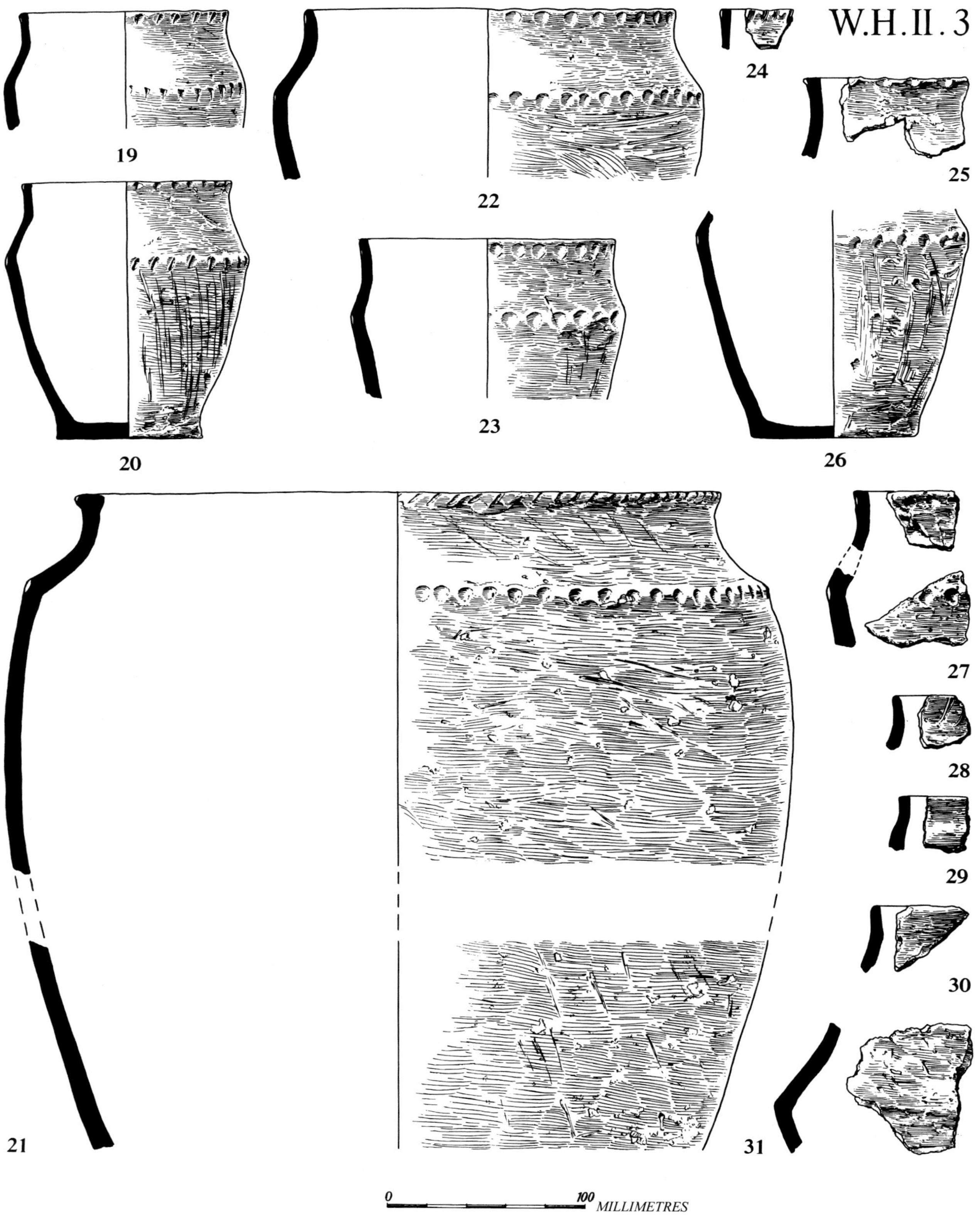

Fig. 3.16 Pottery from Enclosure II Working Hollow 3 (scale 1:3)

exterior burnished, haematite coated. F13.
P18, D00, S04/2.

15. Shoulder sherd from vessel, possibly bowl with rounded body.
Rounded shoulder carination with two horizontal lines of stabbed impressions. Exterior and interior orange; burnished haematite on exterior. F13.
?P15, D60, S04/2.

16. Almost complete profile of carinated bowl with rounded body.
6 sherds. Blunt shoulder carination, rounded body, flat base. Diagonal shallow incised lines above carination. Exterior orange to brown, interior brown; burnished haematite on exterior. F12.
P13, D35, S04/2.

17. Partially complete profile of carinated bowl with rounded body.
5 sherds. Blunt shoulder carination, rounded body. Groups of vertical incised lines alternating with groups of diagonal incised lines above carination. Exterior orange to dark grey, interior orange. F14.
P12, D07, S01.

18. Lower body and base profile of vessel.
Flat base, lower body out-sloping. Undecorated. Exterior and interior dark red to brown; exterior smooth-wiped. F13.
P00, D00, S03.

Fig. 3.16

19. Rim to below shoulder profile of carinated jar.
5 sherds. Rim tip slightly rounded, gentle shoulder carination. 'Stick' impressions on rim and curved incised lines on shoulder. Exterior brown to grey, interior grey to black. F14.
P33, D29, S01.

20. Complete profile of carinated jar
12 sherds. Rim slightly rounded at tip, shoulder carination, fairly tall body, flat base. Fingertip and nail impressions on rim and shoulder carination. Exterior orange to grey, interior grey; vertical grass-wiping on exterior below carination. F41.
P33, D20, S05.

21. Almost complete profile of large carinated jar
Many sherds, Flat-topped T- rim, blunt shoulder carination, tall, rounded body profile. Fingernail impressions on rim and fingertip impressions on shoulder carination. Colour not recorded; exterior smoothed. F41.
P26, D20, S03.

22. Rim to below shoulder profile of carinated jar.
5 sherds. Plain rim, fairly sharp shoulder carination. Fingertip impressions on rim and shoulder carination. Exterior light brown to grey, interior grey. F43.
P26, D20, S01.

23. Rim to below shoulder profile of carinated jar.
6 sherds. Plain rim, gentle shoulder carination. Fingertip impressions on rim and shoulder carination. Exterior brown to grey, interior black; vertical grass wiping on exterior below carination. F41.
P33, D20, S05.

24. Rim sherd from vessel.
Upright rim with fingertip impressions. Colour not recorded. F41.
P00, D21, S01.

25. Rim and neck sherd from vessel.
2 sherds. Upright rim with fingertip impressions. Exterior buff to grey, interior dark grey. F41.
P00, D21, S01.

26. Shoulder and body profile of carinated jar.
2 sherds. Sharp shoulder carination, body inward sloping, flat base. Fingertip and nail impressions on shoulder. Exterior orange to grey, interior dark grey; exterior smooth-wiped. F41.
P33, D22, S03.

27. Rim to below shoulder sherds from carinated jar.
2 sherds. Upright rim, sharp shoulder carination. Fingertip impressions on rim and shoulder. Exterior brown, interior black. F43.
P33, D20, S01.

28. Rim and neck sherd of vessel.
Upright rim with slash decoration. Exterior and interior brown to grey. F13.
P00, D28, S01.

29. Rim and neck sherd of vessel.
Almost straight rim and neck. Undecorated. Exterior and interior black. F32.
P00, D00, S01.

30. Rim and neck sherd of vessel.
Upright rim. Undecorated. Exterior and interior brown to grey; exterior smoothed. F13.
P00, D00, S03.

31. Neck and shoulder sherd from carinated jar.
Part of tall, concave neck, sharp shoulder carination. Undecorated. Exterior brown to grey, interior dark grey. F41.
P25, D00, S01.

Pottery From Pits

Figs. 3.17-3.31

Enclosure I Pit 1

Fig. 3.17

1. Complete profile of large 'situla' jar.
Layer 3.
C 100 sherds, many joining. Flat-topped rim with pronounced external and internal projections, high rounded shoulder, body tapering to a broad flat base with slight external flaring. Undecorated. Exterior and interior light orange buff to red and dark brown. Thin slip on exterior, burnish marks on shoulder and body; interior pitted where grits burnt or dissolved out. F14. PS 108.
P22, D00, S01.

   It may be a ceramic imitation of a situla of late Hallstatt type with high shoulder and short rolled rim *cf.* Kimmig1962-3, 31-106). The Rhineland situlae, copies of imports from the Tessin in the Hallstatt D phase, were current in Hallstatt D2 – early La Téne. Distribution mainly Rhenish but outliers in France and Switzerland. The form lent itself to copying in pottery. A 5th century date is indicated for this vessel.

2. Rim sherd of vessel.
Layer 1.
Plain, upright rim. Undecorated. Exterior and interior dark grey; once haematite coated; rough surfaces and weathered. F31.
P00, D00, S04.

3. Base and lower body profile of jar, possibly globular.
Layer 3.
4 sherds. Flat base with outward sloping body. Undecorated. Exterior and interior red; vegetable impressions on base; surfaces uneven. F43.
?P36, D00, S01.

4. Rim and neck sherd of vessel.
Layer 1.
Rim with slight external flaring. Undecorated. Exterior and interior red. F41.
P00, D00, S01.

5. Rim, neck and shoulder sherd of carinated bowl with furrowed decoration.
Layer 3.
Everted rim,sharp shoulder carination. Decorated on neck by furrows. Colour not recorded. Exterior haematite coated. F12.
P01, D02, S04.
Residual

6. Rim sherd of vessel.
Layer 1.
Slightly inturning rim with fingertip impressions, broad furrow beneath. Exterior and interior black. F32.
P00, D24, S01.

7. Rim and neck sherd of vessel, probably carinated jar.
Layer 3.
Upright rim with slight internal bevel. Fingernail impressions on rim. Exterior and interior grey to buff; exterior shows sweep marks from vegetable wiping, interior fine horizontal marking. F13.
P27, D21, S03.
Residual

Enclosure II Pit 5

Fig. 3.18

1. Almost complete profile of dish.
10 sherds, some joining. T-shaped rim with rounded external and internal projections, fairly shallow body. Undecorated. Exterior and interior brown; smooth; traces of a slip and burnishing on exterior. Poorly fired, fabric friable and soft. F21. PS 36.
P44, D00, S03.

2. Rim to below shoulder profile of vessel, probably pedestal jar.
2 sherds, not joining. Slightly everted rim, rounded shoulder carination; possibly originally had a pear-shaped body and pedestal base. Undecorated. Exterior grey to brown, interior black; both surfaces coated with a slip; burnished. Poorly fired, fabric friable and soft. F21. PS 101.
?P43, D00, S02.

3. Almost complete profile of pedestal jar.
35 sherds, some joining. Everted rim with small external lip, rounded shoulder, pear-shaped body and stout quoit-shaped pedestal base. No decoration. Exterior and interior dark brown; possibly coated with a slip; burnished; interior weathered. Poorly fired so fabric friable and soft. Fabric with sparse coarse shell, fine sand and some vegetable matter: Wilson F33.
P43, D00, S02.

4. Almost complete profile of large `situla' jar.
21 sherds, some joining. Slightly everted rim with small external lip, gentle shoulder carination, tall body. No decoration. Exterior dark grey to buff, interior black; exterior rough, interior pitted and sooty. Fabric with abundant coarse shelly inclusions: Wilson F31. Williams PS 102.
P22, D00, S01.

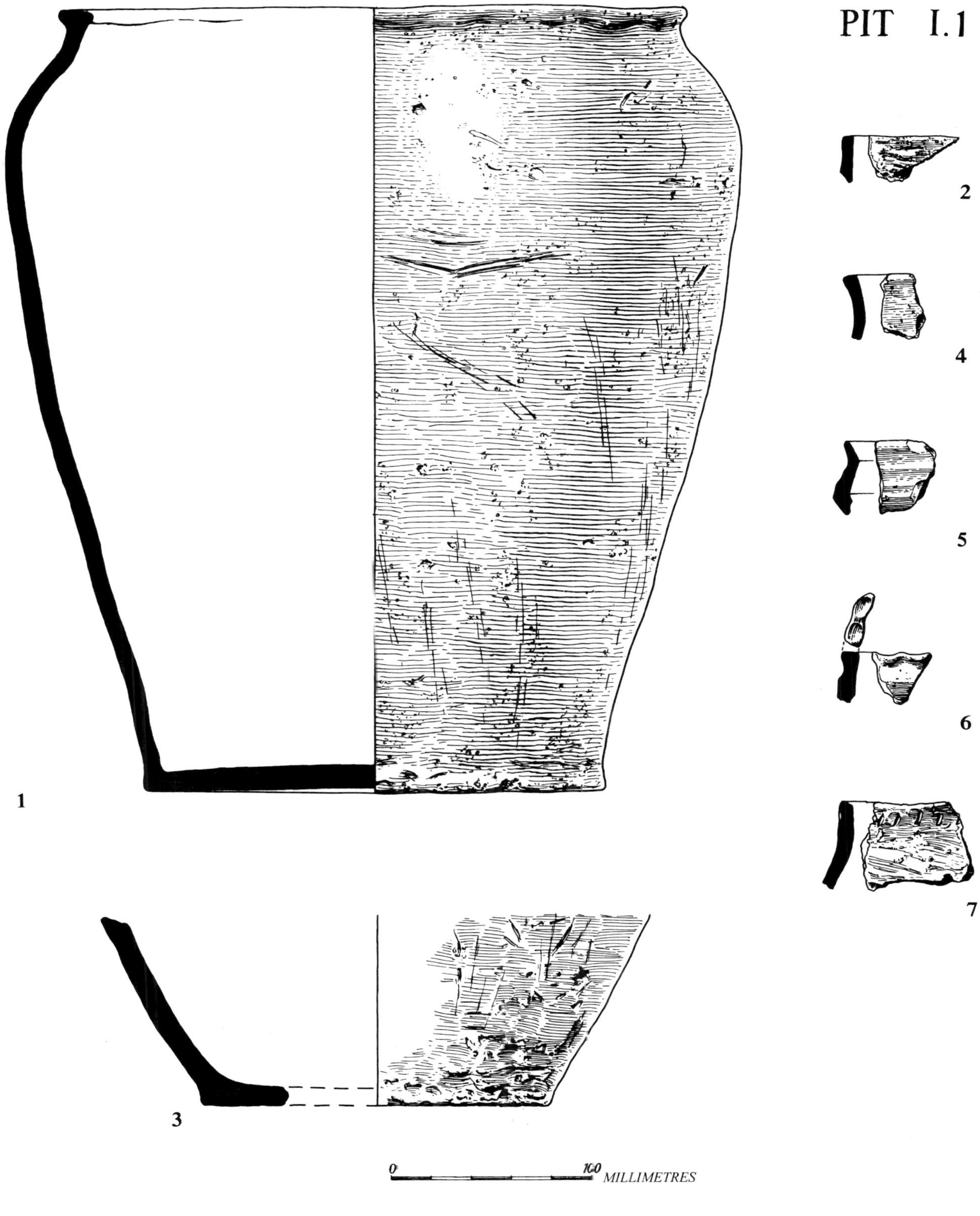

Fig. 3.17 Pottery from Enclosure I Pit 1 (scale 1:3)

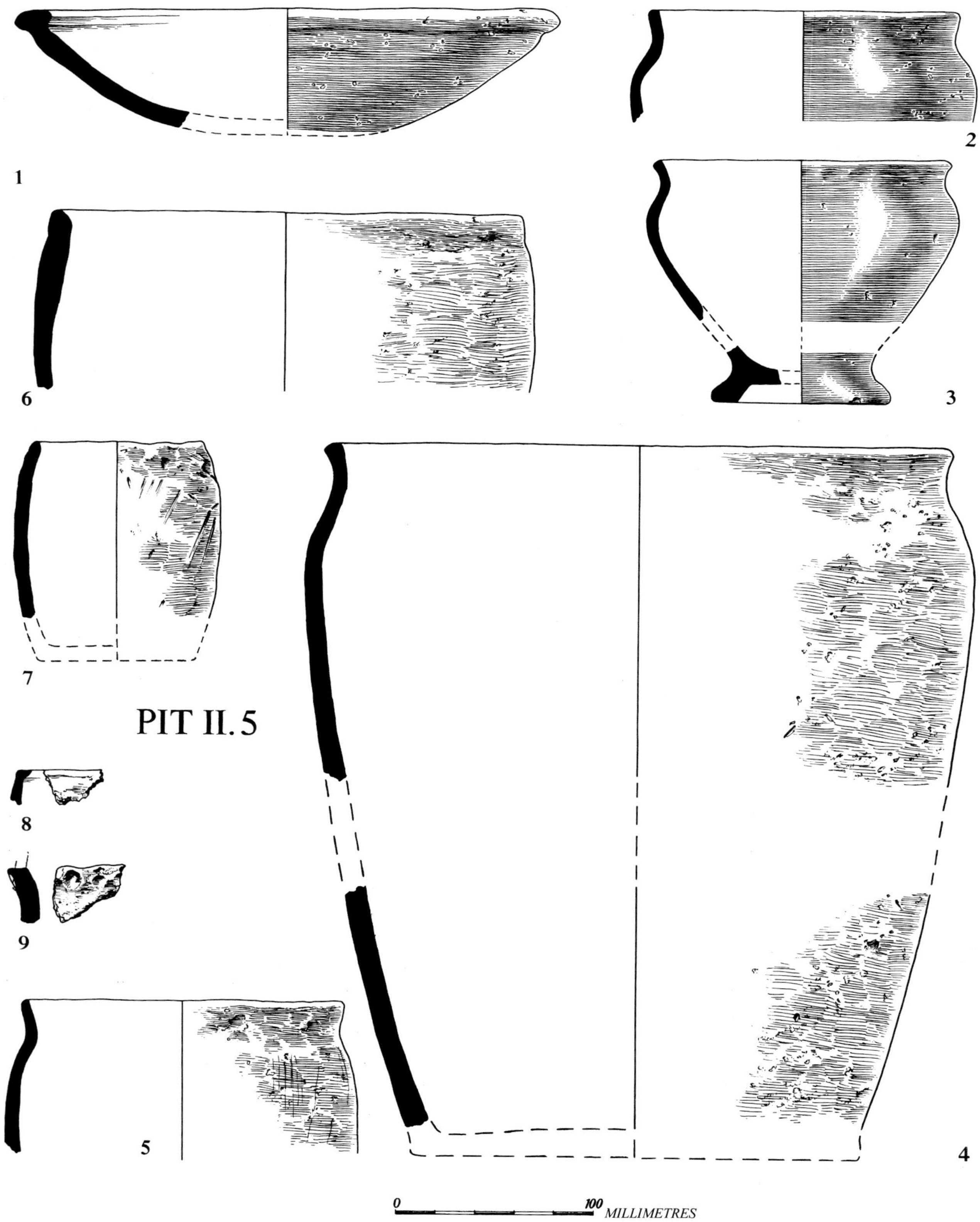

Fig. 3.18 Pottery from Enclosure II Pit 5 (scale 1:3)

5. Rim to below shoulder profile of `situla' jar.
8 sherds, some joining. Everted rim, slight shoulder carination, straight body profile. No decoration. Exterior dark grey to buff, interior black; exterior rough, interior sooty. Probably a cooking pot. Fabric with abundant coarse shelly inclusions: Wilson F31. Williams PS 103.
P22, D00, S01.

6. Rim and body profile of barrel jar.
3 joining sherds. Thick, rounded rim with internal ledge, straight body profile. No decoration. Exterior grey to black, interior red; exterior rough, interior pitted. Fabric with abundant coarse shelly inclusions: Wilson F31. Williams PS 104.
P52a, D00, S01.

7. Almost complete profile of barrel jar.
10 sherds, some joining. Rounded, inturning rim, tall curved body profile. Undecorated. Exterior buff to grey, interior grey. F13. PS 105.
P17, D00, S01.

8. Rim sherd from dish.
Flat-topped rim with internal lip, small groove below rim on exterior. Undecorated. Exterior and interior light brown. F31.
P40, D00, S01.

9. Rim and neck sherd from vessel.
Flat-topped rim with fingertip impressions. Exterior and interior orange; weathered. F42. A rubbish survival from I.A.
P00, D21, S01.

Enclosure II Pit 37

Fig. 3.19

1. Almost complete profile of dish.
Layer 3.
16 sherds, some joining. T- shaped rim with thin external and internal projections, fairly shallow body, possibly a slight footring. Undecorated. Exterior and interior light red; smooth, burnished surfaces. F21. PS 37.
cf. Bretz Mahle, Pl. 121, 2.
P40, D00, S02.

2. Rim sherd from, probably pedestal jar.
Layer 3.
Everted rim with rounded tip, groove on interior. Undecorated. Exterior and interior brown; burnished surfaces. F12.
?P43, D00, S02.

3. Shoulder sherds from jar.
Layer 3.
2 sherds. Rounded shoulder carination, groove at the top. Undecorated. Exterior and interior black. F31.
?P37a, D00, S02.

4. Rim sherds from jar.
Layer 3.
2 sherds, joining. Everted rim with squared tip. Undecorated. Exterior and interior light brown; rough surfaces. F31. PS 39.
P56, D00, S01.

5. Rim and body profile of jar.
Layer 2.
2 sherds. Everted rim with rounded tip, gently curving body profile. Undecorated. Exterior and interior light red, rough surfaces. F31. PS 40.
P56, D00, S01.

6. Almost complete profile of tall `situla' jar.
Layer 4.
Many sherds. Flat-topped rim with protruding external lip, fairly straight neck, gentle shoulder carination, tall body and flat base. Undecorated. Exterior and interior dark grey; rough surfaces. F21. PS 38.
P22, D00, S01.

7. Body sherd from pedestal jar.
Layer 3.
Junction of lower body and pedestal. Undecoratedn. Exterior and interior red brown to black; burnished surfaces. Fairly friable and soft. F13. PS 66.
Similar to Pit II.5, no.3.
P43, D00, S02.

8. Rim to below shoulder profile of 'situla' jar.
Layer 3.
2 sherds. Flat-topped, upright rim, curved shoulder. Undecorated. Exterior and interior red; rough. F31.
Probably same vessel as no. 9 (below).
P22, D00, S01.

9. Lower body and base of 'situla' jar.
Layer 3.
4 sherds. Inward-curving lower body and flat base which thickens towards the centre. Undecorated. Exterior and interior red; rough surfaces; vegetable impressions on underside of base. F31.
Probably the same vessel as no. 8 (above).
P22, D00, S01.

Fig. 3.20

Enclosure II Pit 41

1. Partially complete profile of rounded shoulder jar.
5 sherds, some joining. Everted rim with slight external lip, round shouldered. Undecorated. Exterior brown to black, interior

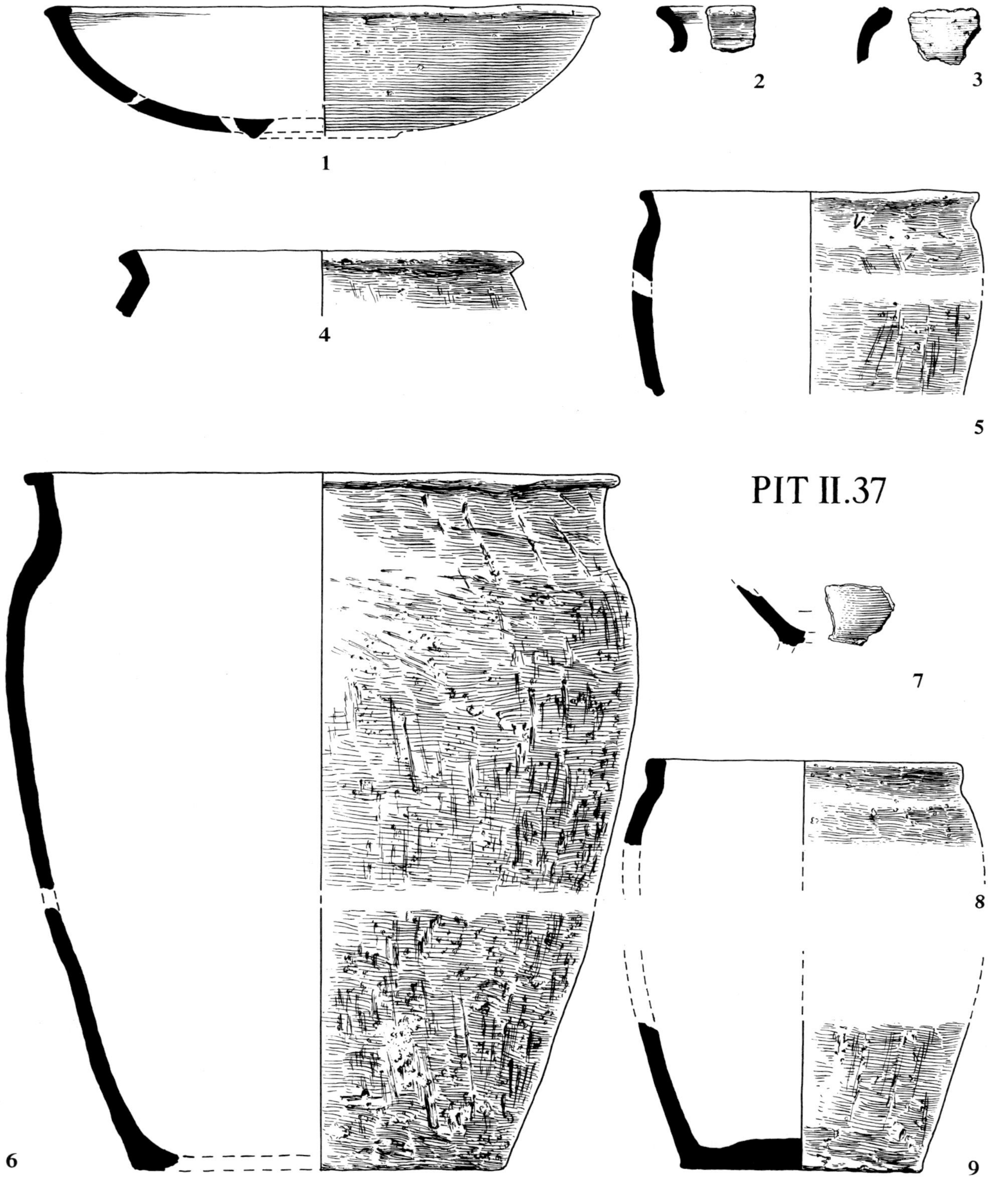

Fig. 3.19 Pottery from Enclosure II Pit 37 (scale 1:3)

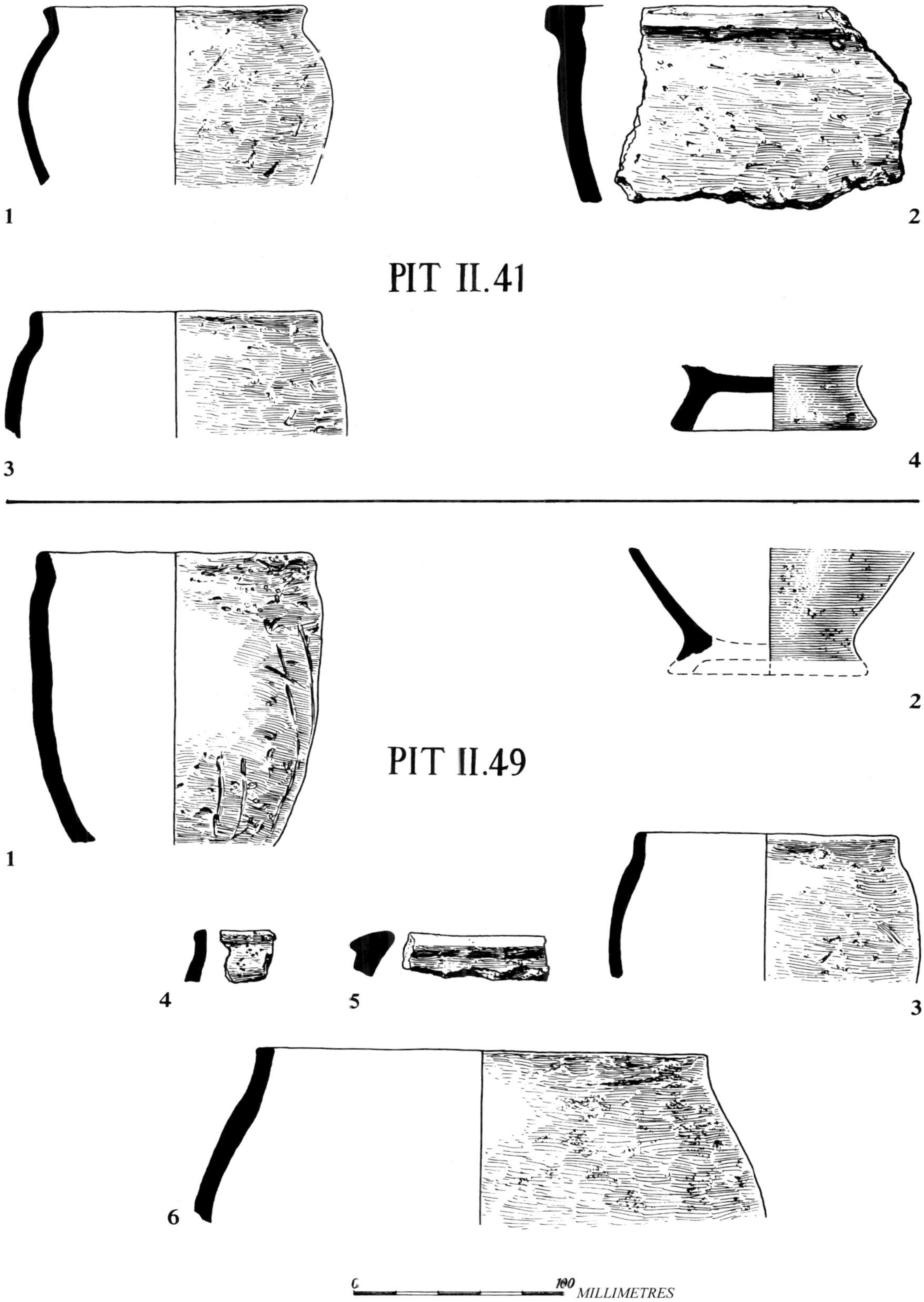

Fig. 3.20 Pottery from Enclosure II Pit 41 and Pit 49 (scale 1:3)

black; burnt and weathered. F11.
P37b, D00, S01.

2. Rim and body sherds from large jar.
9 joining sherds. Heavy, flat-topped rim with squared-off, protruding external lip, short neck, slightly rounded shoulder (less in diameter than the lip). Undecorated. Exterior and interior brown to black. F31.
P46b, D00, S01.

3. Rim and body profile of globular jar.
9 sherds, some joining. Upright rounded rim, gentle shoulder carination. Undecorated. Exterior red to brown, interior brown to black; wiped surface; weathered. F13.
P36a, D00, S03.

4. Base sherds from pedestal jar.
6 joining sherds. Pedestal base. Undecorated. Exterior and interior brown to black; burnished; burnt and weathered. F13.
P43, D00, S02.

Enclosure II Pit 49

1. Partially complete profile of tall jar.
Layer 1.
Many sherds. Short, slightly everted rim, slight shoulder carination, body profile straight, inward curve towards base. Undecorated. Colour not recorded. F31.
P52a, D00, S01.

2. Lower body and base profile of pedestal jar.
Layer 2.
5 joining sherds. Lower body tapering in towards pedestal base. Undecorated. Exterior and interior red to black; exterior burnished; burnt and weathered. F21.
P43, D00, S02.

3. Rim and body profile of globular jar.
Layer 1.
6 sherds, some joining. Short, upright rim, rounded shoulder carination, fairly straight body profile. Undecorated. Exterior black, interior buff to black; burnt. F31.
P36b, D00, S01.

4. Rim and neck sherd from vessel.
Layer 1.
Upright rim with slight, rounded external projection. Undecorated. Exterior black, interior red brown to black; exterior smooth wiped. F31.
P00, D00, S03.

5. Rim sherd of jar.
Layer 2.
Fairly thick, overhanging rim. Undecorated. Exterior and interior red to brown; exterior smooth wiped. F31.
?P22, D00, S03.

6. Rim and body profile of jar.
Layer 1.
Flat-topped, upright rim, slightly rounded shoulder carination, outward-flaring body profile. Undecorated. Colour not recorded. F31.
P37b, D00, S01.

Enclosure II Pit 69/70

Fig. 3.21

1. Rim to upper body and lower body to base profile of jar.
Layer 1.
2 joining sherds form rim and upper body, 1 lower body and base sherd. Flat-topped everted rim, with slight internal lip, outward-flaring, rounded body profile, base very slightly curved. Undecorated. Exterior and interior grey; exterior shows signs of smoothing and vegetation impressions. F42.
P56, D00, S03.

2. Lower body and base profile of jar, probably carinated.
Layer 4.
4 joining sherds. Fairly straight body profile, insloping to flat base with rounded, slightly flaring outside edge. Undecorated. Exterior and interior light brown to grey; exterior smooth wiped. F31.
P27, D00, S03.

3. Rim and neck sherd of 'situla' jar.
Layer 1.
Upright rim with external projection, concave neck. Undecorated. Exterior and interior light grey; smoothed surfaces. F31.
P22, D00, S03.

4. Rim to below shoulder sherd from globular jar.
Layer 1.
Upright rim, short, gently rounded shoulder carination. Undecorated. Exterior and interior light red; smooth surfaces. F21.
P36a, D00, S01.

5. Rim and body sherd from barrel jar.
Layer 1.
Plain, inward curving rim and body. Undecorated. Exterior and interior light brown red, exterior smooth wiped. F21.
P17, D00, S03.

6. Rim sherd from jar.
Layer 4.
Rounded rim with very slight exterior and interior projections, wall flaring. Undecorated. Exterior and interior light red;

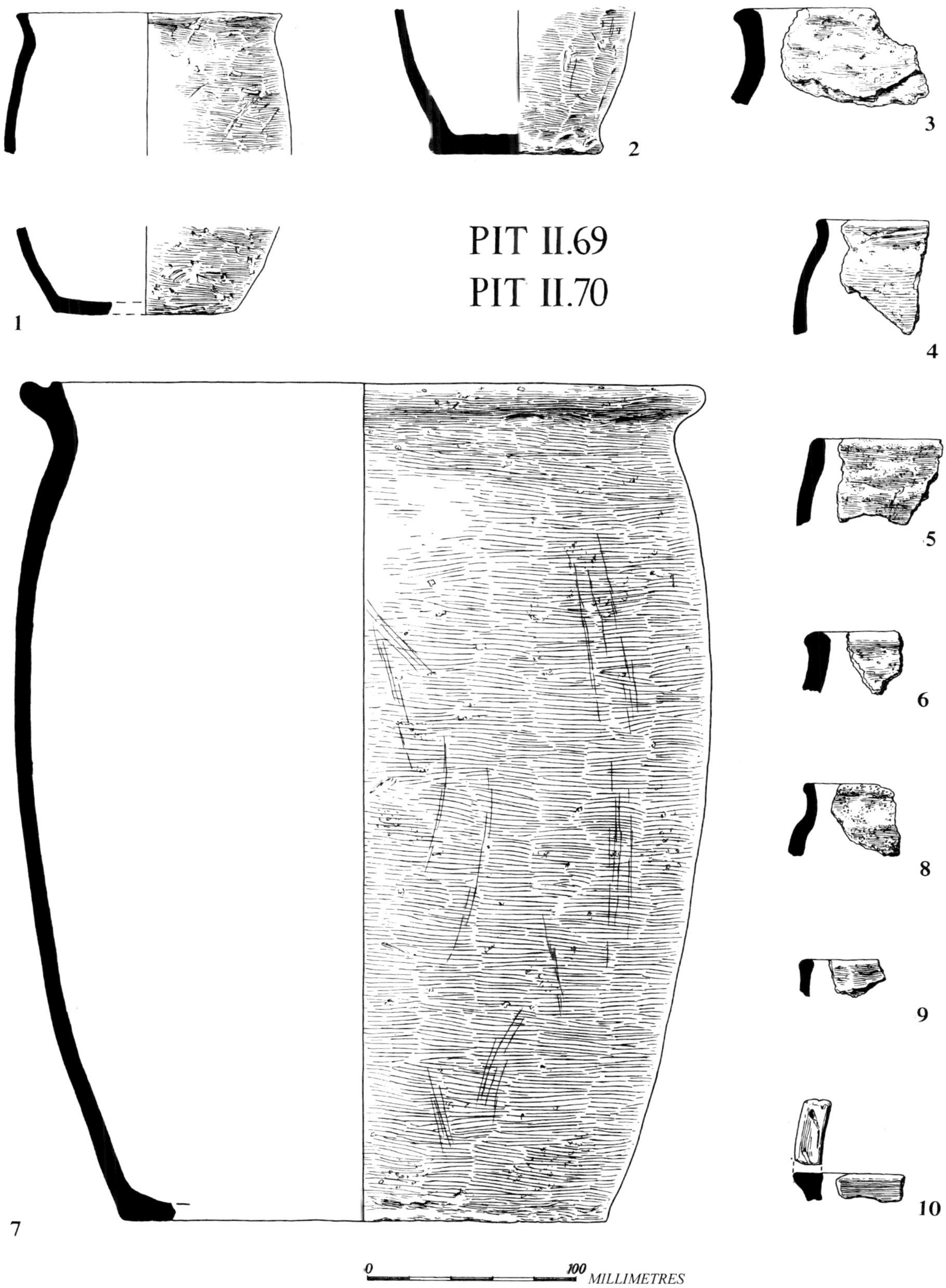

Fig. 3.21 Pottery from Enclosure II Pit 69/70 (scale 1:3)

exterior smooth wiped. F21.
?P52a, D00, S03.

7. Almost complete profile of large barrel jar.
Layer 6.
Many sherds. Rounded, everted rim with pronounced interior ledge, very gentle shoulder carination, tall body with fairly straight walls, insloping lower body and flat base. Undecorated. Exterior and interior buff to grey; exterior wiped. F31. PS 110.
P34, D00, S03.

8. Rim to below shoulder sherd from jar.
Layer 1.
Upright rim with small external lip, rounded shoulder carination. Undecorated. Exterior and interior light brown; exterior slightly burnished. F21.
P56, D00, S01.

9. Rim sherd from vessel.
Layer 4.
Upright rim with rounded tip. Fingertip impressions on rim edge. Exterior and interior dark grey; exterior wiped. F31.
P00, D21, S03.

10. Rim sherd from vessel.
Layer 1.
Flat-topped rim with external and slight internal projections. Incised diagonal lines on rim. Exterior and interior light brown to red. F13.
P00, D27, S01.

Fig. 3.22

Enclosure II Pit 40

1. Rim to below shoulder sherd of jar.
Layer 2.
Upright, flat-topped rim, concave neck, rounded shoulder carination. Undecorated. Exterior brown to black, interior beige. F12.
?P22, D00, S01.

2. Rim and neck sherd of 'situla' jar.
Layer 2.
Upright, flat-topped rim. Undecorated. Colour not recorded. F12.
P22, D00, S01.

3. Neck and shoulder sherds of carinated jar.
Layer 1.
3 joining sherds. Long, sloping neck, shoulder carination. Fingertip and nail impressions on shoulder. Exterior beige to brown, interior black; weathered. F41.
P25, D22, S01.

4. Neck and shoulder sherd from vessel.
Layer 1.
Slightly concave neck, shoulder carination. Fingertip impressions on shoulder. Exterior brown to black, interior black; burnt and weathered. F41.
P27, D22, S01.

5. Neck and shoulder sherd from vessel.
Layer 1.
Straight neck and shoulder carination. Series of horizontal grooves on neck. Colour not recorded; exterior smooth wiped. F11.
P00, D06, S03.

6. Neck and shoulder sherd from vessel, probably carinated jar.
Layer 1.
Rounded shoulder carination. Undecorated. Exterior red to black, interior brown to black; exterior smooth wiped; weathered. F12.
P27, D00, S03.

Enclosure II Pit 47

1. Rim and body sherds from dish.
2 joining sherds. Upright rim, inturned T-shaped tip with slight external and internal projections, carination below rim and insloping walls. Undecorated. Exterior and interior black; exterior wiped, charring on the interior; burnt and weathered. F31.
P40, D00, S03.

Enclosure II Pit 67

1. Rim to below shoulder sherds from pear-shaped jar.
Layer 4.
23 sherds. Small everted rim, concave neck, rounded shoulder. Undecorated. Exterior and interior black; exterior surface burnished; weathered. F12.
P47, D00, S02.

2. Base sherd of vessel.
Layer 1.
Flat base and curved lower body walls. Undecorated. Exterior buff to orange, interior black. F31.
P00, D00, S01.

3. Rim sherd from vessel with everted rim.
Layer 1.
Tall, everted rim. Undecorated. Exterior buff to black, interior buff to orange. F11.
P11, D00, S01.

4. Neck and shoulder sherd from carinated bowl with grooved decoration.
Layer 1.
Sloping neck and shoulder carination. 3 closely spaced furrows on neck. Exterior and interior buff to brown. F11.
P06a, D02, S01.

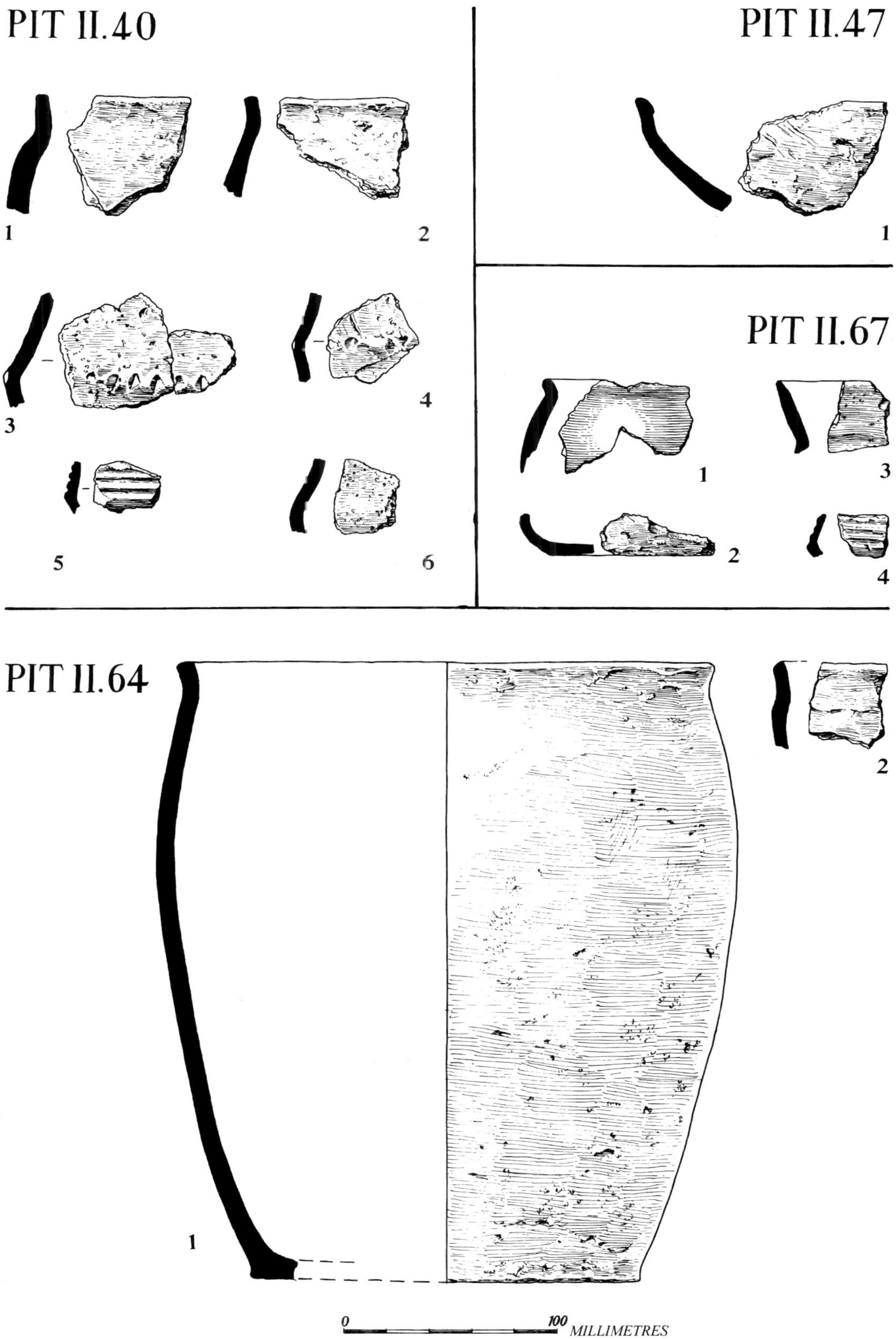

Fig. 3.22 Pottery from Enclosure II Pit 40, Pit 47, Pit 64, Pit 67 (scale 1:3)

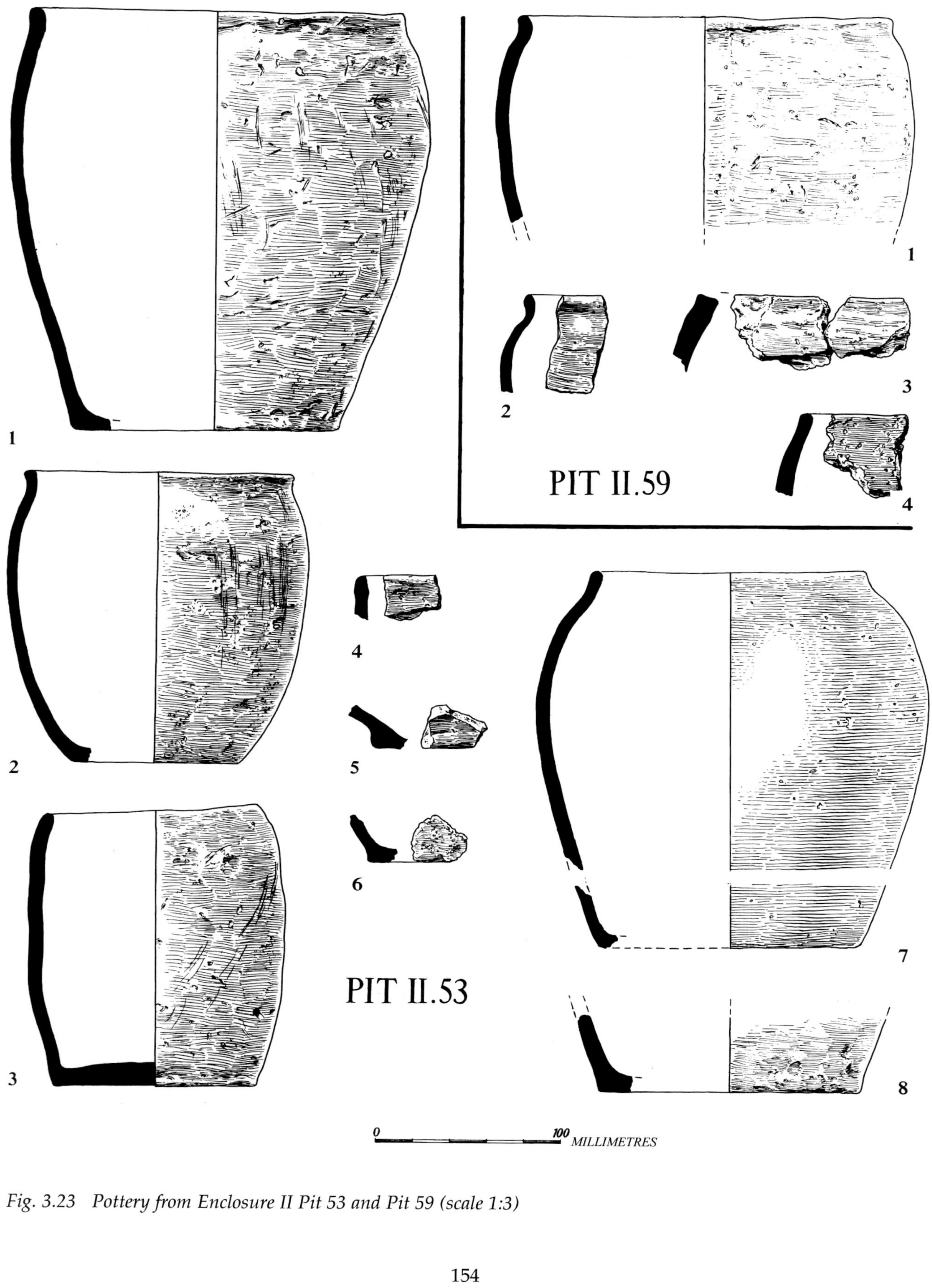

Fig. 3.23 Pottery from Enclosure II Pit 53 and Pit 59 (scale 1:3)

Enclosure II Pit 64

1. Almost complete profile of tall jar.
   Layer 2.
   22 sherds. Short, slightly everted rim, gentle shoulder carination, tall body, lower part tapering towards flat base. Undecorated. Exterior and interior brown to black; interior pitted; weathered and burnt. F21. PS 112.
   P52a, D00, S01.

2. Rim to below shoulder of squat 'situla' jar.
   Layer 2.
   Slightly everted rim, gentle shoulder carination. Undecorated. Exterior and interior black; both surfaces smooth wiped. F33.
   ?P22, D00, S03.

Fig. 3.23

Enclosure II Pit 53

1. Almost complete profile of tall jar.
   Layers 4 and 5.
   Many sherds. Short upright rim, gentle shoulder carination, tall body, lower part sloping inwards to flat base. Undecorated. Colour not recorded; vertical grass-wiping externally. F31.
   P52a, D00, S05.

2. Almost complete profile of tall globular jar.
   Layers 2, 3 and 4.
   6 sherds. Short, upright rim with external lip, rounded shoulder carination, rounded body profile, flat base. Undecorated. Exterior and interior dark brown; exterior slightly burnished. F31.
   P36b, D00, S02.

3. Complete profile of barrel jar.
   Layer 5.
   Many sherds: pot restored. Inturned rim, irregular, sagging body and flat base, thick walls. Undecorated. Exterior and interior red to brown with blackened rim; roughly smoothed with vegetable impressions; poorly fired, crumbly texture. F22.
   P17, D00, S03.

4. Rim sherd from vessel.
   Layer 2.
   Upright rim with uneven finish. Undecorated. Exterior and interior grey; exterior burnished; roughly smoothed. F13.
   P00, D00, S02.

5. Base sherd from vessel, probably bowl with rounded body.
   Layer 5.
   Flat base with short vertical outside edge and flaring wall. Undecorated. Exterior and interior brown; burnished surfaces. F13.
   ?P16, D00, S02.

6. Base sherd from vessel.
   Layer 2.
   Flat base with slight vertical outside edge with upward sloping wall. Undecorated. Exterior and interior brown. F21.
   P00, D00, S01.

7. Almost complete profile of jar.
   Layers 1, 2, 3, 4 and 5.
   Many sherds. Insloping rim, rounded shoulder carination, lower body tapering to base. Undecorated. Exterior and interior light brown to black, with blackened rim; exterior rough, with vegetable markings and finger sweeps, interior is pitted and very burnt towards the bottom. F31. PS 119.
   P37a, D00, S01.
   [A sample of the burnt food remains that were encrusted under rim inside this vessel were retained for analysis.]

8. Lower body and base of vessel.
   Layers 4 and 5.
   7 joining sherds. Flat base with upward sloping walls. Undecorated. Exterior and interior grey; smoothed surfaces. F31.
   P00, D00, S03.

Enclosure II Pit 59

1. Rim and body profile of jar.
   Layer 2.
   28 sherds, many joining. Short everted rim, rounded shoulder carination. No decoration. Exterior and interior light brown with blackened rim; exterior rough, interior pitted with area of burnt food residue encrusted near the bottom. F22.
   P52a, D00, S01.

2. Rim to below shoulder sherd from jar.
   Layer 1.
   Everted rim, concave neck, rounded shoulder carination. Undecorated. Exterior and interior black; exterior burnished. F13.
   P37a, D00, S02.

3. Rim sherds from jar, probably barrel.
   Layer 1.
   2 joining sherds. Thick rim with inward-sloping top, outsloping walls. Undecorated. Exterior and interior brown to red; exterior rough, interior surface eroded. F31.
   P39, D00, S01.

4. Rim sherd from jar, probably barrel.
   Layer 2.
   Rounded, inward sloping rim. Undecorated.

Exterior and interior black; burnished. F21.
P39, D00, S02.

Fig. 3.24

Enclosure II Pit 43

1. Rim, neck and shoulder sherds from pear-shaped jar.
4 joining sherds. Short everted rim, rounded shoulder carination. Undecorated. Exterior brown to black, interior red to brown; wiped surface. F32.
P47, D00, S03.

2. Rim and body sherds from jar.
2 sherds. Short everted rim, concave neck, rounded shoulder carination. Undecorated. Exterior black, interior grey to black; exterior burnished; burnt and weathered. F21.
P52a, D00, S02.

3. Rim sherd from jar.
Upright rim with insloping top. Undecorated. Exterior black, interior red to black; burnt and weathered. F32.
P52b, D00, S01.

Enclosure II Pit 44

1. Rim and body sherd from vessel.
Layer 2.
Slightly everted rim, gentle shoulder carination. Undecorated. Exterior red brown to black, interior black; burnt. F12.
P37a, D00, S01.

Enclosure II Pit 54

1. Rim and body profile of `saucepan' vessel.
Layers 1 and 2.
3 sherds, 2 joining. Thinned, upright rim, fairly straight body profile. Undecorated. Exterior black, interior black to brown; exterior burnished; weathered. F12.
P42, D00, S02.

2. Lower body and base of vessel.
Layer 2.
Flat base with outsloping walls. Undecorated. Exterior and interior red to brown. F32.
P00, D00, S01.

3. Partially complete profile of globular jar.
Layers 1 and 2.
22 sherds, many joining. Slightly everted rim, gentle shoulder carination, tall body with lower walls tapering towards the base. Undecorated. Exterior red to light brown and black, interior brown to black; probable grass wiping on exterior; burnt and weathered. F32.
P36a, D00, S05.

4. Rim sherd from vessel.
Layer 1.
Upright rim with fairly pointed external projection. Undecorated. Exterior red to brown, interior black. F31.
P00, D00, S01.

5. Rim sherd from vessel.
Layer 1.
Upright rim with flaring lip. Undecorated. Exterior buff to brown, interior red. F32.
P00, D00, S01.

6. Rim and body sherd of jar.
Layer 1.
Flat-topped rim, slightly flaring with external projection, gentle shoulder carination. Undecorated. Exterior and interior buff to red. F31.
P52b, D00, S01.

7. Rim and body sherd of c'saucepan' vessel.
Layer 2.
Plain, upright rim, straight body profile. Undecorated. Exterior black to brown, interior black; both surfaces burnished; burnt and weathered. F32.
P42, D00, S02.

8. Rim to below shoulder sherd of vessel.
Layer 2.
Plain, upright rim, slightly concave neck, gentle shoulder carination. Undecorated. Exterior and interior black; exterior wiped. F21.
P00, D00, S03.

Enclosure II Pit 51

1. Rim and body profile of barrel jar.
3 joining sherds. Plain, incurving rim. Undecorated. Exterior brown to black, interior buff to brown and black; exterior surface wiped; burnt and weathered. F21.
P17, D00, S03.

2. Rim and body sherd of globular jar.
Plain, upright rim, gentle shoulder carination. Undecorated. Exterior grey to black, interior grey to brown; weathered. F22.
P36a, D00, S01.

3. Rim and body sherd from vessel.
Upright rim with slight external and internal projection, slight contraction under rim, fairly straight body profile. Undecorated. Exterior

Fig. 3.24 (facing page) Pottery from Enclosure II Pit 43, Pit 44, Pit 51, Pit 54 (scale 1:3)

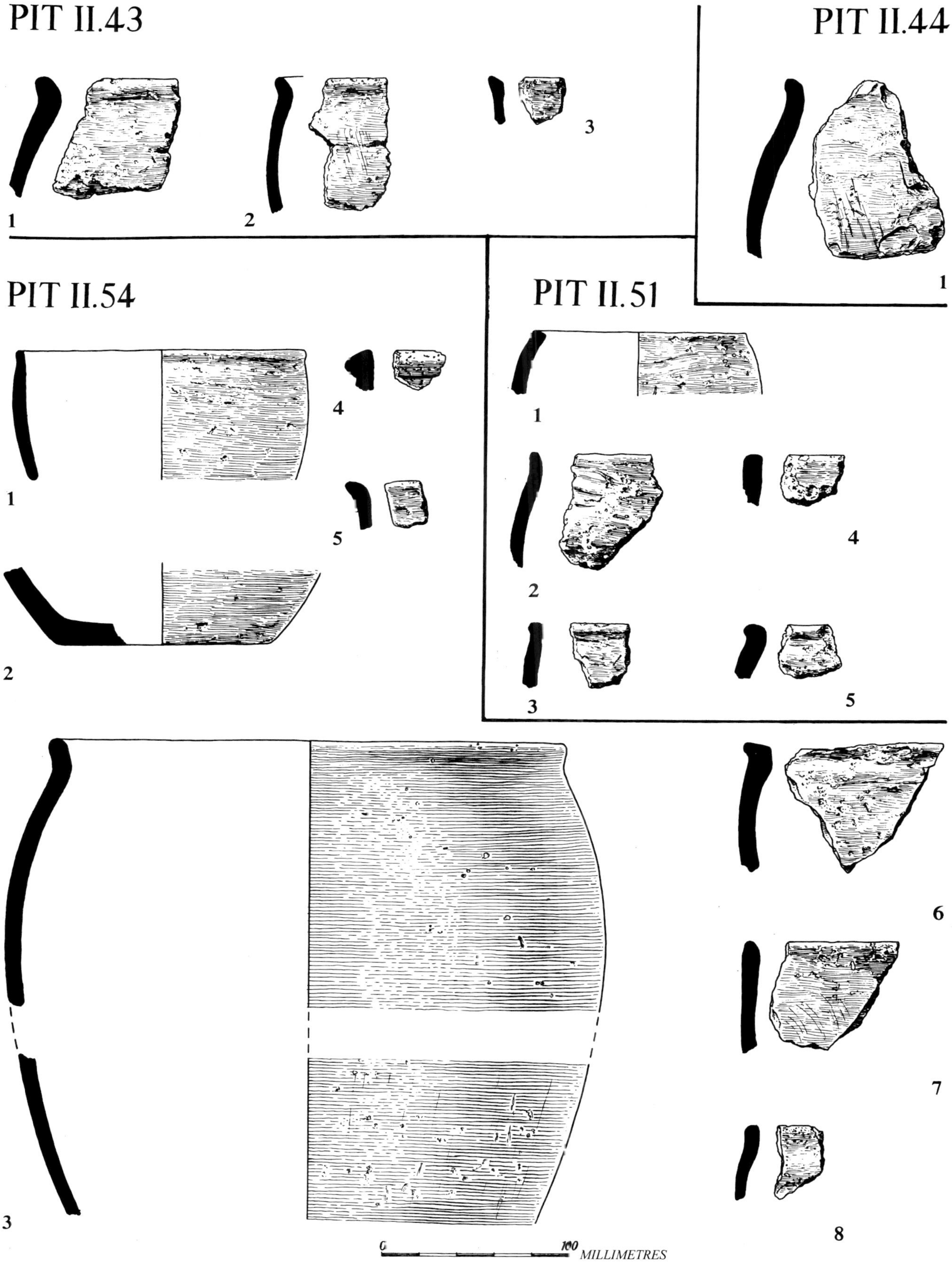
PIT II.43
1
2
3
PIT II.44
1
PIT II.54
1
2
3
4
5
PIT II.51
1
2
3
4
5
6
7
8
0
100
MILLIMETRES

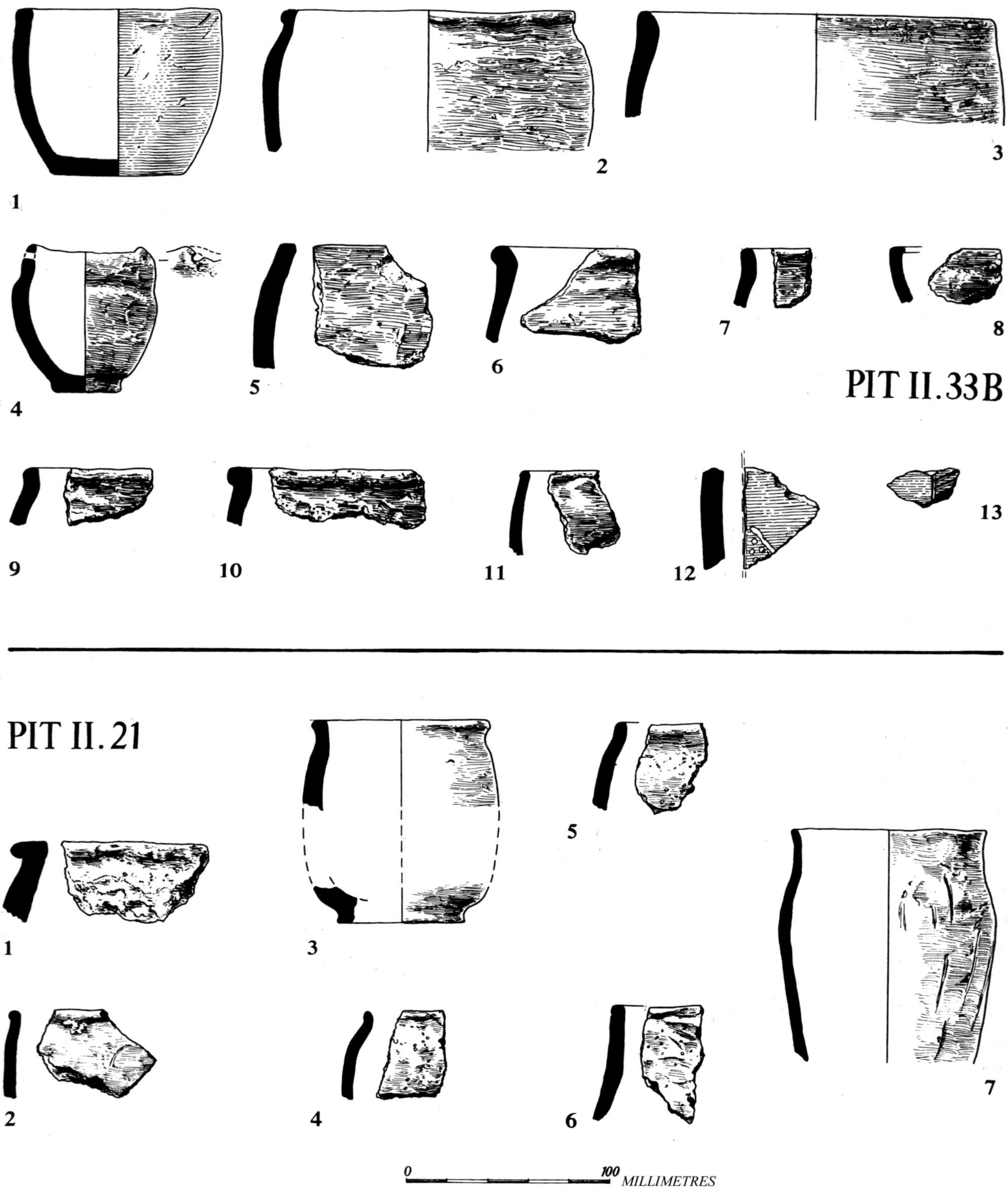

Fig. 3.25 Pottery from Enclosure II Pit 33B and Pit 21 (scale 1:3)

brown to black, interior beige to black; exterior possibly wiped, badly weathered. F12.
P00, D00, S01

4. Rim sherd of vessel.
Upright rim. Traces of finger tip impressions below rim. Exterior brown to orange, interior black; interior charred; burnt and weathered. F31.
P00, D25, S01.

5. Rim sherd of pear-shaped jar.
Rounded rim with external lip, outsloping walls. Undecorated. Exterior red brown to black, interior red to brown; weathered. F31.
P47, D00, S01.

Fig. 3.25

Enclosure II Pit 33B

1. Complete profile of miniature bowl.
Complete pot. Rounded rim, gently curving body and flat base. Undecorated. Colour not recorded; exterior wiped. F44.
P38, D00, S03.

2. Rim and body profile of jar.
2 joining sherds. Rim with rounded external lip, constricted neck, rounded shoulder carination, straight body. Undecorated. Exterior dark brown to black, interior light brown to dark brown; traces of burnishing on exterior surface. F31.
P37b, D00, S02.

3. Rim and body profile of 'saucepan' vessel.
Upright rim with inward-sloping top, almost straight body. Undecorated. Exterior buff, interior orange to red. F32.
P42, D00, S01.

4. Complete profile of miniature barrel jar.
Complete pot. Plain rim with small hole in raised lug, short neck, rounded shoulder carination, body tapering to a flat base with well defined, short vertical external edge. Undecorated. Exterior and interior red to light brown. F42.
P31b, D00, S01.
Possibly a crucible pot.

5. Rim and body sherd from jar.
Flat-topped, incurving rim, curved body. Undecorated. Colour not recorded. F12.
?P55, D00, S01.

6. Rim and body sherd from `saucepan' vessel.
Thick, everted rim with rounded tip, flaring body profile. Undecorated. Exterior patchy black, interior dark grey. F13.
P42, D00, S01.

7. Rim and body sherd from vessel.
Plain, upright rim. Undecorated. Exterior dark brown, interior light brown. F31.
P00, D00, S01.

8. Rim and body sherd from dish.
Flat-topped rim with small internal projection, incurved body profile. Undecorated. Exterior and interior buff to orange; exterior smooth wiped. F33.
P40, D00, S03.

9. Rim and body sherd from vessel.
Upright rim, external edge of tip downwards sloping. Undecorated. Exterior dark brown, interior black. F31.
P00, D00, S01.

10. Rim and body sherds from 'situla' jar.
2 joining sherds. Flat-topped rim with rounded external projection, slightly curved body. Undecorated. Exterior dark brown, interior red to brown. F31.
P22, D00, S01.

11. Rim and body sherd from vessel, probably barrel jar.
Slightly incurving rim, rounded tip with very slight external projection, curved body. Undecorated. Exterior dark brown, interior dark brown to black; exterior wiped. F32.
P39, D00, S03.

12. Body sherd from vessel.
Almost straight body profile. Decorated by incised dots with white inlay with linear border. Colour not recorded. F11.
P00, D11, S01.

13. Body sherd from vessel.
Decorated by hatched area with border. Colour not recorded; exterior haematite coated. F11.
F00, D34, S04.

Enclosure II Pit 21

1. Rim and body sherd from 'situla' jar.
Flat-topped rim with long external projection, outward-sloping body profile. Undecorated. Exterior brown to grey, interior brown to black. F31.
P22, D00, S01.

2. Rim and body sherd from 'saucepan' vessel.
Upright rim with small external lip, almost straight body. Undecorated. Exterior brown to black, interior black; exterior smooth wiped. F22.
P42, D00, S03.

3. Partially complete profile of miniature barrel jar.
   3 sherds, not joining. Slightly everted rim with small external lip, gently rounded shoulder carination, curved body, flat base. Undecorated. Exterior orange to brown, interior dark grey to black; possible smooth wiped areas on exterior surface. F41.
   P31a, D00, S03.

4. Rim and body sherd from pear-shaped jar.
   Short, slightly everted rim, concave neck, rounded shoulder, fairly straight body. Undecorated. Exterior orange to grey, interior orange; exterior wiped. F32.
   P47, D00, S03.

5. Rim and body sherd from globular jar.
   Upright rim, concave neck, gentle shoulder carination, flaring body profile. Undecorated. Exterior and interior beige to brown; exterior wiped. F22.
   P36a, D00, S03.

6. Rim and body sherd from jar.
   Upright rim, tall, straight upper neck, flaring lower neck. Undecorated. Exterior brown to black, interior black. F42.
   P37b, D00, S01.

7. Almost complete profile of `situla' jar.
   7 sherds, some joining. flared rim, straight neck, rounded shoulder carination, insloping body. Undecorated. Exterior black, interior brown to black; surfaces possibly wiped, vertical striations (probably accidental) on exterior. F12.
   P22 (small), D00, S03.

Fig. 3.26

Enclosure II Pit 50

1. Rim and body profile from globular jar.
   Layer 2.
   7 sherds, 2 joining. Insloping rim with rounded external projection, gentle shoulder carination, curved body. Undecorated. Exterior black, interior red brown to buff, exterior possibly wiped, burnt. F31.
   P36b, D00, S01.

2. Rim and body profile of barrel jar.
   Layer 1.
   Plain rim, slightly incurving, slightly incurving body. Undecorated. Exterior black to orange, interior black; both surfaces wiped. F13.
   P17, D00, S03.

3. Lower body and base profile from vessel.
   Layers 1 and 2.
   3 sherds, 2 joining. Insloping lower body profile, flat base. Undecorated. Exterior orange, interior beige to black. F13.
   P00, D00, S01.

4. Rim to below shoulder sherd from jar.
   Layer 2.
   Outward flaring rim, rounded shoulder carination, insloping body profile. Undecorated. Exterior and interior buff to orange; burnt and weathered. F52.
   P37a, D00, S01.

5. Rim and neck sherd from vessel.
   Layer 2.
   Upright rim with fairly pointed external projection. Undecorated. Exterior black, interior buff to black; weathered. F12.
   P00, D00, S01.

6. Rim and neck sherd from vessel.
   Layer 1.
   Everted rim. Undecorated. Exterior and interior brown to black; traces of burning on exterior surface. F13.
   P00, D00, S01.

Enclosure II Pit 52

1. Rim and body sherd from vessel.
   Layer 1.
   Upright rim, outsloping body. Undecorated. Exterior black, interior buff to black; interior pitted. F21.
   P00, D00, S01.

2. Rim and body sherd from vessel, probably barrel jar.
   Layer 1.
   Plain rim, slightly incurving, body. Undecrated. Exterior orange to black, interior brown; weathered and burnt. F31.
   ?P17, D00, S01.

3. Rim and body sherd from vessel.
   Layer 1.
   Slightly everted rim. Undecorated. Exterior and interior black; exterior smooth wiped; fairly weathered. F32.
   P00, D00, S03.

4. Rim sherd from vessel.
   Layer 1.
   Thick, slightly everted rim. Undecorated. Exterior brown, interior black; weathered. F32.
   P00, D00, S01.

5. Rim sherd from vessel.
   Layer 1.
   Short, slightly everted rim. Undecorated. Colour not recorded. F32.
   P00, D00, S01.

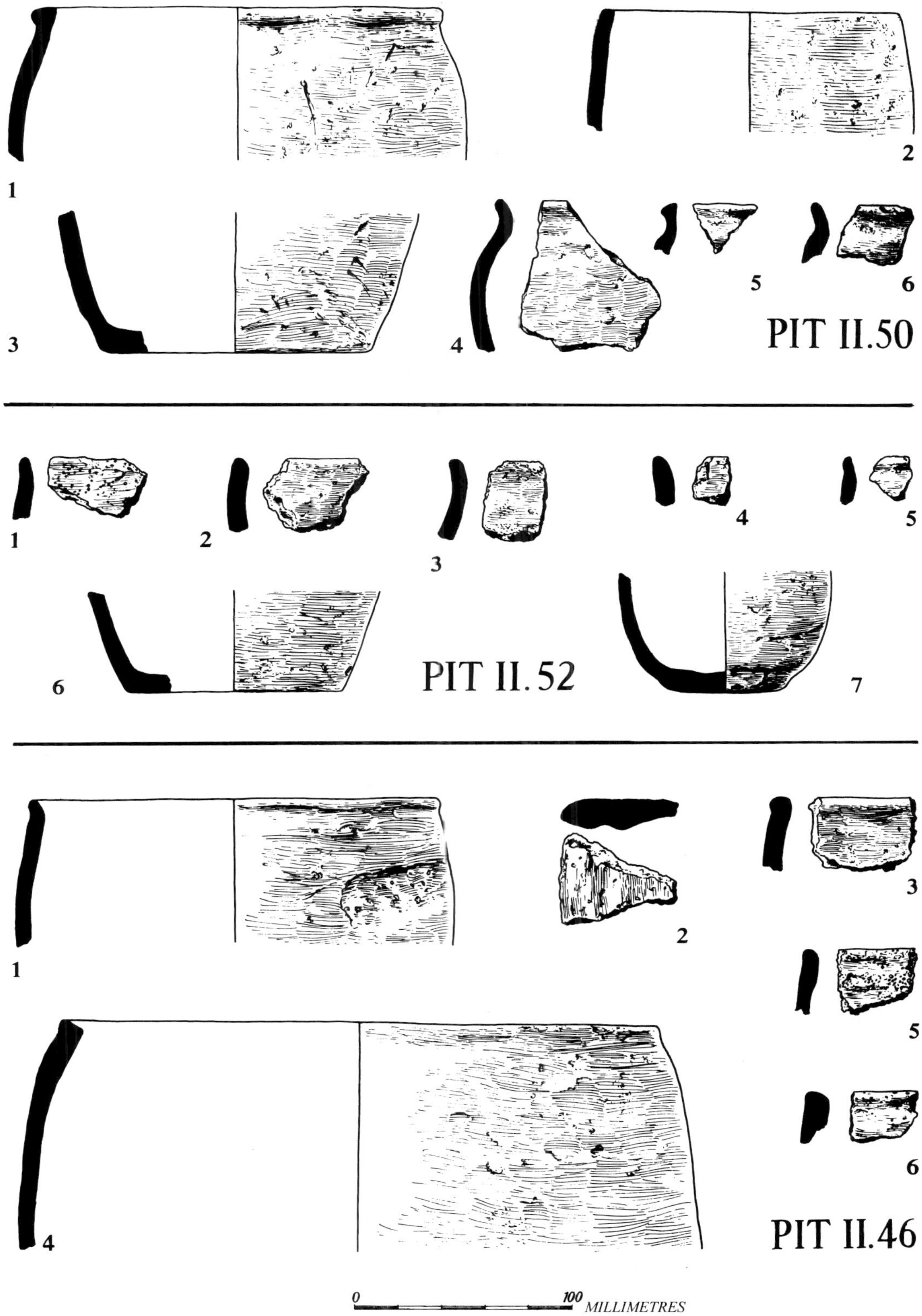

Fig. 3.26 Pottery from Enclosure II Pit 50, Pit 52, Pit 46 (scale 1:3)

6. Lower body and base profile of vessel.
Layer 1.
3 joining sherds. Insloping lower body, flat base. Undecorated. Exterior buff to brown, interior beige to black; exterior wiped; interior weathered. F32.
P00, D00, S03.

7. Lower body and base profile of barrel jar.
Layer 2.
Complete base. Curved lower body, flat base, small diameter. Undecorated. Exterior black, interior brown to black. F21.
P17, D00, S01.

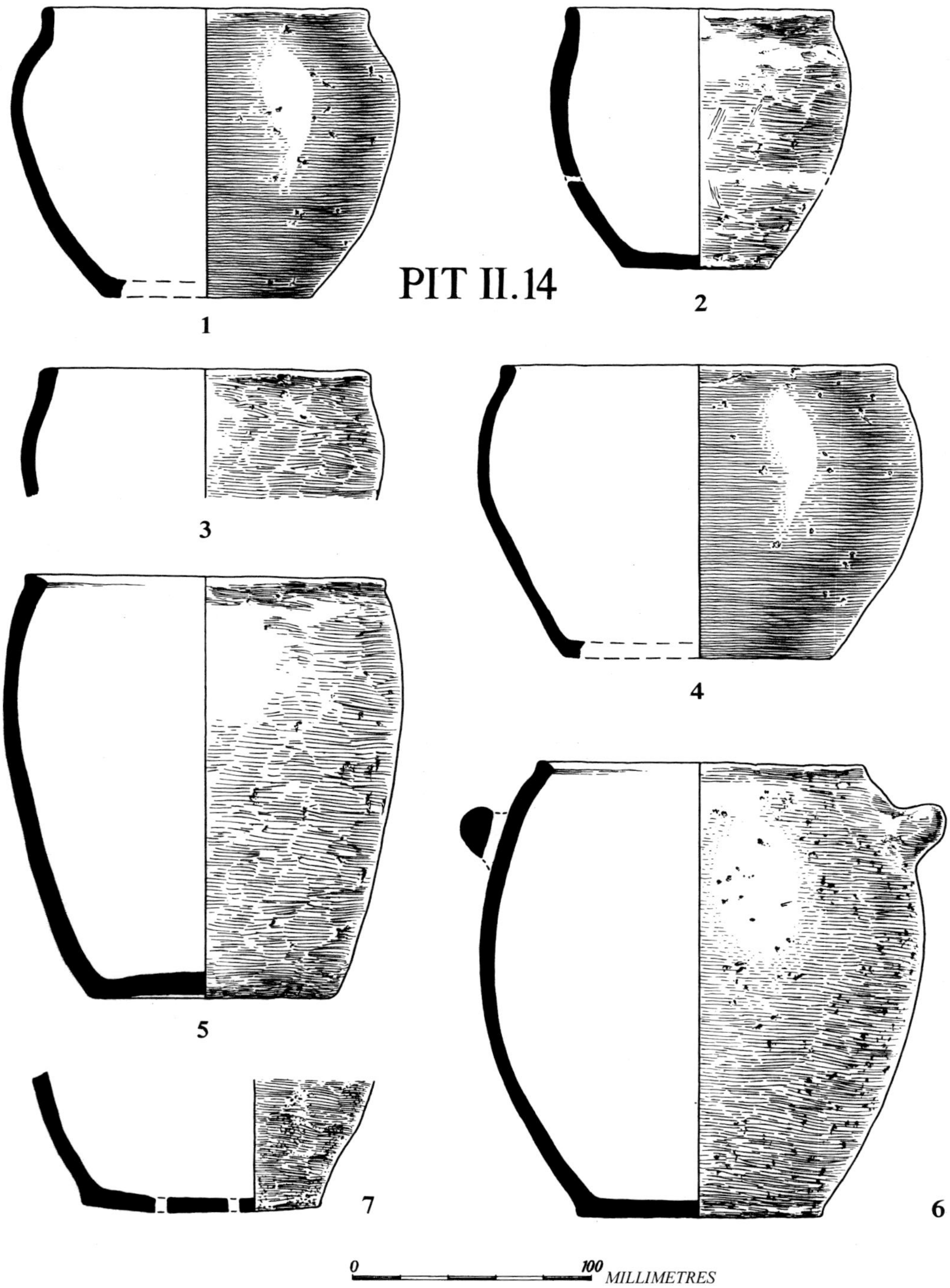

Fig. 3.27 Pottery from Enclosure II Pit 14 (scale 1:3)

Enclosure II Pit 46

1. Rim and body profile of jar.
4 sherds. Short, everted rim, slightly curved body. Undecorated. Exterior and interior black; exterior burnished. F31.
P52a, D00, S02.

2. Lid sherd to fit jar.
Lid with smooth top and uneven underside. Undecorated. Exterior red, interior brown. F31.
P45, D00, S01.

3. Rim and body sherd from vessel.
Rounded, slightly incurved rim with slight external projection, curved body. Undecorated. Exterior black, interior red to brown; exterior wiped; burnt. F22.
P00, D00, S03.

4. Rim and body profile of jar.
17 sherds, some joining. Incurving rim with internal ledge, curved shoulder carination, straight body. Undecorated. Exterior and interior black; burnt and weathered. F31.
P52b, D00, S01.

5. Rim sherd from vessel.
Plain rim, slightly incurving. Undecorated. Interior red to black, interior black, exterior wiped; weathered. F21.
P00, D00, S03.

6. Rim sherd from vessel.
Thick rim, slightly incurving. Undecorated. Exterior and interior black. F31.
P00, D00, S01.

Fig. 3.27

Enclosure II Pit 14

1. Almost complete profile of squat jar.
9 sherds, most joining. Upright rim with very slight external lip, high, rounded shoulder carination, globular body, flat base. Undecorated. Exterior and interior grey to black, burnished black slip on exterior. F12. PS 113.
P37a, D00, S02.

2. Almost complete profile of globular jar.
9 sherds, most joining. Upright rim, rounded shoulder carination, globular body, flat base. No decoration. Exterior and interior light brown to grey, horizontal and vertical wiping on exterior. F21. PS 114.
P36a, D00, S05.

3. Rim to below shoulder profile of jar.
Insloping rim with slight external lip, rounded shoulder carination, inward-sloping body profile. Undecorated. Exterior and interior dark grey; roughly smoothed surfaces. F21. PS 115.
P37b, D00, S03.

4. Almost complete profile of squat jar.
23 sherds, many joining. Flat-topped rim, high, rounded shoulder carination, insloping body, flat base. Undecorated. Exterior and interior light brown; surfaces burnished; burnt. F33. PS 116.
P37b, D00, S02.
Rim dia. 160mm. Height *c* 130mm.

5. Complete profile of tall jar.
Numerous sherds. Incurving rim with internal bevel and slight external lip, gentle shoulder carination, incurving body, slightly concave base. Undecorated. Exterior red brown, interior red, blackened around rim; exterior smoothed and vertically wiped, interior pitted. F13. PS 117.
P52b, D00, S03.
Rim dia. *c*150mm, Height *c*185mm.

6. Complete profile of globular tall jar with a pair of lugs
Numerous sherds. Incurving rim with internal bevel and slight external lip, globular body, flat base. Below rim are a pair of applied lugs with neat vertical perforations and possible string marks. Undecorated. Exterior light brown to black, interior dark brown; exterior smoothed, surfaces burnished and pitted. F31.
P36b, D00, S02.
Rim dia. *c*138mm, Height *c* 198mm.

7. Lower body and base of jar.
5 joining sherds. Insloping lower body profile, slightly sagging base. Drilled perforations 5mm in diameter in base, possibly a strainer. Undecorated. Exterior and interior orange brown; exterior wiped. F21.
P00, D00, S03.

Fig. 3.28

Enclosure II Pit 11

1. Rim and body profile of jar.
21 sherds, many joining. Flat-topped, slightly everted rim, rounded shoulder carination, straight body. Undecorated. Exterior and interior dark brown to red, traces of burnishing on exterior; weathered. F19.
P37b, D00, S02.

2. Rim and body sherds from `situla' jar.
2 sherds, not joining. Insloping rim with long external projection, insloping body. Undecorated. Exterior red, interior dark brown to red. F32.
?P22, D00, S01.

3. Almost complete profile of tall jar.
Numerous sherds. Rounded, everted rim, tall body with curved profile. Undecorated. Exterior dark brown to red, interior red. F13.
P52a, D00, S01.

Enclosure II Pit 55

1. Rim and body profile of barrel jar.
Layer 2.
12 joining sherds. Thinned, incurving rim, rounded shoulder carination, insloping body. Undecorated. Exterior brown to black, interior black. F22.
P51, D00, S01.

2. Rim and neck sherds from vessel, probably pedestal jar.
Layer 1.
2 sherds. Everted rim with rounded tip. Undecorated. Exterior and interior brown to black; exterior burnished. F13.
?P43, D00, S02.

3. Rim sherds of vessel.
Layer 2.
2 sherds. Plain, insloping rim. Undecorated. Exterior black, interior brown, possibly burnt. F31.
P00, D00, S01.

4. Rim and body sherd of jar.
Layer 1.
Upright, rounded rim, rounded shoulder carination. Undecorated. Exterior beige to black, interior beige to brown; weathered and burnt. F21.
P37a, D00, S01.

5. Rim sherd from vessel.
Layer 1.
Thick, everted rim with squared tip. Undecorated. Exterior and interior brown to black; weathered and probably burnt. F13.
P00, D00, S01.

6. Rim and body profile of 'saucepan' vessel.
Layer 1.
10 sherds. Upright rim with internal bevel and slight external lip, straight body. Undecorated. Exterior red brown to black, interior red to brown; exterior wiped; probably burnt. F32.
P42, D00, S03.

Enclosure II Pit 65

1. Rim to body sherd of jar.
Layer 1.
Slightly flared rim with squared tip, almost straight body. Undecorated. Exterior buff brown to black, interior brown to orange red; exterior wiped. F32.
P37a, D00, S03.

2. Rim to body sherd of jar.
Layer 1.
2 joining sherds. Upright, slightly rounded rim, gentle shoulder carination. Undecorated. Exterior and interior orange to black; exterior wiped. F31.
P52a, D00, S03.

Fig. 3.29

Enclosure II Pit 22

1. Partially complete profile of 'saucepan' vessel.
16 sherds, many joining. Slightly incurving rim, groove below tip on exterior, gently curving body, flat base. Decorated below groove by incised 'eyebrow' pattern. Exterior and interior dark brown to black; surfaces burnished. F12.
P50, D30, S02.

2. Almost complete profile of globular jar.
14 sherds. Slightly everted rim, gentle shoulder carination, rounded body profile, flat base. Decorated on body by patterns of incised lines: hatching, curving parallel lines and individual lines. Exterior dark brown to black, interior red orange to brown; exterior burnished. F32.
P36b, D33, S02.

3. Rim and neck sherd of pear-shaped jar.
Gently everted rim, long, concave neck. Undecorated. Exterior buff to red, interior red to black; smooth wiped. F21.
P35, D00, S03.

4. Rim and neck sherd of 'saucepan' vessel.
Short, everted rim. Undecorated. Exterior and interior black; surfaces burnished. F32.
P42, D00, S02.

Enclosure II Pit 18

1. Rim and body profile of jar.
5 sherds, some joining. Upright rim, gently rounded shoulder carination. Undecorated. Exterior red to orange, interior brown to black; possible fingernail marks under rim; traces of burning on exterior. F31.
P52a, D00, S01.

2. Rim and body sherds of `saucepan' vessel.
2 sherds, not joining. Upright rim with slight internal bevel, almost straight body. No decoration. Exterior and interior dark brown to black. F31.
P50, D00, S01.

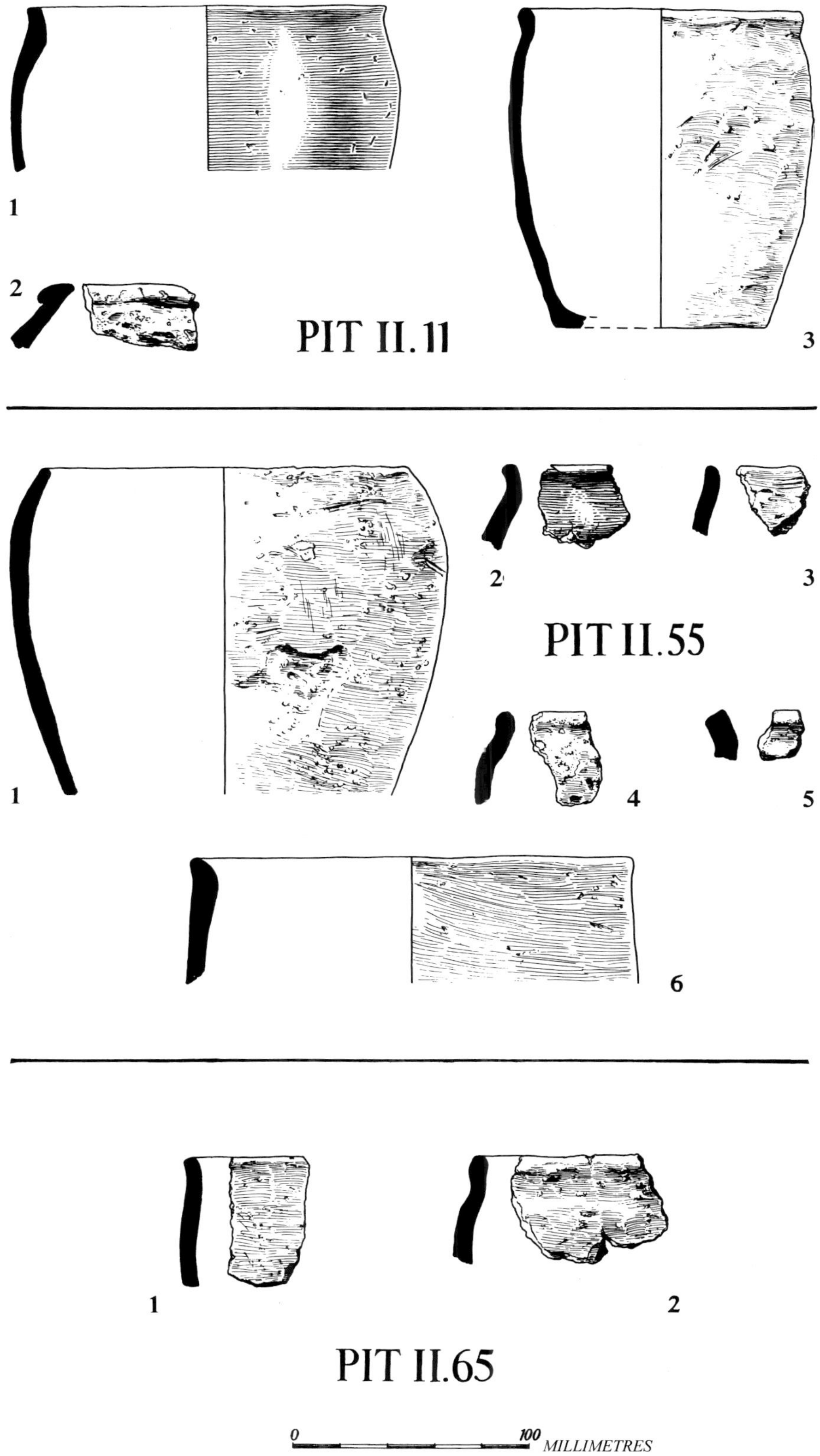

Fig. 3.28 Pottery from Enclosure II Pit 11, Pit 55, Pit 65 (scale 1:3)

3. Rim and body sherd from pear-shaped jar. Short, everted rim, outloping body. Undecorated. Exterior buff to dark brown, interior buff to brown; possible traces of wiping below rim. F12. P47, D00, S01.

4. Rim and body sherd form jar, pear-shaped jar. Tip of rim everted, curved body. Undecorated. Exterior dark brown, interior buff, traces of burnishing on the exterior. F32. ?P47, D00, D01.

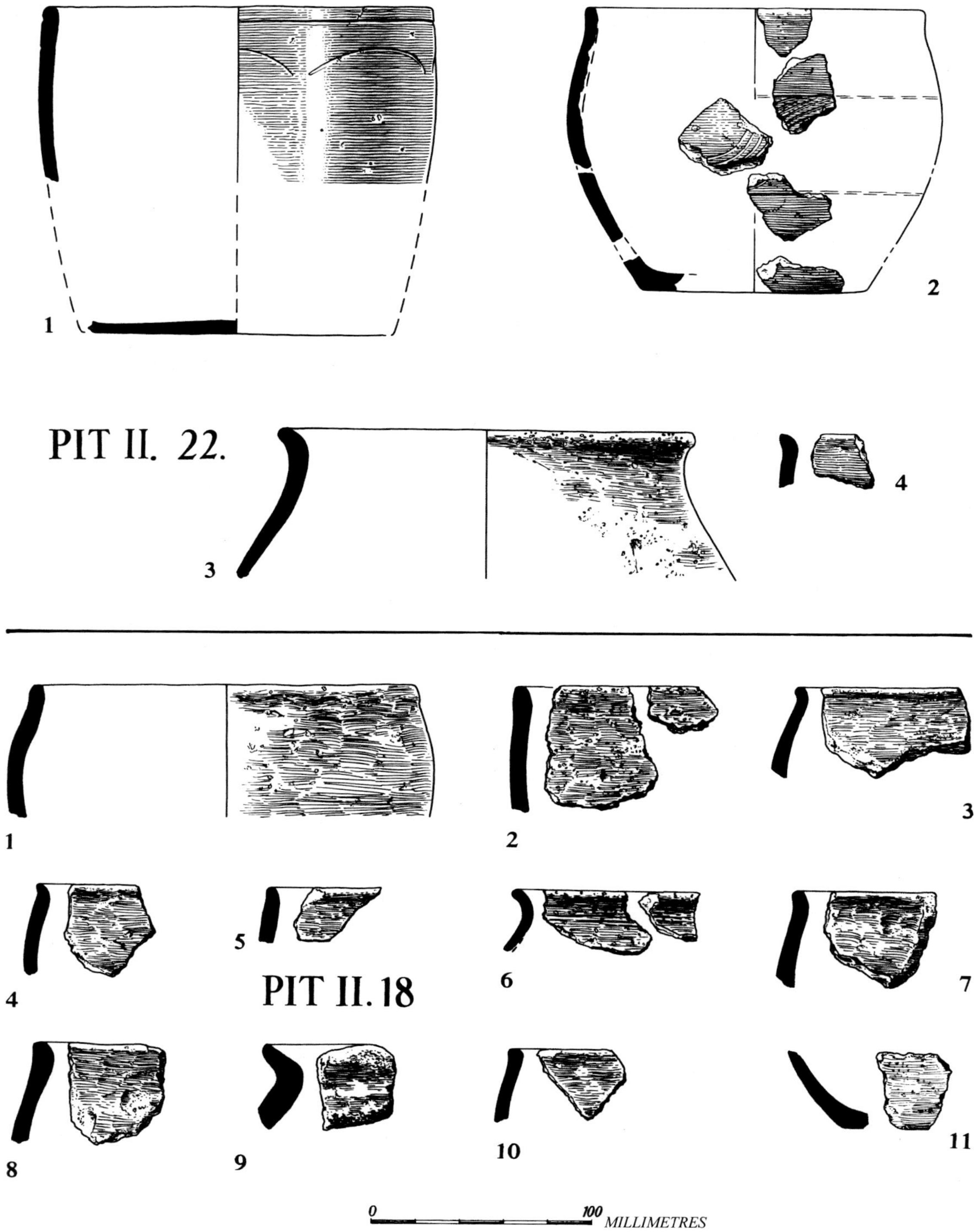

Fig. 3.29 Pottery from Enclosure II Pit 22, Pit 18 (scale 1:3)

5. Rim sherd from vessel.
Plain, insloping rim. Undecorated. Exterior red to dark brown black, interior black. F12.
P00, D00, S01.

6. Rim sherds from pear-shaped jar.
2 sherds, not joining. Gently everted rim with slight external lip. Undecorated. Exterior and interior black, exterior burnished. F31.
P35, D00, S02.

7. Rim and body sherd from vessel, probably globular jar.
Slightly everted rim, outsloping body. Uncorated. Exterior and interior dark brown to black; wiped surfaces. F31.
?P36a, D00, S03.

8. Rim sherd from 'saucepan' vessel.
Short, slightly everted rim, outsloping body. Undecorated. Exterior dark brown to black, interior dark red to brown; wiped surfaces. F32.
P42, D00, S03.

9. Rim sherd from vessel, probably pear-shaped jar.
Thick, everted rim. Undecorated. Exterior and interior red to brown. F15.
P41, D00, S01.

10. Rim sherd from jar.
Inward-sloping rim with slight internal bevel, outcurved body. Undecorated. Exterior dark brown red to black, interior red; surfaces smooth wiped. F32.
P37a, D00, S03.

11. Lower body and base sherd from vessel.
Insloping body, flat base. Undecorated. Exterior dark brown to black, interior red to light brown; exterior surface possibly wiped. F31.
P00, D00, S01.

Fig. 3.30

Enclosure II Pit 2

1. Rim and body sherd from pear-shaped jar.
Upright, rounded rim, outsloping body. Undecorated. Exterior and interior black. F32.
P47, D00, S01.

2. Rim and body sherd from jar.
Upright T-shaped rim with small external and internal projections, slightly concave neck, rounded shoulder carination. Undecorated. Exterior and interior buff to orange; exterior wiped. F31.
P37b, D00, S03.

3. Rim sherd from 'saucepan' vessel.
Plain, upright rim, tip thickened. Undecorated. Exterior light brown to black, interior light brown to dark brown; possibly burnt. F31.
P50, D00, S01.

4. Rim and body sherd from jar.
Plain, upright rim, gentle shoulder carination. Undecorated. Exterior black, interior light brown. F31.
P52a, D00, S01.

Enclosure II Pit 3

1. Rim and body profile from 'saucepan' vessel.
11 sherds, many joining. Incurving, rounded rim with gentle furrow beneath tip on external side, curved body. Undecorated. Exterior black, interior red; exterior wiped; burnt. F31.
P42, D00, S03.

2. Rim and body sherd from pear-shaped jar.
Short, everted rim with squared tip, outsloping body. Undecorated. Exterior and interior black. F15.
P47, D00, S01.

Enclosure II Pit 7

1. Rim and body sherd from jar.
Slightly everted rim, rounded shoulder. Undecorated. Exterior brown to black, interior black; exterior wiped; probably burnt. F21.
P52a, D00, S03.

2. Rim and body sherd from pear-shaped jar.
Thick, slightly incurving rim with rounded external projection, outsloping body. Undecorated. Exterior red to black, interior black. F32.
P47, D00, S01.

3. Rim and body sherd from pear-shaped jar.
Flared rim, with external lip, tall concave neck. Undecorated. Exterior and interior black. F12.
P35, D00, S01.

4. Rim and body sherd from vessel, probably barrel jar.
Plain, insloping rim, curved body. Undecorated. Exterior black, interior grey to black; burnt and weathered. F21.
P39, D00, S01.

5. Rim and body sherd from vessel, probably 'situla' jar.
Everted rim, outsloping body. Undecorated. Exterior black, interior dark grey; burnt and weathered. F32.
?P22, D00, S01.

Enclosure II Pit 9

1. Rim and body sherds from jar.

2 joining sherds. Incurving rim with external projection, curved body. Undecorated. Exterior red to black, interior black; exterior surface grass wiped; burnt. F31.
P52b, D00, S05.

2. Rim sherd from vessel, probably barrel jar. Rounded rim, slightly insloping, curved body. Undecorated. Exterior and interior black; exterior smooth wiped, surfaces pitted. F31.
P39, D00, S03.

3. Rim sherd from vessel.
Flat-topped, incurving rim. Undecorated. Exterior and interior black; exterior wiped; probably burnt. F21.
P00, D00, S03.

4. Rim sherd from jar.
2 sherds, not joining. Curved, everted rim, with interior ledge. Undecorated. Exterior black, interior brown to black; exterior possibly wiped. F21.
P52b, D00, S03.

5. Rim and body sherd from 'situla' jar.
Everted rim, concave neck, rounded shoulder carination. Undecorated. Exterior and interior red to black; burnt. F21.
P22, D00, S01.

Enclosure II Pit 19

1. Rim sherd from vessel.
Upright rim with wide furrow beneath tip on external side. Undecorated. Exterior dark brown to black, interior light to dark brown. F21.
P00, D00, S01.

2. Rim sherd from vessel.
Curved, everted rim. Undecorated. Exterior black, interior red to black. F31.
P00, D00, S01.

3. Rim sherd from vessel.
Upright rim with rounded external projection. Undecorated. Exterior and interior buff to black; exterior wiped. F13.
P00, D00, S03.

4. Base sherd from vessel.
Curved lower body, flat base. Undecorated. Exterior dark brown to black, interior black; traces of burning on interior. F42.
P00, D00, S01.

Enclosure II Pit 24

1. Rim and body sherd from vessel.
Upright, rounded rim. Undecorated. Exterior and interior orange to buff. F31.
P00, D00, S01.

2. Rim and body sherd from vessel.
Upright rim, flaring body. Undecorated. Exterior orange to red, interior brown to black. F21.
P00, D00, S01.

Enclosure II Pit 30

1. Rim and body sherd from jar.
Flat-topped rim with external projection, curved body. Undecorated. Exterior black, interior buff to brown; probably burnt. F31.
P52a, D00, S01.

2. Lower body and base sherd from dish.
Body wide, insloping lower body, flat base. Undecorated. Colour and fabric unrecorded.
P53, D00, S01.

Fig. 3.31

Enclosure II Pit 34

1. Body and base profile of 'situla' jar.
3 sherds, 2 joining. Rounded shoulder carination, insloping body, flat base. Fingernail impressions on shoulder. Exterior buff to orange, interior brown. F31.
P22, D40, S01.

Enclosure II Pit 39

1. Rim sherd from pear-shaped jar.
Layer 1.
Everted rim. Groove below rim on exterior surface. Exterior black, interior red to black; exterior smooth wiped. F32.
P35, D31, S03.

2. Rim sherd from pear-shaped jar.
Layers 2 and 3.
2 sherds. Slightly everted rim. Undecorated. Exterior and interior black; uneven surfaces; burnt and weathered. F12.
P35, D00, S01.

3. Rim sherd from jar.
Layer 2.
Slightly insloping rim, slight external lip with furrow beneath. Undecorated. Exterior black, interior red to orange; exterior burnished. F31.
P52a, D00, S02.

Enclosure II Pit 48

1. Rim and body sherd from globular jar.
Layer 2.
Flat-topped rim, with external projection, outsloping body. Undecorated. Exterior red to black, interior red to brown; possibly burnt. F22.
P36b, D00, S01.

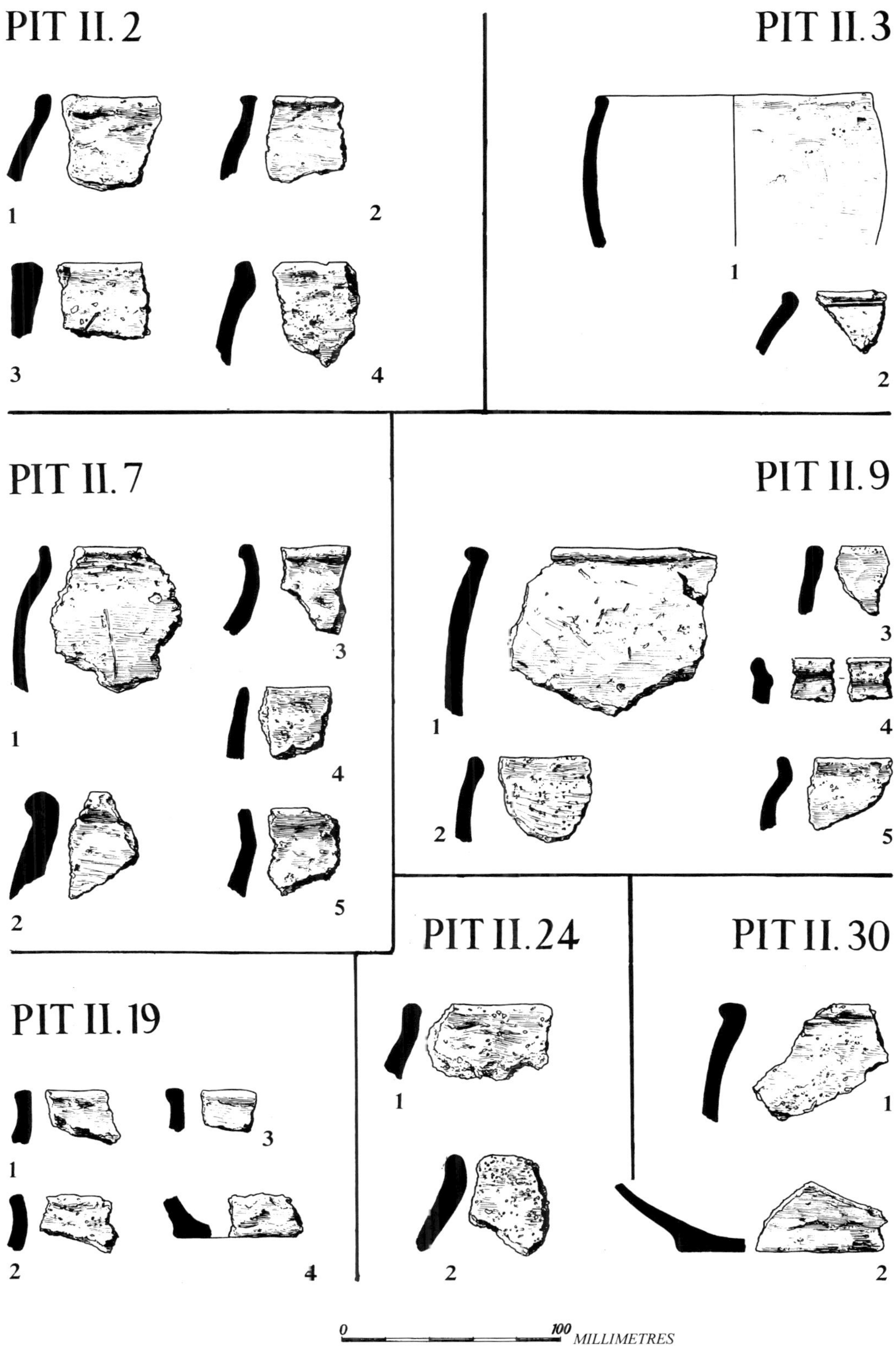

Fig. 3.30 Pottery from Enclosure II Pit 2, Pit 3, Pit 7, Pit 9, Pit 19, Pit 24, Pit 30 (scale 1:3)

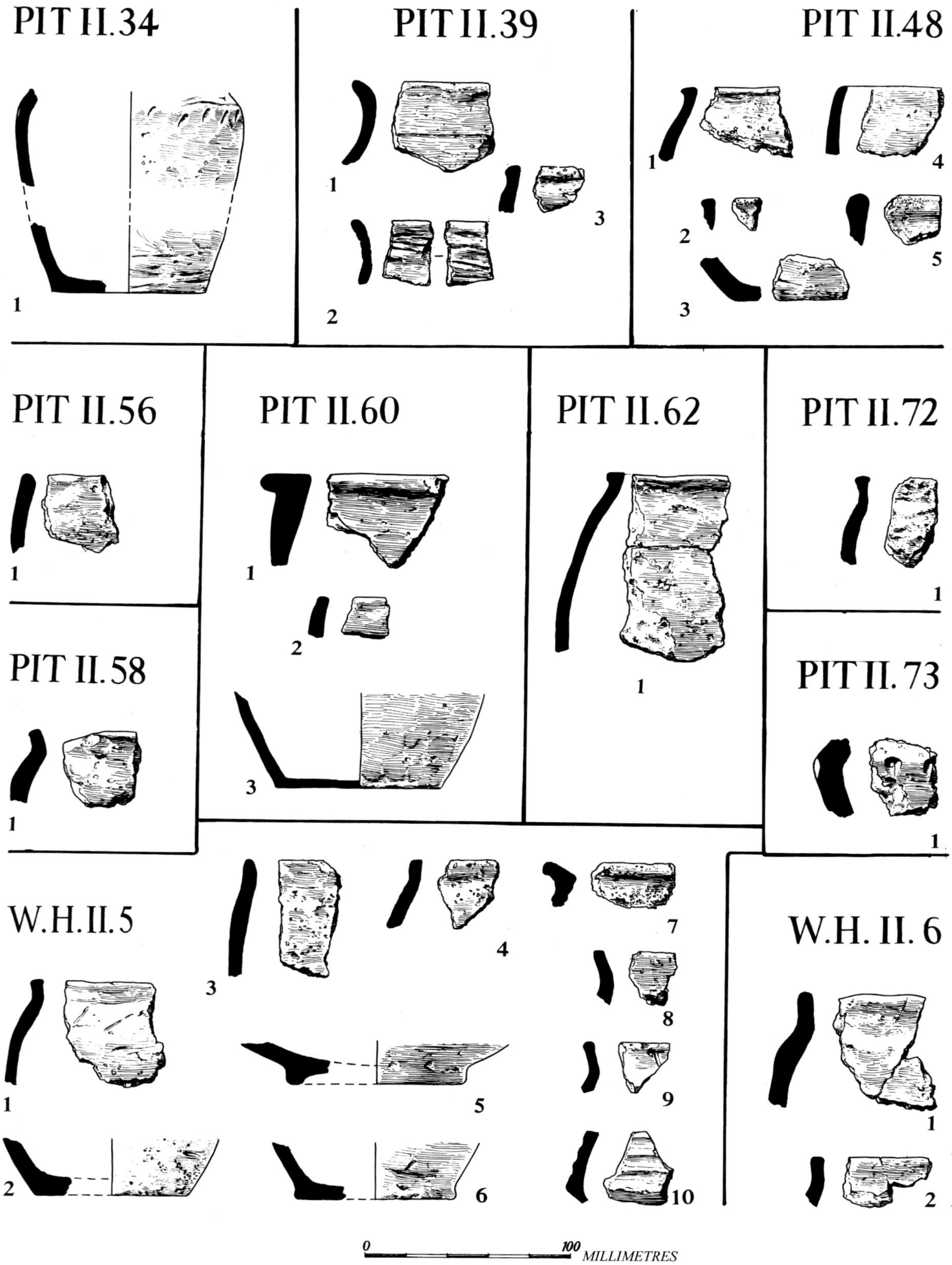

Fig. 3.31 Pottery from Enclosure II Pit 34, Pit 39, Pit 48, Pit 56, Pit 58, Pit 60, Pit 62, Pit 72, Pit 73, Pit 5, Pit 6 (scale 1:3)

2. Rim sherd from vessel.
Layer 1.
Upright rim with slight external lip.
Undecorated. Exterior and interior red. F21.
P00, D00, S01.

3. Lower body and base sherd from vessel.
Layer 2.
Insloping body, flat base. Undecorated.
Exterior buff to black, interior red to buff; probably burnt and weathered. F22.
P00, D00, S01.

4. Rim sherd from barrel jar.
Layer 1.
Upright rim with incurved tip. Undecorated.
Exterior and interior brown to black; exterior wiped. F31.
P17, D00, S03.

5. Rim sherd from vessel.
Layer 1.
Upright rim with rounded tip. Undecorated.
Exterior and interior brown to black. F21.
P00, D00, S01.

Enclosure II Pit 56

1. Rim sherd from vessel.
Plain, slightly incurving rim. Undecorated.
Exterior black, interior red to black; weathered and probably burnt. F31.
P00, D00, S01.

Enclosure II Pit 58

1. Rim and body sherd from vessel.
Layer 1.
Everted rim with squared tip, rounded shoulder carination. Undecorated. Exterior and interior black; exterior wiped; burnt and weathered. F13.
P00, D00, S03.

Enclosure II Pit 60

1. Rim and body sherd from jar.
Layer 2.
Flat-topped rim with long external projection, almost straight upper body.Undecorated.
Exterior black to buff, interior red; exterior and interior wiped; burnt and weathered. F31.
P46b, D00, S03.

2. Rim sherd from vessel.
Layer 1.
Plain, insloping rim. Undecorated. Exterior and interior black; weathered. F31.
P00, D00, S01.

3. Lower body and base sherds from vessel.
Layer 1.
18 sherds, many joining. Insloping lower body, flat base. Undecorated. Exterior brown to black; interior black; burnt and weathered. F31.
P00, D00, S01.

Enclosure II Pit 62

1. Rim and body sherd from globular jar.
Layer 1.
Flat-topped rim, rounded external projection, curved body. Undecorated. Exterior brown to black, interior brown; burnt and weathered. F31.
P36b, D00, S01.

Enclosure II Pit 72

1. Rim and body sherd from globular jar.
Layer 1.
Upright rim with T-shaped tip, rounded shoulder carination. Undecorated. Exterior and interior buff brown to black; weathered and burnt. F12.
P36b, D00, S01.

Enclosure II Pit 73

1. Shoulder sherd from carinated jar.
Layer 1.
Rounded shoulder carination. Decorated on carination by finger tip impressions. Exterior beige to orange red, interior black; burnt. F31.
P27, D22, S01.

Enclosure II Working Hollow 5

1. Rim and body sherds from globular jar.
3 sherds, 2 joining. Flat-topped rim with slight internal lip, rounded shoulder carination. Undecorated. Exterior and interior black; possibly burnt. F31.
P36b, D00, S01.

2. Lower body and base profile from vessel.
Insloping lower body, flat base. Undecorated.
Exterior black, interior dark grey. F12.
P00, D00, S01.

3. Rim and body sherd from vessel, probably barrel jar.
Plain, upright rim, slightly curved body.
Undecorated. Exterior beige to black, interior black; possibly burnt. F31.
P39, D00, S01.

4. Rim and body sherd from vessel.
Upright rim, outsloping body. Undecorated.
Exterior black, interior orange red. F31.
P00, D00, S01.

5. Lower body and base profile of vessel.

Wide body, incurving lower body, rounded footring. Undecorated. Exterior and interior red to black; exterior wiped. F31.
P00, D00, S03.

6. Lower body and base profile of vessel.
Insloping lower body, flat base. Undecorated. Exterior buff to black, interior brown to red, exterior wiped. F31.
P00, D00, S03.

7. Rim sherd from vessel, probably pear-shaped jar.
Everted rim with slight external lip. Undecorated. Colour and fabric not recorded.
P41, D00, S01.

8. Rim sherd from vessel.
Flat top rim, slightly everted. Undecorated. Colour and fabric not recorded.
P00, D00, S01.

9. Rim sherd from vessel.
Everted rim with rounded tip. Undecorated. Exterior and interior dark brown to black; wiped surfaces.F12.
P00, D00, S03.

10. Neck and shoulder sherd from vessel.
Outsloping neck, shoulder carination. Decorated on neck by series of broad shallow furrows. Colour and fabric not recorded.
P00, D02/3, S01.

Enclosure II Working Hollow 6

1. Rim and body sherd from jar.
2 joining sherds. Upright rim, rounded shoulder. Undecorated. Exterior and interior brown to black; exterior smooth wiped; weathered and probably burnt. F13.
P37a, D00, S03.

2. Rim and body sherds from vessel.
2 sherds. Upright rim. Undecorated. Exterior and interior black; weathered and probably burnt. F13.
P00, D00, S01.

Enclosure II Ditches

Fig. 3.32

Enclosure II Ditches

Primary Silt

1. Shoulder profile of carinated bowl.
EII, D6.
Shoulder carination. Undecorated. Exterior and interior black; exterior burnished. F12.
P06b, D00, S02.

2. Rim and body profile of 'saucepan' vessel.
EII, I2.
Flat-topped, upright rim, rounded shoulder carination. Undecorated. Exterior and interior black. F12.
P42, D00, S01.

3. Rim and body sherds from jar or bowl.
EII, K7.
2 sherds. Plain, upright rim neck. Fingertip impressions on rim. Exterior and interior dark grey. F22.
P46a, D21, S01.

4. Shoulder sherds from carinated jar.
EII, J8.
2 sherds. Shoulder carination. Line of overlapping fingertip impressions on shoulder. Exterior dark grey, interior black. F22.
P25, D22, S01.

5. Rim sherd from pear-shaped jar.
EII, H3.
Fairly thick, upright, flat-topped rim. Undecorated. Exterior and interior dark grey. F31.
P35, D00, S01.

6. Rim sherd from `saucepan' vessel.
EII, H2.
Thick, upright, flat-topped rim. Undecorated. Exterior and interior black. F13.
P50, D00, S01.

Secondary Silt

7. Rim and body sherd from vessel.
EII, K5.
Plain, upright rim, almost straight body. Undecorated. Exterior black, interior dark grey. F41.
P32, D00, S01.

8. Rim and body sherd from vessel, probably barrel jar.
EII, K 19B
Incurving rim with rounded, internal lip, straight body. Undecorated. Exterior light brown, interior light brown to grey. F52.
?P17, D00, S01.

9. Rim sherd from vessel.
EII, H2.
Slightly outsloping rim with fairly pointed external projection. Undecorated. Exterior and interior dull orange. F21.
P00, D00, S01.

Final Silt

10. Rim and body sherd from pear-shaped jar.
EII, B2.

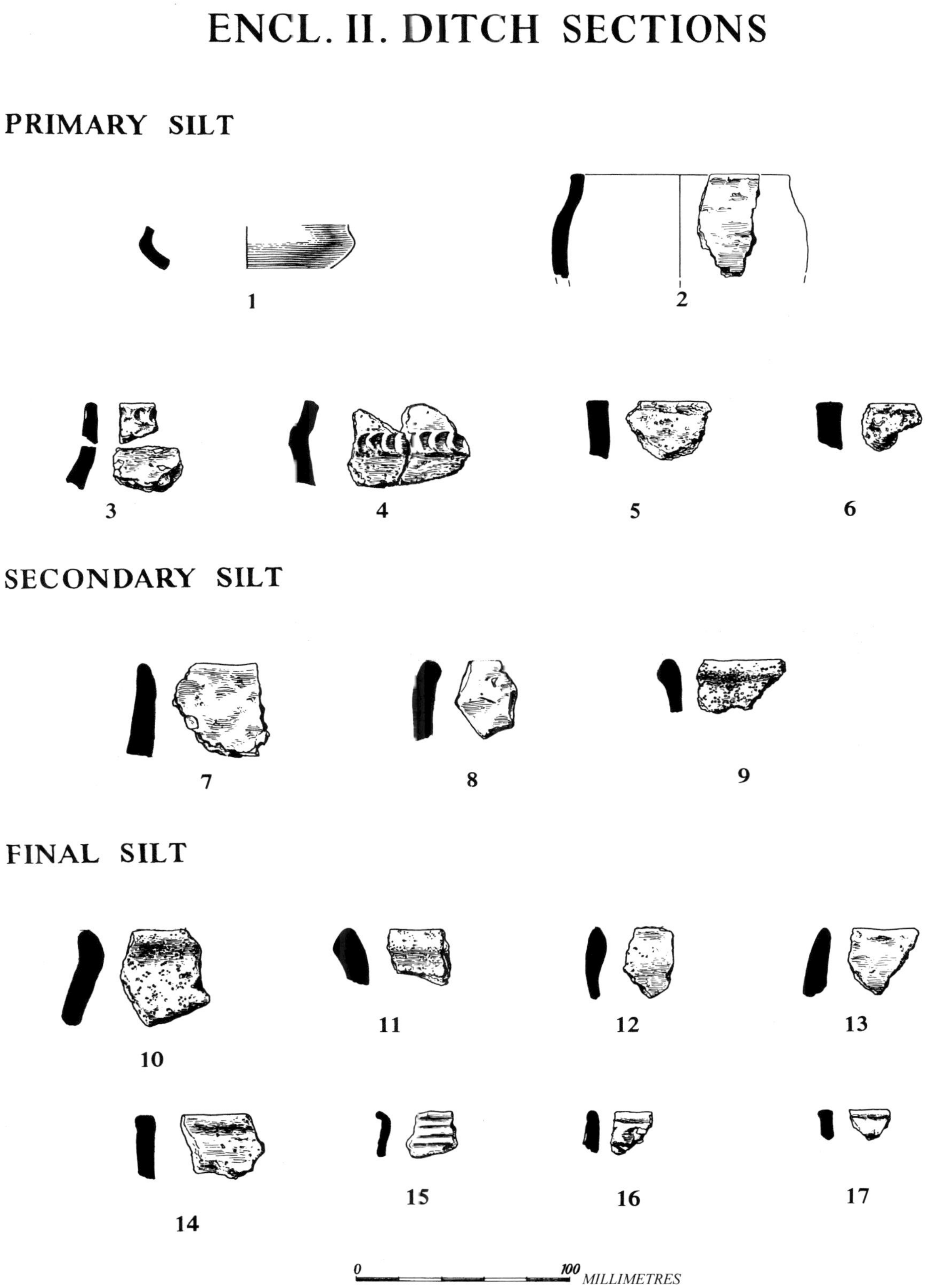

Fig. 3.32 Pottery from Enclosure II Ditch sections (scale 1:3)

Rounded, everted rim, outsloping body. Undecorated. Exterior brown, interior orange brown. F21.
P47, D00, S01.

11. Rim sherd from vessel.
EII, J3.
Thick rim, outcurved. Undecorated. Exterior brown to grey, interior grey. F21.
P00, D00, S01.

12. Rim sherd of dish.
EII, D3.
Slightly incurving rim with thickened tip. Undecorated. Exterior and interior dark grey. F22.
P40, D00, S01.

13. Rim sherd of vessel, probably barrel jar.
EII, K5.
Plain, slightly incurving rim. Undecorated. Exterior and interior black. F21.
?P17, D00, S01.

14. Rim sherd of vessel.
EII, D2.
Flat-topped, upright rim with slight furrow beneath rim on external side. Undecorated. Exterior brown, interior orange. F31.
P00, D00, S01.

15. Rim and neck sherd of carinated bowl with furrowed decoration.
EII, J3.
Thin-walled vessel; small everted rim with rounded tip, outsloping body profile. Series of shallow furrows on neck. Exterior orange, interior grey. F11.
P01, D02/3 S01.

16. Rim sherd of vessel.
EII, J3.
Upright rim with shallow groove below slight external lip. Fingertip impressions on rim. Exterior and interior black. F41.
P00, D21, S01.

17. Rim sherd of vessel.
EII, H2.
Upright rim with slight external and internal projections. Undecorated. Exterior dark grey, interior brown. F13.
P00, D00, S01.

Fig. 3.33

Enclosure III

1. Partially complete profile of jar.
Ditch, M 8.
8 sherds. Small, everted rim, gently rounded body. Undecorated. Exterior and interior black, exterior burnished. F12.
P00, D00, S02.

2. Partially complete profile of globular jar.
Ditch, M 8.
7 sherds. Upright rim with internal ledge, flat base. Undecorated. Exterior and interior black; exterior burnished. F21.
P36a, D00, S02.

3. Rim and body profile of vessel.
Ditch, K, 3-5.
5 sherds. Upright rim, with slight external lip and slight internal ledge, upper body profile straight, lower body profile insloping. Undecorated. Exterior and interior black. F31.
P00, D00, S01.

4. Mid-lower body and base profile of jar.
Ditch, N 5 and 6.
Many sherds. Gently rounded body, flat base. Undecorated. Exterior and interior orange brown to dark grey. F32.
P00, D00, S01.

5. Rim sherd from vessel.
Cutting 30, 2.
Curved, everted rim, with groove under tip on exterior. Undecorated. Colour not recorded; exterior burnished. F12.
P00, D00, S02.

6. Rim sherd from 'saucepan' vessel.
Ditch, N 5.
Thick, upright rim, with rounded internal ledge. Undecorated. Exterior and interior dark grey. F32.
P42, D00, S01.

7. Rim sherd from 'saucepan' vessel.
PH 120, 1 (House 3).
Upright rim, with slightly pointed tip. Undecorated. Colour not recorded; exterior wiped. F12.
P49, D00, S03.
Intrusive.

8. Rim sherd from 'saucepan' vessel.
Cutting 32, 2.
Upright rim with rounded tip. Undecorated. Colour not recorded; exterior wiped. F12.
P49, D00, S03.
Intrusive.

Roman Pottery

9. Almost complete profile of shallow dish.
Section O, Cutting 20, 6.
Plain rim, inward-sloping body, flat base. Undecorated. Exterior and interior black.
Roman coarse ware: F1.

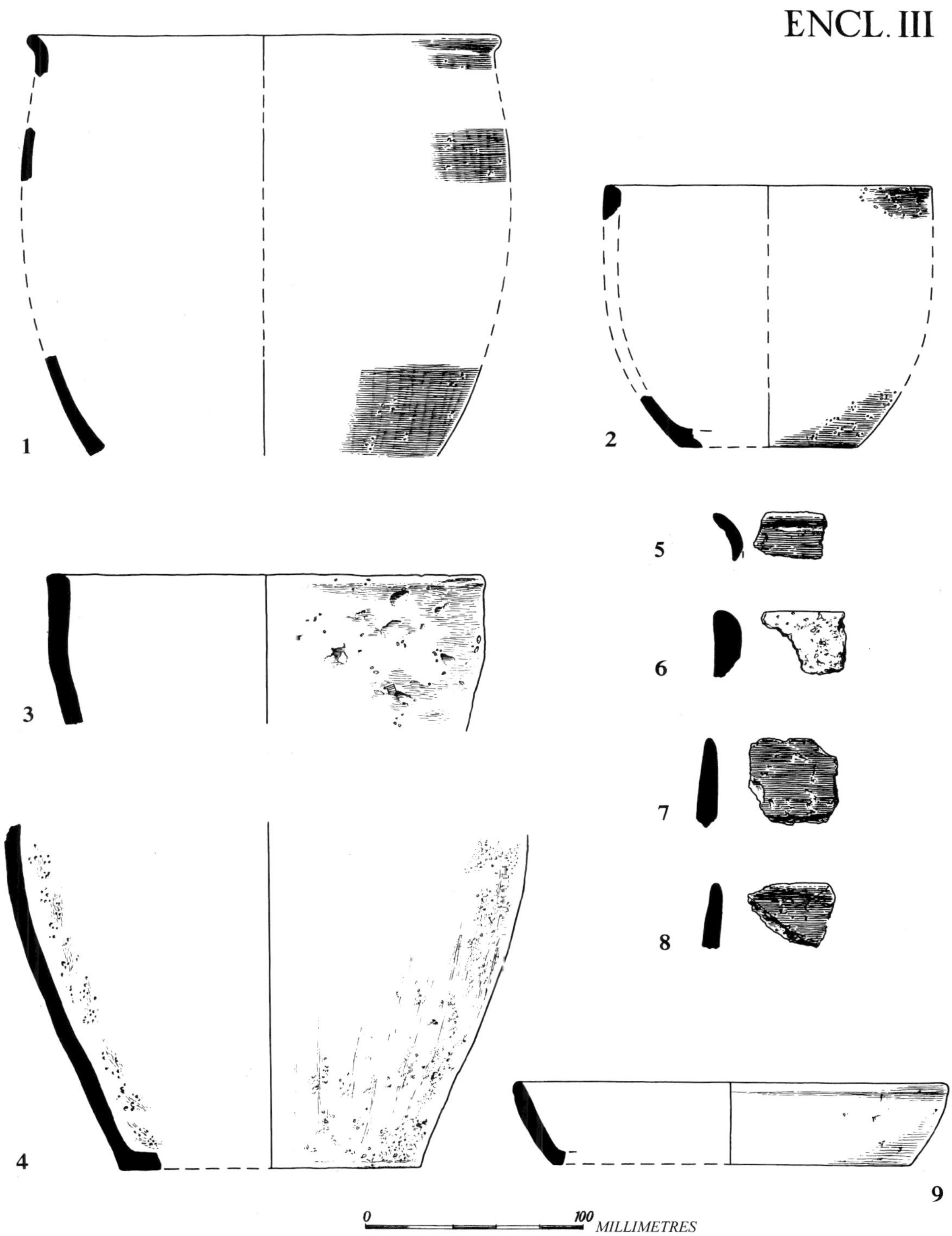

Fig. 3.33 Pottery from Enclosure III (scale 1:3)

Fig. 3.34 Enclosure II House 1: Pottery group

Fig. 3.35 Enclosure II House 2: Bowl no. 11 and no. 25 (Figs 3.7 and 3.8)

Fig. 3.36 Enclosure II House 3: Bowl no. 15 and cup no. 8 (Fig. 3.11)

Fig. 3.37 Enclosure II Pit 5: Pedestal jar no. 3 (Fig. 3.18)

Fig. 3.38 Enclosure II Pit 14: Lugged pot no. 6 (Fig. 3.27)

Chapter 4: The Small Finds

METALWORK

by Christopher Hawkes

Bronze

Fig. 4.1

1. Bronze punch. Length 45mm; stem cracked, surfaces partly corroded. Cross-section rectangular, 5 x 2.5mm at butt, 2.5 x 1.5mm near tip; even taper to tip from butt, but a thickening on one broad face may be remnant of a stop to fix the upper part into a handle.
   Enclosure II Area S1 Pit 69/70

The punch is of Late Bronze Age Ewart Park phase, 9th-8th century BC in Burgess' system (1979, 270, fig. 15A) and associated with pottery dated to the Early Iron Age. Earliest Iron Age sherds were also present, probably derived from deposits associated with House 4, on which the pit impinged. The punch could also have been a residual object dating to the occupation of the house. A similar object from the Isle of Harty hoard in north Kent (Evans 1881, 186, 463, fig. 220 no. 105) was interpreted as a tool for the punching-out of the clay cores of socketed axes, baked hard in casting.

2. Penannular earring. Diameter 15mm, oval section 1mm diameter. Ends slightly tapered, 2 mm apart.
   Enclosure II House 2 PH 233

Production of pliable wire was required for later Bronze Age hooked-and-loop bracelets, like the one from Heathery Burn Cave (Britton 1968) and in the Llangwyllog hoard (*RCAM Anglesey*, pl. 53), both associated with a tanged razor of Class II (Piggott, 1946, 138-9, nos. 43 and 56). A small penannular bracelet from Tan Hill near All Cannings Cross was made of wire of the same diameter (Moore and Rowlands 1972, 64 and pl.16 no. 76) and there are two similar in Ebbesbourne Wake hoard (*ibid.* nos. 16-17).

3. Head and broken shank of a small pin or stud, the head diameter 3.5mm; cylindrical shank diameter 2mm; surviving length 2.5mm.
   Enclosure II House 1 Porch PH 140

Several similar pieces, one a pin with a short tapering shank, were found in the socket of a Hallstatt type iron spearhead, among a group of weapons recovered from the Avon alluvium at the Melksham bypass excavations in 1972 (Gingell 1979, fig. 13, 5a). Gingell did not distinguish their date from that of the spearhead, which is not earlier than Burgess's (1979) Llynfawr phase, late 7th century/ early 6th BC (1979). Yet they resemble pins of the Ewart Park phase (Champion 1980, 218; Needham and Longley 1980, 405), including two from Runnymede Bridge, which also produced a stud similar to this. The type could therefore be of the Ewart Park phase, perhaps as early as 8th century BC.

4. Pin or rivet fragment. Curved head diameter 8mm, bottom flat. Stump of shank, diameter 1.5mm, offset from centre of head.
   Enclosure II House 1 PH 154

The shank was presumably either a pin driven into wood or a rivet driven into leather, the eccentric location of the shank possibly intended to clear the space for inserting a blade into a leather scabbard. Possibly Ewart Park phase.

5. Bracelet fragment of late Hallstatt style. Length 19.5mm, width 9mm, made from a flat-cast rod nick-decorated into a type of bead-and-reel pattern. Broken and flattened in antiquity.
   Enclosure III House 3 PH 3

The bracelet was found in the fill of a much recut posthole complex close to the porch of House 3, the latest of the four houses, and may have been contemporary with the occupation of the building.

6. Bracelet fragment. Length 27mm, width 2.5mm, made from a cast plano-convex rod, with regularly spaced slight swelling mouldings, each decorated with a fine nick at either side. Broken and flattened in antiquity.
   Enclosure II Cutting BV Pit 17

The pottery from the pit suggests that the pit post-dates the bracelet, which was probably incorporated as a residual object relating to the occupation of structures in the vicinity. The bracelet resembles Fig. 4.1, no. 5 from House 3. Similar, mostly fragmentary, bracelets from the site of Mont-Lassois in Burgundy, the 'Oppidum de Vix' (Joffroy 1960, 65-7 and pls. 14-15), are noted for their 'banality' of ornamentation, contrasting with the rich and select ones worn by the 'Lady' buried in the tomb. They are of mostly small internal diameter, less suited to the wrists of adults than to those of girls in their early teens, of which he illustrates three that closely resemble the Longbridge example (pl. 14, nos. 14-16) and two from All Cannings Cross (Cunnington

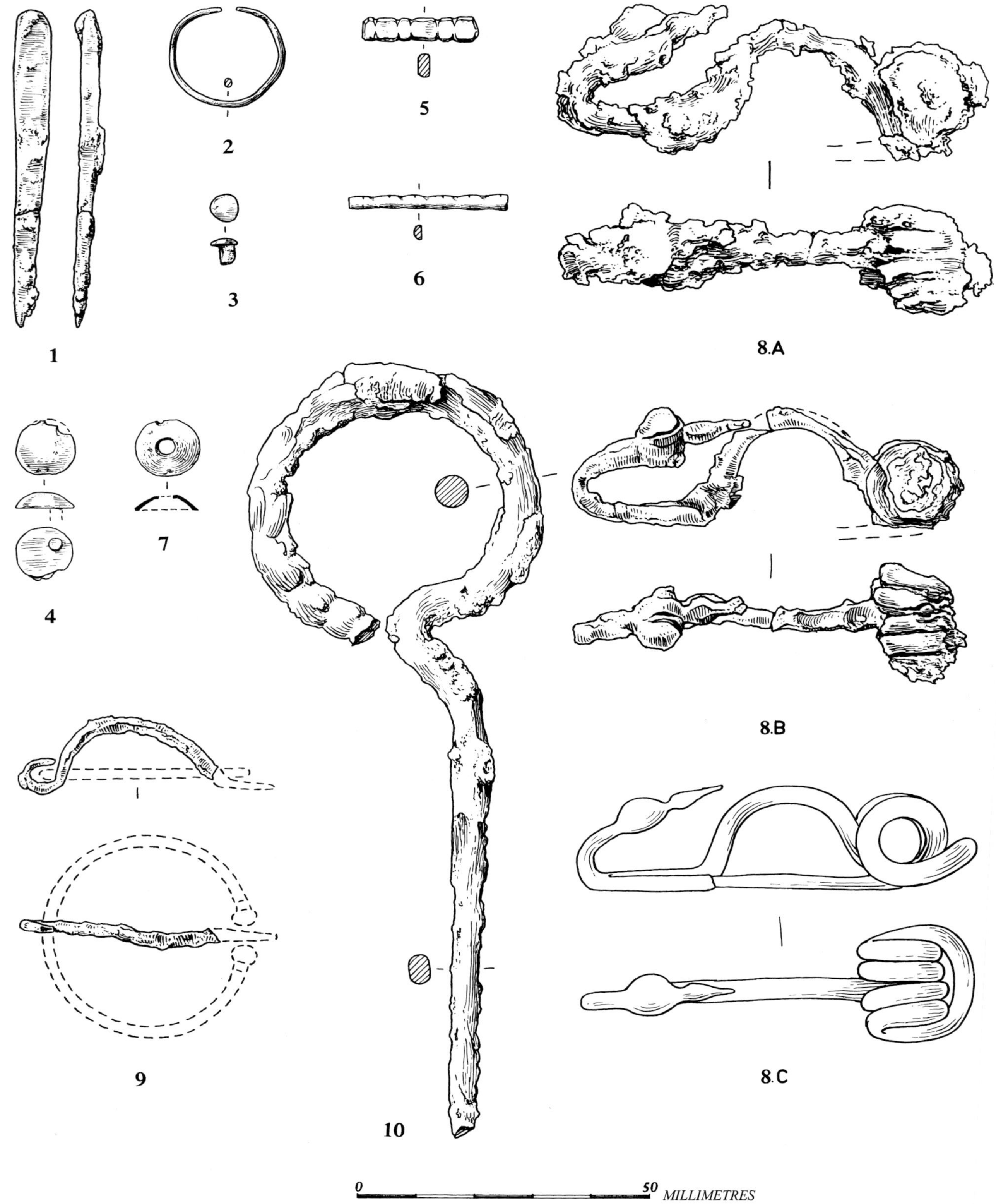

Fig. 4.1 Metalwork

1923, 118-19, pl. 18). The diameters of the Longbridge bracelets could not be determined because they are fragmentary and flattened. Nonetheless they appear to be Final Hallstatt, having ornament formed by a series of matching nicks along their outer edges, giving the effect of flat knobs without casting in relief.

7. Rivet or pinhead with missing central stud; Diameter 8.75mm, perforation for stud 2.5mm, height 2.5mm; Probably for attachment to an iron surface.
 Enclosure II Area S3 Pit 54 (1)

Low bronze bosses on iron were a Hallstatt feature, introduced into Britain (Jope 1961, 309-10, fig. 1, pls. 17-18, 329-30, Mortlake dagger). The mode would have been favoured where bronze for whole surfaces could not be spared. At Maiden Castle comparable collared rivets occur in association with both iron and copper alloy sheet metal, presumably decorative and functional studs used to rivet together components of vessels (Wheeler 1943, 383; Sharples 1991, 154, fig. 129, 1-5). Stanford (1974, 160-1, fig. 74, nos 2-8), dated similar bosses from Croft Ambrey to the 4th century BC and later. The Longbridge boss probably formed part of a cauldron, and the associated pottery in Pit 54 suggests a date *c.* 300 BC.

Iron

Iron Objects of Prehistoric Date

The recovery of a hearth-bottom from WH2 by the fence around House 4, and another hearth-bottom and slag from pits adjacent to Post Hole Complex 5, which dates from the period of the houses, suggest that iron might have been produced on site. The status of the site would make it quite likely. Alternatively iron goods might, in that period, have been imported from workings elsewhere, the goods when worn or broken being returned to the smiths for re-forging.

Fig. 4.1, 8-10

8. Iron brooch with spring of 4 coils, lacking its pin and the chord of its spring. Forged from a single piece of iron. (Previously published in Hull and Hawkes 1987, no. 3623, pp. 76 and 82, pl. 24).
 Enclosure II Area S3 Pit 37 (3)

The reconstruction drawing (Fig. 4.1, 8C) includes a conjecture for the chord. Its four large coils, external chord, bow well arched, catch plain, foot reverted slightly slanting, bearing a disc faintly swelling above, tapered to a tip, identifies it as a standard primary La Téne I type, Hull and Hawkes Iaa (Hull and Hawkes 1987, no. 3623). This primary La Téne I type is recognised to appear within the 5th century BC, *c.* 475 and at latest by 450, and to continue with small variations until sometime after 400 BC. Changes then ensue which in part seem resultant from the Celtic invasions into Italy, but mostly appear to be internal to La Téne I development. The variations relevant here are in the form of the foot, reverted level to parallel the catch, and varied in some to a very slight slant. The standard form prevails in Britain, with a distribution in Kent, Suffolk, Thames Valley, Wiltshire, Dorset, southern Midlands, Gloucestershire (two, one in iron from Crickley Hill), Glamorgan, Herefordshire, Clwyd and Yorkshire/North Humberside. Comparative continental forms in bronze indicate a date between the early-mid 5th century and the early-mid 4th century BC. This applies to any examples in iron despite their apparent rarity. The Longbridge brooch, therefore, would have been deposited within that time, and not after *c.* 400.

The brooch was well stratified in layer 3 of the pit, associated with an iron knife (Fig. 4.2, 7), bone handle (Fig. 4.12, 1) and large pieces of several pottery vessels of early La Tène type (Fig. 3.19, 1-4, 7-9), undoubtedly the best assemblage of this period from the site. Immediately below layer 3 there was an iron sickle of La Téne type (Fig.4.2, 11) and below that a deposit of carbonised grain. The grain was originally radiocarbon dated to the second half of the 5th century BC, providing a deposition date for the brooch (Hull and Hawkes, 1987, 76), but recalibration in 2010 produced a broader range of 810-370 cal BC (see Marshall, Chapter 6). The type occurs in Britain, mostly in bronze, from *c.* 450. The Longbridge Deverill brooch was made, no doubt from locally smelted iron, before 400 and perhaps a little after 450 BC.

9. Penannular iron brooch, ring missing, represented by pin with broken tip; complete end bent back into loop for pivoting on ring; arched shank; surviving length 33mm, original diameter of ring *c.* 35mm. Hull type P1+ (unclassified) (Hull and Hawkes 1987, no. 7135).
 Enclosure II Area S3 Pit 64 (2)

The Longbridge brooch and a bronze example from Swallowcliffe Down (Clay 1925, 74, pl. 7, A3) are wholly in place in the 4th century, and a penannular brooch with doubly moulded terminals and 'emphatically curved pin' from Pit 22 at Maiden Castle (Wheeler 1943, 264-5) should be of the same date. One with a similar pin from Meare, Somerset (Bulleid and Gray 1953, 204-5, pl. 48; Coles 1987) was found in a refuse-deposit that incorporated pottery typical of Meare phase 2 (Avery 1973, 527). Less usual, from a small pit at Winklebury Camp, 12 miles south of Longbridge, is a bronze penannular brooch with a straight pin (Pitt-Rivers 1888, 248-9, pl.147, 11). This pit group contained fingertip-decorated pottery, which suggests a rather earlier date. One at Colchester (Fowler 1960, 172), also with early pottery, has a similar retention of the Aisne type straight pin, but with the bent-out terminals of Fowler Type B (Fowler 1960), as has one from All Cannings Cross (Cunnington 1923, 116, pl.18,1). More usual for Type B (Fowler 1960, 151-2) is a slightly arched pin, but straight ones also follow later, in her series A1 and B1 onwards. Yet the distinctive humped pin was Britain's predominant early form, so that the Longbridge example was standard for its time.

10. Iron ring-headed dress pin; length 135mm, with unusually large head, 50mm in external diameter. The point is damaged. There appear to be textile remains on the top of the ring. Though it is corroded, the apparent form of the terminal is probably correct, and it is moulded into a sort of thistle head.
Enclosure II Area S2 Pit 13 (4)

The pin was found lying flat just above the bottom of Pit 13, on the surface of layer 5, where it was photographed *in situ* in 1958. From the remains of textile on its head it had either been wrapped in cloth, or had its attaching thread or the garment on which it was normally worn buried with it. Therefore it may be another case of the ritual offering of an object still useful and prized by its depositors.

This distinctively British type is directly derived from the Hallstatt swan's neck dress-pin. It retains the swan's neck bend of the neck, for preventing the shank from riding up and out of the garment, but the head is bent right round into a circular ring to which, as the surviving evidence of textile suggests, a tie or decorative streamer may have been attached. The standard account is still Dunning (1934), with a number of iron examples from Wessex, *e.g.* All Cannings Cross (Cunnington 1923, pl. 21, 2-4) and Swallowcliffe Down (Clay 1925, pl. 11, C1). Other examples are a bronze pin from Boscombe Down West (Richardson 1951, fig. 16,12), six in iron from Maiden Castle (Wheeler 1943, fig. 87, 1-6), three from Gussage (Wainwright 1979, 105 fig. 80) and three from Danebury, where they are dated to *c.* 470-360 BC (Ceramic Phase 3) (Cunliffe 1984, 369 fig. 7,25, 2.200-1, 371; Cunliffe and Poole 1991, 351, fig. 7.26, 2.375). The Longbridge pin, with its moulded head was probably quite decorative, and appears by contrast with the others to have been unusually large, capable of fastening a thick outer garment such as a cloak or coat, to which it may have been permanently attached by a thread or thong.

Fig. 4.2

1. Iron rod bent into a half loop, 29mm x 29mm, rectangular section, one end slightly turned over. Original use uncertain.
   Enclosure II Area S3 Pit 39 (1)

2. Fragment of iron nail; length 22mm, circular section, shank bent, pointed at one end and squared off at the head end; traces of bronze stain at the squared end.
   Enclosure II Area S3 Pit 60 (2)

3. Iron angle-bracket or box fitting; length 37mm. A flat, sub-lozenge-shaped plate of thin sheet metal, narrower end bent at right angles to the larger section. Small nail hole at base of right angle bend and larger one near broad end.
   Enclosure II Area S1 House 4

4. Fragment of flat iron strip, very thin, broken at both ends; length 36mm, width 12mm.
   Enclosure II Area S3 Pit 54 (1)

5. Iron tubular socket; surviving length 62mm. Formed by hammering a strip into a hollow cylinder, ends both open. One end running into broken off shank of unidentifiable tool, traces of wood or horn handle fixed in the socket.
   Enclosure II Area S1 Pit 69/70 (1)

6. Iron tool perhaps a punch or fine chisel; surviving length 66mm. Remains of tang and square-sectioned working end.
   Enclosure II Area S3 Pit 36 (3)

7. Large iron knife with broken blade broken; surviving length 129mm. Flat tang, with wood or horn remains, in line with its upper edge, the junction cracked across. In section the blade shows the upper edge barely thicker than the cutting edge. Corrosion may have blunted and thinned the original edge, or it may have been a specialised tool, involving the use of both edges of the blade. Lying close by in the same layer was a bone handle (Fig. 4.4, 1), which probably did not belong to the knife (see Worked Bone and Antler below). Like the sickle (Fig. 4.2,11) and the brooch (Fig. 4.1, 8) from this pit, the knife had been a finely crafted object of some value. Resembles a knife from Danebury (Cunliffe 1984, 350 fig. 7.10, 2.33), and two from Boscombe Down West, with upper edges virtually matching the cutting edge in sharpness (Richardson 1951, 156 fig. 16, 10 and 14).
   Enclosure II Area S3 Pit 37 (3)

8. Tool with broken tang and thick body, possibly a punch; surviving length 52mm.
   Enclosure II Area S1 Pit 2

9. Broken parallel-sided object of uncertain function with forged repair. Perhaps part of sole of a ploughshare. A second piece of iron has been forged onto the first, with the first continuing beneath at a length of 32mm from the irregular break. Maximum length 63mm, width at break 40mm.
   Enclosure II Area S1 Pit 67 (4)

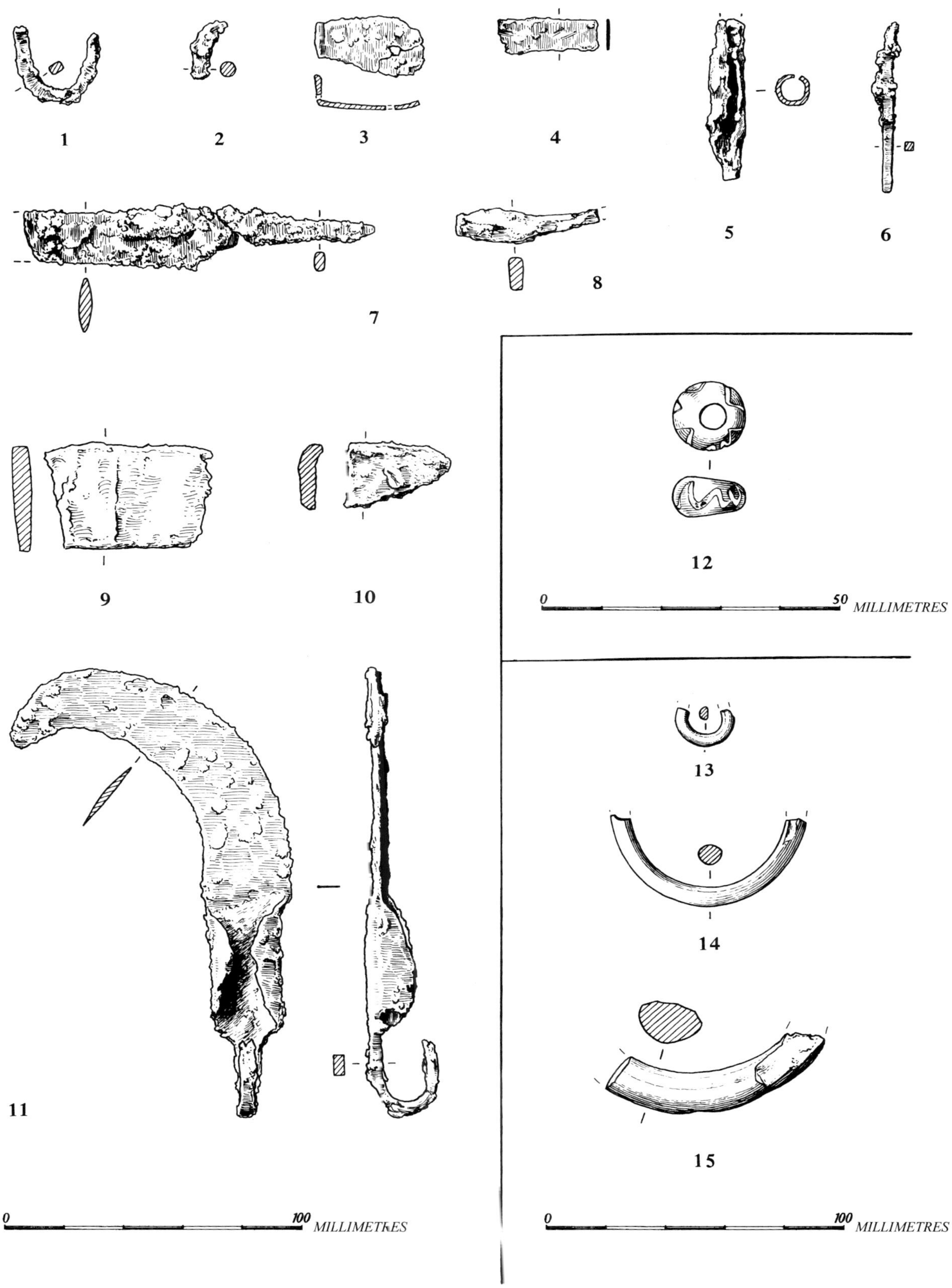

Fig. 4.2 Prehistoric iron objects (nos 1-11); glass bead no. 12; Kimmeridge shale objects (nos 13-15)

10. Broken off tip of straight parallel sided flat forging, possibly a ploughshare tip; maximum length 38mm, width at break 25mm, mean thickness 6mm. Tongue shaped tip, ending in a blunt point with upper edge slightly curved over. A detailed study of Iron Age ploughs carried out by Rees (1979) offers no precise parallels for this small fragment. The tips of complete shares from Danebury (Sellwood 1984, 354-6, fig. 7.14, 270 and 271) seem stouter in construction.
    Enclosure II Area S3 Pit 60 (1)

11. Iron sickle; length 172mm. Curved flat blade with slightly hooked tip, apparently with a cutting edge on either face. The other end has hammered wings to grip a wooden handle, and a thin tang deliberately bent over and hammered down to prevent it pulling out of its socket. Wood traces survive inside the socket, on the entire inside of the curve of the tang, and on the side and back of the bend, so the sickle was hafted when buried.
    Enclosure II Area S3 Pit 37 (4)

The winged variant is best represented in La Tène period Britain, the simple flat tanged type more common on the continent. Simple winged and other forms have been interpreted as billhooks (Déchelette 1914 and reprint, 1381, 1383; 1927, 887-889). It is paralleled by seven of varying sizes from Danebury (Sellwood in Cunliffe 1984, 348 fig. 7.9, 2.12-18) where, however, many others have no hook and two have a flat tang only. Sellwood points out that reaping corn (proper to sickles) would not be the only use of curved-bladed cutting tools, which include pruning hooks and billhooks. Analysing the 24 from Danebury by period, frequency and size, she compares the six from Barbury Castle, one tanged, four winged and one winged with hook (MacGregor and Simpson 1963, 394) and refers in general to Rees (1979, 450-689). Another was found at Fifield Bavant (Clay 1924, 482, pl. xi, 4).

The Longbridge sickle, however, remains distinct of its kind. Its light two-edged blade, with the terminal hafting-hook, which precludes any long handle such as a billhook, is specifically a tool designed for cutting and reaping grass and corn and could not have sustained heavier use without severe damage. Its position in Pit 37, on top of a layer of grain, reinforces this impression of its specific function, and its date is well-defined by its position below a La Tène I brooch (Fig. 4.1,8) and a radiocarbon determination within a range of 770-360 cal BC from the carbonised grain (see Chapter 6).

Such a fine functional tool, complete with handle, can hardly have been lost by accident even deep amongst sacks of grain. It was found lying, as if left as a deliberate offering, on top of the layer of carbonised grain at the bottom of the pit. Perhaps it was so placed on the last remains of the old harvest as a symbol of renewal, to help ensure the success of the new crops. The La Tène I brooch (Fig. 4.1, 8) and the broken knife (Fig. 4.2,7) from layer 3, can also hardly have reached the end of their useful lives, and these were associated with large sherds of broken fineware pottery. The whole assemblage appears a deliberate 'time capsule' of representative finds of the day associated with agriculture. Was Pit 37 the receptacle of a multiple offering of diverse objects at a time of stress, perhaps even of famine, at a time of cultural change, perhaps population change, in the history of the site's occupation?

Miscellaneous Iron Fragments (Not illustrated)

Fragmentary rod, rectangular section; length 38mm, broken in antiquity. Perhaps part of the shank of an awl.
Enclosure II Area S1 Pit 18

Fragment of tang and blade of a flat bladed object such as a spatula or slim knife.
Enclosure II Cutting BXVII Pit 27

Tip of iron nail; length 19mm, round sectioned with remains of wood adhering.
Enclosure II Area S3 Pit 53 (1)

Fragmentary nail or long rivet; length 32mm, round shank, with upper end hammered over.
Enclosure II Area S3 Pit 53 (1)

Flat, slender, fragment of iron; length 31mm. Possibly the tang of a small knife or other fine cutting tool.
Enclosure II Area S3 (2) topsoil)

Iron Objects of Medieval and Post-medieval Date Fig. 4.3, nos 1.7

1. Half of a small pair of cloth shears broken across the rounded spring head; blade slender with narrow flat back, cutting edge still sharp, tip broken; length 130mm.
   Probably 16th-17th century
   Enclosure III Cutting M (Old A II) (4) upper silt of ditch terminal, on north side of causeway

2. Straight bar with rectangular section; length 134mm; top curled to form a swivel-loop, lower end bent backwards 180° to form a hook, ending blunt and pressed tight against the bar for 32mm. Possibly from cart-horse harness.
   Enclosure III Area T Cutting AV (2) topsoil just inside enclosure entrance

3. D-shaped harness-ring, a form still standard on draught-horse harness, but normally in brass; width 40mm
   Enclosure III Cutting O (3) at east end just inside enclosure, c.152mm deep in denuded remains of the internal bank make-up

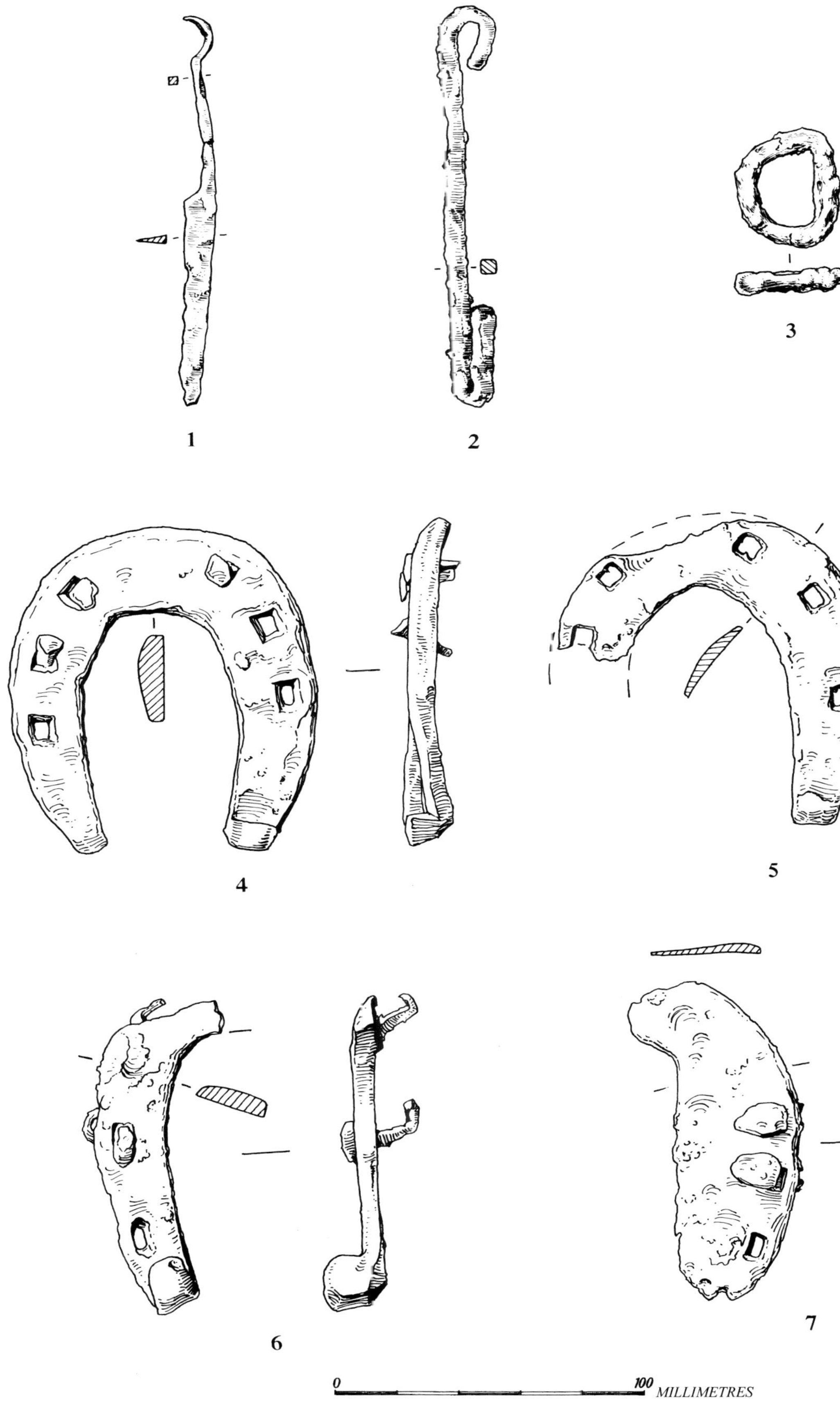

Fig. 4.3 Iron objects of later/post-medieval date

4. Horseshoe; 227g, size 110 x 100mm, lacking one calkin (turned-up terminal), six countersunk squared nail holes, three with flat-headed nails.
   Enclosure III Area T Cutting A 148 (2a) topsoil just inside southern terminal of ditch

5. Incomplete horseshoe; size 102 x 102mm, one surviving calkin and five countersunk squared nail-holes surviving.
   Enclosure III Cutting A XIV (2) topsoil, western area of enclosure

6. Half horseshoe; length 102mm, with very thickcalkin and three surviving rectangular nail holes, two with bent over nails.
   Enclosure III Cutting N (4) upper level of ditch silt, just north of causeway

7. Half oxshoe; length 105mm. Made in two halves to accommodate cloven ox hooves. Three rectangular nail holes, two with oval headed nails.
   Enclosure III Cutting B (1) turf overlying northern corner of ditch

Not illustrated

Heavy small horseshoe; 170gm, size 102 x 89mm, complete but for loss of four nails. Rectangular holes, three on either side, punched through from the front, producing the wavy edge, dated relatively early in Ward-Perkins's (1941) scheme for medieval shoes. Thick and prominent calkins, *c.* 13mm high, the two surviving nails 'fiddle-key' shaped.
Enclosure III Area T Cutting A 101 (1) turf 4.6m inside the entrance

The literature of horseshoes, mainly in England, was started in 1869 by George Fleming. Medieval shoeing was introduced in the early 9th century from the continental west and its adaptation to heavy war horses arrived into England at the Norman Conquest (William Ridgeway 1905). More recent horseshoe studies, begun by Murray (1927, 1937a and b) and continued by Ward and Ward-Perkins (1941), presented chronologies by type, and these confirm a medieval date for the Longbridge examples (on ox-shoes see Ward 1941, pl. xxix and 172, nos 58-60).

A note on Christopher Hawkes' 1988 discussion of the horseshoes added by Sonia Hawkes in 1994 reads:

All of the horseshoes came either from the upper silt of the Enclosure III ditch, which contained Roman pottery, or from the turf or topsoil in the interior of the enclosure, mostly just inside the entrance. The scatter of Romano-British pottery in the ploughsoil over Enclosure II indicates that the area was manured from a local Romano-British farmyard and then ploughed, mainly in the 2nd century AD. Thereafter, as the air-photographs and survey show, all the area to the east of Enclosure III, including the whole of Enclosure II, was covered by medieval ridge and furrow, so from perhaps the 12th century the area was again under plough. No medieval pottery was found on the site to date this phase of activity, possibly because animal fertiliser was not derived from farmyard manure during this period. The next certain date of ploughing is attested by Colt Hoare's visit to the site in 1812: it had been under tillage during the Napoleonic Wars. But according to the Stratton brothers, who began ploughing the site in the 1950s, the downs had been allowed to return to grass for as long as those living locally recalled. The air photographs confirm that there was no ploughing during WWII. The Stratton's first ploughing, a year or two before the start of the excavation, broke up the downland turf that still survived in Enclosure III and overlying the major part of Enclosure I at that time.

The horseshoes could, therefore, have been lost in the early Roman period, the medieval period or later. None is large, however, so none belonged to anything approaching the size of animal developed in the post-medieval period for the plough. The likelihood, therefore, is that they are medieval. None particularly resembles the late Roman shoes from Maiden Castle, but all have counterparts in Ward-Perkins' medieval series. The smallest, no 8, with its wavy outline, looks typologically the earliest and could be 12th century, while the rest might be later medieval. Their accumulation within Enclosure III, which seems not to have been ploughed in the Middle Ages, suggests that this is where the plough teams were turned off the open field to graze. The medieval farm would have been far down in the valley, so this grassy enclosure must have been a very useful place in which to do running repairs to harness and tasks such as removing and discarding loose shoes.

While conceding that the horseshoes are likely to be medieval or later, correspondence in the archive indicates that Sonia Hawkes persevered in her interpretation of Enclosure III as an Iron Age feature until her death. She explained the presence of the horseshoes as indicative of post-Roman reuse of the earthwork.

GLASS AND SHALE

by Christopher Hawkes

Fig. 4.2, nos 12 – 15

Glass

12. Glass bead of ring shape, depth 5mm to 7.5mm; diameter 13mm. Cylindrical perforation diameter 5mm. Glass semi-translucent dark blue, with opaque white marvered trail, irregularly wavy around outside edge. Perhaps 3rd century BC but the type is very long-lived in Britain.
    Enclosure II Cutting H (old BXXII) Ditch (2) upper silt (2)

Kimmeridge Shale

13. Small ring, just over half complete; external diameter 22mm, mean thickness 5mm, plano-convex section; very delicate, well-finished and smoothed.
    Enclosure II/III Area 00 1957 Cutting 103B (2A) Roman ploughsoil, from above the floor of House 3, in SW part of interior, associated with majority of other domestic artefacts

14. Half of a shale ring/bracelet; internal diameter c. 57mm. Almost circular section, very. well-finished and smoothed.
    Enclosure II Cutting BXVI Pit 19

15. Fragment of shale bracelet; internal diameter *c.* 90mm. Roughly cut with faceted inner surface and rather pointed outer face, tool marks only roughly smoothed; possibly broken when not quite finished.
    Enclosure II Cutting BIX Pit 14

Not Illustrated

Complete ring-bead or-pendant, unusually small for the Kimmeridge industry; *c.* 10mm larger has been recorded from the Kimmeridge site (Davies 1936). Enclosure III House 3, 103B (2a) Roman plough soil overlying floor level. This layer contained most of the finds from the house occupation.

WORKED BONE AND ANTLER

by Christopher Hawkes

Fig. 4.4, nos 1 – 11

1. Bone handle; length 95mm, oval section. Curved and polished, incised line around each end. At the narrower end the cancellous tissue is hollowed, with slight iron staining left by the tang of an iron implement. A corresponding hollow at the wider end contains a nail-shaped tang, enclosed within what remains of a short wooden holder, wedged with a bone plug cut flat at the top to lie flush with the top of the handle. The tang protrudes 15mm beyond this, suggesting there was a pommel of perishable material such as leather at this end. The handle may have been from an iron knife, but not the one found in this pit.
   Enclosure II Cutting BXXIII Pit 37 (3)

2. Antler weaving comb; length 125mm. Red deer antler split and roughly shaped, preserving the original rough internal and external surfaces. Fairly crude teeth were cut at the wider end. Teeth and edges polished and worn.
   Enclosure II House 4 PH 208 (from packing at the base)

3. Bone weaving comb; length 128mm. Split and shaped ox metacarpal or metapodial bone. Incised line below teeth, of which there were probably 9 or 10, most entirely broken. Both surfaces well-worked and outer surface polished.
   Enclosure II Cutting BXXIV Pit 39

4. Fragment of red deer antler weaving comb decorated with incised transverse grooves and cross-hatching. Polished and burnt, presumably from contact with burning fabric of House 3. Incised decoration resembles All Cannings Cross pl.12, 7-13 (Cunnington 1923).
   Enclosure III Cutting A148 (2a) topsoil between inner and middle post rows of House 3

5. Small bone spatula, perhaps toilet instrument. Cut very thin, with pierced rounded handle end expanding to a slightly dished oval, like a spoon bowl, but this end broken; surviving length 40mm, but possibly originally *c.* 75mm. Bluish staining. Parallels from All Cannings Cross (Cunnington 1923, pl. 6 nos. 1-7).
   Enclosure III House 3 PH 57

6. Pointed end of bone needle with oval section; length 26mm. Carefully worked and polished.
   Enclosure II Cutting BXXVI Pit 50

7. Fragment of bone tool, probably calf metatarsal or metapodial, split lengthways down the middle, narrow end further split but broken in antiquity; surviving length 105mm. Broad end has transverse perforation, diameter 4mm, which crossed the empty medullary channel, to fasten an inserted suspension handle.
   Enclosure II BXXXIII Pit 69/70

8. Bone gouge or weaving beater, lamb tibia or metapodial, smoothed from use (*cf* Crowfoot, 1945); length 140mm. One end sliced and tapered with the tip worn, broken off and further worn in antiquity. The broken butt end had a transverse perforation, diameter *c* 2mm.
   Enclosure II Area S2/3 (recovered from spoil heap)

9. Bone gouge or weaving beater, distal end of lamb tibia, tip and butt ends broken but not worn; surviving length 93mm.
   Enclosure III House 3 top of (2b) over main ring PHs 123 and 124

10. Bone or red deer antler gouge or weaving beater. Made from a bone split and shaped, butt end squared and tip pointed but broken; surviving length 87mm. Tip end burnt from contact with burning post.
    Enclosure III House 3 PH 109

11. Broken tool made from the radius of sheep or goat, worn smooth with use; surviving length 76mm. The working end of this tool is flattened by friction. It may have been used for

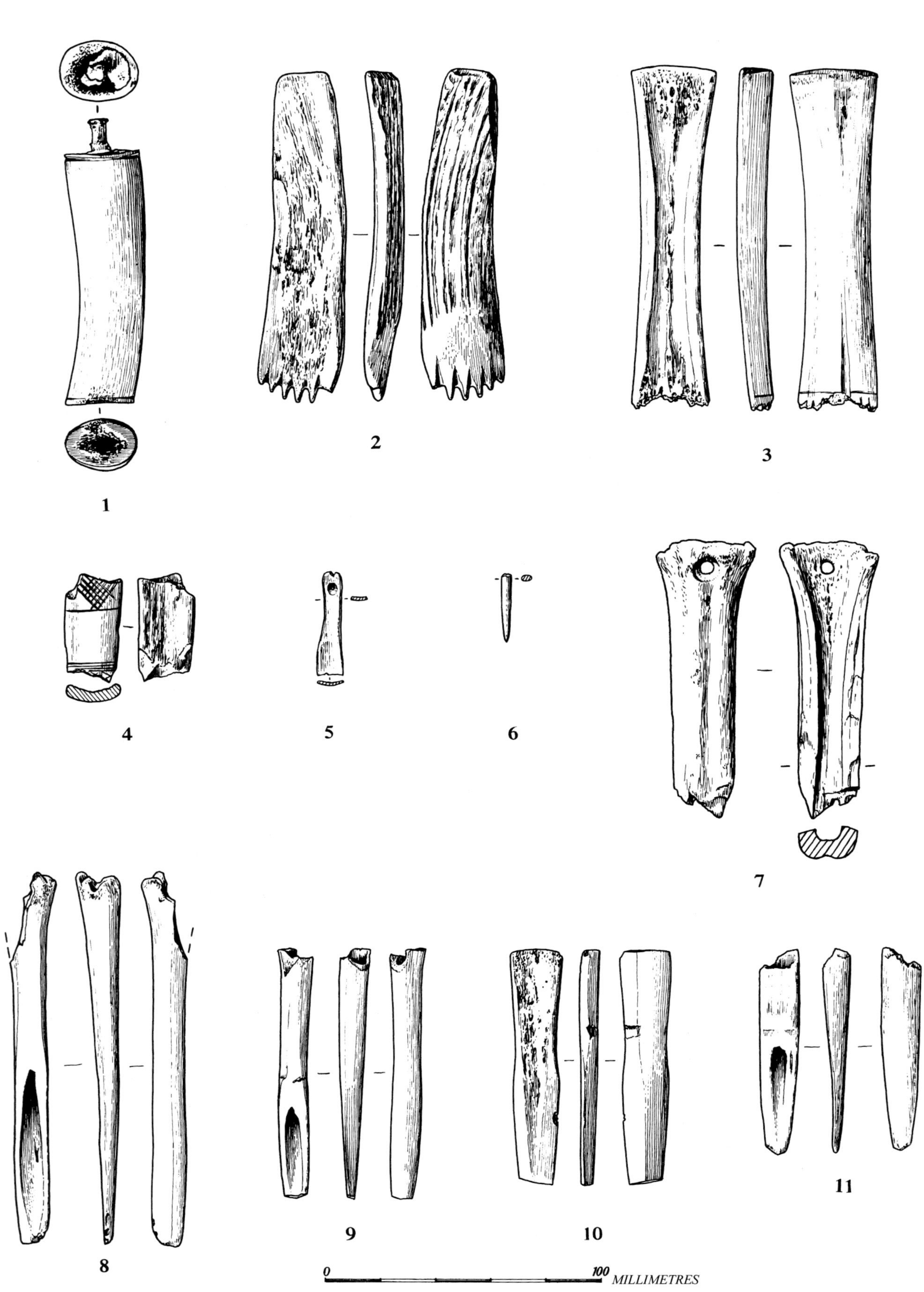

Fig. 4.4 Worked bone and antler

the dressing of hides like another from this area of Enclosure II and two more from House 3, all four being of Class 2 'bone gouges' distinguished by Sellwood (1984, 302ff, 387).
Enclosure II Cutting BV Pit 17

Not illustrated

Broken tip of bone gouge or weaving beater, tibia of sheep or goat, highly polished; surviving length 43mm.
Enclosure II Cutting BV Pit 13

Two fragments of polished and burnt bone, possibly from tools.
Enclosure II House 3 PH 18

Part of polished bone handle of beater or gouge.
Enclosure II Cutting B XXXI (2)

Fig. 4.5, nos 1 – 5

1. Red deer antler, broken in antiquity; length 520mm. Very smooth and polished with use. One tine deliberately cut off in antiquity and the main shaft snapped. Probably most of an antler pick.
Enclosure II House 2, PH 137

2. Cattle or horse rib; length 152mm. Gnawed. No polish or evidence of working.
Enclosure II Cutting H (old BXXII) Ditch (3)

3. Bone implement made from metapodial or metatarsal of a horse. Tip recently broken; surviving length 101mm. No polish or evidence of working.
Enclosure II Cutting BXXIX Pit 58 (located at right shoulder of human skeleton)

4. Horn core from sheep or goat; length 76mm. Smoothed and cut at each end and burnt, possibly in an attempt to harden it (Cunnington 1923, pl. 13, nos. 15 and 18).
Enclosure II House 2 PH 174

5. Tine of red deer antler; length 95mm. Appears to have been broken off the main shaft. Well worn, tip polished and showing many cut marks. Some burning suggests an attempt at hardening.
Enclosure II House 1 PH 165

Discussion
by Michael Smith

Longbridge Deverill produced few pieces of worked bone and antler relative to some other sites in the region, such as All Cannings Cross (Cunnington 1923), which produced no fewer than 528 pieces. It is also notable that characteristic forms from All Cannings Cross, such as the thin perforated blades and the tanged spatulae, were absent at both Longbridge Deverill and Little Woodbury. Those artefacts that do appear, knife handle, gouge, comb and antler point, are common on many sites (Smith 1983).

Knife handles of type Fig. 4.4, 1 many of antler, have also been found at All Cannings Cross, Cold Kitchen Hill (Cunnington and Goddard 1934), Highfield (Stevens 1934) and Swallowcliffe Down (Clay 1925, 1927). This particular artefact is unusual in its complexity of construction and evidence of the use of wood and possibly leather.

The word 'comb' has been used in this report in preference to the more common 'weaving comb' as it has a more neutral connotation of their still debated function. Within the classification scheme devised by Bulleid and Gray (1911) the two Longbridge examples are Type 4. Although the Longbridge examples were clearly made from antler, Newcomer (1974) has pointed out the difficulty in many cases in distinguishing between bone and antler.

Cunnington (1923), St. George Gray (1925, 1926, 1927), Wheeler (1943) and Henshall (1950) argued for a weaving function in association with a loom, but Roth (1934, 132) and Hodder and Hedges (1977) have cast doubts o1n this hypothesis. They could have been used for preparing woollen thread for weaving by combing the tangled mass of wool – the function of a jigging comb. Sellwood's (1984) comprehensive report on 39 combs from Danebury (the assemblage eventually numbered 71) considers the various options, and a large assemblage from Meare Village East (Coles 1987, 105-17) provides useful comparative material. All Cannings Cross, Cold Kitchen Hill, Fifield Bavant Down (Clay 1924), Highfield and Swallowcliffe Down Clay (1925) in Wiltshire also produced numerous combs.

The word 'gouge' is used here in preference to 'weaver's beater', a function that is by no means certain. Sellwood's (1984) analysis of 38 gouges from Danebury provides a simple classification that sets aside previous classification schemes devised by Cunnington (1923, 82) and others. The only two of the Longbridge gouges sufficiently complete to be identified appear to correspond to Sellwood's Class 3 of short-shafted examples. Both Cunnington and Sellwood propose that the variety of gouge forms indicates that they were multifunctional tools, but evidence for an association with weaving, based on use wear analysis, is strong in some cases (Sellwood 1984, 385).

WORKED STONE
by Christopher Hawkes and Sonia Chadwick Hawkes (petrological identifications by F. W. Anderson)

Weights

Fig. 4.6, nos 1 – 4

1. Chalk loomweight, broken across perforation. Rough on the base.
Enclosure II Cutting BXXIII Pit 37 (2)

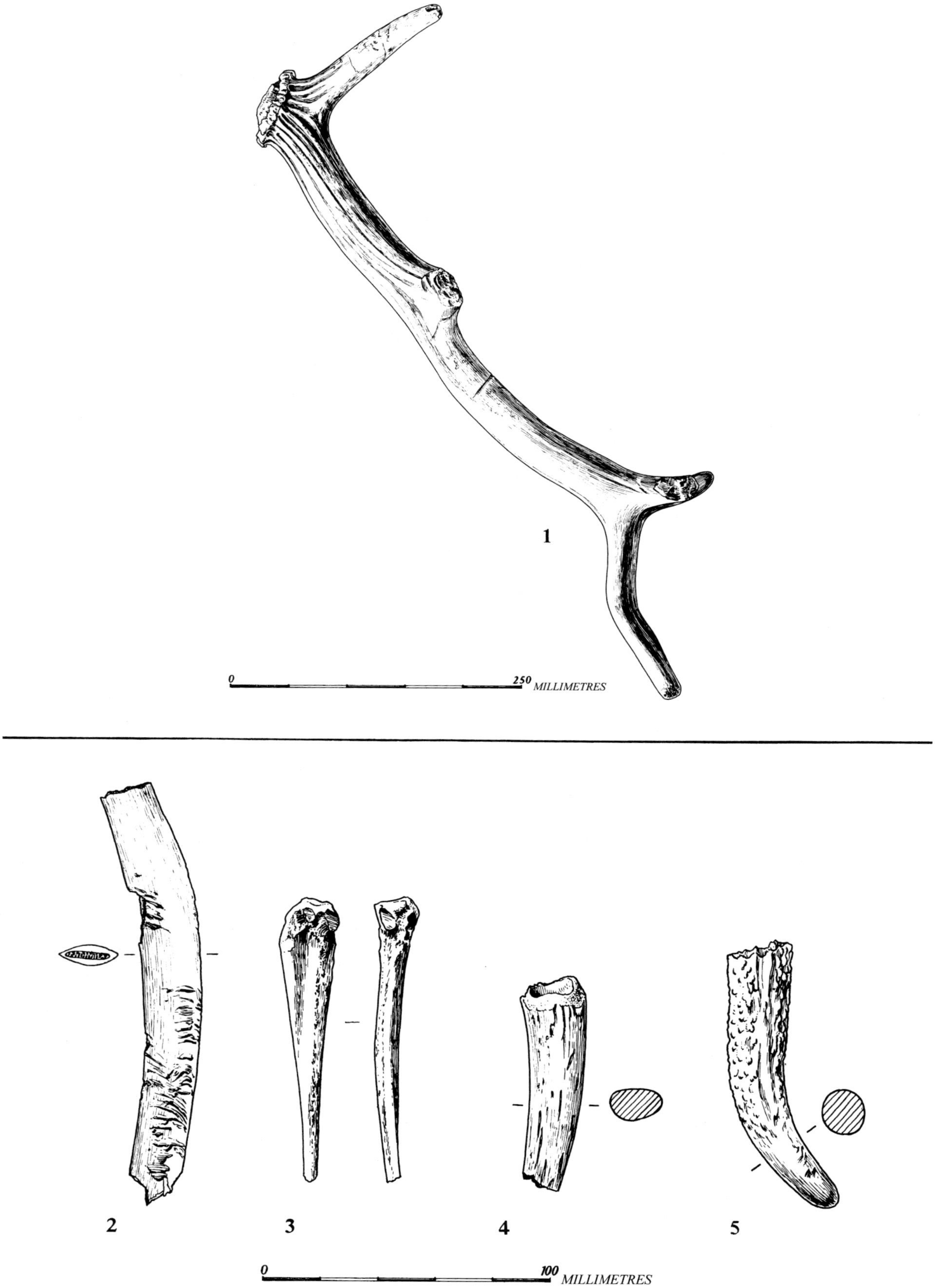

Fig. 4.5 Worked bone and antler

2. Chalk loomweight, broken on one side; length 129mm. Oval chalk nodule with worn perforation at one end. Despite damage, signs of string-wear apparent inside the hole.
Enclosure II Cutting BXXIV Pit 43

3. Chalk weight, roughly oval shape 84mm x 75mm, maximum thickness 29mm. Perforation bored from either side. Rather worn, especially around the edges, but not noticeably inside the perforation.
Enclosure II Cutting BXXIV Pit 43

4. Triangular chalk loomweight, broken at two corners and worn around the edges. Perforation at bottom centre shows distinct

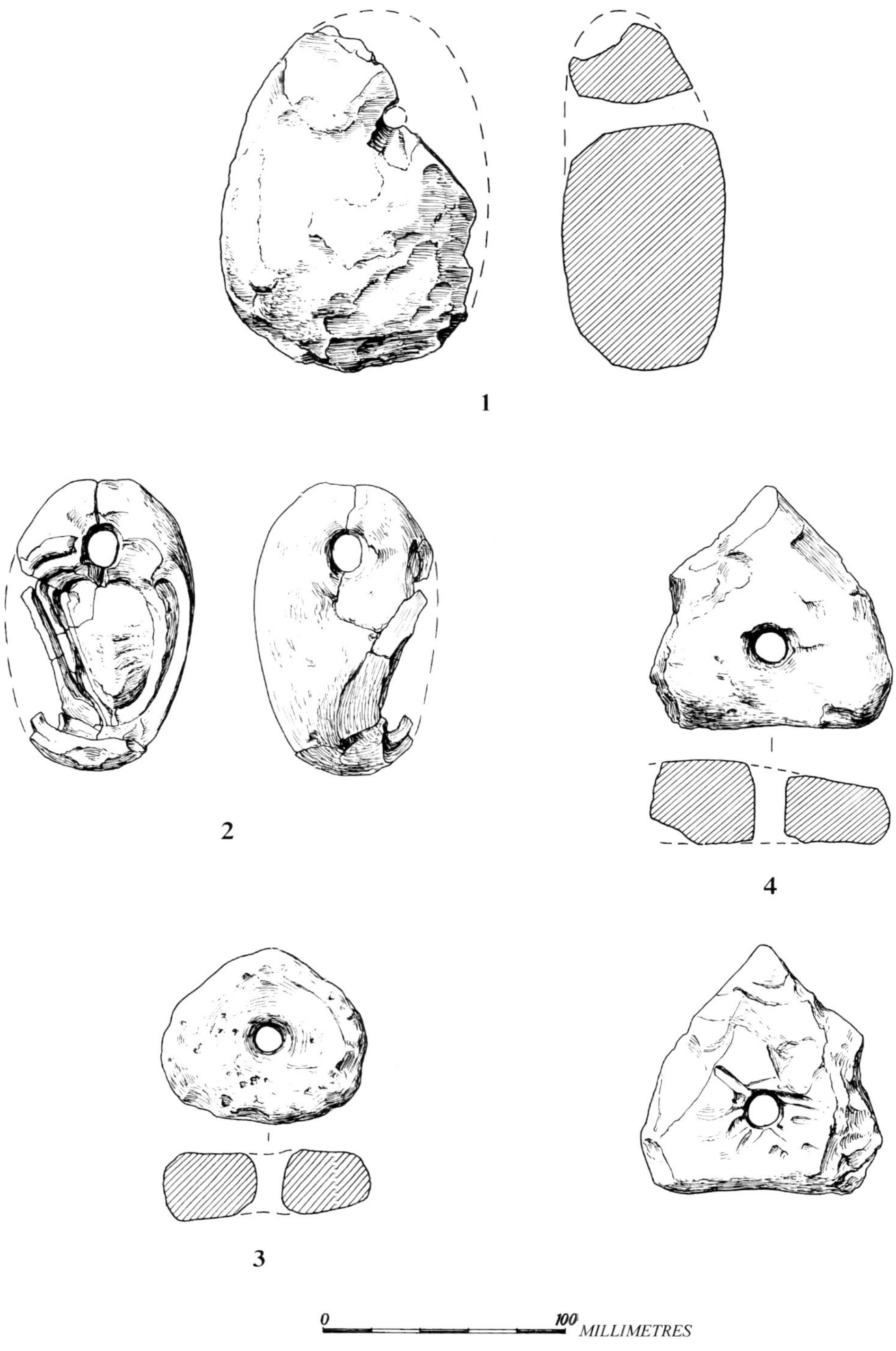

Fig. 4.6 Chalk loomweights (scale 1:3)

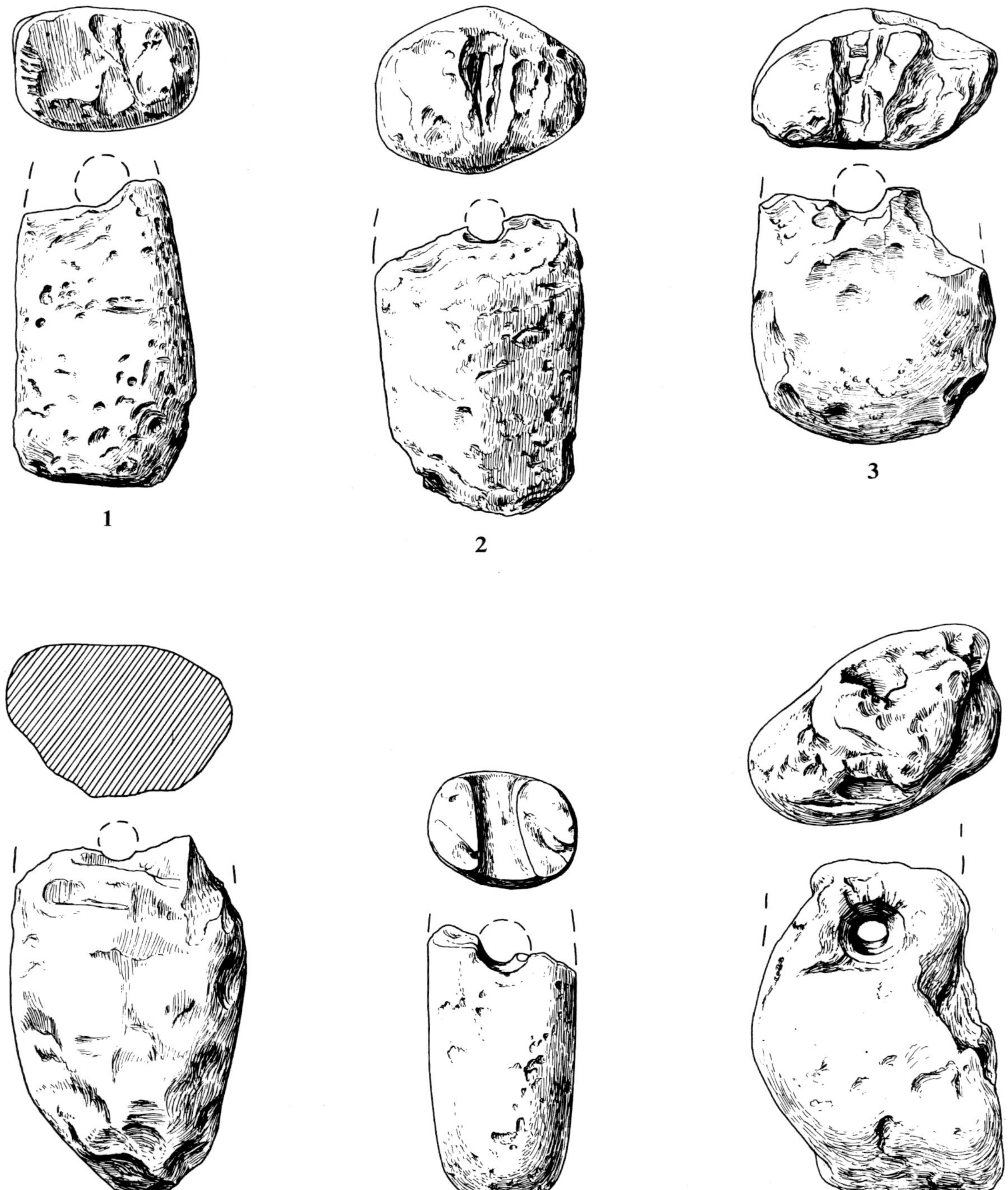

Fig. 4.7 Chalk loomweights (scale 1:3)

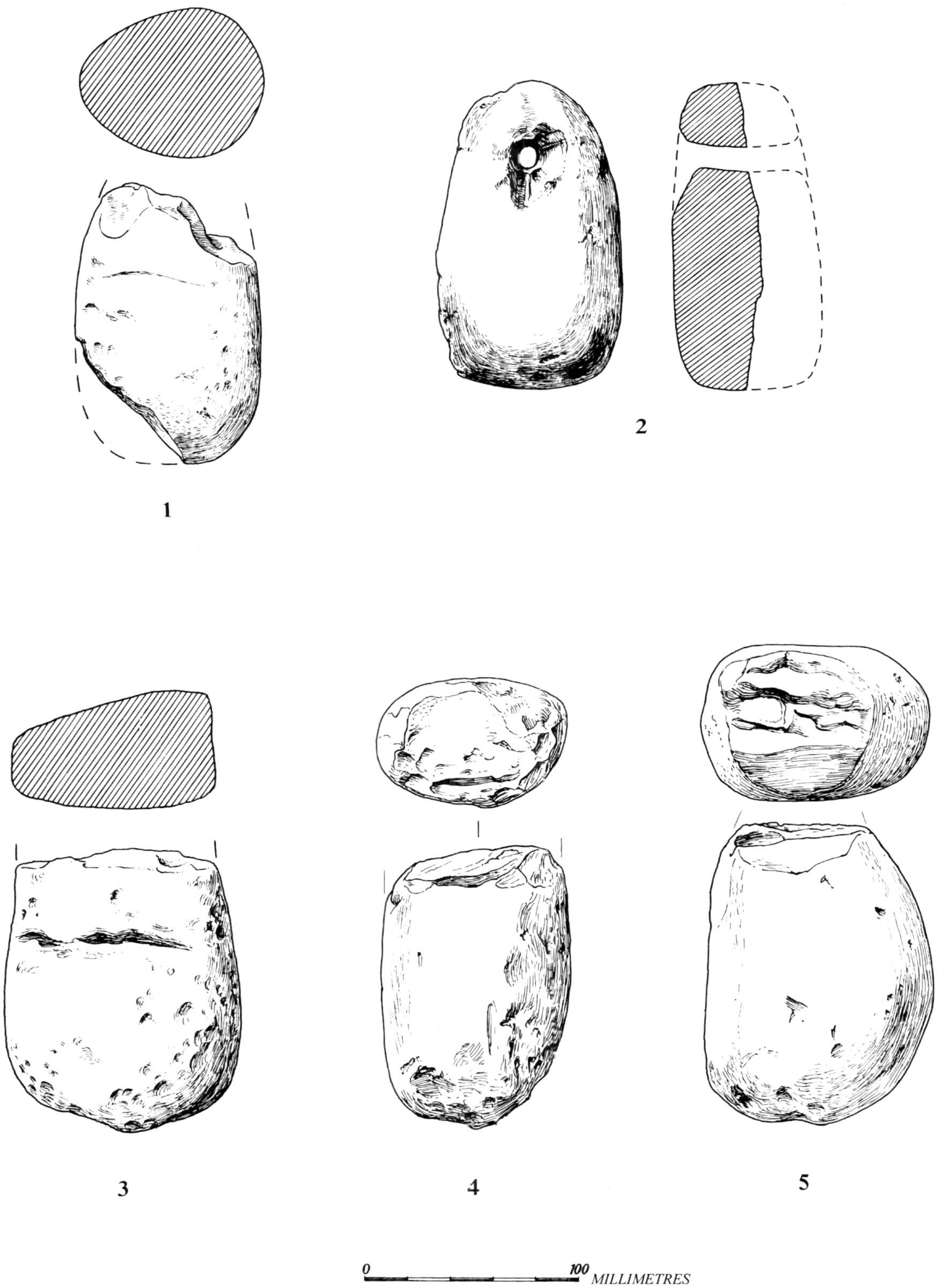

Fig. 4.8 Chalk loomweights (scale 1:3)

string lines. The illustration shows that the strings were attached in four different ways, towards top, bottom and sides of weight.
Enclosure II Cutting BXXX Pit 53

Fig. 4.7 nos 1 – 6

1. Cylindrical chalk loomweight, broken across perforation; surviving length 144mm. Slight string marks at edge of perforation.
   Enclosure II Cutting BVI Pit 1

2. Cylindrical chalk loomweight; surviving length 142mm. Perforation not finished off smoothly, suggesting breakage during manufacture. Surfaces smoothed, so possibly body shaped attempting perforation.
   Enclosure II Cutting BV Pit 7

3. Chalk loomweight, probably originally cylindrical, but broken on one side and across perforation at narrow end; surviving length 120mm. Perforation not finished off smoothly, suggesting breakage during manufacture. Surfaces still rough, so weight may have been discarded before body finished.
   Enclosure II Cutting BXI, Pit 36 (2)

4. Ovoid chalk loomweight, broken across perforation; surviving length 170mm. Surfaces of body rough, but the small patch of the perforation seems finished.
   Enclosure II Cutting BXVI Pit 22

5. Cylindrical chalk loomweight, broken across perforation; surviving length 130mm. Perforation bored from both sides shows slight traces of string-wear.
   Enclosure II Cutting BXXV Pit 39 (1)

6. Chalk loomweight, irregular oval shape; length 158mm. Perforation bored from both sides shows slight traces of string-wear. Tool marks apparent on body.
   Enclosure II Cutting BXXIV Pit 39

Fig. 4.8 nos 1 – 5

1. Sub-cylindrical chalk loomweight, broken below perforation at the narrow end and bottom corner; surviving length 140mm. Surface of body smooth.
   Enclosure II Cutting B XVII (2) (trial trench for ditch, SW area)

2. Sub-cylindrical chalk loomweight, broken in half lengthways; length 150mm. Perforation at narrow end. Distinct string marks around hole. Surface of body worn.
   Enclosure II Cutting BIV Posthole Complex 5

3. Sub-cylindrical chalk loomweight, broken below perforation; surviving length 138mm. Surface of body weathered.
   Enclosure II Cutting BV Posthole Complex 5

4. Roughly cylindrical chalk loomweight, broken below perforation; surviving length 135mm.
   Enclosure II Cutting BXXX Pit 60

5. Ovoid chalk loomweight, ovoid, broken across perforation at narrow end; surviving length 148mm. Perforation incomplete, indicating breakage during manufacture. Very hard chalk, quite heavily burnt.
   Enclosure II Cutting B XXVI Pit 44 (2)

Fig. 4.9 nos 1 – 3

1. Chalk loomweight, sub-triangular; length 156mm, weight 1800g. Small perforation at narrow end, bored from both sides. Traces of string wear on one side.
   Enclosure II Cutting BXVII Pit 27 (trial trench for ditch, SW area)

2. Stone loomweight, sub-triangular; length 200mm, weight 2000g. Broken across perforation with broken piece split lengthways. Perforation bored from both sides. May have broken during manufacture as no traces of wear around the perforation. Slightly micaceous Lower Greensand; discoloured grey by burning, spalled surface.
   Enclosure II Cutting BXXIV Pit 37 (3)

3. Stone loomweight, sub-triangular; length 212mm, weight 2100g. Broken across perforation at narrow end and bottom corner. Traces of wear, particularly below perforation towards the broad end, demonstrate use before breakage, but not direct suspension from the narrow end. Possibly encaged in string when suspended from warp threads. Local Lower Greensand; discoloured and blackened by burning, one side pinkish where flaked.
   Enclosure II Cutting BXXIII Pit 37 (3)

Not illustrated

1. Discoidal chalk loomweight, broken across perforation; diameter 190mm. No clear traces of wear inside perforation.
   Enclosure II Cutting B XXXI (2)

2. Sub-cylindrical chalk loom weight, broken across perforation at narrow end and again below it; surviving length 60mm. Perforation incomplete, indicating breakage during manufacture. Burnt hard chalk.
   Enclosure II Cutting BXXXIII Pit 67 (3)

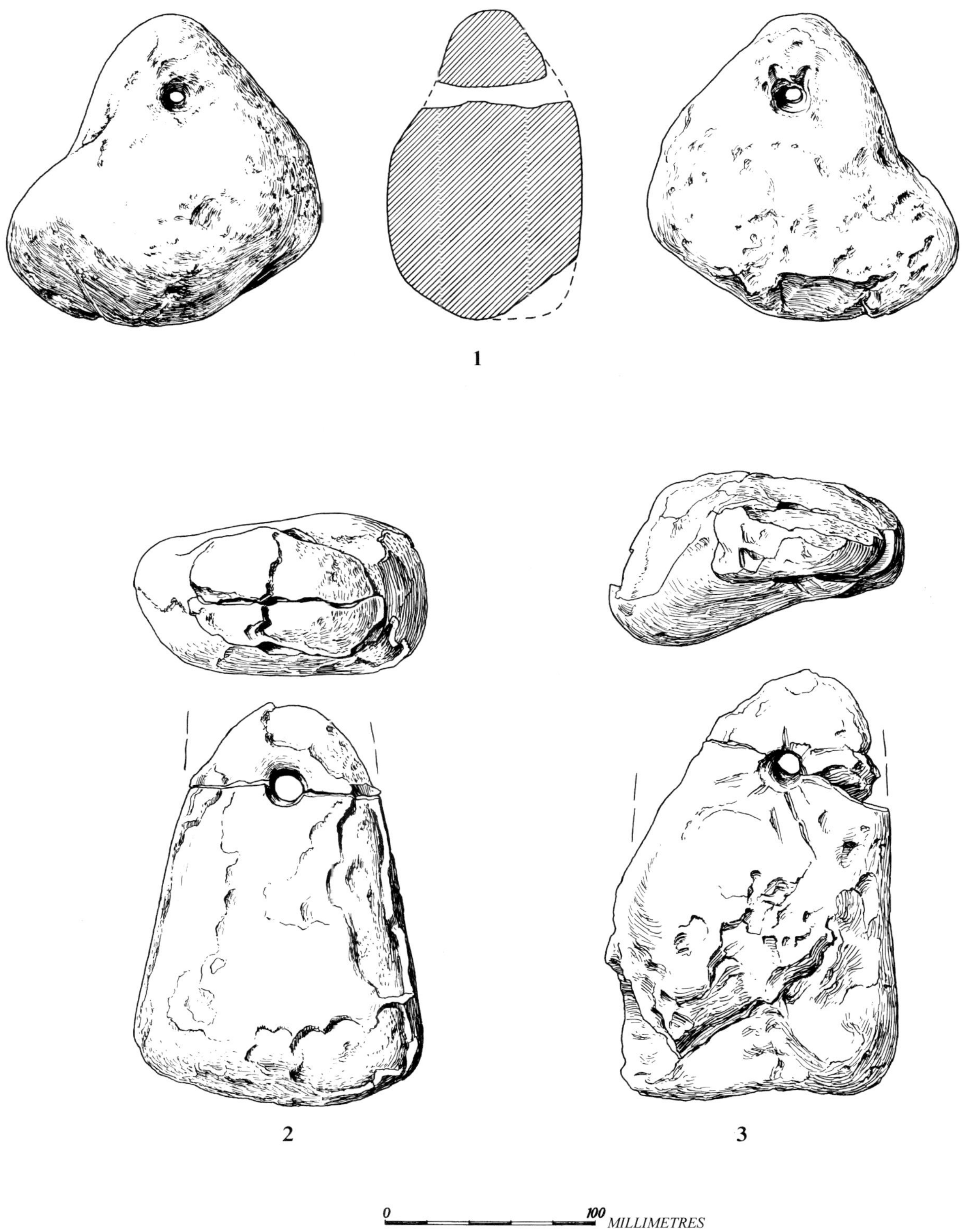

Fig. 4.9 Chalk and Greensand loomweights (scale 1:3)

3. Roughly pear-shaped chalk loomweight, broken across perforation at narrow end; surviving length 150mm. Perforation bored from both sides. Distinct string-marks on edge of perforation.
   Enclosure II Cutting A103 House 3 in topsoil SW of interior

4. Part of chalk loomweight, irregular shape. Perforation bored from both sides.
   Enclosure II Cutting A104 House 3 in topsoil SW of interior

5. Chalk loomweight, roughly quadrangular in section. Broken below perforation, bottom battered and corner broken off; surviving length *c.* 80mm. Hard chalk, slightly burnt.
   Enclosure II Cutting BXXVI Pit 45

6. Discoidal stone loomweight, broken across perforation, surviving length 65mm. Distinct string marks inside perforation and on top of weight. Local Lower Greensand, discoloured by burning.
   Enclosure II Cutting BXXXIII Pit 67

7. Bottom fragment of weight. No other details recorded.
   Enclosure II Cutting A32 Pit 36

Discussion
by Rebecca Annable

The site produced several loomweights and some weights of a more general kind. The preferred material was the locally derived chalk, and the few stone examples are in local Greensand. Many of the weights were broken and worn but their probable shape and function were determinable. The loomweights provide evidence for the existence of upright looms and cloth production on the site and the occurrence of bone combs and spindle whorls fills out the picture. Elaborate string marks and impressions on several of the weights suggest that they may have been used to weight objects other than the loom weft, for example thatch or fish nets. Many of the weights were broken or cracked. This is a common feature of loomweights in general as the heavy stone would knock together while the loom was in motion, causing fracturing and the possible eventual breakage of the object.

Many of the loomweights retained their original perforations, all of which were horizontal and located near the top end. Where the method of perforation was recognisable, the holes were bored from opposite sides to meet in the middle. Several weights had unfinished perforations and were rough on the exterior, which suggests that they were broken in manufacture. Wear marks in the perforations indicate that cords were threaded through the hole to suspend the stone and attach it to the vertical weft of the loom. In addition, string bags may have been used to encase the object and to give greater support during weaving. The possible thatch and fish net weights may also have been encased in a string bag and suspended from the roof area of the houses, or from fishing nets.

Cylindrical weights formed the greater part of the site assemblage, and these were often well made. This is a practical shape, as the straight sides would have been less likely to knock against other weights and cause fracturing. But the area of perforation was usually the vulnerable part and the weights were often broken or cracked at this point. The more irregular shaped weights found at Longbridge are a feature of many sites of the period. Their irregularity may have been due to the difficulties of working stone and/or a general attitude that regularity was not always sufficiently desirable or necessary to expend the additional effort required for precise shaping.

Parallels can be seen throughout areas of England but mainly in the southern part of the country. The sub-triangular shape of the large stone weights from Pit 37 resemble those from Swallowcliffe Down (Clay 1925) and All Cannings Cross (Cunnington 1912) and the long cylindrical-shaped chalk weight from Pit 39 (Fig. 4.7, 5) is paralleled at the site of Fifield Bavant (Clay 1924). Maiden Castle yielded similar shaped weights in Iron Age levels (Wheeler 1943; Laws 1991). A large collection of 256 chalk weights recovered from Danebury encompasses a very wide morphological range that includes the Longbridge varieties (Brown 1984; Laws *et. al.* 1991). The method of horizontal perforation visible in all the weights is paralleled at other Iron Age sites, but this method was not exclusive. Weights with multiple perforations are known at Boscombe Down (Richardson 1952) and Fifield Bavant Down (Clay 1924) and the methods of hanging these weights can only be surmised.

Postholes associated with House 1 (Enclosure II Area S3) and Posthole Complex 5 (Enclosure II Area S2) produced the only loomweight fragments from the domestic areas. All of these are oval or cylindrical in shape, perhaps suggesting that the triangular shape was a later development, as the remaining weights, in a variety of shapes that included triangular, came from pits. Pit 37 (Enclosure II Area S3) yielded two large sub triangular stone weights with very heavy bases (Fig. 4.9, 2 and 3). They were similar in shape and were associated with other notable objects in what clearly represented an act of deliberate deposition. Pit 27 produced a distinctly triangular-shaped weight, which was finely constructed (Fig. 4.9, 1). Pits 39, 44 and 60, all within Area S3 outside House 2, produced cylindrical-shaped weights. An example from Pit 39 was especially finely constructed (Fig. 4.7, 5). The remaining weights from Pits 43 and 53 in Area S3 were fragmentary and, in several cases, it was difficult to determine their original shape. One or two of them may have been weights of a more general kind, for example thatch or fish net weights, especially those from Area A103.

Other Stone Objects

Fig. 4.10 nos 1 – 10

1. Near complete sub-circular sandstone rubber; diameter 103mm, maximum thickness 40mm. Edges slightly damaged and both broad surfaces show signs of wear, but one is more flat and smooth from use. Both have traces of brown staining, and the flatter, smoother surface has lumps of what appears to be haematite adhering. A dark grey brown grit sandstone, possibly Corallian: Bristol Pennant sandstone.
   Enclosure II Cutting BXXIX Pit 66

2. Sandstone rubber; diameter 99mm, maximum thickness 30mm. Edges slightly damaged. It has a pecked grinding surface, possibly modified from a quern. Grey stone, burnt red brown in places. Probably Pennant sandstone or other non-local sandstone.
   Enclosure II Cutting BXXIII west extension (2)

3. Sandstone rubber or sharpening stone; length 80mm, maximum thickness 40mm. One end and one side distinctly flattened by wear. Waterworn stream pebble of very fine grained palaeozoic, grey sandstone.
   Enclosure II Cutting BXXX (1)

4. Chert rubber; diameter *c.* 105mm, maximum thickness 43mm. Edges broken, no finished or worked surfaces. Dark green Chert: Upper Greensand.
   Enclosure II House 4 PH 216

5. Part of sandstone rubber, broken in half but originally circular; diameter 95mm, maximum thickness 40mm. Upper surface well adapted to hand grip, under surface smoothed by grinding. Burnt red in places. Brown sandstone, either Pennant from Bristol Coalfield area or Westbury Iron Ore sandstone. Enclosure III, in depression in southwest corner of trial hole, close to stake holes, associated with fragments of burnt bone

6. Blade end of polished Neolithic stone axe; total length 72mm, blade length 17mm. Very battered. The broken end has been smoothed and evidently been used as a whetstone.
   Enclosure II Cutting BXX backfill from 1958 excavation

In a report on the axe R. W. Sanderson (1975) of the Ancient Monuments Laboratory identified the rock as a thermally metamorphosed gabbro (epidiorite) composed of laths and plates of oligoclase-andesine, containing numerous small prismatic crystals of greenish-brown hornblende, up to *c.* 0.7mm long. Coarse aggregates of similar hornblende enclose residual grains of colourless or neutrally tinted clinopyroxene. The larger plates of hornblende measure *c.* 1.35mm in length. Broken and bent prisms of apatite *c.* 0.64mm long, and large, sometimes skeletal, grains of opaque iron ore are common accessories. The groundmass contains granular aggregates of quartz, small poikilitic plates of biotite and a little sericite. The material is much weathered and there are no matches for this specimen in the AML collection. It is probably one of the epidiorites found in the vicinity of the granite intrusions of Cornwall, but it is not possible to assign it to any of the Stone Axe groups.

7. Hammerstone of Upper Greensand Chert; 70mm x 65mm. Very battered with use.
   Enclosure II House 1 PH 154

8. Hammerstone of Upper Greensand Chert; 75mm x 65mm. Fairly battered.
   Enclosure II House 1 PH 155.

9. Hammerstone of flint, spherical; diameter 65mm. Battered.
   Enclosure II Cutting BXXX Pit 57.

10. Sandstone lamp, roughly hemispherical; 83mm x 73mm x 50mm. Artificially hollowed out in the middle. The hollow shows traces of reddening by burning around the upper edges and adjacent parts. Lower Greensand.
    Enclosure II Cutting BXIV/XX (1)

Not Illustrated

1. Fragment of sandstone, burnt; diameter 193mm, maximum thickness 20mm. One side straight, one surface smoothed and with traces of haematite. Pennant sandstone.
   Enclosure II Pit 44 (2)

2. Fragment of yellow brown shiny stone; length 90mm. One edge appears to have been used for sharpening or polishing. Upper Greensand Chert.
   Unstratified

Fig. 4.11 nos 1 – 7

1. Fragment of rubbing stone; length 82mm, maximum thickness 18mm. Both surfaces flat and worn, but one worked slightly concave as if the broken fragment had been used as a hone. Fine grained red sandstone.
   Enclosure II Cutting BXXVI Pit 45 (3)

2. Fragment of stone; surviving length 55 mm, maximum thickness 14mm. Both surfaces flat and one edge very smooth, probably used as a hone. Fine grey micaceous sandstone.
   Enclosure II Cutting BXXVI Pit 51

3. Stone fragment, possibly used as a hone;

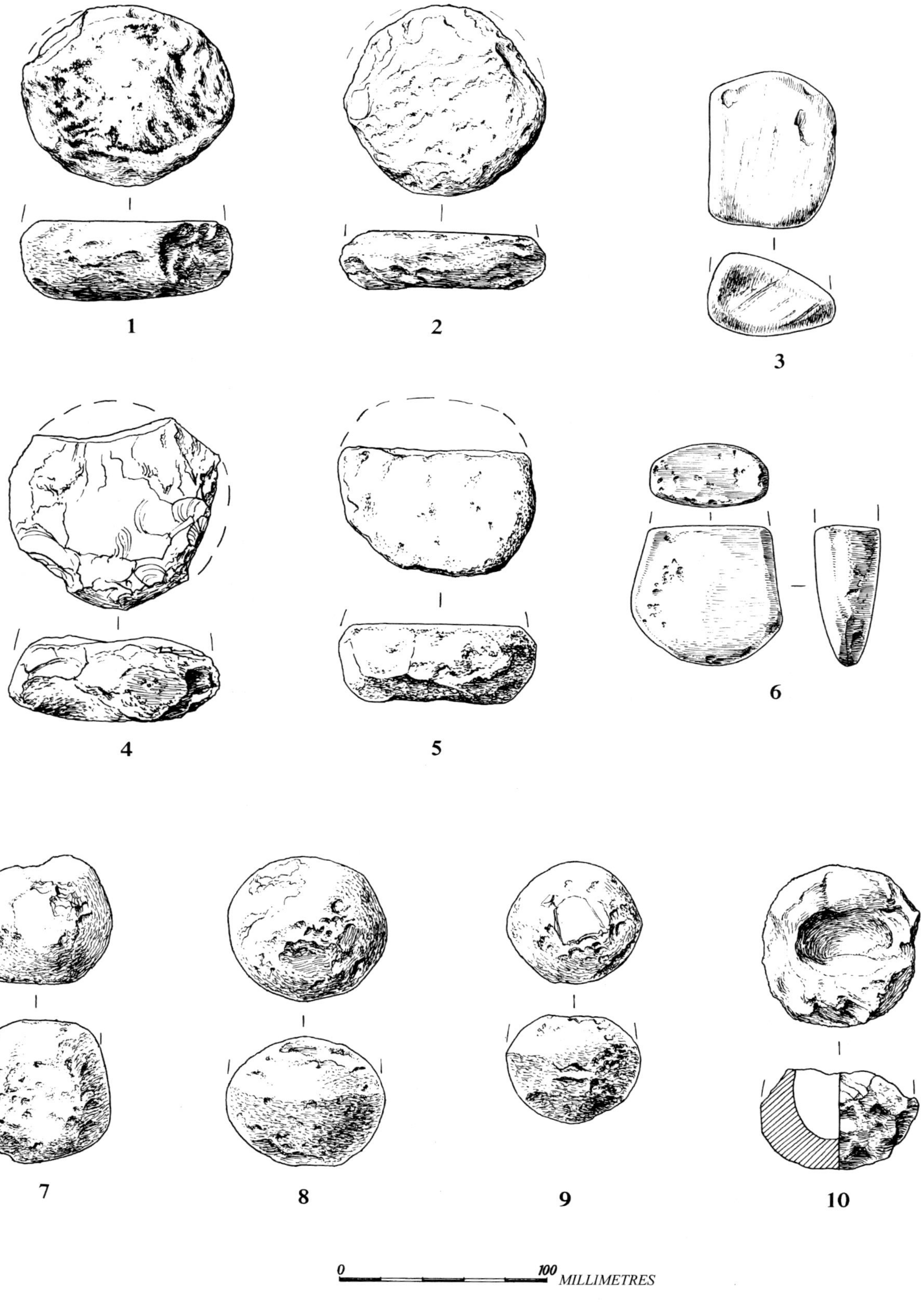

Fig. 4.10 Worked stone (scale 1:3)

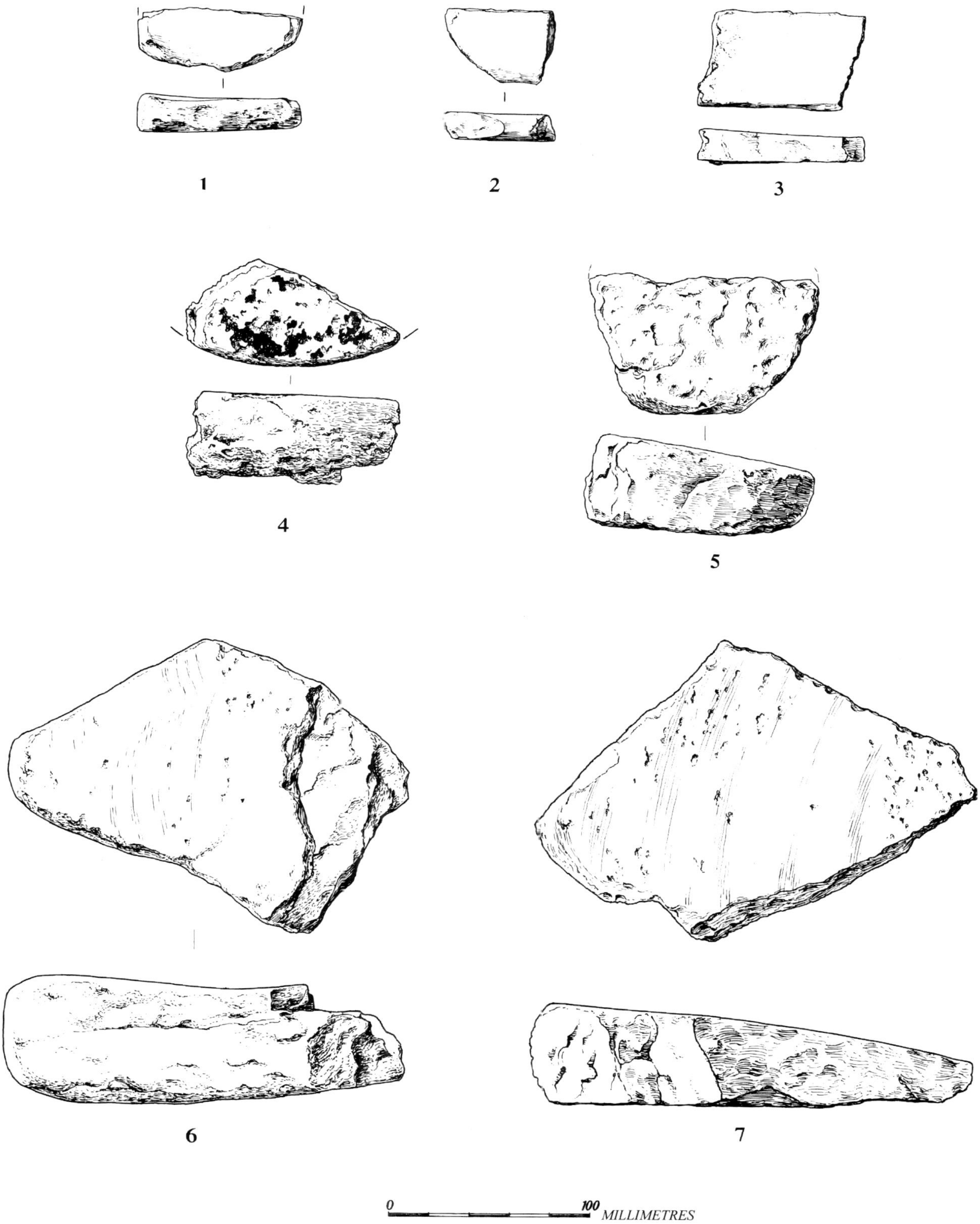

Fig. 4.11 Worked stone

length 75mm, maximum thickness 17mm. One broad surface very smooth. Fine grained red sandstone.
Enclosure II Cutting BXXXIII WH 19

4. Fragment of sandstone rubber; surviving length 100mm, maximum thickness 45mm. Flat grinding surface and worked edge. Broken edges show quite green where not reddened by burning. Grinding surface has pockets and accretions of haematite, so may have been used for grinding haematite, possibly for on-site haematite coated pottery production. Local Lower Greensand.
Enclosure II House 4 PH 218

5. Half a sandstone rubber; diameter 115mm, maximum thickness 48mm. Smoothed grinding surface. Possibly made from a broken quern stone. Lower Greensand.
Enclosure II House 3 PH 10

6. Large fragment from a sandstone saddle quern; surviving length 200mm, maximum thickness 66mm. Two original edges survive and large part of a well worn grinding area, worn concave. Ferruginous brown grit sandstone, burnt grey mauve, probably Pennant sandstone.
Enclosure II Cutting BXXXI (2)

7. Large fragment of lower stone of sandstone rotary quern; surviving length 220mm, maximum thickness 43mm. The grinding surface is very worn, with constant roughening and re-grinding. The broken edge is very thin.
Enclosure II Cutting BXXIII (2) topsoil

Not Illustrated

1. Fragment of lower stone of saddle quern; surviving length 140mm, maximum thickness 50mm. Grinding surface smooth with slight peck marks in surface. Coarse grained stone, burned pink. Not a sandstone, probably Sarsen.
Enclosure II House 3 topsoil in southwest sector

2. Possible fragment of quern. No other details.
Enclosure II House 3 topsoil on south side of house.

SPINDLE WHORLS

by Christopher Hawkes and Sonia Chadwick Hawkes

Fig. 4.12

1. Cylindrical ceramic spindle whorl, cylindrical; diameter 34mm, thickness 31mm. Three rows of fingernail impressed decoration around the outside. Perforation bored from one side, diameter 9mm, tapering to 6.5mm (illustrated end). Exterior orange buff, interior blackish grey; sparse white grits and small red inclusions. Weathered and worn.
Enclosure II House 1 PH 154

2. Cylindrical ceramic spindle whorl; diameter 28mm, thickness 25mm, diameter of hole 5mm. Exterior deep red; gritty fabric with dense rounded inclusions and small flint inclusions, fabric similar to pottery from House 2. Surfaces weathered.
Enclosure II Cutting B XXIV (2) topsoil (probably from House 2)

3. Biconical ceramic spindle whorl; diameter 46mm, thickness 28mm. Perforation bored from one end, diameter 9mm, tapering to 6mm. Exterior buff, though largely burnt to dark grey brown; fine, well levigated fabric with flecks of mica, very sparse, small grits and small red inclusions, fabric similar to House 1 pottery. Smooth surface.
Enclosure II House 1 PH 186

4. Ceramic spindle whorl, roughly biconical; diameter 34mm, maximum thickness 29mm, diameter of hole 4mm. Fine fabric with small white grits; weathered and burnt and cracked with heat.
Enclosure II House 4 PH 200

5. Ceramic spindle whorl, truncated rounded-conical; diameter 34mm, thickness 25mm. Diameter of hole 10mm, tapering to 5mm; wider hole ends with bell-mouth. The shape and bell-mouth recalls the 'Hallstatt' type of continental whorl, found occasionally in Britain, *e.g.* Park Brow (Smith 1927). Exterior deep red brown; very fine white grits, tiny micaceous flecks and tiny well-rounded red and black siliceous or quartzite grits, with flint grit temper.
Enclosure II Cutting BXXIV Pit 40

6. Disc shaped chalk spindle whorl; diameter 34mm, maximum thickness 18mm. Perforation bored from both sides rather irregularly, conically; diameter of larger hole 12mm, tapers to centre, 3 mm, and widens to other end, diameter 10mm. The illustrated side is marked by rubbing from cord or thong. Exterior shows finishing scratches made by a knife.
Enclosure III House 3 (2a) on top of undisturbed level, in entrance area

7. Chalk spindle whorl, roughly biconical; diameter 41mm, thickness 27mm, diameter of hole 7.5mm. Smooth surfaces.
Enclosure III House 3 PH 108, in burnt fill.

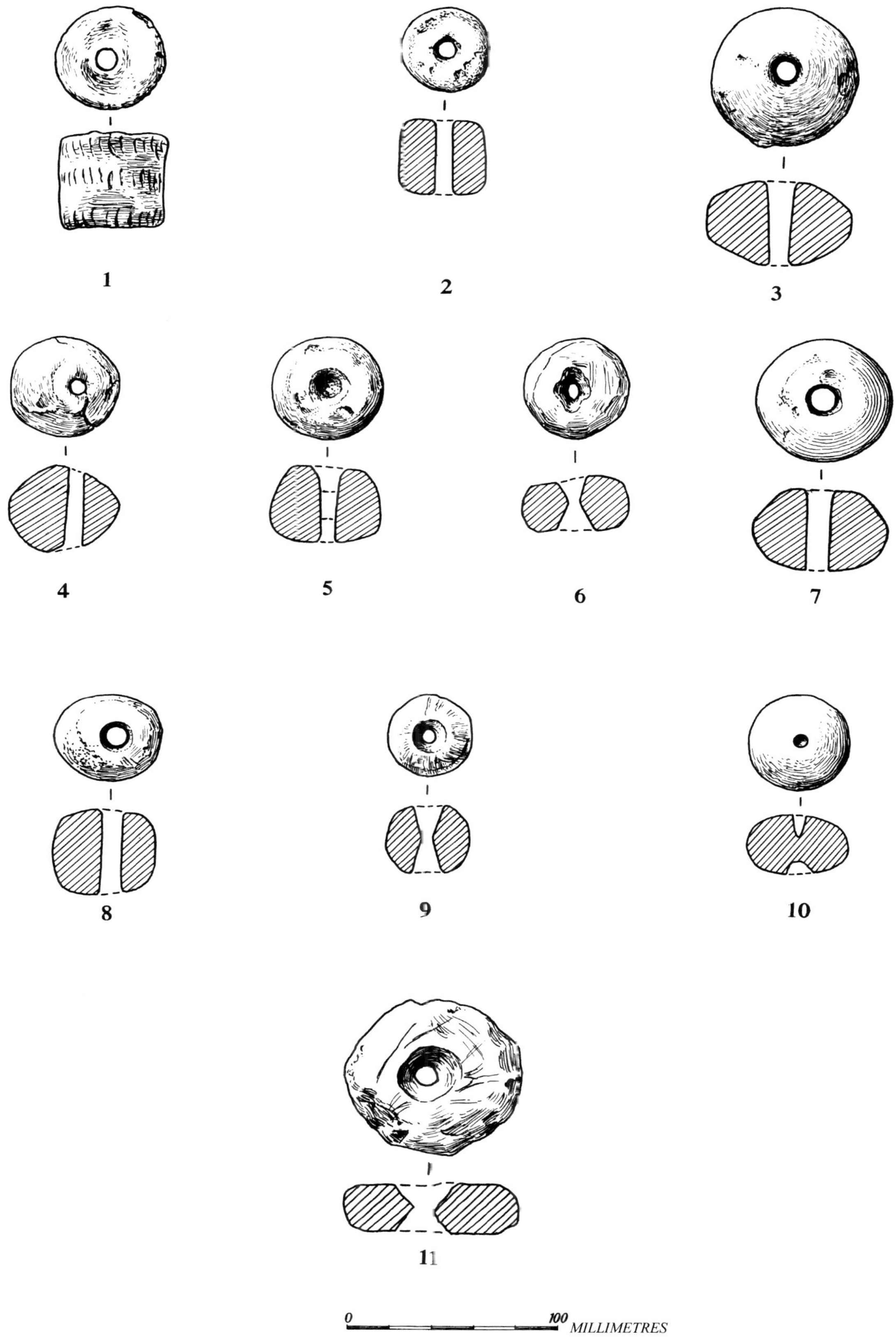

Fig. 4.12 Spindle whorls

8. Chalk spindle whorl, rounded but approaching cylindrical; maximum diameter 35mm, thickness 29mm, diameter of hole 6mm. Exterior shows scratches made by a knife.
Enclosure III House 3 (2a) topsoil on west side of house, between inner and middle rows of postholes

9. Barrel shaped chalk spindle whorl; diameter 27mm, thickness 22mm. Perforation cut conically from both sides; diameter of larger hole 10 mm, tapers to centre, 3mm, and widens to other end, diameter 9mm.
Enclosure II Cutting BXI Working Hollow 2

10. Chalk spindle whorl, flattened spheroid; diameter 32mm, thickness 20mm. Unfinished as perforation not complete.
Enclosure II Cutting BXXX Pit 55 (1)

11. Disc shaped chalk spindle whorl or weight; diameter 57mm, thickness 15mm. Perforated conically from both sides; diameter of larger hole 20mm, tapers to centre, 6mm, and widens to other end, diameter 17mm. Surfaces not badly worn, but one side shows several scratch marks.
Enclosure II House 1 PH 225

Discussion

by Rebecca Annable

The site produced 11 spindle whorls, all complete and well preserved. The materials used in their manufacture were clay, chalk and pottery. The spindle whorls preserve clear evidence of the method of perforation. Most of the bored holes were regular in shape, but some were slightly off-centre or tapering. The perforations of the ceramic whorls would have been created by a stick or similar object punched through from one side when the clay was still wet, forming a cylindrical hole. The chalk whorls were perforated from two sides to meet in the middle, most often producing a double conical hole. The unfinished spindle whorl from Pit 55 (Fig. 4.12, no. 10) illustrates this method.

Most of the spindle whorls were recovered from postholes and topsoil layers in the habitation areas of all four roundhouses. The remainder came from Pits 40 and 55 (Enclosure II Area S3) and Working Hollow 2 (Enclosure II Area S1). The cylindrical, decorated whorl from main ring PH154 of House 1 is reminiscent of cylindrical decorated ceramic loomweights, which are generally found in Bronze Age contexts. However, adjacent PH186 produced a ceramic biconical whorl of common Iron Age form (Poole 1984, fig. 7.46; 1991, fig. 7.43). PH 225 on the other side of the house contained a chalk disc shaped whorl or small weight (Fig. 4.12, 11). The topsoil of House 2 produced a well-preserved cylindrical clay whorl retaining a clear perforation and House 3 produced three chalk whorls, cylindrical and disc-shaped with regular perforations, from topsoil and posthole provenances. A rounded clay whorl with an unusual off-centre perforation (Fig. 4.12, 4) was recovered from main ring PH 200 of House 4. Pit 40 produced the only spindle whorl from the site made from a pottery sherd. Pit 55 and Working Hollow 2 yielded one chalk spindle whorl each. These were spheroid and barrel-shaped respectively. The whorl from Pit 55 was unfinished, with an incomplete perforation.

Spindle whorls are a common find on Iron Age sites. The compact size and shape of the spindle whorl has ensured widespread survival on Iron Age sites, and the same range of shapes appear again and again on many sites. Other Wiltshire sites such as Swallowcliffe (Clay 1925), Boscombe Down West (Richardson 1951) and All Cannings Cross (Cunnington 1923) produced similar examples made from baked clay and stone. Chalk spindle whorls were present at Gussage All Saints, Dorset (Wainwright 1979) and their perforations suggest similar methods of manufacture to the Longbridge whorls. The large assemblage of chalk spindle whorls from Danebury (Brown 1984, 422-5; Laws *et al.* 1991, 397-404) and Maiden Castle (Laws 1991, 212) are mostly disc-shaped, while many of the ceramic versions are biconical.

OBJECTS ASSOCIATED WITH METAL-WORKING AND FIRING

by Christopher Hawkes

Fig. 4.13, nos 1-4

1. Fragment of plain rim of ceramic crucible, probably originally bowl-shaped. Exterior covered with a yellowish glaze-like substance, produced by intensive heating. Interior also 'glazed' but with red and green stains. This substance seems residual from the smelting or melting down of copper alloy, implying some level of on-site production. A similar crucible was found at the early Iron Age site at Long Wittenham, Oxfordshire (Savory 1937, 3-4, fig. 1.3).
Enclosure II Cutting BXXVI Pit 50 (2)

2. Complete profile of crucible or miniature jar. Plain rim with small hole in raised lug, short concave neck, rounded shoulder carination, body profile tapering to a flat base with well defined, short vertical external edge. Exterior and interior red to light brown. Medium sandy fabric with sparse medium/coarse flint: Fabric F42. Also featured in the pottery catalogue, Fig. 3.25, no. 4.
Enclosure II Pit 33B

3. Piece of baked clay, possibly oven floor. Pinkish colour, but turning to grey on the unbroken surface, which is grey (with darker grey patches) possibly due to exposure to hot, dark smoke. Fabric has inclusions of tiny white and black flecks, micaceous or siliceous, with

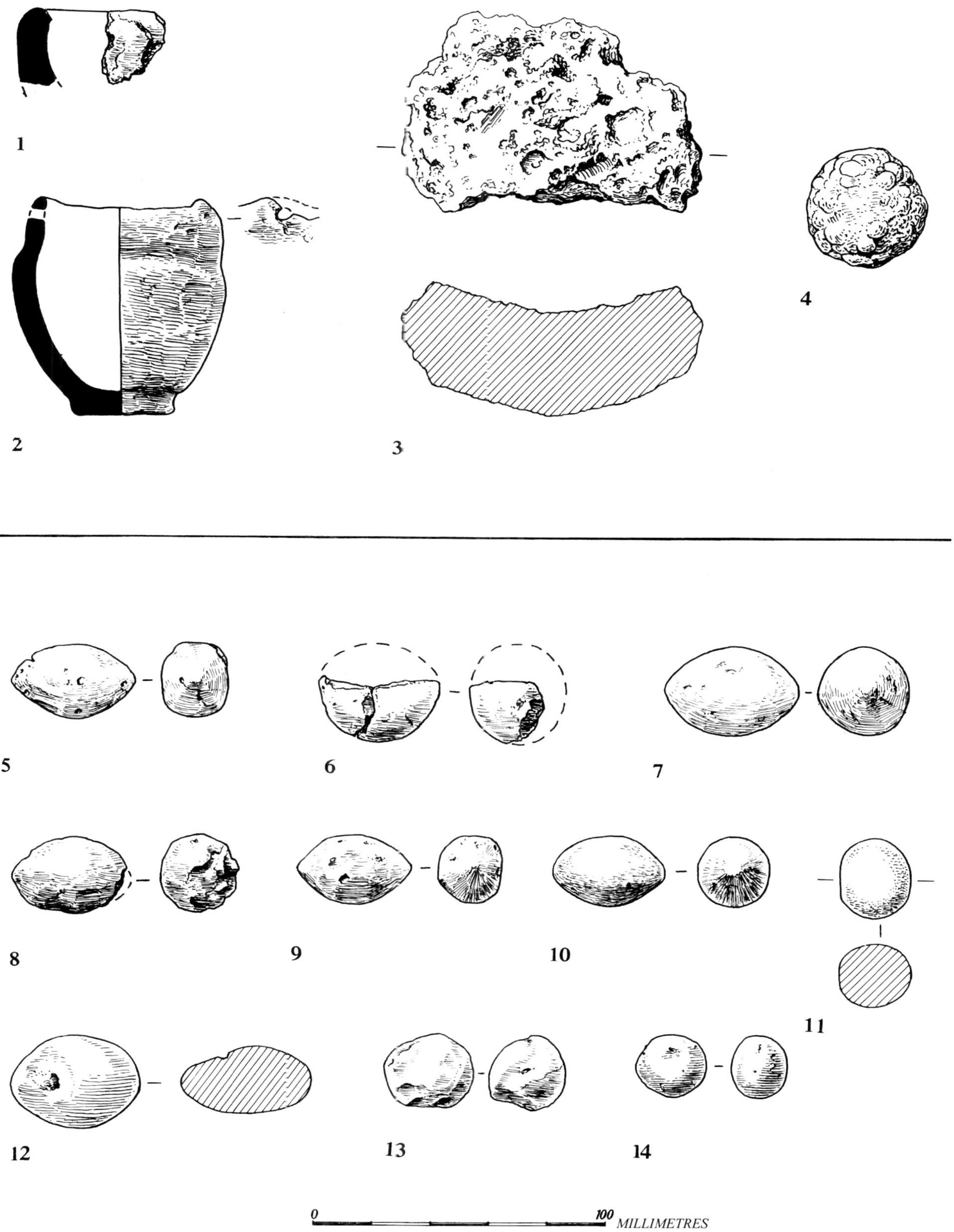

Fig. 4.13 Crucibles and pyrites (nos 1-4); ceramic slingshots (nos 5-14)

temper of black or red burnt and pounded flint which appears in patches on the broken surfaces.
Provenance unrecorded

4. Iron pyrites ball; diameter 41mm. Considerable wear on all surfaces.
Enclosure II Cutting BXXIX Pit 58, placed at right heel of skeleton

FIRED CLAY SLINGSHOTS
by Christopher Hawkes

Fig. 4.13, nos 5-14

5. Ellipsoid slingshot with pointed ends; length 43mm, weight 25g. Pinkish fabric with red streaks (possibly haematite), well-rounded black and white siliceous or quartzite grits, flecks of mica and pounded flint grits; weathered.
Enclosure II Cutting BXXII PH 45

6. Fragments of oval slingshot; length 41mm. Grey brown core, orange surface; sparse white grits, flint inclusions, red inclusions (possibly haematite) and flecks of mica; fairly smooth surface.
Enclosure II House 4 PH 195

7. Ellipsoid slingshot with fairly pointed ends; length 46mm, weight 35g. Pinkish fabric, with red streaks (possibly haematite), well-rounded black and white siliceous or quartzite grits, flecks of mica and pounded flint grits; well preserved.
Enclosure II Cutting BVII Working Hollow I

8. Ellipsoid slingshot, one end fairly pointed, other end damaged; surviving length 38mm, weight 30g. Pinkish orange fabric, with well-rounded black and white siliceous or quartzite grits and flecks of mica; weathered.
Enclosure II Cutting BXXIII Pit 37 (2)

9. Ellipsoid slingshot with fairly pointed ends; length 39mm, weight 25g. Yellow orange fabric, with well-rounded black and white siliceous or quartzite grits, flecks of mica and pounded flint grits.
Enclosure II Cutting BXXXI Pit 63

10. Ellipsoid slingshot with fairly pointed ends; length 40mm, weight 25g. Pinkish fabric with red streaks (possibly haematite), well-rounded black and white siliceous or quartzite grits, flecks of mica and pounded flint grits.
Enclosure II Cutting BXXXI, Pit 63

11. Ceramic slingshot; length 24mm. No other details.

12. Ceramic slingshot; length 44mm. No other details.

13. Ceramic slingshot, irregular shape; length 31mm. Reddish fabric, with white and other siliceous or quartzite grits.
Enclosure II Cutting BXXXIII (1)

14. Ceramic ball, possibly a slingshot, diameter 23mm. Orange fabric, with well-rounded siliceous or quartzite grits, flecks of mica and pounded flint grits.
Enclosure II Cutting BXXXII (2) topsoil

[*Editor's note*] Close parallels for the Longbridge ceramic slingshots are provided by the collections from All Cannings Cross (Cunnington 1923) and Meare (Coles 1987) as well as the hillfort sites of Danebury (Poole 1984, 398-9; 1991a, 370-1) and Maiden Castle (Poole 1991b, 210). Poole proposed that ceramic slingshots, especially the smaller examples, were more likely to have been used for hunting small game than for warfare, for which stone shots would have been better suited (Poole 1991a, 370).

THE DAUB
by Eric Freeman

[*Editor's note*] Eric Freeman's undated daub report was written when he worked for the Ancient Monuments Laboratory. It is essentially a fabric typology, but his more informative observations on fragments of structural daub have been abstracted and included in the Chapter 2 descriptions of the roundhouses.

The daub was divided into five basic types, designated 1, 2/3, 4, 5 and 6. Types 2 and 3 were merged as there were few well-defined points of difference between them.

Type 1, which includes the majority of the samples, is of a dirty white colour when dry (Munsell 10 YR 8/2). It appears to consist of dried chalk mud but it is possible that the chalk was fired before use and applied in the form of a paste of slaked lime. However, simple chemical and visual examination was not capable of distinguishing between these possibilities. Type I fragments frequently show clear impressions of wattle, from which it appears that the poles of the wattle varied from *c.* 5mm to *c.* 40mm. in diameter. Some fragments, in addition to wattle impressions, also show two flat surfaces, roughly parallel to one another and *c.* 40 mm apart.

Type 2/3, the second most abundant type in the collection, is clearly distinct from Type 1, and consisted of burnt, somewhat calcareous clay. In general it survived in smaller pieces than type 1 and, probably as a result of this increased fragmentation, rarely shows wattle impressions. The colour varies within individual pieces from a relatively

Fig. 4.14 Daub showing wattle impressions: (a) House 2 PH 142; (b) House 2 PH 172

unoxidised dark greyish-brown (Munsell 10 YR 4/2) to a more strongly oxidised reddish yellow colour (Munsell 7.5 YR 7/8), Experimental firing of the relatively unoxidised clay reproduced the reddish-yellow colour of the more oxidised material.

Type 4 applies to low density, high porosity materials which contain a high proportion of fine sand/silt. It is predominantly brownish-yellow (Munsell 10 YR 6/6) but also contains relatively unoxidised areas of a dark grey colour (Munsell 10 YR 4/1). The grey areas also developed a brownish-yellow colour upon experimental firing. The Type 4 material contained only a small amount of calcareous matter, and showed no wattle impressions.

Type 5 represents a calcareous clay showing no evidence of burning. It is light grey (Munsell 5 Y 6/1) and contains isolated sub-angular compact cream coloured limestone fragments and small fragments of charcoal. Type 5 material usually

Table 4.1 Daub from House 1

House 1	*Type 1*	*Type 2/3*	*Type 4*	*Type 5*	*Type 6*
PH 165	156 S	--	--	156 m	--
PH 186	--	157	--	–	--
PH 154	--	158 S	--	–	--
PH 237	159	159	--	--	--
PH 225	--	160	--	--	160
PH 42	161m	161 S	--	--	--
PH 154	--	162	--	--	--
PH 63	--	163	--	--	--
PH 151	164	--	--	--	--
PH 165	165	--	--	--	--

Table 4.2 Daub from House 2

House 2	*Type 1*	*Type 2/3*	*Type 4*	*Type 5*	*Type 6*
PH 135	166	--	--	--	166
PH 204	--	167	--	--	--
PH 157	168	168	--	--	168
PH 132	169	--	--	--	--
PH 171	170	--	--	--	--
PH 126	171 J	--	--	171 J	--
PH 182	172 J	--	--	172 J	--
PH 126	173 J	--	--	173 mJ	--
PH 142	174 J	--	--	174 mJ	--
PH 172	175 J	--	--	175 mJ	--

Table 4.3 Daub from House 3

House 1	*Type 1*	*Type 2/3*	*Type 4*	*Type 5*	*Type 6*
PH 11	--	286	--	--	--
PH 47	--	--	--	--	287 S
PH 63	--	288	--	--	--
PH 64	--	--	--	--	289 (?)
PH 70	290	290	--	--	--
PH 71	291	--	--	--	--
PH 124	292	--	--	--	--
PH 103	293 (?)	--	--	--	--
PH 107	--	294 (?)	--	--	--
Cutting 113	--	--	295	--	--
Cutting 104	--	296	--	--	--

Table 4.4 Daub from House 4

House 1	*Type 1*	*Type 2/3*	*Type 4*	*Type 5*	*Type 6*
PH 197	--	279	--	--	--
PH 198	280	--	--	280	--
PH 207	281	--	--	--	--
PH 210	282	--	--	--	--
PH 208	--	283	--	--	--
PH 195	--	284	--	--	--
PH 216	285	285	--	--	--

occurs associated with fine chalk rubble (*ie* Type I) which it encloses in a rather non-uniform way. Experimental firing of Type 5 material produced the colours seen in Type 2/3.

Type 6 material is of a totally different nature to the other four and indicate a much higher degree of firing, which resulted in the formation of a very low density slag-like material with porous particles of *c.* 5-10 mm diameter loosely welded together to form an aggregate, with an overall brown colour (Munsell 7.5 Y 5/2). A certain amount of calcareous matter is present in this category of material.

Table 4.5 Daub from pits and other deposits.

House 1	*Type 1*	*Type 2/3*	*Type 4*	*Type 5*	*Type 6*
P 39	176	--	--	--	--
--	177	177 m	--	--	--
P 37	178	178	--	--	--
P 37	179	--	--	--	--
P 39	180	--	--	--	--
P 52	181	--	--	--	--
P 38	--	182	--	--	--
--	183 J	--	--	183 J	--
P 50	184	--	--	--	--
P 60	185	--	--	--	--
P 57 (2)	--	186	--	--	--
P 7	--	187	--	--	--
P 37 (3)	188	--	--	--	--
P 54 (1)	189	--	--	--	--
P 57 (1)	190	190	--	--	--
P 1 (1)	191	--	191	--	--
P 63 (2)	192	--	--	192 mJ	--
Cutting R (2)	--	--	193 S	--	--
P 59 (1)	194 m	--	--	194	--
P 4	--	--	195	--	--
P 21	196 J	--	--	196 mJ	--
P 47	--	197	--	--	--
B XI (2)	--	--	198	--	--
P 37	--	199	--	--	--
P 21	--	--	--	200 S	--

The distribution of these five types of daub is shown in Tables 4.1-4.5. In all cases, assignment of a sample to its type was performed by comparison to a `standard' marked in the table by an 'S'. The letter 'J' indicates the presence of a junction in the sample between the types so marked. In all other cases the occurrence of two or more types in the same sample merely indicates a mixture of separate fragments of these types under the sample number. Finally, the letter 'm' indicates material constituting only a minor fraction of the overall sample.

Chapter 5: The Environment, Economy and Population

INTRODUCTION

by Lisa Brown

The reports presented in this chapter represent a garnering of the most reliable of the specialist evidence compiled from the various levels of examination, classification and analysis of the animal and human bone, charred organic remains, metalworking debris and natural stone, salvaging what has best stood the test of time. Some of the reports presented below were submitted to Sonia Hawkes as preliminary drafts, and others are little more than collections of notes on material by students or amateur volunteers. The analyses have been updated and enhanced where possible and appropriate, but an attempt has been made to respect the original objectives of the individual authors.

Tylecote's metallurgy report, submitted in 1983, is closest to a finished product but does not go so far as to place the analysed material in the context of the site or regional Iron Age economy. The discussion on the imported and local stone by Sonia Hawkes draws together information from the small finds report (see Chapter 4) and notes made during meetings with the geologist Frederick Anderson.

Graham Morgan was consulted during editing of the charcoal report. He recalls that the tables below were compiled in about 1967 when he was working with F. Richardson at the Ancient Monuments Laboratory, and that he was not commissioned at the time to produce a full report on the charcoal. He adds that, as no specific measurements were available in the records made available to him, it cannot be explicitly demonstrated that any of the charcoal derived from structural elements of the roundhouses. He, therefore, drew no conclusions as to whether the examined material represented structural timbers. However, Sonia Hawkes' comments on the radiocarbon results clearly state that charred oak posts were found *in situ* in postholes associated with Houses 1 and 4 (see Chapter 6).

In 2009 Wendy Smith, then of Oxford Archaeology, kindly reviewed and updated the report by M.E.S. Morrison and Sonia Hawkes on the charred grain from Pit 37, adding a discussion highlighting the significance of the deposit. The animal bones report brings together a context catalogue of tentatively identified bones compiled in 1965 by Betty Westley, along with a preliminary report written on a selection of the material by Ralph Harcourt in 1967. This he revised in 1982, in the light of new methodologies and the publication of his report on the large assemblage from Gussage All Saints (Harcourt 1979), discussing both groups in a regional and wider context. Nonetheless, the analysis is not comprehensive as the smaller bone fragments were discarded without recording at an early stage and the report is now over 25 years out of date.

Of the human remains recovered, only the two significantly complete skeletons from Pits 58 and 62 were recorded and analysed by a specialist in the field, Don Brothwell, who worked with the assistance of B. Denston. His report is undated and there are indications throughout that procedures now regarded as standard were not in use at the time of writing. Brothwell and Denston did not discuss the context or significance of the pit burials. Sonia Hawkes considered these issues and offered somewhat idiosyncratic interpretations, which are not included here. The other human bones were identified and catalogued by Shirley Jarman in 1968, but she had clearly not seen the full assemblage, as fragments identified as human by Betty Westley in 1965 do not appear in her catalogue. Westley's entries have been added to Jarman's catalogue (below) but her identifications cannot be regarded as reliable as she was not a human remains specialist. Of a human burial from Pit 63 catalogued by Westley, for example, there is no mention in Jarman's list, but it appears in the site records for the pit as a 'near complete infant under six months' (Chapter 2 and Appendix 2B).

THE METALWORKING DEBRIS

by Ronald Tylecote

Mrs. Hawkes writes: "I have sorted through the pyrites and slag: clearly most of the former is natural, and any burning accidental, but there is an occasional occurrence of pyrites so burnt and fragmented as to make one wonder whether they were smelting it deliberately."

Metallurgical Analysis

Analysis was carried out at the Ancient Monuments Laboratory (AML). The largest and most convincing group of slag came from Pit 7, which produced an original radiocarbon date of 506-640 BC, recalibrated in 2010 as 830-170 cal BC (NPL-108) (see Chapter 6). The pyrites and slag were found in a number of different contexts.

Identification

WH 2. AML no. 650600. Small smithing hearth bottom *c.* 90mm dia. Sectioned and analysed (Table 5.1).
Pit 7. AML no. 650601. Small hearth bottom *c* 80mm dia. Many broken pieces of slag. Sectioned and analysed (Table 5.1).
Pit 13. AML no. 650602. One piece of slag.
Pit 45. AML no. 650603. Small pieces of slag, possibly from a single smithing hearth bottom, or smelting furnace bottom.
Pit 47. AML no. 50604. Small lump of red sandy material with grey fibrous semi-glossy crystals and brownish-red streak (haematite).
Pit 48. AML no. 650605. Yellowish, ochreous material – cone of weathered radial pyrites.
Pit 53. AML no. 650606. Dark brown glassy fuel ash slag.
Pit 54. AML no. 650607. Small weathered, hollow pyrite nodule crust 4-5mm dia. (Analysis of typical specimen from area shown in Table 5.2).
Pit 56. AML no. 650608. One piece of slag, heavy, with drips, with a wood impression. Clearly high in iron. Tap or furnace smelting slag.
Pit 58. AML no.650609. Natural pyrite nodule with material which could be weathered pyrites with flint adhering. Some is weathered outer crusts of nodules and some looks redeposited from water.
Pit 67. AML no. 650610. One piece probable smithing slag.
B XXII Ditch. AML no. 650611. Fragments of iron-stained ironstone.

Results of analysis

The analyses of the hearth bottoms were undertaken by two methods. The XRF shows the total iron on the surface as Fe_2O_3 since much of it was weathered wüstite and redeposited iron in the form of goethite (FeO.OH). The probe analyses were done on a polished section across the core) to analyse the fayalite-wüstite material, together with any glass phase. These indicate the true proportion of iron present as FeO both in the fayalite and in the wüstite. In the case of the other elements, agreement is as would be expected, with somewhat lower figures in the XRF than in the EPMA (EPMA Energy dispersive: Tylecote and Clough 1983).

Table 5.1 Analyses of smithing hearth bottoms from Longbridge Deverill

	XRF (Wave diap.)		*EPMA (Raster; 200_m).*	
AM Lab. no.	*650601*	*650600*	*650601*	*650600*
SiO2	10.1	16.5	25.8	20.5
TiO2	0.1	0.1	0.3	0.3
Al2O3	0.1	1.2	2.4	1.8
Fe2O3	84.5	75.5	--	--
FeO	--	--	60.3	68.4
MnO	0.1	0.2	n.d.	0.3
MgO	0.7	1.1	1.0	0.8
CaO	2.2	3.8	5.0	4.0
K2O	0.5	0.9	1.9	1.4
P2O5	0.4	0.7	--	--
Total	98.7	100.0	96.7	97.5

Key: -- not sought; n.d. not detected; XRF used sodium biborate fusion technique.

Discussion

The analysed material is predominantly smithing debris but at least one piece of slag (650608) could be from a smelting process. Pyrite nodules are present in both the natural and weathered, but not roasted, status. No other type of iron ore is present. The fact that pyrite, weathered or not, is present does not mean that it has been smithed on the site. In an area on the chalk pyrite nodules are usually so common that they might be lying around without indicating any intention of their being used. On the other hand they would serve as strike-a-lights and might have been collected for this purpose. On the basis of composition alone, however, they *could* have been responsible for the iron that gave rise to the smithing hearth bottoms.

Analyses of the hearth bottoms (Table 5.1) showed that they are very low in lime, alumina and manganese, and high in iron oxide. They are, there-

Table 5.2 Composition of limonitised pyrite nodules from Marlborough, Wilts. (weight %)

Fe2O3	97 - 99%
SiO2	2 - 3%
CaO	0.3 - 0.5%
MgO	0.2 - 0.4%
S	0.2%

Table 5.3 Analyses of Wiltshire iron ore (%)

	Seend D*	*Westbury* D*	K+
FeO	--	49.26	47.25
Fe_2O_3	64.61	--	1.32
SiO_2	18.02	17.10	14.72
Al_2O_3	3.85	14.24	5.46
CaO	0.64	tr.	0.74
MgO	0.20	--	0.36
P_2O_5	0.64	--	tr.
S	--	--	0.05
H_2O	11.85	17.5	--
CO_2	--	17.5	30.01
Total	98.46	98.10	105.62

Key: * (Day and Gale 1981); + (Kendall 1893)

fore, typical of low lime *and* alumina ores and are unlikely to have originated in ores of the Westbury or Seend type (Table 5.3).

Considering that on smelting and smithing substantial contributions of lime are made to the slag from the fuel ash, there is little room for any addition from the ore when the lime in the slag is in the range 2.2–5.0%. On the other hand, the lime and alumina content of the pyrite nodules is very low (Table 5.2) as it is possible that these furnace bottoms are derived from metal smelted from such ores.

Normally, smithing hearth bottoms are formed from smelting slag entrapped in the metal (usually fayalite type slag), oxidised iron (mostly FeO) and fuel ash (50% CaO and 10% K_2O + Na_2O). By composition this material is indistinguishable from smelting slag and it is their small size compared with the larger size of smelting furnace bottoms that tends to suggest that they derive from the smithing process.

Experimental work has been carried out on the smelting of pyrites (Tylecote and Clough 1983). While it is possible to roast them to give iron oxides with sulphur contents as low as 0 46% (and once ignited the process goes spontaneously), this is not really necessary as the availability of naturally limonitized nodules is so great. Such nodules have iron oxide contents in the range 97 – 98% (Table 5.2). In smelting, it is necessary to produce slag to bring the iron particles into intimate contact and, therefore, sand needs to be added to the charge as slagging material (flux).

There is no real objection to the smelting of iron from pyritic ores from the chalk of the south of England but it is, unfortunately, very difficult to prove and this site certainly has not helped us. The presence of a small amount of sulphur in the slag would not confirm the use of pyritic ores, as other ores contain it also. The best way would be to find a suite of the necessary materials: pyrites in various stages of roasting, sand as flux, charcoal as fuel, tap slag, and, of course, the metal itself. But there may be trace elements such as Ni and Cu associated with these ores which might turn up in all the products, particularly the metal. It would be a good idea to test the natural nodules for such elements.

THE IMPORTED AND LOCAL STONE

by Sonia Hawkes

(based on work by Frederick Anderson and Christopher Hawkes)

It is still very vivid to me that, in the first cutting we made across the Enclosure III ditch in 1956, the ganger amongst my West Wiltshire labourers stooped to pick up and thoughtfully rub a piece of pinkish sandstone, uttering the words 'This be furrin stone Miss'. Questioned more closely as to its likely source, he was firm in his opinion that it came from Somerset, and being a builder's labourer of the old school, knowing his materials, his opinion deserves respect. Over the years we became very accustomed to this 'foreign' sandstone, pink, red, brown and grey, which occurred all over the site at all periods of the occupation.

From the postholes of the roundhouses of the early phase of occupation there was, of course, less stone than from the more capacious pits of the later phase. Even so they produced occasional sandstone quern fragments, finished artefacts such as spindle-whorls and loomweights made from chalk and stone rubbers made of the relatively local Upper and Lower Greensand. The real 'foreign' stone, the ferruginous sandstone which had been brought from a considerable distance, was prolific in the fill of later phase pits and ditch fills, and it seemed to us extraordinary that it occurred mostly in broken pieces, apparently as discards from quern-making or just meaningless lumps, and rarely as complete artefacts. The volume of this imported stone seemed far too great for home consumption, and indeed fragments of broken saddle querns that showed signs of wear were not at all common. All this suggested the importation of lumps of unworked stone from a distance to be worked on the site and perhaps traded on as finished saddle querns.

In this respect the site differed from the only remotely comparable other major Iron Age farmstead site excavated within the recent past, at Gussage All Saints in Dorset, where 'since there is a marked absence of waste-stone from the site, it is reasonable to suggest that the saddle querns were produced elsewhere and brought to the site as trade-goods' (Buckley 1979, 89). Gussage seems to have had a resident metalworking industry, producing mainly horse harness (Spratling 1979, 125-149), not found at Longbridge Deverill and, if not produced there, just the sort of thing that would have to have been bought in to the Longbridge economy. Both trade and prestige would have required functional and upmarket horse gear for at least the man in charge at Longbridge. Thus these big and prosperous farmstead sites may each have operated specialist trade economies in addition to basic farming, enabling them to exchange goods with neighbours far and wide.

Very few fragments of rotary querns were found in the excavated area. The large example (Fig .4.11, 7) was turned up by the plough elsewhere in Enclosure II after the end of the excavations, presumably from a pit or a house dating late in the 'B' phase of occupation. It was tentatively identified by D. Grant King (letter 3 December 1966, in archive) as made of Sarsen. Christopher Hawkes, however, in detailed notes shortly after its discovery, described the stone as pinkish brown micaceous sandstone, which suggests a source similar to that of the other 'foreign' stone from the site.

Throughout the excavations, we kept a large sample of stone fragments as well as all complete stone artefacts. Frederick Anderson examined the significant pieces and sorted them for listing. His brief report, below, was written from memory:

The site is at the north-west edge of the Chalk outcrop. To the north-west lie Upper Greensand and Gault which overlap onto the Middle Jurassic strata beyond. The Upper Greensand is used locally for building. Local materials found at the site were Upper Greensand, flint and chert. There was a little Ironstone, probably from Westbury, Wilts. (the Westbury iron ore is Corallian) about 6 miles to the north. There was a little Lower Greensand which may be local or from the Vale of Wardour 10 miles to the south-east, from whence came the few fragments of Purbeck limestone. The bulk of the material seen (mainly quern fragments) consisted of coarse brown sandstone, most probably Pennant sandstone, together with some of a coarser grey gritty sandstone resembling Millstone Grit, both of which must have been imported to the site from the west, as the nearest available source is in the Bristol and Somerset coalfields.

The original lists are lost but brief statistics of the numbers and percentages of the stone samples kept and identified from closed contexts are presented here (Table 5.4). The sample from the 'Phase A' houses is separated from that from the more prolific 'Phase B' because there seems to be a genuine difference in emphasis in the stone imported in the two periods.

Table 5.4 Imported Stone

	PHASE 'A'		*PHASE 'B'*	
Stone Type	*Nos*	*%*	*Nos*	*%*
Upper Greensand	5	25%	93	40%
Lower Greensand	10	50%	49	21%
Sarsen	2	10%	2	0
Purbeck Limestone	0	0%	6	2.6%
Sandstone/Ironstone	3	15%	79	34%
Mudstone	0	0%	3	1.3%
Portland	0	0%	1	0.5%

That ironstone is bracketed with sandstone shows up a major problem. Anderson's lists failed to distinguish between Westbury, Wiltshire, the source of a little ironstone on the site, and Westbury-sub-Mendip, one of his major candidates for the source of the much more prolific sandstone. The abbreviated list failed to distinguish the ironstone so, though there was definitely a little, it was not possible to quantify, although it was certainly far less common in the 'B' phase, at least, than the sandstone. Anderson was uncertain about the provenance of the sandstones, and his major hesitation was between sandstone from Westbury-sub-Mendip and Pennant from the Bristol coalfields, on the grounds that they are very similar.

The bulk of the collection has been discarded but Christopher Hawkes believed that most of the sandstone was not Pennant. Roe's work at South Cadbury Castle, Somerset, cites unsuitability of Pennant stone for querns (Roe 2000) and suggests that all the Longbridge sandstones, and also the so-called Millstone Grit, could have come from the Mendips.

From Mendip, the trade route involved seems more feasible than that from the Bristol coalfield further north. In the Roman period there was a road which ran from Old Sarum (Salisbury) along the Groveley Great Ridge, passing just over 2 miles (5km) south of Longbridge Deverill, and thence out of the chalk country and along the crest of the Mendip hills (Margary 1955, 93-95), passing close to several stone quarries marked on the Ordnance Survey map. Doubtless this road followed a long-established major prehistoric trackway, which, with its side-routes, including the complex of trackways on Longbridge Deverill and Whiten Hill, would have created a complex of Iron Age routeways serving the Iron Age communities in West Wiltshire. The distance as the crow flies from Longbridge Deverill to *e.g.*, Westbury-sub-Mendip is about 25 miles (40km), but the nearest source of Old Red Sandstone, the likeliest identification of the pink 'foreign' sandstones, on the route is little more than half that distance away.

However, whatever the distances involved, transporting heavy stone along such trackways would have been laborious because there was no convenient river system to enable easy carriage of the stone on rafts, even for part of the journey. So the Longbridge people would have had a long and heavy task transporting the raw materials for their quernstone industry overland, involving steep ascents and descents on unmade-up tracks, and the passage of the valleys of the rivers Frome and Wylye. One wonders why the saddle querns were not finished in Somerset rather than transported to Longbridge as rough stones, but such speculation enters the realm of politics, which archaeology alone cannot answer. However, the pottery evidence clearly indicates that Longbridge Deverill was on the extreme western edge of a long lasting style zone, probably a tribal frontier, and it may not have been prudent for members of one major tribal unit to linger longer than necessary in the territory of another.

However it was organised, the transport of the sandstone in quantity from Mendip would have required surplus manpower in the Longbridge community. One imagines that it took place in summer, when the route was reasonably dry, possibly between the hay and corn harvests when the large numbers of pack and or draught animals and carts, which must have been required, could best be spared. The large number of horse bones from the site and the hypothesis that there were wild herds of ponies available to draw on for breaking in as pack or draught animals are relevant to this point (see Animal Bones below). The availability of plentiful timber evidenced in the great roundhouses suggests there would have been no shortage of materials for cart building; and the Longbridge community occupied a favourable geographical position in regard to trade relationships with quarry owners in Mendip territory. The Mendip sandstones offered the best available quernstones to the Iron Age peoples of western Wessex, and clearly the Longbridge Deverill occupants, on the western edge of the chalk plateau, were in the best geographical, and also presumably the best political situation, to exploit their advantage. How far they marketed the finished querns is not known, because too few contemporary sites in their area have been excavated.

In his publications of the Iron Age sites on Fifield Bavant and Swallowcliffe Downs, over 18km distant on the great chalk scarp south of the Nadder valley, and hence in another geographical territory, Clay (1924 and 1925) recorded the stone recovered. Apart from one fragment of red micaceous sandstone from Fifield (Clay 1924, 478-9), all the quernstones were of the local 'green sandstone' brought up from the valley. The fragment of red sandstone quern may have been an outlier from the activities of the Longbridge Deverill traders. It suggests that they may have limited their normal range to the more accessible sites on the Groveley Great Ridge, using, amongst other doubtless innumerable minor track-ways, a continuation of the precursor of the Roman road leading eastwards towards Old Sarum. But certainly even a limited market in such good querns, which presumably commanded a high price, will have greatly increased the prosperity of the Longbridge Deverill community.

The major importation and exploitation of sandstone quernstones from Mendip seems to have been a development in the 'B' phase occupation of the site, but some was certainly being acquired earlier because there were remains of such a quern from House 2. Another hint as to the range of activity at this time is provided by the gritting of pottery with fossil shell, which appeared first in the pottery of House 2 and continued during the following 'B' phase (Williams Fabric J). The fossil shell was imported from a source nearly 16km away, witness the pieces of stone from the Purbeck shell bed which were found on the site (in Hollow 2 and Pits 39, 43, 47, 52, 55), all with the majority of their shell layers ground away. This shell-bed limestone derives from the Vale of Wardour, which lies to the south-west and could be reached by travelling a few miles across the Groveley Great Ridge and down into the Nadder Valley below Fifield and Swallowcliffe. Close by, perhaps at Chilmark, will have been the source of the single piece of Portland stone found at Longbridge. These are comparatively minor items, however, and were surely part of a larger trading activity with that area. As Anderson noted, the Vale of Wardour is one of the nearer sources of Lower Greensand. This occurred in some quantity at Longbridge Deverill and may have been the major source of quernstone in the 'A' phase of occupation before the mass importation of superior stone from Mendip.

The Upper Greensand occurs with the Gault clay all around the edges of the Wessex chalk scarp and was the most commonly used stone at Longbridge for items other than querns. It could have been brought from the Vale of Wardour along with the Lower Greensand or acquired more locally from the Wylye valley just below, from much the same area as the clay source, arguably the Gault, that supplied the pottery used by the Longbridge Deverill community. Since the clay 3km up the Wylye at Crockerton, and medieval pottery made from that clay, have proven not to be a perfect match for the Longbridge pottery it is conceivable that the Late Bronze/Iron Age source was even nearer. One envisages clay and Greenstone both being hauled up to the site by way of the W LIN trackway, which appears on Fig.1.7 (Chapter 1). The distance involved may not have been great but the going would have been steep, though nothing so laborious and time-consuming as the other longer distance routes used for the 'foreign' stones. Dr. Clay commented on the great effort involved in hauling 'local' stone the few miles from the Nadder valley up the scarp to the Iron Age sites on Fifield and Swallowcliffe Downs, and the local situation at Longbridge Deverill would not have been greatly different. Nothing about living on these hilltop sites in the Iron Age was easy as everything from water to stone had to be carried uphill.

Finally, the Ironstone from Westbury, Wiltshire must always have been crucial as the most important source of iron. The fact that, unlike the sandstone, it was not found lying about the site in great quantities probably means that was it was smelted, either there or elsewhere. Iron was certainly worked at Longbridge Deverill, as testified by slag and furnace bottoms (Tylecote, this chapter), but the only excavated evidence was of smithing rather than smelting. Bringing the iron ore stone from Westbury would have involved yet another cross-country journey.

THE CHARCOAL

by Graham Morgan and F. Richardson (Kew Royal Botanic Gardens)

Samples of charred wood taken from the postholes of Houses 1-4 and from 15 pits were submitted for identification. Four species were identified – oak, hawthorn, hazel and ash. Postholes of House 2 and House 4 produced examples of all four species, Houses 2 and 3 only oak, hawthorn and hazel. The predominant species found amongst the pit charcoal was oak, but hazel was also common, while ash was found only in Pit 41.

Tables 5.5–5.9 below present a basic presence/absence indicator for species, along with a broad gauge of the timber size.

Charcoal Analysis by Original Estimated Timber Size

Table 5.5 Charcoal from House 1

Context	*Oak*			*Hawthorn*			*Hazel*			*Ash*		
House 1												
	*	>4"	<4"	*	>4"	<4"	*	>4"	<4"	*	>4"	<4"
PH 63	*	prob	--	--	--	--	--	--	--	--	--	--
PH 127	*	--	prob	--	--	--	--	--	--	--	--	--
PH 139	*	prob	--	*	--	yes	--	--	--	--	--	--
PH 151	--	--	--	*	--	yes	--	--	--	--	--	--
PH 152	*	prob	--	--	--	--	--	--	--	--	--	--
PH 153	*	prob	--	--	--	--	--	--	--	--	--	--
PH 165	*	prob	--	--	--	--	*	--	yes	--	--	--
PH 186	*	prob	--	--	--	--	--	--	--	--	--	--
PH 225	--	--	--	*	--	yes	--	--	--	--	--	--

Table 5.6 Charcoal from House 2

Context	*Oak*			*Hawthorn*			*Hazel*			*Ash*		
House 2												
	*	>4"	<4"	*	>4"	<4"	*	>4"	<4"	*	>4"	<4"
PH 90	--	--	--	--	--	--	*	--	yes	--	--	--
PH 91	--	--	--	*	--	yes	--	--	--	--	--	--
PH 126	--	--	--	--	--	--	*	--	yes	--	--	--
PH 132	*	yes	--	--	--	--	--	--	--	--	--	--
PH 134 CH 214	--	--	--	--	--	--	*	--	yes	--	--	--
PH 134 CH 215	--	--	--	--	--	--	*	--	yes	--	--	--
PH 135 CH 216	--	--	--	--	--	--	*	--	yes	*	--	yes
PH 135 CH 217	--	--	--	--	--	--	*	--	yes	*	--	yes
PH 142	*	prob	--	--	--	--	--	--	--	--	--	--
PH 144	*	prob	--	--	--	--	--	--	--	--	--	--
PH 146	*	yes	--	--	--	--	--	--	--	--	--	--
PH 149	*	--	yes	--	--	--	*	--	yes	--	--	--
PH 157	--	--	--	--	--	--	*	--	yes	--	--	--
PH 170	*	--	prob	--	--	--	*	--	prob	--	--	--
PH 172	*	yes	--	*	--	yes	*	--	yes	--	--	--
PH 174	*	yes	--	--	--	--	*	--	yes	--	--	--
PH 179	*	prob	--	*	--	yes	*	--	yes	*	prob	--
PH 180	*	prob	--	--	--	--	*	--	yes	--	--	--
PH 181	*	prob	--	--	--	--	--	--	--	--	--	--
PH 182	--	--	--	--	--	--	*	--	yes	*	prob	--
PH 213	--	--	--	--	--	--	*	--	yes	--	--	--
PH 229	*	--	prob	--	--	--	*	--	yes	--	--	--
PH 238	--	--	--	*	--	prob	*	--	yes	--	--	--
PH 157	*	prob	--	--	--	--	*	--	yes	--	--	--
PH 171	*	prob	--	--	--	--	--	--	--	--	--	--

Table 5.7 Charcoal from House 3

Context	*Oak*			*Hawthorn*			*Hazel*			*Ash*		
House 3												
	*	>4"	<4"	*	>4"	<4"	*	>4"	<4"	*	>4"	<4"
PH 11	--	--	--	*	--	yes	*	--	yes	--	--	--
PH 106	*	prob	--	--	--	--	--	--	--	--	--	--
PH 107	*	prob	--	--	--	--	--	--	--	--	--	--

Table 5.8 Charcoal from House 4

Context	*Oak*			*Hawthorn*			*Hazel*			*Ash*		
House 4												
	*	>4"	<4"	*	>4"	<4"	*	>4"	<4"	*	>4"	<4"
PH 184	*	prob	--	--	--	--	--	--	--	--	--	--
PH 197	*	yes	yes	--	--	--	--	--	--	--	--	--
PH 198	*	--	yes	--	--	--	--	--	--	--	--	--
PH 199	*	prob	--	--	--	--	--	--	--	--	--	--
PH 208	*	prob	--	*	--	prob	--	--	--	--	--	--
PH 215	*	--	yes	--	--	--	--	--	--	--	--	--
PH 216	*	yes	--	*	--	yes	*	--	yes	*	prob	--

Table 5.9 Charcoal from Pits

Context	*Oak*			*Hawthorn*			*Hazel*			*Ash*		
Pits												
	*	>4"	<4"	*	>4"	<4"	*	>4"	<4"	*	>4"	<4"
P 2	*	--	yes	*	--	yes	*	--	yes	--	--	--
P 5	--	--	--	--	--	--	*	--	yes	--	--	--
P 14	*	prob	--	*	--	prob	*	--	yes	--	--	--
P 29	*	yes	--	--	--	--	--	--	--	--	--	--
P 36 (1)	*	--	yes	*	--	yes	*	--	yes	--	--	--
P 36 (2)	--	--	--	--	--	--	*	--	yes	--	--	--
P 36 (3)	*	prob	--	--	--	--	--	--	--	--	--	--
P 37 (1)	*	prob	--	--	--	--	--	--	--	--	--	--
P 37 (2)	*	prob	--	*	--	yes	*	--	yes	--	--	--
P 37 (4)	--	--	--	--	--	--	*	--	yes	--	--	--
P 38	*	yes	--	--	--	--	*	--	yes	--	--	--
P 39 (1)	--	--	--	--	--	--	*	--	yes	--	--	--
P 39 (2 & 3)	*	prob	--	--	--	--	*	--	yes	--	--	--
P 40	*	--	yes	--	--	--	*	--	yes	--	--	--
P 40	*	prob	--	*	--	yes	--	--	--	--	--	--
P 41	*	prob	--	*	--	yes	--	--	--	*	--	yes
P 42	*	--	yes	--	--	--	*	--	yes	--	--	--
P 43	*	--	yes	--	--	--	--	--	--	--	--	--
P 45 (2)	--	--	--	*	prob	--	--	--	--	--	--	--
P 45 (3)	--	--	--	--	--	--	*	--	prob	--	--	--
P 48 (3)	*	--	yes	--	--	--	*	--	yes	--	--	--
P 59 (1)	*	--	yes	*	yes	--	--	--	--	--	--	--

CHARRED PLANTS: STORED BARLEY GRAIN FROM PIT 37

by M.E.S. Morrison and Sonia Hawkes

(revised by Wendy Smith 2009)

This revised report concerns the recovery of stored grain possibly charred *in situ* within an Iron Age pit. Sampling of archaeobotanical remains was still relatively rare in the 1960s *eg* Martin Jones' (1984, 483) comment on *ad hoc* sampling at 1950s and 1960s British excavations. Although the actual archaeobotanical material could not be consulted directly by the revising author, photographs of the remains and the detailed report made by Morrison in 1967 appear relatively reliable. Every attempt has been made to respect the spirit of Sonia Hawkes' and Morrison's notes and reports on this pit deposit, which still provide clear and useful details some 40 years later. Unfortunately, the photographs of the pit deposit *in situ* and/or during excavations are of poor quality and provide little detail (Fig. 5.1). Where original text has been used in this report, it appears in italics.

A rich assemblage of charred cereal grain, with a few accompanying contaminants (*ie* cereal chaff and weeds of crop) was recovered during the course of excavation of Pit 37, layer 4 in 1960. The pit had been cut through the floor level of House 2 after the structure had been demolished, apparently destroyed by fire, whether accidentally or deliberately. Sonia Hawkes' notes concerning the deposit state:

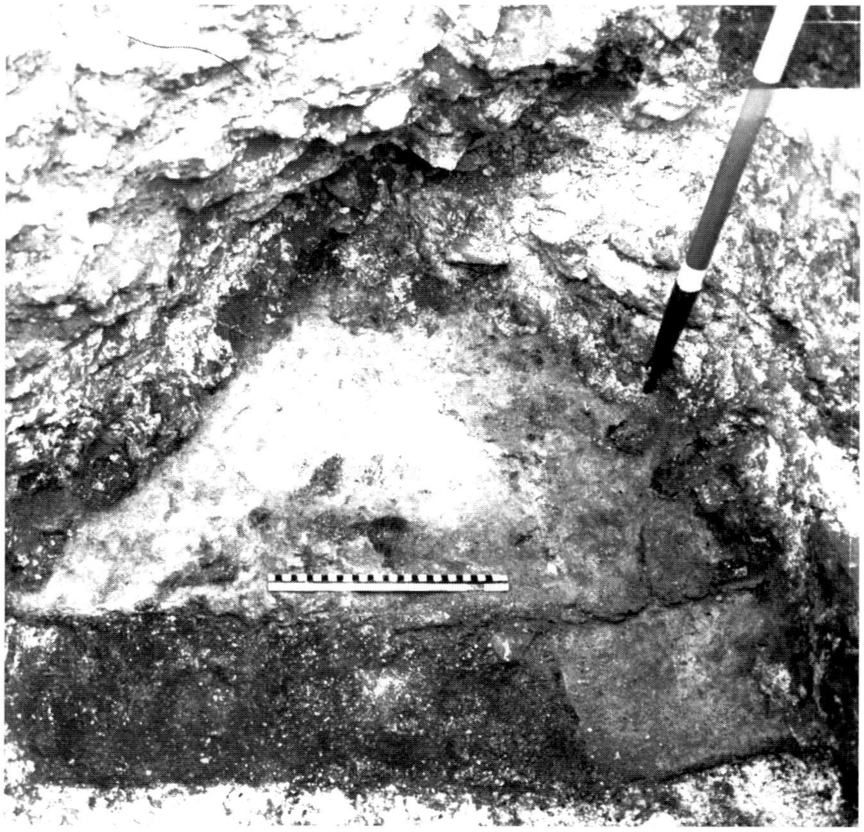

Fig. 5.1 Charred grain deposit on base of Pit 37

...[A] disused grain storage pit about 1.5m deep. The grain lay directly on the chalk bottom to a depth of 25-50mm, below layers of rubbish. Immediately above it, with grain adhering closely to it was the remains of a sack or cover of some kind[.] On top of this deposit lay the blade of an iron sickle, complete with tang, and clearly in good condition when first left in the pit. It seems likely that the grain was the last of the store originally kept in the pit[.] Whether the sickle had been left in the pit by accident when the grain was being stored, or whether it was deliberately placed on top of...the grain as some sort of propitiation or offering remains unanswerable.

Hawkes discusses the assemblage as 'mouldy grain' at various points but this has been deleted from the notes above, since the assemblage was clearly charred and therefore stable. The grain was carefully lifted, together with the fine dust that it accompanied. It was sifted from the fine dust and sub-sampled. Morrison reported on it in February 1967 but did not examine the fine dust for weed seeds and grass seeds. In 1972, the whole sample was weighed in preparation for taking an uncontaminated sample for radiocarbon dating (HAR S253). The original radiocarbon date obtained was 2390 ± 70 BP (440 BC), recently recalibrated at 770-360 cal BC (see Chapter 6).

The recorded weights are as follows (Table 5.10).

Table 5.10 Charred grain from Pit 37

Description	*Dry Weight Carbonised grain*	*Dry Weight Fine dust*
Sub-sample examined by Morrison	0.91 Kg	-
Sub-sample for 14C 0.28 Kg (Harwell Laboratory)	-	
Unexamined residue	0.91 Kg	1.17 Kg
Total	2.00 Kg	1.17 Kg

Morrison originally concluded his report with the following text, but it is perhaps the best introduction to this assemblage and still holds today:

This deposit of carbonised material – the bulk of it barley grain – is, in terms of quantity, perhaps one of the most important finds of carbonised grain in the British Isles. Six large boxes, filled with grain, were sent to me for study. It has, of course, been impossible to examine all this material and the above report is based on sub-sampling, so that in fact only a small fraction of the total deposit has been closely scrutinised. It is certain that further study, especially of the fine carbonised material accompanying the grain, will yield further identifications and these should be of much interest because they should go a long way towards improving our knowledge of the weed flora of the Iron Age.

To our knowledge no further analysis beyond the original work carried out by Morrison in 1967 was conducted. Unfortunately, the original material recovered from the Pit 37 is no longer available for study; nevertheless, the Morrison's 1967 report is, in the opinion of the revising author, largely reliable and still of use. Table 5.10 presents the estimated and/or fully quantified results from the sub-sample examined by Morrison. It is clear from the notes, that this is the only archaeobotanical sample to have been collected from the site.

Barley grain

Morrison identified both naked and hulled barley grain. The identification of naked barley (*Hordeum vulgare* L. var. *nudum*), however, is somewhat suspect since this was based on the observed absence of the palea and lemma and did not consider the possibility that these items of cereal chaff, although fused to the grain, may have burned off during charring. A taphonomic effect that has been demonstrated through experimental work using controlled burning of cereal chaff and grain (*eg* Boardman and Jones 1990). Criteria for the identification of hulled and naked barley is now well recognised (*eg* Jacomet 1987; 2000) and although only a few grains were photographed; they do exhibit the classic 'bevel' shape, with straight, blunt apex characteristic of 'hulled' barley. Moreover, the recovery of naked barley in the British Isles, does seem to be somewhat exclusively limited to early prehistory, especially the Neolithic and Beaker periods (*eg* Murphy unpublished data gathered for *Eastern Regional Review of Archaeobotany*).

Morrison did use both the ratio of twisted to straight grains (but only for those with the palea and lemma fully intact) and the presence of the 'horse-shoe' indentation on the lemma base of some hulled grain as criteria for the identification of a six-rowed (including lax-eared or 4-row barley *sensu* Jacomet 1987; 2006). Morrison goes on to state:

Much firmer grounds for identifying the material to the six-row barley, Hordeum vulgare *L., are provided by the length of the rachis internodes, and the shape of the basal part of the glume.*

A short rachis internode, in approximately the range 1.8 to 2.0mm, with rather broad articulation and unusually heavily pubescent edges, is regarded as characteristic of so-called 'erect six row barley', Hordeum hexastichum. *But a longer rachis internode, in approximately the range 2.7 to 4.0mm, tapering and usually with less hairy edges, is considered to indicate* Hordeum vulgare. *Now, twelve unbroken rachis internodes (Fig. 5.2a) (hulled barley), were found in the fine carbonised debris in the Cow Down material, and these yielded an average length of 3.25mm, the smallest being 3 mm and the largest 4mm and this is substantial evidence for* Hordeum vulgare.

Furthermore, in Hordeum vulgare [meaning the now well-recognised lax 4-row type *sensu* Jacomet (2000, 43)] *the basal part of the glume, on its dorsal face, carries a horseshoe-shaped depression and this is quite well seen on all the preserved glumes of the Cow Down material (Fig. 5.2 b) (barley rachis node). By contrast,* Hordeum hexastichum [now also known as *Hordeum vulgare* L. – but meaning dense six-row type *sensu* Jacomet *is distinguished by having a more or less transverse groove in the corresponding position. These differences are figured by Jessen and Helbaek (1944, fig. 15).*

Because of the various uses to which the different cereals are put, such as baking and brewing, and the different processing involved, the carbonised finds from prehistoric sites cannot give an accurate and unbiased picture of the relative importance of the various cereals throughout the different prehistoric periods. However, it is believed that barley was the most important cereal through much of prehistoric time in Britain and Western Europe.

This deposit was so rich that Morrison did not quantify his sub-sample of the assemblage. However it is possible to estimate the quantity of barley grain by using calculations based on the Iron Age barley from pit deposit 1078 from Danebury hillfort. Here Jones (1984, 492) calculated that 2.2 ±0.95 barley grains were recovered per gram. If we estimate that 46 contaminants identified weigh 10g (which is likely to be overly generous) that leaves approximately 900g of charred barley grain for the sub-sample studied by Morrison. This equates to an assemblage of between 1125 and 2835 barley grains for the sub-sample studied by Morrison – and would equate to between 2475 and 6237 barley grains for the entire sample collected by Sonia Hawkes.

Wheat (*Triticum* spp.)

Fifteen naked grains [*ie* free of surrounding chaff] *of wheat were picked out from a large amount of material* [Morrison recorded dimensions, but this data is now lost]. *It seems likely that our Cow Down wheat is either emmer wheat (*Triticum dicoccum *Schübl.), or Spelt Wheat (*Triticum spelta *L.). The grains or kernels of these are similar but according to Helbaek (1953) Spelt can sometimes be distinguished because the apex of its grain is blunter and the grain more flattened and broader than that of emmer. Nevertheless, Helbaek (1953) admits that '[i]n spite of this one would hardly feel sure of spelt in a deposit with no spikelet parts preserved'. The fine material accompanying the Cow Down grain was closely searched for spikelet parts but unfortunately none was found, aside from those which have been identified as belonging to barley.*

Helbaek's (1953) summary of wheat finds from Early Iron Age sites in southern England shows slightly more evidence of emmer than spelt among the grain impressions in pottery, while in the carbonised material spelt occurs in greater quantities, but there is too little evidence yet for a generalisation on the relative importance of the two types. It is interesting to record that, according to Peterson (1965) spelt is today grown in Europe in mountainous regions of Germany and to a lesser extent in Spain, Switzerland and Italy, where its hardiness enables it to compete with common wheats.

Other Grass (GRAMINEAE) [now renamed POACEAE (Stace 1997, 823)]

A dozen carbonized grass fruits, correctly referred to as caryopses, were found after thoroughly searching through a large amount of the finer carbonised debris accompanying the carbonised grain. However, there are so many grasses in the British Flora that an accurate identification of carbonised specimens is difficult.

Fig. 5.2 Charred grain from Pit 37: (a) hulled barley rachis; (b) barley rachis node; (c) cleaver

Moreover, I do not at present have access to a herbarium collection of British grasses. However, some guidance may be had from Armstrong's (1950) book which contains a key to the commoner British grasses. This key to their identification is based on fruit characteristics and, judging mainly from the size of the carbonised fruits, we may consider the possibility of the following: Lolium perenne *L. ([Perennial] Rye Grass),* Festuca pratensis *Huds. (Meadow Fescue), and Zerna inermis* [now renamed as *Bromopsis inermis* (Leyss.) Holub ssp. *inermis* but still considered naturalised and a casual weed by Stace (1997, 887)]. *Since Zerna* [now renamed *Bromopsis inermis* (Leyss.) Holub ssp. *inermis*] *is usually regarded as a recent introduction it would be as well, for want of better evidence, to exclude it as a possibility in the present context. One of the carbonised fruits bears a strong resemblance to* Anisantha sterilis (L.) Nevski [syn. *Bromus sterilis* L. (Stace 1997, 888)] *(Barren Brome); this has a notably long, slender fruit which has been described and illustrated by Jessen and Helbaek (1944) who found it in the Early Iron Age site at Fifield Bavant in England.*

Galium [Cleaver]

Four carbonised, sub-globose fruits (Fig. 5.2c) (galium spp), measuring approximately 2mm in diameter were discovered after working through a large amount of fine carbonised debris. These fruits almost certainly belong to the genus Galium *of the family* RUBIACEAE. *Strictly speaking they are half-fruits because the fruit of* Galium, *at maturity splits into two one-seeded portions, known in botanical jargon as mericarps. Judging from their size and the wrinkled surface, they can be referred to* Galium erectum *(Erect Hedge Bedstraw)* [now renamed *Galium mollugo* L. ssp. *erectum* Syme (Stace 1997, 647)] *or to* Galium spurium *L. (False Cleavers). Godwin (1956) lists a number of species of* Galium *which have been identified as fossils in the Quaternary Period,* Galium erectum [now renamed *Galium mollugo* L. ssp. *erectum* Syme (Stace 1997, 647) *is not one of these, but Galium spurium is noted, and in fact refers to Helbaek's (1953) find from the Late Bronze Age site at Itford Hill, Sussex. Godwin records that Galium spurium is 'now a rare plant of arable fields in the southern half of England. It has been found from Neolithic and Bronze Age strata in Switzerland and from Iron Age deposits in Bornholm and Gotland in the Baltic'. Clapham, Tutin and Warburg (1952) record that, at the present time,* Galium [mollugo *ssp.*] erectum *occurs throughout lowland Britain, especially on calcareous soils.*

Blackberry (*Rubus* spp.)

Three non-carbonised fruit stones, which can be confidently identified as Rubus fructicosus [*L.*] *agg. (blackberry) were found in the Cow Down material. Their non-carbonised state leaves us in some doubt as to whether or not they properly belong to the find. However, we may note that these fruit-stones turn up frequently in the Quaternary Period and Godwin (1956) states 'There are frequent records in different interglacial deposits, and from Atlantic time onward in the Post-glacial. There are two records suggesting an early Post-glacial status but none for the Late-glacial. The abundance of records of the Roman period certainly indicates the use of blackberries as food'.*

Discussion

In general, the majority of pit deposits encountered at Iron Age archaeological sites tend to be a mixture of cereal grain, cereal chaff and accompanying weeds of crop (*eg* Campbell 2000, 53; Jones 1984, 493-5; van der Veen and Jones 2006). They are typically interpreted as secondary deposition of crop processing waste (*eg* Jones 1984, 493-4; Straker 2000, 86-7) or possibly remains of burning of the pit to clean it prior to use (*eg* Monk 1991, 106; Monk and Fasham 1980, 335-6; van der Veen and Jones 2006, 222). Certainly, ash would have some insecticide properties (Hakbijl 2002).

The recovery of pure (or fairly pure) cereal grain assemblages interpreted as primary deposits from pits is extremely rare in Iron Age England (Campbell 2000, 53; van der Veen and Jones 2006, 223). To date, only four other sites have produced pit deposits widely believed to be actual primary deposits of stored grain charred *in situ* (Campbell 2000, 53; Straker 2000, 205). Pit 1078 from Danebury, Hampshire (Jones 1984, 491-2); pits 5789 (only six-row hulled barley) and 7372, Winnall Down, Hampshire (Monk and Fasham 1980, 333-4and 339-340); Hascombe, Surrey (Murphy 1977, 82-4) and a forthcoming result from an early Iron Age storage pit at Heron Grove, Sturminster Marshall, Wiltshire (Carruthers forthcoming). As Carruthers (2002, 205) suggests, deliberate burning of a stored crop, due to spoilage or an accidental fire, is much less likely than a pit falling out of use. 'Any stored grain remaining in the pit would rot away leaving no trace, but the charred lining would be preserved, particularly if the pit was backfilled within a short space of time' (Carruthers *ibid*). As van der Veen and Jones (2000, 223) have recently advised, although 'on a probabilistic level' grain-rich assemblages are likely to imply large-scale agricultural activities this is an assumption, based on limited data from one site (or even deposit), which may simply be due to chance preservation.

Aside from the rarity of recovering a primary deposit of stored grain preserved through charring, the result from Cow Down is unique in itself. Only Pit 5789 from Winnall Down, Hampshire contains a nearly pure assemblage of barley (1: 0.001 ratios of barley grain to barley chaff for both lower layers and 1: 0.07 and 1: 0.09 ratios of barley grain to weed seeds). Unfortunately such ratios are somewhat difficult to reconstruct for Cow Down because the 'fine ash' was not studied, and as Morrison pointed out at the time, this 'fine ash' material most likely contained a range of weeds of crop. All of the other primary stored grain deposits from Iron Age pits in southern England are either dominated by emmer/spelt wheat or have a mixture of emmer/spelt wheat and barley grain.

Most presume that pits were either unlined (especially if cut from chalk) or lined with cereal chaff, which is also referred to by Varro in *De Re Rustica* 1.57.2 and Pliny in *Nat. Hist. Book XVIII* (cited in Monk and Fasham 1980, 335). Cunliffe (2005, 411) also notes stone-lined pits (*eg* on the Isle of Portland) and wicker-lined pits (*eg* Dane's Camp, Worcestershire; Poxwell, Dorset and Worlebury, Somerset). However, as Cunliffe (*ibid*) notes, 'there is nothing to show that these pits were used for storing grain rather than other commodities'. Sonia Hawkes' notes on the Cow Down pit suggest a cloth lining surrounded the grain. Unfortunately, the 'cloth' was never analysed (or at least there is no specialist report in the site archive) and photographs of the deposit taken during excavation of Pit 37 are unclear. Although hearsay, the preservation of grain stored within a cloth sack of some form is completely unique in the English Iron Age. However, without documentation one cannot rule out the possibility that charred cereal chaff lining the pit, possibly poorly preserved, may have been confused for fabric during excavation.

Finally, the recovery of a sickle placed upon the stored grain is, as Hawkes suggests in her own notes, likely to be ceremonial in nature and clearly falls into the category of a 'structured deposit' (*sensu* Hill 1995). Pit 37, Cow Down may, indeed, form an exact example of 'how ritual relates to everyday life' (Hill 1995, 126).

Conclusions

Pit 37 is a single tantalising archaeobotanical result from an Iron Age settlement. It provides something akin to a 'Pompeii effect', preserving the temporary storage of grain and the care with which the Iron Age residents of Cow Down went to performing that 'everyday' act. The charred remains of the roundhouses, preserving thatch, wattle and daub and possibly other stored crops were not sampled. This was, unfortunately, all too typical of early archaeobotanical work and should be seen as symptomatic of the approach to sampling in the era (*eg* Jones 1984, 483). Some opportunities may have been missed; nevertheless, the clearly careful sampling of Pit 37 and the commissioning of Morrison to analyse the charred cereal remains do suggest concern for recovering archaeobotanical data from the site. Although we may approach the sampling of such a site differently today, Hawkes' careful recovery of this primary deposit of stored grain remains a useful contribution to archaeobotanical studies in Iron Age Britain, even though the analysis of the assemblage from Pit 37 focused on clearly visible remains, excluding material possibly contained within the 'fine ash', such as weeds of crop or fragmented cereal chaff.

Whether the barley recovered from Pit 37 was seed corn or a stored food-stuff for human or animal consumption remains an open question. The debate regarding whether the storage of grain in pits is temporary storage of a product for use (either daily or regular) or storage of surplus (*eg* van der Veen and Jones 2006, 224-5) remains unresolved.

Acknowledgements

M.E.S. Morrison thanked Professor and Mrs. Hawkes for making the material available and for their assistance during the course of the original investigation. W. Smith would like to thank Lisa Brown for discussing details of the site and archive in advance of preparing an updated version of this text and Gill Campbell (English Heritage, Centre for Archaeology) and Vanessa Straker (English Heritage, Regional Advisor for Archaeological Science south-west England) for providing access to their unpublished manuscript reviewing archaeobotanical data for southern England.

THE ANIMAL BONES

Introduction

by Sonia Chadwick Hawkes

From the first season of excavation in 1956 all but the most fragmentary pieces of animal bone were retained but at that time there was no trained specialist available to deal with identification and no official money for analysis. In this and other respects, the excavation was ahead of its time in the quantity of data recorded and kept, by contrast with the lack of specialist expertise in so many areas and the total lack of post-excavation funding.

Despite the lack of funding, in 1961 Dr Ian Cornwall at the London University Institute of Archaeology accepted the animal bones on the off chance that a postgraduate student might be persuaded to study them as a thesis project. The contents of the boxes were listed as to provenance, the bones weighed and despatched in several batches between 1961 and 1965. Several students helped to go through the collection and a volunteer, Betty Westley began a sorting and listing. Following this stage permission was sought and given to discard the fragmentary material, leaving measurable, reconstructable bone worthy of closer study.

Betty Westley's preliminary catalogue of the animal bones represented in each feature was received in January 1965. In 1966, however, she left the Institute and, though Dr Cornwall attempted to finish the work himself, it was never completed. Westley's lists, extracts of which are listed below (Tables 5.21–5.23) are thus not complete. The excavator sent a list of missing items, some but not all of which may have been deliberate discards, to Dr Cornwall in February 1965 but whether they were incorporated in the body of material seen by Harcourt, who wrote the first version of the final bone report shortly after, is unclear. But it can be confidently asserted that Harcourt saw a large and representative of the animal bones from the site.

The major omission is any report on the mollusca. Snail shells were kept by the excavators but no one involved with the study of the animal bones thought them important or felt competent to report on them. The pioneering work of John Evans (1972) on snails appeared after the Longbridge collection was consigned by Harcourt to the storehouses of the Laboratory of the then Inspectorate of Ancient Monuments, where presumably they

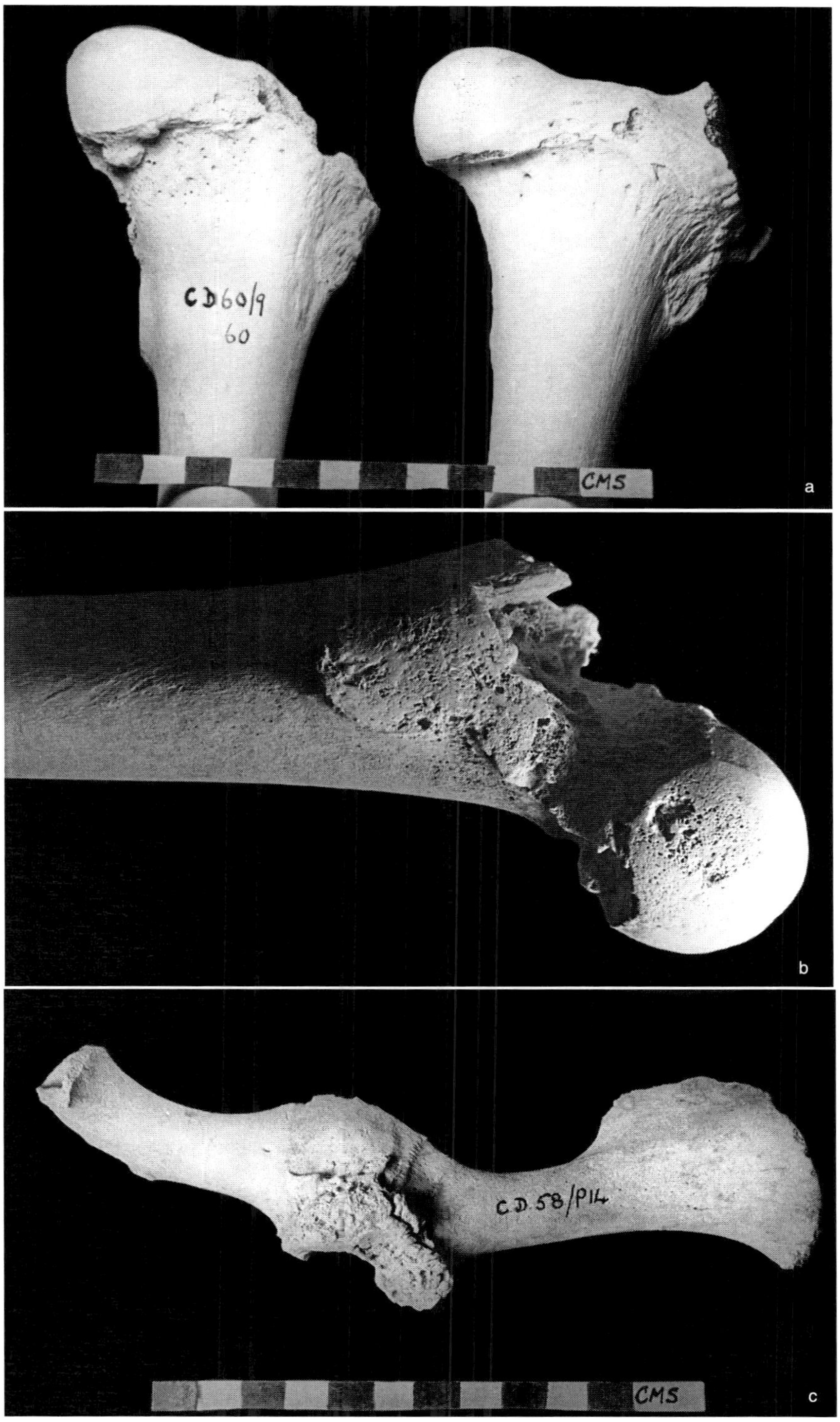

Fig. 5.3 Animal bone: (a) wear on dog femur; (b) exotoses in a dog femur; (c) proliferative bony growth on acetabulum of pig pelvic bone

remain to this day, now in the charge of English Heritage. All of the supervisor's lists and the correspondence dealing with the animal bones is deposited with the rest of the site archive.

In 1967, thanks to John Musty, then a Chief Scientific Officer in charge of the Inspectorate's Conservation and Research Laboratory, the writing of the final report on the animal bones was entrusted to Ralph Harcourt, who completed the first version in 1968. He dealt with the even larger, but similar, assemblage from Gussage All Saints (Harcourt 1979b), and in the light of this, revised his Longbridge report in 1982.

Results *by Ralph Harcourt*

The bones from the site weighed 161kg and were in three groups, one each from the 'A' and 'B' occupation phases and another of uncertain provenance but definitely of Iron Age date. The bulk of the material was from the 'B' phase but, as no differences were found in any morphological aspect of the same species in different groups, all of it has been amalgamated and treated as a single collection except for the estimation of minimum numbers of individuals (Table 5.11) and of the species meat contribution (Table 5.19). The species represented were cattle, sheep, goat, pig, horse, red deer, dog, small rodents, amphibia and bird.

Proximal and distal extremities were measured across articular surfaces and measurement points for other dimensions are indicated in the relevant table for each species.

Ages, when employed at all, were estimated using the 19th century data cited by Silver (1963). As has been set out elsewhere (Harcourt 1979b), the preferred method was to establish age groups and thus a relative and not absolute age structure. This can be done either via the presence or absence of epiphyseal fusion or with the aid of the mandibles, preferably both techniques. Some epiphyses fuse early, some late. Thus unfused early fusing epiphyses must be from young animals and fused late fusing epiphyses must be from fully mature adults. The first category provides a 'not greater than' age and the latter, a 'mot less than' age. All mandibles at the same stage of development were grouped. The number of stages was kept low to avoid the risk of over-classification. Not all individuals at the same stage of dental development are necessarily the same age. The greater the number of stages employed the greater does the chance become of introducing discrepancies. Five stages were used for sheep and cattle.

Table 5.11 Minimum number of individuals

Species/Phase	*A*	*B*	*Undated*	*Totals*
Cattle	5	19	11	35
Sheep	4	27	18	49
Goat	0	0	1	1
Pig	4	12	4	20
Horse	2	7	5	14
Dog	1	4	2	7

Minimum numbers of individuals in each species were established from a direct count of the most commonly occurring specimen

Cattle

The measurements of the long bones (Table 5.12) and the shape of the skulls and horn cores show that these cattle were identical with those described from other Iron Age sites, small beasts, some 1.05 m at the shoulder, the so-called *Bos taurus longifrons* (Jackson 1917, 48). The cranial portions of the eight skulls were found. Three had normal horn cores but the other five indicated the presence of polled beasts; indeed these relative numbers suggest the possibility that polled cattle may have been more abundant than those with horns. The sites of the horn cores were marked in two cases by irregular pits and in the others by small prominences which would have been palpable under the skin but not visible in the living animal.

Age

The unfused epiphyses in the early fusing group, Group I, (juvenile animals), comprised 5% and the fused epiphyses in the late fusing group, Group III, (fully mature) comprised 55% (Table 5.13). The evidence from the mandibles is similar; older beasts were in the majority or are better represented (Table 5.14). When the lower third molar, a very late erupting tooth which survives very well, is considered alone, then the conclusion is strengthened; the heavily worn teeth are much more

Table 5.12 Measurements of the cattle long bones

	N	*O.R. (mm)*	*Height (m)*	*v d D*
Radius tl	5	229-260	-	PL*
Pw	14	60-71	-	-
Dw	12	45-72	-	-
Humerus tl	2 211		-	GLC
Dw	35	060-074	-	BT
Femur tl	1	288	-	-
Tibia tl	4	269-291	-	L1*
Dw	32	42-51	-	-
Metacarpal tl	7	169-175	1.03 - 1.07	GL
Metatarsal tl	8	186-201	1.01-1.09	GL

Key:
tl = total length; pw = proximal width; dw = distal width
N = number of specimens measured; O.R. = observed range;
Ht. = shoulder; v d D = measurement points of von den Driesch (1976, * these strictly apply only to the horse but the nearest equivalents were used for the cattle specimens).
For height estimation the multiplication factor for the steer (Fock 1966) was used (metacarpal: 6.12. metatarsal: 5.45)

Table 5.13 Age at death of cattle and sheep epiphyses

	Cattle	No. specimens	Sheep	No. specimens
Group I	5%	3/65	29%	28/96
Group II	40%	-	47%	-
Group III	55%	3/65	24%	23/96

Group I = juveniles; Group II (derived by subtraction) = intermediate age; Group III = fully mature adults and the age

Table 5.14 Age at death of cattle and sheep. b) mandibles and molars

	Cattle	Sheep		Cattle	Sheep
All stages up to M1 in wear	3	10	1 cusp	3	3
M2 in wear	1	5	2.....	1	6
M3, 1 cusp in wear	0	1	3....	1	9
M3, 2 or 3 cusps in wear	0	6	Well worn	14	17
M3, 3 cusps well worn	6	3			
Mandibles			Molars		

Table 5.15 Measurements of sheep long bones

	N	O.R	Msd Inde	Ht:cm	v d D
Humerus tl	2	120-125	-	-	GLC
dw	20	22-28	-	-	BT
Femur tl	1	149	-	-	GLC
Metacarpal tl	3	116-121	8.5-9.9%	56-59**	GL
dw	3	20-22	-	-	-
Metatarsal tl	4	122-128	7.8-8.1%	57-60**	GL
dw	6	20-21	-	-	-

Key as for Table 5.12
msd=midshaft diametermsd Index=msd.100/tl
**the multiplication factors for height estimation were those of Tsalkin (1961) - Metacarpal: 4.86; Matatarsal: 4.68

numerous than the others (Table 5.14). Some were so heavily worn that the crown had almost disappeared. It seems likely that these came from beasts which were ten years old or more. Thirty-seven specimens were noted from animals of less than four years old as against 89 from those of more than four years old. Of these, 29 were considered on the basis of molar wear to be from cattle of more than five years of age.

In the ruminant the lower third molar (M3) is a tooth that survives very well and is nearly always found in large numbers relative to other specimens. Within the molar group therefore the usual complication of differential survival can be ignored. It will be seen that the number of well-worn molars is more than three times as great as that of any other category.

Sheep

The dimensions of the sheep bones (Table 5.15) show that the animals closely resembled the Soay in build; that is, they were small and slender.

Nine horn cores were found and from the dimensions and shape of these it seems probable that there were horned animals among both ewes and rams, although it is possible that the more slender horns were from wethers. In a horned breed the horns of ewes and of wethers are very similar.

Age

From the evidence of the epiphyses and of the mandibles (Tables 5.13 and 5.14) the youngest age group would seem to be as well represented as the adults. However, in each case the proportions of juvenile animals is inflated to some extent by the relatively large number of the remains of foetal or neonate animals, a common finding with sheep. The number of well-worn molars (Table 5.14) is striking and some, as with the cattle, showed extreme wear. It is possible that some of the animals may have been as much as ten years of age.

The mortality among the lambs in the first twelve months of life is always high so that many of the individuals among the juvenile group could be accounted for by natural death. These small slender sheep would have so little meat on them when very young that to kill them would have been pointless except perhaps in an unusually successful lambing year which itself followed a mild winter so that numbers were high.

Goat

The only bone from this species identified with certainty was a complete metatarsal with the dimensions: 130 tl; 17 pw; 15 msd; 20 pw. The midshaft diameter index was thus 11.5%. In early sheep it is unusual for this value to exceed 9.5%. The differentiation of goat from sheep is not always easy and, when the bones are fragmentary, often impossible.

Pig

The remains of this species were too few and fragmentary for it to be possible to obtain much information of value. Only one specimen was large enough to suggest the presence of wild pig. This was a very large but broken tusk; at its broadest point it had sides of 15 x 22 x 27mm. All age groups were represented from young piglets to fully mature adults with well-worn lower third molars.

Horse

This collection was remarkable for the amount of horse bone present. The animals represented were the small ponies characteristic of the period and the range of their shoulder height was from 1.12-1.22 m (11-12 hands). The measurements are shown in Table 5.16.

Table 5.16 Measurements of horse bones

	N	*O.R.*	*M*	*Sd*	*Cv*	*Ht**	*v d D*
Humerus tl	2	240 & 251	-	-	-	177 & 122	GLC
dw	2	61 % 66	-	-	-	-	BT
Radius tl	1	300	-	-	-	130	GL
Metacarpal tl	10	181-205	198	7.3%	3.6%	116-131	GL
Femur tl	-	334	-	-	-	117	GLC
Tibia tl	2	320 & 332	-	-	-	139 & 144	L1
Metatarsal tl	8	235-259	245	8.8%	3.6%	15-138	GL

Key
M=mean Sd=standard deviation Cv=coefficient of variation
* The mean shoulder height estimated from all bones is 1.24 m (12.5 hands)

Age

Most of the specimens which yielded evidence of age were from young adults. These included cheek teeth, some of which had not erupted and of which others showed only slight wear. There were seven portions of mandible in which a sufficiently full set of incisors survived to allow for ageing; one was from an animal of about 18 months and the other six indicated ages ranging from four to eight years.

There were two bones from those of more than one and a half years and ten from those of nearly four years old. There is, however, no way of knowing whether the middle group came from horses, which were also in the oldest group. In contrast to the cattle and sheep, there was one age group among the horse bone that was conspicuously absent, namely the very young or the foetal. Not a single such specimen was encountered. The probable significance of this is discussed below.

Red Deer

There were very few remains of this species, only some teeth and portions of cast antler from Pit 9.

Dog

Two pits each yielded the almost complete skeleton of a 12-15 months old dog but in one case there was no skull. The rest of the material was rather scatted with only a few specimens found in any single feature. Two skulls were found, one complete and the other nearly so. The skull dimensions are shown in Table 5.17 and of the long bones in Table 5.18.

The dogs fall into the known range for the Iron Age. In terms of shoulder height, conformation and skull shape they would have resembled a Border Collie but it should be emphasised that the citing of such a modern breed implies no resemblance other than in the features quoted. Bones provide no evidence for any other characteristics which are necessary to identify a 'breed', that is, coat colour and length, shape and carriage of ears and tail and even temperament. The breeding of dogs at a settlement such as this could well have been completely uncontrolled except perhaps in terms of numbers of puppies allowed to survive, and their function may simply have been that of village scavengers. Equally they may have served as guard or herd dogs.

Table 5.17 Skull measurements of dogs

I	*III*	*IV*	*IX*	*X*	*XI*	*XII*	*XV*	
174	85	86	86	53	62	35	73	Pit 53
199	95	109	92	64	70	44	-	Pit 60

(1)	I	Occipital protuberance - alveolar
(2)	III	Posterior junction of nasals - alveolar
(30)	IV	Bizygomatic breadth
(13)	IX	Greatest length of palate
(34)	X	Greatest breadth of palate
(15)	XI	Maxillary tooth row
(36)	XII	Width across canines at lateral margin of alveolus
(8)	XV	Mandibular tooth row

The figures in parentheses to the left of the Roman numerals indicate the equivalent measurement points in the system of von den Driesch (1976).

Table 5.18 Measurements of dog long bones

	N	O.R. (m)	Ht (m)	MF
Humerus	2	1.35-1.36	0.44	(tl x 3.43) -26.54
Radius	3	130-152	0.43-0.50	(tl x 3.18) +19.51
Femor	3	144-180	0.44-0.55	(tl x 3.14) -12.96
Tibia	*4*	*154-180*	*0.46-0.53*	*(tl x 2.92) + 9.41*

MF = multiplication factor. Also Humerus + radius combined: (tl x 1.65) -4.32
Femur + tibia: (tl x 1.52) -2.47 (Harcourt 1974). Shoulder height: 16-21 ins.
Msd Index range: 6.6 -8.5%. Mean : 7.7%

Rodents and Amphibia

Numerous bones and skulls of water vole (*Arvicola terrestris*), field vole (*Nicrotus agrestis*) and a few wood mouse (*Apodemus sylvaticus*) were found, mostly in the pits. Many bones of frog and toad were present.

Bird

Most of the skeleton of a young raven was found in Pit 58 from the 'B' phase of occupation.

Pathological alterations and anatomical anomalies

Lesions of osteoarthritis were found in the elbow of one of the dogs and in a bovine femur The head of the femur showed marked wear, the normal rounded profile having become flattened (Fig. 5.3a). Exotoses extended all round the lip of the articular surface and as far down as the lesser trochanter (Fig.5.3b). In the dog, which at some fifteenth months old, was unusually young to be affected with this condition, the humerus and ulna were involved; both showed exotosis and eburnation, a smooth ivory-like surface. A proliferative bony growth, possible neoplastic, filled the acetabulum of the pelvis of a pig. There was very little false joint formation so that in life the leg must have been fixed, with only minimum movement possible (Fig.5.3c). In the femur of a dog there was a healed diagonal midshaft fracture. This had occurred at least one year before as the callus had disappeared almost completely. In four cattle mandibles and one of the sheep there were only five cheek teeth instead of the usual six. Especially in cattle this feature is a common finding from both Iron Age and from Romano-British sites in Britain.

Butchery

Knife marks, which presumably occurred during de-fleshing, were found at the distal extremities of two sheep long bones.

Table 5.19 Species meat contribution

Occupation phase	*Cattle %*	*Sheep %*	*Pig %*	*Horse %*
A	59	5	7	29
B	60	8	6	26
Undated	57	9	3	31

Species meat contribution

On the basis of bone measurements and comparisons with modern breeds of known weight and similar stature (Harcourt 1979b) carcase weight ratios were derived, the sheep being taken as unity; cattle – 10; horse – 12; pig – 1.5 and sheep – 1.

The ratio for each species is multiplied by the minimum number of individuals in each period to give the number of 'meat units' (Sp. mu). This value is then expressed as a percentage of the total meat units (TMU provided by all species combined; that is Sp. Mu x 100/TMU (Table 5.19).

Discussion

by Ralph Harcourt

Like Iron Age sites in general and its near neighbour, Gussage All Saints in particular (Harcourt 1979b), the bone remains of the cattle, sheep and pigs reflect the typical picture of a subsistence economy with all age groups represented and including a substantial proportion of fully mature animals together with a number of old ones.

It is often forgotten that farm stock animals, once commonplace, may be becoming rarer but they are still encountered in those areas where it is not possible to practice intensive agriculture. Cattle, especially cows, are kept until they are ten years or more and, perhaps surprisingly, the same is true of sheep. The oldest sheep kept under farm conditions known to the writer died at the age of 17. There are two small islands off Bergen in Norway where there still exists a small indigenous type of sheep, which live unattended throughout the year with scarcely any supplementary feed. Naerland (1970) refers to one of these animals, a ewe, which although 18 years old was in good condition and possessed a complete set of incisor teeth. This fact, of the potential longevity of farm stock, should be borne in mind when considering the economic interpretations of bone collections from prehistoric sites.

The age structure of the Longbridge Deverill assemblage clearly indicates that the target in stock-keeping was a lifetime exploitation of the various species on a sustained yield basis. For sheep this would constitute milk and wool; for cattle, milk and power and possibly for both species, manure. From the pig nothing but meat is obtained but its high fecundity can mean that this, on a species basis, constitutes a sustained yield. Early stock, it is reasonable to assume, would have been slow to mature and of low fertility by modern standards. These factors compounded by natural losses such as the inevitable perinatal mortality, infectious disease, parasitism, abortions and those caused by drought or cold could mean that the achievement of significant surplus was difficult. Ryder (1981) has recently provided a useful discussion of this and related topics.

Polled skulls have so far been found at four other sites in Wessex – All Cannings Cross (Jackson 1924), Swallowcliffe Down (Jackson 1925-1927), Mount Pleasant and Gussage All Saints (Harcourt 1979 a & b). The character exists nowhere else in Europe except Scandinavia and has not yet been found before the Iron Age or, as far as the writer is aware, outside Wessex. This character is a genetically dominant mutation and it would seem very likely that, in Britain, it arose during the Iron Age and that its presence over a wide area of Wessex is strong evidence for the interchange of cattle between settlements as the mutation is unlikely to have occurred twice in such a small area.

The age structure of the horse population, as has already been remarked, differed in one important respect from that of the sheep and cattle. There were no bones from very young animals. Even the youngest represented were from horses which, though immature, were nevertheless not far from their full stature. This phenomenon was also seen at Gussage All Saints. It was suggested that at both sites horses were acquired by periodic round-ups of a wild or a feral population (Harcourt 1979b). The latter is perhaps the more likely though in this context the difference is not suitable for even light work until about three years old so that if the round-up employed the expenditure of all the necessary care and attention and the long period of non-productivity would be avoided. Moreover, the weaker animals would be weeded out by the usual biological processes of disease, malnutrition and predation.

Such an age structure is not universal for the horse at Iron Age sites either in Wessex or elsewhere. At the present stock-keeping practices vary from one part of the country to another, often with quite a marked difference between two areas not very far apart. This could have been so in prehistoric times. Thus in those areas which could sustain a feral population and where the existence of such a population was not incompatible with agriculture, periodic round-ups could have been the normal practice. Elsewhere there could have been settlements which raised horses in the same way that other species were raised. Another possibility is that within a particular region there may have been settlements in which horse breeding was carried out and others in which it was not, although all would have used horses, that is to say it was a specialist activity. If this latter arrangement existed, then both Longbridge Deverill and Gussage All Saints would appear to have been user settlements, not breeder settlements.

Table 5.20: Fauna

Species	*Fragments*	*% total*
Sheep/Goat	1940	39
Cattle	1993	40
Horse	538	11
Pig	378	8
Dog	103	2
Deer	29	0.6
Rodent	6	0.1
Bird	6	0.1
Frog/Toag	4	0.1
Weasel	1	-
Hare	1	-

Acknowledgements

I am indebted to Don Brothwell for the identification of the bird remains and to F.C. Fraser for confirming the identity of the rodents.

Concluding Discussion

by Sonia Chadwick Hawkes and Betty Wesley

Harcourt's report deals with the collection as a whole, whereas in 1965 Westley listed the material (including human bone) according to feature as a preliminary to further work on the assemblage. The total identified is 5,010, excluding whole skeletons (dog, infant, rodents) that are housed in separate boxes.

Westley wrote:

The identification was carried out by several students who did not record evidence of the age of the animals. To this writer, however, who has dealt with the bulk of it, the food animals appear to have been slaughtered at much the same age as they are butchered today. A sample count showed that about 25% of the sheep/goat bones showed evidence of immaturity such as unfused epiphyses of the longer bones and unworn or deciduous teeth, and this is customary on Iron Age and Roman sites. There are scarcely any infant bones, however, and no evidence of animals killed before their first winter, but this could be because such delicate bones did not survive. Only in one particular, so far, does the material show any considerable departure from the usual form, and that is in the percentage of horse bones, which is much higher than usual. Horse bones have appeared quite rarely on comparable sites investigated, and most of these animals at Longbridge Deverill are young and apparently healthy.

Westley's preliminary observations foreshadowed Harcourt's conclusions. Although the detailed listings are also of interest, to publish the whole of Westley's lists feature by feature would be tedious, but her lists of pit contents compared with the contents of the postholes of the three major houses seem worth setting out. The pits belong late in the occupation of the site, the so-called 'B' phase, and the houses early, to the 'A' phase, and differences resulting from date or function would be interesting to observe.

Animal Bone from Pits in Enclosure II

Table 5.21

Animal Bone from Postholes

Westley listed the bone from some of the postholes belonging to the early Houses 1 and 2 and contemporary posthole complexes. The absolute numbers from each feature being small, they are grouped together to make a larger sample. The same applies to House 3.

Table 5.21 Animal bone from Enclosure II Pits

Pit	*Sheep/goat*	*Cattle*	*Horse*	*Pig*	*Deer*	*Dog*	*Bird*	*Frog/Toad*	*Rodent*
1	26	23	2	5					
2	26	47		13		8			
3	3	9		1					
5	12 (1 Lamb)	140	40	34					
7	143	61	13	19		43			
8	20	8	5	1					
9	2	7	2		antler				
13	65	11	8	2					
14	5	20	6						
18	42	21	9	3		2			
22	45	48	4	8		6			
26	2	4							
31	2	1 (skull)	16						
34	14	16		3					
36	30	4	5	5					
37	21	1	2	11				2	
38	10		1						vole
39	24	9	31 (C)	2		1			
40	11	3		2					
41	40								
42	15								
43	51	26	18	3					
44	18	1							
45	6	16	6	6					
46	19	17	5	1					
47	8	2							
48	2	5	2						vole
49	20	2							
50	60	14	8			8			
51	22	14	6	2					
52	51	62	25						
53	17	8	15	1		C -			
54	78	150	15	13				in daub	voles
55	12	7	1	2		2			
57	10	3	7	4					
58	16	12	14				1 C		
59	42	55	1	1					
60	6	11	13			1 C			
62	16 (2 sheep)	61	36						
63									
67	6	21	3	1					
68	4	3							
69/70	12	51	19						
72		10	12 (1 juvenile)						
Total	1165	981	353	143	1	73	1		

Key: C- Complete

The following postholes produced animal bone:

Posthole Complex Area S2: PH28; PH36; PH48; PH56; PH61; PH97
Posthole Complex North of House 4: PH26; PH73
House 1
- Main ring: PH151; PH152; PH153; PH154; PH235
- Porch: PH139; PH141; PH165; PH167

House 2
- Main Ring: PH90; PH126; PH134
- Outer Ring: PH202
- Interior: PH136

Postholes in the Vicinity of House 1 and 2: PH4; PH18

The character of animal bone assemblages from the pits differs quite markedly from those present in the house features. One obvious explanation is that the pits, once disused, became rapidly filled up with domestic rubbish taken from the midden, and that this rubbish would have included the dismembered and defleshed carcasses of newly slaughtered animals, whereas the living quarters would presumably have been kept relatively clean of such smelly rubbish. Butchery, as we know it, and as it existed in Roman and Saxon times when there were efficient iron tools for cleaving, was non-existent in the early Iron Age. The Longbridge Deverill animal bones were not hacked across nor split; in fact they showed remarkably few cut marks at all, and there would have thus been no handy small joints of meat to be cooked indoors. The skinning, defleshing, boiling and perhaps occasional roasting of whole animals are activities best carried out outdoors.

It was obvious at the time of excavation that some pits, usually large ones such as Pit 5, were densely packed with animal remains, whereas others of equal size, such as Pit 9, yielded virtually none. Though some pits were rich in the bones of one species, *eg* horse bones and skull in Pit 39, there was no evidence at all of ritual sacrifice. Except for burials of the two human females (described and discussed elsewhere) the assemblages appeared to be the disarticulated remains of animals slaughtered for food or, as in the case of the dogs, the lamb and the human infant, useless dead creatures buried in the nearest available pit open at the time.

There is no evidence to show whether the slaughter of food animals was a seasonal or year round activity but since, with the exception of the horses, there is little evidence of young animals being killed, the practice of 'autumn killing' seems as unlikely at Longbridge Deverill as at Gussage All Saints (Harcourt 1979, 160). Instead, beasts may have been fattened and killed as required at any time of the year. Animal husbandry on Longbridge Deverill was competent and domestic beasts seem to have been over-wintered for many seasons. We now know from the work of the Royal Commission that the field system associated with the Longbridge farms was a large one, and there can be no reason to

Table 5.22 Animal bone totals from Houses 1 and 2 and Posthole Complex

Sheep/goat	120 fragments	48.5%
Cattle	59	23.9
Pig	8	15.4
Horse	11	4.5
Deer	16	6.5
Dog	2	0.8
Rodent	1	0.4
Total	247 fragments	

Table 5.23 Animal bone totals from House 3 (Cuttings IV, V, VI, XVI, 94, 109, PH51; PH123; PH124)

Sheep/goat	82 fragments	40.0%
Cattle	59	28.8
Pig	36	17.5
Horse	17	8.3
Deer (antler)	10	4.9
Dog	1	0.5
Total	205 fragments	

suppose that the agricultural method operating differed greatly from the rotation of crops and fallow that served our medieval and recent ancestors so well before the introduction of artificial fertilisers. So presumably there was an adequate production of hay, which, perhaps supplemented by foliage gathered from the surrounding countryside, will have kept the domestic animals going throughout the winter.

The horses seem to represent a different factor. Their bones form the third largest group on the site as a whole and figure prominently in the pits, and obviously horsemeat was a significant part of the diet. Yet no very young animals are represented, suggesting that they were not bred on the farm. This was a novelty to Harcourt and the Excavator in the 1960s, as the interchange of letters in the archive recalls, but it is a phenomenon since recognised at both Gussage All Saints and Pimperne Down, Dorset (Harding, Blake and Reynolds 1993, 55 and 64-71). The obvious answer, even in 1967, was that there must have been herds of ponies running wild on the downs or in the valleys, which would have provided a major resource in terms of meat and horsepower. At Gussage there was evidence both from the horse bones and the horse harness and cart fittings produced on the site that ponies were broken and used to pull wheeled vehicles (Wainwright 1979, 188; Spratling in Wainwright 1979, 125-49).

At Longbridge no horse harnesses were found in the excavated area but the status of the top man of such a large farm, with its imposing roundhouses, suggests a probable chariot owner. So pairs of ponies will have been needed to enable him to clatter along the double-lynchet track across the downs to impress his neighbours in style and, more mundanely, sturdy animals will have been needed to draw farm carts and to serve as pack ponies. Unworked stone was brought in quantity to the site from great distances and strong pack ponies seem the likeliest means of transport. So, at Longbridge, as at Gussage, we must presuppose annual roundups of the biggest and strongest young stallions to be broken for the task that best suited them, and the culling of unsuitable or surplus animals. The pony herds could at all periods have become a menace unless culled. Doubtless the roundups would have been exciting occasions in the life of the farm and very probably the surplus young or mature animals were eaten as well as killed. Horseflesh seems to have provided a significant addition to the meat available to the community. Whether there were horse sacrifices or organised fights between stallions to celebrate the horse cull there is no evidence from Longbridge. But the presence of wild horse herds could possibly explain why, at the end of the first 'A' phase of the Iron Age, the yard and perhaps the vegetable plots of the big farm were enclosed for the first time by Enclosure II, with its surrounding ditch and presumed quickthorn hedge. Wild horse herds could have been on the increase in numbers and causing damage to domestic crops and buildings.

Throughout the history of the site a large percentage of sheep was kept, not for the sake of their meat (Table 5.19) but presumably to supply a big farm and its population with sufficient fleeces and wool for clothes and bedding. The women must have been kept busy processing the wool and, from the distribution of such things as loomweights and spindle whorls, such activities took place in and around the houses. Compared with the pits, the finds from the houses also include fewer cattle and horse bones but more of the raw material in the form of sheep and pig bones, from which tools for working skins and textiles were made. Deer were apparently not hunted on the site, but shed antlers were collected and their distribution, again predominantly in association with the houses, has certainly to do with domestic crafts such as the production of horn tool handles. Such work must have occupied the men whenever they had leisure indoors, so it is not surprising to find antler concentrated in the houses and not the pits.

THE HUMAN REMAINS

Introduction

by Lisa Brown

Longbridge Deverill human remains were never fully analysed or reported. The catalogue (Table 5.24) below is a compilation of occurrences of

Table 5.24 Catalogue of human remains

Provenance	*Details*	*Source*
Pit 1	Postcranial bones: Lower part of left humeral shaft; probably adolescent as the distal condyle was unfused.	Jarman 1968
Pit 5	Cranial bones: near complete occipital bone with part of the right parietal attached; probably male. Four Wormian bones visible in the lambdoid suture.	Jarman 1968
Pit 8	Cranial bone: Fragment of infant occipital bone	Westley 1965
Pit 18	Cranial bones: Antero-sagittal part of a left parietal bone. One Wormian bone visible in the coronal suture.	Jarman 1968
Pit 21	Mandible: Major part of the right half of a lower jaw, posterior part of the horizontal and ascending rami missing. The three molars in position and sockets for the premolars, canine and incisor teeth show that these were lost postmortem. Very small torus mandibularis present on the lingual side of the jaw. Caries - M1 mesial neck; M3 occlusal. Traces of dental calculus visible. Attrition pattern in keeping with young adult c. 20-25 years, and general size of the jaw suggests it is probably female. Molar tooth: One loose left M1. As size and attrition pattern similar to those of the right M1 in the mandibular fragment, this tooth probably belonged to the same specimen.	Jarman 1968
Pit 37	One fragment of human bone (no details provided)	Westley 1965
Pit58	Complete adult inhumation burial	Brothwell
Pit 63	Near complete infant under six months	Westley 1965
Pit 67	Complete adult inhumation burial	Brothwell
Hollow 2	Maxilla: A fragment of the upper jaw with the first premolar in position. The tooth shows slight hyperplasia of the enamel, and traces of dental calculus are present. Postcranial bones: Mid-section of a right femoral shaft.	Jarman 1968

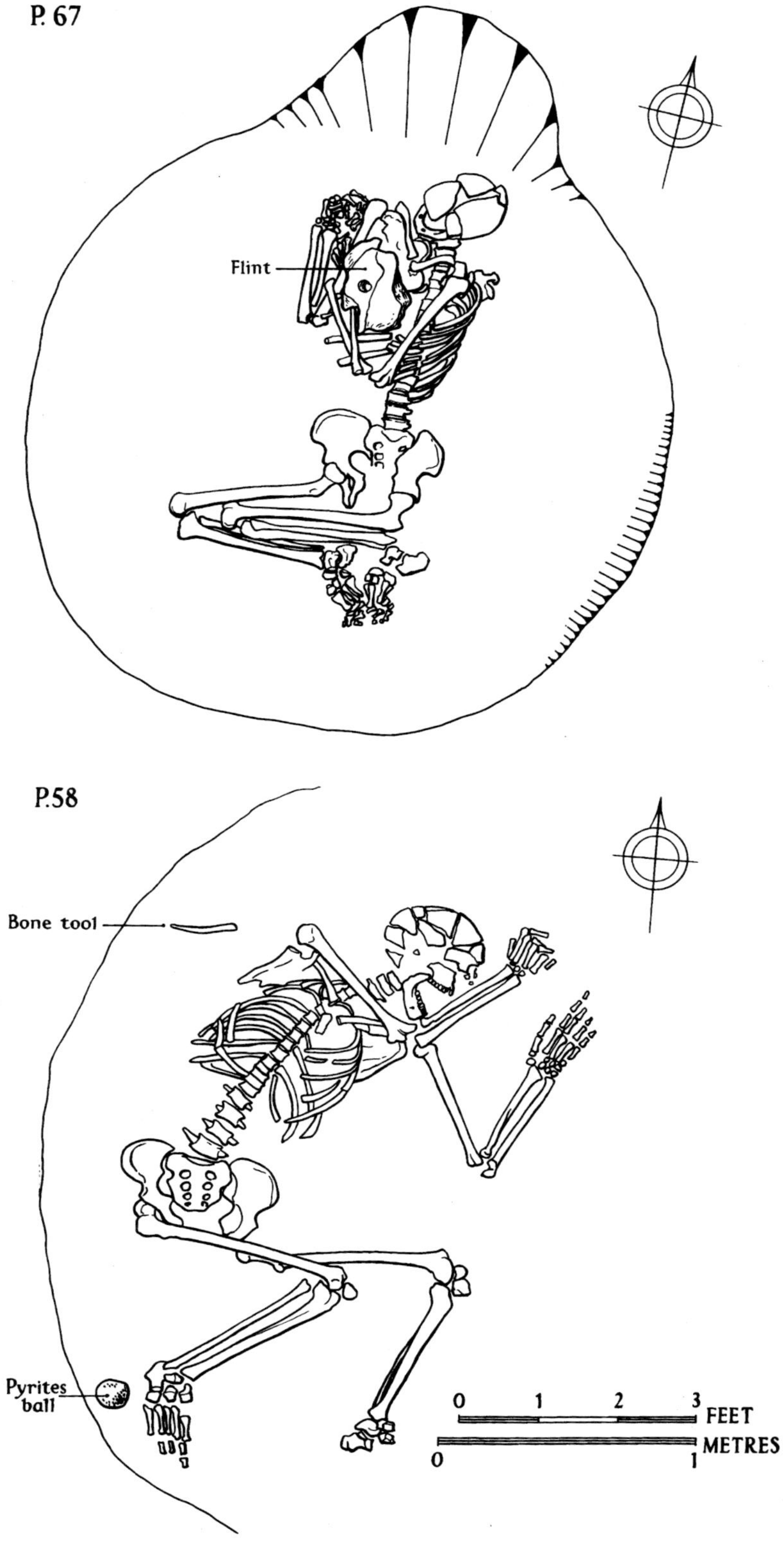

Fig. 5.4 Human burials: Pit 58 and Pit 67

human bone from the site based on all of the available evidence. All of the remains were evidently recovered from features and deposits associated with Enclosure II. The catalogue brings together notes made by Shirley Jarman in May 1968, elements extracted from the animal bone listing compiled by Betty Westley in 1965 and an undated report on two complete human burials in pits P58 and P67 by Don Brothwell and B. Denson. Betty Wesley's information is not entirely reliable, as her preliminary identifications may have been subsequently superseded without documentation.

The report by Brothwell and Denston was probably intended only as a preliminary statement at its time of writing. The report is undated but correspondence in the archive indicates that it was produced when Brothwell was working at the Museum of Archaeology and Ethnology at Cambridge from 1958 to 1961. A method statement was not supplied but it can be assumed that Brothwell's observations are broadly in keeping with the protocols he later described in Digging up Bones (1981). Current practice normally relies on the pubic symphysis for ageing females, but the symphyseal face was not described in this report. No discussion of the wider context of burials was provided, nor of the then existing knowledge of funerary treatment for the early Iron Age period, aspects of analysis that Brothwell would no doubt have addressed had he been provided with a wider brief at the time.

Burials in Pit 58 and Pit 67

by Don Brothwell and B. Denston

The skeletons were in a very good state of preservation, although crushing made it impossible to record all the usual biometric measurements. From an examination of the pelvis, it is clear that both individuals were female, although certain features of the skull of Pit 58 were rather masculine

Fig. 5.5 Burial in Pit 58

(Eu.1.3.227, Duckworth Laboratory, University of Cambridge). Owing to the inability to determine the developmental age of females by changes at the pubic symphysis, only very tentative ages can be suggested. The dental attrition of the Pit 58 skeleton suggests a person of not more than 40 years, but the zedentulous condition of the Pit 62 individual's teeth is strongly suggestive of an elderly individual (Eu.1.3.228, Duckworth Laboratory, University of Cambridge). The skeletal build was light skeletal and thin skull. No evidence is forthcoming from the bones as to the reason for the peculiar circumstances of burial, or for the positioning of the bodies within the grave. The cause of death is unclear but in the case of the Pit 58 skeleton the large abscess cavity could be considered in the context of a possible (although rarely certain) cause of death.

Details of the individual skeletons are presented below. Standard measurements are given in Table 5.25.

Table 5.25 Standard biometric measurements of the Longbridge Deverill skeletons

		Eu.1.3.227 *Pit 58*	*Eu.1.3.228* *Pit 67*
SKULL			
Maximum length	(L)	189	---
Maximum breadth	(B)	133	135
Minimum frontal breadth	(B')	101	93.0
Basi-bregmatic height	(H')	144	---
Basi-nasal length	(LB)	107.5	---
Frontal arc	(S1)	133	---
Frontal chord	(S'1)	115	---
Parietal arc	(S2)	127.5	116
Parietal chord	(S'2)	119.5	104
Occipital arc	(S3)	117	108
Occipital chord	(S'3)	100	90
Total sagittal arc	(S)	380	---
Transverse bregmatic arc	(T')	312	288
Horizontal circumference	(U)	520	---
Upper facial height	(G'H)	75.0	---
Basi-alveolar length	(GL)	96.0?	---
Orbital breadth	(O1)	46.3	---
Orbital height	(O2)	37.0?	---
Foraminal length	(FL)	38.5	---
Foraminal breadth	(FB)	31.7	---
Nasal breadth	(NB)	25.0?	---
Nasal height	(NH')	52.4	---
Bregmatic auricular height	(BOH)	121	---
Bicondylar breadth	(W1)	119.5	113
Condyle length	(CYL)	19.5	18.3
Least ramus breadth	(RB')	31.6	29.1
Bimental breadth	(ZZ)	42.0	39.3
Mandibular angle	(M<)	132_	129_
Projective L.left ramus	(RL)	56.0	51.5
Maximum projective L.mandible	(ML)	108.5	95.5
Bigonial breadth	(GoGo)	---	95.0
LONG BONES			
Femur maximum length	(FeL1)	420 (L)	381 (L)
Femur minimum antero-posterior diameter	(FeD1)	21.0 (L)	21.2 (L)
Femur transverse diameter	(FeD2)	33.7 (L)	34.0 (L)
Tibia maximum length	(TiL1)	343 (R)	299 (R)
Tibia maximum antero-posterior diameter	(TiD1)	33.0 (L)	32.3 (L)
Tibia transverse diameter	(TiD2)	22.0 (L)	20.0 (L)
Humerus maximum length	(HuL1)	295(L)	285 (R)
Humerus maximum diameter	(HuD1)	19.5 (L)	20.0 (L)
Humerus minimum diameter	(HuD2)	17.5 (L)	16.0 (L)
Radius maximum length	(RaL1)	227 (L)	200 (L)
Ulna maximum length	(UlL)	246 (L)	222 (L)

Skeleton Pit 58

Figs 2.26, 5.5 and 5.6

The dentition is as follows:

```
                    EE
                   AAC A
  8 7 6 5 4 3 2 1 | 1 2 3 4 5 6 7 8
-----------------------------------
NP 8 7 6 5 4 3 2 1 | 1 2 3 4 5 6 7 8
       C C                AC   A
```

A = abscess. E = pulp exposure. X = lost ante-mortem.
NP = congenital absence. \ = tooth lost post mortem.
C = caries

Four caries cavities were present in 24 teeth. Five abscesses, two definitely in association with pulp exposure, were present. Alveolar bone destruction through periodontal disease was marked at some teeth. Massive abscessing on the left inner aspect has spread onto the palatal surface of the maxillary bone with subsequent further bone destruction. At least five teeth were lost before death. Some degree of tooth rotation was observed at:

```
5 3 2 | 2 3 5 7
------------------
    2 | 2
```

Fig. 5.6 Burial in Pit 67

Slight enamel hypoplasia was noted in the case of some teeth.

The vertebrae show varying degrees of osteoarthritis [*editor's note: it is possible that the author meant to describe the condition as osteophytosis*], visible as bony 'lipping', but on no vertebra is this severe. The sacrum is normal in conformation, but the dorsal arch of the last lumbar had not united with the body of the vertebra. So-called 'vascular grooves' are present on the posterior aspects of both femora, and the lateral aspects of the tibial shafts.

Skeleton Pit 67

Figs 5.5; 5.7-5.8

Only the mandible was available for dental examination, and it was completely edentulous (the teeth all being lost before death). Slight osteoarthritis was noted on thoracics 3 to 8 and lumbars 2 to 3; whereas a medium degree was recorded on thoracics 10 to 11 and cervicals 6 to 7. Some arthritic deformity was also seen at some articular areas of the ulnae and clavicles, and on one or two phalanges. Vascular grooves were present, as in P58, on both femora and tibiae.

Fig. 5.7 Burial in Pit 67 (detail)

Chapter 6: Radiocarbon Dating and Calibration

INTRODUCTION

by Lisa Brown

Radiocarbon determinations were obtained on ten samples from Longbridge Deverill, nine of charred wood and one of charred grain. The site records and Sonia Hawkes' descriptions of six of the wood samples (Samples 1-3 and 7-9), recovered from postholes associated with the four roundhouses, indicate that they were the remnants of *in situ* charred structural timbers, all oak. These were submitted to the National Physical Laboratory at Teddington (NPL) in 1966 and 1968.

Another wood sample (Sample 4) was taken from a posthole within the circuit of House 2, and may have been a support for an internal dividing wall or furniture. The other two wood samples were a fragment of oak (Sample 5) from Pit 7, located to the south of Posthole Complex 5 in Enclosure II Area S2 (Chapter 2, Fig. 2.58), and a piece of hazel (Sample 6) from Pit 37, which cut through the destruction level of House 2. These, along with the grain sample from Pit 37 in the interior of House 2, were submitted to the Harwell Nuclear Physics Laboratory (HAR) in 1972. Summary details of the samples are presented below in Table 6.1. The dates anticipated by Hawkes (final column) were based largely on ceramic typology and stratigraphic evidence.

The results of all the original radiocarbon measurements were published in *Radiocarbon* (Callow, Baker and Hassall 1966; Callow and Hassall, 1968; 1974). Sonia Hawkes' remarks on the significance of the dates, produced shortly after their release in 1966 and 1973, are summarised below. In 2010 the 10 radiocarbon measurements were calibrated by Peter Marshall of English Heritage's Scientific Dating Team and the report is reproduced in full.

RADIOCARBON RESULTS

by Sonia Chadwick Hawkes

In Table 6.2 the first date in each case is that supplied by the laboratories using the old half-life value of 5570 years (W.F. Libby). The second date is that arrived at by conversion to the most recent half-life value, 5730 (by multiplying the bp results by 1.03 and subtracting 1950).

Table 6.1 Radiocarbon samples submitted 1966-1972

Sample	*ID*	*Lab. No.*	*Excavated*	*Material & context*	*Anticipated date*
1	650087	NPL-104	1960	Charcoal, *Quercus* sp. almost entirely *Q. robur* House 1, PH235 main post-ring. Probably from the post	7th-6th century BC
2	650088	NPL-105	1960	Charcoal, *Quercus* sp. almost entirely *Q. robur* House 1, PH141 main post-ring	7th-6th century BC
3	650089	NPL-106	1960	Charcoal, *Quercus* sp. almost entirely *Q. robur* House 2 PH114 main post-ring, from base of post socket showing circular post shape 10" dia.. Probably small tree trunk	5th century BC
4	650233	NPL-107	1960	Charcoal, *Corylus avellana* PH136, recut posthole in interior of House 2	5th century BC
5	650091	NPL-108	1958	Charcoal, *Quercus robur* Pit 7 Area S2, near PH Complex 5, from well down in fill	3rd - 1st century BC
6	650092	NPL-109	1960	*Corylus avellana.* Pit 37 (3), within House 2, from well down in fill. Pit cut floor level of House 2 and contained much occupation debris from destruction of house, so charcoal may be rubbish survival	3rd - 1st century BC
7	-	HAR-255	1960	Charcoal, *Quercus robur* House 3 PH 104. Base of charred post of main post-ring	5th century BC
8	-	HAR-254	1960	Charcoal, *Quercus robur* House 4 PH 198. Charred post stump, main post-ring	-
9	-	HAR-256	1960	Charcoal, *Quercus robur* House 4 PH 217. Base of charred post	5th century BC
10	-	HAR-253	1957	Carbonised grain, mainly barley Pit 37 (4) Base of pit, below charcoal Sample 6 NPL-109	5th century BC

Table 6.2 Radiocarbon Results (1966 and 1972)

LAB No	Sample	Provenance	Material	OHL bp	bc	NHL	bp	bc
NPL-104	1	House 1 PH235	*Q Robur*	2480 ± 90	530	2554	604 ± 90	740
NPL-105	2	House 1 PH141	*Q Robur*	2580 ± 155	630	2657	707 ± 155	800
NPL-106	3	House 2 PH114	*Q Robur*	2450 ± 90	500	2524	574 ± 90	660-720
NPL-107	4	House 2 PH136	*Corylus avellana*	2370±95	420	2440	490±95	470
NPL-108	5	Pit7	*Q Robur*	2410±140	460	2482	532±140	500-640
NPL-109	6	Pit 37(3)	*Corylus avellana*	2440±90	490	2513	563±90	530-710
HAR-255	7	House 3 PH104	*Q Robur*	2330±60	380	2400	450±60	440
HAR-254	8	House 4 PH198	*Q Robur*	2420 ± 60	470	2492	543±60	510-660
HAR-256	9	House 4 PH217	*Q Robur*	2440±90	490	2513	563±90	530-710
HAR-253	10	Pit 37(4)	Grain	2390±70	440	2462	512±70	490

Significance of Radiocarbon Results

These must be among the first radiocarbon dates for structures belonging to the British early Iron Age, and are extremely valuable. For the houses they confirm the suggestion, already made from archaeological evidence, that the beginnings of the British Iron Age in Wessex should be taken back at least a century earlier than had previously been accepted.

The four houses and Working Hollow 3 (see Chapter 2), along with Pits 7 and 37, form a sequence of early Iron Age structures and features. The radiocarbon dates from House 1 (7th-6th century BC) and House 2 (6th-5th century BC) conform generally well to the archaeological expectations. House 1 belongs probably in the 7th century BC, based on the calibrated radiocarbon dates of 740 cal BC and 800 BC from two burnt oak posts from the outer wall. The date confirmed the tentative conclusions drawn from comparative work on the pottery sequence from this house. House 2 was stratigraphically later than House 1 by perhaps a century or so and had a pottery sequence that did not show any continuity from it. The initial radiocarbon results of 500 BC and 420 BC suggested a construction date in the middle of the 5th century. However, conversion to the more recent half-life value produced a much earlier date of 660-720 BC on the house timber and 470 BC on a post from an internal structure.

The dates for House 3 (5th century BC) also met expectations but the result for House 4, anticipated to be 5th century BC, proved to be somewhat earlier. The date produced by the wood from Pit 37 also seems far too early to accommodate the stratigraphic and artefact evidence, but the 5th century date from the grain on the pit base is appropriate. The pit cut through the destruction level of the interior of House 2 and contained much pottery and debris from that period, so the charcoal from the in the rubbish-filled pit had survived from an earlier period than the pottery.

RADIOCARBON ANALYSIS AND RECALIBRATION

by Peter Marshall (2010)

Six radiocarbon measurements on charcoal from Longbridge Deverill were carried out by the National Physics Laboratory, Teddington, in 1965 and 1966. No quality assurance measurements survive, although known-age and absolute standards were available to the laboratory at this period. The measurements were calculated using the Libby half-life (5568 years) and the counting

Table 6.3 Radiocarbon results 2010

Lab. No.	Sample No.	Material & context	Radiocarbon Age (BP)	$\delta^{13}C$ (‰)	Calibrated date range (95% confidence)
NPL-104	Sample 1	Charcoal, *Quercus* sp. almost entirely *Q. robur*. House 1, PH235	2480±90	-25.0	820-390 cal BC
NPL-105	Sample 2	Charcoal, *Quercus* sp. almost entirely *Q. robur*. House 1, PH141	2580±155	-25.0	1060-380 cal BC
NPL-106	Sample 3	Charcoal, *Quercus* sp. almost entirely *Q. robur*. House 2, PH114	2450±90	-25.0	810-380 cal BC
NPL-107	Sample 4	Charcoal, *Corylus avellana* PH136, recut posthole interior House 2	2370±95	-25.0	790-200 cal BC
NPL-108	Sample 5	Charcoal, *Quercus robur* Enclosure II, Pit 7	2410±140	-25.0	830-170 cal BC
NPL-109	Sample 6	*Corylus avellana*. Enclosure II, Pit 37, layer (3)	2440±90	-25.0	810-370 cal BC
HAR-255	Sample 7	Charcoal, *Quercus robur* House 3, PH 104	2330±60	-25.7	710-210 cal BC
HAR-254	Sample 8	Charcoal, *Quercus robur* House 4, PH198	2420±60	-25.7	780-380 cal BC
HAR-256	Sample 9	Charcoal, *Quercus robur* House 4, PH217	2440±90	-24.7	810-370 cal BC
HAR-253	Sample 10	Carbonised grain, mainly barley Pit 37 layer (4) [below (3) Sample 6 NPL-109]	2390±70	-24.6	770-360 cal BC

error in all cases was increased to allow for uncertainty introduced by 'the De Vries effect'. The samples were prepared according to methods outlined by Callow *et al* (1963) and measured by gas proportional counting (carbon dioxide). Further details of error calculations are provided by Callow *et al* (1965).

The three charcoal and one carbonised grain sample measured at AERE Harwell in 1973 were converted to benzene following the method of Polach and Stipp (1967) and measured by liquid scintillation counting (Otlet and Slade 1974)

Results

The radiocarbon results, given in Table 6.3 and Fig. 6.1 below, are quoted in accordance with the international standard known as the Trondheim convention (Stuiver and Kra 1986). They are conventional radiocarbon ages (Stuiver and Polach 1977).

Calibration

The calibrations of the results, relating the radiocarbon measurements directly to calendar dates were calculated using the calibration curve of Reimer *et al* (2004) and the computer program OxCal v4.0.5 (Bronk Ramsey 1995; 1998, 2001, 2009). The calibrated date ranges cited in Table 6.3 are those for 95% confidence. They are quoted in the form recommended by Mook (1986), with the end points rounded outwards to 10 years. The ranges in Table 6.4 have been calculated according to the maximum intercept method (Stuiver and Reimer 1986) and those in Fig. 6.1 are derived from the probability method (Stuiver and Reimer 1993).

CONCLUSIONS

by Lisa Brown

The recalibrated radiocarbon dates produced in 2010 reflect a problem common to the chronology of

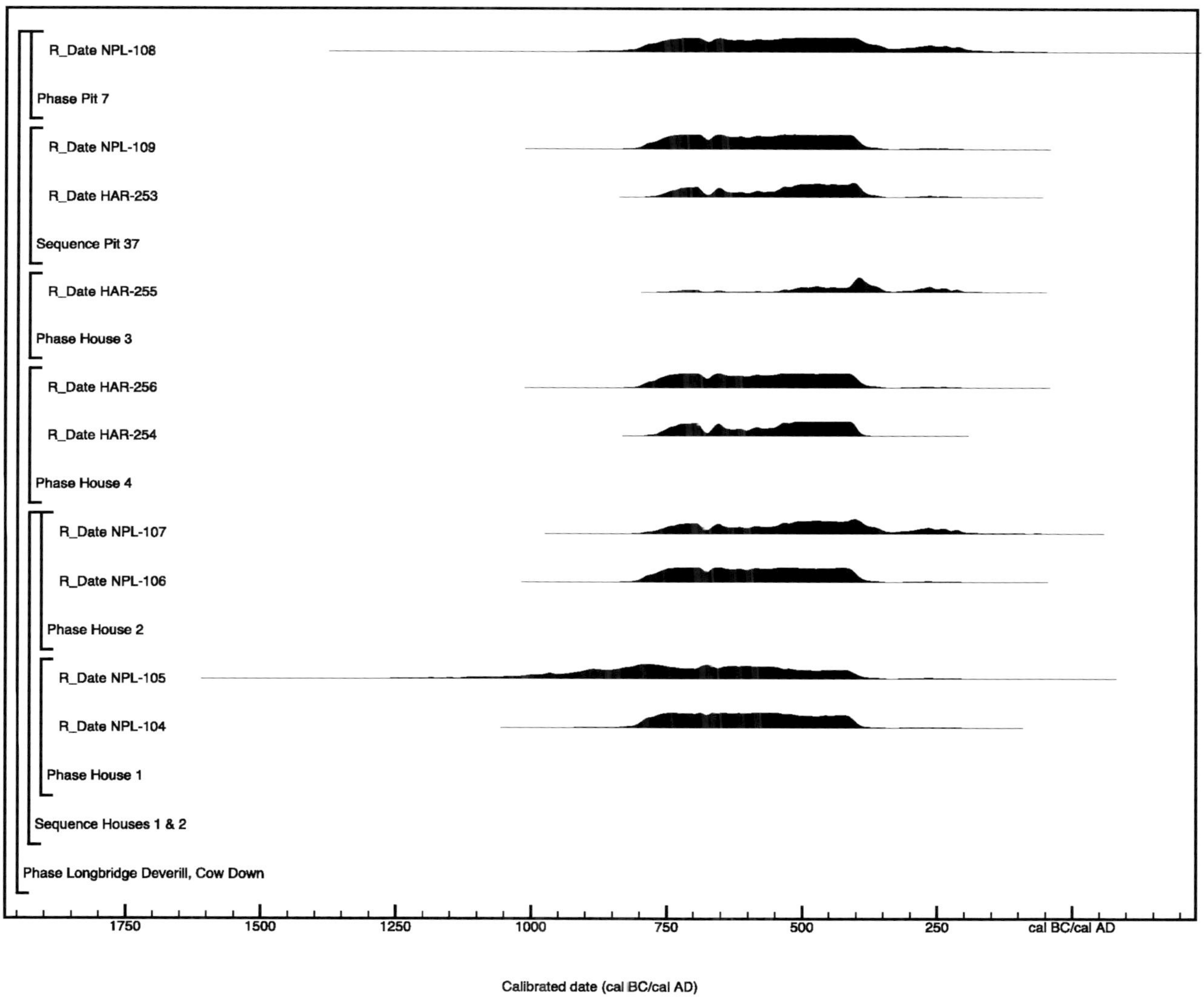

Fig. 6.1 Probability distributions of dates. Each distribution represents the relative probability that an event occurred at a particular time. These distributions are the result of simple radiocarbon calibration (Stuiver and Reimer 1993).

many Iron Age sites – the inherent limitation produced by the wide standard deviation associated with the radiocarbon ages of plateau-affected deposits. The general flatness of the calibration curve applies particularly to the period *c.* 800-400 BC, which is, unfortunately, precisely pertinent to the Longbridge settlement.

The earlier set of radiocarbon determinations available to Hawkes provided her with the scope and confidence to propose a sequence for the roundhouses. However, because the date for Pit 37 posed problems for her she rightly sought explanations in the interpretation of the settlement history and activity provided by stratigraphic, morphological and artefactual evidence. In the light of the calibrated dates (Table 6.4), it is clearly necessary to rely more heavily on these dating strategies than the radiocarbon determinations.

Table 6.4 Radiocarbon measurements calibrated in 1973 and 2010

Lab. No.	*Sample*	*1973 calibration*	*2010 re-calibration*
NPL-104	Sample 1	740	820-390
NPL-105	Sample 2	800	1060-380
NPL-106	Sample 3	660-720	810-380
NPL-107	Sample 4	470	790-200
NPL-108	Sample 5	500-640	830-170
NPL-109	Sample 6	530-710	810-370
HAR-255	Sample 7	440	710-210
HAR-254	Sample 8	510-660	780-380
HAR-256	Sample 9	530-710	810-370
HAR-253	Sample 10	490	770-360

Nonetheless, the calibrated dates do allow for a broad sequence for the roundhouses to be suggested. The stratigraphic evidence clearly demonstrated that House 2 post-dated House 1. The date range of 1060-380 cal BC for House 1 allows it to be the earliest of the four, and the ceramic evidence indicates occupation sometime between the 9th and 7th centuries BC. House 2 was constructed next, sometime between 810-200 BC but, on the ceramic evidence, clearly at the beginning of that period, and not later than the 6th century BC.

The two dates of 810-370 and 780-380 cal BC for House 4 indicate that this structure is likely to have been very close in date to House 2, possibly even contemporary with it. House 4 was the smallest of the four, substantially smaller than the imposing House 2, and may have been either a lower status dwelling or it could served a different, perhaps ancillary, function within the settlement. The character of the relatively small pottery assemblage from House 4, consisting mostly of coarsewares, also suggests a different function or status but, because of the preponderance of coarsewares, does not allow for close ceramic dating beyond that it was unlikely to post-date the 6th century BC.

House 3 appears to have been the latest in the sequence, with a radiocarbon date of 710-210 cal BC. The ceramic assemblage, which included many examples of carinated bowls and a carinated cup of a type dated at Potterne to the 7th-6th century BC (Gingell and Morris 2000, 152) supports a date early within the radiocarbon range. The fact that the construction technique of House 3 is different to that of the other roundhouses could support the case for a later date.

Appendix 1

FIELDWALKING SURVEY 1982-1983

Based on notes by Peggy Guido and Eve Machin

Introduction

The aim of the field-walking exercise undertaken in 1982-3 was to ascertain whether fresh pottery was being pulled up by the plough. The interior of Enclosure II adjacent to Enclosure III was walked, corresponding to much of the area that had been excavated, but including some areas which had not. As finds spots were not distinguished by area the results of the work are of limited value.

Pottery compendium

Fifty sherds of very weathered pottery, most of it quartz and flint-tempered material of Phase A and a few shell-tempered sherds. Most are jar and bowl sherds. No decorated or featured sherds.

A samian ware bowl rim and two small samian body sherds and a rim of a fine black-slipped vessel. Four quartz-tempered Iron Age sherds, all very worn, one a haematite-coated bowl base.

Forty very small weathered sherds of Iron Age 'A' jar and bowl wares. Fifty medium and small weathered sherds, all apparently Iron Age 'A' wares, some from a large jar and one burnt and weathered triple-furrowed bowl shoulder. Thirteen sherds set aside by walkers as featured sherds included a handle in flint-tempered ware, a finger-tipped shoulder sherd from a medium jar and a large sherd, slightly less weathered than the others, which appears to be a broken rim with pinched decoration.

Conclusions

None of the pottery appeared to have been recently pulled up from below the topsoil and it was all very weathered. Despite the very chalky condition of the Down it seems the plough had not recently been going deeper. The preponderance of Iron Age A sherds is puzzling, except of course that Iron Age B fabrics tend to be less well fired and more friable, and so may have decayed in the ploughsoil.

Slag

Some slag was recovered, including a large piece of a hearth bottom, evidence of on-site smithing. The slag presumably came from Iron Age pits.

Stone

Machin and Guido included 'foreign' stone in their collection (important in view of the fact that the stone collected from the excavations had been discarded). This was examined by Fiona Roe, who confirmed that as well as local Greensand there was stone from Mendip, some of which closely resembled that from Cadbury Castle.

Glass

A small bag labelled 'miscellaneous' contained a fragment of pale blue flat, thin glass which might be Roman window glass.

Appendix 2A

STRUCTURAL REMAINS: THE ENCLOSURES AND ROUNDHOUSES

Enclosure I Ditches: Stratigraphy and Finds

Ditch P (Old C I) Figs 2.1; 2.9
Ditch width 2.80 m, depth 1.22 m, inward-sloping sides, V-profile base.
Fill: Layer 2:- brown soil with lumps of chalk and flint: layer 3:- chalky soil with lumps of chalk; layer 4:- loose chalk; layer 5:- chalk and flint rubble.
Bone frags: 12 sheep/goat, 17 cattle, 4 horse.
Pottery: 1 rim sherd and 4 body sherds, fabric 12; 3 rim sherds, 1 base sherd and 17 body sherds, fabric 11; 20 body sherds, fabric 12; 5 body sherds, fabric 13; 2 rim sherds and 20 body sherds, fabric 14; 7 body sherds, fabric 21; 3 body sherds, fabric 22; 1 rim sherd, 1 base sherd and 26 body sherds, fabric 31; 3 body sherds, fabric 32; 4 base sherds and 50 body sherds, fabric 41; 1 rim sherd, 2 base sherds and 11 body sherds, fabric 42; 8 body sherds, fabric 52.

Ditch Q (Old C II) Fig. 2.9
Ditch width. 2.19 m, depth 1.02 m, inward-sloping sides, pointed bottom.
Fill: Layer 2:- chalky soil with small lumps of chalk; layer 3:- dark soil with small lumps of chalk; layer 4:- chalk rubble.
Bone frags: 9 cattle.
Pottery: 1 body sherd, fabric 12; 1 body sherd, fabric 14; 1 rim sherd and 2 body sherds, fabric 21; 1 base sherd and 3 body sherds, fabric 22; 1 base sherd and 16 body sherds, fabric 31; 2 body sherds, fabric 42; 3 body sherds, fabric 51.

Enclosure I Cutting R: Stratigraphy and Finds

Cutting R (Old C III) Fig. 2.9
Fill: Layer 2:- brown soil with lumps of chalk.
Daub: 1 fragment with wattle impression, Freeman type IV.
Bone frags: 11 sheep/goat, 24 cattle, 3 horse, 3 pig.
Pottery (general): 9 body sherds, fabric 13; 1 rim sherd, fabric 21; 11 body sherds, fabric 31; 1 rim sherds and 5 body sherds, fabric 32; 4 base sherds, fabric 41; 15 body sherds, fabric 42.

Enclosure II Ditches: Stratigraphy and finds

Ditch A (Old A 151) Fig. 2.16
Fill: Layer 2:- dark soil; layer 3:- chalky soil with lumps of chalk; layer 4:- chalk rubble with a little chalky soil; layer 5:- large lumps of chalk; layer 6:- chalk rubble; brown soil with small chalk lumps; layer 8:- chalk rubble.

Ditch B (Old A 149) Fig. 2.16 & 2.17
No drawn section.
Small finds: Iron ox shoe (Fig. 3, no. 7).
Pottery: 1 sherd pear-shaped jar, fabric 21 (Fig. 3.32, no. 10)

Ditch C (Old A 147) Fig. 2.16
Fill: Layer 2:- chalky soil with small lumps of chalk; layer 3:- chalky soil with medium lumps of chalk; layer 4:- brown soil; layer 5:- chalky soil with small chalk lumps; layer 6:- chalky soil with medium lumps of chalk; layer 7:- chalky soil with many lumps of chalk; layer 8:- chalk rubble.

Ditch D (Old A 145) Fig. 2.16 & 2.18
Fill: Layer 2:- brown soil; layer 3:- fine dark soil; layer 4:- chalky soil with small lumps of chalk; layer 5:- chalky soil with small and medium lumps of chalk; layer 6:- chalky earth with medium chalk lumps; layer 7:- chalk rubble.
Bone frags: 6 sheep/goat, 19 cattle, 3 horse, 5 pig.
Pottery: 1 body sherd, fabric 41; 1 body sherd, fabric 43, 1 sherdcarinated bowl, fabric 12 (Fig. 3.32, no. 1); 1 sherd dish, fabric 22 (Fig. 3.32, no. 12); 1 sherd vessel, fabric 31 (Fig. 3.32, no. 14).

Ditch E (Old B VIII) Fig. 2.19
Fill: Layer 2:- chalky soil with lumps of chalk; layer 3:- chalk rubble; layer 4:- brown soil; layer 5:- chalk rubble.
Bone frags: 3 sheep/goat, 21 cattle, 1 horse, 2 pig.

Ditch F (Old B XIX) Fig. 2.19
Fill: Layer 2:- brown soil with variously sized lumps of chalk and flint; layer 3:- brown soil with small lumps of chalk; layer 4:- loose chalk; layer 5:- chalky soil with small lumps of chalk; layer 6:- brown soil; layer 7:- chalky soil with small lumps of chalk; layer 8:- chalk rubble with chalk wash beneath.
Bone frags: 7 sheep/goat, 26 cattle, 2 pig, 1 dog.

Ditch G Not illustrated
Fill: Layer 2:- gravelly soil; layer 3:- loose brown soil with small lumps of chalk and flint; layer 4:- grey soil; layer 5:- grey soil with lumps of chalk; layer 6:- grey soil with large lumps of chalk; layer 7:- chalky soil with lumps of chalk.

Ditch H (Old B XXII) Fig. 2.20
Fill: Layer 2:- brown soil:- layer 3:- chalky soil with lumps of chalk.
Bone frags: 31 sheep/goat, 58 cattle, 2 pig.
Small finds: Rib bone (bos) from cow or horse (Fig. 5, no. 2).
Pyrites: 1 complete burnt piece of pyrites, 1 struck fragment.
Miscellaneous finds: Fragments of iron-stained ironstone (analysed by AM Lab.).
Pottery: 1 sherd pear-shaped jar, fabric 31 (Fig. 3.32, no. 5); 1 sherd 'saucepan' vessel, fabric 13 (Fig. 3.32, no. 6); 1 sherd vessel, fabric 21 (Fig. 3.32, no. 9); 1 sherd vessel, fabric 13 (Fig. 3.32, no. 17).

Ditch I (Old B XVII) Fig. 2.20 and 2.21
Fill: Layer 1:- brown soil with small lumps of chalk; layer 2:- brown soil with lumps of chalk; layer 3:- chalky soil with lumps of chalk; layer 4:- chalky soil with medium lumps of chalk; layer 5:- chalk rubble.
Pottery: 1 sherd 'saucepan' vessel, fabric 12 (Fig. 3.32, no. 2);
Bone frags: 4 sheep/goat, 7 cattle, 2 pig.

Ditch J (Old A 19) Fig. 2.22
Fill: Layer 2:- chalky soil with fairly large chalk lumps; layer 3:- chalky soil with small chalk lumps; layer 4:- brown soil; layer 5:- loose chalk; layer 6:- brown soil with chalk lumps; layer 7:- chalk rubble; layer 8:- brown soil; layer 9:- chalk rubble and chalk wash.
Bone frags: 6 sheep/goat, 12 cattle, 1 horse, 4 pig, 3 dog.
Pottery: 1 sherd vessel, fabric 21 (Fig. 3.32, no. 11); 1 sherd carinated bowl, furrowed decoration, fabric 11 (Fig. 3.32, no. 15); 1 sherd vessel, fabric 41 (Fig. 3.32, no. 16).

Ditch K (Old A 19 B) Fig. 2.22 & 2.23
Fill: Layer 2:- brown soil with small chalk lumps; layer 3:- loose chalk; layer 4:- brown soil; layer 5:- chalky soil with numerous chalk lumps; layer 6:- chalky soil with lumps of chalk; layer 7:- chalk rubble and chalk wash.
Bone frags: 17 cattle, 1 horse, 1 dog.
Pottery: 2 sherds jar or bowl, fabric 22 (Fig. 3.32, no. 3); 2 sherds carinated jar, fabric 22 (Fig. 3.32, no. 4); 1 sherd vessel, fabric 41 (Fig. 3.32, no. 7); 1 sherd vessel, probably barrel jar, fabric 52; 1 sherd vessel, probably barrel jar, fabric 21 (Fig. 3.32, no. 13); 5 sherds vessel, fabric 31 (Fig. 3.33, no. 3).

Ditch L (Old A 19 C) Fig. 2.22
Fill: Layer 2:- brown soil; layer 3:- loose chalk; layer 4:- brown soil; layer 5:- chalky soil with small lumps of chalk; layer 5B:- chalky soil with fairly large lumps of chalk; layer 6:- brown soil; layer 7:- chalky soil with lumps of chalk; layer 8:- chalk rubble; layer 9:- chalk rubble and chalk wash.

Enclosure II Cuttings: Finds Summary

Cutting S (Figs 2.1 & 2.11)
Small finds (recovered from dump, Area S2/3): Bone gouge or weaving beater (Fig. 4.4, no. 8).
Pottery (general): 1 body sherd, fabric 12; 1 body sherd, fabric 31; 1 base sherd and 4 body sherds, fabric 41.
– Also see individual features in Areas S1, S2, and S3.

Ditch V Not illustrated (Position shown on Fig. 2.1)
Cutting B II
Bone frags: 28 sheep/goat, 21 cattle, 1 horse, 1 pig, 1 mustelid (weasel?).

Cutting B III
Bone frags: 2 sheep/goat, 7 cattle, 2 pig.

Cutting B XI
Daub: Fragments of daub, Freeman type IV.

Cutting B XIV/XX
Small finds: Sandstone lamp (Fig. 4.10, no. 10).

Cutting B XVII
Bone frags: 6 sheep/goat, 1 cattle, 2 horse, 2 pig.
Small finds: Semi-translucent dark blue glass ring-bead (Fig. 4.2, no. 12); part of chalk loom weight (Fig. 4.7, no. 1).
Pyrites: Several struck and burnt pieces of pyrites.

Cutting B XVIII
Bone frags: 13 sheep/goat, 16 cattle, 7 horse.

Cutting B XX
Small finds: Blade end of polished Neolithic stone axe (Fig. 4.10, no. 6).

Cutting B XXIII
Bone frags: 18 sheep/goat, 17 cattle, 4 horse, 3 pig.
Small finds: Sandstone rubber (Fig. 4.11, no. 2), large fragment of lower stone of sandstone saddle quern (Fig. 4.11, no. 7).

Cutting B XXIV
Bone frags: 26 sheep/goat, 27 cattle, 11 pig, 6 horse.
Small finds: Ceramic spindle whorl (Fig. 4.12, no. 2).

Cutting XXIX
Bone frags: 23 sheep/goat, 38 cattle, 2 horse, 5 pig.

Cutting B XXX
Bone frags: 5 sheep/goat, 29 cattle, 6 horse, 6 pig.
Small finds: Sandstone rubber or sharpening stone (Fig. 4.11, no. 3).

Cutting B XXXI
Small finds: Part of polished bone handle of beater or gouge (not illustrated); part of chalk loom weight (not illustrated), Large fragment of lower stone of a sandstone saddle quern (Fig. 4.11, no. 6).

Cutting B XXXII
Bone frags: 72 sheep/goat, 95 cattle, 15 pig, 12 horse, 12 dog.
Small finds: Ceramic ball, possibly a sling bullet (Fig. 4.13, no 14).

Cutting B XXXIII
Bone frags: 11 sheep/goat, 26 cattle, 10 pig.
Small finds: Ceramic sling bullet (Fig. 4.13, no. 13).

Cutting B XXXIV
Bone frags: 10 sheep/goat, 17 cattle.

Enclosure III Ditches: Stratigraphy and Finds

Ditch M (Old A II) Fig. 2.25
Fill: Layer 2:- brown soil with small lumps of chalk; layer 3:- chalky soil with lumps of chalk; layer 3B:- chalky soil with small lumps of chalk; layer 4:- dark soil with sparse chalk lumps; layer 5:- chalky soil with small lumps of chalk; layer 5B:- chalky soil with large lumps of chalk and flint; layer 6:- brown soil; layer 7:- chalky soil with small lumps of chalk; layer 8:- chalk rubble; layer 8A:- burnt soil; layer 9:- chalk rubble; layer 9B:- burnt soil.
Bone frags: 5 sheep/goat, 3 cattle, 1 horse, 2 pig, 1 bird.
Small finds: Thin iron blade (Fig. 4.3, no. 1).
Pottery: 8 sherds jar, fabric 12 (Fig. 3.33, no. 1); 7 sherds globular jar, fabric 21 (Fig. 3.33, no. 2).

Ditch N (Old A I) Figs 2.25 & 2.26
Fill: Layer 1B:- brown soil; layer 2:- brown soil with small lumps of chalk; layer 3:- chalky soil with lumps of chalk; layer 3B:- fairly large flints; layer 4:- brown soil with chalk lumps; layer 5:- chalky soil with lumps of chalk; layer 6:- chalk rubble; layer 6B:- chalk wash; layer 7:- brown soil.
Bone frags: 5 cattle, 2 horse, 1 fox.
Pottery: many sherds from jar, fabric 32 (Fig. 3.33, no. 4); 1 sherd 'saucepan' vessel, fabric 32 (Fig. 3.33, no. 6).

Ditch O (Old A 20) Figs 2.25 & 2.27
Fill: Layer 2:- brown soil with small lumps of chalk; layer 3:- chalky soil with fairly large lumps of chalk; layer 4:-

loose chalk; layer 5:- brown soil; layer 6:- chalky soil with lumps of chalk; layer 7:- loose chalk and flint; layer 8:- brown soil with lumps of chalk; layer 9:- flints; layer 10:- chalky soil with lumps of chalk; layer 11:- chalk rubble and chalk wash; layers 12 and 13:- chalk wash.
Small finds: Iron harness ring (Fig. 4.3, no. 3).
Pottery: 1 sherd shallow dish, Roman coarse ware F1 (Fig. 3.33, no. 9); 1 body sherd, fabric 2 (Roman) 1 body sherd, fabric 4 (Roman); 2 body sherds, fabric 12; 1 body sherd, fabric 13; 1 body sherd, fabric 14; 12 body sherds, fabric 41; 2 body sherds, fabric 51; 1 body sherd, fabric 52.

Enclosure III Trial Trench Cuttings: Features and Finds *(Figs 2.28 – 2.30)*

[Editor's note: The features exposed in the trial trenches excavated within the interior of Enclosure III are shown in Figs 2.28 – 2.30 but there are no other records of them in the archive. The only finds recorded from this part of the interior of the enclosure were two pottery sherds.]

Trench A 30 Topsoil (Position of trench not recorded)
Pottery: 1 sherd vessel, fabric 12 (Fig. 3.33, no. 5).
Trench A 32 (Position indicated on Fig. 2.24)
Pottery: 1 sherd 'saucepan' vessel, fabric 12 (Fig. 3.33, no. 8).

Enclosure III: Area T Cuttings Finds Summaries

Cuttings in numerical order:
A III, A IV, A IV Ext., A V, A V Ext., A VI, A VI Ext., A VII, A VIII, A XIV, A XV, A XVI.
A 18, A 23, A 30, A 32, A 44, A 51, A 52, A 53, A 54, A 57, A 58, A 59, A 60, A 61, A 62, A 62B, A 63, A 63B, A 64, A 64B, A 65, A 65B, A 66, A 67, A 68, A 77, A 83, A 84, A 85, A 86, A 87, A 88, A 89, A 90, A 91, A 91B, A 92, A 93, A 94, A 94B, A 95, A 96, A 97, A 98, A 99, A 100, A 101, A 101B, A 102, A 102B, A 103, A 103B, A 104, A 104B, A 105, A 106, A 107, A 108, A 109, A 110, A 111, A 111B, A 112, A 113, A 114, A 115, A 119, A122B, A 140, A 143, A 150.
Position of cuttings shown in Fig. 2.5

Enclosure III, topsoil beside entrance.
Small finds: Part of iron horseshoe (Fig. 4.3, no. 6).

Enclosure III, from depression in SW corner of trial hole, close to stakeholes and associated
with fragments of burnt bone.
Small finds: Part of sandstone rubber (Fig. 4.11, no. 5).

A III
Pottery: 1 body sherd, fabric 2 (Roman grey ware); 5 body sherds, fabric 13; 2 body sherds, fabric 42.

A IV
Bone frags: 1 sheep/goat, 3 cattle, 1 horse, 2 pig.
Small finds: Chalk spindle whorl (Fig. 4.12, no. 6).
Pottery: 1 sherd vessel, fabric 32 (Fig. 3.13, no. 60); 1 body sherd, fabric 11; 2 body sherds, fabric 12; 4 body sherds, fabric 13; 5 body sherds, fabric 14; 1 base sherd and 7 body sherds, fabric 31; 3 base sherds and 8 body sherds, fabric 41; 12 body sherds, fabric 42.

A IV Ext.
Pottery: 2 body sherds, fabric 3 (Roman); 3 body sherds, fabric 11; 3 body sherds, fabric 12; 1 base sherd and 3 body sherds, fabric 13; 10 body sherds, fabric 14; 2 body sherds, fabric 31; 1 body sherd, fabric 32; 5 body sherds, fabric 41; 3 body sherds, fabric 42; 5 body sherds, fabric 43.

A V
Bone frags: 2 cattle, 3 horse.
Pottery: 1 sherd vessel, fabric 21 (Fig. 3.13, no. 63); 1 sherd vessel, fabric 31 (Fig. 3.13, no. 64); 1 rim sherd and 11 body sherds, fabric 13; 1 rim sherd and 4 body sherds, fabric 14; 5 body sherds, fabric 42; 1 body sherd, fabric 43.

A V Ext.
Small finds: Iron rod with circular section (Fig. 4.2, no. 2).
Pottery: 1 rim sherd and 12 body sherds, fabric 11; 1 base sherd and 2 body sherds, fabric 12; 34 body sherds, fabric 13; 4 body sherds, fabric 14; 1 rim sherd and 1 body sherd, fabric 21; 2 rim sherds and 8 body sherds, fabric 31; 2 rim sherds, fabric 32; 6 body sherds, fabric 41; 18 body sherds, fabric 42; 8 base sherds and 1 body sherd, fabric 43.

A VI
Bone frags: 5 sheep/goat, 3 cattle, 1 horse, 2 pig.
Pottery: 1 sherd from vessel, fabric 31 (Fig. 3.13, no. 58); 1 body sherd, fabric 13.

A VI Ext.
No finds.

A VII
Pottery: 1 body sherd, fabric 12; 1 body sherd, fabric 14; 2 body sherds, fabric 42; 2 body sherds, fabric 43.

A VIII
No finds.

A XIV
Small finds: Part of iron horseshoe (Fig. 4.3, no. 5).

A XV
Pottery: 2 body sherds, fabric 13; 4 body sherds, fabric 14, 3 body sherds, fabric 42.

A XVI
Bone frags: 1 sheep/goat, 10 red deer (antler and teeth fragments).

A 18
No finds.

A 23
Pottery: 1 body sherd, fabric 12; 1 body sherd, fabric 41.

A 30
Pottery: 1 rim sherd and 2 body sherds, fabric 12.

A 32
Pottery: 1 rim sherd, fabric 12.

A 44
Pottery: 1 body sherd, fabric 41.

A 51 – A 62
No finds.

A 62 B
Pottery: 2 body sherds, fabric 11; 3 body sherds, fabric 12; 5 body sherds, fabric 13; 8 body sherds, fabric 14; 1

body sherd, fabric 21; 2 body sherds, fabric 31; 3 body sherds, fabric 41; 3 body sherds, fabric 42.

A 63
Pottery: 5 body sherds, fabric 14; 1 body sherd, fabric 52.

A 63 B
Pottery: 2 sherds carinated bowl, fabric 11 (Fig. 3.11, no. 12); 1 rim sherd and 11 body sherds, fabric 13; 4 body sherds, fabric 14; 1 body sherd, fabric 21; 1 body sherd, fabric 52.

A 64 – A 64 B
No finds.

A 65
Pottery: 34 sherds, many joining, carinated bowl, fabric 11 (Fig. 3.11, no. 7); 1 sherd carinated jar, fabric 14 (Fig. 3.12, no. 46); 1 body sherd, fabric 11; 1 rim sherd and 2 body sherds, fabric 13; 4 body sherds, fabric 14; 1 body sherd, fabric 31; 13 body sherds, fabric 41; 3 body sherds, fabric 42.

A 65 B
Pottery: 1 sherd carinated bowl, fabric 42 (Fig. 3.11, no. 4); 1 sherd vessel, fabric 42 (Fig. 3.12, no. 36); 2 joining sherds, fabric 42 (Fig. 3.12, no. 37); 4 joining sherds carinated jar, fabric 41 (Fig. 3.12, no. 49); 1 sherd vessel, fabric 31 (Fig. 3.13, no. 59); 1 body sherd, fabric 11; 17 body sherds, fabric 13; 8 body sherds, fabric 14; 1 body sherd, fabric 21; 1 rim sherd and 3 body sherds, fabric 31; 13 body sherds, fabric 41; 1 body sherd, fabric 42; 13 body sherds, fabric 43; 1 base sherd, fabric 52.

A 66
Pottery: 1 base sherd, fabric 31; 2 body sherds, fabric 41; 1 body sherd, fabric 42.

A 67
Pottery: 1 sherd from vessel, fabric 14 (Fig. 3.12, no. 20).

A 68
Pottery: 2 base sherds, fabric 12; 3 body sherds, fabric 41; 1 body sherd, fabric 43.

A 77
No finds.

A 83 – A 85
No finds.

A 86
Pottery: 1 body sherd, fabric 11; 1 body sherd, fabric 13; 1 body sherd, fabric 14; 1 body sherd, fabric 31; 3 body sherds, fabric 41; 7 body sherds, fabric 43.

A 87 – A 88
No finds.

A 89
Pottery: 1 body sherd, fabric 43.

A 90
No finds.

A 91
Pottery: 1 sherd carinated bowl, fabric 11 (Fig. 3.11, no. 5); 3 joining sherds carinated jar, fabric 41 (Fig. 3.12, no. 50); 2 body sherds, fabric 11; 1 body sherd, fabric 12; 15 body sherds, fabric 13; 1 rim sherd, 2 base sherds and 14 body sherds, fabric 14; 1 body sherd, fabric 21; 6 body sherds, fabric 31; 3 base sherds and 19 body sherds, fabric 41; 1 rim sherd, 2 base sherds and 23 body sherds, fabric 42; 3 base sherds and 7 body sherds, fabric 43.

A 91 B
Pottery: 2 body sherds, fabric 11; 2 body sherds, fabric 13; 2 body sherds, fabric 14.

A 92
Pottery: 1 sherd vessel, fabric 42 (Fig. 3.12, no. 21); 1 sherd vessel, fabric 14 (Fig. 3.12, no. 22); 3 sherds vessel, fabric 14 (Fig. 3.12, no. 23); 1 base sherd and 2 body sherds, fabric 31; 5 body sherds, fabric 41.

A 93
Pottery: 1 sherd carinated bowl, fabric 14 (Fig. 3.11, no. 3); 2 joining sherds carinated jar, fabric 42 (Fig. 3.12, no. 28); 1 base sherd and 3 body sherds, fabric 11; 1 rim sherd and 4 body sherds, fabric 13; 1 rim sherd and 4 body sherds, fabric 14; 1 body sherd, fabric 33;

A 94
Small finds: Bone gouge or weaving beater (Fig. 4.4, no. 9).
Bone frags: 42 sheep/goat, 21 cattle, 5 horse, 16 pig.
Pottery: 3 sherds, not joining, carinated bowl, grooved decoration, fabric 11 (Fig. 3.11, no. 1); 1 sherd carinated bowl or cup, fabric 13 (Fig. 3.11, no. 13); 1 sherd large carinated jar with rounded body, fabric 13 (Fig. 3.11, no. 17); 1 sherd vessel, fabric 21 (Fig. 3.12, no. 18); 1 sherd carinated jar, fabric 14 (Fig. 3.12, no. 27); 1 sherd vessel, fabric 43 (Fig. 3.12, no. 39); 3 joining sherds carinated jar, fabric 31 (Fig. 3.12, no. 41); 2 sherds carinated jar, fabric 21 (Fig. 3.12, no. 48); 3 body sherds, fabric 11; 1 body sherd, fabric 12; 4 body sherds, fabric 13; 1 rim sherd and 10 body sherds, fabric 14; 1 body sherd, fabric 21; 7 body sherds, fabric 31; 1 base and 14 body sherds, fabric 41; 2 body sherds, fabric 42; 8 body sherds, fabric 43; 1 base sherd and 1 body sherd, fabric 44;

A 94 B
Pottery: 2 joining sherds carinated bowl or cup rounded body, fabric 13 (Fig. 3.11, no. 14); 2 body sherds, fabric 12; 1 body sherd, fabric 13; 1 body sherd, fabric 14; 1 body sherd, fabric 41; 2 body sherds, fabric 42; 3 body sherds, fabric 43; 1 body sherd, fabric 44

A 95
Pottery: 6 sherds large carinated jar with rounded body, fabric 13 (Fig. 3.11, no. 17); 3 joining sherds carinated jar, fabric 13 (Fig. 3.12, no. 25); 1 sherd from vessel, fabric 41 (Fig. 3.13, no. 57); 2 body sherds, fabric 11; 5 body sherds, fabric 13; 5 body sherds, fabric 14; 8 body sherds, fabric 42; 2 body sherds, fabric 43;

A 96 – A 101 B
No finds.

A 102
Pottery: 1 body sherd, fabric 41.

A 102 B
Pottery: 1 body sherd, fabric 13; 2 body sherds, fabric 31; 4 body sherds, fabric 42.

A 103
Small finds: Part of chalk loom weight (not illustrated); fragment of lower stone of saddle quern (not illustrated).
Pottery: 6 body sherds, fabric 13; 3 body sherds, fabric 42.

A 103 B
Small finds: Kimmeridge shale ring (incomplete) (Fig. 4.2, no. 13).

A 104
Daub: 1 burnt piece of daub, Freeman type II/III.
Small finds: Part of chalk loom weight (not illustrated).
Pottery: 2 body sherds, fabric 11; 3 body sherds, fabric 12; 3 body sherds, fabric 13; 2 rim sherds and 18 body sherds, fabric 14; 3 body sherds, fabric 31; 13 body sherds, fabric 41; 4 body sherds, fabric 42; 6 body sherds, fabric 43; 3 body sherds, fabric 52.

A 104 B – A 105
No finds.

A 106
Small finds: Chalk spindle whorl (Fig. 4.12, no. 8).

A 107- 108
No finds.

A 109
Bone frags: 9 sheep/goat, 7 cattle, 1 horse, 2 pig.

A 110
No finds.

A 111
Pottery: 1 body sherd, fabric 13; 1 body sherd, fabric 24; 2 body sherds, fabric 42.

A 111 B – A 112
No finds.

A 113
Daub: 1 large burnt piece of daub, Freeman type IV.
Small finds: Possible fragment of quern (not illustrated).
Pottery: 1 body sherd, fabric 13; 1 body sherd, fabric 14; 6 body sherds, fabric 41; 1 rim sherd and 1 body sherd, fabric 42;

A 114
Pottery: 1 body sherd, fabric 13.

A 115
Pottery: 3 body sherds, fabric 13; 5 body sherds, fabric 14; 1 body sherd, fabric 41; 2 body sherds, fabric 42.

A 119
Pottery: 1 body sherd, fabric 31.

A 122 B
Pottery: 1 base sherd, fabric 31.

A 140
Pottery: 1 body sherd, fabric 41.

A 148
Small finds: Iron horseshoe (Fig. 4.3, no. 4); fragment of red deer antler weaving comb (Fig. 4.4, no. 4).
Pottery: 3 joining sherds carinated jar, fabric 41 (Fig. 3.12, no. 24); 1 sherd carinated jar, fabric 41 (Fig. 3.12, no. 43); 3 sherds carinated jar, fabric 14 (Fig. 3.12, no. 45); 4 body sherds, fabric 12; 2 rim sherds and 11 body sherds, fabric 13; 1 base sherd, 1 lug handle (*cf.* Fig. 3.10, no. 55) and 18 body sherds, fabric 14; 1 body sherd, fabric 19; 1 body sherd, fabric 21; 1 rim sherd, 1 base sherd and 6 body sherds, fabric 31; 1 rim sherd, fabric 32; 2 rim sherds, 1 base sherd and 42 body sherds, fabric 41; 1 base sherd and 29 body sherds, fabric 42; 6 body sherds, fabric 43;

A 150
No finds.

House 1 Catalogue of postholes and contents
(Fig. 2.35)

[Listed clockwise from the porch area, measurements taken from top of chalk bedrock. Pottery fabrics: Wilson]

Main Ring Postholes

PH 165
Dia. 0.46 m, depth 0.25m; sloping sides, flat bottom. No clear trace of post socket. One large fragment of stone, several local Lower Greensand quern stones and lumps of chalk in the packing.
Fill: Brown earth.
Daub: 55 pieces of cob daub which was partly burnt. Many of the larger pieces showed good wattle impressions. 3 pieces had definite wattle impressions running up and down, Freeman Type I and small amount of Type V.
Charcoal: Oak and hazel charcoal.
Bone frags: 4 sheep/goat, 2 pig, 1 red deer (antler).
Small Finds: Tine of red deer antler (Fig. 4.5, no. 5).
Pottery: 1 rim sherd from carinated bowl with furrowed decoration, fabric 14 (Fig. 3.1, no. 9); 1 sherd from large carinated vessel, fabric 11 (Fig. 3.6, no. 76); 1 sherd from large carinated vessel, fabric 14 (Fig. 3.6, no. 77); 1 rim sherd and 2 body sherds, fabric 11; 1 body sherd, fabric 42.

PH 155
Dia. 0.38 m, depth 0.18 m; vertical sides, flat bottom.
Fill: Brown earth with lumps of Upper Greensand and Chert.
Small Finds: Hammerstone of Upper Greensand Chert (Fig. 4.10, no. 8).
Pottery: 1 body sherd, fabric 14.

PH 151
Dia. 0.51 m, depth 0.21m; vertical sides, flat bottom. Dia. post socket 0.38 m, depth 0.18 m.
Fill: Brown earth. Chalk and flint lumps, and a chip of Upper Greensand Chert in the packing.
Daub: 1 large well preserved piece of cob daub (unburnt) with wattle impressions, Freeman Type I.
Charcoal: Hawthorn charcoal.
Bone frags: 3 sheep/goat, 4 cattle, 1 pig.
Pottery: 21 joining sherds from furrowed keg jar, fabric 11 (Fig. 3.1, no. 1); 1 rim sherd from furrowed keg jar or bowl, fabric 14 (Fig. 3.1, no. 4); 1 sherd from carinated bowl, furrowed decoration, fabric 11 (Fig. 3.1, no. 19); 3 sherds from carinated bowl, furrowed decoration, fabric 14 (Fig. 3.2, no. 20); 4 joining sherds from carinated bowl, furrowed decoration, fabric 11 (Fig. 3.2, no. 23); 2 joining sherds from carinated bowl, furrowed decoration, fabric 11 (Fig. 3.2, no. 24); 6 sherds from carinated bowl,furrowed decoration, fabric 11 (Fig. 3.2, no. 25); 3

joining sherds from carinated bowl, furrowed decoration, fabric 11 (Fig. 3.2, no. 26); 5 joining sherds from carinated bowl, furrowed decoration, fabric 13 (Fig. 3.2, no. 30); 6 sherds from carinated bowl,furrowed decoration, fabric 11 (Fig. 3.2, no. 31); 2 sherds from carinated bowl, furrowed decoration, fabric 13 (Fig. 3.2, no. 36); 7 sherds from large carinated jar, fabric 11 (Fig. 3.3, no. 37); 1 sherd from large carinated jar, fabric 11 (Fig. 3.3, no. 38); 2 joining sherds from large carinated jar, fabric 11, (Fig. 3.3, no. 40); 1 sherd from large carinated jar, fabric 11 (Fig. 3.3, no. 41); 44 sherds from large carinated jar, fabric 11 (Fig. 3.4, nos. 43, 44, 45 and 46); 18 sherds from large carinated jar, fabric 11 (Fig. 3.5, no. 48); 2 joining sherds from large carinated jar, fabric 11 (Fig. 3.5, no. 52); 1 sherd from large carinated jar, fabric 11 (Fig. 3.5, no. 58); 2 sherds from large carinated jar, fabric 11, (Fig. 3.6, no. 75); 1 sherd from thin-walled rounded jar, fabric 11 (Fig. 3.6, no. 81), 2 joining sherds, fabric 41 (Fig. 3.6, no. 87); 1 rim sherd, fabric 42, (Fig. 3.6, no. 89); 1 handle sherd, fabric 42 (Fig. 3.6, no. 90); 1 rim sherd from carinated jar, fabric 42 (Fig. 3.6, no. 92); 73 body sherds, fabric 11; 5 body sherds, fabric 13; 12 body sherds, fabric 14; 1 body sherd, fabric 31; 8 body sherds, fabric 41; 4 body sherds, fabric 42.

PH 152
Dia. 0.46 m, depth 0.23 m; vertical sides, flat bottom. Dia. post socket 0.21m, depth 0.18 m.
Fill: Brown earth. Chalk and flint packing.
Charcoal: Oak charcoal; possibly also Hazel and Salicaceaeae Populus charcoal.
Bone frags: 6 sheep/goat, 4 cattle, 6 (antler) red deer.
Pottery: 1 rim sherd from furrowed keg jar, fabric 11 (Fig. 3.1, No. 3); 1 sherd from carinated bowl with furrowed decoration, fabric 11 (Fig. 3.1, no. 6); 1 sherd from carinated bowl with furrowed decoration, fabric 11 (Fig. 3.1, no 15); 9 sherds from carinated cup with furrowed decoration, fabric 11 (Fig. 3.1, no. 16); 8 sherds from large carinated bowl with furrowed decoration, fabric 11 (Fig. 3.1, no. 18); 5 sherds from carinated bowl with furrowed decoration, fabric 11, (Fig. 3.2, no. 29); 1 sherd from carinated cup with furrowed decoration, fabric 11 (Fig. 3.2, no. 34); 3 sherds from large carinated jar, fabric 11 (Fig. 3.3, no. 37); 1 sherd from large carinated jar, fabric 11 (Fig. 3.3, no. 42); 1 sherd from large carinated jar, fabric 11 (Fig. 3.5, no. 49); 2 joining sherds from large carinated jar, fabric 11 (Fig. 3.5, no. 50); 2 joining sherds from large carinated jar, fabric 11 (Fig. 3.5, no. 51); 17 sherds from large carinated jar, fabric 14 (Fig. 3.5, no. 60); 1 sherd from large carinated jar, fabric 11 (Fig. 3.6, no 61); 2 joining sherds from large carinated jar, fabric 11 (Fig. 3.6, no. 65); 1 sherd from large carinated jar, fabric 11 (Fig. 3.6, no. 66); 4 sherds from large carinated jar, fabric 11 (Fig. 3.6, no. 68); 2 joining sherds from large carinated jar, fabric 11 (Fig. 3.6, no. 69); 1 sherd from large carinated jar, fabric 11 (Fig. 3.6, no. 74); 51 body sherds, fabric 11; 4 body sherds, fabric 13; 8 body sherds, fabric 14; 6 body sherds, fabric 21.

PH 153
Dia. 0.53 m, depth 0.26m; flat bottom. Dia. post socket 0.33 m, depth 0.21m.
Fill: Brown earth. Chalk packing.
Charcoal: Oak charcoal.
Bone frags: 3 sheep/goat, 1 horse.
Pottery: 5 sherds from carinated bowl with furrowed decoration, fabric 13 (Fig. 3.1, no. 7); 4 joining sherds from large carinated jar, fabric 11 (Fig. 3.5, no. 57); 1 sherd from large carinated jar, fabric 11 (Fig. 3.5, no 59); 1 sherd from large carinated jar, fabric 11 (Fig. 3.6, no. 61); 2 joining sherds from large carinated jar, fabric 11 (Fig. 3.6, no. 62); 1 sherd from large carinated jar, fabric 11 (Fig. 3.6, no. 64); 4 joining sherds from large carinated jar, fabric 11 (Fig. 3.6, no. 71); 1 sherd from thin-walled rounded jar, fabric 11 (Fig. 3.6, no. 81); 42 body sherds, fabric 11; 1 body sherd, fabric 13, 1 rim sherd and 9 body sherds, fabric 14; 2 body sherds, fabric 41; 3 body sherds, fabric 42.

PH 154
Dia. 0.41 m, depth 0.23 m; slightly rounded bottom.
Fill: Brown earth with 1 fragment Upper Greensand Chert saddle quern and 1 fragment bruised hammer stone.
Daub: 6 pieces of orange yellow burnt clay daub, straw impressions but no wattle marks, Freeman Type II/III.
Bone frags: 2 sheep/goat, 6 cattle, 4 pig.
Small Finds: Bronze small solid mushroom-shaped cap (Fig. 4.1, no. 4), ceramic spindle whorl (Fig. 4.12, no. 1), hammer stone of Upper Greensand Chert (Fig. 12 no. 7).
Pottery: 28 sherds from carinated bowl, furrowed decoration, fabric 14 (Fig. 3.1, no. 10); 1 body sherd from carinated bowl, furrowed decoration, fabric 14 (Fig. 3.1, no. 11); 3 sherds from large carinated bowl, furrowed decoration, fabric 14 (Fig. 3.1, no. 12); 1 sherd from carinated bowl, furrowed decoration, fabric 14 (Fig. 3.1, no. 17); 24 joining sherds from carinated bowl, furrowed decoration, fabric 14 (Fig. 3.2, no. 20); 13 joining sherds from carinated bowl, furrowed decoration, fabric 11 (Fig. 3.2, no. 27); 1 sherd from carinated bowl, furrowed decoration, fabric 11 (Fig. 3.2, no. 28); 35 sherds from large carinated jar, fabric 11 (Fig. 3.3, no. 39); 15 sherds from large carinated jar, fabric 11 (Fig. 3.4, no. 47); 4 joining sherds from large carinated jar, fabric 11 (Fig. 3.5, no. 53); 2 joining sherds from large carinated jar, fabric 11, (Fig. 3.6, no. 67); 1 sherd from large carinated jar, fabric 11 (Fig. 3.6, no. 70); 6 joining sherds from large carinated jar, fabric 11 (Fig. 3.6, no. 72); 1 sherd from large carinated jar, fabric 11 (Fig. 3.6, no. 73); 18 sherds from large carinated jar, fabric 41 (Fig. 3.6, no. 78); 1 rim sherd, fabric 13 (Fig. 3.6, no. 84), 1 rim sherd, fabric 14 (Fig. 3.6, no. 85); 1 rim sherd, fabric 13 (Fig. 3.6, no 88); 19 body sherds, fabric 11; 1 body sherd, fabric 13; 6 body sherds, fabric 14; 1 body sherd, fabric 41; 1 body sherd, fabric 42.

PH 186
Dia. 0.41 m, depth 0.21m; rounded bottom. Dia. post socket 0.23 m, depth 0.18 m.
Fill: Brown earth with some flints (possibly struck).
Daub: Several pieces of burnt daub, some was yellow and burnt black in places, no definite wattle impressions, Freeman Type II/III.
Charcoal: Oak charcoal.
Small Finds: Ceramic spindle whorl (Fig. 6, no. 3).
Pottery: 1 sherd from carinated bowl, furrowed decoration, fabric 11, (Fig. 3.2, no. 27); 1 sherd from carinated bowl, furrowed decoration, fabric 12 (Fig. 3.2, no. 33); 1 sherd from jar with body rounded out, fabric 14 (Fig. 3.6, no. 79); 2 body sherds, fabric 11.

PH 62 Not illustrated.
Dia. and depth not recorded. Depth of post socket 0.36m. Located centre of the south side.
Fill: Brown earth.

PH 42 Not illustrated
Dia. west 0.33 m, east 0.43 m, depth 0.23 m
Fill: Light brown earth. Some chalk at the bottom, and large flints in the packing at the sides.
Daub: About 40 small pieces of orange clay daub with occasional narrow impressions, and 3 whitish pieces of cob daub, Freeman Type II/III and small amount of Type I.
Pottery: 1 rim sherd from furrowed keg jar, fabric 11 (Fig. 3.1, no. 2); 4 joining body sherds from furrowed keg jar, fabric 14 (Fig. 3.1, no. 5); 2 sherds from large carinated bowl with furrowed decoration, fabric 14 (Fig. 3.1, no. 12); 1 sherd from carinated bowl with furrowed decoration, fabric 11 (Fig. 3.2, no. 32); 3 joining sherds from large carinated jar, fabric 11 (Fig. 3.5, no. 54); 1 sherd from large carinated jar, fabric 11 (Fig. 3.5, no. 55); 2 sherds from large carinated jar, fabric 11 (Fig. 3.5, no. 56); 4 body sherds, fabric 11; 4 body sherds, fabric 14; 3 body sherds, fabric 16.

PH 63 Not illustrated.
Dia. 0.61 m, depth 0.76 m. Dia. post socket 0.38 m, depth 0.13m.
Fill: Dark soil.
Daub: 12 pieces of orange burnt clay daub, burnt black in places, no wattle impressions, Freeman Type II/III.
Charcoal: Fragments of oak charcoal.
Pottery: 1 sherd from carinated cup, furrowed decoration, fabric 11 (Fig. 3.1, no. 14); 4 body sherds, fabric 11; 2 body sherds, fabric 14; 1 body sherd, fabric 42.

PH 69 Not illustrated
Dia. 0.28 m, depth 0.23 m. Depth of post socket 0.31m.
Fill: Dark chalky earth.

PH 235
Dia. 0.41 m, depth 5 in (12.5 cm); flat bottom.
Fill: Grey soil with patches of clay.
Charcoal: Oak charcoal in the fill. Radiocarbon sample NPL-104
Bone frags: 10 red deer.
Small finds: Small chalk weight.
Pottery: 13 joining sherds from carinated bowl, furrowed decoration, fabric 14 (Fig. 3.1, no 8); 11 sherds from carinated bowl, furrowed decoration, fabric 14 (Fig. 3.1, no.13); 1 sherd from carinated cup, furrowed decoration, fabric 11 (Fig. 3.1, no. 14); 1 sherd from possible plain keg jar, fabric 42 (Fig. 3.6, no. 83); 1 sherd from decorated bowl with rounded body, fabric 14, an intruder (Fig. 3.6, no. 91); 2 body sherds, fabric 11; 1 base sherd and 5 body sherds, fabric 13; 5 body sherds, fabric 14; 6 body sherds, fabric 31; 1 body sherd, fabric 41; 6 body sherds, fabric 42.

PH 237 Not illustrated
Dia. 0.38 m, depth 0.41 m. Depth post socket 0.15 m.
Fill: Brown earth with small lumps of chalk and clay.
Daub: 5 small pieces of yellow coloured material and 1 whitish piece of cob daub, Freeman Type I and II/III.
Charcoal: Fragments of charcoal, especially in the top levels.
Pottery: 1 sherd from large jar, fabric 11 (Fig. 3.6, no. 80); 2 body sherds, fabric 11.

PH 77 Not illustrated
D1a. 0.33 m, depth 0.46m. Depth post socket 0.46 m. Clear post core.
Fill: Yellow sandy soil.
Charcoal: Solid charcoal in the centre.

PH 241
Dia. 0.43 m, depth 0.41 m; sloping sides, flat bottom.
Fill: Brown earth with lumps of chalk and flint.
Charcoal: Fragments of charcoal.

PH 242
Dia. 0.43 m, depth 0.31m, irregular sides and bottom.
Fill: Brown earth with lumps of chalk and flint.

PH 225
Dim. 0.46 m, depth 0.33 m; vertical sides, flat bottom.
Dia. post socket 0.33 m, depth 0.28 m.
Fill: Brown earth with stones, including Westbury Ironstone, pebbles and chalk sponge fossils. Chalk packing.
Daub: Small pieces of burnt daub, burnt yellow and black, Freeman Type II/III and VI.
Charcoal: Hawthorn charcoal.
Small Finds: Chalk spindle whorl or weight (Fig. 6, no. 11).
Pottery: 2 joining rim sherds and 15 body sherds (probably from same vessel), fabric 11; 1 rim sherd, 1 base sherd and 13 body sherds (probably from same vessel), fabric 14; 1 body sherd, fabric 41.

PH 127
Dia. 0.46 m, depth 0.31m; sloping sides, rounded bottom.
Dia. post socket 0.26m, depth 0.28m
Fill: Brown earth. Chalk packing.
Charcoal: Oak charcoal.
Bone frags: Miscellaneous.
Pottery: 1 rim sherd and 2 body sherds, fabric 11.

PH 129 (west end of the cutting)
Dia. 0.46 m, depth 0.31m; vertical sides, flat bottom.
Fill: Brown earth with a few lumps of chalk.
Charcoal: Unspeciated fragments.
Pottery: 2 body sherds, fabric 14.

PH 141
Dia. 0.59 m, depth 0.28 m; sloping sides, flat bottom.
Fill: Fine dark soil. Chalk and flint packing.
Charcoal: Fragments of oak charcoal. Radiocarbon sample NPL-105
Bone frags: 6 sheep/goat, 4 pig.

Porch Postholes

PH 167 Not illustrated
Dia. and depth not recorded.
Fill: Dark soil with chalk lumps, large flints, and 1 piece whitish sandstone quern.
Bone frags: 3 sheep/goat, 4 cattle, 2 pig.
Pottery: 2 body sherds from large carinated bowl, furrowed decoration, fabric 14 (Fig. 3.1, no. 12); 3 sherds from carinated bowl, furrowed decoration, fabric 14 (Fig. 3.2, no. 20); 1 sherd from carinated bowl, furrowed decoration, fabric 13 (Fig. 3.2, no. 30); 2 body sherds, fabric 11 (Fig. 3.6, no. 82); 2 body sherds, fabric 11; 1 body sherd, fabric 14.

PH 140 (south side of the cutting) Not illustrated
Dia. 0.41 m, depth 0.41 m. No trace of the post.
Fill: Brown earth.
Bone frags: Burnt fragments, probably pig and sheep.
Small Finds: Bronze head of small pin (Fig. 4.1, no. 3).
Pottery: 2 body sherds, fabric 11; 2 body sherds, fabric 14.

PH 145 Not illustrated
Dia. 0.51 m, depth 0.18 m. Depth of post socket 0.10 m.
Fill: Dark earth with chalk lumps.
Bone frags: Burnt fragments, probably pig and sheep.
Pottery: 1 rim sherd, fabric 42 (Fig. 3.6, no. 86); 1 body sherd, fabric 13; 3 body sherds, fabric 41; 1 body sherd, fabric 42.

PH 139 Not illustrated
Dia. and depth not recorded. Depth of post socket 0.38 m. A recut post hole.
Fill: Chalky earth.
Charcoal: Oak and hawthorn charcoal.
Bone frags: 7 sheep/goat, 2 cattle.
Pottery: 1 sherd from carinated bowl, furrowed decoration, fabric 11 (Fig. 3.2, no. 35); 3 body sherds, fabric 11; 2 body sherds, fabric 14; 1 body sherd, fabric 31; 9 body sherds, fabric 42.

Internal Postholes

PH 224 Not illustrated
Dia. 0.61 m, depth 0.15 m.
Fill: Dark earth with lumps of flint and flecks of burnt clay.
Pottery: 1 rim sherd, fabric 11.

PH 161 D Not illustrated
Dia. 0.33 m, depth 0.13m.
Fill: Brown chalky soil.
Charcoal: Unspeciated fragments.
Pottery: 1 body sherd, fabric 14.

PH 228
Dia. 0.46 m, depth 0.13 m; sloping sides, flat bottom.
Fill: Dark earth with chalk lumps.

PH 234 Not illustrated
Dia. 0.21 m, depth 0.10 m.
Fill: Dark soil with a few chalk lumps.

PH 100 Not illustrated
Dia. 0.53 m, depth 0.41 m.
Fill: Brown earth.

PH 101 Not illustrated
Dia. and depth not recorded. Depth of post socket 0.26 m. Centre cutting.
Fill: Brown earth.

PH 102 Not illustrated
Dia. and depth not recorded. Depth of post socket 0.18 m. A small rounded posthole, north-west of the cutting.
Fill: Brown earth.

PH 103 Not illustrated
Dia. and depth not recorded. Depth of post socket 0.23 m. A small rounded posthole north-west of the cutting.
Fill: Brown earth.

External Postholes

PH 128 Not illustrated
Dia. 0.43m, depth 0.28 m. Depth of post socket 0.26 m.
Fill: Brown earth with chalk lumps.

House 2 Catalogue of postholes and contents (Fig. 2.37 & 2.38)

Measurements taken from top of chalk bedrock

Main Ring Postholes

Clockwise from porch area

PH 132
Dia. 0.48 m, depth 0.43 m; vertical sides, flat bottom. Dia. post socket 0.21 m, depth 0.41 m.
Fill: Dark soil with a few chalk lumps. Chalk packing.
Daub: 1 piece of whitish cob daub, Freeman Type I.
Charcoal: Fragments of oak charcoal.
Pottery: 1 body sherd from carinated jar, fabric 41 (Fig. 3.9, no. 42); 1 rim and 1 body sherd, fabric 13; 1 body sherd, fabric 14.

PH 133
Dia. 0.48 m, depth 0.41 m; almost vertical sides, flat bottom.
Fill: Chalky soil. Heavy stone packing.
Pottery: 1 base and 2 body sherds, fabric 11.

PH 142
Dia. 0.46 m, depth 0.48 m; almost vertical sides, flat bottom. Depth post socket 0.38 m.
Fill: Dark soil. Lumps of chalk at base.
Daub: 21 pieces of chalky cob daub, Freeman Types I and V. Impressions of thin withies about 1 cm long. (Chapter 5, Fig. 5.3.1)
Charcoal: Fragments of oak charcoal.
Pottery: 4 body sherds, fabric 31; 1 rim sherd, fabric 41.

PH 126.
Dia. 0.51 m, depth 0.56 m; flat bottom. Depth post socket 0.48 m.
Fill: Brown soil with a few chalk lumps.
Daub: 40 large pieces of cob daub, many with good wattle impressions *c.* <1 cm long, Freeman Types I and V.
Charcoal: Hazel charcoal.
Bone frags: 4 sheep/goat, 1 cattle, 5 pig.
Pottery: 1 base sherd from carinated bowl, grooved decoration, fabric 11 (Fig. 3.7, no. 5); 1 base sherd from carinated bowl, grooved decoration, fabric 11 (Fig. 3.7, no. 9); 8 sherds from carinated bowl, grooved decoration, fabric 14 (Fig. 3.7, no. 12); 1 sherd from carinated bowl, grooved decoration, fabric 14 (Fig. 3.7, no. 13); 7 sherds from carinated bowl, grooved decoration, fabric 14, (Fig. 3.7, no. 15); 4 sherds from rilled carinated cup, grooved decoration, fabric 13 (Fig. 3.8, no. 18); 1 sherd from large carinated jar, fabric 41 (Fig. 3.8, no. 28); 1 sherd from large carinated jar, fabric 41 (Fig. 3.8, no. 29); 8 sherds from carinated jar, fabric 14 (Fig. 3.9, no. 37); 1 sherd from carinated jar, fabric 41 (Fig. 3.9, no. 40); 3 sherds from carinated jar, fabric 41 (Fig. 3.9, no. 42); 1 sherd from carinated jar, fabric 14 (Fig. 3.10, no. 52); 2 sherds from carinated jar, fabric 41 (Fig. 3.10, no. 53); 1 base sherd, fabric 31 (Fig. 3.10, no. 60); 1 body sherd, fabric 11; 4 body sherds, fabric 14; 1 body sherd, fabric 20; 2 body sherds, fabric 31; 4 body sherds, fabric 41; 3 body sherds, fabric 42.

PH 147
Dia. 0.41 m, depth 0.38 m; almost vertical sides, flat bottom. Dia. post socket 0.26 m, depth 0.33 m.
Fill: Brown soil with a few chalk lumps. Chalk packing.
Charcoal: Unspeciated fragments.
Pottery: 2 sherds from carinated cup, rooved decoration,

fabric 13 (Fig. 3.7, no. 1); 2 sherds from carinated bowl, grooved decoration, fabric 14 (Fig. 3.7, no. 10); 4 sherds from rilled carinated cup, grooved decoration, fabric 13 (Fig. 3.8, no. 18); 2 joining sherds from carinated bowl, rooved decoration, fabric 13 (Fig. 3.8, no. 20); 5 joining sherds from carinated bowl, rooved decoration, fabric 14 (Fig. 3.8, no. 24); 3 sherds from large carinated jar, fabric 41 (Fig. 3.8, no. 28); 1 sherd from carinated jar, fabric 41 (Fig. 3.9, no. 42); 1 sherd probably from carinated jar, fabric 14 (Fig. 3.10, no. 45); 1 sherd probably from carinated jar, fabric 14 (Fig. 3.10, no. 49); 5 joining sherds from carinated jar, fabric 14 (Fig. 3.10, no. 51); 4 sherds from carinated jar, fabric 41 (Fig. 3.10, no. 53); 1 base sherd, probably from carinated jar, fabric 42 (Fig. 3.10, no. 62); 2 body sherds, fabric 11; 6 body sherds, fabric 13; 7 body sherds, fabric 14; 2 body sherds, fabric 31; 2 body sherds, fabric 41; 8 body sherds, fabric 42.

PH 134
Dia. 0.46 m, depth 0.38 m, vertical sides, flat bottom. Dia. post socket 0.28 m, depth 0.31m.
Fill: Brown soil with a few chalk lumps.
Charcoal: Abundant hazel charcoal fragments.
Bone frags: 5 sheep/goat, 6 cattle, 1 horse.
Pottery: 6 sherds from carinated cup, grooved decoration, fabric 13 (Fig. 3.7, no. 1); 4 sherds from carinated bowl, grooved decoration, fabric 13 (Fig. 3.7, no. 2); 1 sherd from carinated bowl, grooved decoration, fabric 11 (Fig. 3.7, no. 6); 1 sherd from carinated bowl, grooved decoration, fabric 11 (Fig. 3.7, no. 8); 1 sherd from carinated bowl, grooved decoration, fabric 14 (Fig. 3.7, no. 10); 1 sherd from carinated bowl, grooved decoration, fabric 14 (Fig. 3.8, no. 23); 5 sherds from carinated jar, fabric 14 (Fig. 3.8, no. 31); 2 joining sherds from carinated jar, fabric 31 (Fig. 3.8, no. 33); 4 joining sherds from carinated jar, fabric 14 (Fig. 3.9, no. 35); 1 sherd from carinated jar, fabric 31 (Fig. 3.9, no. 44); 1 sherd probably from carinated jar, fabric 13 (Fig. 3.10, no. 48); 1 sherd from carinated jar, fabric 41 (Fig. 3.10, no. 53), 1 base sherd and 3 body sherds, fabric 13; 9 body sherds, fabric 14; 3 body sherds, fabric 31; 3 body sherds, fabric 42.

PH 135
Dia. 0.6 m, depth 0.41 m; vertical sides, flat bottom. Dia. post socket 0.38 m, depth 0.38 m.
Fill: Brown soil with a few chalk lumps. Chalk packing.
Daub: 1 large and 2 small fragments of whitish cob daub, Freeman Types I and VI.
Charcoal: Fragments of hazel and ash charcoal.
Small finds: Flint pebble, possibly a sling bullet.
Pottery: 2 sherds from carinated bowl, grooved decoration, fabric 13 (Fig. 3.7, no. 2); 1 sherd carinated bowl, grooved decoration, fabric 11 Fig. 3.7, no. 4); sherds carinated bowl, grooved decoration, fabric 11 (Fig. 3.7, no. 5); 4 sherds carinated bowl, grooved decoration, fabric 11 (Fig. 3.7, no. 9); 11 sherds carinated bowl, grooved decoration, fabric 14 (Fig. 3.7, no. 10); 2 sherds carinated bowl, grooved decoration, fabric 14 (Fig. 3.7, no. 12); 10 sherds carinated bowl, grooved decoration, fabric 14 (Fig. 3.7, no. 13); 4 sherds carinated bowl, grooved decoration, fabric 14 (Fig. 3.7, no. 15); 1 sherd carinated bowl, grooved decoration, fabric 11 (Fig. 3.8, no. 19); 23 sherds carinated bowl, grooved decoration, fabric 14 (Fig. 3.8, no. 23); 4 sherds carinated jar, fabric 41 (Fig. 3.8, no. 34); 1 sherd carinated jar, fabric 41 (Fig. 3.9, no. 36); 1 sherd carinated jar, fabric 41 (Fig. 3.9, no. 39); 2 sherds probably from carinated jar, fabric 41 (Fig. 3.10, no. 46); 1 sherd carinated jar, fabric 14 (Fig. 3.10, no. 52); sherds carinated jar, fabric 41 (Fig. 3.10, no. 53); sherds from probable carinated jar, fabric 43 (Fig. 3.10, no. 58); 9 body sherds, fabric 11; 2 body sherds, fabric 13; 3 base sherds and 13 body sherds, fabric 14; 1 body sherd, fabric 19; 1 base sherd and 5 body sherds, fabric 31; 20 body sherds, 41; 3 rim sherds, 1 base sherd and 3 body sherds, fabric 42.

PH 146
Dia. 0.51 m, depth 0.41 m; vertical sides, flat bottom. Dia. post socket 0.28 m, depth 0.36 m.
Fill: Dark soil with a few chalk lumps. Chalk packing.
Charcoal: Fragments of oak charcoal.
Pottery: 2 sherds carinated bowl, grooved decoration, fabric 14 (Fig. 3.7, no. 12); 2 sherds carinated bowl with grooved decoration, Wilson fabric 14 (Fig. 3.8, no. 23); 1 sherd from large carinated jar, fabric 41 (Fig. 3.8, no. 28); 1 sherd carinated jar, fabric 13 (Fig. 3.9, no. 41); 5 sherds carinated jar, fabric 31 (Fig. 3.9, no. 44); 3 body sherds, fabric 11; 1 base sherd, fabric 13; 2 rim sherds and 5 body sherds, fabric 14; 1 body sherd, fabric 31; 1 body sherd, fabric 42.

PH 144
Dia. 0.43 m, depth 0.48 m; almost vertical sides, slightly rounded bottom.
Fill: Chalky soil with lumps of burnt clay.
Charcoal: Fragments of oak charcoal.
Pottery: 3 sherds carinated bowl, grooved decoration, fabric 11, (Fig. 3.7, no. 7); 8 sherds large carinated jar, fabric 41 (Fig. 3.8, no. 28); 4 sherds carinated jar, fabric 31 (Fig. 3.9, no. 44); 3 body sherds, fabric 13; 2 body sherds, fabric 31; 7 body sherds, fabric 41.

PH 229
Dia. 0.43 m, depth 0.59 m; vertical sides, flat bottom. Depth post socket 0.41 m.
Fill: Loose dark soil. Chalk packing.
Charcoal: Oak and hazel charcoal.
Pottery: 8 sherds, 5 joining carinated jar, fabric 41 (Fig. 3.9, no. 38); 10 sherds carinated jar, fabric 31 (Fig. 3.9, no. 44); 1 rim and 2 body sherds, fabric 13; 2 body sherds, fabric 31; 4 body sherds, fabric 41; 1 rim sherd, fabric 42.

PH 90 Not illustrateds
Dia. 0.41 m, depth 0.51 m. Depth post socket 0.51 m.
Fill: Loose dark soil. Stone packing at the sides.
Charcoal: Fragments of hazel charcoal.
Bone frags: 1 horse, 1 deer (antler fragment).
Pottery: 1 body sherd, fabric 11; 4 body sherds, fabric 14; 2 body sherds, fabric 42.

PH 91 Not illustrated
Dia. and depth not recorded.
Fill: Dark central core. Chalk packing.
Charcoal: Hawthorn charcoal.
Pottery: 2 body sherds, fabric 27; 1 body sherd, fabric 31; 3 body sherds, fabric 32; 7 body sherds, fabric 41.

PH 241 (This PH is illustrated with PH 242 from House 1).
Dia. 0.43 m, depth 0.41 m; sloping sides, flat bottom.
Fill: Brown soil with patches of clay and lumps of chalk and flint. Marked by lumps of charcoal and clay wads. Packing of large chalk lumps and flints.
Charcoal: Unspeciated fragments.
Pottery: 1 body sherd, fabric 11.
Adjoining PH 242 from House 1.

PH 238
Dia. 0.53 m, depth 0.28 m; sloping sides, rounded bottom.
Fill: Brown soil with chalk lumps.
Charcoal: Hawthorn and hazel charcoal.
Pottery: 1 base sherd and 4 body sherds, fabric 11.

PH 239
Dia. 0.63.5 m, depth 0.41 m, rounded bottom.
Fill: Chalky soil with flint and chalk lumps and carbon traces *in situ*.
Pottery: sherd carinated jar, fabric 14 (Fig. 3.9, no. 37). 1 rim sherd, fabric 14; 1 body sherd, fabric 21.

PH 149
Dia. 0.23 m, depth 0.51 m; flat bottom.
Fill: Dark soil with lumps of chalk and flint. Chalk packing on west side and bottom.
Daub: 1 piece of burnt orange daub.
Charcoal: Oak and hazel charcoal.
Pottery: 2 body sherds, fabric 11.

PH 174
Dia. 0.51 m, depth 0.46 m; vertical sides, flat bottom. Dia. post socket 0.23 m, depth 0.31 m. A well-defined post impression
Fill: Dark soil, chalk packing.
Charcoal: Oak and hazel charcoal.
Small finds: Horn core (Fig. 4.5, no. 4).
Pottery: 1 body sherd, fabric 11 (Fig. 3.8, no. 27); 3 body sherds, fabric 14.

PH 175
Dia. 0.56 m, depth 0.43 m; sloping sides, rounded base. Dia. post socket 0.36 m, depth 0.31 m.
Fill: Brown soil. Chalk packing.
Pottery: 1 rim and 1 base sherd, fabric 11.

PH 182
Dia. 0.46 m, depth 0.43 m; vertical sides, flat base. Regularly cut circular post hole. No clear trace of the post.
Fill: Brown soil with lumps of chalk, flint, and some pebbles.
Daub: 38 pieces of chalky cob daub, 2 large pieces with good wattle impressions, very thick daub, Freeman Types I and V.
Charcoal: Hazel and ash charcoal.
Bone frags: Burnt fragments, possibly sheep.
Pottery: 3 sherds carinated bowl, grooved decoration, fabric 11 (Fig. 3.8, no. 16); 1 rim sherd, fabric 11; 1 body sherd, fabric 14.

PH 180
Dia. 0.46 m, depth 0.43 m; vertical sides, rounded bottom.
Fill: Brown soil with chalk lumps. Chalk packing at the sides, no clear trace of the post.
Charcoal: Oak and hazel charcoal.
Pottery: 1 rim sherd and 1 body sherd, fabric 14.

PH 179
Dia. 0.56 m, depth 0.43 m; sloping sides, flat bottom.
Fill: Brown soil with chalk and flint lumps. Some flint and chalk packing, but no clear trace of the post.
Charcoal: Oak, hawthorn, hazel and ash charcoal.
Pottery: 4 sherds, 2 joining from carinated bowl, grooved decoration, fabric 11 (Fig. 3.8, no. 21); 1 body sherd, fabric 14.

PH 112
Dia. 0.41 m, depth 0.46 m; vertical sides, flat bottom. Dia. post socket 0.41 m, depth 0.36 m. An irregularly cut post hole.
Fill: Dark grey soil with chalk and flint lumps. Packing of flint and chalk lumps.
Charcoal: Unspeciated fragments.

PH 113
Dia. 0.48 m, depth 0.51 m; vertical sides, flat bottom. Depth post socket 0.23 m.
Fill: Brown soil. Collapsed chalk and flint packing.
Small finds: Iron fragment (not illustrated).

PH 114
Dia. 0.51 m, depth 0.51 m; slightly sloping sides, flat bottom. Dia. post socket 0.26 m, depth 0.33 m.
Fill: Brown soil with patches of burnt soil. Chalk packing.
Charcoal: Unspeciated fragments.

PH 214
Dia. 0.69 m, depth 0.46 m; vertical sides, almost flat bottom. Dia. post socket 0.38 m, depth 0.46 m.
Fill: Brown soil with a few chalk lumps. Chalk packing, particularly on the north side.
Pottery: 2 body sherds, fabric 13.

PH 213
Dia. 0.53 m, depth 0.51 m; vertical sides, flat bottom.
Fill: Chalky soil.
Charcoal: Hazel charcoal.

PH 157 Not illustrated
Dia. 0.61 m, depth 0.51 m. Depth post socket 0.41 m.
Fill: Brown soil with flint fossils, pebbles and a piece of quern stone.
Daub: 7 pieces of burnt yellow daub (including 1 particularly cindery piece with wattle impressions), Freeman Types I, II/III and VI.
Charcoal: Oak and hazel charcoal.
Pottery: 11 sherds, 5 joining from undecorated carinated bowl, fabric 14 (Fig. 3.8, no. 26); 2 body sherds, fabric 13; 1 body sherd, fabric 31; 1 body sherd, fabric 41; 2 body sherds, fabric 42.

PH 204
Dia. 0.41 m, depth 0.36 m; sloping sides, flat bottom. Dia. post socket 0.23 m, depth 0.31 m.
Fill: Brown soil with small chalk lumps.
Daub: 2 pieces of burnt orange cob daub, Freeman Type II/III.
Charcoal: Fragments of charcoal.
Pottery: 10 sherds, 9 joining from carinated jar, fabric 31 (Fig. 3.8, no. 30); 2 body sherds, fabric 31; 5 body sherds, fabric 41.

PH 203
Dia. 0.28 m, depth 0.18 m; sloping sides, flat bottom.
Fill: Dark soil with a few chalk lumps.
Pottery: 1 body sherd, fabric 14.

PH 172
Dia. 0.92 m, depth 0.46 m; sloping sides, flat bottom. The top of the post hole was very black with charcoal and ash.
Fill: Chalky soil, with patches of burnt soil.
Daub: 39 pieces of chalky cob daub, many with clear

wattle impressions and roughly smoothed surfaces; 1 piece with impressions going up and through, and 1 very thick piece with a cobbled outer surface, Freeman Types I and V (Chapter 5, Fig. 5.3.1).
Charcoal: Fragments of oak, hawthorn and hazel charcoal.
Pottery: 1 sherd carinated bowl, grooved decoration, fabric 14 (Fig. 3.7, no. 13); 1 body sherd, fabric 14; 10 body sherds, fabric 31; 2 base sherds and 1 body sherd, fabric 42.

The External Postholes

PH 226
Dia. 0.53 m, depth 0.71 m; flat bottom.
Fill: Chalky soil.
Small finds: Ceramic spindle whorl.

PH 227
Dia. 0.31 m, depth 0.5 m; flat bottom.
Fill: Dark soil with small chalk lumps.

PH 233
Dia. 0.23 m, depth 0.10 m; sloping sides, flat bottom.
Small Finds: Bronze ear ring (Fig. 4.1, no. 2)
Fill: Dark soil with small chalk lumps.

PH 234
Dia. 0.21 m, depth 0.71 m) flat bottom.
Fill: Brown soil with small chalk lumps.

PH 181 Not illustrated
Dia. 0.31 m, depth 0.13 m.
Fill: Brown soil.
Charcoal: Oak charcoal.
Pottery: 1 body sherd, fabric 41.

Internal Postholes

PH 170
Dia. 0.51 m, depth 0.38 m; vertical sides, rounded bottom.
Fill: Brown soil with lumps of quern stone and chalk.
Daub: Small pieces of daub.
Charcoal: Oak and hazel charcoal.
Pottery: 1 body sherd, fabric 41.

PH 171 Not illustrated
Dia. 0.28 m, depth 0.23 m. Depth post socket 0.23 m.
Fill: Brown soil.
Daub: 10 pieces of yellow cob daub, one or two pieces with flat surfaces, Freeman Type I.
Charcoal: Oak charcoal fragments.

PH 169 Not illustrated
Dia. 0.31 m, depth 0.13 m. Depth post socket 0.13 m.
Fill: Brown soil.

PH 138 Not illustrated
Dia. 0.21 m, depth 0.18 m. Depth post socket 0.15 m.
Fill: Chalky soil.

PH 137 Not illustrated
Dia. and depth not recorded. Depth post socket 0 31 m. A recut post socket.
Fill: Brown soil.
Small Finds: Red deer antler (Fig. 4.5, no. 1).
Pottery: 19 sherds carinated bowl, grooved decoration, fabric 14 (Fig. 3.7, no. 3); 35 sherds carinated bowl, grooved decoration, fabric 11 (Fig. 3.7, no. 6); 5 sherds carinated bowl, grooved decoration, fabric 11 (Fig. 3.7, no. 7); 12 sherds carinated bowl, grooved decoration, fabric 14 (Fig. 3.7, no. 12); 3 sherds carinated bowl, grooved decoration, fabric 14 (Fig. 3.7, no. 15); 2 sherds carinated bowl, grooved decoration, fabric 13 (Fig. 3.8, no. 17); 1 sherd carinated bowl, grooved decoration, fabric 11 (Fig. 3.8, no. 19); 1 sherd carinated bowl, grooved decoration, fabric 11 (Fig. 3.8, no. 22); 10 sherds undecorated carinated bowl, fabric 14 (Fig. 3.8, no. 25); 1 sherd large carinated jar, fabric 41 (Fig. 3.8, no. 28); 1 sherd carinated jar, fabric 42 (Fig. 3.8, no. 32); 1 sherd carinated jar, fabric 31 (Fig. 3.9, no. 44); 1 rim sherd probably from carinated jar, fabric 14 (Fig. 3.10, no. 45); 2 sherds carinated jar, fabric 14 (Fig. 3.10, no. 50); 4 sherds carinated jar, fabric 41 (Fig. 3.10, no. 53); 11 sherds carinated jar, fabric 31 (Fig. 3.10, no. 54); 6 sherds probable carinated jar, fabric 43 (Fig. 3.10, no. 58); 1 sherd from vessel, fabric 41 (Fig. 3.10, no. 59); 1 base sherd, probably from carinated jar, fabric 14 (Fig. 3.10, no. 61); 2 body sherds, fabric 11; 2 body sherds, fabric 12; 1 base sherd and 7 body sherds, fabric 13; 1 base sherd and 7 body sherds, fabric 14; 1 body sherd, fabric 19; 1 body sherd, fabric 27; 10 body sherds, fabric 31; 7 base sherds and 47 body sherds, fabric 41; 1 base sherd and 4 body sherds, fabric 43.

PH 136
Dia. 0.61 m, depth 0.36 m; flat bottom.
Fill: Brown soil with chalk lumps. Chalk packing at the bottom.
Charcoal: Unspeciated fragments.
Bone frags: 14 sheep/goat, 2 cattle, 15 pig, 3 rodent (vole).
Pottery: 2 sherds carinated bowl, grooved decoration, fabric 14 (Fig. 3.7, no. 3); 4 sherds carinated bowl, grooved decoration, fabric 11 (Fig. 3.7, no. 7); 4 sherds carinated bowl, grooved decoration, fabric 14 (Fig. 3.7, no. 12); 4 sherds carinated bowl, grooved decoration, fabric 13 (Fig. 3.8, no. 17); 3 sherds carinated bowl, grooved decoration, fabric 11 (Fig. 3.8, no. 19); 6 sherds undecorated carinated bowl, fabric 14 (Fig. 3.8, no. 25); 5 sherds carinated jar, fabric 14 (Fig. 3.8, no. 31); 19 sherds carinated jar, fabric 14 (Fig. 3.9, no. 43); 1 sherd probably from carinated jar, fabric 14 (Fig. 3.10, no. 47); 3 sherds carinated jar, fabric 14, (Fig. 3.10, no. 50); 1 sherd carinated jar, fabric 14 (Fig. 3.10, no. 52); 4 sherds carinated jar, fabric 41 (Fig. 3.10, no. 53); 2 joining sherds carinated jar, fabric 14 (Fig. 3.10, no. 55); 3 sherds, fabric 41 (Fig. 3.10, no. 59); 7 body sherds, fabric 11; 4 body sherds, fabric 13; 12 body sherds, fabric 14; 3 body sherds, fabric 31; 2 body sherds, fabric 41; 1 rim sherd, 2 base sherd and 5 body sherds, fabric 42; 2 body sherds, fabric 43.

PH 143
Dia. 0.28 m, depth 0.41 m, Almost vertical sides, rounded bottom.
Fill: Chalky soil.
Pottery: 1 sherd carinated bowl, grooved decoration, fabric 13 (Fig. 3.8, no. 17); 1 rim sherd, fabric 31 (Fig. 3.10, no. 57); 1 body sherd, fabric 12; 1 body sherd, fabric 14.

PH 148 Not illustrated
Dia. and depth not recorded. Depth of post socket 0.21 m.
Fill: Brown soil. Chalk packing.

PH 160 Not illustrated
Dia. 0.31 m, depth 0.15 m. Depth of post socket 0.13 m.
Fill: Brown soil.

PH 128
Dia. 0.43 m, depth 0.28 m, Slightly sloping walls, rounded bottom.
Fill: Brown soil with chalk lumps.
Pottery: 2 body sherds, fabric 11; 5 base sherds, fabric 13.

PH 130 Not illustrated
Dia. 0.36 m, depth 0.28 m. Depth of post socket 0.23 m.
Fill: Brown soil.
Pottery: 1 body sherd, fabric 13.

PH 131
Dia. 0.36 m, depth 0.28 m; slightly sloping sides, slightly rounded bottom.
Fill: Brown soil.

PH 159 Not illustrated (in the extension of the cutting)
Dia. 0.46 m, depth 0.13 m. Depth of post socket 0.13 m.
Fill: Brown soil with lumps of flint and chalk.

PH 162
Dia. 0.21 m, depth 0.10 m; vertical sides, flat bottom. Cut by PH 163.
Fill: Chalky soil.
Pottery: 1 rim sherd, fabric 42 (Fig. 3.10, no. 56); 6 body sherds, fabric 41.

PH 163
Dia. 0.26 m, depth 0.15 m; sloping sides, rounded bottom. Cuts PH 162
Fill: Chalky soil.

PH 167
Dia. 0.66 m, depth 0.41 m; vertical sides, flat bottom.
Fill: Chalky soil with large lumps of chalk and flint.
Pottery: 1 sherd carinated bowl, grooved decoration, fabric 14 (Fig. 3.7, no. 12); 5 sherds carinated jar, fabric 41 (Fig. 3.10, no. 53); 2 body sherds, fabric 14; 1 base sherd and 1 body sherd, fabric 31; 5 body sherds, fabric 41; 1 body sherd, fabric 42.

PH 166 Not illustrated
Dia. 0.21 m by 0.28 m, depth 0.31 m. Depth post socket 0.31 m.
Fill: Brown soil.

PH 164
Dia. 0.23 m, depth 0.23 m; vertical sides, flat bottom. Dia. post socket 0.23 m, depth 0.21 m.
Fill: Brown soil. Thin layer of packing.

PH 150
Dia. 0.31 m, depth 0.23 m; flat bottom.
Fill: Chalky soil.

PH 117 Not illustrated
Dia. 0.31 m, depth 0.21 m. Depth post socket 0.21 m.
Fill: Brown soil with lumps of chalk.

PH 118 Not illustrated
Dia. 0.26 m, depth 0.21 m. Depth post socket 0.18 m.
Fill: Brown soil.

PH 119 Not illustrated
Dia. 0.28 m, depth 0.28 m. Depth post socket 0.26 m.
Fill: Brown soil.

PH 123
Dia. 0.28 m, depth 0.33 m; vertical sides, flat bottom.
Fill: Brown soil.
Pottery: 1 body sherd, fabric 41.

PH 122
Dia. 0.28 m, depth 0.26 m; vertical sides, almost flat bottom.
Fill: Brown soil with chalk lumps.

PH 120 Not illustrated
Dia. 0.31 m, depth 0.33 m. Depth post socket 0.31 m.
Fill: Brown soil.

PH 125 Not illustrated
Dia. and depth not recorded. A shallow posthole.
Fill: Brown soil.
Pottery: 1 body sherd, fabric 41.

PH 121 Not illustrated
Dia. 0.33 m, depth 0.26 m. Depth post socket 023 m.
Fill: Brown soil.

PH 115
Dia. 0.33 m, depth 0.18 m; irregular sides and bottom.
Fill: Loose chalk.

PH 116
Dia. 0.31 m, depth 0.31 m; almost flat bottom.
Fill: Loose chalk with patches of burnt clay.

PH 213
Dia. 0.53 m, depth 0.56 m; vertical sides, slightly rounded bottom.
Fill: Chalky soil.

PH 158
Dia. 0.31 m, depth 0.38 m; vertical sides, rounded bottom. Depth post socket 0.33 m.
Fill: Greyish soil with a lump of saddle quern stone. Chalk and flint packing.

PH 178 Not illustrated
Dia. 0.51 m by 0.31 m, depth 0.15 m. Depth post socket o.15 m.
Fill: Brown soil with lumps of burnt clay.

House 3 Catalogue of postholes and contents (Figs 2.45 – 2.47)
Measurements taken from top of chalk bedrock

Main Post Ring Postholes
Listed clockwise from entrance

PH 53 (Cutting A 64B) Not illustrated
Dia. 0.61 m, depth 0.38 m; straight sides, flat bottom. Dia. post socket 0.31 m
Fill: Burnt soil. Collapsed chalk rubble packing, with some flints.
Charcoal: Fragments of unspeciated charcoal at the bottom.

PH 52 (CUTTING A 65)
Dia. (oval) 0.61 m x 0.53 m, depth 0.61 m; straight sides, flat bottom. Dia. post socket 0.38 m depth 0.46 m below

chalk. Collapsed post socket at NW side; sides heavily packed with flints. Evidently this post, like the last, had had all but its burnt stump removed, allowing the packing to collapse.
Upper fill: Dark silty soil with stones at bottom of this layer.
Lower fill: Burnt soil.
Daub: A few fragments of clay daub.
Charcoal: Fragments of charcoal at the bottom.
Bone frags: Miscellaneous.
Pottery: 2 joining body sherds, fabric 13; 2 body sherds fabric 14; 6 undecorated sherds fabrics 42 and 43.

PH 70 (Cutting A 93)
Dia. 0.53 m x 0.69 m, depth 0.64 m; straight sides, flat bottom.
Fill: Dark soil with lumps of chalk. Collapsed chalk packing at bottom and sides. No measurable trace of post, evidently withdrawn after the fire.
Daub: 3 pieces of burnt daub, Freeman Types I and II/III.
Pottery: 1 rim sherd, 1 base sherd and 1 body sherd from bowl, fabric 11; 6 undecorated jar sherds, fabrics 31, 41 and 42.

PH 71 (CUTTING A 93) Not illustrated
Dia. 0.61 m, depth 0.56 m; straight sides, rounded bottom. Chalk packing enclosing remains of post *in situ*, dia. 0.26 m.
Fill: Dark soil.
Daub: 1 large burnt piece, Freeman type I.
Charcoal: Fragments of charcoal.
Bone frags: Miscellaneous.
Pottery: 1 sherd carinated bowl, fabric 14 (Fig. 3.11, no. 11); 2 body sherds from bowls, fabrics 11 and 14; 12 body sherds, fabrics 11, 13, 31 and 41.

PH 124 (Cutting A 148)
Dia. 0.53 m, depth 0.59 m; straight sides, flat bottom. Chalk packing around well-preserved cylindrical post socket, dia. 0.36 m with flat bottom, depth 0.56 m.
Upper fill: Dark muddy soil.
Lower fill: Fine brown soil with patches of clay.
Daub: Several fragments, Freeman Type I.
Charcoal: Unspeciated fragments.
Bone frags: 24 sheep/goat, 7 cattle, 12 pig, 1 dog.
Pottery: 1 neck and shoulder sherd carinated bowl with grooved decoration, fabric 13 (Fig. 3.11, no. 2); 1 shoulder sherd carinated jar, finger nail decoration, fabric 14 (Fig. 3.12, no. 47); 38 body sherds, fabrics 13, 14, 31, 41, 42 and 43.

PH 123 (Cutting A 148)
Dia. oval, max. 0.76 m, depth 0.64 m; straight sides, flat bottom recessed for post. Chalk packing at sides around a well-preserved cylindrical post socket, dia. 0.33 m, with flat bottom: not vertical like the others but showing an outward thrust of about 6 degrees to east.
Upper fill: Dark muddy soil.
Lower fill: 0.5 m of fine dark soil below fine burnt soil.
Charcoal: Unspeciated fragments.
Bone frags: 16 cattle, 3 pig.
Pottery: 3 sherds large carinated jar with rounded body, fabric 13 (Fig. 3.11, no. 17); 1 rim and neck sherd vessel with finger tip and nail decoration, fabric 41 (Fig. 3.12, no. 30); 1 rim and neck sherd carinated jar, finger tip and nail decoration, fabric 13 (Fig. 3.12, no. 31); 1 rim and neck sherd carinated jar, finger tip and nail decoration, fabric 42 (Fig. 3.12, no. 32); 3 rim and neck sherds vessel decorated on rim edge by horizontal lines, fabric 42 (Fig. 3.12, no. 34); 2 joining rim, neck and shoulder sherds carinated jar, fabric 43 (Fig. 3.12, no. 42); 1 shoulder sherd carinated jar, finger tip and nail decoration, fabric 31 (Fig. 3.12, no. 51); 1 shoulder sherd carinated jar, slashed decoration, fabric 41 (Fig. 3.12, no. 54); 1 flat top rim sherd, fabric 41 (Fig. 3.13, no. 62); 2 rim sherds, fabric 42; 34 body sherds, fabrics 13, 31, 41, 42 and 43.

PH 63 (Cutting A 148)
Dia. 0.61 m, depth 0.74 m; straight sides, recessed bottom. Chalk packing at sides and base around a well-preserved cylindrical post socket, dia. 0.38 m with flat bottom, depth 0.61 m.
Fill: Muddy brown soil.
Daub: 2 burnt pieces, Freeman Type II/III.
Charcoal: Unspeciated fragments.
Pottery: 1 base sherd large carinated jar with rounded body, fabric 13 (Fig. 3.11, no. 17); 1 neck and shoulder sherd carinated jar, finger tip and nail decoration, fabric 43 (Fig. 3.12, no. 44); 1 tall, straight shoulder sherd, fabric 11 (*cf.* Fig. 3.11, no. 10); 1 haematite coated shoulder sherd carinated bowl, fabric 11; 1 sherd from tall straight-sided bowl, fabric 13; 2 base sherds from bowl, fabric 14; 21 body sherds, fabrics 41 and 42.

PH 105 (Cutting A 104)
Dia. oval 0.61 x 0.76 m, depth 0.53 m; straight sides, flat bottom. Packing of chalk and large flints at base and sides around a well-preserved cylindrical post socket, dia. 0.31 m, with flat bottom, depth 0.43 m.
Fill: Fine dark burnt soil with patches of clay.
Daub: Fragments of clay daub.
Charcoal: Fragments of charcoal.
Pottery: Most pottery was from the fill, a little in the packing. 2 joining neck sherds with hatched chevron decoration, fabric 41 (Fig. 3.12, no. 19); 2 rim and neck sherds vessel with finger tip decoration, fabric 41 (Fig. 3.12, no. 38); 1 shoulder sherd carinated jar with finger tip decoration, fabric 43 (Fig. 3.12, no. 52); 1 rim and neck sherd, fabric 13 (Fig. 3.13, no. 55); 2 joining rim sherds from bowl, fabric 13; 3 joining rim sherds bowl, fabric 14; 24 body sherds, fabrics 13, 14, 31, 41 and 42.
PH 106 (Cutting A I04)
Dia. oval 0.76 x 0.53 m, max. depth 0.51 m; straight sides, bottom recessed below post. Chalk packing at sides and base around a well-preserved cylindrical post socket, dia. 0.33 m, with flat bottom, depth 0.46 m.
Fill: Dark soil.
Daub: Fragments of daub.
Charcoal: Oak (*Q.R.*) from post.
Pottery: 38 non-joining sherds, fabrics 14, 31, 41, 42 and 43.

PH 107 (Cutting A 104)
Dia. oval 0.84 x 0.66 m, max. depth 0.59 m; irregular sides and bottom recessed for post. Chalk packing at sides and bottom around a well-preserved cylindrical post socket, diam. 0.31 m, with flat bottom, depth 0.51 m.
Fill: Burnt soil with patches of clay.
Daub: 1 piece of clay daub, Freeman Type II/III.
Charcoal: Oak (*Q.R.*) from post.
Pottery: 1 rim sherd and 1 shoulder sherd haematite coated bowl, fabric 11; 2 base sherds from bowl, fabric 13; 1 base sherd from jar, fabric 41; 15 body sherds, fabrics 14, 31, 41, 42 and 43.

PH 121 (Cutting A 103b)
Dia. oval 0.61 x 0.69 m, depth 0.51 m; sloping sides, flat bottom. Chalk packing around post socket, with flat bottom dia. 0.31 m, depth 0.46 m, and slightly tapering sides.
Fill: Powdery burnt soil.
Charcoal: Fragments of charcoal.
Bone frags: Miscellaneous.
Pottery: 2 rim sherds and 1 base sherd haematite coated bowl, fabric 11; 2 non-joining sherds, fabric 43.

PH104 (Cutting 106)
Dia. 0.66 m, depth 0.48 m; sloping sides, flat base. Chalk packing at sides around well-preserved cylindrical post socket, dia. 0.36 m, with flat bottom. depth 0.48 m.
Fill: Dark, powdery burnt soil.
Daub: Fragments of daub.
Charcoal sample: Oak (*Q.R.*) from post; Radiocarbon sample HAR-255
Bone frags: Burnt bone.
Pottery: 7 non-joining sherds, fabrics 31, 41, 42.

PH 103 (Cutting A 106)
Dia. max. 0.69 m, depth 0.38 m; sloping sides, flat base. Chalk packing at sides and base of post socket, with flat bottom dia. 0.33 m, depth 0.33 m, and slightly sloping sides. Amongst the packing was pottery, bone and clay daub.
Fill: Fine burnt soil and ash.
Daub: 8 pieces of burnt daub with straw impressions, probably Freeman Type II/III.
Charcoal: Unspeciated fragments.
Bone frags: Miscellaneous burnt bone.
Pottery: 1 rim sherd bowl, fabric 11; 1 plain rim sherd from jar, fabric 31; 1 body sherd of jar, fabric 41; 1 plain rim sherd from jar, fabric 42; 1 shoulder sherd jar with finger tip decoration, fabric 43.
PH 109 (Cutting A 107) Not illustated
Dia. oval, 0.92 x 0.59 m, depth 0.56 m. Chalk packing at sides around a reasonably central post socket, dia. 0.38 m, depth 0.46 m.
Fill: Burnt soil.
Daub: Fragments of clay daub.
Charcoal: Unspeciated fragments.
Bone frags: Miscellaneous.
Small finds: Bone or red deer antler gouge or weaving beater (Fig. 4.4, no. 10).

PH 108 (Cutting A 107)
Dia. 0.61 m, depth 0.56 m; sloping sides. Chalk packing at sides enclosing a cylindrical post socket, dia. 0.36 m, depth 0.56 m.
Fill: Burnt soil.
Daub: Fragments of daub.
Charcoal: Fragments of charcoal.
Small finds: Chalk spindle whorl (Fig. 4.12, no. 7).

PH 120 (Cutting A 101 B) Not illustrated
Dia. oval, 0.84 m x 0.56 m, depth 0.41 m; flat bottom. Packed at the base with large flints and pieces of sandstone, at sides with flints and chalk rubble, around a flat bottomed cylindrical post socket, dia. 0.36 m, depth 0.38 m.
Upper fill: Muddy soil with flints.
Lower fill: Fine burnt soil.
Daub: Fragments of daub.
Bone frags: miscellaneous.
Pottery: 4 joining rim and shoulder sherds carinated bowl, fabric 11 (Fig. 3.11, no. 6); 1 neck and shoulder sherd haematite coated jar, fabric 11 (fig. 3.11, no. 16); 1 sherd saucepan vessel, fabric 12 (Fig. 3.33, no. 7) intrusive; 1 base sherd with omphalos haematite coated bowl, fabric 11; 1 rim sherd (intrusive), fabric 12; 4 jar sherds, fabrics 42 and 43.

PH 101 (Cutting A 101)
Dia. 0.69 m, depth 0.46 m; sloping sides, flat bottom. Chalk packing at sides of a funnel shaped post socket, dia. 0.23 m at base and 0.38 m at top, depth 0.38 m.
Upper fill: Muddy silt.
Lower fill: Fine, dark burnt soil
Charcoal: Many fragments of unspeciated charcoal.
Bone frags: Miscellaneous burnt bone.
Pottery: In the post socket filling (i), 1 sherd base of fine bowl, fabric 11; in the packing (2), 1 body sherd medium jar, fabric 43.

PH 102 (Cutting A 101 B)
Dia. oval 0.69 m x 0.61 m, depth 0.51 m; irregular sides and bottom. It was packed around with chalk rubble in which the remains of the post was sited in the east side of the post hole and showed a slight slope inwards. The post socket dia. 0.28 m, round-bottomed and depth 0.38 m.
Fill: Fine burnt soil, orange and grey in colour with ash and other burnt remains.
Charcoal: Unspeciated fragments. (The burning in this area must have been intense.)
Pottery: 1 body sherd, fabric 14.

PH 46 (Cutting A 59) Not illustrated
Dia. 0.41 m, depth 0.36 m; straight sides, flat bottom. No clear post socket survived, suggesting that the post had either burned right down into its post hole, as confirmed by the signs of intense heat here, or been withdrawn. The posthole had collapsed chalk packing at sides.
Fill: Fine burnt soil.
Daub: Cindered fragments of daub.
Charcoal: Unspeciated fragments.

PH 47 (Cutting A 101 B)
Dia. 0.53 m, depth 0.51 m; rounded bottom. At the sides a slide of fine chalk rubble around the remains of the post, dia. 0.31 m, which had burned right down into its socket. At the base of the post socket was much charcoal from the post.
Fill: Fine, burnt soil.
Daub: 11 cindered pieces, Freeman Type VI.
Charcoal: Fragments of charcoal.
Bone frags: Miscellaneous burnt bone.
Pottery: 1 rim sherd, fabric 11.

PH 69 (Cutting 89)
Dia. 0.46 m, depth 0.48 m; vertical sides, flat bottom. Dia. of post socket 0.31 m, depth 0.43 m.
Fill: Burnt soil and ash. Chalk packing.
Charcoal: Unspeciated fragments.

PH 64 (Cutting 90)
Dia. 0.46 m, depth 0.59 m; flat bottom. Dia. of post socket 0.33 m, depth 0.59 m
Fill: Fine burnt soil and ash. Chalk packing at sides.
Daub: 5 small pieces of burnt cob daub, orange and black in colour and with no good wattle or straw impressions, probably Freeman Type VI.
Charcoal: Unspeciated fragments.
Pottery: 1 body sherd, fabric 11.

PH 65 (Cutting 90)
Dia. 0.46 m, depth 0.59 m; vertical sides, flat bottom. Dia. post socket 0.31 m, depth 0.59 m.
Fill: Brown soil with patches of clay and ash. Chalk packing at sides.
Pottery: 1 neck sherd from grooved bowl (*cf* Fig. 3.11, no. 2).

PH 57n (Cutting 62 B) Not illustrated
Dia. not recorded, depth 0.41 m.
Fill: Burnt soil. Heavy chalk packing; but no post present.
Charcoal: Fragments of charcoal at the bottom of the fill.
Small finds: Small bone spatula (Fig. 4.4, no. 5).
Pottery: 1 rim and 1 body sherd, fabric 11; 4 body sherds from jars, fabrics 41, 42 and 43.

PH 51 (Cutting 51)
Dia. 0.46 m, depth 0.53 m irregular sides and bottom. Dia. post socket 0.31 m, depth 0.61 m.
Fill: Burnt soil. Chalk packing on east side
Charcoal: Many fragments of unspeciated charcoal at the bottom.
Bone frags: 6 horse.

PH 13 (Cutting 63 B) Not illustrated
Dia. 0.53 m depth not recorded. There was a post in the hole, dia. 0.31 m which reached to the bottom.
Fill: Burnt soil.
Charcoal: Unspeciated fragments.

PH 14 (Cutting IV ext) Not illustrated.
Dia. 0.31 m, depth 0.46 m; perfectly cylindrical with flat bottom. No trace of post socket or packing.
Fill: Orange burnt soil.
Charcoal: Unspeciated fragments.

PH 15 Not illustrated.
Dia. not recorded, depth 0.46 m. No trace of post.
Fill: Packing material.
Adjacent and out of line with the rest of the post holes. Clearly dug out of line and backfilled, while PH 14 was made to the exact size to replace it.

Porch Postholes

PH 4 (N. side inner PH)
Irregular dia., depth 0.76 m; rounded bottom. Post socket dia. 0.18 m x 0.66 m. Chalk packing.
Upper fill: Burnt soil with patches of clay.
Lower fill: Fine dark soil.
Daub: Very small fragments of daub.
Charcoal: Unspeciated fragments.
Bone frags: 36 sheep/goat, 1 cattle.
Small finds: Iron angle bracket (Fig. 4.2, no. 3).
Pottery: 1 rim and neck sherd carinated jar, finger nail decoration, fabric 41 (Fig. 3.12, no. 40); 1 rim sherd, fabric 31; 14 body sherds, fabrics 13, 21, 31, 32, 41 and 52. This post hole cut an earlier version. It was linked tp PH 5by a slot filled with chalk fragments and light brown earth.

PH 5 (N. side outer)
Dia. Oval 0.87 m, depth 0.61 m; vertical sides, almost flat bottom. Post socket dia.0.23 m, and 0.53 m.
Fill: Brown soil with patches of clay. Chalk packing.
Small finds: 2 chalk loom weights (Fig. 4.8, nos. 2 and 3).
Pottery: 1 body sherd, fabric 14.

PH 11 (S. side inner) Not illustrated
Large recut post hole, irregular dia., depth 0.66 m.
Fill: Burnt soil.
Daub: 4 medium sized pieces of burnt cob daub, orange and black in colour, some straw impressions identified on the daub, Freeman Type II/III.
Charcoal: Hawthorn and hazel charcoal.
Pottery: 2 rim sherds and 50 body sherds, fabrics 14, 21, 31, 41, 42, 43.

PH 9 (S. side outer) Not illustrated
Dia. 0.92 m, depth 0.31 m. An impression of the post remained.
Fill: Burnt soil.

PH 16 Not illistrated.
(adjacent to PH 9 and cut by it, but evidently in use at the same time, possibly a twin support post)
Dia. 1 ft 0.46 m, depth 0.23 m. Small post socket, depth 0.23 m below chalk. Remains of a burnt post at the bottom.
Fill: Brown soil.

PH 10 (Between PH 11 and PH 9) Not illustrated
Dia. 0.31 m) depth 0.15 m. Remains of a burnt post at the bottom.
Fill: Chalky soil.
Small finds: Sandstone rubber (Fig. 4.11, no. 5).
Contemporary with main porch structure and perhaps a support post. Cuts a shallow slot which connects PH 9 and PH11.

PH 8 (N. of outer N. porch post) Not illustrated
Dia. 0.61 m, depth 0.18 m. Dia. and depth of post socket not recorded.
Fill: Brown soil.

PH 3 (N. in concentric line from outer porch)
Dia. not recorded, depth 051 m. Large recut post hole.
Fill: Dark soil. Flint packing stones.
Charcoal: Unspeciated fragments.
Small finds: Fragment of bronze bracelet (Fig. 4.1, no. 5).

PH 12 (N. in concentric line from outer porch) Not illustrated
Dia. not recorded, depth 0.31 m.
Fill: Brown soil.

Internal Postholes
(Clockwise from the entrance)

PH 129
Dia. 0.36 m, depth 0.66 m; vertical sides and rounded bottom. Clear trace of post with a flat bottom sunk almost to the base of the hole. Post socket dia.0.26 m and 0.56 m.
Fill: Dark soil. Chalk packing at the sides and bottom.
Pottery: 1 rim sherd carinated jar, finger nail decoration, fabric 13 (Fig. 3.12, no. 26); 2 joining rim sherds carinated jar, finger tip decoration, fabric 43 (Fig. 3.12, no. 29); 1 body sherd haematite coated bowl, fabric 13.

PH 72
Dia. 0.41 m, depth 0.59 m; vertical sides and slightly rounded bottom. Clear trace of post with flat bottom sunk to base. Post-socket dia. 0.31 m and 0.56 m.
Fill: Dark soil. Chalk packing at the sides.
Pottery: 1 rim, neck and shoulder sherd carinated bowl,

fabric 14 (Fig. 3.11, no. 9); 5 joining sherds from carinated bowl with deep, rounded body, fabric 14, (Fig. 3.11, no. 15), 1 rim and 3 base sherds from bowl, fabric 14 (*cf.* Fig. 3.11, no. 9); 1 base sherd from bowl, fabric 11; 4 body sherds, fabric 42; 4 joining sherds jar, finger tip decoration, fabric 43.

PH 66
Dia. 0.38 m, depth 0.33 m; vertical sides and flat bottom. Clear trace of small post in the post hole. Post socket dia. 0.15 m.
Fill: Brown soil with traces of ash. Flint packing stones and chalk lumps at the sides.
Charcoal: Unspeciated fragments.

Internal posts
(Possibly connected with the domestic arrangements – listed in order from porch)

PH 119
Dia. 0.28 m, depth 0.28 m; vertical sides and flat bottom.
Fill: Dark soil.
Daub: Fragments of daub.

PH 130 Not illustrated
Dia. 0.21 m, depth 0.10 m; vertical sides and flat bottom.
Fill: Brown soil.

PH 114
Dia. 0.21 m, depth 0.31 m; vertical sides and flat bottom.
Fill: Brown soil with small lumps of chalk.
Charcoal: Unspeciated fragments.

PH 113
Dia. 0.23 m, depth 0.18 m; vertical sides, rounded bottom.
Fill: Brown soil with small lumps of chalk; flints at the bottom.

PH 117
Dia. 0.21 m, depth 0.31 m; vertical sides, flat bottom. Post socket dia. 0.21 m, depth 0.31 m below chalk.
Fill: Dark soil with small chalk lumps.
The old post cut by it was full of chalky packing material.

PH 76
Dia. 0.23 m by 0.31 m, depth 0.33 m; vertical sides and flat bottom.
Fill: Dark soil with single large flint at the bottom.

PH 77 Not illustrated
Dia. 0.31 m, depth 0.23 m; rounded bottom.
Fill: Dark soil.
Possibly a pair with PH 78.

PH 78
Dia. 0.31 m, depth 0.23 m; rounded bottom.
Fill: Dark soil. Chalk packing on east side.
Possibly a pair with PH 77

PH 132 Not illustrated
Dia. 0.21 m, depth 0.71 m; rounded bottom.
Fill: Brown soil.

PH 133 Not illustrated
Dia. 0.21 m, depth 0.10 m; rounded bottom.
Fill: Brown soil.

PH 131
Dia. 0.23 m, depth 0.13 m; vertical sides, flat bottom.
Fill: Dark soil.

Internal Posts
(these post holes may have contained roof supports)

PH 110 Not illustrated
Dia. 0.31 m, depth 0.18); straight sides and flat bottom.
Fill: Brown soil with chalk lumps.
Charcoal: Unspeciated fragments.

PH 134 Not illustrated
Dia. 0.31 m, depth 0.61 m; vertical sides with pointed bottom.
Fill: Brown soil.

PH 74
Dia. 0.28 m, depth 0.41 m; almost vertical sides and flat bottom. stones.
Fill: Dark soil. Collapsed flint packing

PH 60
Dia. 0.28 m, depth 0.51 m; vertical sides and flat bottom. No post remaining.
Fill: Dark brown soil. Flint packing stones which have subsided.

PH 100 (close to main ring post hole 108, possibly a support post)
Dia. 0.46 m, depth 0.36 m; sloping sides and a roughly flat bottom. Post not remaining.
Fill: Muddy soil. Collapsed flint packing stones.
Posthole seems to have been blocked up before the house was abandoned.

PH 54 (just inside the main ring adjacent to PH 53) Not illustrated
A shallow depression not cut into the chalk. No measurements recorded.
Fill: Dark soil.
Pottery: 2 bowl sherds, fabric 11; 1 sherd (jar?) fabric 13; 14 body sherds, fabrics 31, 41, 42 and 43.

PH 55 (just inside the main ring, adjacent to PH 53) Not illustrated
A shallow depression not cut into the chalk, between the main and outer rings.
Fill: Dark soil.
Pottery: 8 joining sherds carinated cup, fabric 13 (Fig. 3.11, no. 8); 1 rim and neck sherd, finger nail impressions or slashes made by small tool, fabric 42 (Fig. 3.12, no. 33); 1 rim and neck sherd from vessel with finger nail decoration, fabric 42 (Fig. 3.12, no. 35); 1 plain rim sherd from bowl, fabric 14 (*cf* Fig. 3.11, no. 9); 2 body sherds, fabric 11; 1 rim sherd from bowl, fabric 13; 1 base sherd, fabric 14; 4 joining sherds and 2 joining sherds from bases of jars, fabric 43; 11 body sherds, fabrics 14, 31, 42 and 43.

Loom Structure (?)
(This feature is situated inside House 3, between the main ring posts and the support posts of the interior)

G7 (the trench)
0.61 m by 0.71 m, depth 0.38 c); sloping sides and flat bottom.
Fill: Large flints and chalk rubble, tightly packed.

PH 73
Dia. 0.66 m, depth 0.46 m; sloping sides, flat bottom. No trace of post
Fill: Compact dark soil with chalk lumps. A little chalk and flint packing at the sides.
Bone frag: 1 pig.
Pottery: 4 joining base sherds (with perforations) carinated bowl, fabric 11 (Fig. 3.11, no. 6); 1 rim sherd carinated jar, finger tip decoration, fabric 13 (Fig. 3.12, no. 25); 2 joining sherds, rim and shoulder carinated jar, fingertip and nail decoration, fabric 14 (Fig. 3.12, no. 27); 1 shoulder sherd carinated jar, fingertip and nail decoration, fabric 21 (Fig. 3.12, no. 48); 1 rim and neck sherd, fabric 13 (Fig. 3.13, no. 56); 1 shoulder sherd carinated jar, fabric 31 (Fig. 3.13, no. 61); 3 rim sherds and 3 body sherds, fabric 14; 1 shoulder sherd jar with fingertip decoration, fabric 41; 21 body sherds jar, fabric 43; 6 body sherds, fabrics 41, 42 and 43.

PH 62 (west end of trench)
Dia. 0.66 m, depth 0.46 m; sloping sides, flat bottom.; no trace of post.
Fill: Dark soil with chalk lumps. Packing stones at the top and chalk packing at the sides and bottom
Pottery:
PH 62a: 4 joining sherds carinated bowl, fabric 14 (Fig. 3.11, no. 10); 2 joining body sherds, fabric 21 (Fig. 3.12, no. 18); 2 joining shoulder sherds carinated jar, finger tip decoration, fabric 43 (Fig. 3.12, no. 53); 1 rim sherd, 1 neck sherd and 3 joining sherds base of bowl, fabric 14; 2 joining sherds body of thin-walled bowl, fabric 52; 37 body sherds, fabrics 41, 42, 43, 31, 19.
PH 62b: 8 sherds, fabrics 13, 41, and 42.

Outer Ring Postholes

These post holes are not well preserved and often the information is not complete.
(listed clockwise from the porch starting with PH 18)

PH 18 Not illustrated
Dia. 0.61 m x 0.21 m, depth 0.23 m; oval in shape with a rounded bottom. No trace of the post.
Fill: Chalky soil.
Bone frags: 4 sheep/goat.
Small finds: 2 fragments of polished and burnt bone (not illustrated).
Pottery: 1 body sherd, fabric 13; 1 rim sherd, 1 base sherd, and 4 body sherds, fabric 41.

PH 17 Not illustrated
Dia. 0.46 m x 0.21 m, depth 0.23 m; rounded bottom. No trace of the post.
Fill: Chalky soil.
Pottery: 3 body sherds, fabric 42.

PH 147 Not illustrated
Dia. 0.92 m, depth 0.21 m.
Fill: Chalky soil.

PH 126 Not illustrated
Dia. 0.31 m x 0.46 m, depth 0.71 m.
Fill: Brown soil.

PH 115 Not illustrated
Dia. not recorded, depth 0.15 m.
Fill: Chalky soil.

PH 116
Dia. 0.41 m, depth 0.28 m; rounded bottom. No trace of post.
Fill: Muddy soil.

PH 112 Not illustrated
Dia. 0.31 m, depth 0.18 m. No trace of post.
Fill: Compact soil.
Charcoal: Unspeciated fragments.

PH 111 Not illustrated
Dia. 0.26 m, depth 0.76 m; rounded bottom. No trace of post.
Fill: Brown soil.
Charcoal: Unspeciated fragments.

PH 155 Not illustrated
Dia. not recorded, depth 0.21 m.
Fill: Brown soil.

PH 156 Not illustrated
Dia. not recorded, depth 0.15 m.
Fill: Brown soil.
Pottery: 1 body sherd, fabric 11; 1 body sherd, fabric 14; 1 rim sherd, fabric 42.

PH 157 Not illustrated
Dia. not recorded, depth 0.71 m.
Fill: Brown soil.

PH 118
Dia. 0.53 m, depth 0.33 m; circular with flat bottom.
Fill: Muddy soil.

PH 125 Not illustrated
Dia. 0.31 m x 0.46 m, depth 0.15 m.
Fill: Brown soil.

PH 22 Not illustrated
PH diam. not recorded, depth 0.10 m.
Fill: Brown soil.

PH 21 Not illustrated
PH diam. not recorded, depth 0.71 m.
Fill: Brown soil.

PH 20 Not illustrated
Dia. not recorded, depth 0.13 m.
Fill: Brown soil.

PH 19 Not illustrated
Dia. not recorded, depth 0.13 m.
Fill: Brown soil.

PH 50 Not illustrated
Dia. 0.31 m by 0.46 m, depth 0.21 m; sloping sides and flat bottom.
Fill: Brown soil.

Postholes to the outside of the latter external holes

PH 48 Not illustrated
Dia. not recorded, depth 0.28 m.
Fill: Brown soil. Flint packing stones around the top.
Bone frags: 4 sheep/goat, 3 cattle, 2 pig.
Pottery: 5 body sherds, fabric 41.

PH 67 Not illustrated
Dia. 0.36 m, depth 0.33 m; vertical sides and flat bottom. Dia. post socket 0.31 m
Fill: Dark soil. A little chalk packing.

PH 68 Not illustrated
Dia. 0.31 m, depth 0.33 m; vertical sides and flat bottom.
Fill: Light brown loam with chalk and other collapsed packing stones.

Postholes possibly associated with a drying rack.

PH 75
Dia. 0.56 m, depth 0.51 m; vertical sides, slightly rounded bottom. Dia. post socket 0.21 m, depth 0.48 m.
Fill: Brown soil with a few chalk lumps. Chalk packing.
Daub: Several fragments of daub.
Charcoal: Unspeciated fragments.
Pottery: 5 body sherds, fabric 41.

PH 49 Not illustrated
Dia. 0.53 m, depth 0.43 m. Dia. post socket 0.26 m, depth 0.36 m.
Fill: Brown soil. Chalk packing.
Charcoal: Unspeciated fragments.
Pottery: 1 body sherd, fabric 14; 2 body sherds, fabric 21.

PH 2
Dia. 0.61 m, depth 0.28 m; rounded sides and bottom.
Fill: Brown soil with a few chalk lumps, particularly on the sides and bottom.

House 4 – Catalogue of postholes and contents (Fig. 2.52)
Measurements taken from top of chalk bedrock

Main Ring Postholes
listed clockwise from the porch area

PH 200
Dia. 0.46 m, depth 0.23 m; sloping sides, rounded bottom. Dia. post socket 0.21 m, depth 0.15 m.
Fill: Brown soil. Chalk packing.
Charcoal: Fragments
Small finds: Ceramic spindle whorl (Fig. 4.12, no. 4).

PH 199
Dia. 0.51 m, depth 0.26 m; irregular sides and bottom.
Fill: Brown soil. Chalk packing at the sides.
Daub: Small pieces of daub.
Charcoal: Oak charcoal fragments.
Pottery: 2 body sherds, fabric 11, 2 body sherds fabric 41.

PH 198
Dia. 0.41 m, depth 0.21 m; irregular sides, flat bottom. Dia. post socket 0.21 m, depth 0.18 m.
Fill: Brown soil. Chalk packing.
Daub: 6 pieces of whitish cob daub with slight wattle impressions, Freeman Types I and V, Freeman Types I and V.
Charcoal: Large quantity of oak charcoal fragments. Radiocarbon sample HAR-254
Pottery: 14 sherds carinated jar, fabric 22 (Fig. 3.13, no. 1); 5 body sherds, fabric 21; 1 body sherd, fabric 31.

PH 197
Dia. 0.41 m, depth 0.21 m; irregular sides and bottom.
Dia. post socket 0.10 m, depth 0.18 m.
Fill: Brown soil. Chalk packing.
Daub: 1 large piece and several small pieces of burnt yellow clay daub, Freeman Type II/III.
Charcoal: Large quantity of oak charcoal fragments.
Pottery: 1 body sherd, fabric 42.

PH 195
Dia. 0.46 m, depth 0.28 m; vertical sides and flat bottom.
Fill: Brown soil. Large lumps of flint around the sides.
Daub: Small quantity of daub, Freeman Type II/III.
Small finds: Fragments of ceramic sling bullet (Fig. 4.13, no. 6).

PH 196
Dia. 0.61 m, depth 0.38 m; almost flat bottom. No trace of the post.
Fill: Brown soil. Large lumps of flint and chalk
Daub: Small fragments of yellow clay daub.
Charcoal: Small quantity of charcoal.
Pottery: 9 body sherds, fabric 12; 1 base sherd, fabric 13; 3 base sherds and 5 body sherds, fabric 21.

PH 184
Dia. 0.41 m, depth 0.23 m; slightly rounded bottom. Dia. post socket 0.23 m, depth 0.23 m.
Fill: Dark soil and burnt clay. Chalk packing.
Daub: Fragments of daub.
Charcoal: Large quantity of oak charcoal.
Pottery: 1 body sherd, fabric 13.

PH 183
Dia. 0.46 m, depth 0.21 m; almost vertical sides, flat bottom. Dia. post socket 0.21 m, depth 0.15 m.
Fill: Dark soil and burnt clay. Chalk packing, particularly on north side.
Charcoal: Unspeciated flecks.

PH 185
Dia.0.38 m, depth 0.26 m; rounded bottom.
Fill: Brown soil. Lumps of chalk, particularly at the bottom.
Pottery: 1 body sherd, fabric 11.

PH 193
Dia. 0.33 m, depth 0.28 m; irregular sides, flat bottom.
Upper fill: Dark soil.
Lower fill: Grey, chalky soil.
Pottery: 1 body sherd, fabric 13; 2 body sherds, fabric 42.

PH 230
Dia. 0.48 m, depth 0.31 m; almost vertical sides, rounded bottom.
Fill: Brown soil with chalk lumps.

PH 232
Dia. 0.41 m, depth 0.43 c); almost vertical sides, irregular bottom.
Fill: Dark soil with lumps of chalk. Chalk packing.
Charcoal: Fragments of charcoal at the bottom of post socket.
Pottery: 1 body sherd, fabric 13; 1 body sherd, fabric 42.

PH 194
Dia. 0.64 m, depth 0.31 m; irregular sides, rounded bottom.

Fill: Dark soil with lumps of chalk and occasional small flints.
Charcoal: Small quantity of charcoal fragments.

PH 207
Dia. 0.41 m, depth 0.33 m; sloping sides, pointed bottom.
Fill: Dark soil with lumps of chalk. Chalk packing at the sides.
Daub: 2 pieces of daub, 1 yellow and 1 white, Freeman Type I.
Charcoal: Many fragments of charcoal at the bottom of posthole.
Pottery: 35 sherds, many joining from small carinated jar, fabric 41 (Fig. 3.13, no. 5).

PH 208
Dia. 0.51 m, depth 0.36 m vertical sides, flat bottom. Dia. post socket 0.26 m, depth 0.23 m.
Fill: Brown soil. Chalk packing, with large lumps at the sides.
Daub: 9 pieces of yellow daub with wattle impressions, Type II/III.
Charcoal: Oak and hawthorn charcoal.
Small finds: Antler weaving comb (Fig. 4.4, no. 2).
Pottery: 1 body sherd, fabric 11.

PH 209
Dia. 0.46 m, depth 0.48 m vertical sides, flat bottom. Dia. post socket 0.28 m, depth 0.31 m.
Fill: Dark soil with lumps of chalk. Numercus large chalk and flint lumps in the packing, and also a sub-rectangular burnt piece of Westbury Iron Ore Sandstone.

PH 210
Dia. 0.26 m, depth 0.31 m vertical sides, flat bottom. No clear trace of the post
Fill: Brown soil with patches of clay. Chalk packing at the sides.
Daub: 20 pieces of Cob daub, some with a number of flat surfaces on which were wattle impressions, Freeman Type I.
Charcoal: Fragments of charcoal.
Pottery: 1 body sherd, fabric 41 (Fig. 3.13, no. 6); 1 body sherd, fabric 14, 1 body sherd, fabric 42.

The Internal Postholes

PH 231
Dia. 0.31 m, depth 0.23 m; vertical sides, flat bottom.
Fill: Chalky soil with large lumps of chalk.

PH 191 Not illustrated
Dia. 0.33 m, depth 0.10 m.
Fill: Chalky soil.

PH 192
Dia. 0.36 m, depth 0.26 m, sloping sides, flat bottom.
Fill: Brown soil with collapsed packing of flint and chalk.

PH 187
Dia. 0.41 m, depth 0.13 m; sloping sides, almost flat bottom.
Fill: Chalky grey soil.
Pottery: 1 body sherd, fabric 13 (Fig. 3.13, no.3).

PH 188 Not illustrated
Dia. 0.26 m, depth 0.13 m).
Fill: Chalky soil.

PH 211
Dia. 0.41 m, depth 0.31 m vertical sides, flat bottom.
Fill: Brown soil with lumps of chalk and flint.
Pottery: 1 body sherd, fabric 12; 2 body sherds, fabric 14.

PH 220
Dia. 0.36 m, depth 0.23 m; sloping sides, rounded bottom.
Fill: Brown soil with lumps of chalk.

PH 219 Not illustrated
No information recorded.

PH 202
Dia. 0.48 m, depth 0.15 m; sloping sides, flat bottom.
Fill: Dark soil with large lumps of chalk.
Bone frags: 2 horse.

PH 205 Not illustrated
Dia. 0.28 m, depth 0.15 m.
Fill: Fine dark soil.

The External Postholes

PH 240
Dia. 0.26 m, depth 0.10 m; sloping sides, almost flat bottom.
Fill: Dark soil with lumps of chalk.

PH 212 Not illustrated
Dia. 0.31 m, depth 0.21 m.
Fill: Grey brown chalky soil. Some packing stones at the sides.

PH 216
Dia. 0.69 m, depth 0.38 m; almost vertical sides, flat bottom. Dia. post socket 0.48 m, depth 0.33 m. A recut post hole.
Fill: Brown soil with lumps of chalk. Chalk packing.
Daub: 15 small pieces of orange clay daub and 2 whitish pieces of cob daub; no wattle impressions, Freeman Types I and II/III.
Charcoal: Oak, hawthorn, hazel and ash charcoal.
Small finds: Chert rubber
Pottery: 2 joining sherds from probably a carinated bowl, fabric 11 (Fig. 3.13, no. 2); 1 rim sherd from bowl, fabric 12 (Fig. 3.13, no.4); 10 body sherds, fabric 12; 1 body sherd, fabric 41.

PH 218
Dia. 0.81 m, depth 0.53 m vertical sides, flat bottom.
Fill: Large lumps of chalk and flint.
Small finds: Fragment of sandstone rubber (Fig. 4.11, no. 4).

PH 215
Dia. 0.31 m, depth 018 m sloping sides, rounded bottom.
Fill: Grey soil with several lumps of chalk.
Charcoal: Fragments of oak charcoal.

PH 217 Not illustrated
Dia. 0.71 m, depth 0.41 m. Dia. post 0.18 m.
Fill: Dark soil.
Charcoal: Flecks of unspeciated charcoal. Radiocabon sample HAR-256
Pottery: 1 body sherd, fabric 42.

PH 226
Dia. 0.66 m, depth 0.51 m; almost straight sides, flat bottom.
Fill: Large lumps of chalk and flint.

PH 206 Not illustrated
Dia. 0.31 m, depth 0.10 m.
Fill: Dark soil with lumps of chalk at the bottom.

PH 201 Not illustrated
Dia. 0.28 m, depth 0.13 m.
Fill: Dark soil with lumps of chalk.
Pottery: 1 body sherd, fabric 13.

PH 221
Dia. 0.31 m, depth 0.23 m; almost vertical sides, irregular bottom.
Fill: Dark soil with lumps of chalk and flint.

PH 222 Not illustrated
Dia. 0.15 m, depth 0.18 m.
Fill: Dark soil with a few lumps of chalk.
Pottery: 1 body sherd, fabric 11; 1 base sherd, fabric 13.

PH 223
Dia. 0.48 m, depth 0.23 m; sloping sides, irregular bottom.
Fill: Dark soil with large lumps of flint.

PH 236
Dia. 0.33 m, depth 0.18 m; rounded bottom.
Fill: Dark soil with small lumps of chalk.

PH 189 Not illustrated
Dia. 0.26 m, depth 0.10 m.
Fill: Chalky soil.

Appendix 2B

STRUCTURAL REMAINS: THE PITS

Enclosure I

P.1 Fig. 2.9 (section and plan)
Pit dia. 1.67 m, depth 0.92 m; almost vertical sides, flat bottom.
Fill: Layer 1:- dark soil with small lumps of chalk and flint; layer 2:- chalk rubble; layer 3:- brown soil with some chalk and burnt flint lumps; layer 4:- chalk lumps with a little brown earth.
Bone frags: 27 sheep/goat, 4 cattle, 2 rodent (voles).
Pyrites: 1 large piece of struck and burnt pyrites, plus 3 smaller fragments.
Pottery: About 100 sherds of large 'situla' jar, fabric 14 (Fig. 3.17, no. 1); 1 sherd from vessel, fabric 31 (Fig. 3.17, no. 2); 4 sherds possible globular jar, fabric 43 (Fig. 3.17, no. 3); 1 sherd from vessel, fabric 41 (Fig. 3.17, no. 4); 1 sherd carinated bowl, furrowed decoration, fabric 12 (Fig. 3.17, no. 5); 1 sherd from vessel, fabric 32 (Fig. 3.17, no. 6); 1 sherd from vessel, probably carinated jar, fabric 13 (Fig. 3.17, no. 7); 1 body sherd, fabric 11; 19 body sherds, fabric 12; 1 base sherd and 10 body sherds, fabric 21; 6 body sherds, fabric 22; 8 body sherds, fabric 31; 17 body sherds, fabric 41; 1 base sherd and 13 body sherds, fabric 42; 6 body sherds, fabric 51; 1 body sherd, fabric 52.

P.2 Fig. 2.9 (section and plan)
Pit dia. 1.78 m, depth 0.90 m; inward-sloping sides, flat bottom.
Fill: Layer 1:- dark soil with lumps of burnt flint; layer 2:- chalky soil with chalk rubble beneath; layer 3:- dark soil.
Bone frags: 22 sheep/goat, 17 cattle, 8 horse, 4 pig, 1 man (metatarsal).
Pyrites: 2 balls of pyrites, plus 2 fragments.

P.3 Fig. 2.9 (section and plan)
Pit dia. 1.12 m, depth 0.46 m; almost vertical sides, flat bottom.
Fill: Layer 1:- dark brown soil with chalk and flint lumps; layer 2:- chalk rubble.

P.4 Fig. 2.9 (plan)
Pit dia. 1.60 m, depth 0.76 m.
Fill: Layer 1:- loose brown soil with chalk and burnt flint lumps; layer 2:- chalk rubble.
Bone frags: 12 sheep/goat, 1 cattle, 1 pig, 1 dog, 1 frog/toad.
Pyrites: 1 piece of struck and burnt pyrites.

Enclosure II

P.1
Pit dia. 0.97 m, depth 0.38 m; gently inward-sloping sides, flat bottom.
Fill: Layer 2:- fine brown soil with tightly packed heavy flints and small lumps of chalk.
Daub: Freeman Types I and IV.
Bone frags: 26 sheep/goat, 23 cattle, 2 horse, 5 pig, 1 man (infant/adolescent long bone: (Chapter 5).
Small finds: Part of chalk loom weight (Fig. 4.7, no. 1).

P.2
Pit dia. 2.44 m, depth 1.45 m; almost vertical sides, flat bottom.
Fill: Layer 2:- brown soil with small lumps of chalk; layer 3:- chalk rubble; layer 4:- chalky wash; layer 5:- ash; layer 6:- small lumps of chalk; layer 7:- chalky soil and ash.
Charcoal: Oak, hawthorn and hazel charcoal.
Bone frags: 26 sheep/goat, 47 cattle, 13 pig, 8 dog.
Small finds: Iron tool (Fig. 4.2, no. 8).
Pottery: 1 sherd from pear-shaped jar, fabric 32 (Fig. 3.30, no. 1); 1 sherd from jar, fabric 31 (Fig. 3.30, no. 2); 1 sherd 'saucepan vessel', fabric 31 (Fig. 3.30, no. 3); 1 sherd jar, fabric 31 (Fig. 3.30, no. 4); 1 body sherd, fabric 12; 1 body sherd, fabric 13; 1 rim sherd and 10 body sherds, fabric 21; 1 rim sherd and 12 body sherds, fabric 31; 1 rim sherd, 1 base sherd and 3 body sherds, fabric 33.

P.3
Pit dia. 1.12 m, depth 0.41 m; gently inward-sloping sides, sloping bottom.
Fill: Layer 2:- sticky dark brown soil with small lumps of chalk and flint.
Bone frags: 3 sheep/goat, 9 cattle, 1 pig.
Pottery: 11 sherds, many joining, from 'saucepan' vessel, fabric 31 (Fig. 3.30, no. 1); 1 sherd pear-shaped jar, fabric 15 (Fig. 3.30, no. 2); 2 body sherds, fabric 31; 1 rim and 4 body sherds, fabric 33.

P.4
Pit dia. 1.58 m, depth 0.43 m; almost vertical sides, flat bottom.
Fill: Layer 2:- chalky soil; layer 3:- tightly packed chalk rubble; layer 4:- dark grey soil. The rammed layer of chalk lumps with dark soil beneath suggests that this pit had two phases.
Daub: Freeman Type IV.
Miscellaneous finds: 1 large orange clay object.
Pottery: 1 rim and 1 body sherd, fabric 21; 1 base sherd, fabric 32; 1 body sherd, fabric 42; 1 base sherd, fabric 51.

P.5 Not illustrated
Pit dia. 1.60 m, depth 1.75m.
Fill: Brown soil and flints at the top, below which were layers of chalk lumps, organic material and ash. Fill very loose at the bottom, with burnt flints and lumps of chalk.
Charcoal: Hazel charcoal.
Bone frags: 142 sheep/goat, 140 cattle, 40 horse, 34 pig, 1 human (occipital, young adult: see Chapter 5). Remains of one complete lamb, one month (?).
Pyrites: 1 piece of pyrites.
Pottery: 10 sherds, some joining from dish, fabric 21 (Fig. 3.18, no. 1); 2 sherds from vessel, probably pedestal jar, fabric 21 (Fig. 3.18, no. 2); 35 sherds, some joining from pedestal jar, fabric 33 (Fig. 3.18, no. 3); 21 sherds, some joining from large 'situla' jar, fabric 31 (Fig. 3.18, no. 4); 8 sherds, some joining from 'situla' jar, fabric 31 (Fig. 3.18, no. 5); 3 joining sherds from barrel jar, fabric 31 (Fig. 3.18, no. 6); 10 sherds, some joining from barrel jar, fabric 13 (Fig. 3.18, no. 7); 1 sherd from dish, fabric 31 (Fig.

3.18, no. 8); 1 sherd from vessel, fabric 42 (Fig. 3.18, no. 9); 3 body sherds, fabric 12; 1 base sherd and 10 body sherds, fabric 13; 1 body sherd, fabric 14; 1 rim sherd and 4 body sherds, fabric 21; 1 rim sherd, 2 base sherds and 18 body sherds, fabric 31; 1 base sherd and 1 body sherd, fabric 32; 1 base and 4 body sherds, fabric 41; 3 body sherds, fabric 42; 3 body sherds, fabric 52.

P.6 Not illustrated = part of H4
Pit dia. uncertain, depth 2.13 m.

P.7
Pit dia. 1.67 m, depth 1.60 m; rounded sides, fairly flat bottom.
Fill: Layer 2:- brown soil with flints and small lumps of chalk; layer 3:- powdered chalk; layer 4:- chalky soil with lumps of chalk and flint; layer 5:- brown soil with patches of clay; layer 6:- brown soil with lumps of chalk; layer 7:- grey chalky soil with small chalk lumps; layer 8:- chalk rubble.
Daub: 1 crumbled mass of cob daub, Freeman Type II/III.
Bone frags: 143 sheep/goat, 61 cattle, 13 horse, 19 pig, 43 dog.
Small finds: Part of chalk loom weight (Fig. 4.7, no. 2).
Slag: 2 large pieces and 15 smaller fragments of iron slag.
Miscellaneous finds: Small hearth bottom (analysed by AM Lab.).
Miscellaneous finds: 1 piece of burnt clay.
Pottery: 1 sherd jar, fabric 21 (Fig. 3.30, no. 1); 1 sherd pear-shaped jar, fabric 32 (Fig. 3.30, no. 2); 1 sherd pear-shaped jar, fabric 12 (Fig. 3.30, no. 3); 1 sherd from probable barrel jar, fabric 21 (Fig. 3.30, no. 4); 1 sherd from probable 'situla' jar, fabric 32 (Fig. 3.30, no. 5); 2 body sherds, fabric 12; 2 body sherds, fabric 13; 2 base sherds and 4 body sherds, fabric 14; 1 base and 9 body sherds, fabric 21; 6 body sherds, fabric 31; 4 body sherds, fabric 32; 1 base sherd, fabric 41; 2 body sherds, fabric 51.

P.8 Not illustrated
Pit dia. uncertain, depth 0.51 m; flat bottom.
Fill: Dark soil with layer of rammed chalk making a false bottom, below which was another later of dark soil with small lumps of chalk. A hole with dark grey soil (Dia. *c.* 0.41 m was cut through all layers below from the top layer.
Bone frags: 20 sheep/goat, 8 cattle, 5 horse, 1 pig, 1 human (infant occipital).
Pottery: 1 rim sherd and 1 body sherd, fabric 31; 1 body sherd, fabric 42.

P.9
Pit dia. 1.93 m, depth 2.08 m; sloping sides, base wider than top, flat bottom.
Fill: Layer 2:- dark brown soil; layer 3:- chalky soil with small lumps of chalk and flint; layer 4:- loose chalk; layer 5:- chalky soil; layer 6:- loose chalk; layer 7:- chalky soil with very small lumps of chalk; layer 8:- brown soil; layer 9:- chalk wash.
Bone frags: 2 sheep/goat, 7 cattle, 2 horse, 1 deer (roe?) antler fragment.
Pottery: 2 joining sherds jar, fabric 31 (Fig. 3.30, no. 1); 1 sherd from probable barrel jar, fabric 31 (Fig. 3.30, no. 2); 1 sherd from vessel, fabric 21 (Fig. 3.30, no. 3); 2 sherds jar, fabric 21 (Fig. 3.30, no. 4); 1 sherd from 'situla' jar, fabric 21 (Fig. 3.30, no. 5); 3 body sherd, fabric 12; 1 body sherd, fabric 14; 1 body sherd, fabric 15; 4 body sherds, fabric 21; 1 rim sherd and 11 body sherds, fabric 31; 3 body sherds, fabric 32; 2 body sherds, fabric 51.

P.10 Not illustrated
Pit dia. 1.2 m, depth 0.26 m.
Fill: Dark soil with hard packed chalk lumps beneath.
Pottery: 2 base sherds and 17 body sherds, fabric 13; 1 body sherd, fabric 31; 2 body sherds, fabric 41; 1 base sherd and 6 body sherds, fabric 42.

P.11
Pit dia. 1.42 m, depth 0.46 m; almost vertical sides, irregular bottom.
Fill: Layer 2:- small lumps of chalk; layer 3:- brown soil with lumps of chalk and flint; layer 4:- dark ashy soil.
Pottery: 21 sherds, many joining, from jar, fabric 19 (Fig. 3.28, no. 1); 2 sherds, not joining, from 'situla' jar, fabric 32 (Fig. 3.28, no. 2); numerous sherds from tall jar, fabric 13 (Fig. 3.28, no. 3); 1 base sherd and 2 body sherds, fabric 13; 2 rim sherds and 5 body sherds, fabric 21; 6 body sherds, fabric 31; 3 body sherds, fabric 32; 2 body sherds, fabric 52.

P.12 = part of H4

P.13
Pit dia. 0.99 m, depth 0.61 m; irregular sides, fairly flat bottom.
Fill: Layer 2:- small lumps of chalk; layer 3:- brown soil with small lumps of chalk; layer 4:- ash and clay; layer 5:- brown soil with small lumps of chalk.
Bone frags: 65 sheep/goat, 11 horse, 8 cattle, 2 pig.
Small finds: Iron ring-headed pin (Fig. 4.1, no. 10), broken tip of bone gouge or weaving beater (not illustrated).
Slag: 1 piece of slag (analysed by AM Laboratory, Chapter 5).
Pottery: 1 rim sherd, fabric 31.

P.14
Pit dia. 2.64 m, depth 1.58 m; irregular sides and bottom.
Fill: Layer 2:- chalky soil with small lumps of chalk; layer 3:- loose chalk; layer 4:- ash; layer 5:- chalk rubble; layer 6:- ash; layer 7:- brown soil and charcoal; layer 8:- chalky soil with lumps of chalk.
Charcoal: Hazel charcoal and probably oak and hawthorn charcoal.
Bone frags: 5 sheep/goat, 20 cattle, 6 horse.
Small finds: Fragment of a large shale ring (Fig. 4.2, no. 15).
Pottery: 9 sherds, most joining, squat jar, fabric 12 (Fig. 3.27, no. 1); 9 sherds, most joining, from globular jar, fabric 21 (Fig. 3.27, no. 2); 1 sherd jar, fabric 21 (Fig. 3.27, no. 3); 23 sherds, many joining, squat jar, fabric 33 (Fig. 3.27, no. 4); numerous sherds tall jar, fabric 13 (Fig. 3.27, no. 5); numerous sherds globular tall jar with paired lugs, fabric 31 (Fig. 3.27, no. 6); 5 joining sherds jar, fabric 21 (Fig. 3.27, no. 7); 5 body sherds, fabric 13; 1 body sherd, fabric 14; 1 body sherd, fabric 21; 3 base sherds and 5 body sherds, fabric 21; 8 body sherds, fabric 31; 1 base and 3 body sherds, fabric 32; 1 base sherd, fabric 41.

P.15 (Cutting E)
Pit dia. uncertain, depth 0.94 m, inward-sloping sides and sloping bottom.
Fill: Layers 2:- brown soil with chalk lumps; layer 5:-

chalk lumps; layer 6:- brown soil; layer 7:- brown soil with chalk lumps.

P.16 Not illustrated
Pit dia. 0.69 m, depth 0.38 m.
Fill: unrecorded.

P.17
Pit dia. 1.37 m, depth 1.07 m; almost vertical sides, flat bottom.
Fill: Layer 1:- chalky soil; layer 2:- small lumps of chalk; layer 3:- chalky soil; layer 4:- dark soil; layer 5:- loose chalk and flint; layer 6:- dark soil above loose chalk; layer 7:- dark soil; layer 8:- brown soil with small lumps of chalk; layer 9:- dark soil with small lumps of chalk.
Small finds: fragment of bronze bracelet (Fig. 4.1, no. 6), broken tip of bone gouge or weaving beater (Fig. 4.4, no. 11).
Pottery: 2 base sherds and 15 body sherds, fabric 12; 1 body sherd, fabric 13; 1 body sherd, fabric 41; 10 body sherds, fabric 42.

P.18
Pit dia. 2.47 m, depth 1.42 m; roughly cylindrical shape. Adjoining Working Hollow 1.
Fill: Layer 1:- chalky soil with small lumps of chalk; layer 2 (H.1):- small lumps of chalk; layer 3 (H.1):- chalk rubble; layer 4:- brown soil with small lumps of chalk; layer 5:- chalky soil; layer 6:- brown soil with small lumps of chalk; layer 7:- chalky soil with small lumps of chalk; layer 8:- dark soil.
Bone frags: 42 sheep/goat, 21 cattle, 9 horse, 3 pig, 2 dog, 1 human (adult parietal fragment: Chapter 5).
Pottery: 5 sherds, some joining, from jar, fabric 31 (Fig. 3.29, no. 1); 2 sherds, not joining, 'saucepan' vessel, fabric 31 (Fig. 3.29, no. 2); 1 sherd pear-shaped jar, fabric 12 (Fig. 3.29, no. 3); 1 sherd pear-shaped jar, fabric 32 (Fig. 3.29, no. 4); 1 sherd from vessel, fabric 12 (Fig. 3.29, no. 5); 2 sherds pear-shaped jar, fabric 31 (Fig. 3.29, no. 6); 1 sherd probable globular jar, fabric 31 (Fig. 3.29, no. 7); 1 sherd 'saucepan' vessel, fabric 32 (Fig. 3.29, no. 8); 1 sherd pear-shaped jar, fabric 15 (Fig. 3.29, no. 9); 1 sherd jar, fabric 32 (Fig. 3.29, no. 10); 1 sherd from vessel, fabric 31 (Fig. 3.29, no. 11); 2 base sherds and 10 body sherds, fabric 11; 1 base sherd and 20 body sherds, fabric 12; 6 body sherds, fabric 13; 3 base sherds and 12 body sherds, fabric 14; 3 base sherds and 4 body sherds, fabric 21; 15 body sherds, fabric 31; 11 body sherds, fabric 32; 1 body sherd, fabric 33; 1 rim sherd and 27 body sherds, fabric 41; 1 base sherd and 12 body sherds, fabric 42; 2 body sherds, fabric 43; 2 body sherds, fabric 44.

P.19
Pit dia. 2.03x1.22 m, depth 0.87 m; rounded sides, flat bottom.
Cuts Pit 32.
Fill: Layer 1:- brown soil with small lumps of chalk; layer 2:- chalk rubble.
Small finds: One half of a shale ring (Fig. 4.2, no. 14).
Pottery: 1 sherd from vessel, fabric 21 (Fig. 3.30, no. 1); 1 sherd from vessel, fabric 31 (Fig. 3.30, no. 2); 1 sherd from vessel, fabric 13 (Fig. 3.30, no. 3); 1 sherd from vessel, fabric 42 (Fig. 3.30, no. 4); 1 base sherd, fabric 11; 14 body sherds, fabric 12; 7 body sherds, fabric 13; 1 body sherd, fabric 15; 2 base sherds and 23 body sherds, fabric 21; 1 base sherd and 20 body sherds, fabric 31; 4 body sherds, fabric 32; 1 body sherd, fabric 33; 1 base and 2 body sherds, fabric 42.

P.20 Not illustrated
Pit. dia. 1.50 m depth 0.84 m.
Fill: Dark soil with small lumps of chalk.
Pottery: 1 base sherd, fabric 13; 1 base sherd and 3 body sherds, fabric 31; 2 body sherds, fabric 41.

P.21
Pit dia. 1.42 m, depth 1.63 m; irregular sides, flared top, fairly flat bottom.
Fill: Layer 1:- dark grey soil with small lumps of chalk and flint; layer 2:- chalky soil with small lumps of chalk and flint; layer 3:- dark brown soil; layer 3A:- light brown soil; layer 4:- chalky soil with small lumps of chalk.
Daub: Freeman Types I and V.
Bone frags: 1 part of lower mandible of human adult: (Chapter 5).
Miscellaneous finds: Large piece of unbaked clay, soft when found.
Pottery: 1 sherd from 'situla' jar, fabric 31 (Fig. 3.25, no. 1); 1 sherd from 'saucepan' vessel, fabric 22 (Fig. 3.25, no. 2); 3 sherds, not joining, miniature barrel jar, fabric 41 (Fig. 3.25, no. 3); 1 sherd pear-shaped jar, fabric 32 (Fig. 3.25, no. 4); 1 sherd globular jar, fabric 22 (Fig. 3.25, no. 5); 1 sherd from jar, fabric 42 (Fig. 3.25, no. 6); 7 sherds, some joining, 'situla' jar, fabric 12 (Fig. 3.25, no. 7); 1 body sherd, fabric 21; 2 body sherds, fabric 23; 6 body sherds, fabric 31; 5 body sherds, fabric 32; 1 rim sherd, 1 base and 4 body sherds, fabric 41; 1 rim sherd, fabric 42; 2 body sherds, fabric 51.

P.22
Pit dia. 0.97 m, depth 0.76 m; almost vertical sides, flat bottom.
Fill: Layer 2:- chalky soil; layer 3:- dark soil with some fairly large lumps of chalk and flint.
Bone frags: 45 sheep/goat, 48 cattle, 4 horse, 8 pig, 6 dog.
Small finds: Part of chalk loom weight (Fig. 4.7, no. 4).
Pottery: 16 sherds, many joining, 'saucepan' vessel, fabric 12 (Fig. 3.29, no. 1); 14 sherds globular jar, fabric 32 (Fig. 3.29, no. 2); 1 sherd pear-shaped jar, fabric 21 (Fig. 3.29, no. 3); 1 sherd 'saucepan' vessel, fabric 32 (Fig. 3.29, no. 4); 3 base sherds, fabric 11; 3 base sherds, fabric 24; 1 rim and 3 body sherds, fabric 31; 5 body sherds, fabric 32; 3 body sherds, fabric 41.

P.23 Not illustrated
Pit dia. uncertain, depth 0.76 m.
Fill: Dark soil with small lumps of chalk.
Pottery: 2 body sherds, fabric 13; 2 base sherds and 5 body sherds, fabric 32.

P.24 (Cutting F) Not illustrated
Pit dia. uncertain, depth 1.04 m.
Fill: Dark soil with small lumps of chalk.
Pottery: 1 sherd from vessel, fabric 31 (Fig. 3.30, no. 1); 1 sherd from vessel, fabric 21 (Fig. 3.30, no. 2).

P.25 (Cutting F)
Pit dia. 2.44 m, depth 2.05 m, almost vertical sides, sloping bottom.
Fill: Layer 1:- dark soil with flint lumps; layer 2:- brown earth with a few chalk lumps; layer 3:- grey brown soil; layer 4:- chalk lumps; layer 5:- dark organic soil; layer 6:- brown soil with chalk and flint lumps; layer 7:- chalk lumps; layer 8:- dark soil; layer 9:- chalk lumps.
Pottery: 1 body sherd, fabric 13; 3 base sherds, fabric 31; 1 body sherd, fabric 41.

P.26
Pit dia. 1.07 m, depth 0.53 m; almost vertical sides, flat bottom.
Fill: Layer 2:- chalky soil with large lumps of chalk; layer 3:- chalk rubble.
Bone frags: 2 sheep/goat, 4 cattle.
Pottery: 2 base sherds and 2 body sherds, fabric 13; 1 body sherd, fabric 23; 1 rim sherd, fabric 32; 1 body sherd, fabric 41.

P.27
Pit dia. 1.22 m, depth 0.71 m; rounded sides, gently sloping bottom.
Fill: Layer 2:- chalky soil with very small lumps of chalk and flint; layer 3:- chalky soil with medium-sized lumps of chalk and flint; layer 4:- lumps of chalk and flint; layer 5:- chalky soil with chalk rubble.
Small finds: Chalk loomweight (Fig. 4.9, no. 1).
Pottery: 1 rim sherd, fabric 11; 1 body sherd, fabric 12; 3 body sherds, fabric 13; 2 base sherds, fabric 25; 1 body sherd, fabric 31.

P.28
Pit dia. 0.87 m, depth 0.53 m; almost vertical sides, flat bottom.
Fill: Layer 2:- chalky soil with dense small chalk and flint lumps; layer 3:- chalk rubble.
Pottery: 1 rim sherd, fabric 31.

P.29 Not illustrated
Pit dia. 0.66 m, depth 0.46 m; irregular sides and bottom.
Fill: Dark soil with burnt flints.
Charcoal: Oak charcoal.
Pottery: 3 body sherds, fabric 13; 2 body sherds, fabric 14; 2 body sherds, fabric 22; 1 body sherds, fabric 41; 1 body sherd, fabric 44.

P.30
Pit dia. 1.45 m, depth 0.61 m; inward-sloping sides, fairly flat bottom.
Fill: Layer 1:- chalky soil with small lumps of chalk; layer 2:- chalk wash with very small chalk lumps.
Pottery: 1 sherd from jar, fabric 31 (Fig. 3.30, no. 1); 1 sherd dish, fabric unrecorded (Fig. 3.30, no. 2).

P.31
Pit dia. minimum 2.44 m, depth 2.13 m; inward-sloping sides, flat bottom.
Next to H.4 and PH 237.
Fill: Layer 2:- dark soil with small chalk and flint lumps; layer 3:- chalky soil with very small lumps of chalk and flint; layer 4:- loose chalk and flint; layer 5:- small lumps of chalk; layer 6:- dark grey soil; layer 7:- loose chalk; layer 8:- brown soil with some fairly large lumps of chalk.
Bone frags: 2 sheep/goat, 1 cattle skull (fragmentary, small type), 16 horse.
Pottery: 1 body sherd, fabric 12; 2 body sherds, fabric 14; 2 body sherds, fabric 21; 8 body sherds, fabric 31; 9 body sherds, fabric 32.

P.31
Pit dia. 1.17 m, depth 0.43 m; inward-sloping sides, fairly flat bottom.
Fill: Layer 2:- fine dark soil with sparse small chalk lumps.

P.32
Pit dia. uncertain, depth 1.60 m; rounded sides, flared top, flat bottom.
Cut by Pit 19.
Fill: Layer 1:- chalky soil with small lumps of chalk; layer 2:- loose chalk; layer 3:- chalky soil with small lumps of chalk; layer 4:- loose chalk; layer 5:- brown soil with small lumps of chalk; layer 6:- loose chalk; layer 7:- chalky soil; layer 8:- chalk rubble; layer 9:- charcoal.

P.33/33B Not illustrated
Pit dia. uncertain, depth 2.21 m.
Below Working Hollow 2.
Fill: Dark soil with small lumps of chalk.
Small finds: Complete profile of crucible or miniature barrel jar (Fig. 4.13, no. 2), also featured in the pottery catalogue, (Fig. 3.25,no. 4).
Pottery: Complete profile of miniature bowl, fabric 44 (Fig. 3.25, no. 1); 2 joining sherds jar, fabric 31 (Fig. 3.25, no. 2); 1 sherd 'saucepan' vessel, fabric 32 (Fig. 3.25, no. 3); complete profile crucible or miniature barrel jar, fabric 42 (Fig. 3.25, no. 4); 1 sherd jar, fabric 12 (Fig. 3.25, no. 5); 1 sherd 'saucepan' vessel, fabric 13 (Fig. 3.25, no. 6); 1 sherd vessel, fabric 31 (Fig. 3.25, no. 7); 1 sherd dish, fabric 33 (Fig. 3.25, no. 8); 1 sherd vessel, fabric 31 (Fig. 3.25, no. 9); 2 joining sherds 'situla' jar, fabric 31 (Fig. 3.25, no. 10); 1 sherd probable barrel jar, fabric 32 (Fig. 3.25, no. 11); 1 sherd vessel, fabric 11 (Fig. 3.25, no. 12); 1 sherd vessel, fabric 11 (Fig. 3.25, no. 13); 1 body sherd, fabric 11; 3 body sherds, fabric 12; 2 body sherds, fabric 13; 1 body sherd, fabric 14; 1 body sherd, fabric 21; 1 body sherd, fabric 22; 8 body sherds, fabric 31; 1 base sherd and 6 body sherds, fabric 32; 7 body sherds, fabric 41; 5 body sherds, fabric 42; 4 body sherds, fabric 43

P.34
Pit dia. 1.42 m, depth 0.92 m; almost vertical sides, fairly flat bottom.
Fill: Layer 1:- brown earth with small lumps of chalk; lumps of chalk; layer 3:- dark soil; layer 4:- brown soil with small lumps of chalk; layer 5:- dark soil; layer 6:- chalk lumps; layer 7:- dark soil.
Bone frags: 14 sheep/goat, 16 cattle, 3 pig.
Pottery: 3 sherds, 2 joining from 'situla' jar, fabric 31 (Fig. 3.31, no. 1).

P.35 Not illustrated
Pit dia. not recorded, depth 0.71 m; irregular sides and bottom.
Fill: Brown soil with small lumps of chalk.

P.36
Pit dia. 1.42 m, depth 1.53 m; almost vertical sides, fairly flat bottom.
Fill: Layer 1:- chalky soil with small lumps of chalk; layer 2:- brown soil with flint and chalk lumps; layer 3:- chalky soil with small lumps of chalk and flint; layer 3A:- ash and charcoal.
Charcoal: Oak, hawthorn and hazel charcoal.
Bone frags: Layer 1:- 10 sheep/goat, 1 pig, 1 horse; Layer 2:- 4 sheep/goat, 1 cattle, 4 horse, 2 pig; Layer 3:- 16 sheep/goat, 3 cattle, 1 horse, 2 pig.
Small finds: Iron rod, punch or awl (Fig. 4.2, no. 6), part of chalk loom weight (Fig. 4.8, no. 3), part of stone weight (not illustrated).
Pottery: 1 body sherd, fabric 11; 3 rim sherds and 11 body sherds, fabric 12; 12 body sherds, fabric 13; 3 base sherds, fabric 14; 3 body sherds, fabric 19; 14 body

sherds, fabric 21; 5 body sherds, fabric 31; 4 body sherds, fabric 42; 1 body sherd, fabric 51.

P.37
Pit dia. 1.27 m, depth 1.58 m; irregular sides, fairly flat bottom.
Fill: Layer 1:- brown soil with small lumps of chalk and flint; layer 2:- charcoal layer with chalk and flint rubble beneath; layer 2A:- large flints; layer 3:- chalky soil; layer 3A:- chalk rubble; layer 4:- burnt clay on top of greyish fibre remains (cloth?) or mould, and below this a large quantity of carbonised grain.
Daub: 5 scraps of burnt orange daub, 2 pinkish pieces. 1 chalk cob piece with wattle impressions; 6 other pieces, burnt and unburnt, 2 with wattle impressions; Freeman Types I and II/III.
Charcoal: Hawthorn, hazel, and probably oak charcoal.
Bone frags: 21 sheep/goat, 1 cattle, 2 horse, 11 pig, 2 frog/toad, 1 human.
Small finds: Penannular iron brooch (Fig. 4.1, no. 8A), iron knife (Fig. 4.2, no. 7), socketed iron sickle (Fig. 4.2. no. 11), bone tool handle (Fig. 4.4, no. 1), ceramic sling bullet (Fig. 4.13, no. 8), part of chalk loom weight (Fig. 4.8, no. 1); 2 stone loomweights (Fig. 4.9, nos. 2 and 3).
Pottery: 1 sherd carinated cup with grooved decoration, fabric 42 (Fig. 3.7, no. 14); 16 sherds, some joining from dish, fabric 21 (Fig. 3.19, no. 1); 1 sherd vessel, probable pedestal jar, fabric 12 (Fig. 3.19, no. 2); 2 sherds jar, fabric 31 (Fig. 3.19, no. 3); 2 sherds jar, fabric 31 (Fig. 3.19, no. 4); 2 sherds jar, fabric 31 (Fig. 3.19, no. 5); many sherds tall 'situla' jar, fabric 21 (Fig. 3.19, no. 6); 1 sherd pedestal jar, fabric 13 (Fig. 3.19, no. 7); 2 sherds 'situla' jar, fabric 31 (Fig. 3.19, no. 8); 4 sherds 'situla' jar, fabric 31 (Fig. 3.19, no. 9); 2 body sherds, fabric 11; 17 body sherds, fabric 12; 1 rim sherd and 7 body sherds, fabric 13; 1 rim sherd and 35 body sherds, fabric 21; 17 body sherds, fabric 22; 2 body sherds, fabric 26; 39 body sherds, fabric 31; 3 body sherds, fabric 32; 5 body sherds, fabric 41; 1 base sherd and 5 body sherds, fabric 42; 1 body sherd, fabric 52.

P.38
Pit dia. 1.37 m, depth 0.66 m; rounded sides and sloping bottom. Cuts Pit 45.
Fill: Layer 1:- chalky soil with small lumps of chalk; layer 2:- dark soil with small lumps of chalk; layer 3:- chalk rubble.
Daub: 8 pieces of cob daub, one or two with wattle marks; Freeman Type II/III.
Charcoal: Oak and hazel charcoal.
Bone frags: 10 sheep/goat, 1 horse, 1 dog, vole.
Pottery: 1 body sherd, fabric 11; 2 rim sherds and 3 body sherds; 4 body sherds, fabric 14; 6 body sherds, fabric 31; 3 base sherds, fabric 41.

P.39
Pit dia. 1.67 m depth 0.97; irregular sides, fairly flat bottom.
Adjoining Pit 43.
Fill: Layer 1:- chalky soil with lumps of chalk and flint; layer 2:- soft, dark soil; layer 3:- chalky soil with small lumps of chalk; layer 3A:- brown soil; layer 4:- chalk rubble; layer 5:- dark brown soil.
Daub: 32 pieces of cob daub, some Freeman Type I.
Charcoal: Hazel charcoal, and probably oak charcoal.
Bone frags: 24 sheep/goat, 9 cattle, 31 horse (including complete skull from small, young animal), 2 pig, 1 dog.
Small finds: Iron rod bent into a half loop (Fig. 4.2, no. 1), bone weaving comb (Fig. 4.4, no. 3), part of chalk loom weight (Fig.4.7, no. 5), chalk loom weight (Fig. 4.7, no. 6).
Pottery: 1 sherd pear-shaped jar, fabric 32 (Fig. 3.31, no. 1); 2 sherds pear-shaped jar, fabric 12 (Fig. 3.31, no. 2); 1 sherd jar, fabric 31 (Fig. 3.31, no. 3); 3 base sherds and 14 body sherds, fabric 12; 5 body sherds, fabric 13; 7 body sherds, fabric 14; 1 base sherd and 18 body sherds, fabric 21: 1 body sherd, fabric 24; 1 rim sherd and 5 body sherds, fabric 31; 2 rim sherds, 1 base sherd and 15 body sherds, fabric 32; 1 base sherd and 11 body sherds, fabric 41.

P.40
Pit dia. 1.53 m, depth 0.53 m; irregular sides, flat bottom.
Fill: Layer 1:- Dark soil with small lumps of chalk; layer 2:- loose chalky soil with very small chalk lumps.
Charcoal: Oak, hawthorn and hazel charcoal.
Bone frags: 11 sheep/goat, 3 cattle, 2 pig.
Small finds: ceramic spindle whorl (Fig. 4.12, no. 4).
Pottery: 1 sherd from jar, fabric 12 (Fig. 3.22, no. 1); 1 sherd 'situla' jar, fabric 12 (Fig. 3.22, no. 2); 3 joining sherds carinated jar, fabric 41 (Fig. 3.22, no. 3); 1 sherd vessel, fabric 41 (Fig. 3.22, no. 4); 1 sherd vessel, fabric 11 (Fig. 3.22, no. 5); 1 sherd probable carinated jar, fabric 12 (Fig. 3.22, no. 6); 1 rim sherd and 10 body sherds, fabric 11; 2 body sherds, fabric 12; 2 rim sherds and 9 body sherds, fabric 13; 1 rim sherd and 2 body sherds, fabric 14; 1 rim sherd, 1 base sherd and 7 body sherds, fabric 21; 3 body sherds, fabric 31; 1 rim sherd, 1 base sherd and 8 body sherds, fabric 41; 2 body sherds, fabric 42; 3 body sherds, fabric 43.

P.41
Pit dia. 0.87 m, depth 0.36 m; vertical sides, flat bottom.
Fill: Layer 1:- brown soil with small lumps of chalk; layer 2:- lumps of chalk and flint; layer 3:- brown soil with small lumps of chalk.
Charcoal: Hawthorn, ash and probably oak charcoal.
Bone frags: 40 sheep/goat.
Pottery: 5 sherds, some joining, rounded shoulder jar, fabric 11 (Fig. 3.20, no. 1); 9 joining sherds large jar, fabric 31 (Fig. 3.20, no. 2); 9 sherds, some joining, globular jar, fabric 13 (Fig. 3.20, no. 3); 6 joining sherds pedestal jar, fabric 13 (Fig. 3.20, no. 4); 5 body sherds, fabric 12; 1 rim sherd and 10 body sherds, fabric 13; 1 rim sherd, 1 base sherd and 8 body sherds, fabric 21; 2 body sherds, fabric 31; 20 body sherds, fabric 41.

P.42
Pit dia. 1.24 m, depth 0.51 m; inward-sloping sides, flat bottom.
Cuts Pit 43.
Fill: Layer 1:- clay; layer 2:- chalky soil with loose chalk and flint.
Charcoal: Oak and hazel charcoal.
Bone frags: 15 sheep/goat.
Pottery: 2 body sherds, fabric 14; 2 base sherds and 1 body sherd, fabric 21; 2 body sherds, fabric 31; 2 body sherds, fabric 32; 1 body sherd, fabric 42; 1 body sherd, fabric 52.

P.43
Pit dia. 0.76 m, depth 1.04 m; rounded sides and bottom.
Cut by Pit 42.
Fill: Layer 1:- dark brown soil with small lumps of chalk; layer 2:- compact chalky soil; layer 3:- chalk and flint rubble.

Charcoal: Oak charcoal.
Bone frags: 51 fragments, 26 cattle, 18 horse, 3 pig.
Small finds: Chalk loom weight (Fig. 4.6, no. 2), oval chalk weight (Fig. 4.6, no. 3).
Pottery: 4 joining sherds pear-shaped jar, fabric 32 (Fig. 3.24, no. 1); 2 sherds jar, fabric 21 (Fig. 3.24, no. 2); 1 sherd jar, fabric 32 (Fig. 3.24, no. 3); 1 rim sherd, fabric 11; 1 body sherd, fabric 12; 1 rim sherd, fabric 13; 3 base sherds and 13 body sherds, fabric 21; 1 rim sherd, fabric 31; 5 body sherds, fabric 32.

P.44
Pit dia. 1.42 m, depth 1.32 m; almost vertical sides, flat bottom.
Adjoining Pit 47.
Fill: Layer 1:- chalky soil with lumps of chalk; layer 2:- chalk rubble; layer 3:- brown soil.
Bone frags: 18 sheep/goat, 1 cattle.
Small finds: Chalk loom weight (Fig. 4.8, no. 5), fragment of sandstone (not illustrated).
Pyrites: 1 lumps of burnt pyrites.
Pottery: 1 sherd vessel, fabric 12 (Fig. 3.24, no. 1); 1 base sherd, fabric 13; 2 body sherds, fabric 31; 1 base sherd, fabric 32.

P.45
Pit dia. uncertain, depth 0.99 m; irregular sides and bottom.
Cut by Pit 38.
Fill: Layer 1:- chalky soil with small lumps of chalk; layer 2:- chalk rubble; layer 3:- chalky soil with lumps of chalk; layer 3A:- ash; layer 4:- dark soil.
Daub: 2 pieces of cob daub.
Charcoal: Probably hawthorn and hazel charcoal.
Bone frags: 6 sheep/goat, 16 cattle, 6 horse, 6 pig.
Small finds: Chalk loom weight (not illustrated), rubbing stone (Fig. 4.10, no. 1).
Slag: Small pieces of slag, possibly from a single smithing hearth bottom, or smelting furnace bottom (analysed by AM Lab.).
Pottery: 8 body sherds, fabric 13; 1 body sherd, fabric 19; 3 base sherds and 3 body sherds, fabric 21; 1 body sherd, fabric 22; 6 body sherds, fabric 31; 1 body sherd, fabric 32; 2 body sherds, fabric 41; 6 body sherds, fabric 42; 2 body sherds, fabric 51; 2 body sherds, fabric 52.
1 body sherd joins another from Pit 49, which suggests that the two pits were open at the same time.

P.46
Pit diam. 1.27 m, depth 0.41 m, inward-sloping sides and flat bottom. Cuts Pit 47.
Fill: Layer 1:- Chalky soil with small lumps of chalk.
Bone frags: 19 sheep/goat, 7 cattle, 5 horse, 1 pig.
Pottery: 4 sherds from jar, fabric 31 (Fig. 3.26, no. 1); 1 lid sherd to fit jar, fabric 31 (Fig. 3.26, no. 2); 1 sherd from vessel, fabric 22 (Fig. 3.26, no. 3); 17 sherds, some joining, from jar, fabric 31 (Fig. 3.26, no.4); 1 sherd from vessel, fabric 21 (Fig. 3.26, no. 5); 1 sherd from vessel, fabric 31 (Fig. 3.26, no. 6); 1 body sherd, fabric 19; 1 rim sherd and 4 body sherds, fabric 21; 4 body sherds, fabric 22; 1 base sherd and 30 body sherds, fabric 31.

P.47
Pit dia. 1.50 m, depth 0.79 m; almost vertical sides, flat bottom.
Adjoining Pit 44. Cut by Pit 46.
Fill: Layers 2 and 4:- chalky soil with small lumps of chalk; layer 5:- dark soil with small chalk lumps; layer 6:- chalky soil with very small lumps of chalk; layer 7:- loose chalk; layer 8:- dark soil; layer 9:- chalk rubble.
Daub: 2 orange scraps of daub, Freeman Type II/III.
Bone frags: 8 sheep/goat, 2 cattle, 1 pig.
Pyrites: 3 pieces of struck and burnt pyrites.
Miscellaneous finds: Small lump of haematite (analysed by AM Lab.).
Pottery: 2 joining sherds from dish, fabric 31 (Fig. 3.22, no. 1); 2 body sherds, fabric 12; 3 body sherds, fabric 13; 4 body sherds, fabric 14; 2 rim sherds, 3 base sherds and 7 body sherds, fabric 21; 1 body sherd, fabric 31.

P.48
Pit dia. uncertain, depth 1.07 m; irregular sides, flat bottom.
Cut by Pit 51.
Fill: Layer 2:- chalky soil with loose chalk; layer 3:- dark soil.
Daub: 10 burnt pieces of daub.
Charcoal: Oak and hazel charcoal.
Bone frags: 2 sheep/goat, 5 cattle, 2 horse, remains of voles.
Pyrites: Cone of weathered radial pyrites (analysed by AM Lab.).
Pottery: 1 sherd globular jar, fabric 22 (Fig. 3.31, no. 1); 1 sherd vessel, fabric 21 (Fig. 3.31, no. 2); 1 sherd from vessel, fabric 22 (Fig. 3.31, no. 3); 1 sherd barrel jar, fabric 31 (Fig. 3.31, no. 4); 1 sherd vessel, fabric 21 (Fig. 3.31, no. 5); 1 body sherd, fabric 12; 1 body sherd, fabric 21; 2 body sherds, fabric 22.

P.49 Not illustrated
Pit dia. 2.39 m, depth 0.21 m.
Fill: Layer 1:- Dark muddy soil with small chalk and flint lumps; layer 2:- grey soil with lumps of chalk and flint; layer 3:- chalky soil.
Bone frags: 20 sheep/goat, 2 cattle.
Pottery: many sherds tall jar, fabric 31 (Fig. 3.20, no. 1); 5 joining sherds pedestal jar, fabric 21 (Fig. 3.20, no. 2); 6 sherds, some joining, globular jar, fabric 31 (Fig. 3.20, no. 3); 1 sherd vessel, fabric 31 (Fig. 3.20, no. 4); 1 sherd jar, fabric 31 (Fig. 3.20, no. 5); 1 sherd jar, fabric 31 (Fig. 3.20, no. 6); 2 body sherds, fabric 21; 1 base sherd and 1 body sherd, fabric 31; 1 body sherd, fabric 33; 2 body sherds, fabric 42.
body sherd joins another from Pit 45, suggesting both pits were open at the same time.

P.50
Pit dia. 1.17 m, depth 0.94 m; irregular sides and bottom.
Fill: Layer 1 :- chalky soil with small lumps of chalk and flint; layer 2:- clay with fine dark soil beneath; layer 3:- chalky soil with small lumps of chalk.
Daub: 1 largish piece of cob daub, 1 burnt piece with charcoal sticks in; Freeman Type I.
Bone frags: 60 sheep/goat, 14 cattle, 8 horse, 8 dog.
Small finds: Pointed end of bone needle (Fig. 4.4, no. 6), fragment of plain rim from ceramic crucible (Fig. 4.13, no. 1).
Pyrites: 1 small fragment and 1 lump of burnt pyrites; 1 burnt, fragmented ball of pyrites, associated with unburnt flint with pieces of pyrites adhering to one edge.
Pottery: 7 sherds, 2 joining, globular jar, fabric 31 (Fig. 3.26, no. 1); 1 sherd barrel jar, fabric 13 (Fig. 3.26, no. 2); 3 sherds, 2 joining, vessel, fabric 13 (Fig. 3.26, no. 3); 1 sherd jar, fabric 52 (Fig. 3.26, no. 4); 1 sherd vessel, fabric 12 (Fig. 3.26, no. 5); 1 sherd vessel, fabric 13 (Fig. 3.26,

no. 6); 4 body sherds, fabric 13; 5 body sherds, fabric 14; 4 body sherds, fabric 21; 1 rim sherd, 2 base sherds and 9 body sherds, fabric 31; 3 body sherds, fabric 42.

P.51
Pit dia. uncertain, depth 0.82 m; irregular sides and bottom.
Cuts Pit 48 and Pit 64.
Fill: Layer 1:- loose ashy soil; layer 2:- chalky soil with some small lumps of chalk; layer 3:- dark soil with small lumps of chalk and flint.
Bone frags: 22 sheep/goat, 13 cattle, 6 horse, 2 pig.
Small finds: Fragment of stone (Fig. 13, no. 2).
Pyrites: 1 lump of burnt and struck pyrites.
Pottery: 3 joining sherds barrel jar, fabric 21 (Fig. 3.24, no. 1); 1 sherd globular jar, fabric 22 (Fig. 3.24, no. 2); 1 sherd vessel, fabric 12 (Fig. 3.24, no. 3); 1 sherd vessel, fabric 31 (Fig. 3.24, no. 4); 1 sherd pear-shaped jar, fabric 31 (Fig. 3.24, no. 5); 1 body sherd, fabric 12; 2 body sherds, fabric 21; 1 rim sherd and 8 body sherds, fabric 31.

P.52
Pit dia. 1.60 m, depth 0.99 m; inward-sloping sides, flat bottom.
Fill: Layer 1:- chalky soil with lumps of chalk and flint; layer 2:- chalk rubble; layer 3:- dark soil with lumps of chalk.
Daub: 6 pieces of chalky cob daub, with possible impressions of ends of sticks; Freeman Type I.
Bone frags: 51 sheep/goat, 62 cattle, 25 horse.
Pyrites: 1 lump of burnt and struck pyrites.
Pottery: 1 sherd vessel, fabric 21 (Fig. 3.26, no. 1); 1 sherd probable barrel jar, fabric 31 (Fig. 3.26, no. 2); 1 sherd vessel, fabric 32 (Fig. 3.26, no. 3); 1 sherd vessel, fabric 32 (Fig. 3.26, no. 4); 1 sherd vessel, fabric 32 (Fig. 3.26, no. 5); 3 joining sherds, fabric 32 (Fig. 3.26, no. 6); 1 sherd barrel jar, fabric 21 (Fig. 3.26, no.7); 4 body sherds, fabric 12; 1 base sherd and 5 body sherds, fabric 21; 2 body sherds, fabric 31; 3 base sherds and 4 body sherds, fabric 32.

P.53
Pit dia. 1.45 m, depth 0.97 m; irregular sides and bottom.
Fill: Layer 1:- brown soil; layer 2:- chalky soil with small lumps of chalk; layer 3:- chalk rubble; layer 4:- chalky soil with lumps of chalk; layer 5:- dark soil.
Daub: 5 pieces of chalky cob daub.
Bone frags: 17 sheep/goat, 8 cattle, 15 horse, 1 pig, 1 dog (Fig. 2.52 complete skeleton apart from cranium fragment, which could be that found in Pit 60).
Small finds: Chalk loom weight, broken at tip, chalk loom weight, triangular shape (Fig. 4.6, no. 4).
Slag: Glassy fuel ash slag (analysed by AM Lab.).
Pottery: many sherds tall jar, fabric 31 (Fig. 3.23, no. 1); 6 sherds tall globular jar, fabric 31 (Fig. 3 23, no. 2); many sherds barrel jar, fabric 22 (Fig. 3.23, no. 3); 1 sherd vessel, fabric 13 (Fig. 3.23, no. 4); 1 sherd probable bowl with rounded body, fabric 13 (Fig. 3.23, no. 5); 1 sherd vessel, fabric 21 (Fig. 3.23, no. 6); many sherds jar, fabric 31 (Fig. 3.23, no. 7); 7 joining sherds vessel, fabric 31 (Fig. 3.23, no. 8); 1 body sherd, fabric 11; 1 rim sherd, 3 base sherds and 10 body sherds, fabric 13; 2 body sherds, fabric 14; 1 base sherd, fabric 15; 2 rim sherds and 5 body sherds, fabric 21; 1 body sherd, fabric 25; 1 base sherd and 24 body sherds, fabric 31; 3 body sherds, fabric 33; 1 body sherd, fabric 42; 8 body sherds, fabric 52.
As a number of sherds from different layers join, it is likely that all layers were contemporary.

P.54
Pit dia. 1.83 m, depth 1.27 m; irregular sides, rounded bottom.
Fill: Layer 1:- chalky soil with small lumps of chalk and flint; layer 2:- chalky soil with lumps of chalk; layer 3:- dark soil.
Daub: 12 pieces of cob daub, Freeman Type I.
Bone frags: 78 sheep/goat, 150 cattle, 15 horse, 13 pig, 1 rodent (fragment of vole, also complete voles), 1 frog/toad (remains bedded in daub).
Small finds: Bronze small collar (Fig. 4.1, no. 7), fragment of iron strip (Fig. 4.2, no. 4).
Pyrites: 1 small weathered pyrite nodule (analysed by AM lab.); 2 pieces of struck and burnt pyrites; other fragments of pyrites.
Pottery: 3 sherds, 2 joining, 'saucepan' vessel, fabric 12 (Fig. 3.24, no. 1); 1 sherd vessel, fabric 32 (Fig. 3.24, no. 2); 22 sherds, many joining, globular jar, fabric 32 (Fig. 3.24, no. 3); 1 sherd vessel fabric 31 (Fig. 3.24, no. 4); 1 sherd vessel, fabric 32 (Fig. 3.24, no. 5); 1 sherd jar, fabric 31 (Fig. 3.24, no. 6); 1 sherd 'saucepan' vessel, fabric 32 (Fig. 3.24, no. 7); 1 sherd vessel, fabric 21 (Fig. 3.24, no. 8); 1 rim sherd, fabric 11; 1 base sherd, fabric 12; 1 base and 2 body sherds, fabric 13; 1 body sherd, fabric 14; 5 base sherds and 6 body sherds, fabric 21; 1 body sherd, fabric 27; 2 base sherds and 4 body sherds, fabric 31; 1 rim sherd, 3 base sherds and 5 body sherds, fabric 32; 1 body sherd, fabric 43; 1 base sherd, fabric 52.
A number of sherds from different layers join, indicating that all layers were contemporary.

P.55
Pit dia. 1.32 m, depth 0.66 m; almost vertical sides, fairly flat bottom.
Fill: Layer 1:- dark soil with small lumps of chalk and flint; layer 2:- chalk rubble.
Bone frags: 12 sheep/goat, 7 cattle, 1 horse, 2 pig, 2 dog.
Small finds: Chalk spindle whorl (Fig. 4.12, no. 10).
Pyrites: 1 large, unburnt ball of pyrites, half ball of pyrites and outer shell of half ball of pyrites.
Pottery: 12 joining sherds barrel jar, fabric 22 (Fig. 3.28, no. 1); 2 sherds probable pedestal jar, fabric 13 (Fig. 3.28, no. 2); 2 sherds vessel, fabric 31 (Fig. 3.28, no. 3); 1 sherd jar, fabric 21 (Fig. 3.28, no. 3); 1 sherd vessel, fabric 13 (Fig. 3.28, no. 5), 10 sherds 'saucepan' vessel, fabric 32 (Fig. 3.28, no. 6); 1 rim sherd and 2 body sherds, fabric 12; 7 body sherds, fabric 13; 1 body sherd, fabric 14; 6 body sherds, fabric 21; 1 rim sherd and 4 body sherds, fabric 31; 1 base sherd and 8 body sherds, fabric 32; 1 body sherd, fabric 52.

P.56
Pit dia. 1.07 m, depth 0.28 m; rounded sides and bottom.
Fill: Layer 1:- brown soil with small lumps of chalk; layer 2:- chalky soil with flecks of charcoal.
Slag: 1 piece of tap or furnace smelting slag (analysed by AM Lab.).
Pottery: 1 sherd vessel, fabric 31 (Fig. 3.31, no. 1); 1 body sherd, fabric 12; 1 body sherd, fabric 14; 1 body sherd, fabric 21; 3 body sherds, fabric 32.

P.57/B
Pit dia. 2.54 m, depth 1.45 m, irregular sides and bottom.
Fill: Layer 1:- dark soil with small lumps of chalk; layer 2:- chalky soil with lumps of chalk; layer 3:- loose chalk;

layer 4:- chalk rubble.
Daub: 8 small pieces of daub, 6 burnt orange; Freeman Types I and II/III.
Bone frags: 10 sheep/goat, 3 cattle, 7 horse, 4 pig.
Small finds: Flint hammer-stone (Fig. 4.10, no. 9).
Pyrites: 4 pieces of pyrites, showing various degrees of burning, but no trace of real smelting.
Miscellaneous finds: 1 piece of yellow clay, 1 piece of yellowish dried substance, possibly dung.
Pottery: 1 rim sherd and 6 body sherds, fabric 13; 2 body sherds, fabric 14; 1 body sherd, fabric 19; 2 rim sherds and 6 body sherds, fabric 21; 3 rim sherds and 8 body sherds, fabric 31; 2 body sherds, fabric 42.

P.58
Pit dia. 2.03 m, depth 0.48 m; irregular sides and bottom.
Fill: Layer 1:- brown soil with lumps of chalk and flint; layer 2:- loose chalk.
Burial: Adult female skeleton in layer 1.
Skeleton of woman lying on her back, knees drawn up and flattened to the left. Head to the left over shoulder. Right arm across neck and bent at right angle around head, fist clenched tightly; left arm bent back at right angle, palm flat, facing upward. (Chapter 5).
Bone frags: Layer 1:- 13 sheep/goat, 7 cattle, 14 horse; Layer 3:- 3 sheep.goat, 5 cattle, remains of a bird.
Small finds: bone implement, found close to the right shoulder of the skeleton in this pit (Fig. 4.5, no. 3), iron pyrites ball, found close to the right heel of the skeleton in this pit (Fig. 4.13, no. 4).
Pyrites: Natural pyrite nodule mixed up with weathered material which could be weathered pyrites with flint adhering (analysed by AM Lab.).
Pottery: 1 sherd vessel, fabric 13 (Fig. 3.31, no. 1); 1 body sherd, fabric 11; 1 body sherd, fabric 12; 1 rim sherd and 8 body sherds, fabric 13; 7 body sherds, fabric 21; 7 body sherds, fabric 31; 1 body sherd, fabric 32.

Pit 58B
Pit dia. 0.92 m, depth 1.17 m, irregular sides and bottom.
Beneath Pit 58.
Fill: Layer 1:- brown soil; layer 2:- chalky soil with small lumps of chalk; layer 3:- loose dark soil with lumps of chalk and flint.

P.59
Pit dia. 2.90 m, depth 1.42 m; irregular sides, flat bottom.
Cuts Pit 66.
Fill: Layer 1:- loose brown soil with lumps of chalk and flint; layer 2:- chalk and flint rubble; layer 3:- dark soil.
Daub: Freeman Types I and V.
Charcoal: Oak and hawthorn charcoal.
Bone frags: 42 sheep/goat, 55 cattle, 1 horse, 2 pig.
Pyrites: 1 piece of struck and burnt pyrites.
Miscellaneous finds: 5 pieces of baked clay.
Pottery: 28 sherds, many joining, jar, fabric 22 (Fig. 3.23, no. 1); 1 sherd jar, fabric 13 (Fig. 3.23, no. 2); 2 joining sherds jar, probably barrel, fabric 31 (Fig. 3.23, no. 3); 1 sherd jar, probably barrel, fabric 21 (Fig. 3.23, no. 4); 3 body sherds, fabric 13; 1 body sherd, fabric 19; 2 base sherds and 5 body sherds, fabric 21; 3 body sherds, fabric 22; 7 base sherds and 6 body sherds, fabric 31; 1 body sherd, fabric 32; 3 body sherd, fabric 42.

P.60
Pit dia. 2.39 m, depth 0.87 m; irregular sides, flat bottom.
Cuts Pit 60B.
Fill: Layer 1:- dark soil with small lumps of chalk; layer 2:- chalky soil with lumps of chalk; layer 3:- chalk and flint rubble; dark soil with small lumps of chalk.
Daub: 3 pieces of burnt orange daub; Freeman Type I.
Bone frags: Layer 1:- 3 sheep/goat, 3 cattle, 3 horse; Layer 2:- 6 sheep/goat, 1 cattle, 8 horse, 1 dog (cranium, could belong with skeleton from Pit 53); Layer 3:- 8 cattle, 1 horse, 1 pig; Layer 4:- 7 cattle, 1 horse.
Small finds: Fragment of iron (Fig. 4.2, no. 2), iron, broken-off tip of straight parallel-sided flat forging (Fig. 2, no. 10), part of chalk loom weight (Fig. 4.8, no. 4).
Pyrites: 1 small ball of pyrites.
Pottery: 1 sherd jar, fabric 31 (Fig. 3.31, no. 1); 1 sherd vessel, fabric 31 (Fig. 3.31, no. 2); 18 sherds, many joining, vessel, fabric 31 (Fig. 3.31, no. 3); 7 body sherds, fabric 11; 1 rim sherd and 38 body sherds, fabric 13; 2 body sherds, fabric 14; 3 base sherds and 35 body sherds, fabric 21; 2 base sherds and 37 body sherds, fabric 31; 3 body sherds, fabric 32; 7 body sherds, fabric 43.

P.60B
Pit dia. uncertain, depth 0.48 m.
Cut by Pit 60.
Fill: Layer 1:- brown soil with layer of charcoal at the bottom.

P.61
Pit. dia. 1.50 m, depth 0.92 m; irregular sides, rounded bottom.
Fill: Layer 1:- dark soil with very small lumps of chalk; layer 2:- chalky soil with small lumps of chalk; layer 3:- dark soil; layer 4:- chalk rubble.
Pottery: 1 body sherd, fabric 21; 2 body sherds, fabric 33; 1 body sherd, fabric 42.

P.62
Pit dia. 1.25 m, depth 0.41 m; rounded sides and flat bottom.
Fill: Layer 1:- dark brown soil with small lumps of chalk and burnt flint; layer 2:- small lumps of chalk.
Bone frags: 16 sheep/goat (including 2 sheep horn cores), 61 cattle, 36 horse, 1 pig.
Pottery: 1 sherd globular jar, fabric 31 (Fig. 3.31, no. 1); 3 body sherds, fabric 21.

P.63
Pit. dia.1.73 m, depth 0.97 m; gently inward-sloping sides, flat bottom.
Fill: Layer 1:- dark grey soil with lumps of chalk and flint; layer 2:- clay; layer 3:- chalk and flint rubble.
Burial: Skeleton of an infant under 6 months old, almost complete.
Daub: 8 pieces of cob daub, Freeman Types I and V.
Small finds: 2 ceramic sling bullets (Fig. 4.13, nos. 9 and 10).
Pottery: 5 body sherds, fabric 13; 1 body sherd, fabric 14; 4 body sherds, fabric 21; 2 base sherds and 6 body sherds, fabric 31; 5 body sherds, fabric 33.

P.64
Pit dia. uncertain, depth 1.27 m; irregular sides, flat bottom.
Cut by Pit 51.
Fill: Layer 1:- loose chalk; layer 2:- chalky soil with small lumps of chalk; layer 3:- dark soil with lumps of chalk; layer 4:- chalk rubble.
Small finds: Penannular iron brooch (Fig. 4.1, no. 9).
Pottery: 22 sherds from tall jar, fabric 21 (Fig. 3.22, no. 1); 1 sherd squat 'situla' jar, fabric 33 (Fig. 3.22, no. 2); 3

body sherds, fabric 13; 1 body sherd, fabric 14; 3 body sherds, fabric 21; 2 body sherds, fabric 31.

P.65
Pit dia. 1.42 m, depth 0.46 m; gently inward-sloping sides and flat bottom.
Fill: Layer 1:- dark soil with small lumps of chalk; layer 2:- chalk rubble.
Pottery: 1 sherd jar, fabric 32 (Fig. 3.28, no. 1); 2 joining sherds jar, fabric 31 (Fig. 3.28, no. 2); 4 body sherds, fabric 11; 6 body sherds, fabric 13; 5 body sherds, fabric 14; 6 body sherds, fabric 21; 1 base sherd and 16 body sherds, fabric 31; 5 body sherds, fabric 32; 1 body sherd, fabric 52.

P.66
Pit dia. uncertain, depth 0.71 m.
Cut by Pit 59.
Fill: layer 5A:- chalky earth; layer 5:- densely packed chalk lumps; layer 6:- dark soil.
Cuts earlier hollow (layer 4:- chalk and flint lumps).
Small finds: Near complete sandstone rubber (Fig. 4.10, no. 1).
Pottery: 1 base sherd, fabric 13; 1 body sherd, fabric 19; 1 body sherd, fabric 31.

P.67
Pit dia. 1.50 m, depth 0.79 m; irregular sides and flat bottom.
Fill: Layer 1:- dark brown soil with very small lumps of chalk; layer 2:- chalky soil with densely packed lumps of chalk; layer 3:- chalk and flint rubble; layer 4:- loose dark brown soil with occasional burnt flints.
Burial: Adult female skeleton in layer 2.
Buried in crouched position, heels drawn up to femurs, knees and feet side by side. Right arm bent with hand at shoulder, palm upwards, fingers bent. Left arm bent across chest and hand resting across right humerus, fingers touching those of the right hand. The body was resting on right side, but pulled rather on to back. On the chest between the two upper arms was a large fragment of sandstone quern with central socket. The skull was badly crushed, facial region broken; the lower jaw had no teeth and the bone had grown over the roots. The remainder of the bones were in good condition. The position of the burial suggests that the body was tied at the wrists and ankles, and the ankles may have been lashed to the thighs; it is not possible to say whether this occurred before or after death. The slight gap between both wrists and ankles could be accounted for if they had been loosely tied.
Bone frags: 6 sheep/goat, 21 cattle, 3 horse, 1 pig.
Small finds: Iron, broken part of parallel-sided heavy forging (Fig. 4.2, no. 9), part of chalk loom weight (not illustrated), part of stone loom weight (not illustrated).
Slag: 1 piece of slag, probably smithing slag (analysed by AM Lab.).
Pottery: 23 sherds pear-shaped jar, fabric 12 (Fig. 3.22, no. 1); 1 sherd vessel, fabric 31 (Fig. 3.22, no. 2); 1 sherd vessel with everted rim, fabric 11 (Fig. 3.22, no. 3); 1 sherd carinated bowl with grooved decoration, fabric 11 (Fig. 3.22, no. 4); 1 rim sherd and 9 body sherds, fabric 11; 30 body sherds, fabric 13; 3 body sherds, fabric 14; 7 body sherds, fabric 21; 1 rim sherd, 1 base sherd and 9 body sherds, fabric 31; 1 body sherd, fabric 32; 18 body sherds, fabric 42.

P.68
Pit dia. 0.99 m, depth 0.61 m; irregular sides, sloping bottom.
Fill: Layer 1:- brown soil with small lumps of chalk and flint, most numerous at the top of the pit; layer 2:- chalk rubble.
Bone frags: 4 sheep/goat, 3 cattle.
Pottery: 1 rim sherd, fabric 11; 1 body sherd, fabric 21; 1 body sherd, fabric 31; 1 body sherd, fabric 42.

P.69/70
Pit dia. 2.44 m, depth 1.53 m. The relationship between pits 69 and 70 was unclear, although pit 70 probably cut pit 69. The finds from the two features amalgamated.
Fill: Layer 1:- dark loamy soil with lumps of burnt chalk and flint; layer 2:- thin layer of charcoal; layer 3:- dark ashy soil; layer 4:- chalky soil with fairly large lumps of chalk; layer 5:- densely packed chalk; layer 6:- brown soil with lumps of burnt flint; layer 7:- chalk rubble; layer 8:- chalky soil; layer 9:- dark ashy soil with burnt flints.
Bone frags: 12 sheep/goat, 51 cattle, 19 horse, 6 pig.
Small finds: Bronze punch (Fig. 4.1, no. 1), damaged iron socket (Fig. 4.2, no. 5), fragment of bone tool (Fig. 4.4, no. 7).
Pottery: 2 joining sherds jar, fabric 42 (Fig. 3.21, no. 1); 4 joining sherds jar, probably carinated, fabric 31 (Fig. 3.21, no. 2); 1 sherd 'situla' jar, fabric 31 (Fig. 3.21, no. 3); 1 sherd globular jar, fabric 21 (Fig. 3.21, no. 4); 1 sherd barrel jar, fabric 21 (Fig. 3.21, no. 5); 1 sherd jar, fabric 21 (Fig. 3.21, no. 6); many sherds o large barrel jar, fabric 31 (Fig. 3.21, no. 7); 1 sherd from jar, fabric 21 (Fig. 3.21, no. 8); 1 sherd vessel, fabric 31 (Fig. 3.21, no. 9); 1 sherd vessel, fabric 13 (Fig. 3.21, no. 10); 6 body sherds, fabric 11; 4 body sherds, fabric 12; 6 body sherds, fabric 13; 10 body sherds, fabric 14; 5 base sherds and 26 body sherds, fabric 21; 3 rim sherds and 29 body sherds, fabric 31; 1 body sherd, fabric 32; 1 body sherd, fabric 41; 4 base sherds and 28 body sherds, fabric 42;

P.71 Not illustrated
Pit dia. 0.92 m, depth 0.18 m.
Fill: Brown soil.
Pottery: 1 sherd carinated jar, fabric 31

P.72 Not illustrated
Pit dia. and depth not recorded.
Fill: Brown soil.
Bone frags: 10 cattle, 12 horse (1 juvenile).
Pottery: 1 sherd globular jar, fabric 12 (Fig. 3.31, no. 1); 1 rim sherd, fabric 32; 1 body sherd, fabric 42.

P.73 Not illustrated
Pit dia. and depth not recorded.
Fill: Brown soil.
Pottery: 1 body sherd, fabric 11; 1 body sherd, fabric 13; 5 body sherds, fabric 31; 2 body sherds, fabric 42.

Appendix 2C

STRUCTURAL REMAINS: POSTHOLES UNRELATED TO HOUSES 1-4

Enclosure I Trench R

PH 1
Dia. 0.43 m, depth 0.35 m; almost vertical sides, flat base.
Fill: Brown soil with lumps of chalk and flint.

PH 2
Dia. 0.18 m, depth 0.10 m
No other details recorded.

PH 3
Dia. 0.35 m, depth 018 m; almost vertical sides, flat base.
Fill: Dark soil with small lumps of chalk.

PH 4
Dia. 0.38 m, depth 0.21 m; almost vertical sides, flat base.
Fill: Dark soil with small lumps of chalk.
Bone frags: 3 cattle, 1 pig.

PH 5
Dia. 0.38 m, 0.21 m; rounded sides and bottom.
Fill: Buff grey loose soil with lumps of flint and charcoal.

PH 6
Dia. 0.35 m, depth 0.33 m; almost vertical sides and flat bottom.
Fill: Dark soil with small lumps of chalk.

PH 7
Dia. 0.33 m, depth 0.13 m
Fill: Brown soil with small lumps of chalk.

PH 8
Dia. 0.18 m, depth 0.10 m; rounded sides, flat bottom.
Fill: Dark soil.

PH 9
Dia. 0.21 m, depth 0.23 m; rounded sides, flat bottom.
Fill: Dark soil.

PH 10
Dia. 0.28 m, depth 0.13 m; rounded sides and bottom.
Fill: dark soil with small lumps of chalk.

PH 11
Dia. 0.21 m, depth 0.10 m; rounded sides and bottom.
Fill: dark soil.

PH 12
Dia. 0.21 m, depth 0.15 m, almost vertical sides, rounded bottom.
Fill: Dark soil.

PH 13
Dia. 0.21 m, depth 0.75 m
Fill: Dark soil.

Enclosure 2: Posthole Complex 5
Figs. 2.6; 2.58-2.59

PH 10 Not illustrated
Dia. 0.31 m, depth 0.43 m
Fill: Brown soil.

PH 11
Dia. 0.30 m, depth 0.20 m
Fill: Dark soil.

PH 12
Dia. 0.30 m, depth 0.20 m
Fill: Dark soil.

PH 19 Not illustrated
Dia 0.33 m, depth 0.33 m
Fill: Brown soil.

PH 20 Not illustrated
Dia. 0.41 m, depth 0.43 m
Fill: Brown soil.

PH 21 Not illustrated
Dia. 0.68 m, depth 0.48 m
Fill: Chalk rubble.

PH 44
Dia. and depth not recorded.
Fill: Grey soil.

PH 45
Dia. and depth not recorded.
Fill: Dark grey soil with layer of rammed chalk and flint packing at the bottom.
Pottery: 2 sherds, not joining, fabric 32 (Fig. 3.14, no. 16); 3 body sherds, fabric 12; 2 body sherds, fabric 13; 1 body sherd, fabric 42.

PH 46
Dia. and depth not recorded.
Fill: Grey soil with small lumps of chalk, with layer of darker chalky soil beneath.

PH 48
Dia. and depth not recorded.
Fill: Grey soil with chalk rubble beneath.
Pottery: 5 body sherds, fabric 48.

PH 50
Dia. and depth not recorded.
Fill: Grey brown soil.

PH 51
Dia. and depth not recorded.
Fill: Grey brown soil.

PH 52
Dia. and depth not recorded.
Fill: Grey brown soil.

PH 53
Dia. and depth not recorded.
Fill: Grey brown soil.

PH 54
Dia. and depth not recorded.

Fill: Grey brown soil.

PH 55
Dia. and depth not recorded.
Fill: Grey brown soil.
Pottery: 2 joining sherds carinated jar, fabric 41 (Fig. 3.14, no. 12).

PH 56
Dia. and depth not recorded.
Fill: Dark soil with lumps of chalk and flint.
Bone frags: 1 sheep/goat, 2 cattle.

PH 57
Dia. not recorded, depth 0.23 m
Fill: Dark soil with lumps of burnt flint.

PH 58
No details recorded.

PH 61
Dia. and depth not recorded. Shallow
Fill: Dark soil.
Bone frags: 2 cattle, 15 pig (1 large, young animal).
Pottery: 1 rim sherd, fabric 12; 2 body sherds, fabric 41.

PH 80
Dia. and depth not recorded.
Fill: Dark grey soil with small lumps of chalk and flint.
Pottery: 1 sherd, fabric 42 (Fig. 3.14, no. 7); 3 rim sherds, fabric 13; 1 body sherd, fabric 32; 1 rim sherd 1 base sherd and 2 body sherds, fabric 42.

PH 84
Dia. and depth not recorded. Shallow PH.
Fill: Chalky soil.

PH 85
Dia and depth not recorded; vertical sides.
Fill: Brown earth.
Cut by PH 86.

PH 86
Dia. and depth not recorded. Shallow PH.
Fill: Brown earth with chalk packing.
Cuts PH 85.

PH 87
Dia. and depth not recorded.
Fill: Brown soil.

PH 88
Dia. and depth not recorded. Shallow PH with rounded bottom.
Fill: Fine, brown soil.

PH 89
Dia. and depth not recorded.
Fill: Brown soil with collapsed flint packing.

Posthole cluster to the south of Complex 5

[Postholes plans are shown on Fig. 2.65. No section drawings extant.]

PH 16
Dia. 0.33 m, depth 0.12 m
Fill: Dark soil with flints.

PH 28
Dia. 0.35 m, depth 0.38 m
Fill: Dark soil.
Bone frags: 2 sheep/goat, 5 cattle (horn core – *Bos longifrons*).

PH 31
Dia. 0.66 m, depth 0.23 m
Fill: Brown soil.
Pottery: 1 rim sherd and 1 body sherd, fabric 11; 5 body sherds, fabric 13; 1 body sherd, fabric 14; 2 body sherd, fabric 32; 4 body sherds, fabric 41; 5 body sherd, fabric 42.

PH 32
Dia. 0.46 m, depth not recorded.
Fill: Dark soil.
Pottery: 3 sherds, not joining, carinated cup, fabric 14 (Fig. 3.14, no. 1); 1 sherd carinated bowl, fabric 14 (Fig. 3.14, no. 8); 1 base sherd, fabric 12; 4 body sherds, fabric 41; 5 body sherds, fabric 42.

PH 36
Dia. and depth not recorded.
Fill: chalky soil.
Bone frags: 7 sheep/goat, 2 cattle, 1 pig.

PH 39
Dia. and depth not recorded.
Fill: Brown soil.
Pottery: 1 sherd from carinated bowl, fabric 42 (Fig. 3.14, no. 10); 2 sherds, fabric 14 (Fig. 3.14, nos. 5 and 6); 1 body sherd, fabric 13; 3 body sherds, fabric 42; 1 body sherd, fabric 51.

PH 40
Dia. and depth not recorded.
Fill: Brown soil.
Pottery: 2 joining sherds, fabric 42 (Fig. 3.14, no. 4); 1 body sherd, fabric 41.

PH 41
Dia. and depth not recorded.
Fill: Brown soil.

PH 81
Dia. and depth not recorded. Small PH with vertical sides and flat bottom.
Fill: Fine, chalky soil.
Pottery: 1 body sherd, fabric 11.

PH 82
Dia. and depth not recorded. Shallow, irregular PH.
Fill: Brown soil with small lumps of chalk.
Pottery: 1 sherd carinated cup, fabric 52 (Fig. 3.14, no. 2); 1 base sherd and 1 body sherd, fabric 51.

PH 93/94
Dia. and depth not recorded.
Fill: Dark grey soil with small lumps of chalk.
Pottery: 3 body sherds, fabric 13; 2 body sherds, fabric 41; 2 rim sherds, fabric 42; 2 body sherds, fabric 51.

Postholes in Enclosure II Cuttings U and E

[No plan or section drawings extant for postholes in Cutting U. Cutting E PH 34 and 35 illustrated in plan and section on Fig. 2.19]

PH 1 (Cutting U)
Dia. 0.23 m, depth 25.5 m
Fill: Chalky soil.

PH 2 (Cutting U)
Dia. and depth not recorded. Shallow.
Fill: Chalky soil.

PH 3 (Cutting U)
Dia. 0.56 m, depth 0.41 m
Fill: Dark soil with heavy flint packing.

PH 6 (Cutting U)
Dia. 0.36 m, depth 0.21 m; rounded bottom.
Fill: Fine, chalky soil.

PH 7 (Cutting U)
Dia. 0.38 m, depth 0.31 m; rounded bottom.
Fill: Chalky soil.

PH 34 (Cutting E) Section drawing Fig. 2.19
Dia. 0.71 m, depth 0.20 m.
Fill: brown soil with small and large chalk lumps.

PH 35 (Cutting E) Section drawing Fig. 2.19
Dia. 0.38 m; depth 0.23 m.
Fill: Chalk lumps, with a little brown soil at the top.

Postholes within Enclosure II Area S1, S2. S3

[Postholes plans are shown on Figs 2.48-2.49 and 2.65. Section drawings appear on figures as indicated below.]

PH 4 Not illustrated
Dia. not recorded, depth 0.31 m
Pottery: 1 sherd from vessel, fabric 31 (Fig. 3.14, no. 13); 3 body sherds, fabric 13; 1 body sherd, fabric 21; 3 body sherds, fabric 31; 5 body sherds, fabric 32.

PH 5 Fig. 2.48; 2.65
Dia. 0.66 m, depth 0.41 m
Fill: Brown soil with chalk rubble at the bottom.

PH 8 Fig.2.48
Dia. 0.25 m, depth 0.28 m
Fill: Fine, dark soil.

PH 9 Fig. 2.48
Dia. 0.31 m, depth 0.23 m
Fill: Brown soil.

PH 10 Not illustrated
Dia. 0.31 m, depth 0.43 m
Fill: Brown soil.

PH 13 Not illustrated
Dia. 0.15 m, depth 0.75 m
Fill: Chalky soil.

PH 14 Not illustrated
Dia. 0.18 m, depth 0.75 m
Fill: Chalky soil.

PH 15 Not illustrated
Dia. 0.23 m, depth 0.75 m
Fill: Chalky soil.

PH 17 Fig.2.48
Dia. 0.25 m, depth 0.18 m
Fill: Chalky soil.
Pottery: 3 body sherds, fabric 42.

PH 18 Figs 2.65; 2.48
Dia. 0.33 m, depth 0.12 m
Fill: Dark grey soil.
Pottery: 2 sherds from carinated jar, fabric 41; 1 body sherd, fabric 13; 1 rim sherd, 1 base sherd and 2 body sherds, fabric 41.

PH 19 Not illustrated
Dia. 0.33 m, depth 0.33 m
Fill: Brown soil.

PH 20 Not illustrated
Dia. 0.41 m, depth 0.43 m
Fill: Brown soil.

PH 21 Not illustrated
Dia. 0.68 m, depth 0.48 m
Fill: Chalk rubble.

PH 22 Fig. 2.49
Dia. and depth not recorded.
Fill: Dark grey chalky soil.

PH 23 Fig. 2.49
Dia. not recorded, depth 0.20 m
Fill: Dark soil with small lumps of chalk.

PH 24 Fig.2.49
Dia. 0.28 m, depth 0.28 m
Fill: Dark soil with small lumps of chalk.

PH 25 Fig. 2.49
Dia. 0 48 m, depth 0.35 m
Fill: Brown soil.
Pottery: 4 body sherds, fabric 13; 1 body sherd, fabric 23; 5 body sherds, fabric 41.

PH 26 Fig. 2.49
Dia. 0.25 m, depth 0.15 m
Fill: Dark soil.
Bone frags: 2 sheep/goat, 2 cattle.

PH 27 Fig. 2.49
Dia. 0.30 m, depth 0.33 m
Fill: Dark soil with small lumps of chalk.

P 29 Fig. 2.49
Dia. and depth not recorded.
Fill: Chalky soil.

PH 30 Fig. 2.49
Dia. and depth not recorded.
Fill: Chalky soil.

PH 33 Figs. 2.48; 2.65
Dia. 0.3 m, depth 0.20 m
Fill: Dark grey soil.

PH 37 Not illustrated
Dia. and depth not recorded.
Fill: chalky soil.

PH 38 Not illustrated

Dia. 0.38 m, depth 0.38 m
Fill: Dark grey soil.

PH 43 Not illustrated
Dia. and depth not recorded.
Fill: Dark soil with small lumps of chalk.
Pottery: 1 sherd, fabric 42 (Fig. 3.14, no. 11); 2 body sherds, fabric 14.

PH 47 Not illustrated
No details recorded.

PH 49 Not illustrated
Dia. and depth not recorded.
Fill: Grey brown soil with chalk rubble beneath.
Pottery: 1 sherd carinated jar,fabric 21 (Fig. 3.14, no. 15).

PH 59 Fig.2.63
Dia. 0.92 m, depth 0.12 m; irregular sides and bottom.
Adjoining Hollow 8.
Fill: Brown soil with lumps of chalk.

PH 60 Fig.2.48
Dia. not recorded, depth 0.33 m
Fill: Fine, chalky soil.

PH 64 Not illustrated
Dia. 0.33 m, depth 0.12 m
Fill: Light brown soil with small lumps of chalk.

PH 65 Not illustrated
Dia. 0.46 m, depth 0.21 m
Fill: Chalky brown soil.

PH 66 Section Fig.2.63
Dia. 0.71 m, depth 0.48 m; inward-sloping sides, irregular bottom.
Fill: Brown soil with chalk lumps.

PH 67 Fig. 2.32; 2.65
Dia. 0.41 m, depth 0.33 m
Fill: Chalky soil.

PH 68 Not illustrated
Dia. 0.48 m, depth 0.46 m
Fill: Dark brown soil with lumps of chalk.

PH 70 Figs 2.49; 2.64
Dia. 0.43 m, depth 0.23 m
Fill: Brown soil.

PH 71 Fig. 2.63
Dia. 0.71 m, depth 0.23 m
Fill: Brown soil with chalk lumps.
Pottery: 2 body sherds, fabric 31.

PH 72 Not illustrated
Dia. and depth not recorded.
Fill: Brown soil.

PH 73 Fig. 2.49
Dia. 0.31 m, depth 0.25 m
Fill: Grey clayey soil with small lumps of chalk.

PH 74 Fig. 2.49
No details recorded.

PH 75 Fig.2.48-9
Dia. 0.56 m, depth 0.23 m
Fill: Grey clayey soil with some large flints.

PH 76 Fig. 2.48; 2.65
Dia. 0.35 m, depth 0.15 m
Fill: Grey soil.

PH 78 Not illustrated
Dia. and depth not recorded.
Fill: Chalky soil.

PH 79 Fig. 2.49
Dia. and depth not recorded.
Fill: Dark grey soil.

PH 83 Not illustrated
Dia. and depth not recorded.
Fill: Brown soil with small lumps of chalk.
Pottery: 1 rim sherd, fabric 52.

PH 92 Not illustrated
Dia. and depth not recorded.
Fill: Brown soil.
Pottery: 1 body sherd, fabric 11; 2 body sherds, fabric 21; 2 body sherds, fabric 41; 1 base sherd, fabric 42.

PH 95 Not illustrated
Dia. and depth not recorded.
Fill: Dark grey soil with some lumps of chalk and flint.
Pottery: 1 sherd carinated bowl, fabric 42 (Fig. 3.14, no. 3); 2 body sherds, fabric 42.

PH 96 Not illustrated
Dia. not recorded, depth 0.38 m.
Fill: Dark grey soil.

PH 97 Not illustrated
Dia. not recorded, depth 0.38 m.
Fill: Dark soil with large flints and lumps of chalk.
Bone frags: 3 sheep/goat, 13 cattle, 6 horse, 1 pig, 2 dog (large animals).
Pottery: 1 body sherd, fabric 11; 2 body sherds, fabric 14; 4 body sherds, fabric 41.

PH 98 Not illustrated
Dia. and depth not recorded.
Fill: Chalky soil.

PH 99 Not illustrated
Dia. and depth not recorded.
Fill: Brown soil.

PH 104 Not illustrated
Dia. 0.38 m, depth 0.23 m
Fill: Brown soil with chalk rubble at the bottom.

PH 105 Fig. 2.48; 2.65
Dia. 0.25 m, depth 0.18 m
Fill: Brown soil with chalk rubble at the bottom.

PH 106 Fig. 2.48; 2.65
Dia. 0.35 m, depth 0.21 m
Fill: Brown soil with large flints.

PH 107 Not illustrated
Dia. 0.38 m, depth 0.21 m
Fill: Light brown gravelly soil.

PH 108 Not illustrated
Dia. 0.28 m, depth 0.12 m
Fill: Light brown gravelly soil.

PH 109 Not illustrated
Dia. 0.31 m, depth 0.13 m
Fill: Light brown gravelly soil.

PH 110 Fig. 2.32
Dia. not recorded, depth 0.35 m.
Fill: Brown soil with large flints.

PH 111 Fig.2.48
Dia. 0.36 m, depth 0.23 m
Fill: Brown soil with small lumps of chalk and flint.

PH 124 Not illustrated
Dia. and depth not recorded.
Fill: Brown soil.

PH 156 Not illustrated
Dia. 0.43 m, depth 0.41 m
Fill: Chalky soil.

PH 168 Not illustrated
Dia. 0.51 m, depth 0.12 m
Fill: Brown soil.
Pottery: 1 body sherd, fabric 12; 1 body sherd, fabric 21.

PH 173 Fig. 2.32
Dia. 0.46 m, depth 0.41 m
Fill: Chalky soil.
Pottery: 1 sherd rounded bowl, fabric 32 (Fig. 3.14, no. 14); 2 body sherds, fabric 12; 6 body sherds, fabric 32.

PH 176 Fig. 2.32
Dia. 0.26 m, depth 0.21 m
Fill: Brown soil.

PH 177 Fig. 2.32
Dia. 0.46 m, depth 0.21 m
Fill: Brown soil.

PH 190 Not illustrated
Dia. 0.21 m, depth 0.10 m
Fill: Brown soil.

PH 196 Fig.2.48-49; Section Fig. 2.52 (with PH 195, of House 4).
Dia. 0.61 m, depth 0.35 m
Fill: Chalky soil with large flints and small lumps of chalk.

Postholes outside Enclosure III Area T

[Figure numbers refer to illustrations on plan. No section drawings extant.]

PH 17 (A 32) Fig. 2.30
Depth 0.15 m

PH 18 (A 32) Fig. 2.20
Depth 0.12 m

PH 19 (A 32) Fig. 2.30
Depth 0.75 m

PH 20 (A 31) Fig. 2.29
Depth 0.10 m

PH 21 (A 31) Fig. 2.29
Depth 0.18 m

PH 22 (A 28) Fig. 2.30
Depth 0.23 m

PH 23 (A 28) Fig. 2.30
Depth 0.21 m

PH 24 (A 28) Fig.2.30
Depth 0.25 m

PH 25 (A 28) Fig. 2.30
Depth 0.41 m

PH 26 (A 28) Fig. 2.30
Depth not recorded.
Bone frags: 2 sheep/goat, 2 cattle.

PH 27 (A 28) Fig. 2.30
Depth 0.10 m

PH 28 (A 27) Fig. 2.30
Depth not recorded.

PH 29 (A 27) Fig. 2.30
Depth 0.20 m

PH 30 (A 27) Fig. 2.30
Depth 0.25 m

PH 31 (A 25) Fig. 2.29
Depth 0.5 m

PH 32 (A 25) Fig. 2.29
Depth 0.12 m

PH 33 (A 25)) Fig. 2.29
Depth 0.10 m

PH 34 (A 26) Fig. 2.30
Depth 0.12 m

PH 35 (A 26) Fig. 2.30
Depth 0.10 m

PH 36 (A 26) Fig. 2.30
Depth not recorded.

PH 37 (A 26) Fig.2.30
Depth 0.12 m

PH 38 (A 26) Fig. 2.29
Depth 0.12 m

PH 39 (A 35) Fig. 2.29
Depth 0.12 m

PH 40 (A 34) Fig. 2.29
Depth 0.23 m

PH 41 (A 34) Fig. 2.28
Depth 0.15 m

PH 42 (A 38) Fig. 2.28
Depth 0.23 m

PH 43 (A 45) Fig. 2.29
Depth 0.12 m

PH 44 (A 45) Fig. 2.29
Depth 0.15 m

PH 45 (A 46) Fig. 2.28
Depth 0.15 m

Appendix 2D

STRUCTURAL REMAINS: WORKING HOLLOWS

Enclosure I Cutting R

H 1 Fig. 2.9 (Plan and Section)
Diameter 0.74 m, depth 0.18 m. Filled with brown soil with small lumps of chalk.

Enclosure II Cutting E

H 7 Fig. 2.19
Depth 0.46 m. Filled with halky soil with lumps of chalk.

Enclosure II Area S1, S2, S3

H 1 Fig. 2.48-2.49; Sections Fig. 2.55; Fig. 2.63-2.64 (sections)
Diameter 3.86 m, depth 0.23 m – 0.48 m.
Adjoining Pit 18
Fill: Layer 2:- brown soil with lumps of chalk; layer 3:- chalk rubble.

H 2 Fig. 2.48-2.49; Section Fig. 2.64
Depth 0.26 m.
Fill: Dark soil.
Pottery: 3 body sherds, fabric 21.

H 3 Fig. 2.48-2.49; Section Fig. 2.64
Depth 0.21 m.
Fill: Brown soil.
Pottery: 1 body sherd, fabric 13; 1 body sherd, fabric 21; 2 body sherds, fabric 31; 1 body sherd, fabric 41.

H 4 Figs. 2.32; 2.33; 2.36; Section Fig. 2.55
Adjacent to Pit 31.
Depth 0.41 m.
Fill: Layer 2:- dark soil with small chalk and flint lumps; layer 3:- chalky soil with very small lumps of chalk and flint; layer 4:- loose chalk and flint.

H 5 Fig. 2.63 (section)
Hollow dia. 2.39 m, depth 0.15 m.
Fill: Brown soil with lumps of chalk.

H 6 Fig. 2.32; 2.33; Fig. 2.63 (section)
Hollow dia. 0.87 m, depth 0.28 m.
Fill: Brown soil.
Pottery: 1 body sherd, fabric 13; 2 body sherds, fabric 21; 5 body sherds, fabric 42.

H 8 [number duplicated] (Area S1 west of House 4) Figs. 2.49-2.49 (Depth 0.08 m.
Fill: Not recorded.

H 8 [number duplicated] (Area S2 next to PH 59) Fig. 2.65; Fig. 2.63 (section)
Hollow dia. 1.65 m, depth 0.31 m.
Adjoining PH 59.
Fill: Layer 1:- dark soil with lumps of chalk; layer 2:- chalky soil with lumps of chalk.
Pottery: 1 rim sherd, fabric 13; 1 base sherd and 6 body sherds, fabric 31; 3 body sherds, fabric 42; 3 body sherds, fabric 44.

H 9 (Area S3, within House 1) Fig. 2.32; Fig. 2.65
Depth 0.21 m.
Fill: Ashy soil.

H 10 (Area S2) Fig. 2.65
Depth 0.26 m.
Fill: Clayey soil with lumps of chalk.

H 11 [number duplicated] (Area S2- next H 10) Fig. 2.65
Depth 0.21 m.
Fill: Dark soil.

H 11 [number duplicated] (Area S3) Fig. 2.32; Fig. 2.65
Depth 0.10 m.
Fill: Brown soil.

H 13 Not illustrated
(Records state 'Near Pit 4' but not show on plans).
No record

H 14 Not illustrated.
No record.

H 15 (Area S3) Fig. 2.65
Depth 0.26 m.
Fill: Grey soil with lumps of chalk and flint.
H 16 Not illustrated
Depth 0.21 m
Fill: Brown soil.

H 17 (within House 2) Fig. 2.32, Fig. 2.36
Depth 0.08 m.
Fill: Dark soil.
Pottery: 3 body sherds, fabric 25; 4 body sherds, fabric 32; 1 body sherd, fabric 33.

H 18 Not illustrated
Dia.0.61 m, depth 0.08 m.
Fill: Not recorded.

H 19 Fig. 2.48-2.49
Dia. 0.71 m, depth 0.18 m.
Fill: Dark soil with large lumps of chalk and flint.
Small finds: Fragment of stone, probably used as a hone (Fig. 13, no. 3).
Pottery: 5 body sherds, fabric 14; 5 body sherds, fabric 31; 1 base sherd, fabric 33; 3 body sherds, fabric 52.

Appendix 3A

SCIENTIFIC ANALYSIS OF THE POTTERY

Selection of Pottery Samples for Analysis

by Sonia Hawkes

Introduction: Problems for Solution

Problem 1

There are fine wares, mostly rilled (furrowed) bowl sherds, from Houses 1, 2, 3, 4, Pit complex 5, WH3, and Enclosure II Ditch filling; also scattered other locations. Does the fabric of these bowl wares vary: (a) within the location of each of the bowl sherds, and (b) from one location to another?

NB (a) The archaeological expectation is that the series as a whole, allowing for time gaps within it, spans at least three centuries of absolute time.
(b) The series of bowl forms represented, though retaining throughout the concept of a drinking bowl or cup, and also retaining the haematite coating that simulates bronze, yet shows distinct variations, mostly in the height and angle of eversion of the rim, but also in the number and quality of execution of the rillings (furrows).

Problem 2

House 1, unlike the other houses, produced not only a series of the bowls/cups (considered under problem 1) but also large jars with incised and white inlaid ornament, cut into their surface, which itself has been haematite-coated. Their fabric appears very similar to that of the bowls/cups and though their mean thickness of wall may be somewhat greater, it approximates closely to that of the larger bowl/cup specimens. Is this visual observation confirmed by the fabric analysis? Sparse inclusions of grit from pounded flint can be seen in the jar sherds, yet these can also be seen in the larger bowl sherds. As a whole, this House 1 pottery gives the impression of a single 'service', for people whose ideal was a 'service' in bronze, so were upper class people, supplied by specialist potters.

We must append to Problem 2 the identification of the white material inlaid in the decoration of the jars. On the similar looking material so inlaid at All Cannings Cross, Cunnington (1923, 197-8) wrote a special note. The material must have been applied as a paste before the firing of the jars and she describes some perforated pot bases encrusted inside with a white material, residue of ancient contents – in some cases exuded through the perforations on to the outside, and sometimes not confined to the base but present on the whole interior. She states that analysis shows the material 'to consist of calcium carbonate, with a considerable quantity of calcium phosphate, traces of iron oxide and alumina, and a small amount of finely-divided silica (does not show any organised structure under the microscope)'. She therefore says, 'It is probable that the deposit is a bone residue'. Its appearance 'almost exclusively on vessels with perforated bases' makes her think it was placed in these 'to drain off superfluous fluid'; so her Note 1 (Cunnington 1923, 97) indicates the probability that the vessels were 'used in the preparation of the inlay for the ornamented pottery'. Having previously surmised that these pottery jars were made on site from clay brought from a distance, she suggests that this inlay preparation confirms that they were made on site. She gives the analysis results obtained by her chemist on six samples of the inlay, from six fragments: nos. 1-3 were 'practically identical' with the deposit on the perforated pots; no. 4 had the calcium phosphate in small amount only, nos 5-6 had none of it.

Firing of the jar could remove or at least would diminish the phosphate, diminished no doubt already by the burning of bones to use in the material *i.e.* the heat treatment would send a lot of it off as volatile phosphorus. So the conclusion seems to have been that the inlay was mostly chalk powdered in with bone ash; the chalk gave the white colouration, the bone ash also the necessary glutinous adhesiveness. On the continent, white inlay was similarly used in the same broad period – Late Bronze to Hallstatt Iron Age, notably in Switzerland (lakeside dwelling sites) and adjacent east French and south-west German areas – though the tradition goes right back to the Neolithic. Problem 2a is therefore whether anything more can be said from the Longbridge samples, to add to or modify the findings from All Cannings Cross, or anywhere else, so that Longbridge results could be offered as definitive.

Problem 3

In Houses 1-4 and WH3 we have variable quantities of medium to coarse fabrics in addition to the fine bowl wares. Were they using the same clay with different temper?

Problem 4

With Pit 37, 41 and 5 we start the 'B' or Middle Iron Age series of fabrics. Superficially all the fabrics appear different from what has gone before. Is this confirmed by analysis?

Problem 5

The latest pit on the site is Pit 22, and perhaps contemporary is the pottery from Enclosure III primary ditch silt. Between Pit 37 *etc.* (apparently 5th century BC) and Pit 22 (apparently 2nd century BC), we have a limited series of transitional forms. At some point we should perhaps test whether the fabrics in these three centuries vary at all significantly.

Problem 6

How many, if any of these wares, were industrial products imported from a distance? It has been suggested, for example, that the so-called scratched-cordoned bowls, were just such a group. We have, unfortunately, only the one sherd from this phase, sample no. 35. It would be interesting to know how it compares with similar bowl fabrics from Gussage and Danebury.

Catalogue of sherds submitted for analysis

[Editor's note. In the catalogue below the entries are as follows:

Fabric and sample number (see Williams below). Context. Illustration no. Sherd description]

Enclosure II, House I

Furrowed bowls, haematite coated

A1. PH63. Black furrowed bowl, ?burnt but shiny exterior
A2. PH139. Base of fine furrowed bowl, weathered
A3. PH151. Base of furrowed bowl, surfaces weathered
K4. PH151. Base of coarse furrowed bowl, visible flint inclusions.
A5. PH152. Base of fine furrowed bowl, exterior polished haematite
A6. PH152. Base of thick furrowed bowl or large jar
B7. PH154. Base of fine furrowed bowl, slightly burnt, purplish haematite internal and external
B8. PH154. Rim and neck of furrowed bowl, blackened
B9. PH154. Rim and neck of large, thick furrowed bowl, visible flint
B10. PH154. Neck of furrowed bowl, burnt, blackened, surfaces abraded
B11. Topsoil. Rim and neck of large furrowed bowl, abraded, visible flint
B12. Topsoil. Shoulder of furrowed bowl, haematite-coated surfaces
B35. PH235. Sherd of scratched-cordoned bowl, intrusive in this period (*NB* potentially the latest haematite type from the site)

Large fine ware jars, haematite coated, excised geometric patterns and white inlay decoration

A13. PH154. Fig. 3.4, no. 47. Body sherd with border stripe
A14. PH151. Fig. 3.4, no. 44. Body sherd, blackened by fire
A15. PH151/2. Fig. 3.5, no. 56. Blackened body sherd
A16. PH151. Fig. 3.5, no. 58. Blackened body sherd with border stripe
A17. PH151/2. Fig. 3.3, no. 37. Neck angle, haematite external surface, blackened inside
A18. PH 152. Weathered body sherd, visible flint
A19. PH154. Weathered body sherd
A20. PH152/3. Fig. 3.5, no. 50. Weathered body sherd with diagonal stripe.
A21. PH152/3. Blackened sherd, stab pattern, border stripe, white inlay
A22. PH42. Blackened body sherd
B23. PH151. Fig. 3.5, no. 52. Body sherd, some haematite, partly blackened.
A24. PH165. Fig. 3.6, no. 76. Neck sherd, slightly weathered
A25. PH129. Body sherd, haematite and border stripe with white inlay
A26. PH237. Fig. 3.6, no. 80. Two decorated body sherds, ?white inlay, haematite surface

Jars in coarser fabric

H27. PH154. Fig 3.6, no. 78. Base, heavy gritting and flint, haematite coated external
H28. PH235. Body sherd of thick coarse gritted jar, ?same vessel as above
H29. PH151. Coarse body sherd of jar with finger-tip decoration.
K30. PH151. Body sherds from 'gritty' jar, possibly haematite coated exterior
H31. PH153. Shoulder of very coarse gritted jar, weathered
H32. PH225. Upper body of medium coarse storage jar, ?second period.
H33. PH151. Medium coarse handle fragment
K34. PH235. Rim of a barrel shaped vessel or bowl

Enclosure II, Pit 5

I36. Pot 2. Fig 3.18, no.1. Rim of shallow bowl, shell gritted, smooth surface

Enclosure II, Pit 37

I37. Fig. 3.19, no.1. Body sherd shallow bowl, shell gritted, smooth coated
I38. Fig. 3.19, no. 6. Body sherd of large flint gritted store jar
J39. Fig. 3.19, no. 4. Body sherd of large black jar
J40. Fig. 3.19, no 5. Buff sherd, body of flint gritted coarse jar
J41. Fig. 3.19, no 7. Body sherd, buff flint gritted jar

Enclosure II, Pit 22

C42. Fig. 3.29, no. 1. Body sherd, black 'saucepan' pot
J43. Fig. 3.29, no. 3. Body sherd, black decorated bowl

Enclosure II, House I

B44. PH 151. Fig. 3.1, no. 1. Base sherd from haematite-coated jar with furrowed rim
I45. PH 151. Rim sherd, medium coarse ware
I46. PH 152. Base sherd from friable coarse vessel

Enclosure II, House 2

B47. PH 134. Fig. 3.7, no. 1. Sandy textured tall necked haematite-coated bowl
B48. PH 134. Fig. 3.7, no. 2. Furrowed sherd from sandy textured haematite-coated bowl/cup
B49. PH 137. Fig. 3.7, no.15. Rim sherd of tall-necked furrowed haematite-coated bowl
B50. B XXIV PH 136. Fig. 3.7, no. 7. Neck sherd of furrowed bowl
B51. PH 126. Fig. 3.7, no. 13. Furrowed shoulder, probably from bowl
B52. PH 137. Fig. 3.7, no. 9. Rim sherd from tall necked furrowed bowl
B53. B XXIV PH 136. Fig. 3.8, no. 25. Rim sherd from tall necked bowl
B54. PH 126. Fig. 3.7, no. 12. Plain body sherd from tall necked furrowed bowl
A55. PH 137. Fig. 3.7, no. 10. Plain body sherd from tall necked furrowed bowl
B56. PH 135. Furrowed sherd from tall necked bowl
-57. PH 126. Base sherd from tall necked furrowed bowl
F58. PH 135. Sherd from very large coarse bowl

Enclosure II, House 2

Jars in coarser fabrics

J59. PH 137. Fig. 3.9, no. 44. Big fingertip dec. jar, smooth fabric, ?shell/limestone temper
J60. PH 137. Fig. 3.10, no. 54. Fingertip dec. jar, smooth texture, ?shell/limestone temper
H61. PH 126. Fig. 3.9, no. 37. Medium coarse jar, ?flint/limestone temper
J62. PH 147, PH 134. Fig. 3.8, no. 33. Small fingertip dec. jar, apparently shell tempered
H63. PH 229. Fig. 3.9, no. 38. Big, coarse, fingertip dec. store jar, visible flint grit
J64. PH 204. Fig. 3.8, no. 30. Small fingertip dec. jar, medium coarse, ?shell/limestone

K65. PH 136. Base of large coarse fingertip dec. jar, quartz, flint/ ?limestone grit

Enclosure II, Pits 37 and 41

D66. Pit 37, layer 3. Sherd of fine pedestal jar (*cf. e.g.* from Pit 50)
D67. Pit 41, layer 1. Fig. 3.20, no. 4. Sherd from fine pedestal jar, as above
D68. Pit 41, layer 1. Fig. 3.20, no. 1. Sherd from medium jar
D69. Pit 41, layer 1. Fig. 3.20, no. 3. Sherd from medium jar

Purbeck Shell Bed Samples

C.D. 60. SF No. 15
C.D. 58 B X WH2

Samples Primarily for Heavy Mineral Analysis

Enclosure II, House 2

B70. PH 146. Base sherd from bowl
B71. PH 146. Base and rilled shoulder sherd
H72. PH 136. Base of bowl
B73. PH 137. Neck and shoulder of bowl
H74. PH 137. Rim sherd from bowl
J75. PH 137. Base-shoulder sherd from bowl

Enclosure II, House 1

A76. PH 63, prob. Fig. 8. Base sherds from bowl
B77. B XIV (2), prob. Fig. 8. Base sherds from bowl
H78. PH 167, prob. Fig. 3.1, no. 12. Base of large bowl
B79. PH 167, prob. Fig. 3.2, no. 20. Body sherd from large bowl
B80. PH 167, prob. Fig. 3.2, no. 30. Neck/body sherd, fine furrowed bowl
K81. Pit 37, layer 1. Rilled sherd

Samples for Thin-section Analysis:

B83. PH 128. Bowl base. To discover if PH belongs to House 1 or 2
A84. House3, Cutting 94,(2b). Bowl sherd. furrowed
A85. House3, Cutting 65(2b), Fig. 3.11, no. 7. Bowl sherd, body
B86. House3, Cutting 94B(2b) Fig. 3.11 no. 17. Sherd from large haematite coated jar
H87. House 4, PH 207. Sherd from finger-tip decorated medium jar
J88. House 4, PH 198. Sherd from large finger-tip decorated jar with tall rim
H89. House 4, B XXXVIII. Body sherd from medium jar
H90. House 4, PH 216. Bowl sherd

Enclosure II, Pit 5. Supplementary Series

I101. Pot 3, Fig. 2. Rim sherd, black burnished jar
J102. Pot 7, Fig. 4. Body sherd from large, coarse, pear-shaped jar
J103. Pot 5, Fig. 5. Rim sherd from small medium cooking pot
J104. Pot 6, Fig. 6. Body sherd, thick store jar
-105. Pot 4, Fig. 7. Sherd from small barrel-shaped jar
J106. Pot 8. Sherd fine pedestal jar, fabric close to 'A' wares(?)
J107. Pot 9. Medium store jar

Enclosure I

I108. Pit 1, layer 3: Fig. 3.17, no. 1. Body sherd, large situlate jar
I109. Pit 2, layer 2: Rim sherd, small medium jar

Enclosure II, Pits

J110. Pit 69/70, layer 6. Sherd of large store jar
I111. Pit 49, layer 2, Figure 3.20, no. 2. Pedestal jar sherd
I112. Pit 64, layer 2, Figure 3.22 no. 1. Rim of large store-jar
B113. Pit 14. Fig. 3.27, no. 1. Rim of burnished black bowl/jar
I114. Pit 14, Fig. 3.27, no. 2. Base of medium jar
J115. Pit 14. Fig. 3.27, no. 3. Body sherd from medium jar
B116. Pit 14. Fig. 3.27, no. 4. Body, smooth, hard-fired, squat jar
-117. Pit 14. Fig. 3.27, no. 5. Body sherd from high shouldered jar
I118. Pit 14. Fig.3.27, no 7. Body sherd from jar, perforated base
J119. Pit 53, layers 4/5, Fig. 3.23, no. 1. Large store jar
I120. Pit 53, layers 4, Fig. 3.23, no. 2. Black medium jar
J121 Pit 53, layer 5, Fig. 3.23, no. 7. Globular medium jar
E122 Pit 11. Sherd from 'saucepan' pot, fine dark ware

Enclosure III, Ditch Cuttings

-123. Cutting II, layer 8, primary silt. Fine, black 'saucepan' pot
I124. Cutting I, layer 5, secondary silt. Base sherd of medium jar

Petrological Examination of Iron Age Pottery

by David Williams

Introduction

One hundred and fourteen sherds were submitted for thin-section fabric analysis. All the samples were initially examined with the aid of a binocular microscope, and the majority were thin-sectioned (T/S), and studied under the petrological microscope. This allowed a number of fabric groupings to be made based on the type of inclusion present in the pottery, and also suggestions as to their likely areas of origin. In addition, an X-ray diffraction examination was made on the white inlay present on the outer surface of some of the sherds. Munsell colour charts are referred to in describing the surface colour of the sherds, as well as free descriptive terms.

Fabric A
Samples T/S: 1, 3, 5, 13, 15, 16, 17, 20, 21, 22, 24, 26, 55, 84, 85 (visual classification: 2, 6, 14, 19, 25, 57, 76).
The sherds appear in a fine, fairly hard, smooth sandy fabric, tending towards reddish-buff or dark grey (2.5YR N4/) in colour. The majority show signs of being haematite coated, and consist predominately of furrowed bowls and large fine ware jars.

In thin section the sherds in this group contain numerous subangular grains of quartz, average size 0.10mm and below, iron ore and flecks of mica. Also present are grains of collophane, and some rounded and sub-rounded dark reddish-brown grains of what may be limonite (altered glauconite), though precise identification is difficult due to the heavy staining of many of the grains. If altered glauconite is present in these sherds it could mean a fairly local origin for the pottery, as this is a mineral which is commonly found in the Upper Greensand, deposits of which are situated close to the Cow Down site. However, an alternative local clay source worth considering is the Gault Clay to the north-west of the site.

A sample of Gault was obtained from the neighbourhood of the Crockerton medieval kiln (Hurst 1968), some 1.5 miles from Cow Down, together with samples of pottery from the kiln. The sample of Gault was baked and then sectioned for study under the petrological microscope in the same way as the pottery. In thin section both the sample of Gault and pottery from the kiln revealed a matrix of clay which contained uniform inclusions of subangular quartz grains, average size 0.10 mm and below, and flecks of mica. Also present in both sections are a number of grains of collophane, which may be associated with phosphatic nodules present in the Gault (Reid 1903, 39). The mineralogy thus suggests that the local Gault was used in the production of the Crockerton medieval wares. The inclusions of quartz in those sherds making up Fabric A Iron Age wares are of a similar size to those in the Gault and pottery sections from Crockerton, and may suggest an origin for this group in that area, though the latter do seem to lack the dark reddish-brown grains present in Fabric A, and collophane is a fairly common mineral.

Fabric B
Samples T/S: 7, 8, 9, 11, 18, 23, 35, 44, 49, 50, 51, 52, 53, 54, 56, 71, 73, 77 (10, 12, 47, 48, 70, 79, 80, 83, 86, 113, 116).
Hard, fairly smooth sandy fabric, containing a scatter of small flint. The colour varies from reddish-brown (2.5YR 5/4) to dark grey (2.5Y N4/). The majority of the sherds show signs of being haematite coated. A number of furrowed bowls are represented, together with a variety of large jars. Sample 35 is a scratched cordon bowl.

The sherds in this fabric group appear slightly coarser than those of Fabric A, though there are petrological similarities between both groups. In thin section the sherds of Fabric B contain a groundmass of numerous subangular quartz grains, average size 0.10 mm and below, with a scatter of larger grains ranging up to 0.60 mm in size, together with flecks of mica and the occasional fragment of flint. Collophane and dark brown grains of (?) limonite are also present, though in lesser numbers than for Fabric A. A fairly local source may again be indicated.

Fabric C
Samples T/S: 42, 123.
Fairly hard, smooth black sandy fabric. Both are 'saucepan' pots. Thin sectioning reveals a scatter of subangular quartz grains in the size range 0.20-.40 mm, together with collophane and possibly some (?) limonite. A fairly local source may be indicated.

Fabric D
Samples T/S: 66, 67, 68, 69.
Fine, smooth sandy fabric, dark grey (5YR 4/1) in colour. Samples 66 and 67 are from pedestal jars, the remainder are from undesignated jars. Thin sectioning shows frequent well-sorted quartz grains, average size 0.20 mm, and some grains of collophane. Once again a fairly local source may be indicated, though it is difficult to be precise on this point.

Fabric E
Sample T/S: 122.
Much abraded sandy sherd, reddish-brown (2.5YR 4/4) in colour. This sample is from a 'saucepan' pot. Thin sectioning shows a scatter a subangular quartz grains, average size 0.10-.20 mm. It is difficult to predict possible sources when dealing with such common minerals.

Fabric F
Sample T/S: 58.
Fairly hard, sandy fabric, light reddish-buff in colour. The sample is from a large coarse bowl. In thin section this sherd is seen to contain frequent quartz grains below 0.20 mm.

Fabric G
(117, not sectioned).
Hard, very sandy fairly smooth fabric, dark grey (10YR 4/) in colour. This sample is from a high shouldered jar.

Fabric H
Samples T/S: 27, 28, 29, 31, 32, 33, 61, 63, (72, 74, 78, 87, 89, 90).
Thick, rough crumbly sandy fabric with frequent inclusions of flint. Reddish-brown (2.5YR 5/4) to greyish brown (10YR 5/2) in colour. The group consists of medium-coarse bowls and jars. As anticipated from a site situated on the chalk, this group is characterized by its flint content. In thin section large fragments of flint, up to 1.50 mm across, occur throughout the clay matrix. Also present are frequent ill-sorted subangular grains of quartz ranging up to 1.30 mm in size, together with a little collophane. The inclusions suggest a fairly local source.

Fabric I
Samples T/S: 36, 37, 38, 45, 46, 101, 108, 112, 120, (111, 114, 118, 124).
Soft, fairly smooth and soapy to the touch, containing inclusions of ooliths scattered throughout the fabric. The sample sherds range in colour from reddish-yellow (5YR 6/6) to dark grey (7.5YR N3/). The forms consist of large storage jars and coarse bowls. Thin sectioning reveals the ooliths more clearly, and it is possible to see their concentric structure within the limestone body. Also present in most cases are fossiliferous shell, limestone and a scatter of quartz grains. The presence of ooliths points to the Jurassic Ridge as a likely source for the temper. The nearest Jurassic outcrop to Cow Down lies some five miles west of the site.

Fabric J
Samples T/S: 39, 40, 41, 43, 59, 60, 62, 64, 75, 103, 104, 106, 110, 119 (88, 102, 107, 109, 115, 121).
All the sample sherds are characterized by visible shell inclusions scattered throughout the fabric. There is a wide range of surface colours. The overwhelming form represented in the group is a fairly coarse jar. In thin section it is possible to see some recrystallization of calcite in the shell suggesting that it is fossiliferous. Also present are small quantities of limestone, while samples 41, 43, 64, 75 and 106 in particular contain frequent quartz grains. The presence of fossiliferous shell suggests the Jurassic Ridge as a likely source for the temper.

Fabric K
Samples T/S: 4, 30, 34, 65, 81.
There is a wide range of surface colours and forms. All the sherds contain visible inclusions of flint. In thin section the fabric is characterized by the presence of limestone. Flint, quartzite, mica and quartz appear in all the sections, though the latter's size and quantity does vary, so

perhaps this should not be looked upon as a 'homogeneous' group. The limestone content is 'undistinguished' and as such it is difficult to suggest a likely origin for the sherds.

Conclusions

If the collophane/possible limonite noted in certain thin sections suggests that the vessels concerned might have been made from the local Gault/Upper Greensand, then it seems likely that all the fine wares and about half of the coarse wares from the earlier deposits (Houses I and II) were made at or near the site. Moreover, Houses I and II share common origins for much of the pottery; Fabrics A, B, H, and K contain samples from both Houses.

The petrological results of the haematite wares from Cow Down and Eldon's Seat, Dorset, where local production was also suggested (Cunliffe and Phillipson 1968, 206-207), indicates in both cases a domestic industry producing for local requirements. This view contrasts with the analysis of haematite pottery from Meon Hill and All Cannings Cross, where owing to the presence of ferruginous grit, those wares were not thought to have been made at either site and, moreover, were suspected of having a common origin (Liddell 1937, 23).

The situation of a number of local centres producing haematite wares on the one hand, and some mechanism of trade on the other hand which allowed a few of these distinctive wares to enjoy a relatively wide distribution, seems to be confirmed by the analysis of haematite pottery from Gussage All Saints (Wainwright 1979). At this site the majority of haematite wares were considered mineralogically to have been made locally; however, there were a small number characterized by oolithic inclusions which were in all probability made at some distance from the site.

An Examination of the White Inlay on the Pottery

An X-ray power diffraction examination was made on a sample of white inlaid decoration taken from a large haematite-coated jar (for an explanation of the method involved see Bimson (1969). The pattern formed from this sample reasonably matched the A.S.T.M. Calcite standard, as in the residues found adhering inside certain pieces from All Cannings Cross (File no. 5-0586). No indication of the presence of phosphate was given, (Cunnington 1923, 33), though the exposure may have been too faint to pick up an amount below 10%. In view of this possibility a phosphate spot test was also undertaken (Schwarz 1967), but recorded a negative result, indicating that phosphate was not present in the sample. In this respect it is apparent that the Cow Down sample is similar to nos. 5 and 6 from All Cannings Cross (Cunnington 1923, 198), which also showed the white inlay on certain Iron Age vessels to be composed almost entirely of calcite.

Heavy Mineral Analysis of Haematite-Coated Sherds
by P.T. Partridge

Five sherds were subjected to heavy mineral analysis: an example of a furrowed bowl from each of Houses 1-3, and two sherds from House 1 representing the large haematite-coated jars. In addition, the three sherds from House 1 were also examined in thin section.

Results

Heavy mineral analysis, the results of which are presented in Table 3A.1 (nos. 8-12) and graphically represented in Table 3A.2 (nos. 5 and 6) suggested that the same source of clay was used throughout the Iron Age occupation of the site. The similarities between all the sherds analysed also indicates that both the bowls and jars derived from the same production source. The thin sections, summarised in Table 3, confirmed these findings, as the fabrics of the bowl and jars examined from House 1 were found to be similarly characterised by small angular quartz grains and sandstone inclusions.

The Longbridge Deverill evidence may be compared with examination of haematite-coated furrowed bowls from a number of sites in Wessex, the results of which are summarised in the accompanying Tables. The heavy mineral assemblages from this site compare closely with those from the neighbouring Wiltshire sites of All Cannings Cross and Swallowcliffe Down. This suggests the exploitation of one major source, the Gault, possibly with some degree of centralised production in the locality. In sharp contrast, however, is the assemblage from the

Table 3A.1 Results of heavy mineral analysis

No.	Site	Sherd	Grains
1	All Cannings Cross	1B	219
2	All Cannings Cross	2A	469
3	Swallowcliffe Down	2A	353
4	Meon Hill	P336	33
5	Poundbury	Unmarked	292
6	Marnhull	Pit 124	107
7	Eldon's Seat	ES '63 D7	214
8	Longbridge Deverill	1 Ph 152 (bowl)	75
9	Longbridge Deverill	1 Ph 151 (jar)	256
10	Longbridge Deverill	1 Ph 152 (jar)	280
11	Longbridge Deverill	2 Ph 137	190
12	Longbridge Deverill	3 '57 932B Ho. 3	231
13	Shipstal Point	Sand	580

Key A = Abundant; C = Common; R = Rare

Table 3A.2 Percentage of heavy minerals

No.	Zircon	Tourmaline	Rutile	Garnet	Andalusite	Kyanite
1	48.4	2.7	11.4	22.8	5.5	5.9
2	53.9	8.7	14.2	12.6	4.7	1.1
3	58.4	2.5	11.9	9.3	6.8	0.3
4	60.6	21.2	9.1	0.0	3.0	3.0
5	58.9	7.2	15.7	14.7	1.0	1.4
6	71.0	7.5	13.1	2.8	4.7	0.0
7	10.7	86.4	0.9	0.9	0.0	0.0
8	60.0	5.3	16.0	9.3	1.3	1.3
9	52.7	6.2	19.9	16.4	1.2	1.6
10	60.7	3.6	11.4	20.4	0.7	0.0
11	54.7	10.0	13.7	16.3	1.6	0.0
12	65.8	5.2	7.8	16.9	0.9	0.9
13	10.5	73.4	4.5	0.2	4.8	1.5

Purbeck site of Eldon's Seat, Encombe, where the high tourmaline content is precisely reflected in the nearby Tertiary sands (Table 3A.2, no. 2).

This hypothesis accords with the concept of regional 'style zones' in Iron Age Britain, where 'areas in which the types constituting the style were commonly in use' (Cunliffe 1976). Cunliffe recognises in the Wessex region two groups with a considerable degree of contact and overlap: the All Cannings Cross group centred in Wiltshire and the Kimmeridge-Caburn group from Dorset. In the context of locally organised communities it may also be significant that thin sections reveal clear differences in the fabrics of sherds from two Hampshire sites, Meon Hill near Stockbridge and St. Georges Street, Winchester.

A programme of detailed petrological research will help to substantiate these conclusions, and contribute to our understanding of relationships between Iron Age communities. The potential of such an approach has already been realised in the work on movement of Later Iron Age wares, such as Glastonbury ware (Peacock 1964).

Table 3A.3 Thin-section study: summary

Site	*Composition of Inclusions*				*Texture (average.size)*		
	Quartz	*Sandstone*	*Flint*	*Limestone*	*0-0.025*	*0.025-0.075*	*0.075+*
Longbridge	A	C	-	-	Yes	-	-
Meon Hill	A	-	C	-	-	Yes	-
Wincester	A	-	C	-	Yes	-	-
Marnhull	A	R	-	-	Yes	-	-
Eldon's Seat	A	-	R	R	-	-	Yes

Key A = Abundant; C = Common; R = Rare

Appendix 3B

ANALYSIS OF THE FABRIC GROUPS

The pottery assemblages from the contexts as recorded have been considered on the basis of the 14 groups recognised by Wilson. The pottery is grouped by fabrics in context of discovery, with inferences drawn for relative chronology. Tables 3B1a-3B11 below present the totals by sherd count of pottery by fabric and context within the following archaeological groupings:

Enclosure I – all pottery
Enclosure II – Houses 1,2,4; pits; postholes; hollows; working hollows; Cuttings
Enclosure III – House 3 Cuttings; House 3 postholes; earthworks (bank and Ditch)

Enclosure I

Table 3B.1a: Enclosure I – total sherds 408

Context	*Pottery Fabrics*													
Enclosure I	1	2	3	4	5	6	7	8	9	10	11	12	13	14	Total
01 Pit 1	—	1	1	21	—	6	—	13	9	1	19	1	7	14	93
02 Pit 2	—	21	5	20	6	3	—	7	18	3	39	—	—	1	123
03 Pit 3	—	—	—	—	4	—	—	—	—	—	15	—	—	—	19
04 Pit 4	—	1	—	5	2	—	—	—	6	—	—	—	—	—	14
05 Top Layer	—	—	—	1	1	—	—	—	—	—	—	—	—	2	4
06 Cutting P	—	—	—	—	—	—	—	—	4	—	—	—	—	11	15
07 Cutting R	2	—	9	—	—	—	—	1	11	6	4	—	—	15	48
08 Enclosure I	—	—	8	19	1	4	—	3	17	—	18	8	3	11	92

Enclosure II

Table 3B.1b: Enclosure II House 1 – total sherds 422

Context	*Pottery Fabrics*														
House 1	1	2	3	4	5	6	7	8	9	10	11	12	13	14	Total
09 PH 42	--	5	--	--	7	--	--	--	--	--	1	--	--	--	13
10 PH 63	--	4	--	--	2	--	--	--	--	--	--	--	--	1	7
11 PH 127	--	2	--	--	--	--	--	--	--	--	--	--	--	--	2
12 PH 129	--	--	--	--	1	--	--	--	--	--	--	--	--	--	1
13 PH 139	--	3	--	--	2	--	--	--	1	--	--	--	--	9	15
14 PH 140	--	2	--	--	2	--	--	--	--	--	--	--	--	--	4
15 PH 145	--	--	--	--	--	--	--	--	--	--	3	--	--	1	4
16 PH 151	--	86	--	--	15	--	--	--	1	--	9	--	--	3	114
17 PH 152	--	78	--	--	11	--	--	5	--	--	--	--	--	--	94
18 PH 153	--	39	--	--	10	--	--	--	--	--	2	--	--	3	54
16/17 PH 151/2	--	1	--	--	--	--	--	--	--	--	--	--	--	--	1
16/18 PH 151/3	--	1	--	--	--	--	--	--	--	--	--	--	--	--	1
17/18 PH 152/3	--	1	--	--	--	--	--	--	--	--	--	--	--	--	1
19 PH 154	--	27	3	--	11	--	--	--	--	--	4	--	--	1	46
20 PH 155	--	--	1	--	--	--	--	--	--	--	--	--	--	--	1
21 PH 161	--	--	--	--	1	--	--	--	--	--	--	--	--	--	1
22 PH 165	--	4	--	--	2	--	--	--	--	--	--	--	--	1	7
23 PH 167	--	2	--	--	1	--	--	--	--	--	--	--	--	--	3
24 PH 186	--	2	--	1	1	--	--	--	--	--	--	--	--	--	4
25 PH 224	--	1	--	--	--	--	--	--	--	--	--	--	--	--	1

26 PH 225	--	2	--	--	2	--	--	--	--	--	1	--	--	--	5
27 PH 235	--	3	6	--	7	--	--	--	6	--	2	--	--	7	31
10/27 PH63/235	--	1	--	--	--	--	--	--	--	--	--	--	--	--	1
28 PH 237	--	1	--	--	--	--	--	--	--	--	--	--	--	--	1
29 PH 241	--	1	--	--	--	--	--	--	--	--	--	--	--	--	1
30 B XIV 2	--	2	--	--	--	--	--	--	--	--	--	--	--	--	2
31 B XXIV 2	--	--	--	--	1	--	--	--	--	--	--	--	--	--	1
32 B XXV 2	--	1	--	--	--	--	--	--	--	--	--	--	--	--	1
33 B XXVII 1	--	2	--	--	--	--	--	--	--	--	--	--	--	--	2
34 B XXVII 2	--	--	--	--	1	--	--	--	--	--	--	--	--	--	1

Table 3B.1c: Enclosure II House 2 – total sherds 500

Context	*Pottery Fabrics*														
House 2	1	2	3	4	5	6	7	8	9	10	11	12	13	14	Total
35 PH 90	--	1	--	--	3	--	--	--	--	--	--	--	--	2	6
36 PH 91	--	--	--	--	--	--	--	--	--	2	2	--	--	--	4
37 PH 123	--	--	--	--	--	--	--	--	--	--	1	--	--	--	1
38 PH 125	--	--	--	--	--	--	--	--	--	--	1	--	--	--	1
39 PH 126	--	2	--	--	11	--	--	--	3	--	6	--	--	3	25
40 PH 128	--	2	1	--	--	--	--	--	--	--	--	--	--	--	3
41 PH 130	--	--	1	--	--	--	--	--	--	--	--	--	--	--	1
42 PH 132	--	--	1	--	--	--	--	--	--	--	1	--	--	--	2
43 PH 133	--	1	--	--	--	--	--	--	--	--	--	--	--	--	1
44 PH 134	--	1	6	--	12	--	--	--	3	--	--	--	--	3	25
45 PH 135	--	6	2	--	21	--	--	--	4	--	24	--	--	3	60
46 PH 136	--	7	1	--	26	--	--	--	3	--	3	--	2	7	49
47 PH 137	--	4	11	2	14	1	--	--	14	--	54	--	5	1	106
48 PH 142	--	--	--	--	--	--	--	--	4	--	--	--	--	--	4
49 PH 143	--	--	--	1	1	--	--	--	1	--	--	--	--	--	3
50 PH 144	--	--	3	--	--	--	--	--	2	--	10	--	--	--	15
51 PH 145	--	--	1	--	--	--	--	--	--	--	--	--	--	--	1
52 PH 146	--	3	2	--	6	--	--	--	1	--	1	--	--	1	14
53 PH 147	--	2	5	--	7	--	--	--	2	--	2	--	--	8	26
54 PH 149	--	2	--	--	--	--	--	--	--	--	--	--	--	--	2
55 PH 156	--	1	--	--	1	--	--	--	--	--	--	--	--	2	4
56 PH 157	--	--	2	--	1	--	--	--	1	--	1	--	--	2	7
57 PH 162	--	--	--	--	--	--	--	--	--	--	6	--	--	1	7
58 PH 167	--	--	--	--	2	--	--	--	--	--	1	--	--	--	3
59 PH 170	--	--	--	--	--	--	--	--	--	--	1	--	--	--	1
60 PH 172	--	--	--	--	2	--	--	--	7	--	--	--	--	3	12
61 PH 174	--	--	--	--	2	--	--	--	--	--	--	--	--	--	2
62 PH 175	--	2	--	--	--	--	--	--	--	--	--	--	--	--	2
63 PH 179	--	1	--	--	1	--	--	--	--	--	--	--	--	--	2
64 PH 180	--	--	--	--	2	--	--	--	--	--	--	--	--	--	2
65 PH 181	--	--	--	--	--	--	--	--	--	--	1	--	--	--	1
66 PH 182	--	2	--	--	1	--	--	--	--	--	--	--	--	--	3
67 PH 203	--	--	--	--	1	--	--	--	--	--	--	--	--	--	1
68 PH 204	--	--	--	--	--	--	--	--	4	--	5	--	--	--	9
69 PH 214	--	--	2	--	--	--	--	--	--	--	--	--	--	--	2
70 PH 229	--	--	2	--	--	--	--	--	3	--	5	--	--	1	11
71 PH 238	--	3	--	--	--	--	--	--	--	--	--	--	--	--	3
72 PH 239	--	--	--	--	1	--	--	1	--	--	--	--	--	--	2
Mixed	--	1	2	--	11	--	--	--	4	--	7	--	--	1	26
73 Pit 43	--	--	1	--	--	--	--	--	--	--	--	--	--	--	1
74 B XXIV	--	1	1	--	2	--	--	--	--	--	--	--	--	--	4
75 B XXIV 2	--	2	8	1	8	1	--	--	1	--	8	--	--	12	41
76 B XXVIII 2	--	--	2	--	--	--	--	--	1	--	--	--	--	2	5

Table 3B.1d: Enclosure II House 4 – total sherds 72

Context	Pottery Fabrics														
House 4	1	2	3	4	5	6	7	8	9	10	11	12	13	14	Total
77 PH 184	--	--	1	--	--	--	--	--	--	--	--	--	--	--	1
78 PH 185	--	1	--	--	--	--	–	--	--	--	--	--	--	--	1
79 PH 187	--	--	1	--	--	--	--	--	--	--	--	--	--	--	1
80 PH 193	--	--	1	--	--	--	--	--	--	--	--	--	--	2	3
81 PH 197	--	--	--	--	--	--	--	--	--	--	--	--	--	1	1
82 PH 198	--	--	--	1	--	9	--	--	1	--	--	--	--	--	11
83 PH 199	--	2	--	--	--	--	--	--	--	--	1	--	--	--	3
84 PH 201	--	--	1	--	--	--	--	--	--	--	--	--	--	--	1
85 PH 207	--	--	--	--	--	--	--	--	--	--	2	--	--	--	2
86 PH 208	--	1	--	--	--	--	--	--	--	--	--	--	--	--	1
87 PH 210	--	--	--	--	1	--	--	--	--	--	1	--	--	1	3
88 PH 211	--	--	--	1	1	--	--	--	--	--	--	--	--	--	2
89 PH 216	--	1	--	1	20	--	--	--	--	--	1	--	--	--	23
90 PH 217	--	--	--	--	--	--	--	--	--	--	--	--	--	1	1
91 PH 222	--	1	1	--	--	--	--	--	--	--	--	--	--	--	2
92 PH 232	--	--	1	--	--	--	--	--	--	--	--	--	--	1	2
93 Gully 1	--	1	--	--	1	--	--	--	--	--	--	--	--	--	2
94 Gully 2	--	--	1	--	--	--	--	--	--	--	--	--	--	--	1
95 Gully 3	--	--	--	--	2	--	--	--	--	--	--	--	--	--	2
96 B XXXIII	--	--	--	--	--	--	--	--	--	--	1	--	--	--	1
97 B XXXIII 2	--	--	--	--	--	--	--	--	2	--	--	--	--	--	2
98 B XXXIII/IV	--	--	--	1	--	–	--	--	1	--	4	--	--	--	6

Table 3B.1e: Enclosure II Pits – total sherds 2049

Context	Pottery Fabrics														
Pits	1	2	3	4	5	6	7	8	9	10	11	12	13	14	Total
99 Pit 2	--	--	2	1	--	--	--	11	15	1	--	--	1	--	31
100 Pit 3	--	--	--	1	--	--	--	--	8	--	--	--	--	--	9
101 Pit 4	--	--	--	--	--	--	--	2	--	1	--	--	1	2	6
102 Pit 5	--	1	12	3	1	1	--	7	27	3	6	3	--	4	68
103 Pit 7	--	--	2	4	6	--	--	12	7	4	1	--	2	1	39
104 Pit 8	--	--	--	--	--	--	--	--	2	--	--	--	--	1	3
105 Pit 9	--	--	--	4	1	--	--	8	14	2	--	--	2	--	31
106 Pit 10	--	--	19	--	--	--	--	--	1	--	2	--	--	7	29
107 Pit 11	--	--	4	--	1	--	--	7	6	5	--	2	--	--	25
108 Pit 12	--	--	--	2	--	--	--	--	--	--	--	--	--	6	8
109 Pit 13	--	--	--	--	--	--	--	–	1	--	--	--	--	--	1
110 Pit 14	--	--	6	1	1	--	--	13	14	4	1	--	--	--	40
111 Pit 16	--	--	--	--	--	--	--	--	--	--	--	--	--	--	--
112 Pit 17	--	--	1	17	--	--	--	--	--	-	1	--	--	10	29
113 Pit 18	--	--	--	--	--	--	--	1	--	5	1	--	--	--	7
113 Pit 18/WH.I	--	5	6	4	5	--	--	9	4	11	--	--	--	--	44
114 Pit 19	--	1	8	15	--	--	--	27	23	4	--	--	--	3	81
115 Pit 20	--	--	1	--	--	--	--	--	4	--	2	--	--	--	7
116 Pit 21	--	--	--	5	1	3	--	1	7	7	7	--	2	1	34
117 Pit 22	--	3	--	3	--	--	3	1	4	13	3	--	--	--	30
118 Pit 23	--	--	2	--	--	--	--	--	--	7	--	--	--	--	9
119 Pit 24	--	--	--	--	--	1	--	--	1	--	--	--	--	--	2
120 Pit 25	--	--	1	--	--	--	--	--	3	--	1	--	--	--	5
121 Pit 26	--	--	4	--	--	1	--	--	--	1	8	--	--	--	14
122 Pit 27	--	1	3	1	--	--	--	2	1	--	--	--	--	--	8
123 Pit 28	--	--	--	--	--	--	--	--	1	--	--	--	--	--	1
124 Pit 29	--	--	3	--	2	2	--	--	--	--	1	--	2	--	10
125 Pit 30	--	--	--	--	--	--	--	--	1	--	--	--	--	--	1

126 Pit 31	--	--	--	1	2	--	--	2	8	9	--	--	--	--	22
127 Pit 34	--	1	--	5	3	--	--	--	4	--	1	--	1	8	23
128-9 Pits 36-B	--	1	12	14	6	--	--	14	5	--	--	--	1	4	57
130 Pit 37	--	2	11	18	3	17	--	56	53	3	5	1	--	6	175
131 Pit 38	--	1	4	5	--	--	--	--	6	--	3	--	--	--	19
132 Pit 39	--	--	5	18	7	--	1	19	7	18	12	--	--	--	87
133 Pit 40	--	12	11	3	3	--	--	9	4	--	13	--	3	2	60
134 Pit 41	--	--	14	5	--	--	--	10	3	--	20	--	--	--	52
135 Pit 42	--	--	--	--	2	--	--	3	2	2	--	1	--	1	11
136 Pit 43	--	1	4	1	--	--	--	17	1	7	--	--	--	--	31
137 Pit 44	--	--	1	6	--	--	--	--	2	1	--	--	--	--	10
138 Pit 45	--	--	8	--	1	1	--	7	7	1	2	2	2	6	37
139 Pit 46	--	--	--	--	1	5	--	6	35	--	--	--	--	--	47
140 Pit 47	--	--	3	2	4	--	--	14	2	--	--	--	--	--	25
141 Pit 48	--	--	--	1	--	5	--	3	1	--	--	--	--	--	10
142 Pit 49	--	--	--	--	--	--	--	3	6	--	--	--	--	2	11
143 Pit 50	--	--	7	1	5	--	--	4	17	--	--	1	--	3	38
144 Pit 51	--	--	--	2	--	1	--	3	11	--	--	--	--	--	17
145 Pit 52	--	--	--	4	--	--	--	8	3	9	--	--	--	--	24
146 Pit 53	--	1	18	1	2	1	--	11	28	--	--	8	--	1	71
147 Pit 54	--	1	3	7	1	--	--	13	8	12	--	1	1	--	47
148 Pit 55	--	--	9	4	1	1	--	7	4	10	--	1	--	--	37
149 Pit 56	--	--	--	1	1	--	--	1	1	3	--	--	--	--	7
150 Pit 57	--	--	7	--	3	--	--	8	11	--	--	--	--	2	31
151 Pit 58	--	1	10	1	--	--	--	7	4	1	--	--	--	--	24
152 Pit 59	--	--	4	--	1	5	--	8	13	1	--	--	--	3	35
153 Pit 60	--	7	45	--	2	--	--	35	45	3	--	--	2	--	139
154 Pit 61	--	--	--	--	--	--	--	1	2	--	--	--	--	1	4
155 Pit 62	--	--	--	--	--	--	--	3	2	--	--	--	--	--	5
156 Pit 63	--	--	5	--	1	--	--	4	12	--	--	--	--	--	22
157 Pit 64	--	--	3	--	1	--	--	4	3	--	--	--	--	--	11
158 Pit 65	--	4	7	--	4	--	--	6	18	6	--	1	--	--	46
159 Pit 66	--	--	1	--	1	--	--	--	1	--	--	--	--	--	3
160 Pit 67	--	12	30	1	4	--	--	7	12	1	--	--	--	18	85
161 Pit 68	--	1	--	--	--	--	--	1	1	--	--	--	--	1	4
162/3 Pits 69/70	--	6	7	4	10	--	--	34	37	1	4	--	--	35	138
164 Pit 72	--	--	--	1	--	--	--	--	--	1	--	--	--	1	3
165 Pit 73	--	1	1	--	--	--	--	--	5	--	--	--	--	2	9

Table 3B.1f: Enclosure II Postholes – total sherds 174

Context	*Pottery Fabrics*														
Postholes	1	2	3	4	5	6	7	8	9	10	11	12	13	14	Total
166 PH 4	--	--	3	--	--	--	--	1	3	7	--	--	--	--	14
167 PH 17	--	--	--	--	--	--	--	--	--	--	--	--	--	3	3
168 PH 18	--	--	1	--	--	--	--	--	--	--	6	--	--	--	7
169 PH 25	--	--	4	--	--	1	--	--	--	--	5	--	--	--	10
170 PH 31	--	2	5	--	1	--	--	--	--	2	4	--	--	5	19
171 PH 32	--	--	--	1	7	--	--	--	--	--	4	--	--	5	17
172 PH 39	--	--	1	--	2	--	--	--	--	--	--	--	1	4	8
173 PH 40	--	--	--	--	--	--	--	--	--	--	1	--	--	2	3
174 PH 43	--	--	--	--	2	--	--	--	--	--	--	--	--	1	3
175 PH 45	--	--	2	3	--	--	--	--	--	2	--	--	--	1	8
176 PH 48	--	--	--	--	--	--	--	--	--	--	5	--	--	--	5
177 PH 49	--	--	--	--	--	--	--	1	--	--	--	--	--	--	1
178 PH 55	--	--	--	--	--	--	--	--	--	--	1	--	--	--	1
179 PH 61	--	--	--	1	--	--	--	--	--	--	2	--	--	--	3
180 PH 71	--	--	--	--	--	--	--	--	2	--	--	--	--	--	2
181 PH 79	--	--	--	--	--	--	--	--	--	--	--	3	--	--	3
182 PH 80	--	--	3	--	--	--	--	--	--	1	--	--	--	5	9

183 PH 81	--	1	--	--	--	--	--	--	--	--	--	--	--	--	1
184 PH 82	--	--	--	--	--	--	--	--	--	--	--	--	2	--	2
185 PH 83	--	--	--	--	--	--	--	--	--	--	--	1	--	--	1
186 PH 92	--	1	--	--	--	--	--	2	--	--	2	--	--	1	6
187/8 PH 93-94	--	--	3	--	--	--	--	--	--	--	2	--	2	2	9
189 PH 95	--	--	--	--	--	--	--	--	--	--	--	--	--	3	3
190 PH 97	--	1	--	--	2	--	–	--	--	--	4	--	--	--	7
191 PH 168	--	--	--	1	--	--	--	1	--	--	--	--	--	--	2
192 PH 173	--	--	--	2	--	--	--	--	--	7	--	--	--	--	9
193 PH 196	--	--	1	9	--	--	--	8	--	--	--	--	--	--	18

Table 3B.1g: Enclosure II Hollows – total sherds 54

Context	Pottery Fabrics														
Hollows	1	2	3	4	5	6	7	8	9	10	11	12	13	14	Total
194 H.6	--	--	1	--	--	--	--	2	--	--	--	--	--	5	8
195 H.8	--	--	1	--	--	--	--	--	7	--	--	--	3	3	14
196 H.13	--	--	--	--	--	--	--	--	--	--	--	--	--	2	2
197 H.17	--	--	--	--	--	--	--	3	1	4	--	--	--	--	8
198 H.19	--	--	--	--	5	--	--	--	14	--	--	3	--	--	22

Table 3B.1h: Enclosure II Working Hollows – total sherds 708

Context	Pottery Fabrics														
Working Hollows	1	2	3	4	5	6	7	8	9	10	11	12	13	14	Total
199 WH 1	--	12	16	23	15	--	--	1	17	3	28	--	4	14	133
200 WH 2	--	4	10	7	7	2	--	4	25	18	8	1	6	7	99
201 WH 3	1	21	71	--	46	–	--	11	49	7	80	--	29	23	338
200/1 WH 2/3	--	--	--	2	6	--	--	--	--	--	4	--	--	--	12
202 WH 4	--	--	--	2	4	2	--	31	10	6	--	--	--	6	61
203 WH 5	--	2	--	1	--	--	--	10	34	--	--	--	--	1	48
204 WH 6	--	--	7	–	--	--	--	2	2	1	--	5	--	--	17

Table 3B.1i: Enclosure II Cuttings – total sherds 288

Context	Pottery Fabrics														
Cuttings	1	2	3	4	5	6	7	8	9	10	11	12	13	14	Total
205 B2	--	--	--	--	--	--	--	1	--	--	--	--	--	--	1
206 D2	--	--	--	3	--	1	--	--	4	--	2	--	1	3	14
207 D3	--	--	1	--	--	14	--	1	7	--	--	--	--	--	23
208 D4	--	--	--	--	1	--	--	--	--	1	--	--	--	--	2
209 D6	--	--	--	--	--	--	--	--	--	--	1	1	--	--	2
210 F5	--	--	--	--	--	--	--	--	1	--	--	--	15	--	16
211 H1	--	--	--	--	1	--	--	--	--	--	--	--	6	--	7
212 H2	--	--	5	--	--	--	--	22	5	--	--	--	--	3	35
213 H3	--	--	6	--	2	--	--	1	3	--	3	--	--	15	30
214 I1	--	--	--	2	--	1	--	--	1	--	1	--	--	--	5
215 I2	--	--	3	1	--	--	--	4	--	--	--	--	--	--	8
216 I3	--	--	--	--	--	--	--	1	--	--	1	--	--	8	10
217 I4	--	3	--	--	1	--	--	--	4	--	20	--	--	--	28
218 I5	--	--	1	--	--	--	--	--	--	--	--	--	--	--	1
219 J3	--	1	4	8	--	--	--	4	4	--	17	--	--	--	38
220 J4	--	--	2	2	4	--	--	2	--	1	--	1	--	--	12
221 J6	--	--	--	--	--	--	--	--	--	--	--	--	1	--	1
222 J8	--	--	--	--	--	--	--	--	--	--	4	--	--	--	4
223 K2	--	--	--	--	--	--	--	--	--	--	3	--	2	--	5

224 K3	--	--	--	--	2	--	--	2	9	--	--	2	--	5	20
225 K5	--	--	--	4	2	--	--	2	--	--	1	--	6	--	15
226 K6	--	--	--	3	--	--	--	--	--	--	--	--	--	1	4
227 K7	--	--	--	--	2	1	--	--	--	--	--	--	--	--	3
228 L3	--	--	--	--	1	--	--	--	--	--	--	--	--	--	1
229 L5	--	--	--	--	--	--	--	--	1	--	--	--	--	--	1
230 L8	--	--	--	--	--	--	--	--	1	1	--	--	--	--	2

Enclosure III

Table 3B.1j: Enclosure III, House 3 Cuttings – total sherds 681

Context	*Pottery Fabrics*														
House 3 Cuttings	1	2	3	4	5	6	7	8	9	10	11	12	13	14	Total
231 C 62B	--	4	7	3	13	--	--	1	3	--	3	--	--	3	37
232 C 63	--	--	10	--	9	--	--	--	--	--	--	2	--	--	21
233 C 63B	--	1	2	--	--	--	--	1	--	--	--	--	--	--	4
234 C 65	--	2	3	--	5	--	--	--	1	--	13	--	--	3	27
235 C 65B	--	--	7	--	8	--	--	1	3	--	14	1	13	2	49
236 C 66	--	--	--	--	--	--	--	--	1	--	2	--	--	1	4
237 C 67	--	--	--	--	1	--	--	--	--	--	--	--	--	--	1
238 C 68	--	--	--	2	--	--	--	--	--	--	3	--	1	--	6
239 C 86	--	1	1	--	1	--	--	--	1	--	3	--	7	--	14
240 C 89	--	--	--	--	--	--	--	--	--	--	--	--	1	--	1
241 C 91	--	1	7	1	11	--	--	--	--	--	9	--	5	3	37
242 C 91B	--	2	6	--	2	--	--	--	3	--	2	--	--	4	19
243 C 92	--	--	--	--	4	--	--	--	3	--	5	--	--	1	13
244 C 93	--	4	6	--	8	--	--	1	3	--	11	--	5	19	57
245 C 94	--	6	11	1	27	--	--	1	8	--	--	--	11	2	67
246 C 94B	--	--	1	2	1	--	--	--	--	--	1	--	4	2	11
247 C 95	--	2	4	--	5	--	--	--	--	--	1	--	2	4	18
248 C 95 2B	--	--	1	--	--	--	--	--	--	--	--	--	--	--	1
249 C 96	--	--	--	--	--	--	--	--	--	--	4	--	--	--	4
250 C 101	--	1	--	--	--	--	--	--	--	--	--	--	--	--	1
251 C 102	--	--	--	--	--	--	--	--	--	--	1	--	--	--	1
252 C 102B	--	--	1	--	1	--	--	--	2	--	--	--	--	4	8
253 C 103	--	1	7	--	3	--	--	--	--	--	--	--	--	3	14
254 C 104	--	--	3	3	17	--	--	--	3	--	9	--	6	4	45
255 C 104 2A	--	2	--	--	3	--	--	--	--	--	4	--	--	--	9
256 C 111	--	--	--	--	--	--	--	--	--	--	--	--	--	1	1
257 C 113	--	--	--	--	1	--	--	--	--	--	6	--	--	--	7
258 C 113 2A	--	--	--	--	1	--	--	--	--	--	--	--	--	--	1
259 C 114	--	--	1	--	--	--	--	--	--	--	--	--	--	--	1
260 C 115	--	--	--	--	2	--	--	--	--	--	1	--	--	2	5
261 IV	--	1	4	2	5	--	--	--	8	1	11	--	--	12	44
262 IV EXT	2	3	4	3	10	--	--	--	2	1	5	--	5	3	38
263 V	--	--	4	--	--	--	--	--	--	--	--	--	1	5	10
264 V EXT	--	13	14	1	9	--	--	2	7	2	5	--	8	17	78
265 VI	--	--	1	2	--	--	--	--	--	--	--	--	--	1	4
266 VI EXT	--	--	1	--	--	--	--	--	2	--	1	--	1	--	5
267 VII	--	--	--	1	1	--	--	--	--	--	--	--	1	1	4
268 XV	--	--	2	--	9	--	--	--	--	--	--	--	--	3	14

Table 3B.1k: House 3, Postholes – total sherds 413

Context	Pottery Fabrics													
House 3														
Post Holes	1	2	3	4	5	6	7	8	9	10	11	12	13	14	Total
269 PH 4	--	--	--	--	--	--	--	1	1	--	5	1	--	--	8
270 PH 5	--	--	--	--	1	--	--	--	--	--	--	--	--	--	1
271 PH 51	--	--	1	--	--	--	--	--	--	--	--	--	--	--	1
272 PH 52	--	--	1	--	1	--	--	--	--	--	--	--	1	1	4
273 PH 54	--	2	1	--	--	--	--	--	2	--	1	--	4	7	17
274 PH 55	--	2	2	--	4	--	--	--	1	--	3	--	7	6	25
275 PH 56	--	--	--	--	3	--	--	--	--	1	--	--	--	--	4
276 PH 57	--	--	--	--	--	--	--	--	--	--	2	--	1	1	4
277 PH 62	--	--	1	--	6	--	--	--	1	--	8	1	3	9	29
278 PH 62a	--	--	--	--	1	--	--	--	--	--	--	--	1	--	2
279 PH 63	--	2	1	--	1	--	--	--	--	--	--	--	1	--	5
280 PH 63 1	--	--	--	--	--	--	--	--	--	--	4	--	--	8	12
281 PH 64	--	1	--	--	--	--	--	--	--	--	--	--	--	--	1
282 PH 65	--	--	1	--	--	--	--	--	--	--	--	--	--	--	1
283 PH 70	--	2	--	--	--	--	--	--	1	--	2	--	--	1	6
284 PH 71	--	2	3	--	2	--	--	--	--	--	3	--	--	--	10
285 PH 72	--	--	4	--	3	--	--	--	--	--	--	--	1	2	10
286 PH 73	--	--	2	--	6	--	--	--	3	--	2	--	11	3	27
287 PH 73/120	--	1	--	--	--	--	--	--	--	--	--	--	--	--	1
288 PH 73/S3	--	--	--	--	--	--	--	--	--	--	--	--	1	--	1
289 PH 102	--	--	--	--	--	--	--	--	--	--	--	--	1	--	1
290 PH 103	--	--	--	--	--	--	--	--	--	--	--	--	1	--	1
291 PH 104	--	--	--	--	--	--	--	--	2	--	1	--	--	1	4
292 PH 105	--	3	7	--	11	--	--	--	1	--	9	--	4	2	37
293 PH 105 1	--	--	1	--	1	--	--	--	--	--	2	--	--	--	4
294 PH 106	--	--	--	--	--	--	--	--	1	--	7	--	2	10	20
295 PH 106 1	--	10	5	--	1	--	--	--	--	--	--	--	--	--	16
296 PH 107	--	2	1	--	1	--	--	--	4	--	1	--	3	5	17
297 PH 111	--	--	1	--	--	--	1	--	--	--	--	--	--	1	3
298 PH 113	--	--	1	--	--	--	--	--	--	--	--	--	--	1	2
299 PH 115	--	--	3	--	3	--	--	--	--	--	--	--	--	--	6
300 PH 120	--	1	--	--	--	--	--	--	--	--	--	--	1	1	3
301 PH 120 1	--	1	--	--	--	--	--	--	--	--	--	--	--	--	1
302 PH 121	--	3	--	--	--	--	--	--	--	--	--	--	2	--	5
303 PH 123	--	--	5	--	--	--	--	--	7	--	6	--	6	14	38
304 PH 123 1	--	1	5	--	--	--	--	--	1	--	3	--	--	--	10
305 PH 123 2	--	--	--	--	--	--	--	--	--	--	--	--	--	1	1
306 PH 124	--	--	--	--	1	--	--	--	--	--	--	--	--	--	1
307 PH 124 1	--	--	6	--	6	--	--	--	6	--	8	--	9	11	46
308 PH 128	--	--	1	--	--	--	--	--	--	--	--	--	--	--	1
309 PH 129	--	--	1	--	--	--	--	--	--	--	--	--	2	2	5
310 PH 148	--	--	3	--	11	--	--	--	--	--	--	--	--	--	14
311 PH 132 b	--	--	--	--	--	--	--	1	--	--	--	--	--	--	1
312 PH 49	--	--	--	--	1	--	--	1	--	--	--	--	--	--	2
313 PH 75	--	--	--	--	--	--	--	--	--	--	5	--	--	--	5

Table 3B.11: Enclosure III earthworks – total sherds 275

Context	*Pottery Fabrics*													
Enclosure III	1	2	3	4	5	6	7	8	9	10	11	12	13	14	Total
314 PH 120	--	--	--	1	--	--	--	--	--	--	--	--	--	--	1
315 Pit? 11	--	--	--	--	2	--	--	1	1	--	8	--	9	13	34
316 S 7	--	--	--	--	--	--	--	--	--	--	--	--	--	1	1
317 C 122B	--	--	--	--	--	--	--	--	1	--	--	--	--	--	1
318 C 140	--	--	--	--	--	--	--	--	--	--	1	--	--	--	1
319 C 145 D	--	--	--	--	--	--	--	--		--	1	--	1	--	2
320 C 148	--	--	10	4	12	--	--	1	8	1	47	--	--	30	113
321 C III	1	--	5	--	--	--	--	--	--	--	--	--	--	2	8
322 S 3	--	1	--	--	1	--	--	--	3	--	1	--	--	11	17
322/235 S 3/65B	--	--	3	--	--	--	--	--	--	--	--	--	--	--	3
323 M 5	--	6	2	3	--	--	--	--	2	5	--	--	6	--	24
324 M 8	--	--	--	7	--	--	--	4	--	--	--	--	--	--	11
325 N 5	--	--	--	--	--	--	--	1	--	2	--	--	--	--	3
326 O 6	1	--	--	--	2	--	--	--	--	--	--	--	1	--	4
327 O 8	2	--	--	--	--	--	--	--	--	--	1	--	--	--	3
328 Surface	34	--	--	--	--	--	--	--	--	--	--	--	--	--	34
329 C 20	--	--	1	2	--	--	--	--	--	--	11	1	--	--	15

Bibliography

ALCOCK, L. 1971: *Arthur's Britain: History and Archaeology AD 367-634* (London).

ALEXANDER, J. 1964: The pins of Jugoslav early Iron Age. *Proc. Prehist. Soc.* 30, 159.

ARMSTRONG, S.F. 1950: *British Grasses and Their Employment in Agriculture* 3rd ed. (Cambridge).

A.S.T.M. *American Society for Testing Materials.*

AVERY, M. 1973: *Caesar and Cassivellaunu.* unpubl. typescript: May 1973, 527.

BARRETT, J. and BRADLEY, R. (eds) 1980: *Settlement and Society in the Later British Bronze Age* (Oxford: BAR Brit Ser 83).

BEAVEN, E.S. 1947: *Barley: Fifty Years of Observation and Experiment* (London).

BELL, G.H.D. 1965: The comparative phylogeny of the temperate cereals. In Hutchinson, J. *Essays on crop plant evolution* (Cambridge), 70-102.

BERSU, G. 1940: Excavations at Little Woodbury: Part 1. *Proc. Prehist. Soc.* 6, 30-111.

BIMSON, M. 1969: The examination of ceramics by X-ray power diffraction. *Studies in Conservation* 14, 85-89.

BOARDMAN, S. and JONES, G. 1990: Experiments on the effects of charring on cereal plant components. *Journal Archaeological Science* 17, 1–11.

BONNEY, D. 1979: Early boundaries and estates in southern England. In Sawyer, P. (ed.) *English Medieval Settlement* (London).

BOWEN, H.C. 1975: Air Photography and the development of the landscape in central parts of southern England. In Wilson, D.R. (ed.) *Aerial Reconnaissance for Archaeology* (London: CBA Res. Rep. 12, 103-18).

BRAILSFORD, J.W. 1948: Excavations at Little Woodbury, part II. *Proc. Prehist. Soc.* **14**, 1-23.

BREWSTER, T.C.M. 1963: *The Excavation of Staple Howe* (Scarborough).

BRITTON, D. with LONGWORTH, I.H. 1968: Late Bronze Age finds in the Heathery Burn Cave, Co Durham. *Inventaria Archaeologia.* (London: British Museum 9th set, GB55).

BRONK RAMSEY, C. 1995: Radiocarbon calibration and analysis of stratigraphy: The OxCal program. *Radiocarbon* 37 (2) 425-430.

BRONK RAMSEY, C. 1998: Probability and dating. *Radiocarbon* 40, 461–74.

BRONK RAMSEY, C. 2001: Development of the radiocarbon calibration program OxCal. *Radiocarbon* 43, 355-63.

BRONK RAMSEY, C. 2007: Deposition Models for Chronological Record. *Quaternary Science Reviews*, INTIMATE, special issue.

BRONK RAMSEY, C. 2009: Bayesian analysis of radiocarbon dates *Radiocarbon* 51, 337-60.

BROTHWELLl, D. 1981: *Digging up Bones* 3rd ed. (New York).

BROWN, L. 1984: Objects of stone. In Cunliffe, B. Vol.2, 407-26.

BROWN, L. 1995: An investigation of the validity of ceramic phases 4 and 5. In Cunliffe, B. *Danebury an Iron Age hillfort in Hampshire Vol. 6. A hillfort community in perspective* (York: CBA Res. Rep. 102, 246-8).

BROWN, L. 2000: The later prehistoric pottery. In Cunliffe, B. and Poole, C. *The Danebury Environs Roman Programme: The Prehistory of a Wessex Landscape Vol 2-Part 6, Houghton Down, Stockbridge, Hants. 1994* (Oxford: Engl. Heritage and Oxford Univ. Comm. Archaeol. Monogr. 49,75-102).

BROWN, L. 2008: The pottery. In Cunliffe, B. and Poole, C. *The Danebury Environs Programme: A Wessex Landscape During the Roman Era, Vol 2 – Part 6, Flint Farm, Goodworth, Clatford, Hants, 2004* (Oxford: Engl. Heritage and Oxford Univ. Comm. Archaeol. Monogr. 71, 63-74)

BULLEID, A. and GRAY, H.St.G. 1911: *The Glastonbury Lake Village Vol. 1* (Glastonbury).

BULLEID, A and GRAY, H.St.G. 1953: *The Meare Lake Village Vol 2* (Taunton).

BURGESS, C.B. 1979: A find from Boyton, Suffolk and the end of the Bronze Age in Britain and Ireland. In Burgess, C.B. and Coombs, D. (eds), 269-82.

BURGESS, C.B. and Coombs, D. (eds) 1979: *Bronze Age Hoards: some finds old and new* (Oxford: BAR Brit. Ser. 67).

BUCKLEY, D.G. 1979: The Stone. In Wainright, G.J. 1979, 89-97.

CALKIN, J.G. 1955: Kimmeridge coal-money: the Romano-British shale armlet industry. *Proc. Dorset Natur. Hist. and Archaeol. Soc.* 75, 45-71.

CALLOW, W. J., BAKER, M.J. and Pritchard, D.H. 1963: National Physical Laboratory Radiocarbon Measurements I. *Radiocarbon* 5, 34-8.

CALLOW, W.J., BAKER, M.J. and Hassall, G.I. 1965: National Physical Laboratory Radiocarbon Measurements III. *Radiocarbon* 7, 156-61.

CALLOW, W.J., BAKER, M.J. and HASSALL, G.I. 1966: National Physical Laboratory Radiocarbon Measurements IV. *Radiocarbon* 8, 340-47.

CALLOW, W.J. and HASSALL, G.I. 1968: National Physical Laboratory Radiocarbon Measurements V. *Radiocarbon* 10, 115-18.

CAMPBELL, G. 2000: Plant utilization: The evidence from charred plant remains. In Cunliffe, B. and Poole, C. *The Danebury Environs Programme: The Prehistory of a Wessex Landscape. Vol 1: Introduction* (Oxford: Engl. Heritage and Oxford Univ. Comm. Archaeol. Monogr. 49,45-59).

CARRUTHERS, W. 1991: The carbonised plant remains from Rowden, in Woodward, P.J. (ed.)

The South Dorset Ridgeway Survey and Excavations 1977-84. Dorset Natur. Hist. and Archaeol. Soc. Monog. 8, Dorchester, 106-11.

CARRUTHERS, W. 2002: The charred and mineralised plant remains, in Valentin, J. and Robinson, S. (eds) Excavations in 1999 on Land Adjacent to Wayside Farm, Nursteed Road, Devizes. *Wiltshire Archaeol Mag* 95, 202-7.

CHAMPION, T.C. 1976: *The Earlier Iron Age in the Region of the Lower Thames: Insular and External Factors* (Oxford: Institute of Archaeology, unpubl. DPhil. thesis).

CHAMPION, T.C.1980: Settlement and environment in later Bronze Age Kent. In Barrett, J.C. and Bradley, R. (eds), 223-46.

CLAPHAM, A., TUTIN, T.G. and WARBURG, E.F. 1952: *Flora of the British Isles* (Cambridge: Cambridge University Press).

CLAY, R.C.C. 1924: An Early Iron Age site on Fifield Bavant Down. *Wiltshire Archaeol. Mag.* 42, 457.

CLAY, R.C.C. 1925: An inhabited site of La Tene I date on Swallowcliffe Down. *Wiltshire Archaeol. Mag.* 43, 59-93.

COE, D. and NEWMAN, R. 1993: Excavation of an Early Iron Age building and Romano-British enclosure at Brighton Hill South, Hampshire *Proc. Hanmpshire Field Club and Archaeol. Soc.* 48, 5-26.

COLES, J.M. 1987: *Meare Village East: the excavations of A. Bulleid and H. St. George Gray 1932-1956* (Exeter: Somerset Levels Papers 13).

COLT HOARE, R. 1812: *The Ancient History of South Wiltshire Vol 1* (London).

COWEN, J.D. 1967: The Hallstatt sword of bronze: on the continent and in Britain. *Proc. Prehist. Soc.* 33, 377- 454.

CRAWFORD, O.G.S. and Wheeler, R.E.M. 1921: The Llynfawr and other hoards of the Bronze Age. *Archaeologia* 71, 133-40.

CROWFOOT, G.M. 1945: The 'bone gouges' of Maiden Castle and other sites. *Antiquity* 19, 157-8.

CUNLIFFE, B. 1957: In R. B. Pugh and Elizabeth Crittall (eds). *Victoria History of the Counties of England: History of Wiltshire Vol.1.*

CUNLIFFE, B. 1984: *Danebury: an Iron Age Hillfort in Hampshire. Vol. 1, The Excavations 1969-78: the site. Vol. 2, The finds (*London: CBA Res. Rep. 52).

CUNLIFFE, B. 1984: Danebury: an Iron Age Hillfort in Hampshire. Volume 2, The Excavations, 1969-78: the finds (London: CBA Res. Rep. 52).

CUNLIFFE, B. 2000: *The Danebury Environs Programme: The Prehistory of a Wessex Landscape. Vol 1: Introduction (*Oxford: Engl. Heritage and Oxford Univ. Comm. Archaeol. Monog. 48).

CUNLIFFE, B. 2005: *Iron Age Communities in Britain* 4th ed. (London).

CUNLIFFE, B. and O'CONNOR, B. 1979: The Late Bronze Age hoard from Danebury, Hampshire. In Burgess, C.B and Coombs, D. (eds), 235-44.

CUNLIFFE, B. and PHILLIPSON, D.W. 1968: Excavations at Eldon's Seat, Encombe, Dorset. *Proc. Prehist. Soc.* 34, 191-237.

CUNLIFFE, B. and POOLE, C. 1991: *Danebury: an Iron Age Hillfort in Hampshire. Vol. 4, The Excavations 1979-1988: the site; Vol. 5, The Excavations 1979-1988: the finds* (London: CBA Res Rep 73).

CUNNINGTON, M.E. 1912: A Late Celtic inhabited site at All Cannings Cross. *Wiltshire Archaeol. Mag.* 37, 526-39.

CUNNINGTON, M.E. 1923: *The Early Iron Age inhabited site of All Cannings Cross Farm, Wiltshire,* (Devizes).

CUNNINGTON, M.E. 1932: Romano-British Wiltshire *Wiltshire Archaeol. Mag.* 45, 166-216.

CUNNINGTON, M.E. and GODDARD, E.H. 1934: *The Devizes Museum Catalogue, Part II* (Devizes).

DAVIES, H. 1936: The shale industries at Kimmeridge, *Dorset. Archaeol. Journal* 93, 200-19.

DAY, R. and GALE, K. 1981: Wiltshire iron 1855-1949. *Journal of the Historical Metallurgy Soc.* 15 (1), 18-38.

DÉCHLETTE, J. 1927: *Manuel d'archéologie préhistorique, celtique et gallo-romaine 1908-1914,* rééditions 1927 (Paris), 887-889.

DIXON , P.W 1976: Crickley Hill 1969-1972. In Harding D.W. (ed.) *Hillforts: Late Prehistoric earth works in Britain and Ireland* (London).

DUNNING, G.C. 1934: The swan's neck and ring-headed pin of the Early Iron Age in Britain. *Archaeol. Journal* 91, 269-95.

DUNNING, G.C. 1959: The distribution of socketed axes of Breton type. *Ulster Journal of Archaeology* 22, 53-5.

EVANS, J. 1881: *The Ancient Bronze Implements, Weapons and Ornaments of Great Britain and Ireland* (London).

EVANS, J.G. 1972: *Land Snails in Archaeology* (London).

FASHAM, P.J., KEEVILL, G., COE, D., and NEWMAN, R. 1995: *Brighton Hill South (Hatch Warren): An Iron Age Farmstead and Deserted Medieval Village in Hampshire.* (Salisbury: Trust for Wessex Archaeology).

FASHAM, P.J, FARWELL, D.E. and WHINNEY , R.J.B. 1989: *The Archaeological Site at Easton Lane Winchester* (Winchester: Hampshire Field Club Archaeol. Soc.Monogr. 6).

FITZPATRICK, A.P. 1994: Outside in: The structure of an early Iron Age house at Dunston Park, Thatcham, Berkshire. In Fitzpatrick, A.P. and Morris, E.L. (eds.) *The Iron Age In Wessex: Recent Work* (Salisbury: Trust for Wessex Archaeology, 68-72).

FITZPATRICK, A.P. 1997: Everyday life in Iron Age Wessex. In Gwilt , A. and Haselgrove, C. (eds) *Reconstructing Iron Age Societies: new Approaches to the British Iron Age.* (Oxford: Oxbow Monogr. 71, 73-86).

FLEMING, G. 1869: Horse-shoes and Horse-shoeing: Their Origin, History, Uses and Abuses (London).

FOCK, J. 1966: *Metrische Untersuchungen an Metapodien einger europäischen Rinderrassen.* (Munich: Dissertation).

FOWLER, G. 1950: A Romano-British village near Littleport, Cambs. *Proc.Cambridge Antiquarian Soc.* 43, 7-20.

FOWLER, E.1960: The origins and development of the penannular brooch in Europe, *Proc. Prehist. Soc.* 26, 149-77.

FOWLER, P., MUSTY, J. and TAYLOR, C. 1965: Some earthwork enclosures in Wiltshire *Wiltshire Archaeol. Mag.* 60, 52-74.

FOX, C.F. 1927: A La Téne I brooch from Wales: with notes on the typology and distribution of these brooches in Britain. *Archaeologia Cambrensis* 82, 67-112.

FOX, C.F. 1958: *Pattern and Purpose· A Survey of Early Celtic Art in Britain* (Cardiff).

FOX, C.F. and HYDE, H.A. 1939: A second cauldron and an iron sword from the Llyn Fawr hoard, Rhigos, Glamorganshire. *Antiquaries Journal* 19, 369-404.

FREIDEN, N. 1982: *The Early Iron Age in the Paris Basin: Hallstatt C and D.* (Oxford: BAR Int. Ser. 131).

FRERE, S.S. (ed.) 1958: Problems of the iron age in Southern Britain; papers given at a CBA conference Dec. 12-14, 1958 (London: Institute of Archaeology Occ. Pap. 11 (1960)).

GINGELL, C. and GINGELL, J. 1981: Excavation of a medieval Highworth Circle at Stratton St Margaret. *Wiltshire Archaeol. Mag.* 74/75, 61-8.

GINGELL, C. 1979: The Bronze and Iron Age Hoard from Melksham and another Wiltshire find. In Burgess, C. and Coombs, D. (eds), *Bronze Age Hoards: Some Finds Old and New* (Oxford: BAR Brit. Ser. 67, 245-52).

GINGELL, C. and MORRIS, E.L. 2000: Pottery. In Lawson, A.J. *Potterne 1982-5: Animal Husbandry in Later Prehistoric Wiltshire.* (Salisbury: Wessex Archaeol. Rep. 17, 135-66).

HULL, M.R. and HAWKES, C.F.C. 1987: Corpus of ancient brooches in Britain: pre-Roman bow brooches (Oxford: BAR Brit. Ser. 168).

GODWIN, H. 1956: *The History of the British Flora: A Factual Basis for Phytogeography* (Cambridge: Cambridge University Press).

GOVER, J., ALLEN-MAWER and STENTON, F. 1939: *The Place Names of Wiltshire* (Cambridge).

GODWIN, H. 1956: *The history of British flora* (Cambridge: Cambridge University Press).

GRAY, H. St.G. 1925: Excavations at Ham Hill, south Somerset (part 1). *Proc. Somersetshire Archaeol. Natur. Hist. Soc.* 70, 104-16.

GRAY, H. St.G. 1926 :Excavations at Ham Hill, south Somerset (part 2).). *Proc. Somersetshire Archaeol. Natur. Hist. Soc.* 71, 57-76.

GRAY, H. St.G. 1927: Excavations at Ham Hill, south Somerset (part 3). *Proc. Somersetshire Archaeol. Natur. Hist. Soc.* 72, 55-68.

GUIDO, M. 1978: *The Glass Beads of the of the Prehistoric and Roman Periods in Britain and Ireland* (London: Society Antiquaries Res. Rep. 35).

GUILBERT, G. 1981: Double-ring roundhouses, probable and possible, in prehistoric Britain. *Proc. Prehist. Soc.* 47, 299-317.

GWILT, A and HASELGROVE, C. (eds) 1997: *Reconstructing Iron Age Societies: New Approaches to the British Iron Age.* (Oxford: Oxbow Monogr. 71).

HAKBIJL, T. 2002: The traditional, historical and prehistoric use of ashes as an insecticide, with an experimental study on the insecticidal efficacy of washed ash. *Environmental Archaeology* 7, 13-22.

HARCOURT, R.A. 1974: The dog in prehistoric and early historic Britain *Journal. Archaeol. Science* 1, 151-75.

HARCOURT, R.A. 1979a: The Animal bones. In Wainwright, G.J. 1979. *Mount Pleasant, Dorset: Excavations 1970-71.* (London: Society Antiquaries Res. Rep. 37).

HARCOURT, R.1979b: The Animal Bones. In Wainwright, G.J. 1979, 150-60.

HARDING, D.W. 1972: *The Iron Age in the Upper Thames Basin* (Oxford).

HARDING. D.W. 1974: *The Iron Age in Lowland Britain.* (London).

HARDING, D.W. and BLAKE, I.M. 1963: An Early Iron Age Settlement in Dorset. *Antiquity* 37, 63-4.

HARDING, D.W., BLAKE, I.M. and REYNOLDS, P.J. 1993: *An Iron Age Settlement in Dorset: Excavation and Reconstruction* (Edinburgh. University Dept. of Archaeology Monogr. Ser. 1).

HAWKES, S.C. 1994: Longbridge Deverill Cow Down, Wiltshire, House 3: a major roundhouse of the Early Iron Age. *Oxford Journal Archaeol.* 13, 49-70.

HAWKES, C.F.C. 1940: A site of the Late Bronze-Early Iron Age transition at Totternhoe. *Bedfordshire Antiquaries Journal* 20, 487-91.

HAWKES, C.F.C. 1976: St. Catharine's Hill, Winchester: the Report of 1930 re-assessed. In Harding, DW, (ed.) *Hillforts. Later Prehistoric Earthworks in Britain and Ireland* (London).

HAWKES, C.F.C. and HULL, M.R. 1947: *Camulodunum* (Oxford: Soc. Antiq. Res. Rep. 14).

HELBAEK, H. 1952: Spelt (Triticum spelta L.) in Bronze Age Denmark. *Acta Archaeologica* 23, 97-115.

HELBAEK, H. 1953: Early crops in southern Britain. *Proc. Prehist. Soc.* 18, 194-233.

HENSHALL, A.S. 1950: Textiles and weaving appliances in prehistoric Britain. *Proc.Prehist. Soc* 16, 130-62.

HILL, J.D. 1995: *Ritual and Rubbish in the Iron Age of Wessex: A Study on the Formation of a Specific Archaeological Record.* (Oxford: BAR, Brit. Ser. 242).

HINTON, P. 1982: Carbonised seeds. In Drewitt, P. (ed.) Later Bronze Age downland economy and excavations at Black Patch, East Sussex. *Proc.Prehist. Soc.* 48, 382-90.

HODDER, I. and HEDGES, J.W. 1977: Weaving combs, their typology and distribution with some introductory remarks on date and function. In Collis, J. (ed.). *The Iron Age in Britain: a review* (Sheffield), 17-31.

HODSON, F.R. 1968: The La Téne cemetery at Munsingen-am-Rain. *Acta Bernensia* 5, 197.

HODSON, F.R.1971: Three Iron Age brooches from Hammersmith. In Sieveking, G.deG. (ed.). *Prehistoric and Roman Studies* (London).

HOOKE, D. 1988: Regional variation in southern and central England in the Anglo-Saxon period and its relationship to land units and settlement. Iin Hooke, D. (ed). *Anglo-Saxon Settlements* (Oxford).

HULL, M.R. and HAWKES, C.F.C. 1987: *Corpus of Ancient Brooches in Britain: Pre-Roman bow brooches* (*Oxford:* BAR Brit. Ser. 168).

HURST, D.G. 1968: Post-medieval Britain in 1967. *Post-Medieval Archaeol.* 2, 187-188.

JACKSON, J.W. 1917: The wild animals; the domestic animals. In Bulleid, A. and Gray, H. St.G. *The Glastonbury Lake Village* (Glastonbury), 641.

JACKSON, J.W. 1924: Notes on animal remains found at All Cannings Cross, Wilts. In Cunnington, M.E., *The Early Iron Age inhabited site at All Cannings Cross Farm, Wiltshire* (Devizes), 43-50.

JACKSON, J.W. 1925: Report on the animal remains. In Clay, R.C.C., An inhabited site of La Téne I date on Swallowcliffe Down. *Wiltshire Archaeol. Mag.* 43, 90.

JACKSON, J.W. 1948: The animal remains from Little Woodbury. *Proc. Prehist. Soc.* 14, 19.

JACOBSTHAL, P. 1944/1969: *Early Celtic Art* (Oxford).

JACOMET, S. 1987: *Prähistorische Getreidefunde: Eine Anleitung zur Bestimmung prähistorishcher Gersten- und Weizen- Funde* (Basel: Botanisches Institut der Universität Abteilung Pflanzensystsematik und Geobotanik).

JACOMET, S. (ed.) 2000: Identification of cereal remains from archaeological sites, 2nd ed. (Basel: Archaeobotany Lab, IPAS, Basel University).

JEFFERIES 1979: The Pits. In Wainwright, G.J 1979, 9-15.

JESSEN, K. and HELBAEK, H. 1944: Cereals in Great Britain and Ireland in prehistoric and early historic times. *Det Kongelige Danske Videnskabernes Selskab, Biologiske Skrifter* 3, 1-68.

JOFFROY, R. 1960: L'Oppidum de Vix et la civilisation hallstattienne dans l'Est de la France. Paris: *Publications de l'Université Dijon),* 20.

JONES, M. 1984: The plant remains. In Cunliffe, B.1984, vol. 2, 483-95.

JOPE, E.M. 1961: Daggers of the early Iron Age in Britain. *Proc. Prehist. Soc.* 27, 307-43.

JOPE, E.M. and HAWKES, C.F.C. 1983: Celtic Studies, Oxford, July 1983. Report of 7th International Congress. *Antiquity* 58, 90-4.

KEELEY, L.H. 1980: *Experimental Determination of Stone Tool Uses: a Microwear Analysis* (Chicago).

KEELEY, L.H. and NEWCOMER, M.H. 1977: Microwear Analysis of Experimental Flint Tools: a Test Case. *Journal of Archaeological Science.* 4(1), 29-62.

KENDALL, J.D. 1893: *Iron ores of Great Britain and Ireland* (London).

KIMMIG, W. 1962-3: Bronzesitulen aus dem Rheinischen Gebirge, Hunsrück-Eifel-Westerwald. *Bericht der Romisch-Germanischen Kommission,* 31-106

RCHM 1937: An Inventory of the Ancient Monuments in Anglesey. *The Royal Commission on Ancient and Historical Monuments in Wales and Monmouthshire* (Cardiff).

LAWS, K. 1991: The chalk. In Sharples, N.M. *Maiden Castle: Excavations and field survey 1985-6* (London: English Heritage Archaeol. Rep.19).

LAWS, K., BROWN, L. and ROE, F. 1991: Objects of stone, in Cunliffe, B. and Poole, C. 1991, 382-404

LIDDELL, D.M.1933: Excavations at Meon Hill. *Proc. Hampshire Field Club Archaeol. Soc.* 12, 127-62.

LIDDELL, D.M. 1935: Report on the Hampshire Field Club's excavation at Meon Hill. *Proc. Hampshire Field Club Archaeol. Soc.* 13, 7-54.

LOBJOIS, G. 1969: La necropole de Pernant (Aisne). *Celticum* 18, 1-284.

LOVELL, J., HAMILTON-DYER, S., LOADER, E, MCKINLEY, J. 1999: Further investigations of an Iron Age and Romano-British farmstead on Cockey Down, near Salisbury, *Wiltshire Archaeol. Mag.*, 92, 33-8.

MACGREGOR, M.and SIMPSON, D.D.A 1963: A group of iron objects from Barbury Castle, Wilts. *Wiltshire Archaeol. Mag.* 58, 394-482.

MARGARY, I.D. 1955: *Roman Roads in Britain* (London).

MCOMISH, D., FIELD, D. and BROWN, G. 2011: The late Bronze Age and early Iron Age Midden Site at East Chisenbury, Wiltshire. *Wiltshire Archaeol. Mag.* 103, 35-101.

MOORE, C.N. and ROWLANDS, M. 1972: *Metalwork in Salisbury Museum* (Salisbury).

MONK, M. 1991: The archaeobotanical work carried out for the M3 Project - a retrospective view. In Fasham, P.J. and Whinney, R.J.B. (eds.) *Archaeology and the M3: The Watching brief, The Anglo-Saxon settlements at Abbots Worthy and Retrospective Sections.* (Winchester: Trust for Wessex Archaeology and Hampshire Field Club Archaeological Society Monogr 7, 105–10).

MONK, M. and FASHAM, P.J. 1980: Carbonised plant remains from two Iron Age Sites in Central Hampshire. *Proc. Prehist. Soc.* 46, 321-344.

MOOK, W.G. 1986: Recommendations/resolutions adopted by the twelfth international radiocarbon conference. *Radiocarbon* 28, 799.

MURPHEY, P. 1977: *Early Agriculture and Environment on the Hampshire Chalklands circa 800 BC–400 AD.* (Southampton: Univ. of Southampton: unpubl. M.Phil. thesis).

MURRAY, R.W. 1927: *An Enquiry Regarding the date of Some old English Horseshoes, the Origin and History of the English Horse-shoe, Dating Old English Horseshoes, the Cult of the Horseshoe* (Cotteswold).

MURRAY, R.W 1937a: An enquiry regarding the date of some old English horseshoes. *Journal British Archaeol. Assoc.* 1, 1-33.

MURRAY, R.W. 1937b: Dating old English horseshoes. *Journal British Archaeol. Assoc.* 2, 133-44.

NAERLAND, G. 1970: Sheep Husbandry in Norway. *Veterinary Record* 86, 130.

NEEDHAM, S. and LONGLEY, D. 1980: *Runnymede Bridge, Egham: a late Bronze Age riverside settlement.* In Barrett J. and Bradley, R. (eds), 397-436.

NEWCOMER, M.H. 1974: Study and replication of bone tools from Ksor Akil, Lebanon. *World Archaeology* 6, 134.

OSWALD, A.1997: A doorway on the past: practical and mystic concerns in the orientation of roundhouse doorways. In Gwilt, A. and Haselgrove, C. 1997, 87-95.

OTLET, R.L. and SLADE, B.S.1974: Harwell radiocarbon measurements I. *Radiocarbon* 16, 178–191.

PARKER PEARSON, M. 1996: Food, fertility and front doors: houses in the first millenium BC. In Champion, T.C. and Collis, J. (eds.). *The Iron Age in Britain and Ireland: Recent Trends* (Sheffield) 117-32.

POLACH, H.A. and STIPP, J.J. 1967: Improved synthesis techniques for methane and benzene radiocarbon dating. *Journal Applied Radiation and Isotopes* 18, 359-364.

POOLE, C. 1991a: Objects of baked clay. In Cunliffe, B. and Poole, C. 1991 vol. 2 (London: CBA Res Rep 73), 370-81.

POOLE, C. 1991b: The small objects of clay and daub. In Sharples, N.M. *Maiden Castle: Excavations and field survey 1985-6*. (London: Engl. Heritage Archaeol. Rep. 19), 209.

PAULI, L. 1971: *Die Golaseccakultur und Mitteleuropa: Ein Beitrag zur Geschichte des Handels über die Alpen* (Hamburg).

PAYNE, F.G. 1947: The plough in ancient Britain. *Archaeol. Journal* 104, 82-111.

PEACOCK, D.P.S. 1969: A contribution to the study of Glastonbury ware from south-western Britain. *Antiquaries Journal* 49, 41-61.

PETERSON, R.F. 1965: *Wheat: Botany, Cultivation and Utilization* (London).

PIGGOTT, C.M.1946: Late Bronze Age razors of the British Isles. *Proc. Prehist. Soc.* 12, 121-41.

PITT RIVERS, A.H.L.F. 1888: *Excavations in Cranborne Chase Vol.2* (London).

PITT RIVERS, A.H.L.F. 1898: *Excavations in Cranborne Chase Vol. 4* (London).

POPE, R.E. 2008: Roundhouses: 3,000 years of prehistoric design. *Current Archaeology* 222, 14-21.

POPE, R. 2007: Ritual and roundhouses: a critique of recent ideas on the use of domestic space in later Prehistory. In Haselgrove, C. and Pope, R. (eds) *The Earlier Iron Age in Britain and the Near Continent* (Oxford).

RAYMOND, F. 2010: Pottery. In McOmish, D., Field, D and Brown, G. 2010, 35-101.

REES, S.E. 1979: Agricultural Implements in Prehistoric and Roman Britain (Oxford: BAR 69).

REIMER, P.J., BAILLIE, M.G.L., BARD, E., BAYLISS, A., BECK, J.W., BERTRAND, C., BLACKWELL, P.G., BUCK, C.E., BURR, G., CUTLER, K.B., DAMON, P.E., EDWARDS, R.L., FAIRBANKS, R.G., FRIEDRICH, M., GUILDERSON, T.P., HUGHEN, K.A., KROMER, B., MCCORMAC, F.G., MANNING, S., BRONK RAMSEY, C., REIMER, R.W., REMMELE, S., SOUTHON, J.R., STUIVER, M., TALAMO, S., TAYLOR, F.W., VAN DER PLICHT, J., and WEYHENMEYER, C.E. 2004: IntCal04 Terrestrial radiocarbon age calibration, 0–26 Cal Kyr BP. *Radiocarbon* 46 (3), 1029-58.

REID C 1903: Geology of the country around Salisbury. *Memoirs. Geological. Survey UK*, Sheet 298.

REYNOLDS, P.J. 1979: *Iron Age Farm: The Butser Experiment*, (London: British Museum).

RICHARDSON, K.M. 1951: The excavation of Iron Age villages on Boscombe Down West. *Wiltshire Archaeol. Mag.* 54, 123-68.

RIDGEWAY, W. 1905: *The Origin and Influence of the Thoroughbred Horse* (Cambridge).

ROE, F.E.S. 2000: Worked Stone. In Barrett, J.C., Freeman, P.W.M. and Woodward, A., *Cadbury Castle, Somerset: The later prehistoric and early historic archaeology* (London: English Heritage Archaeol. Rep. 20, 262-7).

ROTH, H.L. 1934: *Studies in primitive looms* (Halifax: repr. Bankfield Museum).

ROWLETT, R.M. 1966: Review: the La Tene Cultures of Eastern Yorkshire by Ian Stead. *Antiquity* 40, 133-6.

RYDER, M.L. 1981: The history of sheep breeds in Britain. In Thirsk J(ed). *Agrarian History of England and Wales, Vol.* 11640–1750 (Cambridge).

SANDERSON, R.W. 1975: Ancient Monuments Laboratory Report ENQ 2453.

SAVORY, H.N. 1937: An early Iron Age site at Long Wittenham, Berks. *Oxoniensia* 2, 1-11.

SELLWOOD, L., 1984, Objects of bone and antler. In Cunliffe, B. Vol. 2 (London: CBA Res. Rep..52, 371-395).

SHARPLES, N. 2010: Social Relations in Later Prehistory Wessex in the First Millennium BC (Oxford).

SMITH, K. 1977: The excavation of Winklebury Camp, Basingstoke, Hampshire *Proc. Prehist. Soc.* 43, 31-129.

SPRATLING, M. 1979: The debris of metalworking. In Waiwright 1979, 125-53.

STACE, C.A. 1997: New Flora of the British Isles. 3rd ed. (Cambridge).

STANFORD, S.C. 1974: *Croft Ambrey* (Hereford).

STEVENS, F. 1934: The Highfield pit dwellings, Fisherton, Salisbury. *Wiltshire Archaeol. Mag.* 46, 579-624.

STUIVER, M., and KRA, R.S.1986: Editorial comment. *Radiocarbon* 28(2B) ii.

STUIVER, M. and POLACH, H.A. 1977: Reporting of C14 data. *Radiocarbon* 19, 355–63.

STUIVER, M., and REIMER, P.J. 1986: A computer program for radiocarbon age calculation. *Radiocarbon* 28, 1022-30.

STUIVER, M., and REIMER, P.J. 1993: Extended C14 database and revised CALIB 3.0 C14 age calibration program. *Radiocarbon* 35, 215-30.

TYLECOTE, R.F. and CLOUGH, R.E. 1983: Recent bog iron ore analyses and the smelting of pyrites nodules. *Offa*, Band 40, 115-118.

TYLECOTE, R.F. 1987: *The Early History of Metallurgy in Europe* (London).

VAN DER VEEN, M. and JONES, G. 2006: A reanalysis of agricultural production and consumption: Implications for understanding the British Iron Age. *Vegetation History and Archaeobotany* 15, 217-28.

VCH, 1957 *A History of Wiltshire, vol I* Victoria History of the Counties of England (London).

VCH, 1959 *A History of Wiltshire vol 4,* Victoria History of the Counties of England (London).

VIOLLIER, D. 1911: *Les Sepultres du Second Age du Fer sur le Plateau Suisse* (Geneva).

VON DEN DRIESCH, A. 1976: *A Guide to the Measurement of Animal Bones from Archaeological Sites.* (Cambridge: Harvard Univ., Peabody Museum of Archaeology and Ethnology).

WADDINGTON, K. 2008: The politics of the everyday: exploring 'midden' space in Late Bronze Age Wiltshire. In Maltby, M. and Morris, J. (eds) *Integrating Ssocial Environmental Archaeologies: Reconsidering Deposition.* (Oxford: BAR Int. Ser. 2077, 103-18).

WADDINGTON, K. 2010: New perspectives in later prehistory. In Davis, O.P., Sharples, N.M. and Waddington, K.E. (eds). *Changing perspectives on the first millennium BC* (Oxford), 1-10.

WAINWRIGHT, G.J. 1979: *Gussage All Saints. An Iron Age Settlement in Dorset* (London).

WALSHE, D., OSGOOD, R. and BROWN, M.2012: Archaeology as Rehabilitation. *British Archaeology* Jan/Feb 2012, 40-43.

WARD PERKINS, J.B. 1941: The Iron Age horseshoe, *Antiquaries Journal* 21, 144-9.

WEBLEY, L. 2007: Using and abandoning roundhouses: a reinterpretation of the evidence from Late Bronze Age-Early Iron Age southern England. *Oxford Journal Archaeol.* 26, 127-44.

WHEELER, R.E.M. and RICHARDSON, K.M. 1957: *Hillforts of Northern France.* (Oxford: Soc. Antiq. Res. Rep. 19).

WHEELER, R.E.M. 1943: Maiden Castle, Dorset (Oxford: Soc. Antiq. Res. Rep. 12).

WHITTLE, A.1984: The Pits. In Cunliffe, B. 1984 vol. 52, 131.

WINHAM, R.P. 1985: Pit 5548. In Fasham , P.J. *The Prehistoric Settlement at Winnall Down, Winchester* (Winchester: Hampshire Field Club Archaeol. Soc. Monogr. 5, 22-5).

ZAHLHAAS, G. 1972: Der Bronzeeimer von Waldalgesheim. In Otto-Herman *et al* 1972, Frühlatène-Studien. *Hamburger Beiträge Archäol* 1(2), 1971 (1972) 85-179, 115-129.

Index